Microsoft Office
2013

A SKILLS APPROACH

Cheri Manning

Catherine Manning Swinson
Triad Interactive, Inc.

MICROSOFT OFFICE 2013: A SKILLS APPROACH
Published by McGraw-Hill Education, 2 Penn Plaza, New York, NY 10121. Copyright © 2014 by
McGraw-Hill Education. All rights reserved. Printed in the United States of America. No part of this publication
may be reproduced or distributed in any form or by any means, or stored in a database or retrieval system, without the
prior written consent of McGraw-Hill Education, including, but not limited to, in any network or other electronic
storage or transmission, or broadcast for distance learning.

Some ancillaries, including electronic and print components, may not be available to customers outside the
United States.

This book is printed on acid-free paper.

3 4 5 6 7 8 9 0 RMN/RMN 1 0 9 8 7 6 5 4

ISBN 978-0-07-351645-5
MHID 0-07-351645-7

Senior Vice President, Products & Markets: *Kurt L. Strand*
Vice President, Content Production & Technology Services: *Kimberly Meriwether David*
Director: *Scott Davidson*
Senior Brand Manager: *Wyatt Morris*
Executive Director of Development: *Ann Torbert*
Development Editor: *Alan Palmer*
Development Editor: *Allison McCabe*
Digital Development Editor: *Kevin White*
Marketing Manager: *Tiffany Russell*
Lead Project Manager: *Rick Hecker*
Buyer: *Nichole Birkenholz*
Design: *Lisa King*
Cover Image: © *Burazin/Photographer's Choice/Getty Images*
Content Licensing Specialist: *Joanne Mennemeier*
Media Project Manager: *Brent dela Cruz*
Typeface: *10.5/13 Garamond Premier Pro Regular*
Compositor: *Laserwords Private Limited*
Printer: *R. R. Donnelley*

All credits appearing on page or at the end of the book are considered to be an extension of the copyright page.

Library of Congress Cataloging-in-Publication Data
Manning, Cheryl.
   Microsoft Office 2013 : a skills approach / Cheri Manning, Catherine Manning Swinson, (Triad Interactive, Inc.).
      pages cm
   Includes index.
   ISBN-13: 978-0-07-351645-5 (alk. paper)
   ISBN-10: 0-07-351645-7 (alk. paper)
   1. Microsoft Office. 2. Business—Computer programs. I. Swinson, Catherine Manning. II. Title.
   HF5548.4.M525M3492 2014
005.5—dc23   2013017732

The Internet addresses listed in the text were accurate at the time of publication. The inclusion of a website does not
indicate an endorsement by the authors or McGraw-Hill Education, and McGraw-Hill Education does not guarantee
the accuracy of the information presented at these sites.

brief contents

contents

excel 2013

chapter **3**
Using Formulas and Functions   EX-102

chapter **4**
Formatting Worksheets and Managing the Workbook   EX-152

access 2013

Contents

powerpoint 2013

preface

How well do you know Microsoft Office? Many students can follow specific step-by-step directions to re-create a document, spreadsheet, presentation, or database, but do they truly understand the skills it takes to create these on their own? Just as simply following a recipe does not make you a professional chef, re-creating a project step by step does not make you an Office expert.

The purpose of this book is to teach you the skills to master Microsoft Office 2013 in a straightforward and easy-to-follow manner. But *Microsoft® Office 2013: A Skills Approach* goes beyond the **how** and equips you with a deeper understanding of the **what** and the **why.** Too many times books have little value beyond the classroom. The *Skills Approach* series has been designed to be not only a complete textbook but also a reference tool for you to use as you move beyond academics and into the workplace.

WHAT'S NEW IN THIS EDITION

This edition of the *Skills Approach* text includes a Let Me Try exercise and student data file for each skill. These exercises are the same as the simulated Let Me Try exercises in SIMnet 2013. We included the student data files to give students the opportunity to explore the skill in the live application in addition to practicing it in a simulated environment (SIMnet).

The Let Me Try exercises are not intended as a running project or case study. Each Let Me Try data file is independent of the others, so the skills may be taught in any order.

ABOUT TRIAD INTERACTIVE

Triad Interactive specializes in online education and training products. Our flagship program is SIMnet—a simulated Microsoft Office learning and assessment application developed for the McGraw-Hill Companies. Triad has been writing, programming, and managing the SIMnet system since 1999.

Triad is also actively involved in online health education and in research projects to assess the usefulness of technology for helping high-risk populations make decisions about managing their cancer risk and treatment.

about the authors

CHERI MANNING

Cheri Manning is the president and co-owner of Triad Interactive. She is the author of the Microsoft Excel and Access content for the *Skills Approach* series and SIMnet. She has been authoring instructional content for these applications for more than 12 years.

Cheri began her career as an Aerospace Education Specialist with the Education Division of the National Aeronautics and Space Administration (NASA), where she produced materials for K–12 instructors and students. Prior to founding Triad, Cheri was a project manager with Compact Publishing, where she managed the development of McGraw-Hill's Multimedia MBA CD-ROM series.

CATHERINE MANNING SWINSON

Catherine Manning Swinson is the vice president and co-owner of Triad Interactive. She is the author of the Microsoft Word and PowerPoint content for the *Skills Approach* series and SIMnet. She also authors SIMnet content for Microsoft Outlook, Windows, and Internet Explorer. She has been authoring instructional content for these applications for more than 12 years.

Catherine began her career at Compact Publishing, one of the pioneers in educational CD-ROM-based software. She was the lead designer at Compact and designed every edition of the *TIME Magazine Compact Almanac* from 1992 through 1996. In addition, she designed a number of other products with Compact, including the *TIME Man of the Year* program and the *TIME 20th Century Almanac.*

acknowledgments

CONTRIBUTORS

Kelly Morber, *Saints Philip and James School, English teacher and Malone University, master's degree candidate*
Timothy T. Morber, MEd, LPCC-S, *Malone University*

TECHNICAL EDITORS

Menka Brown
Piedmont Technical College

Sylvia Brown
Midland College

Mary Locke
Greenville Technical College

Daniela Marghitu
Auburn University

Judy Settle
Central Georgia Technical College

Pamela Silvers
Asheville-Buncombe Technical College

Candace Spangler
Columbus State Community College

Debbie Zaidi
Seneca College

REVIEWERS

Our thanks go to all who participated in the development of *Microsoft Office 2013: A Skills Approach.*

Sven Aelterman
Troy University

Nick Agrawal
Calhoun Community College

Laura Anderson
Weber State University

Viola Bain
Scott Community College

Greg Ballinger
Miami Dade College

Bill Barzen
Saint Petersburg College

Julia Bell
Walters State Community College

Don Belle
Central Piedmont Community College

Judy Boozer
Lane Community College

Ben Brah
Auburn University

Sheryl Starkey Bulloch
Columbia Southern University

Kate Burkes
Northwest Arkansas Community College

Michael Callahan
Lone Star College

Patricia Casey
Trident Technical College

Wally Cates
Central New Mexico Community College

Jimmy Chen
Salt Lake Community College

Sharon Cotman
Thomas Nelson Community College

Susan Cully
Long Beach City College

Jennifer Day
Sinclair Community College

Ralph De Arazoza
Miami Dade College

Bruce Elliot
Tarrant County College

Bernice Eng
Brookdale Community College

Penny Fanzone
Community College of Baltimore County

Valerie Farmer
Community College of Baltimore County

Jean Finley
Asheville-Buncombe Technical Community College

George Fiori
Tri-County Technical College

Deborah Godwin
Lake-Sumter Community College

Cathy Grant-Churchwell
Lane Community College

Diana Green
Weber State University

Joseph Greer
Midlands Technical College

Debra Gross
Ohio State University

Rachelle Hall
Glendale Community College

Dexter Harlee
York Technical College

Marilyn Hibbert
Salt Lake Community College

Judy Irvine
Seneca College

Sherry E. Jacob
Jefferson Community & Technical College

Linda Johnsonius
Murray State University

Rich Klein
Clemson University

Kevin Lee
Guilford Technical Community College

Mohamed Lotfy
Regis University

Carol Martin
Central Pennsylvania Community College

Sue McCrory
Missouri State University

Ken Moak
Tarrant County College

Cecil Morris
American Intercontinental University

Kathleen Morris
University of Alabama

Patrick J. Nedry
Monroe County Community College

Mitchell Ober
Tulsa Community College

Ashlee Pieris
Raritan Valley Community College

Pamela Silvers
Asheville–Buncombe Technical Community College

W. Randy Somsen
Brigham Young University–Idaho

Bonnie Smith
Fresno City College

Randy Smith
Monterey Peninsula College

Nathan Stout
University of Oklahoma

Carl Struck
Suffolk Community College

Song Su
East Los Angeles College

Kathleen Tamerlano
Cuyahoga Community College

Margaret Taylor
College of Southern Nevada

Debby Telfer
Colorado Technical University

David Trimble
Park University

Georgia Vanderark
Stark State College

Philip Vavalides
Guilford Technical Community College

Dennis Walpole
University of South Florida

Michael Walton
Miami Dade College

Paul Weaver
Bossier Parish Community College

Nima Zahadat
Northern Virginia Community College

Debbie Zaidi
Seneca College

Matthew Zullo
Wake Tech Community College

Instructor Walkthrough

Microsoft Office 2013: A Skills Approach

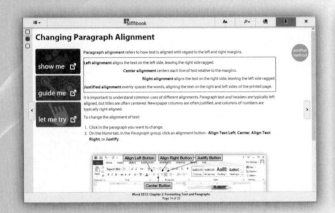

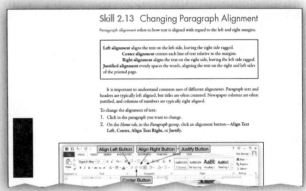

》 **1-1 Content in SIMnet for Office 2013**

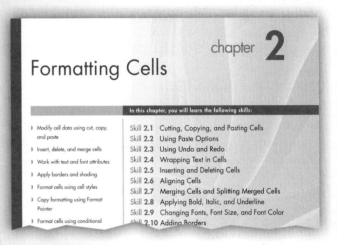

》 **At-a-glance Office 2013 skills**

Quick, easy-to-scan pages, for efficient learning

》 **Introduction—Learning Outcomes are clearly listed.**

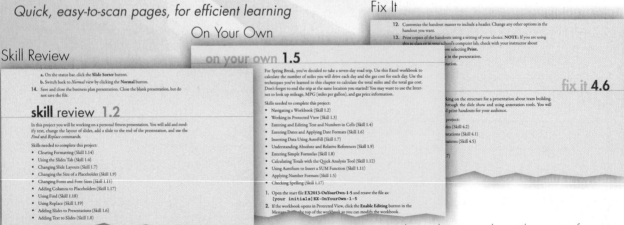

》 **Diverse end-of-chapter projects**

Projects that relate to a broad range of careers and perspectives, from nursing, education, business, and everyday personal uses.

Features

From the Perspective of…

from the perspective of . . .

PROJECT MANAGER

I inherited a database from the person who had my job before me. I am not a database expert, so before I attempted any data entry, I made sure I understood the structure of the database. I used the Relationships window to see how the tables relate to one another. I also switched the Navigation Pane organization to show the tables and related views, so I could see which forms and reports go with which tables. After spending some time exploring the database objects, I felt much more comfortable about using the database. I'm really glad I didn't jump in and start making changes right away.

Tips and Tricks

tips & tricks

Be careful when using the *Undo* and *Redo* commands in Excel. In other Office applications, undo and redo actions are confined to the file you are currently working on—even if you have multiple files open. However, in Excel, the undo–redo list of actions includes all the open workbooks. This means that if you are working on multiple Excel files at the same time, using the *Undo* command can actually undo an action in one of the other open workbooks.

another **method**

» To undo an action, you can also press Ctrl + Z.

» To redo an action, you can also press Ctrl + Y.

Tell Me More

tell me **more**

To group all the sheets in your workbook together, right-click any sheet tab and then click **Select All Sheets**.

To ungroup sheets, right-click one of the grouped sheet tabs and then click **Ungroup**. If all of the sheets in your workbook are grouped together, you must use this method to ungroup them.

let me **try**

Open the student data file **EX4-06-PurchaseOrders** and try this skill on your own:

1. Group sheets *PO June* and *PO July*.
2. Change the text in cell **F3** to: **Quantity Ordered**
3. Ungroup the sheets.

Another Method

another **method**

Use the keyboard shortcuts for the *Cut, Copy,* and *Paste* commands:

» Cut = Ctrl + X

» Copy = Ctrl + C

» Paste = Ctrl + V

Use the command from the right-click menu:

» The *Cut* and *Copy* commands are available from the menu when you select data then right-click.

» To paste, you can right-click within a field and select **Paste**.

let me **try**

If the database is not already open, open the data file **AC1-Appointments** and try this skill on your own:

1. Open the *Customers* table in Datasheet view.

Let Me Try

let me **try**

Open the student data file **EX3-07-Customers** and try this skill on your own:

1. Enter a formula in cell **C5** to display the text from cell **C2** so the first letter in each word is capitalized.
2. Enter a formula in cell **D5** to display the text from cell **D2** so all the letters display in upper case.
3. Enter a formula in cell **E5** to display the text from cell **E2** so all the letters display in lower case.
4. Save the file as directed by your instructor and close it.

» **Instructor materials available on the online learning center, www.mhhe.com/office2013skills**

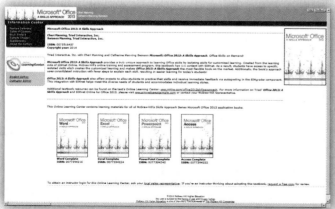

- Instructor Manual
- Instructor PowerPoints
- Test Bank

SIMnet for Office 2013 Online Training & Assessment

❱ Includes:

- Microsoft® Office Suite
- Computer Concepts
- Windows 7
- Internet Explorer 9

EASY TO USE

SIMnet is McGraw-Hill's leading solution for training and assessment of Microsoft Office skills and beyond. Completely online with no downloads for installation (besides requiring Adobe Flash Player), SIMnet is accessible for today's students through multiple browsers and is easy to use for all. Now, SIMnet offers SIMbook and allows students to go mobile for their student learning. Available with videos and interactive "Guide Me" pages to allow students to study MS Office skills on any device. Its consistent, clean user interface and functionality will help save you time and help students be more successful in their course.

LIFELONG LEARNING

SIMnet offers lifelong learning. SIMnet is designed with features to help students immediately learn isolated Microsoft Office skills on demand. Students can use SIMSearch and the Library to learn skills both in and beyond the course.

It's more than a resource; it's a tool they can use throughout their entire time at your institution.

MEASURABLE RESULTS

SIMnet provides powerful, measureable results for you and your students. See results immediately in our various reports and customizable gradebook. Students can also see measurable results by generating a custom training lesson after an exam to help determine exactly which content areas they still need to study. Instructors can use the dashboard to see detailed results of student activity, assignment completion, and more. SIMnet Online is your solution for helping students master today's Microsoft Office Skills.

SIMNET FOR OFFICE 2013

. . . **Keep IT SIMple!** To learn more, visit www.simnetkeepitsimple.com and also contact your McGraw-Hill representative.

Essential Skills for Office 2013

In this chapter, you will learn the following skills:

- Learn about Microsoft Office 2013 and its applications Word, Excel, PowerPoint, and Access
- Demonstrate how to open, save, and close files
- Recognize Office 2013 common features and navigation elements
- Modify account information and the look of Office
- Create new files
- Use Microsoft Help

skills

introduction

This chapter introduces you to Microsoft Office 2013. You will learn about the shared features across the Office 2013 applications and how to navigate common interface elements such as the Ribbon and Quick Access Toolbar. You will learn how to open and close files as well as learn how to work with messages that appear when you first open files. You will become familiar with the Office account and learn how to modify the account as well as the look of Office 2013. Introductory features such as creating and closing files and using Office Help are explained.

Skill 1.1 Introduction to Microsoft Office 2013

Microsoft Office 2013 is a collection of business "productivity" applications (computer programs designed to make you more productive at work, school, and home). The most popular Office applications are:

Microsoft Word—A word processing program. Word processing software allows you to create text-based documents, similar to how you would type a document on a typewriter. However, word processing software offers more powerful formatting and design tools, allowing you to create complex documents, including reports, résumés, brochures, and newsletters.

FIGURE OF 1.1
Microsoft Word 2013

Microsoft Excel—A spreadsheet program. Originally, spreadsheet applications were viewed as electronic versions of an accountant's ledger. Today's spreadsheet applications can do much more than just calculate numbers—they include powerful charting and data analysis features. Spreadsheet programs can be used for everything from personal budgets to calculating loan payments.

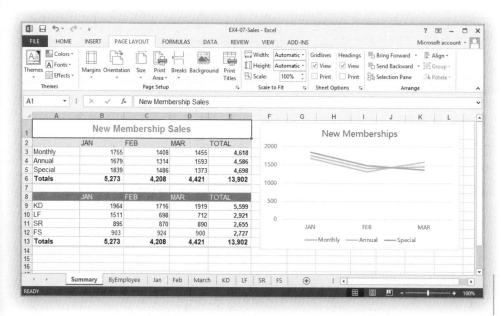

FIGURE OF 1.2
Microsoft Excel 2013

Microsoft PowerPoint—A presentation program. Such applications enable you to create robust, multimedia presentations. A presentation consists of a series of electronic slides. Each slide contains content, including text, images, charts, and other objects. You can add multimedia elements to slides, including animations, audio, and video.

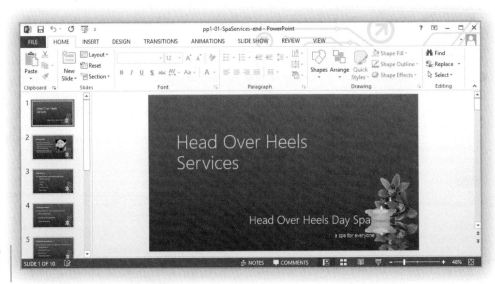

FIGURE OF 1.3
Microsoft PowerPoint 2013

Microsoft Access—A database program. Database applications allow you to organize and manipulate large amounts of data. Databases that allow you to relate tables and databases to one another are referred to as *relational* databases. As a database user, you usually see only one aspect of the database—a *form.* Database forms use a graphical interface to allow a user to enter record data. For example, when you fill out an order form online, you are probably interacting with a database. The information you enter becomes a record in a database *table.* Your order is matched with information in an inventory table (keeping track of which items are in stock) through a *query.* When your order is filled, a database *report* can be generated for use as an invoice or a bill of lading.

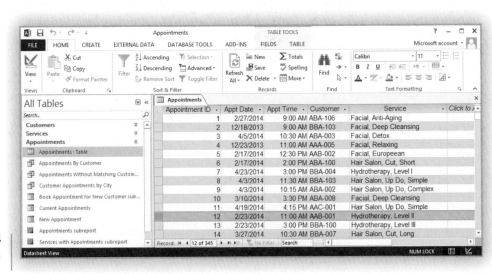

FIGURE OF 1.4
Microsoft Access 2013

To open one of the Office applications using the Windows 8 operating system:

1. Display the **Start screen.**

2. In the *Pinned Apps* section, click the tile of the application you want to open.

To open one of the Office applications using the Windows 7 operating system:

1. Click the Windows **Start** button (located in the lower left corner of your computer screen).

2. Click **All Programs.**

3. Click the **Microsoft Office** folder.

4. Click the application you want to open.

tips & tricks

You can download a free trial version of Microsoft Office from Microsoft's Web site (http://office.microsoft.com). The trial allows you to try the applications before buying them. When your trial period ends, if you haven't purchased the full software license yet, you will no longer be able to use the applications (although you will continue to be able to open and view any files you previously created with the trial version).

tell me **more**

There are two main versions of Microsoft Office, each offering a different way to pay for the program:

Office 365—This version allows you to download and install Office and pay for it on a yearly or monthly subscription basis. It includes full versions of the different Office applications along with online storage services for your files. When the next version of Office is released, the subscription can be transferred to the new version. If you do not want to install the full version of Office on your computer, you can access limited versions of each application online with an Office 365 subscription.

Office 2013—This version allows you to install Office and pay for it once, giving you a perpetual license for the programs. This means that when the next version of Office is released, you will need to purchase the application suite again. You can associate a Windows Live account with Office 2013, giving you access to online storage for your files.

If you are a home user, business, or a student, there are different purchasing options for both Office 365 and Office 2013. Both versions require that you are running the Windows 7 or Windows 8 operating system.

Skill 1.2 Opening Files

Opening a file retrieves it from storage and displays it on your computer screen. The steps for opening a file are the same for Word documents, Excel spreadsheets, PowerPoint presentations, and Access databases.

To open an existing file from your computer:

1. Click the **File** tab to open Backstage view.
2. Click **Open.**
3. The *Open* page displays listing the recently opened files by default.
4. Click **Computer.**
5. A list of folders you have recently opened files from appears on the right. Click a folder to open the **Open** dialog with that folder displayed.

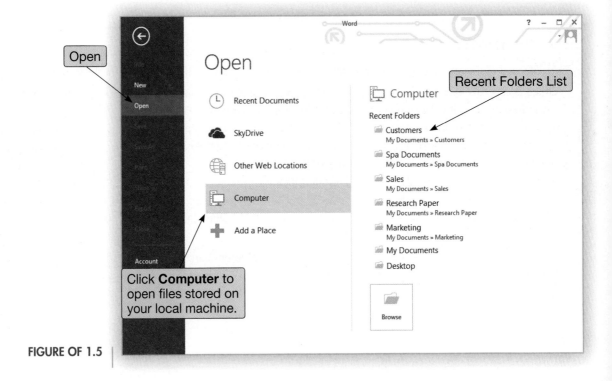

6. Select the file name you want to open in the large list box.
7. Click the **Open** button in the dialog.

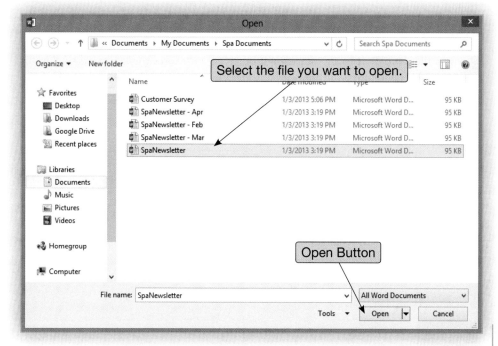

FIGURE OF 1.6

tips & tricks

If you do not see the folder containing the file you want to open, click the **Browse** button. The *Open* dialog will open to your *Documents* folder. Navigate to the location where the file you want to open is located, select the file, and click **Open.**

tell me **more**

The screen shot shown here is from Word 2013 running on the Microsoft Windows 8 operating system. Depending on the operating system you are using, the *Open* dialog will appear somewhat different. However, the basic steps for opening a file are the same regardless of which operating system you are using.

another **method**

To display the *Open* page in Backstage view, you can also press ⌨Ctrl + ⌨O on the keyboard.

To open the file from within the *Open* dialog, you can also:

❯ Press the ⌨←Enter key once you have typed or selected a file name.

❯ Double-click the file name.

let me try

Try this skill on your own:

1. Open the student data file **of1-SpaNewsletter.**
   NOTE: You may see a yellow security message at the top of the window. See the skill *Working in Protected View* to learn more about security warning messages.
2. Keep the file open to work on the next skill.

Skill 1.3 Closing Files

Closing a file removes it from your computer screen and stores the last-saved version for future use. If you have not saved your latest changes, most applications will prevent you from losing work by asking if you want to save the changes you made before closing.

To close a file and save your latest changes:

1. Click the **File** tab to open Backstage view.

2. Click the **Close** button.

3. If you have made no changes since the last time you saved the file, it will close immediately. If changes have been made, the application displays a message box asking if you want to save the changes you made before closing.

Click **Save** to save the changes.

Click **Don't Save** to close the file without saving your latest changes.

Click **Cancel** to keep the file open.

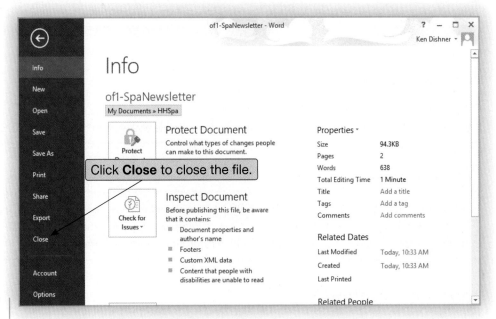

FIGURE OF 1.7

another **method**

To close a file, you can also press (Ctrl) + (W) on the keyboard.

let me **try**

If necessary, open the student data file **of1-SpaNewsletter** and try this skill on your own:
    Close the file.

Skill 1.4 Getting to Know the Office 2013 User Interface

THE RIBBON

If you have used a word processing or spreadsheet program in the past, you may be surprised when you open one of the Microsoft Office 2013 applications for the first time. Beginning with Office 2007, Microsoft redesigned the user experience—replacing the familiar menu bar/toolbar interface with a new Ribbon interface that makes it easier to find application functions and commands.

The **Ribbon** is located across the top of the application window and organizes common features and commands into tabs. Each **tab** organizes commands further into related **groups**.

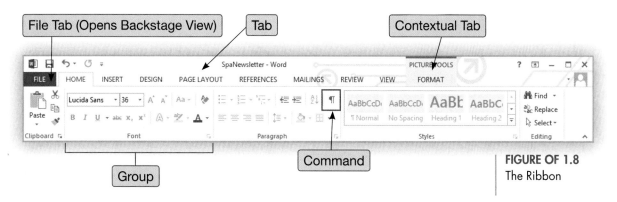

FIGURE OF 1.8
The Ribbon

When a specific type of object is selected (such as a picture, table, or chart), a contextual tab will appear. **Contextual tabs** contain commands specific to the type of object selected and are only visible when the commands might be useful.

Each application includes a **Home tab** that contains the most commonly used commands for that application. For example, in Word, the *Home* tab includes the following groups: *Clipboard, Font, Paragraph, Styles,* and *Editing,* while the Excel *Home* tab includes groups more appropriate for a spreadsheet program: *Clipboard, Font, Alignment, Number, Styles, Cells,* and *Editing.*

tips & tricks

If you need more space for your file, you can minimize the Ribbon by clicking the **Collapse the Ribbon** button in the upper-right corner of the Ribbon (or press (Ctrl) + (F1)). When the Ribbon is minimized, the tab names appear along the top of the window (similar to a menu bar). When you click a tab name, the Ribbon appears. After you select a command or click away from the Ribbon, the Ribbon hides again. To redisplay the Ribbon permanently, click the **Ribbon Display Options** button in the upper-right corner of the window and select **Show Tabs and Commands.** You can also double-click the active tab to hide or display the Ribbon.

BACKSTAGE

Notice that each application also includes a **File tab** at the far left side of the Ribbon. Clicking the *File* tab opens the **Microsoft Office Backstage view,** where you can access the commands for managing and protecting your files, including *Save, Open, Close, New,* and *Print.* Backstage replaces the Office Button menu from Office 2007 and the *File* menu from previous versions of Office.

To return to you file from Backstage view, click the **Back** button located in the upper left corner of the window.

KEYBOARD SHORTCUTS

Many commands available through the Ribbon and Backstage view are also accessible through keyboard shortcuts and shortcut menus.

Keyboard shortcuts are keys or combinations of keys that you press to execute a command. Some keyboard shortcuts refer to F keys or function keys. These are the keys that run across the top of the keyboard. Pressing these keys will execute specific commands. For example, pressing the F1 key will open Help in any of the Microsoft Office applications. Keyboard shortcuts typically use a combination of two keys, although some commands use a combination of three keys and others only one key. When a keyboard shortcut calls for a combination of key presses, such as (Ctrl) + (V) to paste an item from the *Clipboard,* you must first press the modifier key (Ctrl), holding it down while you press the (V) key on the keyboard.

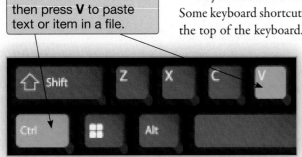

Press and hold **Ctrl** and then press **V** to paste text or item in a file.

FIGURE OF 1.9

tell me **more**

Many of the keyboard shortcuts are universal across all applications—not just Microsoft Office applications. Some examples of universal shortcut keys include:

(Ctrl) + (C) = Copy

(Ctrl) + (X) = Cut

(Ctrl) + (V) = Paste

(Ctrl) + (Z) = Undo

(Ctrl) + (O) = Open

(Ctrl) + (S) = Save

SHORTCUT MENUS

Shortcut menus are menus of commands that display when you right-click an area of the application window. The area or object you right-click determines which menu appears. For example, if you right-click in a paragraph, you will see a shortcut menu of commands for working with text; however, if you right-click an image, you will see a shortcut menu of commands for working with images.

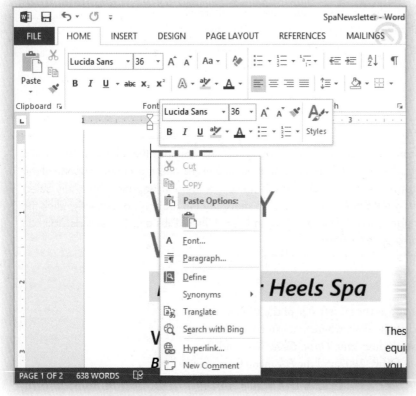

FIGURE OF 1.10
Right-Click Shortcut Menu

THE MINI TOOLBAR

The Mini toolbar gives you access to common tools for working with text. When you select text and then rest your mouse over the text, the Mini toolbar fades in. You can then click a button to change the selected text just as you would on the Ribbon.

another method

To display the Mini toolbar, you can also right-click the text. The Mini toolbar appears above the shortcut menu.

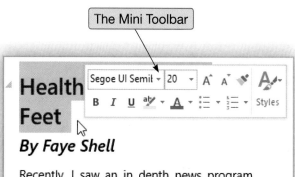

FIGURE OF 1.11

QUICK ACCESS TOOLBAR

The Quick Access Toolbar is located at the top of the application window above the *File* tab. The Quick Access Toolbar, as its name implies, gives you quick one-click access to common commands. You can add commands to and remove commands from the Quick Access Toolbar.

To modify the Quick Access Toolbar:

1. Click the **Customize Quick Access Toolbar** button located on the right side of the Quick Access Toolbar.

2. Options with checkmarks next to them are already displayed on the toolbar. Options with no checkmarks are not currently displayed.

3. Click an option to add it to or remove it from the Quick Access Toolbar.

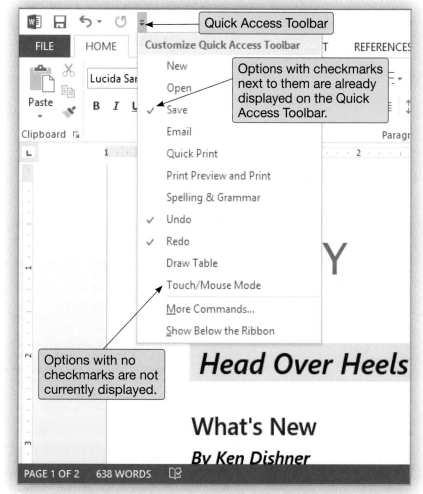

FIGURE OF 1.12

tips & tricks

If you want to be able to print with a single mouse click, add the *Quick Print* button to the Quick Access Toolbar. If you do not need to change any print settings, this is by far the easiest method to print a file because it doesn't require opening Backstage view first.

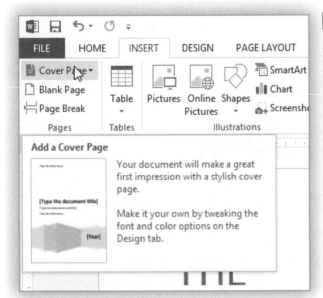

FIGURE OF 1.13
Cover Page
Enhanced ScreenTip

ENHANCED SCREENTIP

A **ScreenTip** is a small information box that displays the name of the command when you rest your mouse over a button on the Ribbon. An **Enhanced ScreenTip** displays not only the name of the command, but also the keyboard shortcut (if there is one) and a short description of what the button does and when it is used. Certain Enhanced ScreenTips also include an image along with a description of the command.

USING LIVE PREVIEW

The **Live Preview** feature in Microsoft Office 2013 allows you to see formatting changes in your file before actually committing to the change. When Live Preview is active, rolling over a command on the Ribbon will temporarily apply the formatting to the currently active text or object. To apply the formatting, click the formatting option.

Use Live Preview to preview the following:

Font Formatting—Including the font, font size, text highlight color, and font color

Paragraph Formatting—Including numbering, bullets, and shading

Quick Styles and Themes

Table Formatting—Including table styles and shading

Picture Formatting—Including correction and color options, picture styles, borders, effects, positioning, brightness, and contrast

SmartArt—Including layouts, styles, and colors

Shape Styles—Including borders, shading, and effects

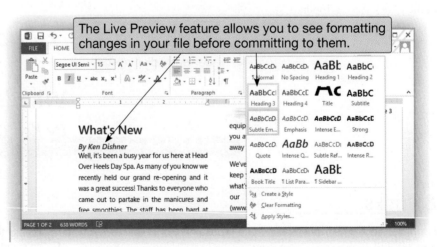

The Live Preview feature allows you to see formatting changes in your file before committing to them.

FIGURE OF 1.14

You can enable and disable some of the user interface features through the *Options* dialog.

1. Click the **File** tab to open Backstage view.

2. Click **Options.**

3. Make the changes you want, and then click **OK** to save your changes.

⟩ Check or uncheck **Show Mini toolbar on selection** to control whether or not the Mini toolbar appears when you hover over selected text. (This does not affect the appearance of the Mini toolbar when you right-click.)

⟩ Check or uncheck **Enable Live Preview** to turn the live preview feature on or off.

⟩ Make a selection from the *ScreenTip style* list:

- **Show feature descriptions in ScreenTips** displays Enhanced ScreenTips when they are available.

- **Don't show feature descriptions in ScreenTips** hides Enhanced ScreenTips. The ScreenTip will still include the keyboard shortcut if there is one available.

- **Don't show ScreenTips** hides ScreenTips altogether, so if you hold your mouse over a button on the Ribbon, nothing will appear.

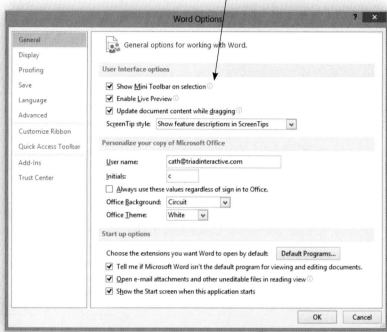

You can enable and disable some of the user interface features through the *Options* dialog.

FIGURE OF 1.15

let me try

Open the student data file **of1-SpaNewsletter** and try this skill on your own:

1. Explore the Ribbon. Click on different tabs and note how commands are arranged together in groups.
2. Click the picture to display the *Picture Tools* contextual tab.
3. Click the **File** tab to display Backstage view. Click the **Back** button to return to the file.
4. Right-click an area of the file to display the shortcut menu.
5. Explore the Mini Toolbar at the top of the shortcut menu. Click away from the menu to hide it.
6. Click the **Customize Quick Access Toolbar** arrow to display the menu of items that can be displayed on the Quick Access Toolbar. Note the ones with checkmarks are the items currently displayed.
7. Click the **Insert** tab. In the *Pages* group, roll your mouse over the **Cover Page** button to display the Enhanced ScreenTip.
8. Click the **File** tab.
9. Click **Options** to open the *Options* dialog.
10. Disable **Live Preview.**
11. Change the ScreenTips so they don't show feature descriptions.
12. Close the file.

Skill 1.5 Using the Start Page

When you launch an Office 2013 application you are first taken to the **Start page**. The *Start* page gives you quick access to recently opened files and templates for creating new files in each of the applications.

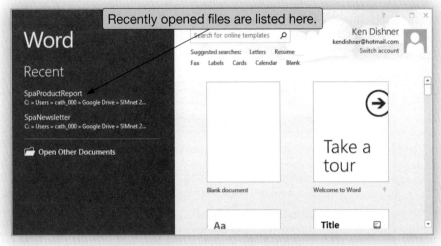

Recently opened files are listed here.

FIGURE OF 1.16

To open a recent file from the *Start* page:

1. Launch the application.
2. The *Start* page displays.
3. Click a file in the left pane to open the file.

tips & tricks

If you do not see the file you want to open in the list of recent files, click **Open Other Documents** at the bottom of the left pane. This will display the *Open* page that includes buttons for finding and opening files from other locations such as your computer or your SkyDrive.

tell me **more**

In previous versions of Office when you launched an application, a blank file opened ready for you to begin working. If you want to start a new blank file, click the blank file template in the list of templates. It is always listed as the first option.

let me **try**

To try this skill on your own:
1. Launch **Microsoft Word.**
2. If you have files listed under *Recent,* click a file to open it.
3. Close the file.

from the perspective of . . .

A BUSY PARENT

Learning Microsoft Office was one of the best things I did to help manage my family's busy lifestyle. I use Word to write up and print a calendar of everyone's activities for the week. I keep a handle on the family finances with a budget of all expenses in an Excel spreadsheet. I've even learned how to use Excel to calculate loan payments and found the best offer when I had to buy a new family car. I used PowerPoint to create a presentation for my family of our summer vacation pictures. Once I became more familiar with Access, I used it to help organize my family's busy schedule. I created a database with one table for activities, another for parent contact information, another one for carpooling, and another one for the schedule. Being able to organize all the information in a database has been invaluable. I always thought Office was only for businesses, but now I can't imagine running my household without it!

Skill 1.6 Changing Account Information

Office 2013 includes an **Account page** that lists information for the user currently logged into Office. This account information comes from the Microsoft account you used when installing Office. From the *Account* page, you can update your user profile, including contact and work information. You can also change the picture associated with the user account.

To change the user information

1. Click the **File** tab.
2. Click **Account.**
3. The current user profile is listed under *User Information.*
4. Click the **Change photo** link.

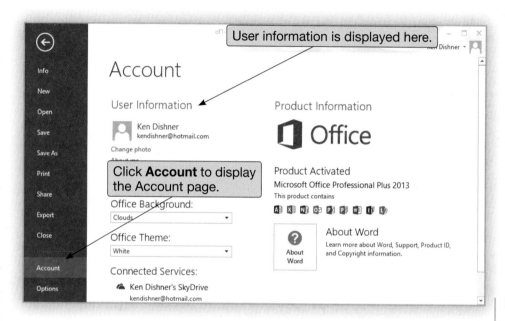

FIGURE OF 1.17

5. The *Profile* page on *live.com* is displayed in the browser window.
6. Click the **Change Picture** link.
7. On the *Picture* page, click the **Browse** button.
8. Navigate to the location of the picture you want to use for you profile and select it.
9. Click the **Open** button.
10. The picture appears on the page. Click the **Save** button to save the profile change.

From the *Profile* page, you can also edit your contact information and work information. Click the **Edit** link under each section to display the edit page. Fill in the form with your information and click the **Save** button.

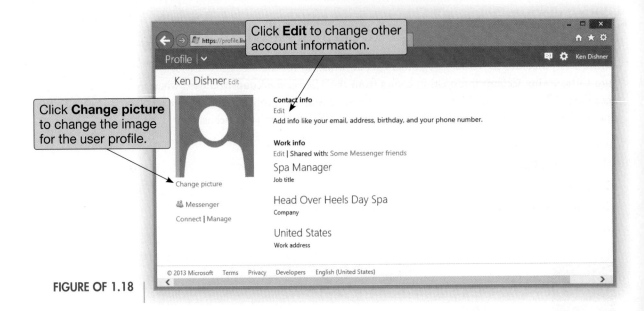

FIGURE OF 1.18

tell me **more**

Depending on the version of Office 2013 you have, you can have multiple accounts use the same installation of Office. When you switch accounts, any personalization that person has done to Office will be applied. The account will also have access to that person's SkyDrive account and all files that have been saved there. To learn more about SkyDrive, see the skill *Saving Files to a SkyDrive*.

another **method**

To change the user photo, you can also click the arrow next to the user name in the upper right corner of the window and click the **Change photo** link.

let me **try**

Open the student data file **of1-SpaNewsletter** and try this skill on your own:

1. Open the **Account** page in Backstage view.
   NOTE: If you are using this in class or in your school's computer lab, check with your instructor about permissions before completing the following steps.
2. Change the photo for the user account.
3. Change the picture using a photo of your choice.
4. Save the changes to the picture.
5. Close the browser window.
6. Keep this file open for working on the next skill.

Skill 1.7 Changing the Look of Office

In addition to managing the Office account, you can also control the look of Office from the *Account* page. Changing the Office background changes the background image that displays in the upper right corner of the window near the user profile. Changing the Office theme changes the color scheme for Office, affecting the look of the Ribbon and dialogs.

To change the look of Office:

1. Click the **File** tab to open Backstage view.
2. Click **Account.**
3. Click the **Office Background** drop-down list and select an option to display as the background.
4. Click the **Office Theme** drop-down list and select a color option for your applications.

FIGURE OF 1.19

let me try

If necessary, open the student data file **of1-SpaNewsletter** and try this skill on your own:

1. Open the **Account** page in Backstage view.
   NOTE: If you are using this in class or in your school's computer lab, check with your instructor about permissions before completing the following steps.
2. Change the Office background to the **Circuit** background.
3. Change the Office color to **Light Gray.**
4. Close the file.

Skill 1.8 Working in Protected View

When you download a file from a location that Office considers potentially unsafe, it opens automatically in **Protected View**. Protected View provides a read-only format that protects your computer from becoming infected by a virus or other malware. Potentially unsafe locations include the Internet, e-mail messages, or a network location. Files that are opened in Protected View display a warning in the Message Bar at the top of the window, below the Ribbon.

To disable Protected View, click the **Enable Editing** button in the Message Bar.

Click **Enable Editing** to begin working on the file.

FIGURE OF 1.20

tips & tricks

To learn more about the security settings in Office 2013, open the Trust Center and review the options. We do not recommend changing any of the default Trust Center settings.

another method

You can also enable editing from the Info page in Backstage.
1. Click the **File** tab to open Backstage.
2. Click **Info.**
3. The Info page provides more information about the file. If you are sure you want to remove it from Protected View, click the **Enable Editing** button.

let me try

Open the student data file **of1-SpaNewsletter** and try this skill on your own:
1. If you downloaded the file from the Internet, the file will open in Protected View.
2. Click the **Enable Editing** button to begin working with the file.
3. Close the file.

Skill 1.9 Picking Up Where You Left Off

When you are working in a long document or a presentation and reopen it to work on it, you may not remember where you were last working. Office 2013 includes a new feature that automatically bookmarks the last location that was worked on when the file was closed.

To pick up where you left off in a document or presentation:

1. Open the document or presentation.
2. A message displays on the right side of the screen welcoming you back and asking if you want to pick up where you left off. The message then minimizes to a bookmark tag.
3. Click the **bookmark tag** to navigate to the location.

FIGURE OF 1.21

tips & tricks

The bookmark tag only displays until you navigate to another part of the document. If you scroll the document, the bookmark tag disappears.

tell me **more**

This feature is only available in Word and PowerPoint. Excel and Access do not give you the option of picking up where you left off when you open a file.

let me try

Open the student data file **of1-09-SpaNewsletter** and try this skill on your own:
1. Navigate to the location where the last location the file was at when last closed.
2. Close the file.

Skill 1.10 Creating a New Blank File

When you first open an Office application, the *Start* page displays giving you the opportunity to open an existing file or create a new blank file or one based on a template. But what if you have a file open and want to create another new file? Will you need to close the application and then launch it again? The New command allows you to create new files without exiting and reopening the program.

To create a new blank file:

1. Click the **File** tab to open Backstage view.
2. Click **New.**
3. The first option on the *New* page is a blank file. Click the **Blank document** thumbnail to create the new blank file.

FIGURE OF 1.22

tell me **more**

In addition to a blank file, you can create new files from templates from the *New* page.

another **method**

To bypass the Backstage view and create a new blank file, press Ctrl + N on the keyboard.

let me try

Open the student data file **of1-SpaNewsletter** and try this skill on your own:
1. Create a new blank file.
2. Close the file but do not save it.

Skill 1.11 Using Help

If you don't know how to perform a task, you can look it up in the **Office Help** system. Each application comes with its own Help system with topics specifically tailored for working with that application.

To look up a topic using the Microsoft Office Help system:

1. Click the **Microsoft Office Help** button. It is located at the far right of the Ribbon.

2. Click in the *Search online help* box and type a word or phrase describing the topic you want help with.

3. Click the **Search** button.

4. A list of results appears.

5. Click a result to display the help topic.

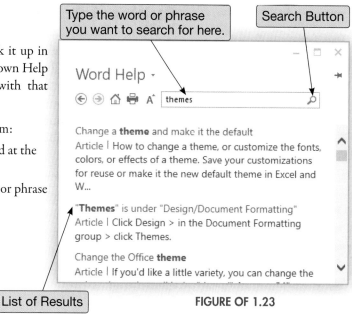

Type the word or phrase you want to search for here.

Search Button

List of Results

FIGURE OF 1.23

Help Button

FIGURE OF 1.24

tips & tricks

To search for topics in Microsoft Office Help, you must have an active Internet connection. If you are working offline (not connected to *Office.com*), Help is still available, but it is limited to information about finding buttons of the Ribbon.

tell me **more**

The Help toolbar is located at the top of the Help window. This toolbar includes buttons for navigating between screens, changing the size of text, and returning to the *Help Home* page. Click the **printer icon** on the toolbar to print the current topic. Click the **pushpin icon** to keep the Help window always on top of the Microsoft Office application.

another **method**

To open the Help window, you can also press (F1) on the keyboard.

let me **try**

Open the student data file **of1-SpaNewsletter** and try this skill on your own:

1. Click the **Microsoft Office Help** button.
2. Search for topics about **themes.**
3. Click a link of your choice.
4. Close the **Help** window.
5. Keep this file open for working on the next skill.

Skill 1.12 Working with File Properties

File Properties provide information about a file such as the location of the file, the size of file, when the file was created and when it was last modified, the title, and the author. Properties also include keywords, referred to as **tags**, that are useful for grouping common files together or for searching. All this information about a file is referred to as **metadata**.

To view a file's properties, click the **File** tab to open Backstage view. Properties are listed at the far right of the *Info* tab. To add keywords to a file, click the text box next to *Tags* and type keywords that describe the file, separating each word with a comma. The Author property is added automatically using the account name entered when you installed and registered Office. You can change the author name or add more names by editing the Author property.

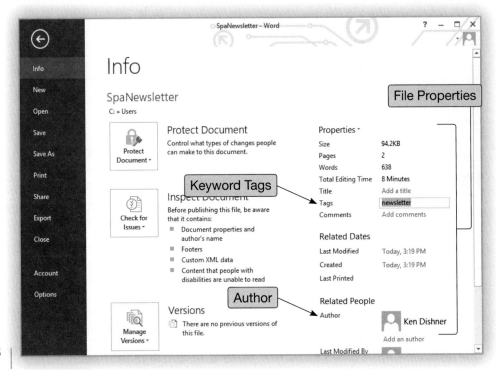

FIGURE OF 1.25

tips & tricks

Some file properties are generated automatically by Windows and cannot be edited by the user, such as the date the file was created and the size of the file.

let me try

If necessary, open the student data file **of1-SpaNewsletter** and try this skill on your own:
1. Add a tag to the document that reads **newsletter.**
2. Keep this file open for working on the next skill.

Skill 1.13 Saving Files to a Local Drive

As you work on a new file, it is displayed on-screen and stored in your computer's memory. However, it is not permanently stored until you save it as a file to a specific location. The first time you save a file, the *Save As* page in Backstage view will display. Here you can choose to save the file to your SkyDrive, your local computer, or another location.

To save a file to a local drive:

1. Click the **Save** button on the Quick Access Toolbar.
2. The *Save As* page in Backstage view appears.
3. On the left side of the page, click **Computer** to save the file to a local drive.
4. Word displays a list of recent folders; select a folder where you want to save the file.

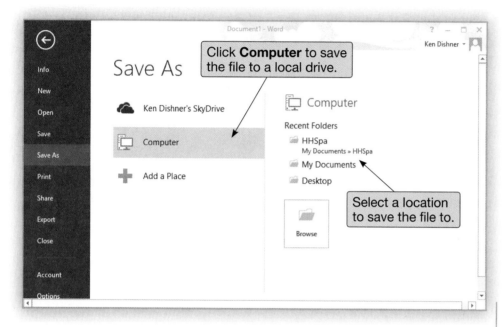

FIGURE OF 1.26

5. The *Save As* dialog opens.
6. If you want to create a new folder, click the **New Folder** button near the top of the file list. The new folder is created with the temporary name *New Folder*. Type the new name for the folder and press **Enter.**
7. Click in the **File name** box and type a file name.
8. Click the **Save** button.

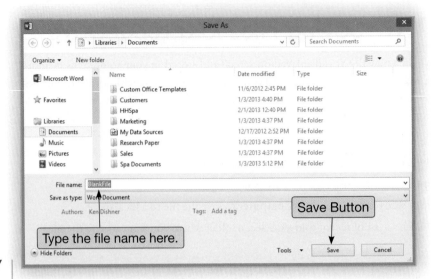

FIGURE OF 1.27

The next time you save this file, it will be saved with the same file name and to the same location automatically.

As you are working with files, be sure to **save often!** Although Office 2013 includes a recovery function, it is not foolproof. If you lose power or your computer crashes, you may lose all the work done on the file since the last save.

tips & tricks

If the location where you want to save the file is not listed under *Recent Folders,* click the **Browse** button to open the *Save As* dialog. Navigate to the location where you want to save the file.

another method

To save a file, you can also:
- Press Ctrl + S on the keyboard.
- Click the **File** tab, and then select **Save.**
- Click the **File** tab, and then select **Save As.**

let me try

Try this skill on your own:
1. Create a new blank file.
2. Save the file to the **My Documents** folder on your computer. Name the file **BlankFile.**
3. Close the file.

Skill 1.14 Saving Files to a SkyDrive

SkyDrive is Microsoft's free cloud storage where you can save documents, workbooks, presentations, videos, pictures, and other files and access those files from any computer or share the files with others. When you save files to your SkyDrive, they are stored locally on your computer and then "synched" with your SkyDrive account and stored in the "cloud" where you can then access the files from another computer or device that has SkyDrive capability.

To save a file to your SkyDrive:

1. Click the **File** tab.
2. Click **Save As.**
3. Verify the SkyDrive account is selected on the left side of the page.
4. Under *Recent Folders,* click the **SkyDrive** account you want to save to.
5. The *Save As* dialog opens to your SkyDrive folder location on your computer.
6. Click in the **File name** box and type a file name.
7. Click the **Save** button.

FIGURE OF 1.28

tips & tricks

By default, your SkyDrive includes folders for documents, pictures, and files you want to make public. You can save your files in any of these folders or create your own. To create a new folder in your SkyDrive, click the **New Folder** button near the top of the file list. The new folder is created with the temporary name *New Folder*. Type the new name for the folder and press ⏎ Enter.

tell me **more**

When you are working on an Excel or Word file that has been saved to your SkyDrive, others can work on the file at the same time you are working the file. The application will mark the area being worked on as read only so others cannot modify the same information you are working on. However, if you are sharing a PowerPoint presentation, only one user at a time can work on the presentation.

let me try

If necessary, open the student data file **of1-SpaNewsletter** and try this skill on your own:

1. Save the file to the **Documents** folder on your SkyDrive. **NOTE:** If you are using this in class or in your school's computer lab, check with your instructor before completing this step.
2. Keep this file open for working on the next skill.

Skill 1.15 Saving Files with a New Name

When working on files you may want to save a file but not overwrite the original file you opened. In this case, you should save the file with a new name. When you save a file with a new name, the original file still exists in its last saved state and the new file you save will include all the changes you made.

To save a file with a new name:

1. Click the **File** tab.

2. Click **Save As.**

3. Select a location to save the file, either your SkyDrive or your local drive.

4. In the *Save As* dialog, click in the **File name** box, type a new name for the file, and click **Save.**

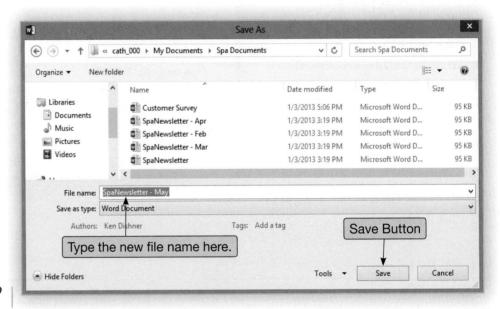

FIGURE OF 1.29

tell me **more**

Beginning with Office 2007, Microsoft changed the file format for Office files. If you want to share your files with people who are using Office 2003 or older, you should save the files in a different file format.

1. In the *Save As* dialog, click the arrow at the end of the *Save as type* box to expand the list of available file types.

2. To ensure compatibility with older versions of Office, select the file type that includes 97-2003 (for example, Word 97-2003 Document or Excel 97-2003 Workbook).

let me **try**

If necessary, open the student data file **of1-SpaNewsletter** and try this skill on your own:

1. Save the file to the **Documents** folder on your computer with the name **SpaNewsletter.**

2. Keep this file open for working on the next skill.

Skill 1.16 Closing the Application

When you close a file, the application stays open so you can open another file to edit or begin a new file. Often, when you are finished working on a file, you want to close the file and exit the application at the same time. In this case, you will want to close the application.

To close an application:

1. Click the **Close** button in the upper-right corner of the application.
2. If you have made no changes since the last time you saved the file, it will close immediately. If changes have been made, the application displays a message box asking if you want to save the changes you made before closing.
   Click **Save** to save the changes.
   Click **Don't Save** to close the file without saving your latest changes.
   Click **Cancel** to keep the file open.

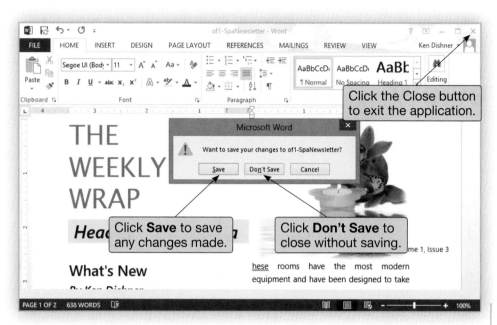

FIGURE OF 1.30

another **method**

To close the application, you can also:

❱ Right-click the title bar and select **Close.**

❱ Click the application icon in the upper-left corner of the application and select **Close.**

let me **try**

If necessary, open the student data file **of1-SpaNewsletter** and try this skill on your own:

Close the application.

key terms

Microsoft Word
Microsoft Excel
Microsoft PowerPoint
Microsoft Access
Ribbon
Tab
Groups
Contextual tabs
Home tab
File tab
Backstage
Keyboard shortcuts
Shortcut menus
Mini toolbar

Quick Access Toolbar
ScreenTip
Enhanced ScreenTip
Live Preview
Start page
Account page
Protected View
New command
Office Help
File Properties
Tags
Metadata
SkyDrive

concepts review

1. Microsoft _____ is a spreadsheet program.
   a. Word
   b. Excel
   c. Access
   d. PowerPoint

2. Click the _____ tab to display Backstage view.
   a. File
   b. Home
   c. View
   d. Contextual

3. To display a shortcut menu _____ an area of the file.
   a. left-click
   b. right-click
   c. double-click
   d. None of the above

4. If you have downloaded a file from the Internet and it opens in Protected View, you should never open the file.
   a. True
   b. False

5. The _____ is located across the top of the application window and organizes common features and commands into tabs.
   a. menu bar
   b. toolbar
   c. title bar
   d. Ribbon

6. The _____ provide(s) information about a file such as the location of the file, the size of file, when the file was created and when it was last modified, the title, and the author.

   a. file properties

   b. user profile

   c. account information

   d. Options dialog

7. When you save files to your SkyDrive, they are available to access from other computers that have SkyDrive capability. If you are working on an Excel or Word file, others can be working on the same file at the same time you are working on the file.

   a. True

   b. False

8. You can change user information from the _____ page in Backstage view.

   a. Account

   b. Options

   c. Share

   d. Info

9. To paste an item from the *Clipboard,* use the keyboard shortcut _____.

   a. Ctrl + C

   b. Ctrl + X

   c. Ctrl + V

   d. Ctrl + P

10. The _____ gives you quick one-click access to common commands and is located at the top of the application window above the *File* tab.

   a. Ribbon

   b. Quick Access Toolbar

   c. Options dialog

   d. Backstage view

word 2013

Getting Started with Word 2013

In this chapter, you will learn the following skills:

❭ Enter, select, and delete text

❭ Use the spelling and grammar features

❭ Use Undo and Redo

❭ Find and replace text in a document

❭ Cut, copy, and paste text

❭ Apply different paste options

❭ Use the Clipboard

❭ Change how the document displays in the window

❭ View Document Statistics

skills

introduction

This introductory chapter will teach students some of the basic editing features of Microsoft Word 2013, such as entering, selecting, and deleting text. Students will also learn how to correct spelling and grammar errors; find and replace text; and use the cut, copy, and paste commands. In addition, students will learn how to look up document statistics and to change the magnification of a document by using the *Zoom* feature.

Skill 1.1 Introduction to Word 2013

Microsoft Office Word 2013 is a word processing program that enables you to create many types of documents including letters, résumés, reports, proposals, Web pages, blogs, and more. Word's advanced editing capabilities allow you to quickly and easily perform tasks such as checking your spelling and finding text in a long document.

Robust formatting allows you to produce professional documents with stylized fonts, layouts, and graphics. Building Blocks and Quick Styles allow you to insert complex desktop publishing elements into your document. Printing and file management can be managed directly from the Word window. In short, everything you need to create polished professional and personal documents is available in Microsoft Word.

You can create a wide variety of documents with Microsoft Office Word 2013.

FIGURE WD 1.1

Here are some basic elements of a Word document:

Font—also called the typeface, refers to a set of characters of a certain design. You can choose from several preinstalled fonts available.

Paragraph—groups of sentences separated by a hard return. A hard return refers to pressing the (←Enter) key to create a new paragraph. You can assign a paragraph its own style to help it stand out from the rest of the document.

Styles—complex formatting, including font, color, size, and spacing, that can be applied to text. Use consistent styles for headings, body text, notes, and captions throughout your document. Styles also can be applied to tables and graphics.

Tables—used to organize data into columns and rows.

Graphics—photographs, clip art, SmartArt, or line drawings that can be added to documents.

tips & tricks

Microsoft Office 2013 includes many other features that can further enhance your documents. If you would like to learn more about these features, click the **Help** icon ? in the upper-right corner of the Word window or visit Microsoft Office online through your Web browser.

tell me **more**

Some basic features of a word processing application include:

❯ *Word Wrap*—places text on the next line when the right margin of the page has been reached.

❯ *Find and Replace*—searches for any word or phrase in the document. Also, allows all instances of a word to be replaced by another word.

❯ *Spelling and Grammar*—checks for errors in spelling and grammar and offers solutions to the problem.

❯ *Document Formatting*—allows the enhancement of the appearance of the document.

Skill 1.2 Entering and Deleting Text

The basic function of a word processing application like Microsoft Word is to create written documents. Whether the documents are simple, such as a letter, or complex, such as a newsletter, one of the basic tasks you will perform in Word is entering text. **Word wrap** is a feature in Microsoft Word that automatically places text on the next line when the right margin of the document has been reached. There is no need to press `← Enter` to begin a new line in the same paragraph. Only press `← Enter` when you want to create a break and start a new paragraph.

To enter text in a document:

1. Place the cursor where you want the new text to appear.

2. Begin typing.

3. When the cursor reaches the end of the line, do not press `← Enter`. Keep typing and allow word wrap to move the text to the next line.

If you make a mistake when entering text, you can press the `← Backspace` key to remove text to the left of the cursor, or press the `Delete` key to remove text to the right of the cursor.

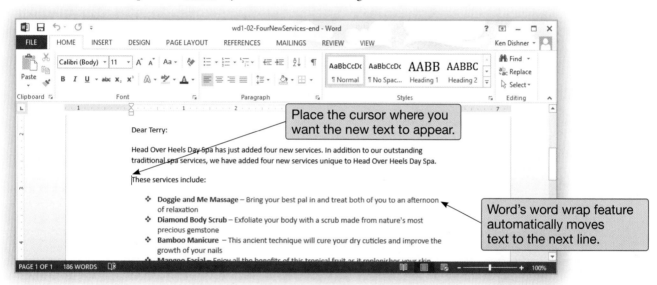

FIGURE WD 1.2

tips & tricks

If you want to edit text you have typed, click in the text to place the cursor anywhere in the document. When you begin typing, the new text will be entered at the cursor point, pushing out any existing text to the right. You can also use the arrow keys to move the cursor around in the document and then begin typing.

tell me **more**

The cursor indicates the place on the page where text will appear when you begin typing. There are a number of cursors that display, but the default text cursor is a blinking vertical line.

let me **try**

Open the student data file **wd1-02-FourNewServices** and try this skill on your own:

1. Place your cursor at the end of the first paragraph and type the following text: `In addition to our outstanding traditional spa services, we have added four new services unique to Head Over Heels Day Spa.`

2. Save the file as directed by your instructor and close it.

Skill 1.3 Selecting Text

When you select text in a document, a shaded background appears behind the selected text. You can then apply commands to the text as a group, such as changing the font or applying the bold effect.

There are several methods for selecting text in a document:

❯ Click and drag the cursor across the text.

❯ To select a single word: double-click the word.

❯ To select a paragraph: triple-click a word in the paragraph you want to select.

❯ To select a line of text: point to the left margin next to the line you want to select. When the cursor changes to an arrow, click once to select the line of text.

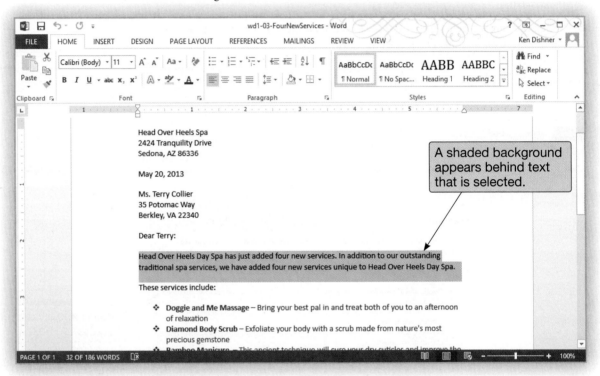

FIGURE WD 1.3

tips & tricks

To select all the text in the document, you can press Ctrl + A on the keyboard or triple-click the left margin of the document.

another method

To select a paragraph of text, you can also double-click in the left margin next to the paragraph you want to select.

let me try

Open the student data file **wd1-03-FourNewServices** and try this skill on your own:

1. Select the word **Sedona**.
2. Select the line **2424 Tranquility Drive**.
3. Select the **first paragraph of text**.
4. Close the file.

Skill 1.4 Checking Spelling and Grammar as You Type

Microsoft Word can automatically check your document for spelling and grammar errors while you type. Misspelled words, words that are not part of Word's dictionary, are indicated by a wavy red underline. Grammatical errors are similarly underlined in blue and are based on the grammatical rules that are part of Word's grammar checking feature. When you right-click either type of error, a shortcut menu appears with suggestions for correcting the error and other options.

To correct a misspelled word underlined in red:

1. Right-click the misspelled word.
2. Choose a suggested correction from the shortcut menu.

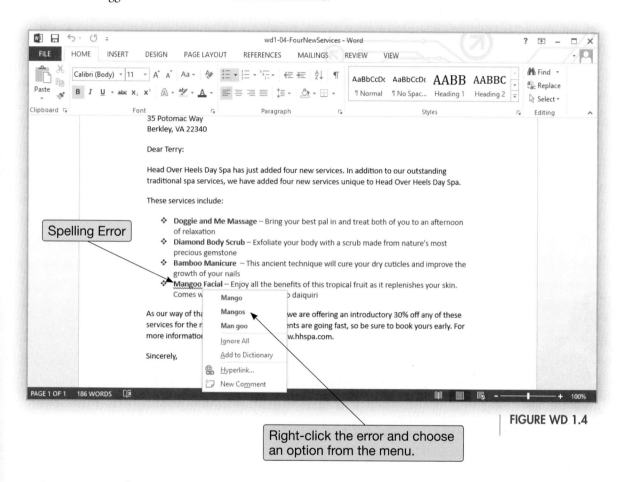

FIGURE WD 1.4

Right-click the error and choose an option from the menu.

tips & tricks

Although checking spelling and grammar as you type is a useful tool when creating documents, there are times when you may find it distracting. You can choose to turn off checking spelling errors or grammar errors as you type. To turn the *Check Spelling as you type* and *Check Grammar as you type* features on and off:

1. Click the **File** tab.
2. Click the **Options** button.
3. In the *Word Options* dialog, click the **Proofing** button.
4. In the *When correcting spelling and grammar in Word* section, deselect the **Check spelling as you type** option for **Spelling Error** or the **Mark grammar errors as you type** option for grammatical errors.

tell me **more**

Word will not suggest spelling corrections if its dictionary does not contain a word with similar spelling, and Word will not always be able to display grammatical suggestions. In these cases, you must edit the error manually. If the word is spelled correctly, you can choose the **Add to Dictionary** command on the shortcut menu. When you add a word to the dictionary, it will no longer be marked as a spelling error.

let me **try**

Open the student data file **wd1-04-FourNewServices** and try this skill on your own:

1. Using the right-click method, replace the misspelled word **mangoo** with the correction **mango.**
2. Save the file as directed by your instructor and close it.

from the perspective of . . .

ADMINISTRATIVE ASSISTANT

It seems like every time I write up a memo or a letter, I use all the basic Word skills I learned when I first started using Word. Shortcuts like triple-clicking to select a paragraph of text and cutting and pasting to move text around in a document are tricks I use over and over every day. My boss has terrible eyesight, so every time I get a document in from him I have to take the zoom on the document down from 180% to 100% before I send it out. And trust me, I don't know where I would be without Word's Spelling and Grammar check, but no matter what, I always give my documents another read before sending them out to clients.

Skill 1.5 Checking Spelling

Regardless of the amount of work you put into a document, a spelling error or typo can make the entire document appear sloppy and unprofessional. All the Office applications include a built-in spelling checker. In Word, the *Spelling & Grammar* command analyzes your entire document for spelling errors. Spelling errors are presented in the *Spelling* task pane, enabling you to make decisions about how to handle each error or type of error in turn.

To check a file for spelling errors:

1. Click the **Review** tab. In the *Proofing* group, click the **Spelling & Grammar** button.

2. The first spelling error appears in the *Spelling* task pane.

3. Review the spelling suggestions and then select an action:

   - Click **Ignore** to make no changes to this instance of the word.

   - Click **Ignore All** to make no changes to all instances of the word.

   - Click **Add** to make no changes to this instance of the word and add it to the main dictionary, so future uses of this word will not show up as misspellings. When you add a word to the main dictionary, it is available for all of the Office applications.

   - Click the correct spelling in the list of suggestions, and click **Change** to correct just this instance of the misspelling in your document.

   - Click the correct spelling in the list of suggestions, and click **Change All** to correct all instances of the misspelling in your document.

4. After you select an action, the spelling checker automatically advances to the next suspected spelling error.

5. When the spelling checker finds no more errors, it displays a message telling you the check is complete. Click **OK** to close the dialog and return to your file.

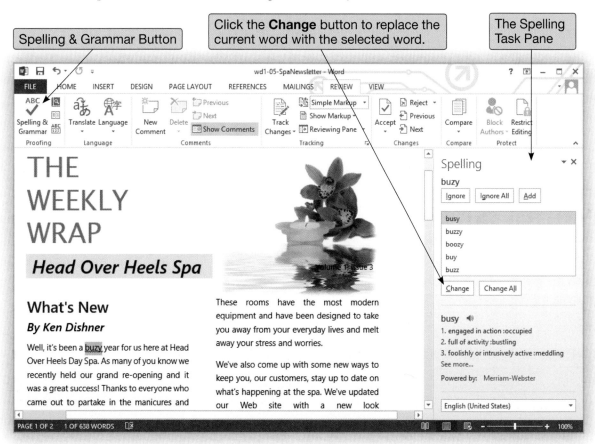

FIGURE WD 1.5

tips & tricks

❭ Whether or not you use the Spelling tool, you should always proofread your files. Spelling checkers are not infallible, especially if you misuse a word, yet spell it correctly—for instance, writing "bored" instead of "board."

❭ If you have repeated the same word in a sentence, Word will flag the second instance of the word as a possible error. In the *Spelling* task pane, the *Change* button will switch to a *Delete* button. Click the **Delete** button to remove the duplicate word.

tell me **more**

When you select an option in the list of suggestions, Word displays a list of words that have the same meaning as the selected word along with an audio file of the pronunciation of the word.

another **method**

To open the *Spelling* task pane, you can also press the (F7) key.

let me **try**

Open the student data file **wd1-05-SpaNewsletter** and try this skill on your own:

1. Open the **Spelling** task pane.
2. Change the word **buzy** to the suggestion **busy**.
3. Save the file as directed by your instructor and close it.

Skill 1.6 Using Undo and Redo

If you make a mistake when working, the Undo command allows you to reverse the last action you performed. The Redo command allows you to reverse the *Undo* command and restore the file to its previous state. The Quick Access Toolbar gives you immediate access to both commands.

To undo the last action taken, click the **Undo** button on the Quick Access Toolbar.
To redo the last action taken, click the **Redo** button on the Quick Access Toolbar.

To undo multiple actions at the same time:

1. Click the arrow next to the *Undo* button to expand the list of your most recent actions.
2. Click an action in the list.
3. The action you click will be undone, along with all the actions completed after that. In other words your document will revert to the state it was in before that action.

Click the **Undo** button to undo the last action taken.

Click the **Redo** button to redo the last action taken.

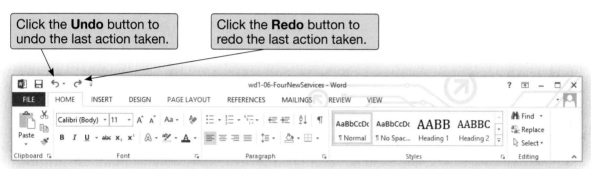

FIGURE WD 1.6

another **method**

To undo an action, you can also press (Ctrl) + (Z) on the keyboard.
To redo an action, you can also press (Ctrl) + (Y) on the keyboard.

let me **try**

Open the student data file **wd1-06-FourNewServices** and try this skill on your own:

1. In the first paragraph, select the word **unique**. Press the **Delete** key to delete the word.
2. Click the **Undo** button to restore the word to the document.
3. Click the **Redo** button to remove the word again.
4. Save the file as directed by your instructor and close it.

Skill 1.7 Finding Text

The **Find** command allows you to search a document for a word or phrase. In past versions of Microsoft Word, searching for text was performed through the *Find and Replace* dialog. In Word 2010, Microsoft introduced the *Navigation* task pane as the default method for searching for text in a document. When you search for a word or phrase in a document using the *Navigation* task pane, Word highlights all instances of the word or phrase in the document and displays each instance as a separate result in the pane.

To find a word or phrase in a document:

1. On the *Home* tab, in the *Editing* group, click the **Find** button.
2. The *Navigation* task pane appears.
3. Type the word or phrase you want to find in the *Search Document* box at the top of the task pane.
4. As you type, Word automatically highlights all instances of the word or phrase in the document and displays any results in the task pane.
5. Click a result to navigate to that instance of the word or phrase in the document.

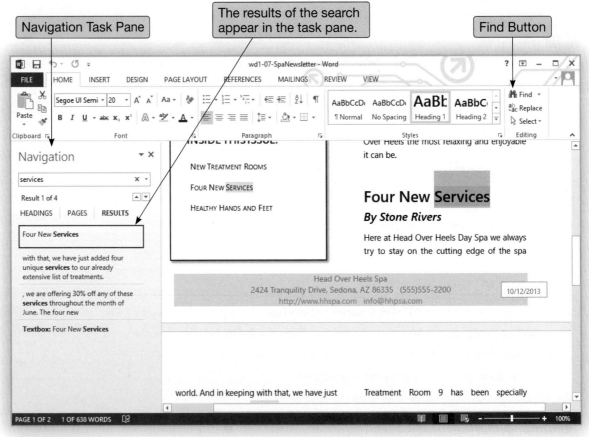

FIGURE WD 1.7

tips & tricks

If you are more comfortable using the *Find and Replace* dialog, you can still use it to search for text in your document. To open the *Find and Replace* dialog, start on the *Home* tab. In the *Editing* group, click the **Find** button arrow and select **Advanced Find...** The *Find and Replace* dialog opens with the *Find* tab displayed. Use the dialog to search for text just as you would in previous versions of Word.

tell me **more**

❭ The magnifying glass in the *Search Document* box gives you access to more search options. You can choose to only search specific elements in your document, such as tables, graphics, footnotes, or comments.

❭ Clicking the **X** next to a search word or phrase will clear the search, allowing you to perform a new search.

another **method**

To display the *Navigation* task pane with the *Results* section displayed, you can also:

❭ Click the **Find** button and select **Find** on the menu.

❭ Press (Ctrl) + (F) on the keyboard.

let me **try**

Open the student data file **wd1-07-SpaNewsletter** and try this skill on your own:

1. Open the **Navigation** task pane with the *Results* section displayed.
2. Search the document for instances of the word **services**.
3. Close the file.

Skill 1.8 Replacing Text

The **Replace** command in Word allows you to locate specific instances of text in your document and replace them with different text. With the *Replace* command, you can replace words or phrases one instance at a time or all at once throughout the document.

To replace instances of a word in a document:

1. On the *Home* tab, in the *Editing* group, click the **Replace** button.
2. Type the word or phrase you want to change in the *Find what* box.
3. Type the new text you want in the *Replace with* box.
4. Click **Replace** to replace just that one instance of the text.
5. Click **Replace All** to replace all instances of the word or phrase.
6. Word displays a message telling you how many replacements it made. Click **OK** in the message that appears.
7. To close the *Find and Replace* dialog, click the **Cancel** button.

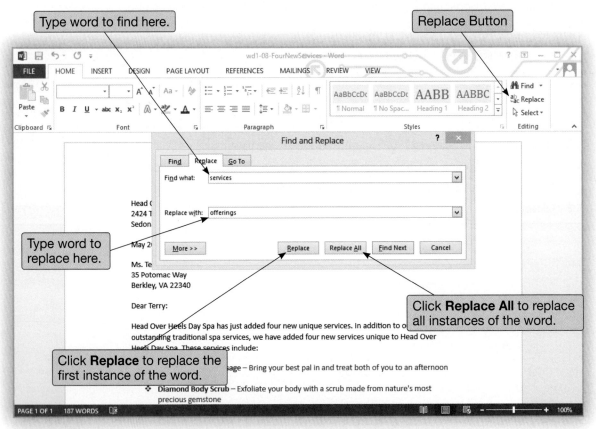

FIGURE WD 1.8

tips & tricks

In addition to text, the *Replace* command can also operate on formatting characters such as italicized text and paragraph marks. The *More >>* button in the *Find and Replace* dialog displays additional options, including buttons that allow you to select formatting and other special characters in the document.

tell me **more**

The *Go To* tab in the *Find and Replace* dialog allows you to quickly jump to any page, line, section, comment, or other object in your document.

another **method**

To open the *Find and Replace* dialog with the *Replace* tab displayed, you can also press (Ctrl) + (H) on the keyboard.

let me **try**

Open the student data file **wd1-08-FourNewServices** and try this skill on your own:

1. Open the **Find and Replace** dialog with the *Replace* tab displayed.
2. Replace all instances of **services** with **offerings**.
3. There will be 5 replacements. Click **OK** to close the message box.
4. Save the file as directed by your instructor and close it.

Skill 1.9 Using Copy and Paste

The **Copy** command places a duplicate of the selected text or object on the *Clipboard* but does not remove it from your document. You can then use the **Paste** command to insert the text or object into the same document, another document, or another Microsoft Office file, such as an Excel workbook or a PowerPoint presentation.

To copy text and paste it into the same document:

1. Select the text to be copied.
2. On the *Home* tab, in the *Clipboard* group, click the **Copy** button.
3. Place the cursor where you want to insert the text from the *Clipboard*.
4. On the *Home* tab, in the *Clipboard* group, click the **Paste** button.

These same steps apply whether you are copying and pasting text, pictures, shapes, video files, or any type of object in a Word file.

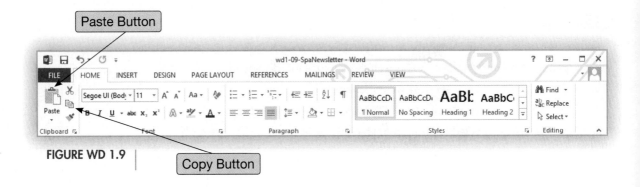

FIGURE WD 1.9

another **method**

To apply the *Copy* or *Paste* command, you can also use the following shortcuts:

Copy = Press Ctrl + C on the keyboard, or right-click and select **Copy**.

Paste = Press Ctrl + V on the keyboard, or right-click and select **Paste**.

let me **try**

Open the student data file **wd1-09-SpaNewsletter** and try this skill on your own:

1. In the first sentence of the first paragraph, select the text **Head Over Heels Day Spa** and copy it to the *Clipboard*.
2. Place the cursor before the word **staff** in the same paragraph. Paste the copied text. Be sure to check for the proper spacing between words.
3. Save the file as directed by your instructor and close it.

Skill 1.10 Using Cut and Paste

The *Copy* command is great if you want to duplicate content in your document, but what if you want to move content from one place to another? The **Cut** command is used to move text and other objects within a file and from one file to another. Text, or an object that is cut, is removed from the file and placed on the **Clipboard** for later use. You can then use the *Paste* command to insert the text or object into the same document, another document, or another Microsoft Office file.

To cut text and paste it into the same document:

1. Select the text to be cut.

2. On the *Home* tab, in the *Clipboard* group, click the **Cut** button.

3. Place the cursor where you want to insert the text from the *Clipboard*.

4. On the *Home* tab, in the *Clipboard* group, click the **Paste** button.

Paste Button   Cut Button

FIGURE WD 1.10

another method

To apply the *Cut* or *Paste* command, you can also use the following shortcuts:

▶ *Cut* = Press Ctrl + X on the keyboard, or right-click and select **Cut**.

▶ *Paste* = Press Ctrl + V on the keyboard, or right-click and select **Paste**.

let me try

Open the student data file **wd1-10-SpaNewsletter** and try this skill on your own:

1. In the *What's New* article, cut the sentence **And have you seen our new treatment rooms?** Be sure to include the space after the question mark.

2. Later in the same paragraph, place the cursor before the sentence that begins with **We added another four rooms**.

3. Paste the cut sentence.

4. Save the file as directed by your instructor and close it.

Skill 1.11 Using Paste Options

When you cut or copy an item, whether it be a piece of text, a chart, or an image, Word gives you a variety of ways to paste the item into your document. The *Paste* button has two parts—the top part of the button pastes the topmost contents of the *Clipboard* into the current file. If you click the bottom part of the button (the *Paste* button arrow), you can control how the item is pasted.

Each type of object has different **paste options**. For example, if you are pasting text, you may have options to keep the source formatting, merge the formatting of the source and the current document, or paste only the text without any formatting. Move your mouse over the icon for each paste option to see a preview of how the paste would look, and then click the **icon** for the paste option you want.

To paste text using paste options:

1. Place your cursor where you want to paste the text.
2. On the *Home* tab, in the *Clipboard* group, click the **Paste button arrow**.
3. Roll your mouse over each of the paste options to see how the text will appear when pasted.
4. Click an option to paste the text.

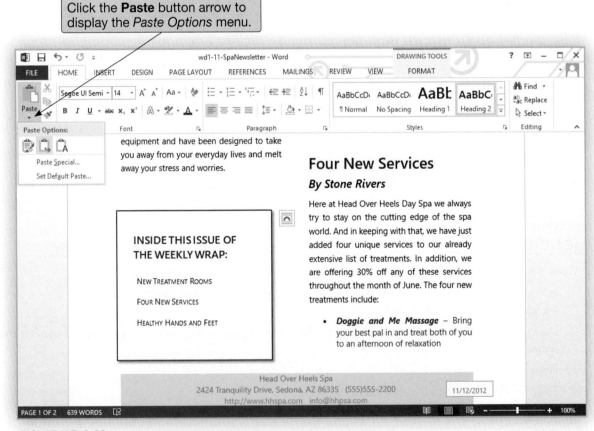

Click the **Paste** button arrow to display the *Paste Options* menu.

FIGURE WD 1.11

tips & tricks

When you paste text using the **Paste** button, Word pastes the text using the source formatting.

tell me **more**

There are three paste options for pasting text:

▶ *Source Formatting*—pastes the text and any formatting that was applied to the copied text.

▶ *Merge Formatting*—pastes the text to match the formatting of the surrounding text.

▶ *Keep Text Only*—pastes the text without any formatting that was applied to the copied text.

another **method**

To paste text using paste options, you can also right-click and select an option under *Paste Options* on the menu.

let me **try**

Open the student data file **wd1-11-SpaNewsletter** and try this skill on your own:

1. Select the newsletter title **THE WEEKLY WRAP**, and copy the text to the *Clipboard*.
2. Place the cursor before the colon in the *Inside this Issue of* text box.
3. Paste the text using the **Merge Formatting** paste command.
4. Save the file as directed by your instructor and close it.

Skill 1.12 Using the Clipboard

When you cut or copy items, they are placed on the *Clipboard*. The icons in the *Clipboard* identify the type of document from which each item originated (Word, Excel, Paint, etc.). A short description or thumbnail of the item appears next to the icon, so you know which item you are pasting into your document. The *Clipboard* can store up to 24 items for use in the current document or any other Office application.

To paste an item from the *Clipboard* into a document:

1. Place your cursor where you want to paste the item.
2. On the *Home* tab, in the *Clipboard* group, click the **Clipboard** dialog launcher.
3. The *Clipboard* task pane appears.
4. To paste an item from the *Clipboard* into your document, click the item you want to paste.

Click the dialog launcher to open the *Clipboard* task pane.

Copied items appear in the *Clipboard*, with the most recent at the top of the list.

FIGURE WD 1.12

tips & tricks

The *Clipboard* is common across all Office applications—so you can cut text from a Word document and then paste that text into an Excel spreadsheet or copy a chart from Excel into a PowerPoint presentation.

tell me **more**

❯ To remove an item from the *Clipboard*, point to the item, click the arrow that appears, and select **Delete**.

❯ To add all the items in the *Clipboard* at once, click the **Paste All** button at the top of the task pane.

❯ To remove all the items from the *Clipboard* at once, click the **Clear All** button at the top of the task pane.

another **method**

To paste an item, you can also point to the item in the *Clipboard* task pane, click the arrow that appears, and select **Paste**.

let me **try**

Open the student data file **wd1-12-SpaNewsletter** and try this skill on your own:

1. Display the **Clipboard**.

2. In the first sentence of the *What's New* article, select the text **Head Over Heels Day Spa** and copy it to the *Clipboard*.

3. Click the picture of the flower at the top of the document to select it. Click the **Copy** button to copy it to the *Clipboard*.

4. Place the cursor before the word **staff** in the first paragraph of the *What's New* article. Paste the copied text from the *Clipboard*.

5. Save the file as directed by your instructor and close it.

Skill 1.13 Zooming a Document

When you first open a document, you may find that the text is too small to read, or that you cannot see the full layout of a page. Use the zoom slider in the lower-right corner of the window to zoom in and out of a document, changing the size of text and images on-screen. Zooming a document only affects how the document appears on-screen. It does not affect how the document will print.

To zoom in on a document, making the text and graphics appear larger:

❱ Click and drag the **zoom slider** to the right.

❱ Click the **Zoom In** button (the button with the plus sign on it) on the slider.

To zoom out of a document, making the text and graphics appear smaller:

❱ Click and drag the **zoom slider** to the left.

❱ Click the **Zoom Out** button (the button with the minus sign on it) on the slider.

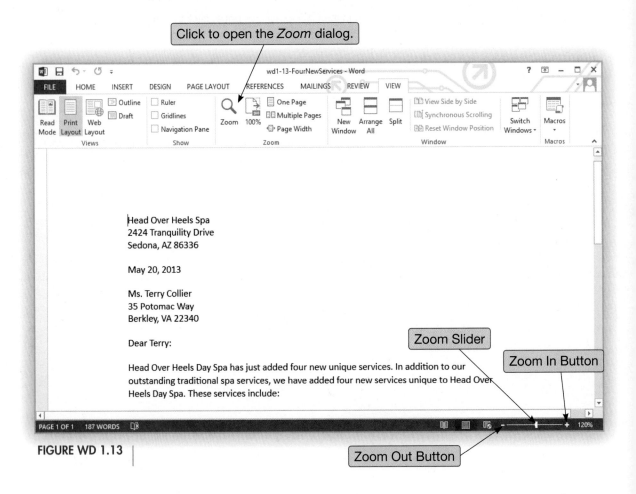

FIGURE WD 1.13

tips & tricks

As you move the slider, the zoom level displays the percentage the document has been zoomed in or out. When zooming a document, 100% is the default zoom level. If you change the zoom percentage and then save and close the document, the next time you open the document, it will display at the last viewed zoom percentage. If you work on a large monitor at a high resolution and need to display your document at a higher zoom percentage, it is a good idea to return the document back to 100% before sending it out to others.

tell me **more**

You can use the *Zoom* dialog to apply a number of display presets:

❯ *Page width*—changes the zoom so the width of the page including margins fills the screen.

❯ *Text width*—changes the zoom so the width of the page not including margins fills the screen.

❯ *Whole page*—changes the zoom so the entire page, both vertically and horizontally, displays on the screen. This is a helpful view when working with a page's layout.

❯ *Many pages*—changes the zoom to display anywhere from one to six pages on the screen at once.

another **method**

You also can change the zoom level through the *Zoom* dialog. To open the *Zoom* dialog:

1. Click the **zoom level number** next to the zoom slider OR click the **View** tab. In the *Zoom* group, click the **Zoom** button.
2. Click a **zoom preset** or type the **zoom percentage** in the *Percent* box.
3. Click **OK**.

let me **try**

Open the student data file **wd1-13-FourNewServices** and try this skill on your own:

1. Change the zoom level of the document to 90%.
2. Change the zoom level of the document back to 100%.
3. Close the file.

Skill 1.14 Using Word Count

Have you ever had to write a 250-word essay or submit a 3,000-word article? You don't need to guess if your Word document is long enough (or too long). Word's **Word Count** feature provides the current statistics of the document you are working on, including the number of pages, number of words, number of characters (with and without spaces), number of paragraphs, and number of lines.

To view document statistics:

1. From the *Review* tab, in the *Proofing* group, click the **Word Count** button.
2. The *Word Count* dialog opens and displays the statistics for the document.
3. By default, the document statistics include the text in text boxes, footnotes, and endnotes. To exclude text in these areas, click the **Include textboxes, footnotes, and endnotes** check box to remove the checkmark.
4. Click **Close** to close the dialog.

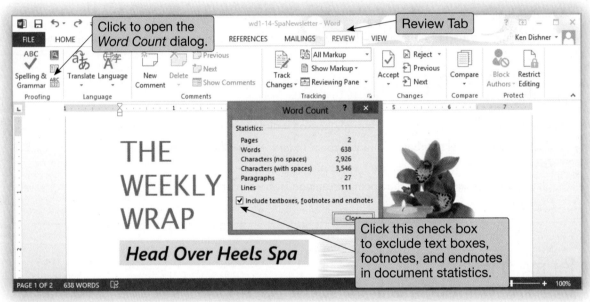

FIGURE WD 1.14

tips & tricks

The number of words and the number of pages in the document are also displayed as part of the document properties available from the *Info* tab in Backstage view. They are also displayed on the status bar at the bottom of the Word window.

another method

To open the *Word Count* dialog, you can also click **Words** on the status bar at the bottom of the Word window.

let me try

Open the student data file **wd1-14-SpaNewsletter** and try this skill on your own:

1. Open the **Word Count** dialog.
2. Note the number of words in the newsletter along with other document statistics.
3. Close the **Word Count** dialog.
4. Close the file.

word 2013   chapter 1 Getting Started with Word 2013

Font
Paragraph
Styles
Tables
Graphics
Word wrap
Undo
Redo
Find

Replace
Copy
Paste
Cut
Clipboard
Paste options
Icon
Zoom slider
Word Count

concepts review

1. To select a paragraph of text, you can _____.

   a. single-click the paragraph

   b. double-click the paragraph

   c. triple-click the paragraph

   d. click in the left margin next to the paragraph

2. Grammatical errors in a document are represented by a _____.

   a. red wavy underline

   b. blue wavy underline

   c. green wavy underline

   d. purple wavy underline

3. The feature in Word that automatically places text on the next line when the right margin of the document has been reached is called _____.

   a. styles

   b. zoom slider

   c. word wrap

   d. status bar

4. To copy text to the Clipboard and remove it from the document, you would use the _____ command.

   a. Copy

   b. Cut

   c. Undo

   d. Redo

5. To paste text with the original formatting of the copied text, you would use the _____ paste option.

   a. Keep Source Formatting

   b. Merge Formatting

   c. Keep Text Only

   d. None of these

6. To replace all instances of a word with another word, you would use the _____ command.

    a. Find

    b. Replace

    c. Replace All

    d. Paste All

7. The primary method for finding text in a document is to use the _____.

    a. Find and Replace dialog

    b. Navigation pane

    c. Clipboard pane

    d. Go To dialog

8. To change one instance of a misspelled word, click the _____ in the *Spelling* task pane.

    a. Add button

    b. Change button

    c. Change All button

    d. Spelling button

9. To magnify the text on-screen, making the text appear larger, you would use the _____.

    a. Zoom Out button

    b. Zoom In button

    c. Page Width command

    d. 100% command

10. In addition to the number of words in a document, the Word Count dialog also displays _____.

    a. the number of tables

    b. the number of charts

    c. the number of pages

    d. the number of images

In this project you will be editing the text of a brochure for Suarez Marketing.

Skills needed to complete this project:

- Zooming a Document (Skill 1.13)
- Entering and Deleting Text (Skill 1.2)
- Selecting Text (Skill 1.3)
- Checking Spelling and Grammar as You Type (Skill 1.4)
- Using Cut and Paste (Skill 1.10)
- Using Word Count (Skill 1.14)

1. Open the **WD2013-SkillReview-1-1** document.

2. Save this document as: **[your initials]WD-SkillReview-1-1**

3. Change how the document is displayed on your computer by clicking the **zoom slider** and dragging it to the 90% magnification.

4. Add text to the document.

   a. Place the cursor on the empty line following the phone number.

   b. Type the following heading: `Mission Statement`

   c. Press **Enter**.

   d. Type the following text: `I am dedicated to listening to your needs and providing you with prompt and excellent service to exceed your expectations.`

5. Select and delete text from the document.

   a. In the paragraph under the *Experience* heading, select the text **hard earned** by clicking and dragging the mouse across the words. Be sure to include the space after the word *earned*.

   b. Press the **Delete** key to remove the text.

6. Check spelling and grammar as you type. Notice how words that Word does not recognize are underlined in red and potential grammar errors are underlined in blue.

   a. Right-click the word **markats** in the *Why I Do What I Do* section. A list of suggested changes is shown.

   b. Click **markets**. Word corrects the spelling of this word.

   c. Right-click the word **communication** in the *Why I Do What I Do* section.

   d. Click **Communication**.

7. Cut and paste text from one part of the document to another.

   a. Select the text **"Putting your needs first"** at the end of the document.

   b. On the *Home* tab, in the *Clipboard* group, click the **Cut** button to remove the text and copy it to the *Clipboard*.

   c. Navigate back to the top of the first page and place the cursor on the empty line before the phone number.

   d. On the *Home* tab, in the *Clipboard* group, click the **Paste** button to paste the text. If an empty line is pasted in with the text, delete the empty line.

8. View the statistics for the document.

   a. Click the **Review** tab.

   b. In the *Proofing* group, click the **Word Count** button.

   c. Review the number of pages, words, and paragraphs in the document. Click the **Close** button to close the *Word Count* dialog.

9. Save and close the document.

skill review 1.2

In this project you will be editing an employment offer from Modern Dynamics International.

Skills needed to complete this project:

- Finding Text (Skill 1.7)
- Replacing Text (Skill 1.8)
- Checking Spelling (Skill 1.5)
- Using Copy and Paste (Skill 1.9)
- Using Paste Options (Skill 1.11)
- Using Undo and Redo (Skill 1.6)

1. Open the **WD2013-SkillReview-1-2** document.

2. Save this document as: **[your initials]WD-SkillReview-1-2**

3. Use the *Navigation* pane to find a word in the document.

   a. On the *Home* tab, in the *Editing* group, click the **Find** button. The *Navigation* pane is displayed on the right side of the Word window. *Ctrl + F* also will open the *Find* feature in the *Navigation* pane.

   b. In the *Search Document* box type: `Vision`

   c. Press **Enter**. Only one occurrence is found.

   d. In the document, select the entire line by clicking to the left of the lettered item outside of the left margin. The entire line will be selected.

   e. Press **Delete** to delete this line.

   f. Click the **X** in the upper-right corner of the *Navigation* pane to close it.

4. Use the **Find and Replace** feature to replace **MoDyInt** with **Modern Dynamics International**.

   a. Press **Ctrl + Home** to move to the top of the document.

   b. On the *Home* tab, in the *Editing* group, click the **Replace** button. The *Find and Replace* dialog will open. *Ctrl + H* also will open the *Find and Replace* dialog.

   c. In the *Find what* box type: `MoDyInt`

   d. In the *Replace with* box type: `Modern Dynamics International`

   e. Click the **Replace** button. The first occurrence of this word is selected in the document.

   f. Click **Replace** to replace **MoDyInt** with **Modern Dynamics International**. The next occurrence will be selected.

   g. Click **Replace All** to replace all occurrences in the document.

   h. Click **OK** to finish the find and replace process.

   i. Click **Close** to close the *Find and Replace* dialog.

5. Spell check the entire document.

   a. Press **Ctrl** + **Home** to move to the top of the document.

   b. Click the **Review** tab.

   c. Click the **Spelling & Grammar** button in the *Proofing* group. The *Spelling* task pane will open.

   d. For the first error, fix the misspelling to read **historically**.

   e. For the second error, ignore the error and do not change the spelling of the last name *Lumita*.

   f. Click **OK** when finished.

6. Copy and paste text.

   a. Triple-click in the last paragraph of the letter to select it. The paragraph begins with *We are excited about you joining.*

   b. On the *Home* tab, in the *Clipboard* group, click the **Copy** button.

   c. Navigate to the beginning of the document and place the cursor at the beginning of the first paragraph. The paragraph begins with *I am pleased to formally extend to you.*

   d. On the *Home* tab, in the *Clipboard* group, click the **Paste** button arrow and select **Keep Text Only** to paste the paragraph without formatting.

7. Click the **Undo** button on the *Quick Access Toolbar* to undo the previous command.

8. Save and close the document.

challenge yourself 1.3

In this project you will be editing the *Notice of Privacy Practices* document from Courtyard Medical Plaza.

Skills needed to complete this project:

- Zooming a Document (Skill 1.13)
- Entering and Deleting Text (Skill 1.2)
- Selecting Text (Skill 1.3)
- Using Cut and Paste (Skill 1.10)
- Replacing Text (Skill 1.8)
- Checking Spelling (Skill 1.5)

1. Open the **WD2013-ChallengeYourself-1-3** document.

2. Save this document as: **[your initials]WD-Challenge-1-3**

3. Change the zoom level to view the document at 120% magnification.

4. Enter and delete text in the document.

   a. On the fourth line on the first page, select **Courtyard Medical Plaza** and delete this entire line.

   b. Click in front of *Notice of Privacy Practices* on the first line of the document, and type Courtyard Medical Plaza and press **Enter**.

   c. Click at the end of the first numbered item on the first page.

   d. Press **Enter**.

   e. Type the following text: tell you about your rights and our legal duties with respect to your protected health information, and

f. If Word automatically capitalized *tell,* change it back to lowercase.

g. Click at the end of the second bulleted item.

h. Replace the period with a semicolon, space once, and type and

i. Press **Enter** and type the following text: `Information about your relationship with Courtyard Medical Plaza such as medical services received, claims history, and information from your benefits plan sponsor or employer about group health coverage you may have.`

5. Cut and paste text in the document.

   a. Select the paragraph in all caps that starts *THIS NOTICE DESCRIBES*

   b. Cut the paragraph and paste it above the heading *Notice of Privacy Practices.*

6. Use Find and Replace.

   a. Use *Find and Replace* to replace **protected health information** with **PHI**. Ignore any occurrences of this information in headings (all caps bolded text). Click **Find Next** to skip an occurrence.

   b. Use *Find and Replace* to replace all instances of **Privacy and Compliance Office** with **Office of Privacy & Compliance**.

   c. Use the *Find* feature to find the word **utilization**.

7. Check the spelling and grammar on the entire document.

   a. Ignore the section heading text that is marked as a potential grammatical error (e.g., *Your*).

   b. Ignore all proper nouns.

   c. Ignore the lowercase letters at the beginning of the numbered list.

8. Save and close the document.

challenge yourself 1.4

In this project you will be editing a personal training program document from American River Cycling Club.

Skills needed to complete this project:

- Zooming a Document (Skill 1.13)
- Entering and Deleting Text (Skill 1.2)
- Selecting Text (Skill 1.3)
- Checking Spelling and Grammar as You Type (Skill 1.4)
- Replacing Text (Skill 1.8)
- Using Copy and Paste (Skill 1.9)
- Using Paste Options (Skill 1.11)
- Using Undo and Redo (Skill 1.6)
- Checking Spelling (Skill 1.5)
- Using Word Count (Skill 1.14)

1. Open the **WD2013-ChallengeYourself-1-4** document.

2. Save this document as: **[your initials]WD-Challenge-1-4**

3. Change the zoom level to view the document at 120%.

4. In the *Training Intensity and Heart Rate* section, select and delete the **second paragraph**.

5. Use the right-click method to fix the **grammar error** in the **second bulleted item** in the *General Guidelines* section.

6. Replace all occurrences of **heartrate** (one word) with **heart rate** (two words).

7. Copy the heading **General Guidelines** to the *Clipboard*.

8. Paste the text at the end of the *More about Long Rides* heading. Use the **Keep Text Only** paste option.

9. Use the **Undo** command to remove the pasted text.

10. Check the spelling and grammar on the entire document. Ignore the word *criterium*.

11. Use the *Word Count* dialog to review the number of words, paragraphs, and pages in the document.

12. Save and close the document.

on your own 1.5

In this project you will be editing the online learning plan for Fairlawn Community College.

Skills needed to complete this project:

- Zooming a Document (Skill 1.13)
- Replacing Text (Skill 1.8)
- Entering and Deleting Text (Skill 1.2)
- Selecting Text (Skill 1.3)
- Finding Text (Skill 1.7)
- Using Copy and Paste (Skill 1.9)
- Using the Clipboard (Skill 1.12)
- Using Undo and Redo (Skill 1.6)
- Checking Spelling (Skill 1.5)
- Using Word Count (Skill 1.14)

1. Open the **WD2013-OnYourOwn-1-5** document.

2. Save this document as: **[your initials]WD-OnYourOwn-1-5**

3. Change the zoom level to your preference.

4. Replace occurrences of **online learning** with **OL**. Make sure you look at the context of the sentence to make sure the replacement is appropriate. Do not make this replacement in headings.

5. In the *Planning Process* section, select and delete the last paragraph and the four bulleted items beneath it.

6. Locate **learning management system** in the body of the document and put the acronym in parentheses after these words. Use proper spacing.

7. In the *PURPOSE OF THIS PLAN* section, type the following as the first sentence in the paragraph: The Online Learning Task Force was formed in February 2005 to develop an Online Learning Strategic Plan for Fairlawn Community College.

8. Copy several pieces of text to the *Clipboard*. Paste a text piece into the document and then undo the action.

9. The current success rate for online courses is 72 %. Find and make this change.

10. Check the spelling and grammar on the entire document and make appropriate changes.

11. Check the number of words and pages in the document.

12. Save and close the document.

fix it 1.6

In this project you will be editing a disclosure letter from Placer Hills Real Estate.

Skills needed to complete this project:

- Zooming a Document (Skill 1.13)
- Entering and Deleting Text (Skill 1.2)
- Selecting Text (Skill 1.3)
- Replacing Text (Skill 1.8)
- Using Cut and Paste (Skill 1.10)
- Checking Spelling and Grammar as You Type (Skill 1.4)
- Checking Spelling (Skill 1.5)
- Using Word Count (Skill 1.14)

1. Open the **WD2013-FixIt-1-6** document.

2. Save this document as: `[your initials]WD-FixIt-1-6`

3. Change the zoom level to your preference.

4. Change the inside address of this block format business letter to:

   ```
   David and Sharon Wing
   4685 Orange Grove Rocklin,
   CA 97725
   ```

5. Make the necessary change to the salutation of the letter.

6. Find and replace all occurrences of **release** with **disclosure**.

7. Add the following sentence as the first sentence in the last body paragraph.
   ```
   Please complete the enclosed disclosure statement by
   March 1, 2014 and return it to me.
   ```

8. Whenever a letter refers to an attached or enclosed document, it is proper to include an Enclosure notation below the reference initials. Cut the word **Enclosure** and paste it in the proper place.

9. Proofread the document carefully and make any necessary spelling and grammar changes.

10. Check the number of words in the document.

11. Save and close the document.

chapter 2

Formatting Text and Paragraphs

In this chapter, you will learn the following skills:

❱ Apply fonts and style to text

❱ Copy and paste formatting using the Format Painter

❱ Use bulleted and numbered lists to organize information

❱ Use Quick Styles and text effects to format text

❱ Change paragraph alignment and spacing to effectively use white space

❱ Set and use tabs and indents to improve document layout

skills

introduction

This chapter will cover character and paragraph formatting and alignment to enhance the presentation, professionalism, and readability of documents. Students will apply fonts and styles, incorporate lists, use Quick Styles, change paragraph alignment and spacing, and use tabs and indents.

Skill 2.1 Using Bold, Italic, and Underline

You can call attention to text in your document by using the **bold,** *italic,* or <u>underline</u> effects. These effects are called character effects because they are applied to individual characters or words rather than paragraphs. Remember that these effects are used to emphasize important text and should be used sparingly—they lose their effect if overused.

You can apply these effects using similar steps:

1. Select the text you want to emphasize.
2. On the *Home* tab, in the *Font* group, click the button of the effect you want to apply:

   B **Bold**—gives the text a heavier, thicker appearance.

   I **Italic**—makes text slant to the right.

   <u>U</u> ▾ Underline—draws a single line under the text.

Some of the other character effects available from the Ribbon include:

   a̶b̶c̶ **Strikethrough**—draws a horizontal line through the text.

   x₂ **Subscript**—draws a small character below the bottom of the text.

   x² **Superscript**—draws a small character above the top of the text.

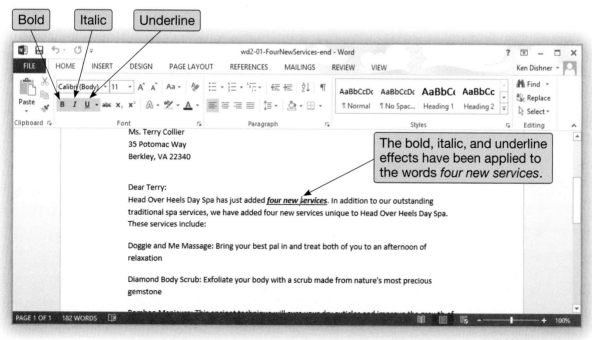

FIGURE WD 2.1

tips & tricks

The *Font* dialog contains other character formatting options not available from the Ribbon. These effects include **Shadow** and **Outline** among others. To open the *Font* dialog, on the *Home* tab, in the *Font* group, click the dialog launcher. Select an option in the *Effects* section and click **OK** to apply the character effect to the text.

tell me **more**

When text is bolded, italicized, or underlined, the button appears highlighted on the Ribbon. To remove the effect, click the highlighted button, or press the appropriate keyboard shortcut.

another **method**

❯ The following keyboard shortcuts can be used to apply the bold, italic, and underline effects:
  - Bold = Ctrl + B
  - Italic = Ctrl + I
  - Underline = Ctrl + U

❯ To access the bold, italic, or underline commands, you can also right-click the selected text and click the **Bold** or **Italic** button on the Mini toolbar.

❯ To apply an underline style, click the **Underline** button arrow and select a style.

let me **try**

Open the student data file **wd2-01-FourNewServices** and try this skill on your own:

1. Select the text **four new services** in the first paragraph.

2. Apply the **Bold, Italic,** and **Underline** character formatting to the text.

3. Save the file as directed by your instructor and close it.

Skill 2.2 Changing Fonts

A **font**, or typeface, refers to a set of characters of a certain design. The font is the shape of a character or number as it appears on-screen or in a printed document.

To change the font:

1. Select the text to be changed.

2. On the *Home* tab, click the arrow next to the *Font* box.

3. As you roll over the list of fonts, the Live Preview feature in Word changes the look of the text in your document, giving you a preview of how the text will look with the new font applied.

4. Click a font name from the menu to apply it to the text.

Word offers many fonts. **Serif fonts**, such as Cambria and Times New Roman, have an embellishment at the end of each stroke. **Sans serif fonts**, such as Calibri and Arial, do not have an embellishment at the end of each stroke. Sans serif fonts are easier to read on-screen and should be used for the main body text for documents that will be delivered and read electronically, such as a blog. Serif fonts are easier to read on the printed page and should be used for documents that will be printed, such as a report.

> Cambria is a serif font. Calibri is a sans serif font.

FIGURE WD 2.2

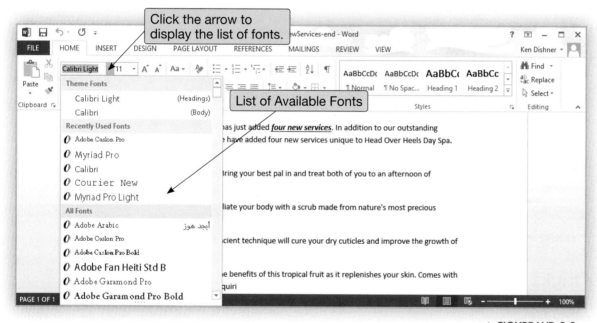

FIGURE WD 2.3

tips & tricks

If you want to change the font of an individual word, you can place your cursor in the word you want to modify, then select the new font.

another method

To change the font you can also right-click the text, click the arrow next to the *Font* box on the Mini toolbar, and select a font from the list.

let me try

Open the student data file **wd2-02-FourNewServices** and try this skill on your own:

1. Select **the address** at the top of the document.

2. Change the font to **Calibri.**

3. Save the file as directed by your instructor and close it.

Skill 2.3 Changing Font Sizes

When creating a document it is important to not only choose the correct font, but also to use the appropriate font size. Fonts are measured in **points**, abbreviated "pt." On the printed page, 72 points equal one inch. Different text sizes are used for paragraphs and headers in a document. Paragraphs typically use 10 pt., 11 pt., and 12 pt. fonts. Headers often use 14 pt., 16 pt., and 18 pt. fonts.

To change the size of the text:

1. Select the text to be changed.
2. On the *Home* tab, in the *Font* group, click the arrow next to the *Font Size* box.
3. Scroll the list to find the new font size.
4. Click the size you want.

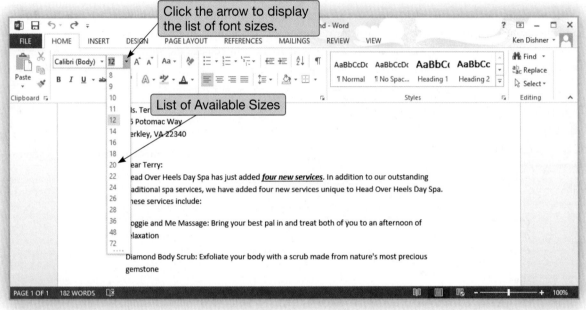

FIGURE WD 2.4

tips & tricks

Sometimes when you are formatting text, you may not be sure of the exact size you want your text to be. You can experiment with the look of text in your document by incrementally increasing and decreasing the size of the font. Use the **Grow Font** A˄ or **Shrink Font** A˅ button, available in the *Font* group, to change the font size by one increment.

another method

To change the font you can also right-click the text, click the arrow next to the *Font Size box* on the Mini toolbar, and select a font size from the list.

let me try

Open the student data file **wd2-03-FourNewServices** and try this skill on your own:

1. Select **the date.**
2. Change the font size to **12 pt.**
3. Save the file as directed by your instructor and close it.

word 2013   chapter 2 Formatting Text and Paragraphs

Skill 2.4 Changing Text Case

When you type on a keyboard you use the (↑ Shift) key to capitalize individual letters and the (Caps lock) key to type in all capital letters. Another way to change letters from lowercase to uppercase, and vice versa, is to use the *Change Case* command. When you use the **Change Case** command in Word, you are manipulating the characters that were typed, changing how the letters are displayed. There are five types of text case formats you can apply to text:

Sentence case—formats text as a sentence with the first word being capitalized and all remaining words beginning with a lowercase letter.

lowercase—changes all letters to lowercase.

UPPERCASE—changes all letters to uppercase, or capital letters.

Capitalize Each Word—formats text so each word begins with a capital letter.

tOGGLE cASE—formats text in the reverse of the typed format, converting uppercase letters to lowercase and lowercase letters to uppercase.

To apply text case formatting to text:

1. Select the text you want to change.
2. On the *Home* tab, in the *Font* group, click the **Change Case** button.
3. Select a text case option from the menu to apply it to the text.

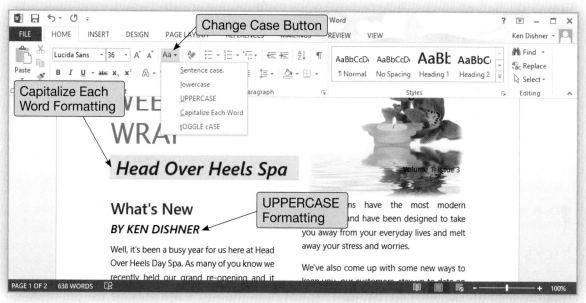

FIGURE WD 2.5

tips & tricks

Headers and titles often use the *Capitalize Each Word* format. One way to ensure that your headers and titles are consistent in text case is to use the *Change Case* command.

tell me **more**

From the *Font* dialog, you can apply the *All caps* or *Small caps* character formatting to text. Although the *All caps* command has the same effect as the *UPPERCASE* case command, *All caps* applies character formatting, while *UPPERCASE* changes the underlying text that was typed.

let me try

Open the student data file **wd2-04-SpaNewsletter** and try this skill on your own:

1. Select the **what's new** article title.
2. Use the **Change Case** command to capitalize each word.

3. Select the text **by ken dishner** below the *What's New* article title.
4. Use the **Change Case** command to change the text to all uppercase letters.
5. Save the file as directed by your instructor and close it.

Skill 2.5 Changing Font Colors

In the past, creating black-and-white documents was the standard for most business purposes. This was mostly because printing color documents was cost prohibitive. Today, color printing is more affordable and accessible. Business documents typically include graphics, illustrations, and color text. Adding color to text in your document adds emphasis to certain words and helps design elements, such as headers, stand out for your reader. It is important to be selective when adding color to your document. Using too many colors can often be distracting to the reader.

To change the color of the text:

1. Select the text to be changed.
2. On the *Home* tab, in the *Font* group, click the arrow next to the *Font Color* button.
3. Click the color you want from the color palette.

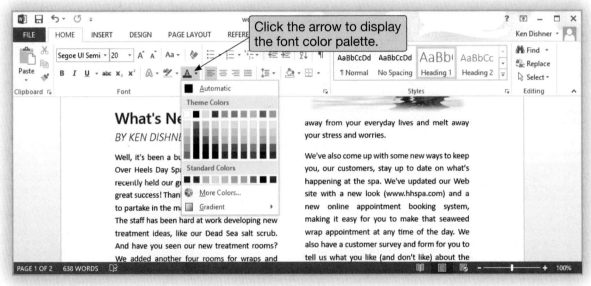

Click the arrow to display the font color palette.

FIGURE WD 2.6

tips & tricks

When you change the color of text, the *Font Color* button changes to the color you selected. Click the **Font Color** button to quickly apply the same color to other text in the document.

tell me **more**

A color theme is a group of predefined colors that works well together in a document. You can apply a color theme to change the color of a number of elements at once. When you change the color theme, the color palette changes and displays only colors that are part of the color theme.

another **method**

You can change the font color from the Mini toolbar. To display the Mini toolbar, right-click in the text you want to change. Click the arrow next to the *Font Color* button and select the color you want.

let me **try**

Open the student data file **wd2-05-SpaNewsletter** and try this skill on your own:

1. Select the text **BY KEN DISHNER** below the *What's New* article title.
2. Change the text to the **Dark Blue** standard color.
3. Save the file as directed by your instructor and close it.

Skill 2.6 Applying Highlights

Text in a Word document can be highlighted to emphasize or call attention to it. The effect is similar to that of a highlighting marker. When text is highlighted, the background color of the selected area is changed to make it stand out on the page.

Highlighting is very useful when you are sharing a document with coworkers or reviewers. It calls the other person's attention to elements that most need his or her attention. However, highlighting can sometimes be distracting as well. Be careful when using the highlighter in Word; only use it for small amounts of text.

To highlight text in a document:

1. Select the text to be highlighted.
2. On the *Home* tab, in the *Font* group, click the arrow next to the *Text Highlight Color* button.
3. Click the color you want to use.

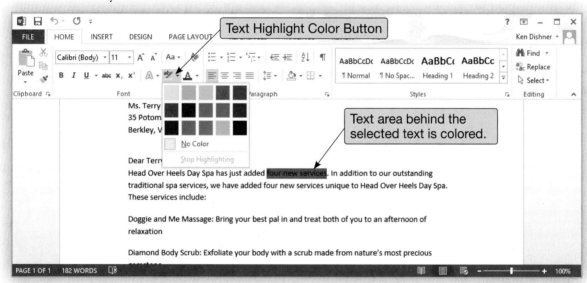

FIGURE WD 2.7

tips & tricks

Be careful when selecting colors to use for highlighting. If both the color of the text and the highlight color are dark, the text will be hard to read. If the highlight color is too light, it may not give the text enough emphasis.

tell me **more**

Rather than applying highlighting to text you have already selected, you can use the highlighter to apply highlighting to text throughout your document. Click the **Text Highlight Color** button without selecting any text first. Your cursor changes to a highlighter shape. Click and drag across text with the highlighter cursor to highlight text. To change your cursor back, click the **Text Highlight Color** button again.

another **method**

You can highlight text from the Mini toolbar. First, select the text you want to highlight; right-click the selected text to display the Mini toolbar. Click the arrow next to the *Text Highlight Color* button and select the color you want.

let me **try**

Open the student data file **wd2-06-FourNewServices** and try this skill on your own:

1. Select the text **four new services** in the first paragraph.
2. Apply the **Pink** highlighting to the text.
3. Save the file as directed by your instructor and close it.

Skill 2.7 Applying Text Effects

Sometimes you will want to draw attention to text you have added to your document. You could format the text using character formatting and changing the font color, or if you want the text to really stand out, use **text effects**. As with other robust text formatting options, be sure to limit the use of text effect to a small amount of text—like a newsletter banner or report title. Overuse of text effects can be distracting to your readers.

Text effects are predefined graphic styles you can apply to text. These styles include a combination of color, outline, shadow, reflection, and glow effects.

To apply text effects:

1. Select the text you want to apply the text effects to.

2. On the *Home* tab, in the *Font* group, click the **Text Effects** button.

3. Select a pre-designed option from the gallery.

Click the Text Effects button and select a predesigned option from the gallery.

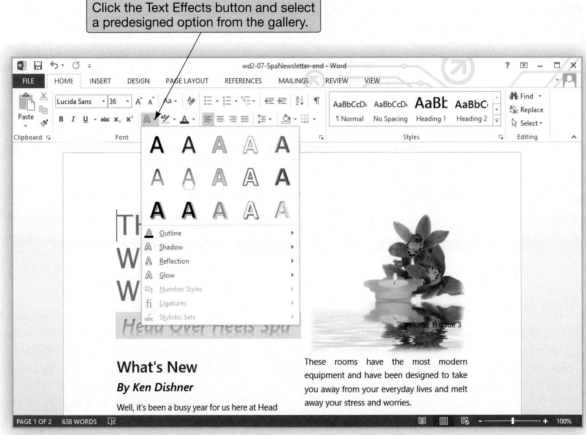

FIGURE WD 2.8

tips & tricks

You can adjust individual effects from the *Text Effects* gallery. Point to a menu item listed below the pre-designed effects in the gallery to display sub-galleries for each effect option. You can then select an option form the sub-gallery to adjust that individual effect. In Word 2013, Microsoft added the ability to control number styles, ligatures, and style sets of text through the *Text Effects* gallery.

tell me **more**

When you add text to a document using the text effects command, it is treated as formatted text. The *WordArt* gallery allows you to add text to a document using the same styles, but when you add WordArt to a document it is treated as a drawing object. Clicking on WordArt in a document will display the *Drawing* contextual tab. Clicking on text with text effects applied will not display the *Drawing* contextual tab.

another **method**

You can also apply text effects through the *Font* dialog:

1. On the *Home* tab, in the *Font* group, click the **Dialog launcher.**
2. In the *Font* dialog, click the **Text Effects...** button.
3. Click the **Text Effects** button at the top of the dialog to select options to apply to text.

let me **try**

Open the student data file **wd2-07-SpaNewsletter** and try this skill on your own:

1. Select the text **Head Over Heels Spa** under the newsletter title *The Weekly Wrap*.
2. Apply the **Gradient Fill–Olive Green, Accent 1, Reflection** text effect to the text. It is the second item in the second row of the gallery.
3. Save the file as directed by your instructor and close it.

Skill 2.8 Using Format Painter

When you want to copy text from one part of your document to another, you use the **Copy** and **Past**e commands. What if you don't want to copy the text but instead copy all the formatting from text in one part of your document to text in another part of your document? The Format Painter tool allows you to copy formatting styles that have been applied to text. You can then "paste" the formatting, applying it to text anywhere in the document.

To use *Format Painter:*

1. Select the text that has the formatting you want to copy.

2. On the *Home* tab, in the *Clipboard* group, click the **Format Painter** button.

3. Select the text that you want to apply the formatting to.

4. The formats are automatically applied to the selected text.

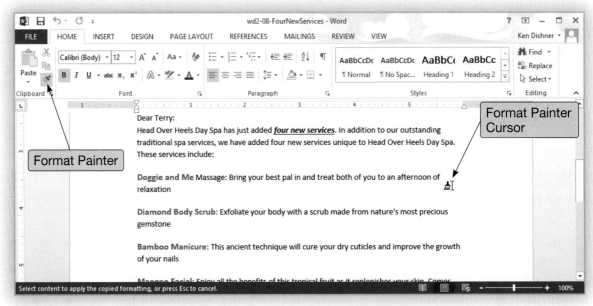

FIGURE WD 2.9

tips & tricks

If the text you are copying the formatting from is formatted using a paragraph *style,* then you don't need to select the entire paragraph. Just place the cursor anywhere in the paragraph and click the **Format Painter** button. To apply the same paragraph style formatting to another paragraph, click anywhere in the paragraph to which you want to apply the formatting.

tell me **more**

If you want to apply the formats more than once, double-click the **Format Painter** button when you select it. It will stay on until you click the **Format Painter** button again or press (Esc) to deselect it.

another **method**

To activate *Format Painter,* you can right-click the text with formatting you want to copy and click the **Format Painter** button on the Mini toolbar.

let me **try**

Open the student data file **wd2-08-FourNew Services** and try this skill on your own:

1. Use the **Format Painter** to copy the formatting of the text **Doggie and me.**

2. Apply the copied formatting to the text **Massage:.**

3. Save the file as directed by your instructor and close it.

Skill 2.9 Clearing Formatting

After you have applied a number of character formats and effects to text, you may find that you want to return your text to its original formatting. You could perform multiple undo commands on the text, or you could use the *Clear Formatting* command. The **Clear Formatting** command removes any formatting that has been applied to text, including character formatting, text effects, and styles, and leaves only plain text.

To remove formatting from text:

1. Select the text you want to remove the formatting from.
2. On the *Home* tab, in the *Font* group, click the **Clear Formatting** button.

FIGURE WD 2.10

tips & tricks

If you clear the formatting from text and then decide that you want to keep the formatting that was removed, you can use the **Undo** command to apply the previous formatting to the text.

another method

To clear the formatting from text, you can also:

1. On the *Home* tab, in the *Styles* group, click the **More** button.
2. Click **Clear Formatting.**

tell me more

The *Clear Formatting* command does not remove highlighting that has been applied to text. In order to remove highlighting from text, you must click the **Text Highlighting Color** button and select **No Color.**

let me try

Open the student data file **wd2-09-SpaNewsletter** and try this skill on your own:

1. Select the text **By Ken Dishner** below the *What's New* article title.
2. Clear the formatting from the text.
3. Save the file as directed by your instructor and close it.

Skill 2.10 Creating Bulleted Lists

When typing a document you may want to include information that is best displayed in list format rather than paragraph format. If your list does not include items that need to be displayed in a specific order, use a bulleted list to help information stand out from surrounding text. A **bullet** is a symbol that is displayed before each item in a list. When a bullet appears before a list item, it indicates that the items in the list do not have a particular order to them.

To create a bulleted list:

1. Select the text you want to change to a bulleted list. In order to appear as separate items within a bulleted list, each item must be followed by a hard return (press (← Enter)).

2. On the *Home* tab, in the *Paragraph* group, click the **Bullets** button.

3. Click outside the list to deselect it.

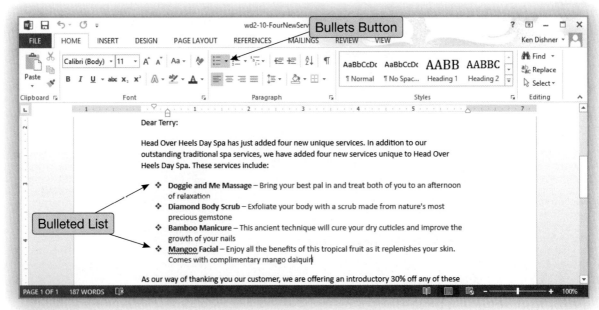

FIGURE WD 2.11

tips & tricks

▸ Sometimes you will want to add more items to an existing list. Place your cursor at the end of a list item and press (← Enter) to start a new line. A bullet will automatically appear before the list item.

▸ You can turn off the **Bullets** formatting feature by pressing (← Enter) twice.

tell me **more**

To change the bullet type, click the **Bullets** button arrow and select an option from the *Bullet Library*. You can create new bullets by selecting **Define New Bullet**...

another **method**

You can start a bulleted list by:

▸ Typing an asterisk, a space, and your list item, then pressing the (← Enter) key.

You can convert text to a bulleted list by right-clicking the selected text, pointing to **Bullets,** and selecting an option.

let me **try**

Open the student data file **wd2-10-FourNew Services** and try this skill on your own:

1. Select the text for the **four new services** in the letter.

2. Apply the **four diamond** bullet style to the text.

3. Save the file as directed by your instructor and close it.

Skill 2.11 Creating Numbered Lists

Some lists, such as directions to complete a task, need to have the items displayed in a specific order. **Numbered lists** display a number next to each list item and display the numbers in order. Numbered lists help you organize your content and display it in a clear, easy-to-understand manner.

To create a numbered list:

1. Select the text you want to change to a numbered list. As with bulleted lists, in order to appear as separate items within a numbered list, each item must be followed by a hard return (press (← Enter)).

2. Click outside the list to deselect it.

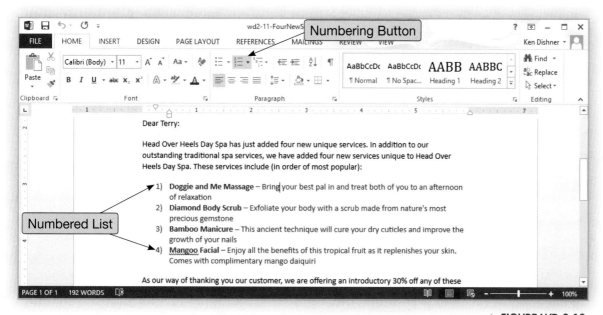

FIGURE WD 2.12

tips & tricks

▶ Sometimes you will want to add more items to an existing list. To add another item to the list, place your cursor at the end of an item and press (← Enter) to start a new line. The list will renumber itself to accommodate the new item.

▶ You can turn off the numbering feature by pressing (← Enter) twice.

another method

You can start a numbered list by:

▶ Typing a 1, a space, and your list item, then pressing the (← Enter) key.

▶ Clicking the **Numbering** button, typing your list item, then pressing the (← Enter) key.

You can convert text to a numbered list by right-clicking the selected text, pointing to **Numbering,** and selecting an option.

tell me **more**

To change the numbering list type, click the **Numbering** button arrow and select an option from the *Numbering Library.* You can create new numbered list styles by selecting **Define New Number Format...**

let me try

Open the student data file **wd2-11-FourNewServices** and try this skill on your own:

1. Select the text for the four new services in the letter.

2. Apply the **1), 2), 3)** number style to the text.

3. Save the file as directed by your instructor and close it.

Skill 2.12 Using Quick Styles

A **Quick Style** is a group of formatting, including character and paragraph formatting, that you can easily apply to text in your document. Quick Styles can be applied to body text, headers, quotes, or just about any type of text you may have in your document.

It is a good idea to use Quick Styles to format text in your documents. When you use Quick Styles to format text, you can quickly change the look of that style across your document by changing the document's theme. Certain Quick Styles, such as headings, are also used by other features in Word, such as creating a table of contents and the Navigation task pane.

To apply a Quick Style to text:

1. Select the text you want to change.

2. On the *Home* tab, in the *Styles* group, click the **More** button .

3. Select a **Quick Style** from the *Quick Styles* gallery.

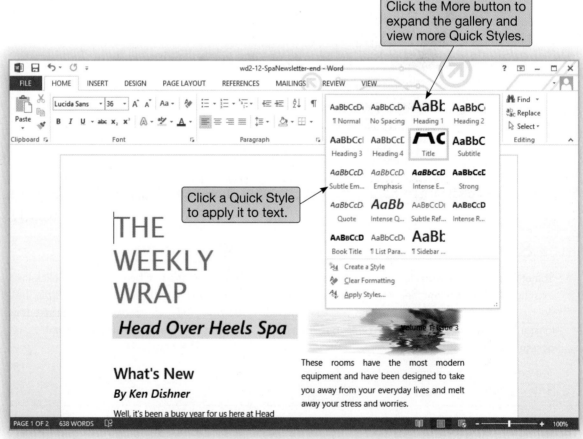

Click the More button to expand the gallery and view more Quick Styles.

Click a Quick Style to apply it to text.

FIGURE WD 2.13

tell me **more**

When you select a new Quick Style, it replaces the style for the text. If you want to clear all the formatting for text, open the *Quick Styles* gallery and select **Clear Formatting.**

another **method**

The *Styles* group on the *Home* tab displays the latest Quick Styles you have used. If you want to apply a recently used Quick Style, you can click the option directly from the Ribbon without opening the *Quick Styles* gallery.

let me **try**

Open the student data file **wd2-12-SpaNewsletter** and try this skill on your own:

1. Select the **What's New** article title.
2. Apply the **Heading 1** Quick Style to the text.
3. Save the file as directed by your instructor and close it.

from the perspective of . . .

COLLEGE GRADUATE

When creating my résumé to send out to potential employers, I always make sure I use the right combination of fonts and styles to create the most eye-catching and professional document. I use tab stops and indents to align text just the way I want it and add space before and after paragraphs to control the layout on the page. I learned my lesson with the first résumé I sent out. Apparently, using a different color font for each section and applying an "eye popping" text effect to my name was not the way to land an interview at the firm I applied to.

Skill 2.13 Changing Paragraph Alignment

Paragraph alignment refers to how text is aligned with regard to the left and right margins.

Left alignment aligns the text on the left side, leaving the right side ragged.
Center alignment centers each line of text relative to the margins.
Right alignment aligns the text on the right side, leaving the left side ragged.
Justified alignment evenly spaces the words, aligning the text on the right and left sides of the printed page.

It is important to understand common uses of different alignments. Paragraph text and headers are typically left aligned, but titles are often centered. Newspaper columns are often justified, and columns of numbers are typically right aligned.

To change the alignment of text:

1. Click in the paragraph you want to change.
2. On the *Home* tab, in the *Paragraph* group, click an alignment button—**Align Text Left, Center, Align Text Right,** or **Justify.**

FIGURE WD 2.14

another **method**

The following keyboard shortcuts can be used to apply horizontal alignment:

▶ Align Left = `Ctrl` + `L`

▶ Center = `Ctrl` + `E`

▶ Align Right = `Ctrl` + `R`

▶ Justify = `Ctrl` + `J`

let me **try**

Open the student data file **wd2-13-SpaNewsletter** and try this skill on your own:

1. Select **all the text** in the *What's New* article. The article includes three paragraphs of text.
2. Change the paragraph text so it is **justified.**
3. Save the file as directed by your instructor and close it.

Skill 2.14 Changing Line Spacing

Line spacing is the white space between lines of text. The default line spacing in Microsoft Word 2013 is 1.08 spacing. This gives each line the height of single spacing with a little extra space at the top and bottom. This line spacing is a good choice to use for the body of a document. Other commonly used spacing options include single spacing, double spacing, and 1.5 spacing.

To change line spacing:

1. Select the text you want to change.
2. On the *Home* tab, in the *Paragraph* group, click the **Line Spacing** button.
3. Select the number of the spacing you want.

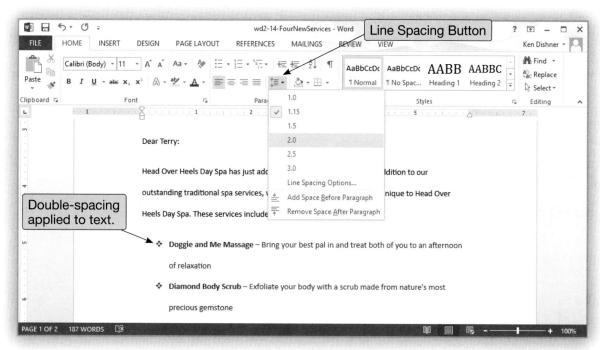

FIGURE WD 2.15

tell me **more**

In Word 2007, Microsoft changed the default line spacing from single space to 1.15 lines. In Word 2013, this default has been changed to 1.08 lines. This new default line spacing is designed to help with readability of online documents on a number of devices, including traditional desktop and laptop computers, tablets, and smart phones.

another **method**

❯ To apply single spacing, you can also press Ctrl + 1 on the keyboard.

❯ To apply double spacing, you can also press Ctrl + 2 on the keyboard.

let me **try**

Open the student data file **wd2-14-FourNewServices** and try this skill on your own:

1. Press Ctrl + A on the keyboard to select **all the text** in the document.
2. Change the line spacing from double spaced to **1.15 spacing.**
3. Save the file as directed by your instructor and close it.

Skill 2.15 Revealing Formatting Marks

When creating a document it is important to use consistent formatting, such as a single space after the period at the end of a sentence. As you create a document, Word adds **formatting marks** that are hidden from view. For example, a paragraph mark, ¶, is created every time the `← Enter` key is pressed. When creating professional documents, it is considered bad practice to use extra line breaks to add space between paragraphs in a document. By displaying formatting marks, you can quickly see where these extra line breaks occur in your documents and then easily delete them.

To display formatting marks in a document:

1. On the *Home* tab, in the *Paragraph* group, click the **Show/Hide** button.

2. The formatting marks are displayed in the document.

3. Click the **Show/Hide** button again to hide the formatting marks. Formatting marks include symbols that represent spaces, nonbreaking spaces, tabs, and paragraphs. Table 2.1 shows examples of formatting marks.

TABLE WD 2.1 Formatting Marks

CHARACTER	FORMATTING MARK
Space	·
Nonbreaking Space	○
Tab	→
Paragraph	¶

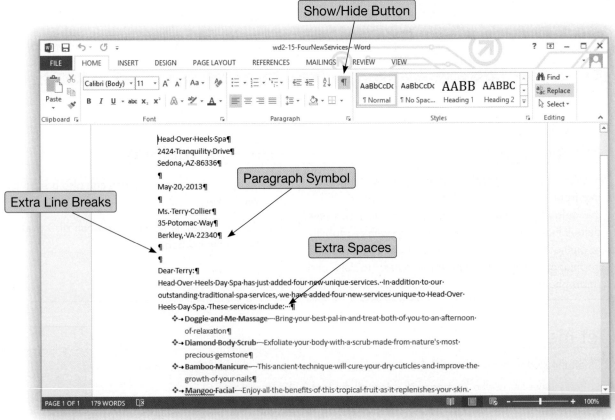

FIGURE WD 2.16

tips & tricks

You can choose to always show specific formatting marks on-screen even when the **Show/Hide** button is inactive. To show specific formatting marks:

1. Click the **File** tab and select **Options.**
2. In the *Word Options* dialog, click the **Display** category.
3. Select the formatting marks you want to display in the *Always show these formatting marks on the screen* section.
4. Click **OK.**

tell me **more**

❯ Formatting marks appear on-screen, but they do not appear in the printed document.

❯ A nonbreaking space is a space between two words that keeps the words together and prevents the words from being split across two lines.

another **method**

To show formatting marks, you can press (Ctrl) + (↑ Shift) + (8).

let me **try**

Open the student data file **wd2-15-FourNewServices** and try this skill on your own:

1. Show the formatting marks in the document.
2. Remove any extra blank lines in the document.
3. There should only be one space after a period and no spaces after punctuation at the end of a line. Remove the extra spaces from the document.
4. Hide the formatting marks.
5. Save the file as directed by your instructor and close it.

Skill 2.16 Adding Space Before and After Paragraphs

The default spacing after paragraphs in Word is 8 pt. This setting results in a very evenly spaced document, with some space between paragraphs to set them apart. To help differentiate between paragraphs even more, you can add space before a paragraph. If you want to tighten up a document, you can remove space after the paragraph.

To increase the space before a paragraph and to decrease the space after a paragraph:

1. Click in the paragraph you want to change.

2. On the *Home* tab, in the *Paragraph* group, click the **Line Spacing** button.

3. Choose one of the following options:

❭ Click **Add Space Before Paragraph** to add space above the first line of the paragraph.

❭ Click **Remove Space After Paragraph** to remove space from below the last line of the paragraph.

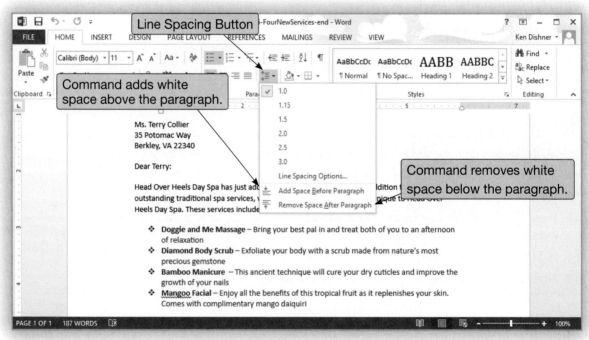

FIGURE WD 2.17

tips & tricks

After you have added space before a paragraph, the command on the menu changes to *Remove Space Before Paragraph* so you can easily remove the space you added. Similarly, when you remove space after a paragraph, the command changes to **Add Space After Paragraph** to add back in the space you removed.

tell me **more**

Many of the Quick Styles available in the *Styles* group on the *Home* tab include spacing before and after paragraphs. Use Quick Styles to add text that includes text and paragraph formatting.

let me try

Open the student data file **wd2-16-FourNewServices** and try this skill on your own:

1. Add space before the **first paragraph in the letter.**

2. Save the file as directed by your instructor and close it.

Skill 2.17 Changing Indents

When you create a document, the margins control how close the text comes to the edge of a page. But what if you don't want all your paragraphs to line up? Indenting paragraphs increases the left margin for a paragraph, helping it stand out from the rest of your document.

To change the indentation of a paragraph:

1. Place the cursor anywhere in the paragraph you want to change.

2. To increase the indent of the paragraph by one level, on the *Home* tab, in the *Paragraph* group, click the **Increase Indent** button.

3. To reduce the indent of the paragraph and bring it closer to the edge of the page by one level, click the **Decrease Indent** button.

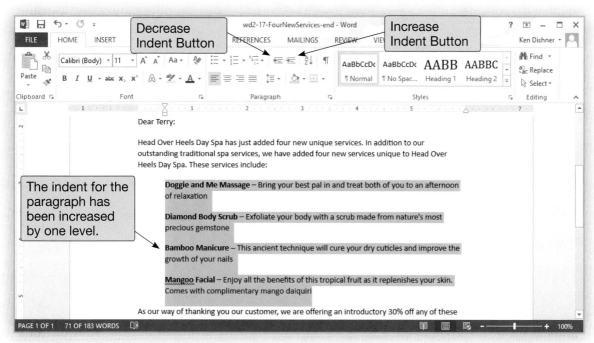

FIGURE WD 2.18

tell me **more**

The *Indent* commands indent all lines in a paragraph the same amount. If you want only the first line of a paragraph to be indented and the remainder of the paragraph to be left-aligned, use a **First Line Indent.** If you want the first line of a paragraph to be left-aligned and the remainder of the paragraph to be indented, use a **Hanging Indent.** In the *Format Paragraph* dialog, you can precisely set options for first line indents and hanging indents. To open the *Format Paragraph* dialog, click the **Dialog Launcher** in the *Paragraph* group on the *Home* tab or in the *Paragraph* group on the *Page Layout* tab.

tips & tricks

You can increase indents by one increment (one tenth of an inch) rather than by one level:

1. Click the **Page Layout** tab.

2. In the *Paragraph* group, click the arrows next to *Left* and *Right* to move paragraphs by one increment for each click.

let me try

Open the student data file **wd2-17-FourNew Services** and try this skill on your own:

1. Select the text for the **four new services** in the letter.

2. Increase the indent for the text by one level.

3. Save the file as directed by your instructor and close it.

Skill 2.18 Displaying the Ruler

When working with documents, it is helpful to display the **ruler**. The ruler displays horizontally across the top of the window just below the Ribbon and vertically along the left side of the window. The ruler gives you a quick view of the margins and position of elements in your document. From the ruler you can also control other document layout controls such as tabs, first line indents, and hanging indents.

To display the ruler:

1. Click the **View** tab.
2. In the *Show* group, click the check box next to **Ruler** so a checkmark appears.
3. To hide the ruler, click the check box again so the checkmark disappears.

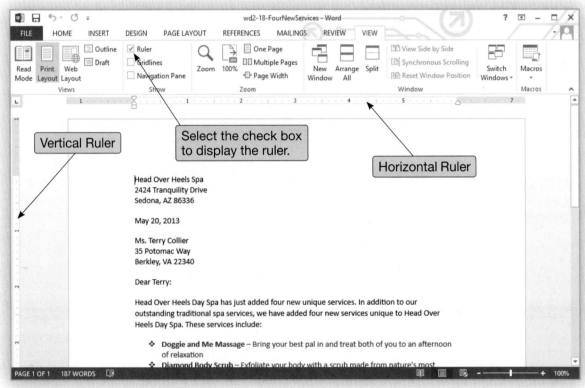

FIGURE WD 2.19

tips & tricks

Double-click the ruler to open the *Page Setup* dialog where you can control page layout elements such as margins and page orientation.

tell me **more**

Gridlines are a series of vertical and horizontal lines that divide the page into small boxes, giving you visual markers for aligning graphics, tables, and other elements on the page.

let me **try**

Open the student data file **wd2-18-FourNewServices** and try this skill on your own:

1. Show the ruler and then hide the ruler again.
2. Close the file.

word 2013   chapter 2 Formatting Text and Paragraphs

Skill 2.19 Using Tab Stops

A **tab stop** is a location along the horizontal ruler that indicates how far to indent text when the Tab key is pressed.

There are five types of tab stops:

- **Left**—Displays text to the right of the tab stop
- **Center**—Displays text centered over the tab stop
- **Right**—Displays the text to the left of the tab stop
- **Decimal**—Aligns the text along the decimal point
- **Bar**—Displays a vertical line through the text at the tab stop

To set a tab stop:

1. Select the paragraph in which you want to set a tab stop.
2. Click the **tab selector** at the far left of the horizontal ruler until it changes to the type of tab you want.
3. Click the horizontal ruler where you want to set a tab stop.

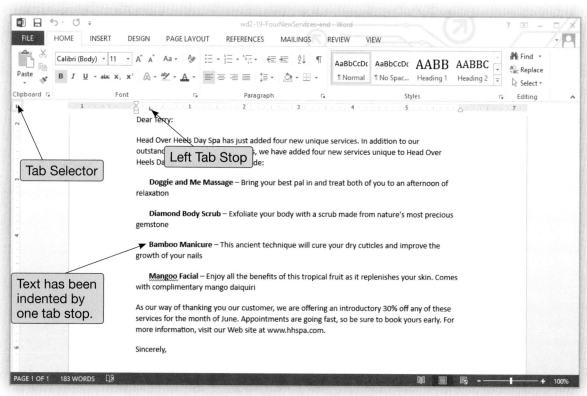

FIGURE WD 2.20

tips & tricks

To clear a tab stop:
Drag the tab marker down from the horizontal ruler to remove it.

To move a tab stop:
Drag the tab marker to the right or left along the horizontal ruler to its new position.

tell me **more**

The tab selector also includes two options for adding indents to your document. The **First Line Indent** controls where the first line of a paragraph begins. The **Hanging Indent** controls where the remainder of the paragraph is indented.

another **method**

You can set tab stops in the *Tabs* dialog:

1. Double-click the ruler to open the *Tabs* dialog.
2. In the *Tab stop position:* box, type the number of where you want the tab stop to appear.
3. Click a radio button in the *Alignment* section.
4. Click **OK.**

let me **try**

Open the student data file **wd2-19-FourNewServices** and try this skill on your own:

1. Select the text for the **four new services** in the letter.
2. Add a **left tab stop** at the **.25" mark** on the ruler.
3. Use the (Tab ⇄) key to indent each of the following by one tab stop: **Doggie and Me Massage:, Diamond Body Scrub, Bamboo Manicure,** and **Mangoo Facial.**
4. Save the file as directed by your instructor and close it.

Bold
Italic
Underline
Font
Serif fonts
Sans serif fonts
Points
Change Case command
Highlighting
Text effects

Format Painter
Bullet
Numbered list
Quick Style
Paragraph alignment
Line spacing
Formatting marks
Ruler
Tab stop

concept review

1. A _____ font has an embellishment at the end of each stroke to lead the eye from one character to the next.

   a. sans serif

   b. serif

   c. theme

   d. heading

2. Use the _____ command to copy the styles from one word to another.

   a. text effects

   b. styles

   c. Format painter

   d. Text Highlighting Color

3. _____ tab stops display the text to the left of the tab stop.

   a. Left

   b. Right

   c. Center

   d. Decimal

4. Use the _____ command to change text from uppercase to having each word capitalized.

   a. Change Font

   b. Grow Font

   c. Shrink Font

   d. Change Case

5. To evenly space words, aligning the text on the right and left sides of the printed page use the _____ command.

   a. Align Left

   b. Center

   c. Align Right

   d. Justify

6. To display a list of items that do not need to be in a certain order, use a _____.

    a. bulleted list

    b. numbered list

    c. multilevel list

    d. justified list

7. Use _____ to ensure parts of your document, such as headings, all use the same formatting.

    a. Quick Styles

    b. Text Effects

    c. Font Styles

    d. Character Styles

8. The _____ command displays hidden formatting marks in a document, including paragraph and space marks.

    a. Clear Formatting

    b. Styles

    c. Format Painter

    d. Show/Hide

9. To call attention to text by coloring the background behind the text, use the _____ command.

    a. Font Color

    b. Text Highlight Color

    c. Text Effects

    d. Styles

10. Use _____ to apply combinations of shadows, outlines, and glows to text with one command.

    a. Font Color

    b. text Highlighting Color

    c. Text Effects

    d. character effects

In this project you will be editing the **WD2013-SkillReview-2-1** document from Suarez Marketing.

Skills needed to complete this project:

* Clearing Formatting (Skill 2.9)
* Changing Fonts (Skill 2.2)
* Changing Font Sizes (Skill 2.3)
* Changing Line Spacing (Skill 2.14)
* Revealing Formatting Marks (Skill 2.15)
* Using Quick Styles (Skill 2.12)
* Adding Space Before and After Paragraphs (Skill 2.16)
* Using Bold, Italic, and Underline (Skill 2.1)
* Changing Font Colors (Skill 2.5)
* Using Format Painter (Skill 2.8)
* Apply Text Effects (Skill 2.7)
* Creating Numbered Lists (Skill 2.11)
* Changing Indents (Skill 2.17)
* Creating Bulleted Lists (Skill 2.10)
* Changing Paragraph Alignment (Skill 2.13)

1. Open the **WD2013-SkillReview-2-1** document.
2. Save this document as: **[your initials]WD-SkillReview-2-1**
3. Clear the formatting on text.
   a. Select the **first two lines of text** in the document.
   b. On the *Home* tab, in the *Font* group, click the **Clear Formatting** button.
4. Change the font and size on **all of the text** in the body of the document.
   a. Press Ctrl + A to select **all text** in the body of the brochure.
   b. On the *Home* tab, in the *Font* group, click the arrow next to the *Font* box.
   c. Choose **Calibri** as the font to use on the selected text.
   d. In the *Font* group, click the arrow next to the **Font Size** box.
   e. Choose **11** as the font size.
5. Change the line spacing for each paragraph.
   a. With the entire document still selected, in the *Paragraph* group, click the **Line and Paragraph Spacing** button.
   b. Click **1.15** to change the line spacing.
6. On the *Home* tab, in the *Paragraph* group, click the **Show/ Hide** button to reveal formatting marks in the document.

7. Delete all of the extra blank lines between paragraphs in the document. Click the **Show/Hide** button again to hide the formatting marks.

8. Use Quick Styles to apply a heading format to a section heading in the document.

   a. Select the **Mission Statement** heading on the first page.

   b. On the *Home* tab, in the *Styles* group, click the **Heading 1** style. The Heading 1 style is applied to the selected section heading.

   c. Apply the *Heading 1* style to the following lines of text:
   - **Experience**
   - **Why I Do What I Do**
   - **What Clients are Saying**
   - **Professional Credentials**
   - **Education & Training**
   - **The Suarez Marketing Belief System**

9. Change the spacing before paragraph on the selected heading.

   a. Select the **Mission Statement** heading on the first page.

   b. Click the **Line and Paragraph Spacing** button.

   c. Select the **Remove Space Before Paragraph** option.

   d. Use this method to remove space before all the headings in the brochure.

10. Change the character formatting, font, and color of text.

    a. Select the text **Maria Suarez** at the top of the document.

    b. On the *Home* tab, in the *Font* group, click the **Bold** button.

    c. In the *Font* group, click the arrow next to the **Font** box and select **Cambria.**

    d. In the *Font* group, click the **Font Color** button and select **Blue-Gray, Text 2** (it is the fourth color in the first row under *Theme Colors*).

11. Use the **Format Painter** to change the format of text.

    a. With the text **Maria Suarez** still selected, on the *Home* tab, in the *Clipboard* group, click the **Format Painter** button.

    b. Select the text **Suarez Marketing** to apply the copied formatting.

12. Apply text effects to text.

    a. Select the tag line **"Putting Your Needs First"**

    b. On the *Home* tab, in the *Font* group, click the **Text Effects** button.

    c. Select the **Fill–Blue, Accent 1, Shadow** effect (it is the second option in the first row of the gallery).

13. Add a numbered list to and decrease the indent on a section of the brochure.

    a. In the *Why I Do What I Do* section, select all of the text.

    b. On the *Home* tab, in the *Paragraph* group, click the **Numbering** button. Numbering is applied to this section and it is indented.

    c. Click the **Decrease Indent** button once to change the left indent to 0".

14. Add a bulleted list to and decrease the indent on a section of the brochure.

    a. In the *The Suarez Marketing Belief System* section, select all of the text.

    b. On the *Home* tab, in the *Paragraph* group, click the **Bullets** button. Bullets are applied to this section and it is indented.

    c. Click the **Decrease Indent** button once to change the left indent to 0".

15. Apply a Quick Style to and change the paragraph alignment on selected text.

    a. In the *What Clients Are Saying* section, select **the first quote and include the quotation marks.**

    b. On the *Home* tab, in the *Styles* group, apply the **Quote** style. You will have to click the **More** button to locate this style.

    c. Use the **Format Painter** to apply this format to the **second quote in this section.**

    d. Select–**Allison Palmer, Creve Couer, MO.**

    e. On the *Home* tab, in the *Paragraph* group, click the **Align Right** button.

    f. Select and right align–**Scott Morris and Associates, St. Louis, MO.**

16. Save and close the document.

skill review 2.2

In this project you will be editing the **WD2013-SkillReview-2-2** document from Tri-State Book Festival.

Skills needed to complete this project:

- Changing Fonts (Skill 2.2)
- Changing Font Sizes (Skill 2.3)
- Changing Line Spacing (Skill 2.14)
- Revealing Formatting Marks (Skill 2.15)
- Using Quick Styles (Skill 2.12)
- Applying Highlights (Skill 2.6)
- Changing Font Colors (Skill 2.5)
- Changing Paragraph Alignment (Skill 2.13)
- Creating Bulleted Lists (Skill 2.10)
- Using Bold, Italic, and Underline (Skill 2.1)
- Using Format Painter (Skill 2.8)
- Displaying the Ruler (Skill 2.18)
- Using Tab Stops (Skill 2.19)
- Changing Indents (Skill 2.17)
- Changing Text Case (Skill 2.4)

1. Open the **WD2013-SkillReview-2-2** document.

2. Save this document as: **[your initials]WD-SkillReview-2-2**

3. Change font, font size, and line spacing on the entire document.

    a. Press **Ctrl + A** to select the entire document.

    b. On the *Home* tab, in the *Font* group, click the arrow next to the **Font** box.

    c. Choose **Arial** as the font to use on the selected text.

    d. In the *Font* group, click the arrow next to the **Font Size** box.

    e. Choose **11** as the font size.

    f. In the *Paragraph* group, change the line spacing to **2.0.**

4. On the *Home* tab, in the *Paragraph* group, click the **Show/Hide** button to reveal formatting marks in the document.

5. Delete all of the extra blank lines between paragraphs in the document. Click the **Show/Hide** button again to hide the formatting marks.

6. Apply a style to text and change paragraph alignment.

   a. Select the text **Tri-State Book Festival** at the top of the document.

   b. On the *Home* tab, in the *Styles* group, select the **Title** style. You might have to click the **More** button to locate this style.

   c. In the *Paragraph* group, click the **Center** button to center align the text on the page.

7. Apply highlighting to text.

   a. In the second paragraph, select the text **Tuesday, August 23.**

   b. On the *Home* tab, in the *Font* group, click the **Text Highlight Color** button. Select the **Yellow** option.

8. Change the color of text.

   a. Select the line of text that reads **Fiction Writers Association of the Tri-State Region.**

   b. On the *Home* tab, in the *Font* group, click the **Font Color** arrow.

   c. Select the **Dark Blue** option under *Standard Colors.*

9. Add bullets and apply character formatting to selected lines of text.

   a. Select the **five lines of text** under *Agency Name:.*

   b. On the *Home* tab, in the *Paragraph* group, click the **Bullets** button arrow.

   c. Select the **open circle bullet.**

   d. On the *Home* tab, in the *Font* group, click the **Bold** button.

10. Use Format Painter to copy and paste styles.

    a. With the bulleted list you just created still selected, on the *Home* tab, in the *Clipboard* group, double-click the **Format Painter** button.

    b. Apply the styles to the following lines:
    - **Non-smoking**
    - **Smoking**
    - **King**
    - **Two Doubles**
    - **Flying: Arrival time: _____**
    - **Driving**
    - **Yes, I would like to participate in the cooking demonstration.**
    - **No, I will not be participating in the cooking demonstration.**

11. Set a tab stop and use the tab to indent lines of text.

    a. If the ruler is not displayed, click the **View** tab. In the *Show* group, click the **Ruler** check box so a checkmark appears in the box.

    b. Place the cursor at the beginning of the line **I need a shuttle to Westfield Hotel & Spa from the airport.**

    c. Add a left tab stop at **1.25″**.

    d. Press the (Tab ⇄) key on the keyboard.

    e. Apply the same tab to the line that reads **I need directions to Westfield Hotel & Spa from:. _____**

12. Apply bullets and indents to text.

   a. Place the cursor at the beginning of the line **I need a shuttle to Westfield Hotel & Spa from the airport.**

   b. On the *Home* tab, in the *Paragraph* group, click the **Bullets** button arrow.

   c. Select the **open circle** option.

   d. In the *Paragraph* group, click the **Decrease Indent** button.

   e. Apply the same bullet style to the text **I need directions to Westfield Hotel & Spa from:. _____**

13. Change font case text.

   a. Select the line of text that reads **Fax or E-Mail This Form to.**

   b. On the *Home* tab, in the *Font* group, click the **Change Case** button and select **UPPERCASE.**

14. Save and close the document.

challenge yourself **2.3**

In this project you will be editing the **WD2013-ChallengeYourself-2-3** document from Spring Hills Community.

Skills needed to complete this project:

- Using Bold, Italic, and Underline (Skill 2.1)
- Changing Fonts (Skill 2.2)
- Changing Font Sizes (Skill 2.3)
- Changing Line Spacing (Skill 2.14)
- Revealing Formatting Marks (Skill 2.15)
- Changing Text Case (Skill 2.4)
- Using Quick Styles (Skill 2.12)
- Changing Paragraph Alignment (Skill 2.13)
- Using Format Painter (Skill 2.8)
- Adding Space Before and After Paragraphs (Skill 2.16)
- Creating Bulleted Lists (Skill 2.10)
- Changing Indents (Skill 2.17)
- Creating Numbered Lists (Skill 2.11)

1. Open the **WD2013-ChallengeYourself-2-3** document.

2. Save this document as: **[your initials]WD-Challenge-2-3**

3. Change font, font size, line spacing, and paragraph spacing on entire document.

   a. Select all the text in the document.

   b. Change the font to **Calibri** and the size to **11 pt.**

   c. Change the line spacing to **1.15 spacing.**

4. Display the paragraph marks for the document and delete all of the extra blank lines between paragraphs in the document. When you are finished, hide the paragraph marks.

5. Customize the title of the document.

    a. Apply the **Document Heading** style to the title of the document.

    b. Change the font size to **18 pt.**

    c. **Center** the title.

6. Customize the first section heading in the document (*Tips for staying safe*).

    a. Apply the **Document Section** style to the text.

7. Use the **Format Painter** to apply the formatting of the first section heading to the other two section headings in the document.

8. Use the **Add Space Before Paragraph** command to add space above each section heading in the document.

9. Change the case of all the section headings to **Capitalize Each Word.**

10. Apply character formatting.

    a. Select the text **basic safety strategy** in the first paragraph.

    b. Bold and italicize the text.

11. Convert the text in the **Basic Tips For Staying Safe** section to a bulleted list.

    a. Select all the lines in this section.

    b. Apply the **closed circle bullet** style.

    c. Decrease the indent of the bulleted list so the bullets are at the left margin.

12. Convert the text in the **What Electronics Are Being Targeted** section to a numbered list.

    a. Select all the five targeted electronic items in this section.

    b. Apply the **1.,2.,3.** number format to the text.

13. Save and close the document.

challenge yourself **2.4**

In this project you will be editing the **WD2013-ChallengeYourself-2-4** document from Fairlawn Community College.

Skills needed to complete this project:

- Changing Fonts (Skill 2.2)
- Changing Font Sizes (Skill 2.3)
- Changing Line Spacing (Skill 2.14)
- Revealing Formatting Marks (Skill 2.15)
- Applying Text Effects (Skill 2.7)
- Using Bold, Italic, and Underline (Skill 2.1)
- Changing Font Colors (Skill 2.5)
- Clearing Formatting (Skill 2.9)
- Using Quick Styles (Skill 2.12)
- Using Format Painter (Skill 2.8)
- Displaying the Ruler (Skill 2.18)
- Using Tab Stops (Skill 2.19)
- Creating Bulleted Lists (Skill 2.10)

1. Open the **WD2013-ChallengeYourself-2-4** document.

2. Save this document as: **[your initials]WD-Challenge-2-4**

3. Change the font on the entire document to **Calibri** and **12 pt**.

4. Change the line spacing for the entire document to **1.5** line spacing.

5. Display the paragraph marks for the document.

   a. Delete all of the extra blank lines between paragraphs in the document.

   b. There should only be one space between sentences and no spaces after a period in the last sentence in a paragraph. Fix all the spacing issues in the document.

   c. When you are finished, hide the paragraph marks.

6. Apply text effects to the title of the document and change the size of the text.

   a. Select the text **Fairlawn Community College Social Software Strategic Initiative** at the top of the document.

   b. Apply the **Fill–Blue, Accent 1, Shadow** text effect to the text. It is the second option in the first row of the gallery.

   c. Change the text size to **18 pt.**

7. Underline, change the color, and clear formatting from text.

   a. Select the first heading section (**Strategic Goal: Student Success**) in the document.

   b. Underline the text.

   c. Change the color of the text to **Blue-Gray–Text 2.**

   d. Clear the formatting from the text.

8. Customize the section headings of the document.

   a. Apply the **Heading 2** Quick Style to the first section heading (**Strategic Goal: Student Success**) in the document.

   b. Use the **Format Painter** to apply this formatting to the remaining headings in the document (**Initiative: Collaboration using Social Software:, Background:, Scope:, Deliverables:, Benefits:, Risks:, and Timeline:**).

9. Set tab stops in the document.

   a. Display the ruler.

   b. Select all the text in the document.

   c. Set a left tab stop at the **.25"** mark.

   d. Using the (Tab ⇥) key, indent the first paragraph under each section to the **.25"** tab stop.

10. Convert text to a bulleted list.

    a. Select the list items in the **Background** section (**Our basic Blog, Wiki, Discussion Board tools**).

    b. Apply the **open circle bullet** style to the list.

11. Save and close the document.

on your own 2.5

In this project you will be editing the **WD2013-OnYourOwn-2-5** document from Pennmark Management Company.

Skills needed to complete this project:

- Clearing Formatting (Skill 2.9)
- Changing Fonts (Skill 2.2)
- Changing Font Sizes (Skill 2.3)
- Changing Line Spacing (Skill 2.14)
- Displaying the Ruler (Skill 2.18)
- Using Tab Stops (Skill 2.19)
- Revealing Formatting Marks (Skill 2.15)
- Using Quick Styles (Skill 2.12)
- Changing Text Case (Skill 2.4)
- Changing Paragraph Alignment (Skill 2.13)
- Applying Highlights (Skill 2.6)
- Using Bold, Italic, and Underline (Skill 2.1)
- Using Format Painter (Skill 2.8)
- Adding Space Before and After Paragraphs (Skill 2.16)
- Creating Numbered Lists (Skill 2.11)

1. Open the **WD2013-OnYourOwn-2-5** document.
2. Save this document as: **[your initials]WD-OnYourOwn-2-5**
3. Select the entire document and make the following formatting changes:
   a. Clear all formatting.
   b. Change the font to **Arial** and **11 pt.**
   c. Change the line spacing to **1.15** spacing.
   d. Set a left tab at **3.5".**
4. Delete all extra blank lines in the document.
5. Select the first line of the document and make the following changes:
   a. Apply the **Heading 1** style.
   b. Change the case to **UPPERCASE.**
   c. Right-align the heading.
6. Select the next line of the document (**Contractor's Questionnaire**) and apply the **Heading 2** style.
7. In the next line of the document, apply a highlight of your choice to the text **Please read carefully.**
8. Select the *Contractor's Information* line in the document. Bold and italicize the text. Change the font color to **Blue–Gray, Text 2.**
9. Apply the formatting from **Contractor's Information** heading to the following lines (the last three lines in the document): **Signature of Applicant, Company,** and **Date of Application.**
10. Add space before each of the following lines: **Signature of Applicant, Company,** and **Date of Application.**

11. Press `Tab` to move the last three lines of text to the **3.5″** tab stop.

12. Select the items under *Contractor's Information* (from **Applicant:** to **Geographical Area of Operation:**) and change the line spacing to **2.0.**

13. Convert the **questions in the questionnaire** to a numbered list and change the line spacing to **2.0.**

14. Select the **entire document** and change the paragraph alignment to **Justify.**

15. Save and close the document.

fix it **2.6**

In this project you will be editing the **WD2013-FixIt-2-6** document. This document is a résumé of an applicant for a project assistant position.

Skills needed to complete this project:

- Clearing Formatting (Skill 2.9)
- Revealing Formatting Marks (Skill 2.15)
- Changing Fonts (Skill 2.2)
- Changing Font Sizes (Skill 2.3)
- Using Quick Styles (Skill 2.12)
- Changing Paragraph Alignment (Skill 2.13)
- Adding Space Before and After Paragraphs (Skill 2.16)
- Changing Font Colors (Skill 2.5)
- Using Format Painter (Skill 2.8)
- Displaying the Ruler (Skill 2.18)
- Using Tab Stops (Skill 2.19)
- Using Bold, Italic, and Underline (Skill 2.1)
- Creating Bulleted Lists (Skill 2.10)
- Changing Indents (Skill 2.17)
- Changing Text Case (Skill 2.4)
- Changing Line Spacing (Skill 2.14)

1. Open the **WD2013-FixIt-2-6** document.

2. Save this document as: `[your initials]WD-FixIt-2-6`

3. Clear the formatting from all the text in the document.

4. Reveal the formatting marks in the document and remove any extra line spaces.

5. Change the font and font size for the text in the document.

6. Select the **name at the top of the document** and apply a **Heading 1** Quick Style of your choice. Center the text.

7. Place your cursor in the first line of the address and remove the space after the paragraph.

8. Select the first section heading (**Summary**) and apply a **Heading 2** Quick Style of your choice and then change the font color of the text.

9. Use the **Format Painter** to copy and paste the formatting from the first section heading to the other section headings (**Computer Skills, Experience,** and **Education**).

10. Display the ruler and set a .75" tab stop to indent the first paragraph under the **Summary** section.

11. In the *Experience* section, bold the **dates** and italicize the **position titles and the company name.**

12. Change the items under *Computer Skills* into a bulleted list using a round filled circle bullet style.

13. Apply the same bulleted list style to items listed under each job experience.

14. Increase the indent on the lines under each degree by one level (the **school name** and the **GPA**).

15. Change the text case on both instances of **Gpa** to be **UPPERCASE.**

16. Adjust the line spacing and remove space before and after paragraphs to fit the text on one page.

17. Save and close the document.

chapter 3

Formatting and Printing Documents

In this chapter, you will learn the following skills:

» Add consistency to document fonts and colors by using themes

» Use headers and footers to display page numbering and the date/time

» Control document layout by adjusting margins and using page breaks

» Enhance document formatting by using page borders, watermarks, and hyperlinks

» Use building blocks, Quick Parts, and property controls to save time and provide consistency for

» Print multiple copies of a document and specific pages within a document

skills

introduction

This chapter provides you with the skills needed to format and print documents. The first step is to apply and work with document themes. Once you have applied themes, you will add document elements, including headers, footers, page numbers, and automatic dates. Next, you will add building blocks and property controls as well as hyperlinks. You'll learn how to modify the layout of a document by adding breaks and adjusting the margins. You will add a cover page and page borders to add graphic elements to the document. Finally, you will preview and print the document, including printing multiple copies and specific page ranges.

Skill 3.1 Applying Document Themes

A **theme** is a group of formatting options that you apply to an entire document. Themes include font, color, and effect styles that are applied to specific elements of a document. Theme colors control the colors available from the color palette for fonts, borders, and backgrounds. Theme fonts change the fonts used for built-in styles—such as Normal style and headings. Theme effects control the way graphic elements in your document appear. Applying a theme to your document is a quick way to take a simple piece of text and change it into a polished, professional-looking document.

FIGURE WD 3.1

To apply a theme to a document:

1. Click the **Design** tab.
2. In the *Document Formatting* group, click the **Themes** button.
3. Click a theme option to apply it to your document.

tips & tricks

To reset the theme to the original theme that came with the document's template, click the **Themes** button and select **Reset to Theme from Template.**

tell me **more**

You can modify any of the existing themes and save it as your own custom theme. The file will be saved with the *thmx* file extension. The theme will be saved in the *Document Themes* folder and will be available from Excel, PowerPoint, and Outlook as well as Word.

let me try

Open the student data file **wd3-01-SpaProductsReport** and try this skill on your own:

1. Change the theme of the document to the **Office** theme.
2. Save the file as directed by your instructor and close it.

Skill 3.2 Applying Style Sets

Each theme comes with a number of style sets you can choose from. A **style set** changes the font and paragraph formatting for an entire document. Style sets apply formatting based on styles. So, in order to see your changes, the text in your document must be formatted using styles. To learn more about applying styles to text, see *Using Quick Styles* in Chapter 2. The *Style Set* gallery displays thumbnails of how the text will appear when the style set is applied.

To change the style set:

1. Click the **Design** tab.
2. In the *Document Formatting* group, click the **More** button to open the *Style Set* gallery.
3. Click a style set from the gallery to apply it to the document.

FIGURE WD 3.2

tips & tricks

Click the **More** button in the *Style Set* gallery to see more options to choose from.

tell me **more**

The first thumbnail in the *Style Set* gallery displays the style set that is currently in use for the document.

let me try

Open the student data file **wd3-02-SpaProductReport** and try this skill on your own:

1. Apply the **Shaded** style set to the document.
2. Save the file as directed by your instructor and close it.

Skill 3.3 Using Color Themes

When creating a document, it can sometimes be difficult to choose colors that work well together. Documents can end up monochromatic or with too many colors that don't work well together. A **color theme** is a set of colors that are designed to work well together in a document. A color theme will change the color of text, tables, and drawing objects in a document. When you apply a theme to a document it includes a color theme, which has default theme colors for document elements. You can change the color theme without affecting the other components of the theme.

To apply a color theme to a document:

1. Click the **Design** tab.
2. In the *Document Formatting* group, click the **Colors** button.
3. Click a color theme option to apply it to your document.

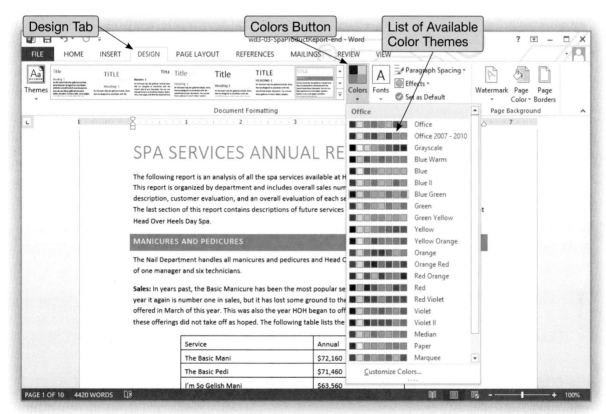

FIGURE WD 3.3

tell me **more**

When you change the color theme for a document, the color options for document elements will change. The theme colors will appear in the *Font Color* menu, as well as in the *Table Styles* and *Shape Styles* galleries. Choose your colors from these preset theme colors to ensure your document has a consistent color design.

let me try

Open the student data file **wd3-03-SpaProductReport** and try this skill on your own:

1. Change the color theme to the **Blue Green.**
2. Save the file as directed by your instructor and close it.

Skill 3.4 Using Font Themes

There are thousands of fonts for you to choose from to use in your documents. Some fonts are designed to work well as header text, such as Calibri Light and Cambria, and others are designed to work well as body text, such as Calibri. When you apply a theme to a document, this includes a font theme, which includes default fonts for body text and header text. As with color themes, you can change the font theme without affecting the other components of the theme.

To apply a font theme to a document:

1. Click the **Design** tab.

2. In the *Document Formatting* group, click the **Fonts** button.

3. Click a font theme option to apply it to your document.

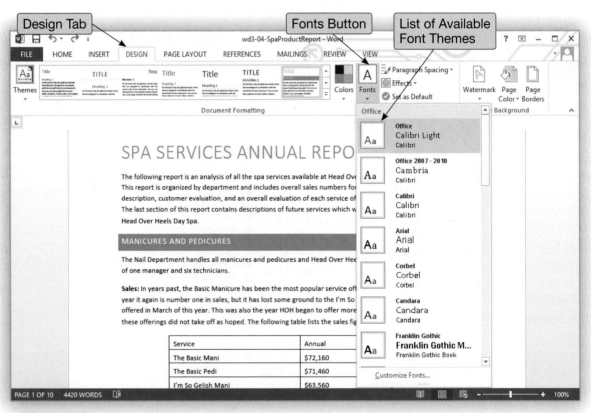

FIGURE WD 3.4

tell me **more**

let me **try**

Skill 3.5 Creating Watermarks

A **watermark** is a graphic or text that appears as part of the page background. Watermarks appear faded so the text that appears on top of the watermark is legible when the document is viewed or printed.

There are three categories of watermarks:

Confidential—Includes the text "Confidential" or "Do Not Copy" in different layouts.
Disclaimers—Include the text "Draft" or "Sample" in different layouts.
Urgent—Includes the text "ASAP" or "Urgent" in different layouts.

To add a watermark to a document:

1. Click the **Design** tab.
2. In the *Page Background* group, click the **Watermark** button and select an option from the gallery.

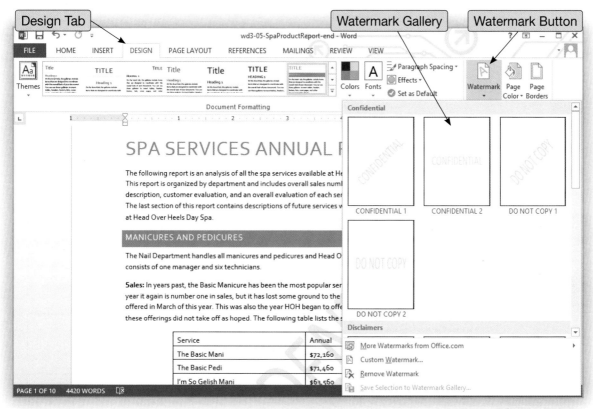

FIGURE WD 3.5

tips & tricks

You do not have to use one of the built-in watermarks from the *Watermark* gallery. You can create your own custom watermark, displaying whatever text or image you like. Click the **Custom Watermark...** command to open the *Printed Watermark* dialog and choose different options for the text watermark. You can add pictures as watermarks from this dialog. When you add a picture as a watermark, it appears faded so any text on top of it is still legible.

let me try

Open the student data file **wd3-05-SpaProduct Report** and try this skill on your own:

1. Apply the **Confidential 1** watermark to the document.
2. Save the file as directed by your instructor and close it.

Skill 3.6 Adding Headers

A **header** is text that appears at the top of every page, just below the top margin. Typically, headers display dates, page numbers, document titles, or authors' names. Word 2013 comes with a number of predesigned headers that you can add to your document and then modify to suit your needs.

To add a header to a document:

1. Click the **Insert** tab.
2. In the *Header & Footer* group, click the **Header** button and select a header format from the gallery.
3. Word displays the *Header & Footer Tools* contextual tab and inserts a header with content controls for you to enter your own information. Click a content control and enter the information for your header.
4. To close the header and return to your document, click the **Close Header and Footer** button on the contextual tab.

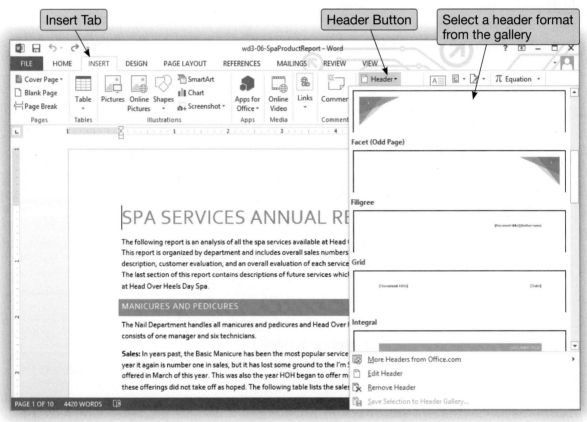

FIGURE WD 3.6

If the first page of your document is a title page, you won't want the header text to display on the page. To display a header on the first page of the document that is different from the header in the rest of the document, display the *Header & Footer Tools* tab. In the *Options* group, select the **Different First Page** check box.

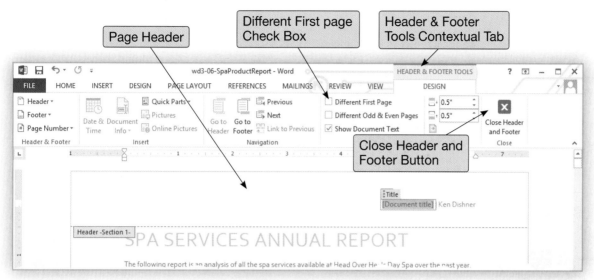

tips & tricks

Headers appear faded out in *Print Layout* view. If you want to edit a header, double-click it and make your changes. Click the **Close Header and Footer** button to return to the document.

another method

You can also add headers through the *Building Blocks Organizer*.

let me try

Open the student data file **wd3-06-SpaProductReport** and try this skill on your own:

1. Add a header to the document using the **Filigree** style.
2. Click the **[Document title]** control and type **Spa Services Annual Report**
3. Have the header display differently on the first page of the document.
4. Close the header and footer.
5. Scroll to the top of page 2 to see the header.
6. Save the file as directed by your instructor and close it.

Skill 3.7 Adding Footers

A **footer** is text that appears at the bottom of every page, just below the bottom margin. Typically, footers display dates, page numbers, or disclaimers. Word 2013 comes with a number of predesigned footers that you can add to your document and then modify to suit your needs.

To add a footer to a document:

1. Click the **Insert** tab.

2. In the *Header & Footer* group, click the **Footer** button and select a footer format from the gallery.

3. Word displays the *Header & Footer Tools* contextual tab and inserts a footer with content controls for you to enter your own information. Click a content control and enter the information for your footer.

4. To close the header and return to your document, click the **Close Header and Footer** button on the contextual tab.

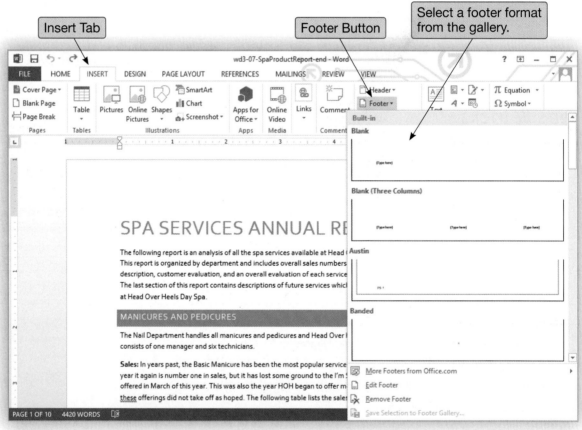

FIGURE WD 3.8

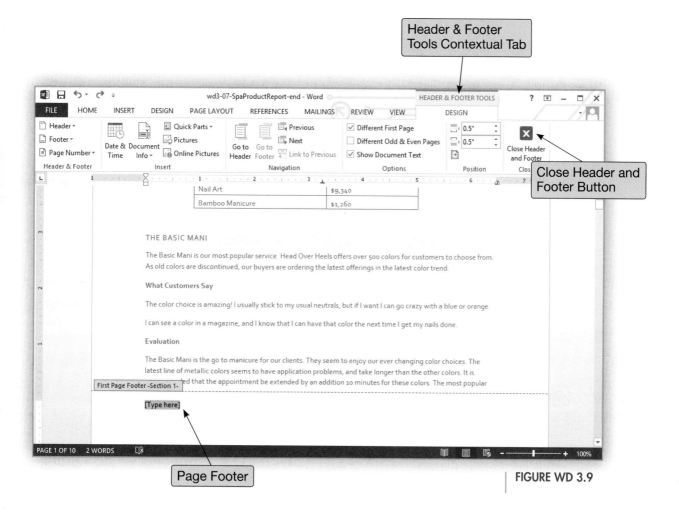

FIGURE WD 3.9

tips & tricks

When you add a header or footer to your document, the *Design* tab under *Header & Footer Tools* displays. This is called a contextual tab because it only displays when a header or footer is the active element. Click the **Design** tab to modify the header or footer properties.

another method

You can also add footers through the *Building Blocks Organizer*.

let me try

Open the student data file **wd3-07-SpaProductReport** and try this skill on your own:

1. Add a footer to the document using the **Blank** style.
2. Click the **[Type here]** control and type **Not for disclosure outside Head Over Heels Day Spa**.
3. Close the header and footer.
4. Save the file as directed by your instructor and close it.

Skill 3.8 Adding an Automatic Date Stamp

In addition to information such as the company name and page numbers, headers and footers typically include the current date. You could manually type the date in the header or footer and then update the date every time you work on the document, or you could add an **automatic date stamp.** This pulls the current date from the computer's system clock and displays the date in the document. The date is then automatically updated when the computer's date changes.

To add an automatic date stamp to the header of a document:

1. Double-click the header to switch to header view.
2. Under the *Header & Footer Tools,* in the *Insert* group, click the **Date & Time** button.
3. In the *Date and Time* dialog, select a date format in the *Available formats* list.
4. Select the **Update automatically** check box.
5. Click **OK.**
6. To close the header and return to your document, click the **Close Header and Footer** button on the contextual tab.

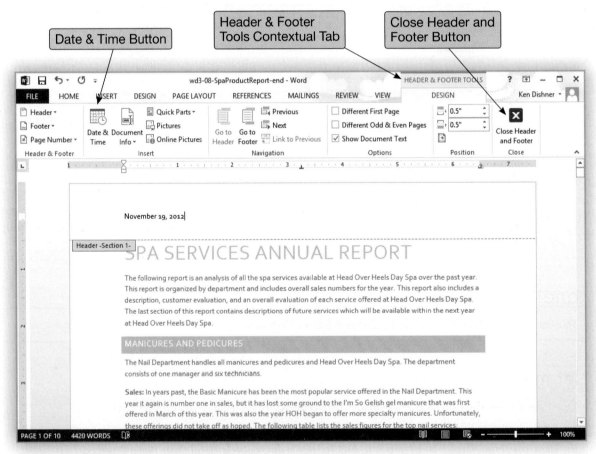

FIGURE WD 3.10

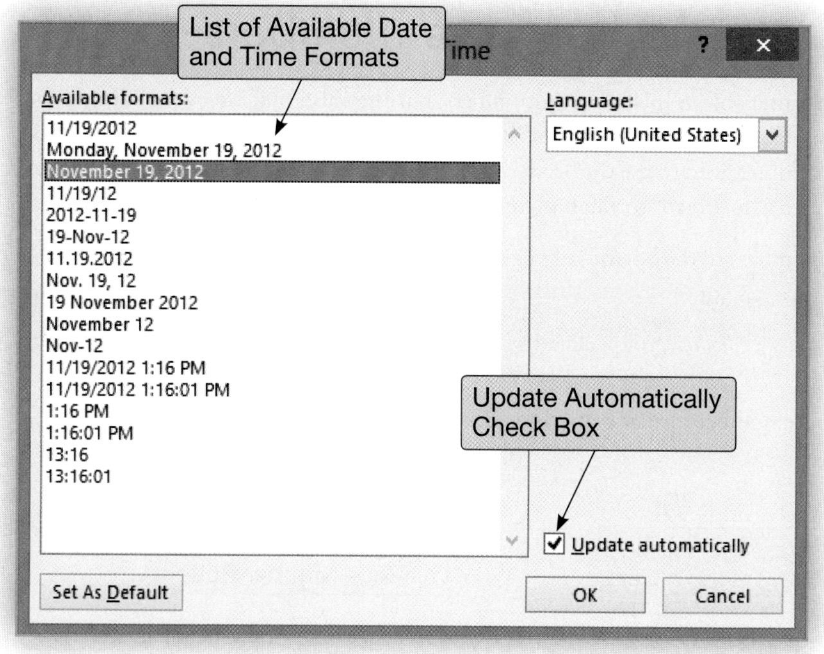
List of Available Date and Time Formats
Time
Available formats:
11/19/2012
Monday, November 19, 2012
November 19, 2012
11/19/12
2012-11-19
19-Nov-12
11.19.2012
Nov. 19, 12
19 November 2012
November 12
Nov-12
11/19/2012 1:16 PM
11/19/2012 1:16:01 PM
1:16 PM
1:16:01 PM
13:16
13:16:01
Language:
English (United States)
Update Automatically Check Box
Update automatically
Set As Default
OK
Cancel

FIGURE WD 3.11

tips & tricks

To update the date in your document, click the date and then select the **Update automatically** check box. Word will automatically display the computer's current date. If you did not select the *Update automatically* check box when you inserted the date, the computer will not automatically update the date in your document.

another method

You can also use *Quick Parts* to add the date and time to the header or footer of your document:

1. Double-click the header to make it active.
2. Under the *Header &Footer Tools,* in the *Insert* group, click the **Quick Parts** button and select **Field**...
3. In the *Field* dialog, click the **CreateDate** or the **Date** field.
4. Select a format for the date.
5. Click **OK.**

let me try

Open the student data file **wd3-08-SpaProductReport** and try this skill on your own:

1. Double-click the header area to switch to header view.
2. Open the **Date and Time** dialog.
3. Add a date that will update automatically the uses the format **Month Day, Year.** For example, January 1, 2014**.**
4. Close the header and footer.
5. Save the file as directed by your instructor and close it.

Skill 3.9 Inserting Page Numbers

Headers and footers often include page numbers, but they also include other information, such as author name, date, and document title. If all you want to do is add page numbers to a document, you don't need to use the header and footer feature. Instead, you can insert simple page numbers to a document through the *Page Number* gallery.

To add page numbers to the bottom of pages of a document:

1. Click the **Insert** tab.
2. In the *Header & Footer* group, click the **Page Number** button. Point to **Bottom of Page.**
3. Click a page number format from the gallery.

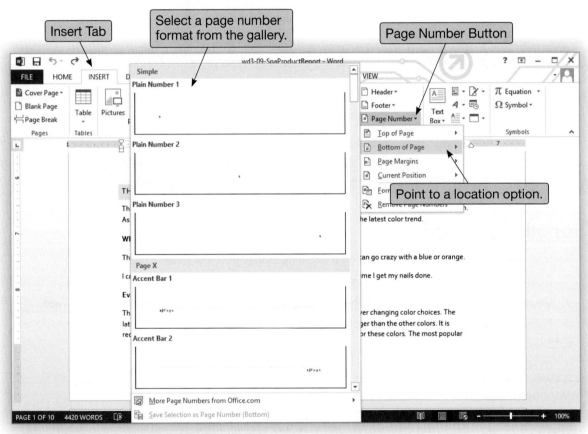

FIGURE WD 3.12

To remove a page number:

1. On the *Header & Footer Tools Design* tab, in the *Header & Footer* group, click the **Page Number** button.
2. Select **Remove Page Numbers.**

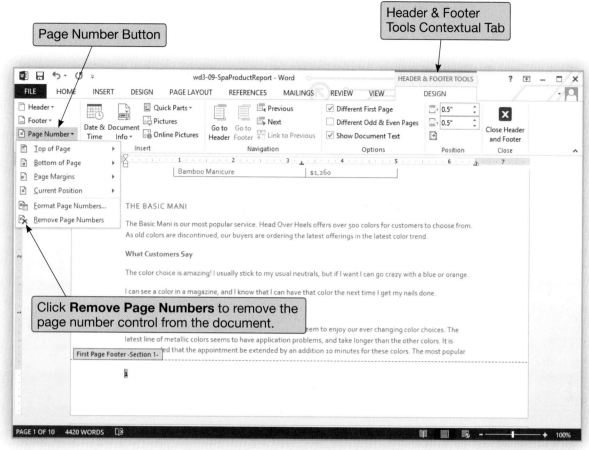

Page Number Button

Header & Footer Tools Contextual Tab

Click **Remove Page Numbers** to remove the page number control from the document.

FIGURE WD 3.13

tips & tricks

When adding page numbers to a document, you should always use Word's built-in building block. If you type page numbers into your document manually, they will not update when you add or remove pages.

tell me more

Traditionally, page numbers appear in the header or footer of the document. However, you can choose to display page numbers in the margin or at the current location of the cursor in the document.

another method

You can also add a page number through the *Building Blocks Organizer.*

let me try

Open the student data file **wd3-09-SpaProductReport** and try this skill on your own:

1. Add a page number to the bottom of the page using the **Plain Number 1** format.

2. Remove the **page number.**

3. Save the file as directed by your instructor and close it.

Skill 3.10 Inserting Building Blocks

A **building block** is a piece of content that is reusable in any document. Building blocks can be text, such as AutoText, or they can include graphics, such as a cover page. You can insert building blocks from specific commands on the Ribbon or from the **Building Blocks Organizer**. The *Building Blocks Organizer* lists the building blocks in alphabetical order by which gallery they appear in and includes *Bibliographies, Cover Pages, Equations, Footers, Headers, Page Numbers, Table of Contents, Tables, Text Boxes,* and *Watermarks.*

To insert a building block from the *Building Blocks Organizer:*

1. Click the **Insert** tab.
2. In the *Text* group, click the **Quick Parts** button and click **Building Blocks Organizer**...
3. Select a building block in the list and click the **Insert** button.

FIGURE WD 3.14

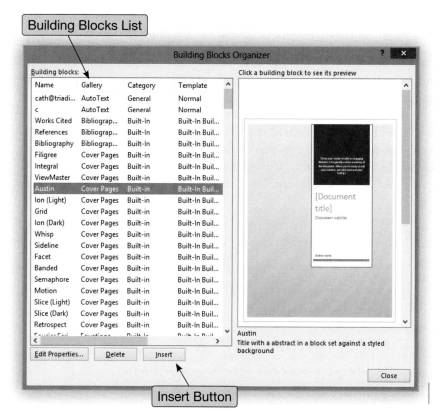

Building Blocks List

Insert Button

FIGURE WD 3.15

tips & tricks

If you find that the list of building blocks is too long, you can remove building blocks you don't use. To remove a building block from the *Building Blocks Organizer,* select a building block and click the **Delete** button. Be aware that the *Building Blocks Organizer* is used across all of Word 2013. If you delete a building block from the *Building Blocks Organizer,* it will no longer be available when you are working on other documents.

tell me **more**

You can sort the list of building blocks by clicking the *Name, Gallery, Category,* or *Template* button at the top of the *Building Blocks Organizer.* You can also modify the properties of a building block, changing properties such as the name or which gallery the building block appears in.

let me try

Open the student data file **wd3-10-SpaProductReport** and try this skill on your own:

1. Open the **Building Blocks Organizer**... dialog.
2. Insert a cover page using the **Austin building block.**
3. Save the file as directed by your instructor and close it.

Skill 3.11 Inserting Property Controls

A **property control** is an element you can add to your document to save time entering the same information over and over again. When you insert a property control and then replace the text with your own information, any time you add that control again it will include your custom text. Property controls can be used as shortcuts for entering long strings of text that are difficult to type. For example, instead of typing the company name Head Over Heels Day Spa, you can insert the *Company* property control. Word will add the text to the document and update the text automatically if any changes are made to the property control. By using property controls, you can be assured that all the information throughout the document is consistent.

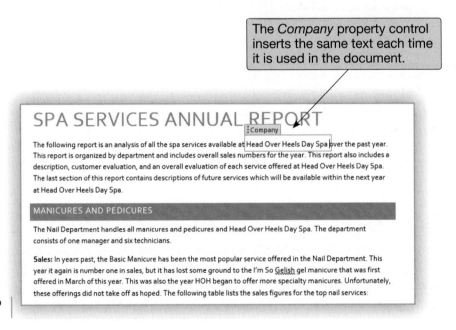

The *Company* property control inserts the same text each time it is used in the document.

FIGURE WD 3.16

To add a property control to a document:

1. Click the **Insert** tab.
2. In the *Text* group, click the **Quick Parts** button, point to **Document Property,** and select a control.
3. Type your text in the control. When you insert a property control, you may need to add a space between the control and the surrounding text.
4. Select the same control from the *Document Property* menu to add the same text to the document.

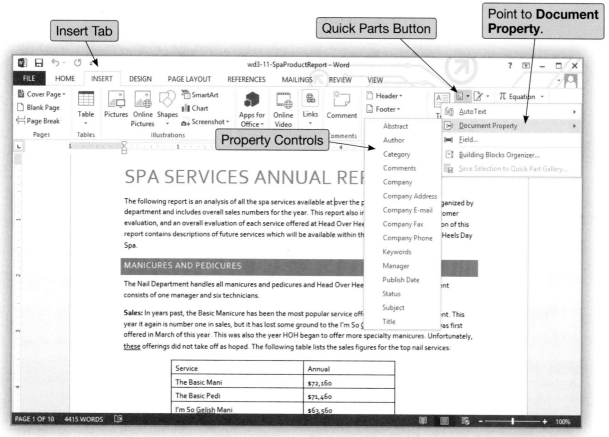

FIGURE WD 3.17

tips & tricks

If you need to update a property control, you only need to type the change once in the document. As you update any property control, all the other controls created from the same property control will update.

tell me more

Many of the built-in property controls, such as company name and author, pull their information from the document's properties. If you add a property control and modify the information, the document's related property will be updated as well.

let me try

Open the student data file **wd3-11-SpaProductReport** and try this skill on your own:

1. Click between the words **at** and **over** in the first sentence of the first paragraph of the document.
2. Insert a **document property** property control.
3. Type **Head Over Heels Day Spa.** Add a space between the property control and the surrounding text to fix any spacing issue.
4. Save the file as directed by your instructor and close it.

Skill 3.12 Inserting Hyperlinks

A **hyperlink** is text or a graphic that, when clicked, opens another page or file. You can use hyperlinks to link to a section in the same document, to a new document, or to an existing document, such as a Web page.

To insert a hyperlink:

1. Select the text or graphic you want to use as the link.
2. Click the **Insert** tab.
3. In the *Links* group, click the **Add a Hyperlink** button to open the *Insert Hyperlink* dialog.
4. Select an option under *Link to* and select the file to which you want to link.
5. Type the text of the link in the *Text to display* box.
6. Click **OK** to insert the hyperlink into your document.

FIGURE WD 3.18

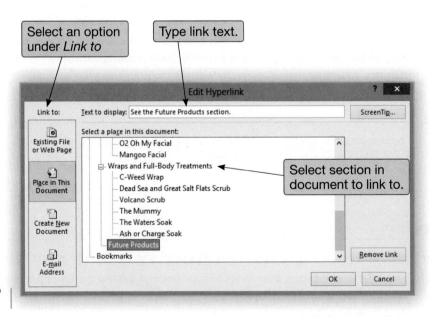

FIGURE WD 3.19

To edit a hyperlink, right-click the link and select **Edit Hyperlink**... from the menu. Make any changes in the *Edit Hyperlink* dialog.

To remove a hyperlink, right-click the link and select **Remove Hyperlink** from the menu.

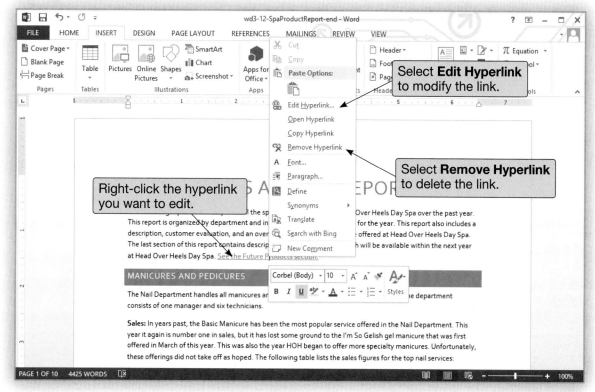

FIGURE WD 3.20

tell me **more**

Some hyperlinks include ScreenTips. A ScreenTip is a bubble that appears when the mouse is placed over the link. Add a ScreenTip to include a more meaningful description of the hyperlink.

another **method**

To open the *Insert* Hyperlink dialog, you can:

❱ Right-click the text or object you want as the link and select **Hyperlink**... from the shortcut menu.

❱ Press (Ctrl) + (K) on the keyboard.

let me **try**

Open the student data file **wd3-12-SpaProductReport** and try this skill on your own:

1. Place the cursor at the end of the first paragraph. Press the spacebar one time.
2. Open the **Insert Hyperlink** dialog.
3. Add a link to the **Future Products** section of the document.
4. Change the link text to read **See the Future Products section** and add the hyperlink**.**
5. Save the file as directed by your instructor and close it.

Skill 3.13 Adjusting Margins

Margins are the blank spaces at the top, bottom, left, and right of a page. Word's default margins are typically 1 inch for the top and bottom and 1 inch for the left and right. Word 2013 comes with a number of predefined margin layout options for you to choose from, including normal, narrow, wide, and mirrored.

To adjust the margins for a document:

1. Click the **Page Layout** tab.
2. In the *Page Setup* group, click the **Margins** button, and select an option for the page layout.

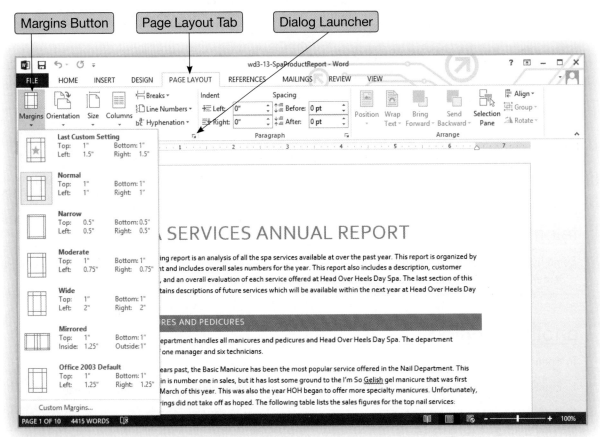

FIGURE WD 3.21

If you don't want to use one of Word's preset margins, you can set your own margin specifications in the *Page Setup* dialog.

To set custom margins:

1. On the *Page Layout* tab, in the *Page Setup* group, click the dialog launcher.
2. The *Page Setup* dialog opens.
3. Click the up and down arrows next to each margin (*Top, Bottom, Left,* and *Right*) to adjust the width and height of the margins.
4. Click **OK** to close the dialog.

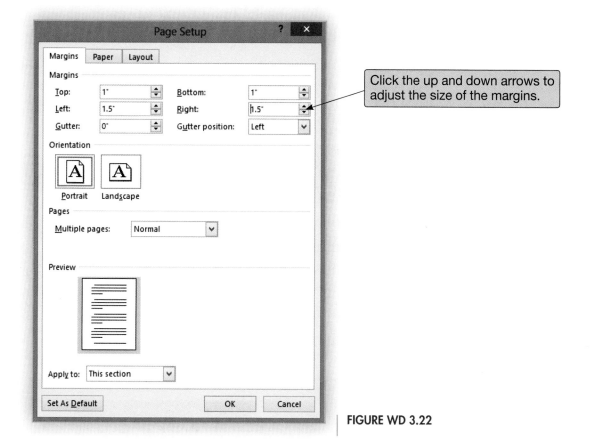

> Click the up and down arrows to adjust the size of the margins.

FIGURE WD 3.22

tips & tricks

While most documents you create will use the *Normal* or *Moderate* settings for margins, some documents will require either less or more space around the text. If you have a large exhibit or table, you may want to make the margins narrow so the content will still fit in portrait orientation. On the other hand, if you are writing a letter, you may want to increase your margins to accommodate preprinted stationery.

tell me **more**

A gutter is additional space you can add to one side of the document when you plan to have the document bound. You can enter the amount of extra space you need for binding in the *Gutter* box in the *Page Setup* dialog. You can then choose how your document will be bound—along the left side or along the top.

another **method**

❱ To open the *Page Setup* dialog, you can also click the **Margins** button and select **Custom Margins...**

❱ To adjust margins in the *Page Setup* dialog, you can also type the number in the box.

let me **try**

Open the student data file **wd3-13-SpaProductReport** and try this skill on your own:

1. Change the margins for the document to use the **Wide** margin settings.
2. Open the **Page Setup** dialog.
3. Change the left margin to **1.5"**. Change the right margin to **1.5"**.
4. Save the file as directed by your instructor and close it.

Skill 3.14 Inserting Page Breaks

When text or graphics have filled a page, Word inserts a soft page break and goes on to a new page. However, at times you may want to manually insert a **hard page break**—forcing the text to a new page no matter how much content is on the present page. Typically hard page breaks are used to keep certain information together.

To insert a hard page break:

1. Click the **Page Layout** tab.
2. In the *Page Setup* group, click the **Breaks** button, and select **Page.**

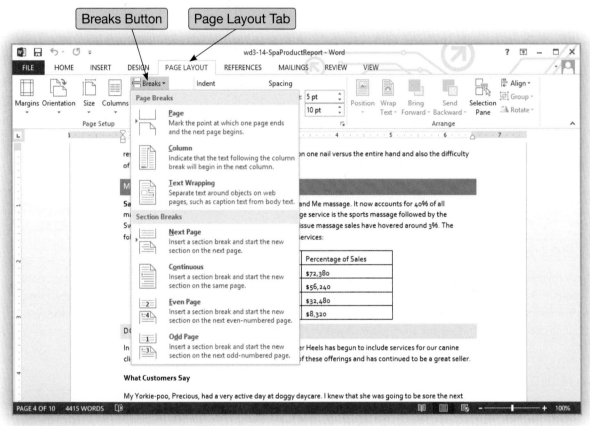

FIGURE WD 3.23

When you insert a page break, any remaining content in the document appears at the top of the next page. If you want an empty page to appear after the break, you can insert a blank page. When you insert a blank page, Word places a hard break, followed by a blank page, followed by the remaining content of the document.

To insert a blank page:

1. Click the **Insert** tab.
2. In the *Pages* group, click the **Blank Page** button.

tips & tricks

If you want to remove a hard page break, switch to *Draft* view so you can see where the break is. Place your cursor below the break and press **Delete** on the keyboard.

tell me **more**

There are two basic types of breaks you can add to a document:

Page Break—These breaks create visual breaks in your document but keep the content in the same section. Page breaks include *Page, Column,* and *Text Wrapping.*

Section Breaks—These breaks create new sections in your document. Section breaks include *Next Page, Continuous, Even Page,* and *Odd Page.*

another **method**

To insert a hard page break:

❯ On the *Insert* tab, in the *Pages* group, click the **Page Break** button.

❯ Press (Ctrl) + (←—Enter) on the keyboard.

let me **try**

Open the student data file **wd3-14-SpaProductReport** and try this skill on your own:

1. Place the cursor at the end of the paragraph before the **Massage Services** section. It is located near the top of page 4.
2. Insert a **page break.**
3. Save the file as directed by your instructor and close it.

Skill 3.15 Adding Page Borders

Page borders are graphic elements that can give your document a more polished look. **Page borders** draw a decorative graphic element along the top, right, bottom, and left edges of the page. Borders can be simple lines or 3-D effects and shadows. You can modify borders by changing the style and color. You can apply a border to the entire document or parts of a section.

To add a border to a document:

1. Click the **Design** tab.
2. In the *Page Background* group, click the **Page Borders** button.
3. The *Borders and Shading* dialog opens with the *Page Border* tab displayed.
4. Click a setting for the border.
5. Select a style, color, and width for the page border.
6. The *Preview* area shows how the border will look.
7. Click **OK** to accept your changes and add the page border to the document.

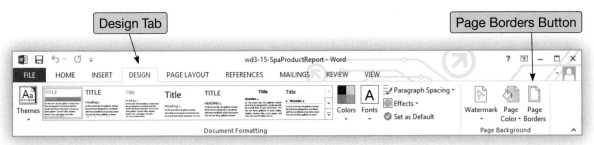

FIGURE WD 3.24

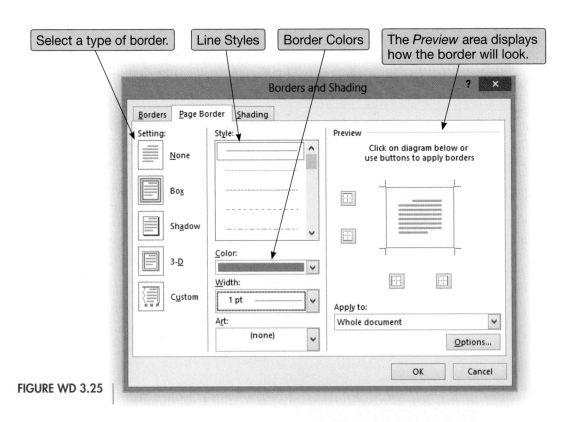

FIGURE WD 3.25

word 2013   chapter 3 Formatting and Printing Documents

tips & tricks

You can further adjust the look of page borders from the *Borders and Shading* dialog:

❱ Click on the **Preview** area diagram to add or remove parts of the border.

❱ Click the **Art** drop-down menu to select graphic elements for the border.

another method

You can also open the *Borders and Shading* dialog from the *Home* tab. In the *Paragraph* group, click the arrow next to the *Borders* button and select **Borders and Shading…**

let me try

Open the student data file **wd3-15-SpaProductReport** and try this skill on your own:

1. Open the **Borders and Shading** dialog.
2. Change the border to use the **Box** style. Apply the **Aqua, Accent 1** color. Change the width of the border to **1 pt.**
3. Save the file as directed by your instructor and close it.

from the perspective of . . .

MARKETING MANAGER

When writing a report, I use Word's built-in themes and style sets to create a cohesive document. A cover page and page borders add visual zing to my report that really grabs the attention of my readers. Before I send it out for review, I always add a footer and watermark to the report to let others know not to share the information outside our organization. Using the *Company* property control has been invaluable, especially when I realized I misspelled our company name in the report! And when it comes to printing, I am often printing at least 10 copies to hand out, but then can easily reprint an individual page when minor edits come in from my boss—which they always do.

Skill 3.16 Adding a Cover Page

When creating documents such as reports, proposals, or business plans, it is a good idea to include a **cover page** that contains the title of the document and the date. You can also add other information such as a subtitle, a short description of the document, and company information. Word 2013 comes with a number of prebuilt cover pages that you can quickly and easily add to your documents.

To add a cover page:

1. Click the **Insert** tab.
2. In the *Pages* group, click the **Cover Page** button and select an option.
3. Word inserts a cover page with content controls for you to enter your own information. Click a content control and enter the information for your document.

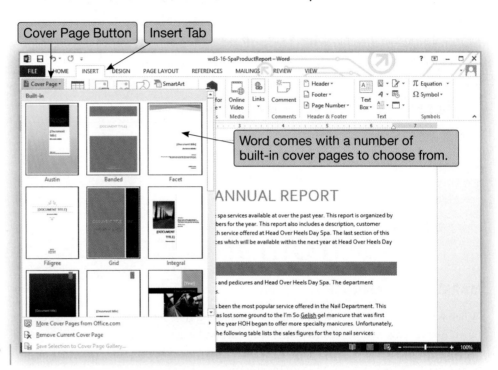

Cover Page Button   Insert Tab

Word comes with a number of built-in cover pages to choose from.

FIGURE WD 3.26

tips & tricks

Most content controls include instructions for adding text to the cover page. However, some content controls, such as the author, do not include text and are hidden from view. One way to see all the fields available in a cover page is to use the *Select All* command by pressing Ctrl + A on the keyboard.

tell me **more**

When you click a date content control, you will notice a calendar icon next to the text area. Click the icon to display the calendar to select a date to add to the cover page.

let me try

Open the student data file **wd3-16-SpaProductReport** and try this skill on your own:

1. Insert a cover page using the **Facet** style.
2. Delete the **Subtitle** content control from the cover page.
3. In the **Email address** content control, add the text **kdishner@hhspa.com.**
4. Save the file as directed by your instructor and close it.

word 2013   chapter 3 Formatting and Printing Documents

Skill 3.17 Previewing and Printing a Document

In Word 2013, all the print settings are combined in a single page along with a preview of how the printed document will look. From the *Print* page in Backstage view, you can preview and print all the pages in your document.

To preview and print a document:

1. Click the **File** tab to open Backstage view.
2. Click **Print.**
3. At the right side of the page is a preview of how the printed document will look. Beneath the preview there is a page count. If there are multiple pages, click the next and previous arrows to preview all the pages in the document.
4. Verify that the correct printer name is displayed in the *Printer* section.
5. Click the **Print** button to print.

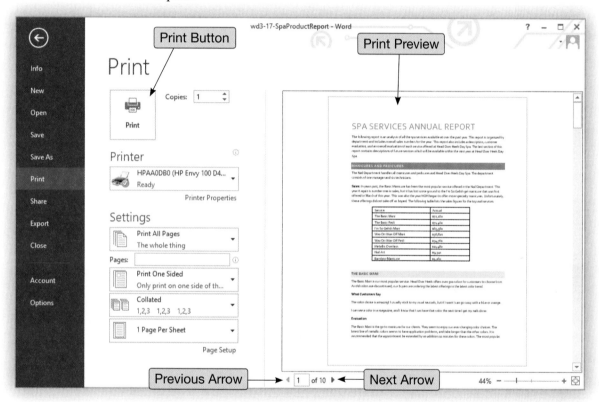

FIGURE WD 3.27

another **method**

To display the *Print* page, you can also press [Ctrl] + [P].

let me **try**

Open the student data file **wd3-17-SpaProductReport** and try this skill on your own:

1. Display the **Print** page in Backstage view.
2. Click the next and previous arrows to view how the document will look when it is printed.
3. Print the document. **NOTE:** If you are using this in class or in your school's computer lab, check with your instructor about printing permissions before completing this step.
4. Save the file as directed by your instructor and close it.

Skill 3.18 Printing Multiple Copies of a Document

When creating documents, sometimes you will only need one printed copy, but other times you will need to print more than a single copy. From the *Print* page in Backstage view, you can print multiple copies of a document.

To print multiple copies a document:

1. Click the **File** tab to open Backstage view.
2. Click **Print.**
3. Type the number of copies you want to print in the **Copies** box.
4. Click the **Print** button to print.

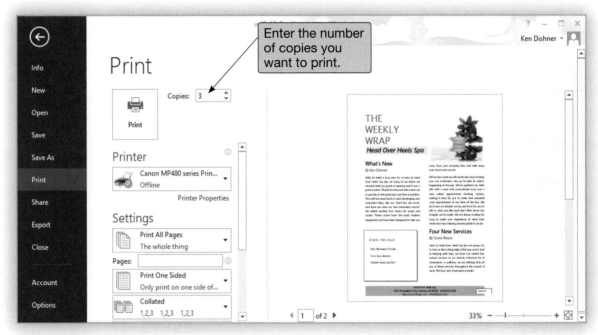

FIGURE WD 3.28

another **method**

You can also change the number of copies to print by clicking the up and down arrows next to the *Copies* box.

let me **try**

Open the student data file **wd3-18-SpaNewsletter** and try this skill on your own:

1. Display the **Print** page in Backstage view.
2. **Print** three copies of the document. **NOTE:** If you are using this in class or in your school's computer lab, check with your instructor about printing permissions before completing this step.
3. Save the file as directed by your instructor and close it.

Skill 3.19 Printing Page Ranges

When designating which pages to print, you can print a range of pages or individual pages. To print sequential pages type the number of the first page you want to print, followed by a hyphen, followed by the last page you want to print. For example, if you want to print pages 3 through 8 in your document, type **3-8** in the *Pages* box. To print individual pages, type each page number you want to print separated by a comma or semicolon. For example, if you want to print page 3, page 5, page 8, and page 10, type **3,5,8,10** in the *Pages* box.

To print specific pages in a document:

1. Click the **File** tab to open Backstage view.
2. Click **Print.**
3. In the *Settings* section, click in the **Pages** box and type the range of pages you want to print.
4. Click the **Print** button to print.

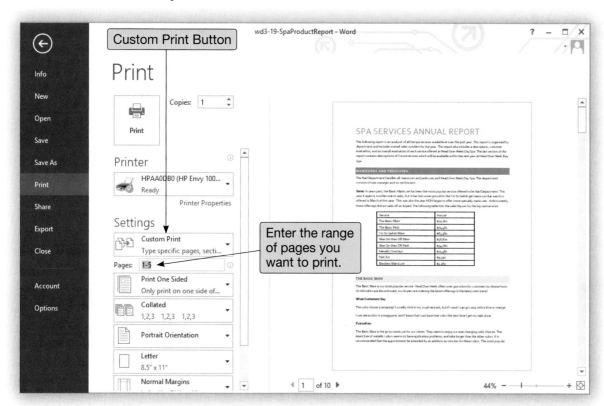

FIGURE WD 3.29

tell me **more**

When you enter a range of pages in the *Pages* box, the first button under *Settings* automatically changes to *Custom Print*.

let me try

Open the student data file **wd3-19-SpaProductReport** and try this skill on your own:

1. Display the **Print** page in Backstage view.
2. Print the first five pages of the document.
3. Now print pages 3 and 5. **NOTE:** If you are using this in class or in your school's computer lab, check with your instructor about printing permissions before completing this step.
4. Save the file as directed by your instructor and close it.

key terms

Theme
Style set
Color theme
Font theme
Watermark
Header
Footer
Automatic date stamp
Building block

Building Blocks Organizer
Property control
Hyperlink
ScreenTip
Margins
Hard page break
Page borders
Cover page

concepts review

1. A group of formatting elements you apply to a document is known as a _____.

a. building block

b. property control

c. theme

d. style

2. A _____ changes the font and paragraph formatting for an entire document based on styles.

a. font theme

b. style set

c. color theme

d. effects theme

3. A _____ is a graphic or text that appears as part of the page background and is usually faded in appearance.

a. watermark

b. cover page

c. margin

d. property control

4. Text that appears at the top of every page, just below the top margin is known as the _____.

a. header

b. footer

c. title

d. cover page

5. A piece of content that is reusable in any document, such as a cover page or a watermark, is known as a _____.

a. property control

b. building block

c. field

d. style set

6. A _____ is an element you can add to your document to save time entering the same information over and over again.

   a. style set

   b. theme

   c. property control

   d. building block

7. The blank spaces at the top, bottom, left, and right of a page are known as _____.

   a. margins

   b. borders

   c. page breaks

   d. columns

8. A _____ is text or a graphic that, when clicked, opens another page or file.

   a. building block

   b. field

   c. property control

   d. hyperlink

9. To force text on to a new page, insert a _____.

   a. cover page

   b. page border

   c. page break

   d. column

10. To print only the third and fifth page in a document, type _____ in the *Pages* box on the *Print* page.

   a. 3-5

   b. 3,5

   c. 3:5

   d. 35

skill review 3.1

In this project you will be formatting and printing a brochure for Suarez Marketing.

Skills needed to complete this project:
- Applying Document Themes (Skill 3.1)
- Applying Style Sets (Skill 3.2)
- Using Color Themes (Skill 3.3)
- Using Font Themes (Skill 3.4)
- Inserting Property Controls (Skill 3.11)
- Adjusting Margins (Skill 3.13)
- Inserting Page Breaks (Skill 3.14)
- Adding Page Borders (Skill 3.15)
- Adding Headers (Skill 3.6)
- Previewing and Printing a Document (Skill 3.17)
- Printing Multiple Copies of a Document (Skill 3.18)

1. Open the **WD2013-SkillReview-3-1** document.
2. Save this document as: **[your initials]WD-SkillReview-3-1**
3. Apply a theme to a document and change the style set.
   a. Click the **Design** tab.
   b. In the *Document Formatting* group, click the **Themes** button and select **Ion.**
   c. In the *Style Set* gallery, click the **Lines (Simple)** option.
4. Change the color theme.
   a. On the *Design* tab, in *Document Formatting* group, click the **Colors** button.
   b. Select the **Blue Warm** color theme.
5. Change the font theme.
   a. On the *Design* tab, in *Document Formatting* group, click the **Fonts** button.
   b. Select the **Corbel** font theme.
6. Add a company property control.
   a. Place the cursor in the empty line below *Maria Suarez.*
   b. Click the **Insert** tab.
   c. In the *Text* group, click the **Quick Parts** button. Point to *Document Property* and select **Company.**
   d. If a company name appears in the property control, delete the name. Type **Suarez Marketing** in the control. Click outside the control to deselect it.
7. Change the margins for the document.
   a. Click the **Page Layout** tab. In the *Page Setup* group, click the **Margins** button and select **Moderate.**
   b. In the *Page Setup* group, click the dialog launcher to open the *Page Setup* dialog.
   c. Type **.9″** in the *Left* box. Type **.9″** in the *Right* box. Click **OK.**

8. Add a page break.

    a. Click before the heading *Professional Credentials.*

    b. On the *Page Layout* tab, in the *Page Setup* group, click the **Breaks** button and select **Page.**

9. Add a page border to the document.

    a. Navigate to the top of the document.

    b. Click the **Design** tab. In the *Page Background* group, click the **Page Borders** button.

    c. Under *Setting,* change the option to **Box.** Click the **Color** arrow and select **Gray–50%, Accent 6** (it is the last option in the first row under *Theme Colors*). Click the **Width** arrow and select **1 ½ pt.** Click **OK.**

10. Add a header to the document.

    a. Click the **Insert** tab.

    b. In the *Header & Footer* group, click the **Header** button and select **Filigree** header option.

    c. On the *Design* tab, click the **Close Header and Footer** button.

11. Print multiple copies of the document.

    a. Click the **File** tab and click **Print.**

    b. Click the **Copies** up arrow two times, so **3** appears in the box.

    c. Click the **Print** button. **NOTE:** If you are using this in class or in your school's computer lab, check with your instructor about printing permissions before completing this step.

12. Save and close the document.

skill review 3.2

In this project you will be formatting and editing a paper on alternate assessments for students.

Skills needed to complete this project:

- Applying Document Themes (Skill 3.1)
- Applying Style Sets (Skill 3.2)
- Adding Footers (Skill 3.7)
- Inserting Property Controls (Skill 3.11)
- Inserting Page Numbers (Skill 3.9)
- Inserting Hyperlinks (Skill 3.12)
- Creating Watermarks (Skill 3.5)
- Inserting Page Breaks (Skill 3.14)
- Adding a Cover Page (Skill 3.16)
- Previewing and Printing a Document (Skill 3.17)
- Printing Page Ranges (Skill 3.19)

1. Open the **WD2013-SkillReview-3-2** document.

2. Save this document as: **[your initials]WD-SkillReview-3-2**

3. Apply a theme to a document and change the style set.

    a. Click the **Design** tab.

    b. In the *Document Formatting* group, click the **Themes** button and select **Mesh.**

    c. In the *Style Set* gallery, click the **Basic (Simple)** option.

4. Add footer text.

   a. Click the **Insert** tab.

   b. In the *Header & Footer* group, click the **Footer** button and select **Blank (Three Columns).**

   c. Click the [**Type here**] control at the far left side.

   d. Type `Alternate Assessment`

   e. Click the [**Type here**] control in the middle and press **Delete.**

5. Insert a property control.

   a. In the footer, click the [**Type here**] control at the far right side.

   b. Click the **Insert** tab.

   c. In the *Text* group, click the **Quick Parts** button, point to **Document Property,** and select **Author.**

   d. Type `Kelly Morehead`

   e. Click the **Header & Footer Tools Design** tab.

   f. Click the **Close Header and Footer** button.

6. Insert page numbers and display a different first page for the header.

   a. Click the **Insert** tab.

   b. In the *Header & Footer* group, click the **Page Number** button, point to **Top of Page,** and select **Plain Number 3.**

   c. On the *Header & Footer Tools Design* tab, in the *Options* group, select the **Different First Page** check box.

   d. Click the **Close Header and Footer** button.

7. Add a hyperlink to another place in the document.

   a. Navigate to the **Modified Achievement Standards** section.

   b. Place the cursor after the third sentence (ending in *to receive an alternate assessment.*) and press the spacebar one time.

   c. Click the **Insert** tab.

   d. In the *Links* group, click the **Hyperlink** button.

   e. Under *Link to* select **Place in This Document.**

   f. Select **Student Eligibility.**

   g. In the *Text to display* box, type (`See the Student Eligibility section`)

   h. Click **OK.**

8. Add a watermark to the document.

   a. Click the **Design** tab.

   b. In the *Page Background* section, click the **Watermark** button and select **DRAFT 1.**

9. Insert a page break.

   a. Navigate to the **Conclusion** heading and place the cursor at the beginning of the line.

   b. Click the **Page Layout** tab.

   c. In the *Page Setup* group, click the **Breaks** button and select **Page.**

10. Add a cover page.

   a. Click the **Insert** tab.

   b. In the *Pages* group, click the **Cover Page** button and select **Banded.**

   c. Select the [**Document Title**] control and type **Alternate Assessment**

   d. Select the [**Company address**] control and press **Delete.**

11. Preview and print a specific page range.

    a. Click the **File** tab.

    b. Click **Print. NOTE:** If you are using this in class or in your school's computer lab, check with your instructor about printing permissions before completing this step.

    c. Use the next and previous arrows to page through the preview of the document.

    d. In the *Pages* box, type **2-6.**

    e. Verify the name of your printer appears under *Printer.*

    f. Click the **Print** button. **NOTE:** If you are using this in class or in your school's computer lab, check with your instructor about printing permissions before completing this step.

12. Save and close the document.

challenge yourself **3.3**

In this project you will be formatting and editing a document for the Tri-State Book Festival.

Skills needed to complete this project:

- Applying Document Themes (Skill 3.1)
- Applying Style Sets (Skill 3.2)
- Using Color Themes (Skill 3.3)
- Using Font Themes (Skill 3.4)
- Adding Headers (Skill 3.6)
- Adding Footers (Skill 3.7)
- Inserting Property Controls (Skill 3.11)
- Adjusting Margins (Skill 3.13)
- Inserting Page Breaks (Skill 3.14)
- Adding Page Borders (Skill 3.15)
- Previewing and Printing a Document (Skill 3.17)
- Printing Multiple Copies of a Document (Skill 3.18)

1. Open the **WD2013-ChallengeYourself-3-3** document.
2. Save this document as: **[your initials]WD-ChallengeYourself-3-3**
3. Apply a theme to a document and change the style set.

    a. Apply the **Facet** theme to the document.

    b. Change the style set to **Shaded.**

4. Change the color theme to **Blue Warm.**
5. Change the font theme to **Century Gothic.**
6. Add a header to the document.

    a. Add a header using the **Banded** format.

    b. Change the header so the first page is different from the rest of the document.

    c. Close the **Header and Footer** contextual tab.

7. Add a footer and a property control.

    a. Add a footer using the **Blank** format.

    b. Replace the [**Type here**] control with an author property control.

    c. Close the **Header and Footer** contextual tab.

8. Change the margins for the document to the following:
   - *Top:* **1.1"**
   - *Bottom:* **1.1"**
   - *Left:* **1.25"**
   - *Right:* **1.25"**

9. Place the cursor above the *Tuesday October 11* heading in the *Agenda* section. Add a page break. Delete the extra line above the heading.

10. Add a page border to the document with the following settings:
    - *Setting:* **Box**
    - *Style:* **Solid line** (default option)
    - *Color:* **Blue, Accent 3**
    - *Width:* **1 pt**

11. Print two copies of the document. **NOTE:** If you are using this in class or in your school's computer lab, check with your instructor about printing permissions before completing this step.

12. Save and close the document.

challenge yourself 3.4

In this project you will be editing the text of a safety memo from the Spring Hills Association.

Skills needed to complete this project:

- Applying Document Themes (Skill 3.1)
- Applying Style Sets (Skill 3.2)
- Using Color Themes (Skill 3.3)
- Adding Footers (Skill 3.7)
- Adding Headers (Skill 3.6)
- Adding an Automatic Date Stamp (Skill 3.8)
- Inserting Hyperlinks (Skill 3.12)
- Creating Watermarks (Skill 3.5)
- Inserting Page Breaks (Skill 3.14)
- Adding a Cover Page (Skill 3.16)
- Previewing and Printing a Document (Skill 3.17)
- Printing Multiple Copies of a Document (Skill 3.18)
- Printing Page Ranges (Skill 3.19)

1. Open the **WD2013-ChallengeYourself-3-4** document.

2. Save this document as: **[your initials]WD-ChallengeYourself-3-4**

3. Apply a theme to a document and change the style set.

   a. Apply the **Wisp** theme to the document.

   b. Change the style set to **Lines (Simple)**.

4. Change the color theme to **Green.**

5. Add a footer using the **Ion (Light)** format. Close the **Header & Footer** contextual tab.

6. Add a header using the **Facet (Even Page)** format and display a different first page for the header.

7. Add an automatic date stamp to the right side of the header using the **MM/DD/YYYY** format. Be sure the date will update automatically. Close the **Header & Footer** contextual tab.

8. Add a hyperlink to another place in the document.

   a. Navigate to the **Our Safety Vision** section.

   b. Place the cursor after the second sentence (ending in *overlapping shifts.*) and press the spacebar one time.

   c. Add a hyperlink to the **Full Time Officers** section of the document. Have text for the link read (See the list of officers)

9. Add a watermark using the **SAMPLE 1.**

10. Insert a page break before the **Our Safety Vision** section.

11. Add a cover page.

    a. Insert a cover page using the **Retrospect** design.

    b. Change the **Document subtitle** to read **KEEPING OUR COMMUNITY SAFE**

    c. Delete the **COMPANY ADDRESS** control on the cover page.

12. Print three copies of the second, third, and fourth pages of the document. **NOTE:** If you are using this in class or in your school's computer lab, check with your instructor about printing permissions before completing this step.

13. Save and close the document.

on your own 3.5

In this project you will be editing the text of a brochure for Suarez Marketing.

Skills needed to complete this project:

- Applying Document Themes (Skill 3.1)
- Applying Style Sets (Skill 3.2)
- Using Color Themes (Skill 3.3)
- Using Font Themes (Skill 3.4)
- Inserting Page Numbers (Skill 3.9)
- Adding an Automatic Date Stamp (Skill 3.8)
- Adjusting Margins (Skill 3.13)
- Inserting Page Breaks (Skill 3.14)
- Adding Page Borders (Skill 3.15)
- Adding a Cover Page (Skill 3.16)
- Previewing and Printing a Document (Skill 3.17)
- Printing Multiple Copies of a Document (Skill 3.18)
- Printing Page Ranges (Skill 3.19)

1. Open the **WD2013-OnYourOwn-3-5** document.

2. Save this document as: **[your initials]WD-OnYourOwn-3-5**

3. Apply a theme of your choice to the document.

4. Change style set, color theme, and font theme.

5. Add a page number to the bottom of the document. Use a format of your choice.

6. Add an automatic date stamp to the footer of the document. Use a format of your choice.

7. Adjust the margins for optimal layout.

8. Insert page breaks so no heading section is broken across a page. **NOTE:** Depending on the margin settings you used, you may not need to insert a page break.

9. Add a page border of your choice. Modify the color and width of the border.

10. Add a cover page of your choice to the document. Enter document information and delete controls that are not used.

11. Print two copies of the document. **NOTE:** If you are using this in class or in your school's computer lab, check with your instructor about printing permissions before completing this step.

12. Save and close the document.

fix it **3.6**

In this project you will be editing the text of a brochure for Suarez Marketing.

Skills needed to complete this project:

- Inserting Page Numbers (Skill 3.9)
- Adding Footers (Skill 3.7)
- Adding an Automatic Date Stamp (Skill 3.8)
- Applying Document Themes (Skill 3.1)
- Applying Style Sets (Skill 3.2)
- Using Font Themes (Skill 3.4)
- Adjusting Margins (Skill 3.13)
- Inserting Page Breaks (Skill 3.14)
- Creating Watermarks (Skill 3.5)
- Previewing and Printing a Document (Skill 3.17)
- Printing Multiple Copies of a Document (Skill 3.18)

1. Open the **WD2013-FixIt-3-6** document.

2. Save this document as: **[your initials]WD-FixIt-3-6**

3. The author David Gonzalez typed his name and a page number at the top of each page. Delete this line from the top of each page. There are five instances of this mistake. **NOTE:** After you have deleted the first two instances of this mistake, the remaining instances will no longer appear at the top of the following pages.

4. Add the **Plain Number 3** page number to the top of **pages 2 through 5.**

5. Add a footer to the document using the **Facet (Even Page)** design.

6. Click after the author's name in the footer and insert an automatic time stamp using the **Month Day, Year** format (January 1, 2014). Close the **Header & Footer Tools** contextual tab.

7. Change the document theme to **View.**

8. Change the style set to **Basic (Simple).**

9. Change the font theme to **Office.**

10. Change the margins to use the **Normal** preset.

11. Insert a page break before the *V. Collect and evaluate the result* section.

12. Add a watermark using the **CONFIDENTIAL 1** format.

13. Print three copies of the document. **NOTE:** If you are using this in class or in your school's computer lab, check with your instructor about printing permissions before completing this step.

14. Save and close the document.

chapter 4

Working with Pictures, Tables, and Charts

In this chapter, you will learn the following skills:

❭ Insert pictures from an online source or from a file

❭ Resize, move, and change the layout of pictures

❭ Apply Quick Styles to objects

❭ Insert SmartArt, shapes, WordArt, and an online video

❭ Create a table

❭ Enter data in a table

❭ Modify the structure of a table

❭ Sort data in a table

❭ Add borders to a table

❭ Create and modify a chart

skills

introduction

This chapter provides you with the skills to add and modify pictures, graphic elements, tables, and charts. You will learn to insert pictures from an online source as well as from your own computer. Once you have added pictures to a document, you will manipulate them by resizing, positioning, and changing the text wrapping. You will then stylize pictures using Quick Styles. You will learn about other graphic objects you can add to documents including shapes, WordArt, and SmartArt diagrams. You will create and enter data in a table and then modify the table by adding and deleting rows and columns. You will change the display of data in a table by merging and splitting cells and sorting the data within a table. You will modify the look of a table by applying a table Quick Style and then changing the display of table borders. Finally, you will add a chart to a document and then modify the look of that chart.

Skill 4.1 Inserting Online Pictures

A new feature in Word 2013 is the ability to add **online pictures.** You can search for pictures from *Office.com Clip Art,* through a *Bing Image Search,* or from your SkyDrive. When you search on *Office.com,* you will be searching through Microsoft Office's royalty-free **clip art** collection. Word will display results of **clips** for you to use in your document. These clips refer to files from another source and include photographs and illustrations. If you use the *Bing Image Search,* you will be searching for images from across the Internet. Searching for images on your SkyDrive will return images that you have added to your SkyDrive for use in document.

To insert clip art from *Office.com*:

1. Click the **Insert** tab.
2. In the *Illustrations* group, click the **Online Pictures** button.

| Insert Tab | Online Pictures Button | **FIGURE WD 4.1** |

3. The *Insert Pictures* dialog opens.
4. Type a word describing the clip you want to search for in the **Office.com Clip Art** box and click the **Search** button.

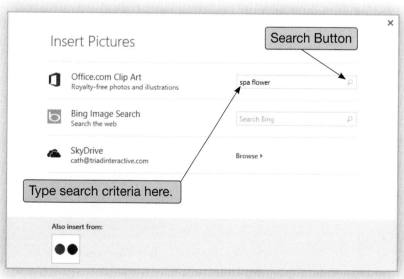

FIGURE WD 4.2

5. Word displays thumbnail results that match the search criteria.
6. Click a thumbnail to select it, and click the **Insert** button to add the image to your document.

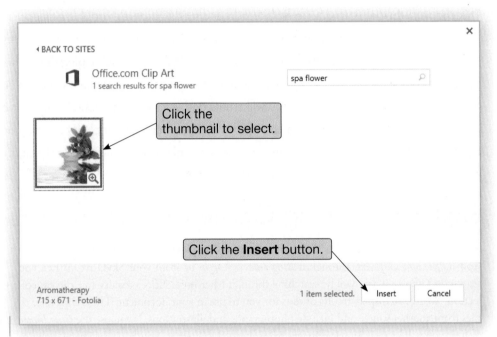

FIGURE WD 4.3

tips & tricks

If you use the *Office.com Clip Art* search, all the results that are returned are royalty-free images. This means you can use them freely in your document without worry of violating a copyright on an image. If you use the *Bing Image Search*, you will be searching the Internet for images and the results may not include images that are royalty free. You should only use images in your documents that you know you have the proper rights to use.

tell me more

In previous versions of Word, you searched for clips using the *Clip Art* task pane. In Word 2013, the *Clip Art* task pane has been replaced with the *Online Pictures* dialog. In the *Clip Art* task pane, you had the ability to filter the search results by type of image—photograph or illustration. The Online Pictures dialog does not have this feature.

let me try

Open the student data file **wd4-01-SpaNewsletter** and try this skill on your own:

1. Place the cursor at the end of the title **The Weekly Wrap.**
2. Open the **Insert Pictures** dialog.
3. Search **Office.com Clip Art** for **spa flower.**
4. Insert the picture of the purple flower with a candle. *Note:* If you do not see an image of a purple flower with a candle, insert an image of your choice.
5. Save the file as directed by your instructor and close it.

Skill 4.2 Resizing Pictures

When you first add an image to a document, you may find it is not the right size. The image may be too large for the page, or it may be too small for the page layout. You can resize images in a document by either manually entering the values for the size of the picture or by dragging a **resize handle** on the image to resize it.

To resize a picture by manually entering values:

1. Select the picture you want to resize.
2. Click the **Picture Tools Format** tab.
3. In the *Size* group, type a value in the *Width* or *Height* box to resize the picture.
4. Press ⏎ Enter to resize the picture.

To resize a picture by dragging:

1. Select the picture you want to change.
2. To resize a picture, click a **resize handle** and drag toward the center of the image to make it smaller or away from the center of the image to make it larger.

FIGURE WD 4.4

tips & tricks

When resizing by dragging, be sure to use one of the resize handles on the four corners of the picture to maintain the aspect ratio of the picture. If you use a resize handle along one of the sides of the picture, you will be resizing the width of the picture only. If you use a resize handle along the top or bottom of the picture, you will be resizing the height of the picture only.

When you enter a value in the *Width* or *Height* box on the Ribbon, the value in the other box will change to maintain the aspect ratio for the picture.

tell me more

When resizing a picture, you will most likely want the aspect ratio of the picture to stay the same. This means that as the width is increased or decreased, the height of the image is increased or decreased proportionally. If the aspect ratio did not remain the same, the image would appear stretched when you resized it.

let me try

Open the student data file **wd4-02-SpaNewsletter** and try this skill on your own:

1. Select the image of the flowers and candle.
2. Resize the image so it is **2.82"** in height and **3"** in width.
3. Save the file as directed by your instructor and close it.

Skill 4.3 Changing Picture Layouts

When you first add a picture to your document, Word inserts the picture at the insertion point and displays the picture in line with the text. This causes the picture to be treated as its own paragraph. But what if you want the text in your document to wrap around the picture? Word comes with a number of layout options for you to choose from. When a picture is selected, you will see the **Layout Options** button. This button gives you one-click access to text layout options for the picture.

To adjust the layout of a picture:

1. Click the image to select it.
2. Click the **Layout Options** button.
3. Select a wrapping option.

FIGURE WD 4.5

tips & tricks

As you roll the mouse over each layout option, Live Preview will display how the document will look with the text wrapping applied.

another method

To change the layout of pictures, you can also click the **Picture Tools Format** tab. In the *Arrange* group, click the **Wrap Text** button and select an option.

let me try

Open the student data file **wd4-03-SpaNewsletter** and try this skill on your own:

1. Select the image of the flowers and candle.
2. Change the layout option of the image of the flowers and candle so it appears behind text.
3. Save the file as directed by your instructor and close it.

Skill 4.4 Moving Pictures

When you first add an image to a document, you may find it is not positioned where you want it. You can change the position of images by dragging and dropping the image where you want it on the page.

Word 2013 now includes alignment guides for helping with picture layout. When you drag a picture, you will see horizontal and vertical green lines called the **alignment guides**. They appear when the picture's edge is aligned with another element on the page.

To move pictures in a document:

1. Select the picture you want to move.

2. Rest your mouse over the picture.

3. When the cursor changes to the **move cursor**, click and drag the image to the new location.

4. When an alignment guide appears aligning it with the desired element on the page, release the mouse button to snap the image in place and align it on the page.

FIGURE WD 4.6

tips & tricks

To turn off alignment guides, click the **Picture Tools Format** tab. In the *Arrange* group, click the **Align** button and select **Use Alignment Guides** so a checkmark does not appear next to the menu item.

let me try

Open the student data file **wd4-04-SpaNewsletter** and try this skill on your own:

1. Move the image of the flowers and candle to the upper right corner of the page, so the bottom of the image is aligned with the bottom of the gray banner (Volume 1, Issue 3).

2. Save the file as directed by your instructor and close it.

Skill 4.5 Inserting a Picture

You can insert pictures that you created in another program into your document. There are a number of graphic formats you can insert into a Word document. Some of the more common file types include JPEG, PNG, BMP, and GIF. By default, Word inserts images as embedded objects, meaning they become part of the new document. Changing the source file will not change or affect the newly inserted image.

To insert a picture from a file:

1. Click the **Insert** tab.

2. In the *Illustrations* group, click the **Pictures** button.

FIGURE WD 4.7

3. The *Insert Picture* dialog opens.

4. Navigate to the file location, select the file, and click **Insert.**

To delete a picture, select it and press the **Delete** key on the keyboard.

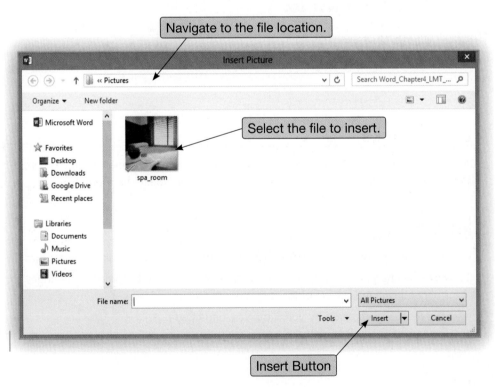

FIGURE WD 4.8

tell me **more**

When you insert a picture to a document, the *Format* tab under *Picture Tools* displays. This tab is called a contextual tab because it only displays when a picture is the active element. The *Format* tab contains tools to change the look of the picture, such as picture style, brightness and contrast, cropping, and placement on the page.

another **method**

To insert the file from the *Insert Picture* dialog, you can also click the **Insert** button arrow and select **Insert.**

let me **try**

Open the student data file **wd4-05-SpaNewsletter** and try this skill on your own:

1. Place the cursor at the end of the **Four New Services** article (below the *Mangoo Facial* bullet on page 2 of the student data file).
2. Open the **Insert Picture** dialog.
3. Navigate to the location where you saved the data files for this book.
4. Insert the **spa_room** picture.
5. Save the file as directed by your instructor and close it.

from the perspective of . . .

A COMMUNITY NEWSPAPER INTERN

When I first started working for the newspaper, articles were text with all the photographs arranged either above or below the text of the article. The text was well formatted, but didn't convey the information in an exciting, visual manner. We do the layout in Word for delivery either in print or online. So, one of the things I thought of was adding video to the online version of the newspaper. I can search for online videos and embed them in articles to be viewed by our readers. I also love playing with Word's picture layout and design tools, so now the newspaper layout has a more dynamic flow.

Skill 4.6 Positioning Pictures

When you first add a picture to your document, Word inserts the picture at the insertion point and displays the picture in line with the text. More often than not, you will want to place the picture somewhere else on the page. Word comes with a number of preset image positions that place the picture at a specific location on the page with text wrapping applied.

To position a picture on a page with text wrapping:

1. Click the **Picture Tools Format** tab.
2. In the *Arrange* group, click the **Position Object** button.
3. In the *With Text Wrapping* section, select an option. The image is placed on the page according to the option you chose.

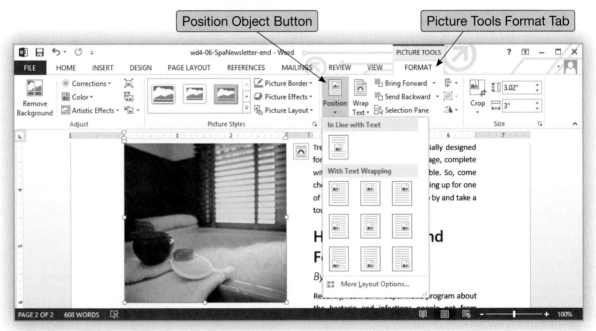

FIGURE WD 4.9

tips & tricks

When you position a picture, the location you choose is for the page the picture is on. If you want the picture to appear on another page, move the picture to that page and then use the **Position Object** command to place it.

another method

You can also position pictures on the page from the *Page Layout* tab. In the *Arrange* group, click the **Position Object** button and select an option.

let me try

Open the student data file **wd4-06-SpaNewsletter** and try this skill on your own:

1. Select the picture on page 2 of the student data file.
2. Position the picture so it is in the middle of the page aligned along the left side.
3. Save the file as directed by your instructor and close it.

Skill 4.7 Applying Quick Styles to Pictures

Quick Styles are a combination of formatting that gives elements of your document a more polished, professional look without a lot of work. Quick Styles for pictures include a combination of borders, shadows, reflections, and picture shapes, such as rounded corners or skewed perspective. Instead of applying each of these formatting elements one at a time, you can apply a combination of elements at one time using a preset Quick Style.

To apply a Quick Style to a picture:

1. Select the picture you want to apply the Quick Style to.
2. Click the **Picture Tools Format** tab.
3. In the *Picture Styles* group, click the **More** button.
4. In the *Picture Quick Styles* gallery, click an option to apply it to the picture.

Choose a formatting style from the *Picture Quick Styles* gallery.

Picture Tools Format Tab

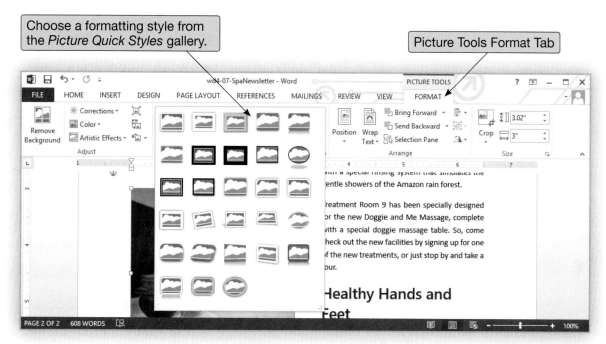

FIGURE WD 4.10

tell me **more**

The same steps for applying Quick Styles to pictures can be used to apply Quick Styles to other drawing objects, such as shapes.

another **method**

To apply a Quick Style to a picture, you can also right-click the picture, click the **Picture** button, and select a Quick Style from the gallery.

let me try

Open the student data file **wd4-07-SpaNewsletter** and try this skill on your own:

1. Select the picture on page 2 of the student data file.
2. Apply the **Reflected Rounded Rectangle** Quick Style to the picture (it is the fifth option in the first row of the gallery).
3. Save the file as directed by your instructor and close it.

Skill 4.8 Inserting SmartArt

SmartArt is a way to make your ideas visual. Where documents used to have plain bulleted and ordered lists, now they can have SmartArt, which are visual diagrams containing graphic elements with text boxes in which you can enter your information. Using SmartArt not only makes your document look better, but it helps convey the information in a more meaningful way.

To add SmartArt to a document:

1. Click the **Insert** tab.
2. Click the **SmartArt** button.

FIGURE WD 4.11

3. In the *Choose a SmartArt Graphic* dialog, click a **SmartArt** option and click **OK.**
4. The Smart Art is added to your document.
5. Click in the first item of the *SmartArt Text* pane and type your first item.
6. Enter the text for each item.
7. Click outside the SmartArt graphic to hide the *Text* pane.

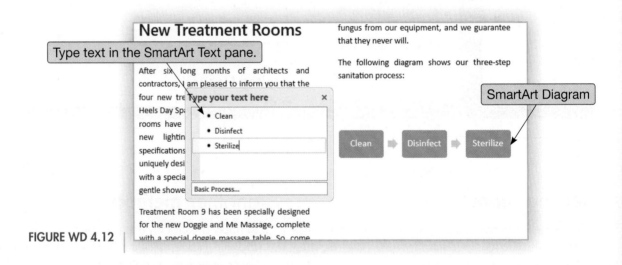

FIGURE WD 4.12

There are eight categories of SmartArt for you to choose from:

List—Use to list items that do not need to be in a particular order.

Process—Use to list items that do need to be in a particular order.

Cycle—Use for a process that repeats over and over again.

Hierarchy—Use to show branching, in either a decision tree or an organization chart.

Relationship—Use to show relationships between items.

Matrix—Use to show how an item fits into the whole.

Pyramid—Use to illustrate how things relate to each other with the largest item on the bottom and the smallest item on the top.

Picture—Use to show a series of pictures along with text in the diagram.

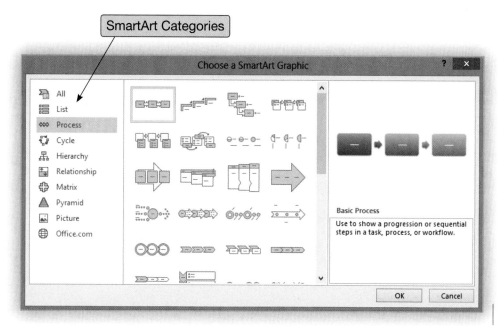

FIGURE WD 4.13

tips & tricks

When choosing a SmartArt diagram, it is important that the diagram type suits your content. In the *Choose a SmartArt Graphic* dialog, click a SmartArt type to display a preview of the SmartArt to the right. The preview displays not only what the diagram will look like, but also includes a description of the best uses for the diagram type.

another method

To enter text in SmartArt, you can click in a text box on the SmartArt diagram and type your text.

let me try

Open the student data file **wd4-08-SpaNewsletter** and try this skill on your own:

1. Place the cursor at the end of the *Healthy Hands and Feet* article (at the end of the second column on the second page).
2. Open the **Choose a SmartArt Graphic** dialog box.
3. Insert a **Basic Process** diagram.
4. Enter **Clean** in the first box.
5. Enter **Disinfect** in the second box.
6. Enter **Sterilize** in the third box.
7. Click outside the diagram to deselect it.
8. Save the file as directed by your instructor and close it.

Skill 4.9 Inserting a Shape

A **shape** is a drawing object that you can quickly add to your document. Word comes with a number of shapes for you to choose from, including lines, block arrows, callouts, and basic shapes such as smiley faces, rectangles, and circles.

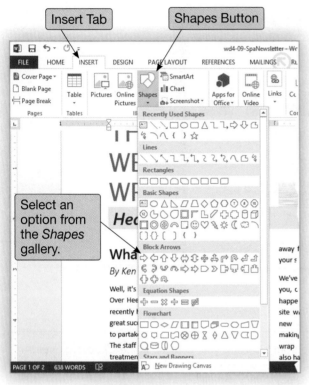

FIGURE WD 4.14

To add a shape to a document:

1. Click the **Insert** tab.
2. In the *Illustrations* group, click the **Shapes** button and select an option from the *Shapes* gallery.
3. The cursor changes to a crosshair.
4. Click and drag anywhere on the document. As you are dragging, you will see an outline of the shape. When the shape is the size you want, release the mouse button.

tell me **more**

When you insert a shape into a document, the *Drawing Tools Format* tab displays. This is called a contextual tab because it only displays when a drawing object is the active element. The *Format* tab contains tools to change the look of the shape, such as shape styles, effects, and placement on the page. You can apply Quick Styles to shapes by selecting an option in the *Shape Quick Styles* gallery in the *Shape Styles* group. Click the **More** button for the gallery to expand it and view all the Quick Style options you can apply to shapes.

let me **try**

Open the student data file **wd4-09-SpaNewsletter** and try this skill on your own:

1. Add a **12-Point Star** shape next the *What's New* article title.
2. Save the file as directed by your instructor and close it.

Skill 4.10 Adding WordArt to Documents

Sometimes you'll want to call attention to text you have added to your document. You could format the text by using character effects, or if you want the text to really stand out, use **WordArt**. WordArt Quick Styles are predefined graphic styles you can apply to text. These styles include a combination of color, fills, outlines, and effects.

To add WordArt to a document:

1. Click the **Insert** tab.
2. In the *Text* group, click the **Insert WordArt** button and select a Quick Style from the gallery.
3. Replace the text *Your Text Here* with the text for your document.

After you have added WordArt to your document, you can modify it just as you would any other text. Use the *Font* box and *Font Size* box on the *Home* tab to change the font or font size of WordArt.

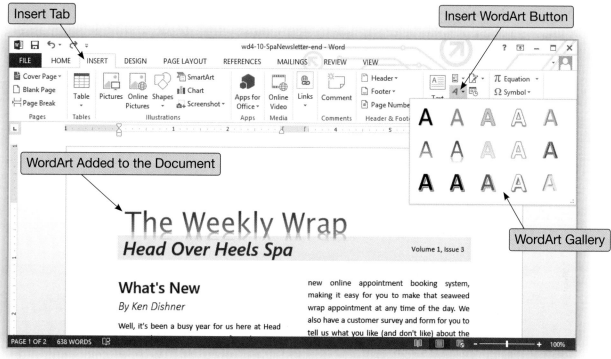

FIGURE WD 4.15

tell me **more**

In Word 2010, WordArt was changed to allow a wide range of stylization. In previous versions of Microsoft Word, WordArt came with a predefined set of graphic styles that could be formatted, but on a very limited basis.

let me **try**

Open the student data file **wd4-10-SpaNewsletter** and try this skill on your own:

1. Place the cursor at the top of the document.
2. Add WordArt to the document using the **Gradient Fill–Blue, Accent 1, Reflection** style.
3. Replace the text *Your Text Here* with **The Weekly Wrap.**
4. Save the file as directed by your instructor and close it.

Skill 4.11 Adding an Online Video

Today documents are not only printed and read, but often they are delivered and primarily viewed in an electronic format. A new feature in Word 2013 is the ability to add **online video** to a document. You can use Microsoft's *Bing Video Search* to search for videos online and then add them to your documents.

To add an online video to a document:

1. Click the **Insert** tab.
2. In the *Media* group, click the **Online Video** button.

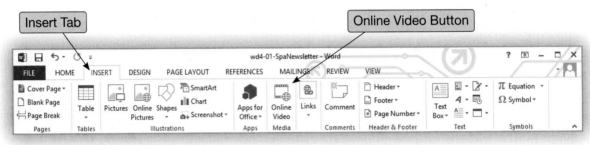

FIGURE WD 4.16

3. The *Insert Video* dialog opens.
4. Type a word describing the video you want to search for in the **Bing Video Search** box and click the **Search** button.

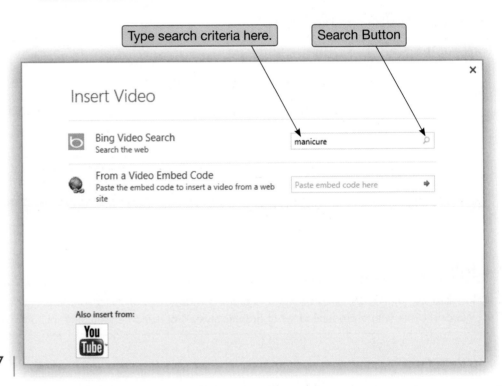

FIGURE WD 4.17

5. Word displays thumbnail results that match the search criteria.
6. Click a thumbnail to select it and click the **Insert** button to add the video to your document.

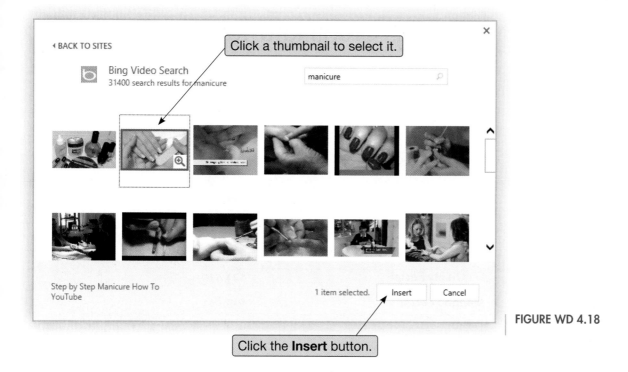

FIGURE WD 4.18

tips & tricks

To play a video in a document, click the **Play** button. However, not all videos allow you to play the video from the document. If you cannot play the video inside the document, right-click the video and select **Open in Browser** to play the video in your Web browser.

tell me **more**

You can also search for videos to add to documents directly from *YouTube* or embed a video from a Web site by entering a video embed code.

let me try

Open the student data file **wd4-11-SpaProductReport** and try this skill on your own:

1. Place the cursor in the blank line under the first paragraph in the **Basic Mani** section.
2. Open the **Insert Video** dialog.
3. Search for a video about **manicure.**
4. Insert the **Step by Step Manicure How To** video. It is the selected thumbnail in Figure 4.18. *Note:* If you do not see the same thumbnails as in the figure, insert an online video of your choice.
5. Save the file as directed by your instructor and close it.

Skill 4.12 Creating a Table

A **table** helps you organize information for effective display. Tables are organized by **rows**, which display horizontally, and **columns**, which display vertically. The intersection of a row and column is referred to as a **cell**. Tables can be used to display everything from dates in a calendar to sales numbers to product inventory.

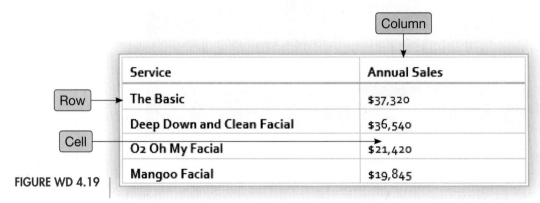

FIGURE WD 4.19

To create a simple table:

1. Click the **Insert** tab.
2. Click the **Table** button.
3. Select the number of cells you want by moving the cursor across and down the squares.
4. When the description at the top of the menu displays the number of rows and columns you want, click the mouse.
5. The table is inserted into your document.

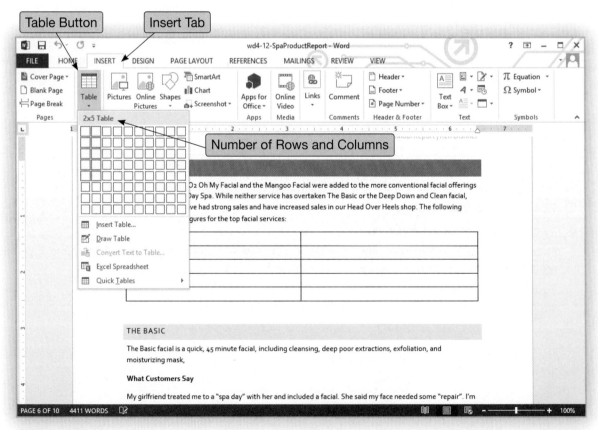

FIGURE WD 4.20

word 2013   chapter 4 Working with Pictures, Tables, and Charts

tips & tricks

Rather than inserting a table and then adding data, you can convert existing text into a table. After selecting the text to be converted, click the **Table** button and click **Insert Table...** The number of rows and columns will automatically be determined by the tabs and paragraphs in the selection.

tell me **more**

Word 2013 comes with a number of Quick Tables building blocks. These templates are preformatted for you and include sample data. To insert a Quick Table, click the **Tables** button, point to **Quick Tables,** and select a building block option from the gallery. After you insert a Quick Table, just replace the sample data with your own.

another **method**

To insert a table, you can also:

1. Click the **Table** button and select **Insert Table...**
2. In the *Insert Table* dialog box, enter the number of rows and columns for your table.
3. Click **OK.**

let me **try**

Open the student data file **wd4-12-SpaProductReport** and try this skill on your own:

1. Navigate to the *FACIALS* section of the document and place the cursor on the blank line under the first paragraph of the section.
2. Insert a table that has **two columns** and **five rows.**
3. Save the file as directed by your instructor and close it.

Skill 4.13 Working with Tables

Once you have inserted a blank table, you will need to enter data. When entering data in a table, it is a good idea to use the first row as a heading row by typing a short description of the content for the column in each cell. After you have labeled each column, continue entering the data into your table.

To enter data in a table:

1. Place the cursor in the cell where you want to enter the data.

2. Type the data just as you would in normal text.

3. Press ⟨Tab ⇄⟩ to move to the next cell and enter more data.

4. When you reach the last cell in the last row of a table, pressing [Tab] on the keyboard will create a new row in the table.

5. Continue pressing ⟨Tab ⇄⟩ until all data are entered.

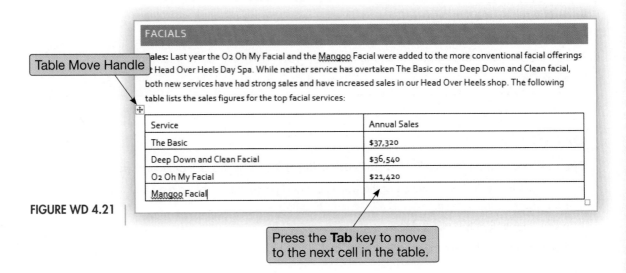

Table Move Handle

Press the **Tab** key to move to the next cell in the table.

FIGURE WD 4.21

After you have entered data in a table, you will most likely want to manipulate all or part of the table. You can select individual rows or columns to work with or the entire table:

❯ To select a row, point to the left side of the row you want to select. When the cursor changes to a white arrow 𝄃, press the mouse button. The selected row will appear highlighted.

❯ To select a column, point to the top of the column you want to select. When the cursor changes to a black, down-pointing arrow ⬇, press the mouse button. The selected column will appear highlighted.

❯ To select the entire table, click the **table move handle** that appears at the upper left corner of the table when it is active.

tell me **more**

another **method**

To select parts of a table, you can also:

1. Click the **Table Tools Layout** tab.
2. In the *Table* group, click the **Select** button and select an option.

let me **try**

Open the student data file **wd4-13-SpaProductReport** and try this skill on your own:

1. Navigate to the empty table in the *FACIALS* section (it is located on page 6 of the student data file).
2. Practice selecting a row, a column, and the entire table.
3. Enter the following information in the table. Press the [Tab ⇄] key to move between cells in the table.

SERVICE	ANNUAL SALES
The Basic	$37,320
Deep Down and Clean Facial	$36,540
O2 Oh My Facial	$21,420
Mangoo Facial	$19,845

4. Save the file as directed by your instructor and close it.

Skill 4.14 Inserting Rows and Columns

Once you have created a table, you often find you need more rows or columns. In Word 2013, you can now quickly add rows and columns to tables with **Insert Controls**. Insert Controls appear when you roll your mouse over the left edge of a row or the top edge of a column.

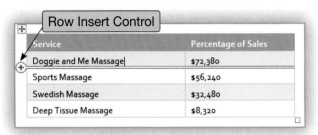

FIGURE WD 4.22

To add a new row using an Insert Control:

1. Roll your mouse along the left side of the table.
2. When the **Insert Control** appears where you want to add the new row, click the **control.**

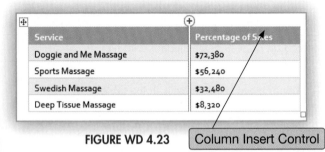

FIGURE WD 4.23

To add a new column using an Insert Control:

1. Roll your mouse along the top of the table.
2. When the **Insert Control** appears where you want to add the new column, click the **control.**

tips & tricks

A quick way to insert a new row at the end of a table is to place the cursor in the last cell in the last row and then press the [Tab ⇆] key. A new row is automatically added to the table, with your cursor in its first cell.

another method

- To insert an additional row and column, you can also click the **Table Tools Layout** tab. In the *Rows & Columns* group, click the **Insert Above** or **Insert Below** buttons to insert a new row. Click the **Insert Left** or **Insert Right** buttons to insert a new column.

- You can also insert rows and columns by right-clicking in a cell, pointing to **Insert** and selecting **Insert Rows Above, Insert Rows Below, Insert Columns to the Left,** or **Insert Columns to the Right.**

- You can also insert rows and columns by right-clicking in a cell, clicking the **Insert** button on the Mini toolbar, and selecting an option.

let me try

Open the student data file **wd4-14-SpaProductReport** and try this skill on your own:

1. Navigate to the table in the *FACIALS* section.
2. Insert a new row between the first and second row in the table.
3. Insert a new column on the right side of the table.
4. Save the file as directed by your instructor and close it.

Skill 4.15 Deleting Columns, Rows, and Cells

After you have added information to your table, you may find that you no longer want to include everything you added. Even if you delete the text in a table row or column, the empty row or column still remains. To remove the row or column from the table, you must delete the row or column, not just the text. When you delete a row or column from a table, the content along with the table element is removed.

To delete a row or column:

1. Select the row or column you want to delete.
2. The Mini toolbar displays.
3. Click the **Delete** button and select an option.

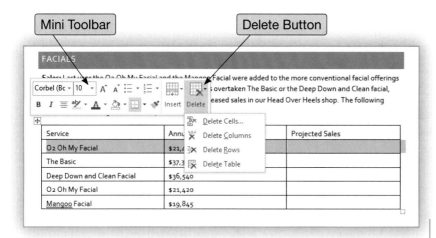

FIGURE WD 4.24

tips & tricks

You can also delete individual cells from a table. When you delete a cell, the *Delete Cells* dialog appears. Here you can choose to shift the cells to the left or up. You can also choose to delete the entire row or column the cell belongs to.

another method

To delete rows and columns you can also:

❱ Select the row or column you want to delete. Right-click in the row or column, and select **Delete Row** or **Delete Column.**

❱ Click in the row or column you want to delete. Click the **Table Tools Layout** tab. In the *Rows & Columns* group, click the **Delete** button and select an option.

let me try

Open the student data file **wd4-15-SpaProductReport** and try this skill on your own:

1. Navigate to the table in the *FACIALS* section.
2. Delete the **second row** in the table.
3. Delete the **Projected Sales** column.
4. Save the file as directed by your instructor and close it.

Skill 4.16 Sizing Tables, Columns, and Rows

When you insert a table, it covers the full width of the page and the columns and rows are evenly spaced. Once you have entered your data, you will probably find the table is larger than it needs to be and the columns and rows need adjusting. You can resize your table using Word's *AutoFit* commands.

To adjust the width and height of cells using the *AutoFit* command:

1. Click in the table you want to resize.
2. Click the **Table Tools Layout** tab.
3. In the *Cell Size* group, click the **AutoFit** button.
4. Select **AutoFit Contents** to resize the cell to fit the text of the table. Select **AutoFit Window** to resize the table to the size of the page.

Rather than using the *AutoFit* command, you can specify a width and height for table cells from the Ribbon.

To adjust the width and height of cells:

1. Click in the row or column you want to resize.
2. On the *Table Tools Layout* tab, in the *Cell Size* group, adjust the numbers for the **Table Row Height** and **Table Column Width** by clicking the up and down arrows in the control box.

To resize all the rows in a table so they have the same height, in the *Cell Size* group click the **Distribute Rows** button. Click the **Distribute Columns** to resize all the columns in a table so they have the same width.

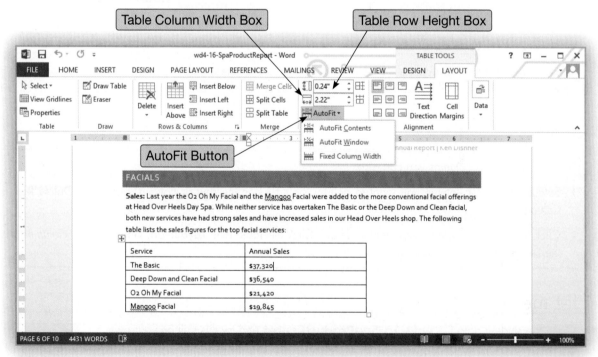

FIGURE WD 4.25

tips & tricks

Once you have resized a table, you will probably want to position it better on the page. You can do this by using the **table move handle** tool that appears at the top-left corner of the table when the mouse pointer is placed over the table. Click the move handle and drag the table to where you want it.

tell me **more**

Each cell is set up as one line, but if you type more data than will fit in one line, Word will automatically wrap and create another line within the cell, making the row taller. If this happens, all the cells in that row will be affected.

another **method**

To resize a table, you can also:

1. Select the table you want to resize.
2. When the **resize handle** appears at the bottom-right corner of the table, click and drag it until you achieve the desired size. This method can also be used to resize columns and rows.

let me **try**

Open the student data file **wd4-16-SpaProductReport** and try this skill on your own:

1. Navigate to the table in the *FACIALS* section.
2. Use the **AutoFit** command to resize the table so it fits the window.
3. Save the file as directed by your instructor and close it.

Skill 4.17 Merging and Splitting Cells

When you first create a table, it is a grid of rows and columns. But what if you want to display your content across columns or across rows? For instance, if the first row of your table includes the title for the table, then you will probably want to display the title in a single cell that spans all the columns of the table. In this case, you will want to *merge* the cells in the first row into one cell. On the other hand, if you have a cell that contains multiple values, you may want to *split* the cell so it can display each value in a separate row or column. Use the **merge cells** and **split cells** commands to customize the layout of tables. Merging cells entails combining multiple cells into one; splitting a cell divides the cell into multiple cells.

To merge cells in a table:

1. Select the cells you want to merge into one.
2. Click the **Table Tools Layout** tab.
3. In the *Merge* group, click the **Merge Cells** button.

To split a cell in a table:

1. Select the cell you want to split.
2. In the *Merge* group, click the **Split Cells** button.
3. In the *Split Cells* dialog box, enter the number of columns and rows.
4. Click **OK** to split the cell.

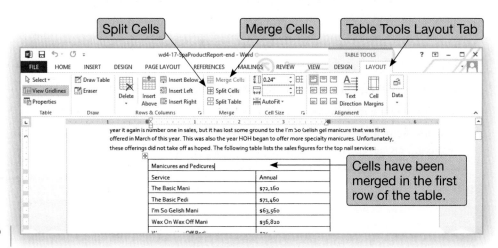

FIGURE WD 4.26

tips & tricks

In addition to splitting cells, you also split a table, creating two tables from one. To split a table into two tables:

1. Place the cursor in the row where you want to split the table.
2. In the *Merge* group, click the **Split Table** button.

another **method**

❱ To merge cells, you can right-click the selected cells and select **Merge Cells** from the menu.

❱ To split cells, you can right-click a cell and select **Split Cells...** from the menu.

let me **try**

Open the student data file **wd4-17-SpaProductReport** and try this skill on your own:

1. Navigate to the table in the *MANICURES AND PEDICURES* section.
2. Split the first row of the table into two columns and one row.
3. Merge the cells in the first row of the table.
4. Save the file as directed by your instructor and close it.

Skill 4.18 Sorting Data in Tables

After you have entered data in a table, you may decide it needs to be displayed in a different order. **Sorting** rearranges the rows in your table by the text in a column or columns. Word allows you to sort data based on the first character of each entry. You can sort in alphabetical or numeric order, in either ascending (A–Z) or descending (Z–A) order.

To sort a column alphabetically:

1. Click the **Table Tools Layout** tab.
2. In the *Data* group, click the **Sort** button.

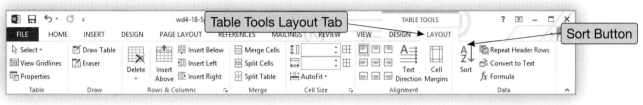

FIGURE WD 4.27

3. The *Sort* dialog box opens.
4. Click the **Sort by** arrow and select a field to sort by.
5. The *Ascending* radio button is selected by default.
6. If your table has a header row that you do not want to include in the sort, select the **Header row** radio button.
7. Click **OK** to sort the text in the table.

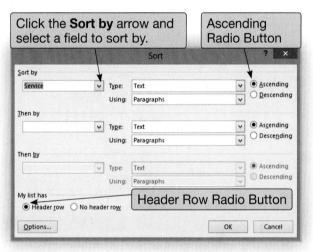

FIGURE WD 4.28

tips & tricks

You can sort by text, number, or date. You can refine the sort by choosing additional fields to sort by:

▶ If you want to sort the text in reverse order, from Z to A, click the **Descending** radio button.

▶ Word can sort upper- and lowercase letters differently. Click the **Options...** button in the *Sort* dialog box and then click the **Case sensitive** check box in the *Sort Options* dialog box.

another method

To open the *Sort* dialog box, from the *Home* tab, in the *Paragraph* group, click the **Sort** button.

let me try

Open the student data file **wd4-18-SpaProduct Report** and try this skill on your own:

1. Navigate to the table in the *MANICURES AND PEDICURES* section.
2. Open the **Sort** dialog.
3. Sort the table in descending order based on the content of the **Annual** column. Be sure not to include the header row in the sort.
4. Save the file as directed by your instructor and close it.

Skill 4.19 Applying Table Quick Styles

Just as you can apply complex formatting to paragraphs using Quick Styles for text, you can apply complex formatting to tables using Quick Styles for tables. Using Quick Styles for tables, you can change the text color along with the borders and shading for a table, giving it a professional, sophisticated look without a lot of work.

To apply a Quick Style to a table:

1. Click the **Table Tools Design** tab.
2. In the *Table Styles* group, click the **More** button.
3. Select a Quick Style from the *Quick Styles* gallery.

By default, the Word *Table Styles* gallery displays styles that include header rows, banded rows, and first column layouts. Depending on the information in your table, you may not want to format your table using all these options. If you want to change the options that display in the gallery, check or uncheck the options in the *Table Styles Options* group.

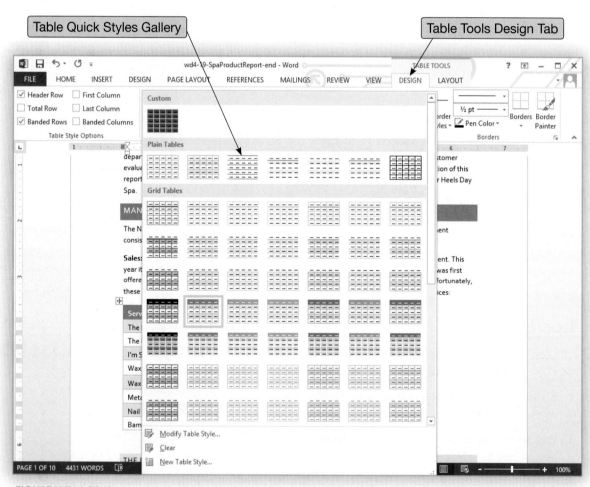

FIGURE WD 4.29

tips & tricks

To create your own table style, click the **More** button and select **New Table Style...** In the *Create New Style from Formatting* dialog box, you can create a new table style based on an existing table style, changing options such as gridlines and shading to suit your needs. When you save the style, it will appear in the *Table Styles* gallery.

tell me **more**

In addition to applying a Quick Style to a table, you can change the shading, or background color, applied to the table. Adding shading to a table helps it stand out on a page. To apply shading to a table, click the **Shading** button in the *Table Styles* group. A palette of colors displays. Select a color to change the background color for the table.

another **method**

The *Table Styles* group on the Ribbon displays the latest Quick Styles you have used. If you want to apply a recently used Quick Style, you can click the option directly from the Ribbon without opening the *Quick Styles* gallery.

let me **try**

Open the student data file **wd4-19-SpaProductReport** and try this skill on your own:

1. Navigate to the table in the *MANICURES AND PEDICURES* section.
2. Change the *Quick Style* gallery display so formats with **first column** formatting do not display.
3. Apply the **Grid Table 4–Accent 1** Quick Style to the table (it is the second option in the fourth row under *Grid Tables*).
4. Save the file as directed by your instructor and close it.

Skill 4.20 Adding Borders to a Table

When you first create a table, it uses the simple grid style. You can apply a Quick Style to your table to quickly add formatting, but what if you want to further adjust the look of a table after applying the Quick Style? You can choose different shading for your table and add and remove borders to change the look of the entire table or just parts of the table.

To change the borders for a table:

1. Select the table you want to change.
2. Click the **Table Tools Design** tab.
3. In the *Borders* group, click the **Borders** button arrow.
4. Click a border option to apply it to the table.

If your table does not show borders, you can display **gridlines** to give you a visual guide. The gridlines appear as a dotted line on screen but do not print as part of the final document. To display gridlines, click the **Borders** button and select **View Gridlines.**

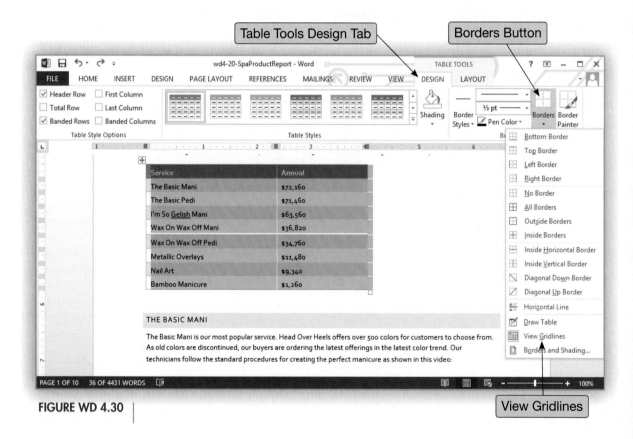

FIGURE WD 4.30

tips & tricks

The **Border Styles** button allows you format specific borders in your table.

1. On the *Table Tools Design* tab, in the *Borders* group, click the **Border** Styles button.
2. Select an option from the gallery.
3. The *Border Painter* becomes active.
4. Click and drag the mouse across the border you want to change to apply the border style.

another **method**

You can change the borders of a table by clicking the *Home* tab. In the *Paragraph* group, click the arrow next to the *Borders* button and select an option.

You can change borders and shading through the *Borders and Shading* dialog box. To open the *Borders and Shading* dialog box:

❱ From the *Home* tab or from the *Design* tab, click the arrow next to the *Borders* button and select **Borders and Shading...**

❱ Right-click on the table and select **Borders and Shading...** from the menu.

let me **try**

Open the student data file **wd4-20-SpaProductReport** and try this skill on your own:

1. Select the table in the *MANICURES AND PEDICURES* section.
2. Apply an **outside border** to the table.
3. Save the file as directed by your instructor and close it.

Skill 4.21 Creating a Chart

Charts allow you to take raw data and display them in a visual way. A **chart** takes the values you have entered in a spreadsheet and converts them to graphic representation. In Word, you can create a wide variety of charts, including bar charts, pie charts, column charts, and line charts.

To add a chart to a document:

1. Click the **Insert** tab.
2. In the *Illustrations* group, click the **Add a Chart** button.

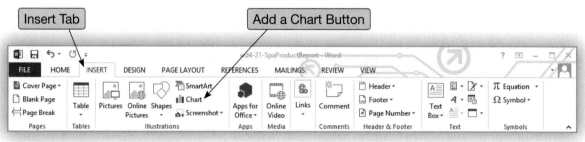

FIGURE WD 4.31

3. In the *Insert Chart* dialog, click a chart type category to display that category in the right pane.
4. Click a chart type in the right pane to select it.
5. Click **OK** to add the chart to the document.

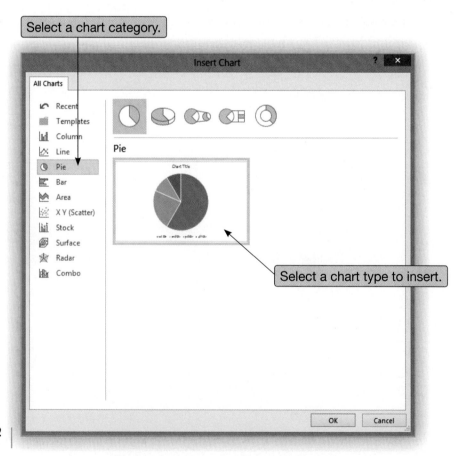

FIGURE WD 4.32

Word automatically opens the *Chart in Microsoft Word* dialog. Think of this dialog as a simplified spreadsheet where you can enter the data for your chart. The dialog opens with sample data entered for you.

1. Replace the sample data with your own data.
2. Click the **Close** button to return to Word to see your finished chart.

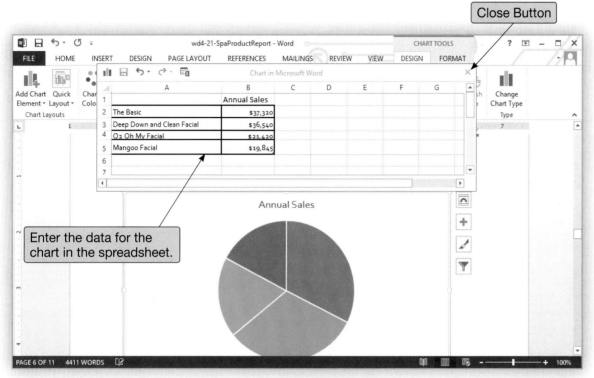

FIGURE WD 4.33

tell me **more**

As you enter data in the *Chart in Microsoft Word* dialog, Word will update the chart as you enter data and move from cell to cell in the spreadsheet.

let me **try**

Open the student data file **wd4-21-SpaProductReport** and try this skill on your own:

1. Navigate to the *FACIALS* section and place your cursor on the empty line.
2. Insert a **pie chart** into the document.
3. Enter the following information for the chart:

	ANNUAL SALES
The Basic	$37,320
Deep Down and Clean Facial	$36,540
O2 Oh My Facial	$21,420
Mangoo Facial	$19,845

4. Close the *Chart in Microsoft Word* dialog.
5. Save the file as directed by your instructor and close it.

Skill 4.22 Modifying a Chart

When you insert a chart, Word displays the chart based on the chart type and the document's theme. But what if you want to change the look of your chart? Word includes a number of chart styles for you to choose from. These styles are a combination of chart layout styles and formatting options.

To change the style of a chart:

1. Select the chart you want to change.
2. Click the **Chart Styles** button on the right side of the chart.
3. Scroll the list of styles. Click a style to apply it to the chart.

To hide and show chart elements, such as the chart title and legend, click the **Chart Elements** button and select and deselect options to show and hide them on the chart.

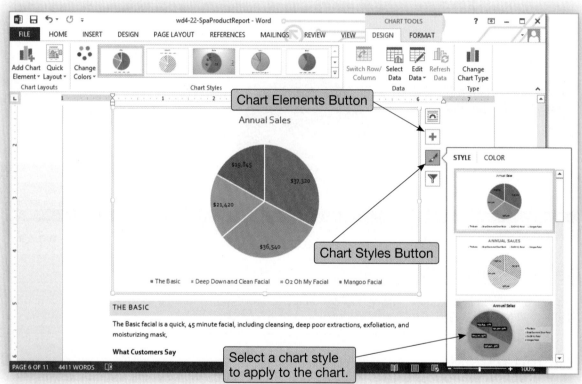

FIGURE WD 4.34

tips & tricks

To change the color of the chart, click the **Color** button in the *Chart Styles* pane. Word displays a number of color sets for you to choose from. These color sets are based on the color theme applied to the document. Select a color set to apply to the chart.

another method

To change the chart style, you can also:

1. Click the **Chart Tools Design** tab.
2. In the *Chart Styles* group, click the style you want to use, or click the **More** button to see all of the chart styles available.

let me try

Open the student data file **wd4-22-SpaProductReport** and try this skill on your own:

1. Navigate to the *FACIALS* section of the document and select the chart.
2. Apply the **Style 3** chart style to the chart.
3. Save the file as directed by your instructor and close it.

Online picture	Online Video
Clip art	Table
Clips	Row
Resize handle	Column
Layout Options	Cell
Alignment guides	Insert Control
Move cursor	Merge cells
Quick Styles	Split cells
SmartArt	Sorting
Shape	Gridlines
WordArt	Chart

concepts review

1. To add clip art to a document, click the _____ button.

   a. Insert Picture

   b. Online Picture

   c. Online Video

   d. Insert Shape

2. To have text wrap around an image, select the image and click the _____ button.

   a. Layout Options

   b. Group

   c. Align

   d. Rotate

3. When you move an image on a page, special green lines called _____ appear, helping you align the image to other elements on the page.

   a. grids

   b. guides

   c. anchors

   d. handles

4. A(n) _____ is a combination of formatting, including color, shadows, and reflections, that you apply to pictures.

   a. Picture Effect

   b. Artistic Effect

   c. Quick Style

   d. Style Set

5. Visual diagrams containing graphic elements with text boxes for you to enter your information in are called _____.

   a. charts

   b. SmartArt

   c. WordArt

   d. tables

6. _____ allows you to quickly add rows and columns to tables.
   a. An Alignment Guide
   b. An Insert Control
   c. A header row
   d. The merge cells command

7. You can add online pictures from _____.
   a. *Office.com*
   b. *Bing Image Search*
   c. your SkyDrive
   d. All of the above

8. To display the content of multiple cells in a single cell that spans several columns, you should _____ the cells
   a. merge
   b. split
   c. insert
   d. autofit

9. Preset drawing objects, such as block arrows and callouts, that you can quickly add to your document are called _____.
   a. clips
   b. shapes
   c. pictures
   d. SmartArt

10. _____ are organized by rows, which display horizontally, and columns, which display vertically.
    a. Charts
    b. Tables
    c. Diagrams
    d. None of the above

projects

skill review 4.1

In this project you will be editing the *WD2013-SkillReview-4-1* document from Suarez Marketing.

Skills needed to complete this project:

- Inserting Online Pictures (Skill 4.1)
- Resizing Pictures (Skill 4.2)
- Changing Picture Layouts (Skill 4.3)
- Moving Pictures (Skill 4.4)
- Inserting SmartArt (Skill 4.8)
- Creating a Table (Skill 4.12)
- Working with Tables (Skill 4.13)
- Inserting Rows and Columns (Skill 4.14)
- Merging and Splitting Cells (Skill 4.17)
- Sizing Tables, Columns, and Rows (Skill 4.16)
- Applying Table Quick Styles (Skill 4.19)
- Adding Borders to a Table (Skill 4.20)
- Inserting a Picture (Skill 4.5)
- Positioning Pictures (Skill 4.6)

1. Open the **WD2013-SkillReview-4-1** document.

2. Save this document as: **[your initials]WD-SkillReview-4-1**

3. Insert an online picture in the document.

    a. Place the cursor in the blank line above the **What Clients are Saying** heading.

    b. Click the **Insert** tab.

    c. In the *Illustrations* group, click the **Online Pictures** button.

    d. In the *Office.com Clip Art* search box, type **customer service** and click the **Search** button.

    e. Find the photograph of the **woman with the cash register.** Click the **image** to select it and click the **Insert** button.

4. Resize a picture.

    a. With the picture selected, on the *Picture Tools Format* tab, in the *Size* group, type **1.5"** in the *Height* box and press ⏎ Enter .

5. Change the layout on a picture.

    a. With the picture selected, click the **Layout Options** button.

    b. Select the **Square** wrapping option.

    c. Click outside the *Layout Options* box to hide it.

6. Move a picture.

   a. Click and drag the picture up and to the right.

   b. Using the guides, place the picture so it is aligned just under the horizontal line in the *Why I Do What I Do* section and aligned with the right side of the text in the document.

7. Insert a *SmartArt* diagram.

   a. Place the cursor in the empty line in the *Suarez marketing process* section.

   b. Click the **Insert** tab.

   c. In the *Illustrations* group, click the **Insert a SmartArt Graphic** button.

   d. Click the **Cycle** category and click the **Segmented Cycle** option. Click **OK.**

   e. In the upper left segment, type `Analyze Needs`.

   f. In the upper right segment, type `Design Project`.

   g. In the lower segment, type `Implement Campaign`.

   h. Click outside the diagram to deselect it.

8. Add a table to the document and enter text into the table.

   a. Place the cursor in the empty line at the end of the document.

   b. Click the **Insert** tab.

   c. In the *Tables* group, click the **Add a Table** button and select a **2 × 1** (two columns and one row) table.

   d. Type the information below into the table. Press **Tab** to move forward from cell to cell. Press **Tab** at the end of a row to insert a new row.

Commitment	To the needs of the client
Communication	Seek first to listen
Trust	Begins with open communication
Integrity	Doing the right thing
Customers	Always come first
Teamwork	Working together for success
Success	Results with integrity
Creativity	Ideas before results
Win-Win	Is always the goal

9. Insert a row.

   a. Place the cursor in the first row of the table.

   b. Click the **Table Tools Layout** tab.

   c. In the *Rows & Columns* group, click the **Insert Rows Above** button.

   d. Type `Suarez Marketing Beliefs`

   e. Apply the following formatting to the text:

      i. Font: **Calibri Light**

      ii. Size: **14 pt**

      iii. Color: **Blue, Accent 5**

10. Merge cells in a table.

   a. Select the first row in the table.

   b. Click the **Table Tools Layout** tab.

   c. In the *Merge* group, click the **Merge Cells** button.

11. Change the height of rows in a table.

   a. Select the table.

   b. On the *Table Tools Layout* tab, in the *Cell Size* group, click the **Height box up arrow** until **0.3"** appears in the box.

12. Apply a Quick Style to the table.

   a. Click the **Table Tools Design** tab.

   b. In *Table Style Options* group, click the **First Column** check box so it is deselected.

   c. In the *Table Styles* group, click the **More** button.

   d. In the *List Tables* section, select the **List Table 2–Accent 5** Quick Style (it is the second to last style in the first row).

13. Apply a border to the table.

   a. On the *Table Tools Design* tab, in the *Borders* group, click the **Borders** button.

   b. Select **Outside Border.**

14. Insert a logo from a location on your computer.

   a. Navigate to the beginning of the document and place the cursor above the name **Maria Suarez.**

   b. Click the **Insert** tab.

   c. In the *Illustrations* group, click the **Pictures** button.

   d. In the *Insert Picture* dialog, browse to your student data file location, select the **Suarez_logo** file, and click the **Insert** button.

15. Position the logo on the page.

   a. On the *Picture Tools Format* tab, in the *Arrange* group, click the **Position** button.

   b. Select the **Position in Top Right with Square Text Wrapping** option (it is the third option in the first row under *With Text Wrapping*).

16. Save and close the document.

skill review 4.2

In this project you will be editing the *WD2013-SkillReview-4-2* document for the Tri-State Book Festival.

Skills needed to complete this project:

- Adding WordArt to Documents (Skill 4.10)
- Changing Picture Layouts (Skill 4.3)
- Inserting a Shape (Skill 4.9)
- Applying Quick Styles to Pictures (Skill 4.7)
- Creating a Chart (Skill 4.21)
- Modifying a Chart (Skill 4.22)
- Working with Tables (Skill 4.13)
- Deleting Columns, Rows, and Cells (Skill 4.15)
- Merging and Splitting Cells (Skill 4.17)

- Inserting Rows and Columns (Skill 4.14)
- Sorting Data in Tables (Skill 4.18)
- Applying Table Quick Styles (Skill 4.19)
- Inserting Online Pictures (Skill 4.1)
- Resizing Pictures (Skill 4.2)
- Moving Pictures (Skill 4.4)

1. Open the **WD2013-SkillReview-4-2** document.

2. Save this document as: **[your initials]WD-SkillReview-4-2**

3. Add WordArt to a document.

   a. Place the cursor at the top of the document.

   b. Click the **Insert** tab.

   c. In the *Text* group, click the **Insert Word Art** button.

   d. Select the **Gradient Fill–Teal, Accent 1, Reflection** WordArt style (it is the second option in the second row of the gallery).

   e. Type **Tri-State Book Festival**.

4. Change the layout of the WordArt.

   a. Click the **Layout Options** button.

   b. Select the **In Line with Text** option.

   c. Click outside the *Layout Options* box to hide it.

5. Insert a shape.

   a. Click the **Insert** tab.

   b. In the *Illustrations* group, click the **Shapes** button and select **Vertical Scroll** option in the *Stars and Banners* section.

   c. The cursor changes to a crosshair cursor.

   d. Click to the right of the WordArt text you added to add the scroll shape (the drawing should be 1.25" in height and 1.13" in width).

   e. If necessary, move the scroll shape so the bottom is aligned with the bottom of the WordArt and it appears within the blue page border.

6. Apply a Quick Style to a picture.

   a. If necessary, select the scroll shape at the top of the document.

   b. On the *Drawing Tools Design* tab, in the *Shape Styles* group, click the **More** button.

   c. In the *Shape Quick Styles* gallery, select **Colored Outline–Blue, Accent 3** (it is the fourth option in the first row).

7. Add a pie chart to the document.

   a. Place the cursor on the empty line below the line *The following chart shows the breakdown of authors by genre:*.

   b. Click the **Insert** tab.

   c. In the *Illustrations* group, click the **Add a Chart** button.

   d. In the *Insert Chart* dialog, click the **Pie** category on the left.

   e. Verify the **Pie** option (the first option) is selected.

   f. Click **OK**.

   g. In the *Chart in Microsoft Word* dialog, change the data in the chart to match Figure WD 4.35.

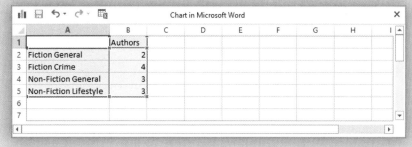

FIGURE WD 4.35

    h. Click the **Close** button in the *Chart in Microsoft Word* dialog.

8. Modify the look of the chart.

    a. Click the **Chart Styles** button.

    b. Scroll the list of chart styles and rest your mouse over each style to see the name of the style. Select the **Style 6** option.

    c. Click outside the chart to deselect it.

9. Delete rows from tables.

    a. Navigate to *AGENDA* section.

    b. In the first table, select the row with the text **Monday October 10.**

    c. Click the **Table Tools Layout** tab.

    d. In the *Rows & Columns* group, click the **Delete** button.

    e. Click **Delete Rows.**

    f. Repeat these steps to delete the first row of the other two tables in this section.

10. Merge cells in a table.

    a. In the *Monday October 10* table, select the **Cocktail reception and dinner cell** and the **two empty cells** to the right.

    b. On the *Table Tools Layout* tab, in the *Merge* group, click the **Merge Cells** button.

11. Insert a row to a table.

    a. In the *Monday October 10* table, place the cursor in the **4:00–5:00 cell.**

    b. Move the cursor to the left until you see the **Insert Row** button above the cell.

    c. Click the **Insert Row** button to add a new blank row.

    d. In the blank cell under *Time,* type **2:00–3:00**

    e. In the blank cell under *The Westfield Theater,* type **Keynote and Welcome**

12. Sort data in a table.

    a. In the *Monday October 10* table, select all the rows except the first row.

    b. On the *Table Tools Layout* tab, in the *Data* group, click the **Sort** button.

    c. Verify the column will sort in ascending order, by the first column, using the text in the cells. Click **OK.**

13. Apply Quick Styles to tables.

    a. Select the **Monday October 10** table.

    b. Click the **Table Tools Design** tab.

    c. In the *Table Styles* group, click the **More** button.

    d. In the *Grid Tables* section, click the **Grid Table 5 Dark–Accent 2** option (it is the third option in the third row under *Grid Tables*).

    e. Apply this table Quick Style to the other two tables in the *AGENDA* section.

FIGURE WD 4.36

14. Insert an online picture.

   a. Place the cursor at the beginning of the first paragraph in the *AUTHORS* section.

   b. Click the **Insert** tab.

   c. In the *Illustrations* group, click the **Online Pictures** button.

   d. In the *Office.com Clip Art* search box, type `stack of books` and click the **Search** button.

   e. Find the photograph of the **spiraling stack of books** (see Figure WD 4.36). **NOTE:** If you do not see the same image as in the figure, insert an online picture of your choice.

   f. Click the **image** to select it and click the **Insert** button.

15. Resize a picture and change the layout.

   a. With the picture selected, on the *Picture Tools Format* tab, in the *Size* group, type **2.5"** in the *Height* box and press `← Enter`.

   b. Click the **Layout Options** button.

   c. Select the **Square** option in the *With Text Wrapping* section.

16. Save and close the document.

challenge yourself **4.3**

In this project you will be editing the *WD2013-ChallengeYourself-4-3* document from Greenscapes landscaping company.

Skills needed to complete this project:

- Inserting Online Pictures (Skill 4.1)
- Resizing Pictures (Skill 4.2)
- Changing Picture Layouts (Skill 4.3)
- Moving Pictures (Skill 4.4)
- Inserting SmartArt (Skill 4.8)
- Inserting a Picture (Skill 4.5)
- Positioning Pictures (Skill 4.6)
- Creating a Table (Skill 4.12)
- Working with Tables (Skill 4.13)
- Sorting Data in a Table (Skill 4.18)
- Inserting Rows and Columns (Skill 4.14)
- Merging and Splitting Cells (Skill 4.17)
- Sizing Tables, Columns, and Rows (Skill 4.16)
- Applying Table Quick Styles (Skill 4.19)
- Adding Borders to a Table (Skill 4.20)

FIGURE WD 4.37

1. Open the **WD2013-ChallengeYourself-4-3** document.

2. Save this document as: **[your initials]WD-ChallengeYourself-4-3**

3. Insert an online picture in the document.

   a. Place the cursor on the blank line at the end of the *Our Philosophy* section.

   b. Search for images of a **landscaped garden** on the *Office.com Clip Art* site.

   c. Insert the photograph of the **Landscaped garden and lawn** (see Figure WD 4.37). **NOTE:** If you do not see the same image as in the figure, insert an online picture of your choice.

4. Resize the picture so it is **1.25"** in height.

5. Apply the **Square** layout option to the picture.

6. Move a picture so it is aligned under the *Our Philosophy* heading with the paragraph text displayed to the right. Use the guides so the top of the pictured is aligned with the top of the paragraph text and the left side of the picture is aligned with the left side of the heading text.

7. Insert a *SmartArt* diagram.

    a. Place the cursor in the empty line after the first paragraph in the *Leaf Removal* section.

    b. Insert a **Basic Process** SmartArt diagram.

    c. Enter **Blow and Rake** in the first box.

    d. Enter **Gather and Haul Away** in the second box.

    e. Enter **Compost** in the third box.

8. Insert a logo from a location on your computer.

    a. Navigate to the *Services* section of the document. Place the cursor before the *Lawn Care* heading.

    b. Insert the **greenscapes_logo** picture from you student data file location.

9. Change the position of the logo so it appears in the **top left corner of the page with square wrapping.**

10. Add a table to the document and enter text into the table.

    a. Place the cursor at the end of the document.

    b. Insert a table with the following information:

Lawn Maintenance	Fertilization, Insect and Disease Control	$ 99.00 per treatment
Shrub and Tree Maintenance	Pruning, Fertilization, Insect and Disease Control	$ 125.00 per hour
Leaf Removal	Composting included	$ 25.00 per hour
Lawn Care	Mowing, Edging, Weed-eating	$ 25.00 per service (weekly) $ 18.00 per service (bi-weekly)
All Four Services	15% Customer Discount	
Specialty Services	As Requested	Call for a quote

11. Sort data in the table

    a. Select the first four rows of the table.

    b. Sort the text in the selected row in ascending order based on the first column.

12. Insert a row and merge cells.

    a. Insert a new row above the first row in the table.

    b. Type **Greenscapes' Services and Pricing** in the first cell.

    c. Change the font of the text to be **Calibri, 16 pt.**

    d. Merge the three cells in the first row of the table.

13. Change the height of the first row in the table to be **0.4"** tall.

14. Apply a Quick Style to the table.

    a. Change the table Quick Styles to show styles without the first column formatted.

    b. Apply the **Grid Table 5 Dark–Accent 3** Quick Style to the table (it is the fourth option in the third row of the *Grid Tables* section).

15. Apply a border to the table.

    a. Select the table.

    b. Apply **all borders** to the table.

16. Save and close the document.

challenge yourself 4.4

In this project you will be editing the *WD2013-ChallengeYourself-4-4* document from the Spring Hills Community.

Skills needed to complete this project:

- Adding WordArt to Documents (Skill 4.10)
- Changing Picture Layouts (Skill 4.3)
- Creating a Chart (Skill 4.21)
- Modifying a Chart (Skill 4.22)
- Working with Tables (Skill 4.13)
- Inserting Rows and Columns (Skill 4.14)
- Deleting Columns, Rows, and Cells (Skill 4.15)
- Sorting Data in Tables (Skill 4.18)
- Applying Table Quick Styles (Skill 4.19)
- Inserting Online Pictures (Skill 4.1)
- Resizing Pictures (Skill 4.2)
- Positioning Pictures (Skill 4.6)
- Applying Quick Styles to Pictures (Skill 4.7)

1. Open the **WD2013-ChallengeYourself-4-4** document.

2. Save this document as: **[your initials]WD-ChallengeYourself-4-4**

3. Add WordArt to a document and change the layout options.

    a. Place the cursor at the top of the document.

    b. Insert WordArt using the **Fill–Green Accent 1, Shadow** style (it is the second option in the first row of the WordArt gallery).

    c. Change the WordArt text to **Spring Hills Community Safety Strategies**.

    d. Change the layout of the WordArt to be in line with the text.

4. Add a chart to the document.

    a. Place the cursor on the blank line after the first paragraph in the *What Electronics Are Being Targeted* section.

    b. Insert a **Clustered Column** chart.

    c. Change the data in the chart to match Figure WD 4.38.

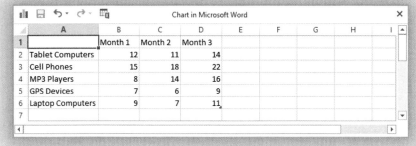

FIGURE WD 4.38

5. Modify the look of the chart.

   a. Apply the **Style 3** Quick Style to the chart.

   b. Hide the **chart title** on the chart.

6. Insert a column to a table.

   a. Place the cursor in the table at the end of the document (in the *Future Safety Modifications* section).

   b. Add a column to the right of the existing column.

7. Insert a row and enter data in a table.

   a. Insert a row above the first row in the table.

   b. In the first cell of the new row, type **Modification**

   c. In the second cell of the new row, type **Status**

   d. Add the status for each modification as shown in Figure WD 4.39.

Modification	Status
New security officer positions	Approved
New security gates	In Progress
Electric security vehicles	Approved
Security card entrance for all garages	In Progress
Increased security cameras	Approved
Reinforcements to perimeter fence	Approved
Weekly security meetings with staff	Approved
Increased security budget	Denied

FIGURE WD 4.39

8. Delete rows from tables.

   a. Select the last row in the table.

   b. Delete the row.

9. Sort data in a table.

   a. Select all the rows in the table except the first row.

   b. Sort the table in ascending order based on the text in column 2.

10. Apply a Quick Styles to tables.

   a. Change the table Quick Styles to show styles without the first column formatted.

   b. Apply the **Plain Table 1** style to the table (it is the second option in the *Plain Tables* section).

11. Insert an online picture.

    a. Place the cursor at the end of the first paragraph in the *Security Staff* section.

    b. Search for images of a **security guard** on the *Office.com Clip Art* site.

    c. Insert the illustrated picture of **Security guard at a gate** (see Figure WD 4.40).
    NOTE: If you do not see the same image as in the figure, insert an online picture of your choice.

12. Resize the picture so the height is **1.2"**.

13. Position the picture using the **Position in Middle Left with Square Text Wrapping** option.

14. Apply the **Center Shadow Rectangle** Quick Style to the picture.

15. Save and close the document.

on your own 4.5

In this project you will be editing the *WD2013-OnYourOwn-4-5* document. This document contains data results for a behavior change project.

Skills needed to complete this project:

- Inserting Online Pictures (Skill 4.1)
- Resizing Pictures (Skill 4.2)
- Changing Picture Layouts (Skill 4.3)
- Moving Pictures (Skill 4.4)
- Applying Quick Styles to Pictures (Skill 4.7)
- Creating a Table (Skill 4.12)
- Working with Tables (Skill 4.13)
- Inserting Rows and Columns (Skill 4.14)
- Merging and Splitting Cells (Skill 4.17)
- Sorting Data in Tables (Skill 4.18)
- Applying Table Quick Styles (Skill 4.19)
- Creating a Chart (Skill 4.21)
- Modifying a Chart (Skill 4.22)

1. Open the **WD2013-OnYourOwn-4-5** document.

2. Save this document as: **[your initials]WD-OnYourOwn-4-5**

3. Search for pictures of students raising hands on *Office.com Clip Art* and insert a picture of your choice.

4. Resize the picture so it fits well in the document.

5. Change the layout options on the picture to wrap with the text.

6. Move the picture so it appears to the right of the first paragraph of the document.

7. Apply a Quick Style of your choice to the picture.

8. Create a new table in the *Observation Phase* section and cut and paste the text from the section into the table. Do not include the Totals in the table. Delete all extra tabs and blank lines that remain after cutting the text.

9. Create a new table in the *Implementation Phase* section and cut and paste the text from the section into the table. Do not include the Totals in the table. Delete all extra tabs and blank lines that remain after cutting the text.

10. Insert a new row to the top of the *Implementation Phase table*. In the second cell of the new row, enter **Raises Hand**. In the third cell of the new row, enter **Does Not Raise Hand**. In the fourth cell of the new row, enter **Percentage**.

11. Insert a new row to the top of the *Observation Phase* table. Cut the text **Observation Phase** and paste it into the first cell of the new table. Merge the cells in the new row.

12. Insert a new row to the top of the *Implementation Phase* table. Cut the text **Implementation Phase** and paste it into the first cell of the new table. Merge the cells in the new row.

13. Sort the data in the *Implementation Phase* table so the dates appear in ascending order.

14. Apply a Quick Style of your choice to the **Observation Phase** table and the **Implementation Phase** table.

15. Create a **pie chart** using the information in the Totals rows in each table. Add the charts below the *Totals* row for each table.

16. Modify the charts so the titles do not appear on the chart.

17. The final document should look similar to Figure WD 4.41 (your document may vary). Save and close the document.

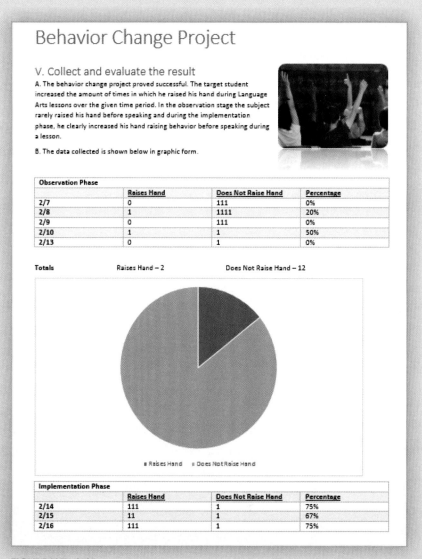

Behavior Change Project

V. Collect and evaluate the result

A. The behavior change project proved successful. The target student increased the amount of times in which he raised his hand during Language Arts lessons over the given time period. In the observation stage the subject rarely raised his hand before speaking and during the implementation phase, he clearly increased his hand raising behavior before speaking during a lesson.

B. The data collected is shown below in graphic form.

Observation Phase

	Raises Hand	Does Not Raise Hand	Percentage
2/7	0	111	0%
2/8	1	1111	20%
2/9	0	111	0%
2/10	1	1	50%
2/13	0	1	0%

Totals   Raises Hand – 2   Does Not Raise Hand – 12

▪ Raises Hand   ▪ Does Not Raise Hand

Implementation Phase

	Raises Hand	Does Not Raise Hand	Percentage
2/14	111	1	75%
2/15	11	1	67%
2/16	111	1	75%

FIGURE WD 4.41

fix it 4.6

In this project you will be correcting the *WD2013-FixIt-4-6* document from Suarez Marketing.

Skills needed to complete this project:

- Positioning Pictures (Skill 4.6)
- Inserting SmartArt (Skill 4.8)
- Resizing Pictures (Skill 4.2)
- Changing Picture Layouts (Skill 4.3)
- Moving Pictures (Skill 4.4)
- Applying Quick Styles to Pictures (Skill 4.7)
- Working with Tables (Skill 4.13)
- Inserting Rows and Columns (Skill 4.14)
- Deleting Columns, Rows, and Cells (Skill 4.15)
- Sizing Tables, Columns, Rows (Skill 4.16)
- Merging and Splitting Cells (Skill 4.17)
- Sorting Data in Tables (Skill 4.18)
- Applying Table Quick Styles (Skill 4.19)
- Adding Borders to a Table (Skill 4.20)

1. Open the **WD2013-FixIt-4-6 document.**
2. Save this document as: **[your initials]WD-FixIt-4-6**
3. Position a picture.
   a. Select the **Suarez Marketing** logo in the middle of the first page.
   b. Position the picture to be in the upper right corner of the page with square wrapping.
4. Insert a *SmartArt* diagram.
   a. Navigate to *The Suarez* Process section.
   b. Place the cursor in the blank line above the bulleted list. Insert a **Segmented Cycle** diagram.
   c. Cut and paste the items from the bulleted list into the segments of the diagram. Remove any extra blank lines.
5. Resize and change the layout of a picture.
   a. Select the large photograph of the woman with a cash register.
   b. Change the size of the picture to be **1.75"** tall and **1.75"** wide.
   c. Change the layout option of the picture to use the **Tight** text wrapping option.
6. Move the picture to right side of the document using guides to align the picture with the right edge of the text. Have the picture display just below the blue horizontal line in the *What I Do What I Do* section.
7. Apply the **Soft Edge Rectangle** Quick Style to the picture (it is the sixth option in the *Picture Quick Styles* gallery).

8. Insert a row in a table.

    a. Navigate to the table at the end of the document.

    b. Insert a new row at the bottom of the table.

    c. Cut and paste the **Win-Win** text into the first cell of the new row.

    d. Cut and paste the **Is always the goal** text into the second cell of the new row.

9. Delete a row in a table.

    a. This table includes a duplicate row of information.

    b. Find the duplicated information and delete one of the rows.

10. Use the **AutoFit** command to resize the table columns to fit the window.

11. **Merge** the two cells in the first row of the table.

12. Sort the table so the first column displays in alphabetical order. Be sure not to include the first row in the sort.

13. Apply the **Grid Table 1 Light–Accent 5** Quick Style to the table (it is the sixth option in the first row in the *Grid Tables* section). Be sure the **First Column Table Style Option** is not part of the design.

14. Apply an **outside border** to the table.

15. Save and close the document.

chapter 5

Working with Reports, References, and Mailings

In this chapter, you will learn the following skills:

- Use Autocorrect
- Check for grammar errors
- Replace words using the Thesaurus
- Use the Tabs dialog and add tab leaders
- Insert and update a table of contents, footnotes, and endnotes
- Use a report reference style, add citations, and create a bibliography
- Mark words in a document to create an index
- Display a document in different views
- Create a new document from a template
- Use mail merge to create mailings
- Create envelopes and labels

skills

introduction

In this chapter you will learn the skills to create reports and mailings. First you will learn to use some of Word's valuable tools for writing documents, including AutoCorrect, Grammar check, and the Thesaurus. You will add a number of reference elements to a report, including a table of contents, footnotes, and captions. You will learn about reference styles and add citations and then create a bibliography from citations you have added. You will mark entries and create an index for a document from those entries. You will also learn about the different views in Word and ways you can display your documents. In the second part of this chapter, you will create a new form letter from a template and then create a mail merge from that letter. Finally, you will learn how to create and print envelopes and labels.

Skill 5.1 Using AutoCorrect

While you are typing, Word's **AutoCorrect** feature analyzes each word as it is entered. Each word you type is compared to a list of common misspellings, symbols, and abbreviations. If a match is found, AutoCorrect automatically replaces the text in your document with the matching replacement entry. For example, if you type "teh," AutoCorrect will replace the text with "the."

You can create your own AutoCorrect entries, as well as modify pre-existing ones. Auto-Correct also allows you to check for common capitalization errors. If you find yourself making spelling errors that AutoCorrect does not recognize, you can add your own entries to the AutoCorrect replacement list.

To add a new entry to the AutoCorrect list:

1. Click the **File** tab.
2. Click the **Options** button.
3. In the *Word Options* dialog, click the **Proofing** button.
4. Click the **AutoCorrect Options...** button.

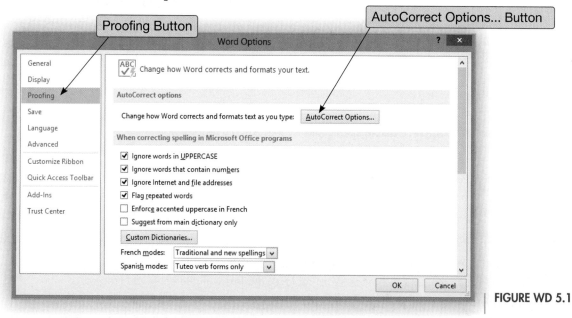

FIGURE WD 5.1

5. Type your commonly made mistake in the *Replace* box.

6. Type the correct spelling in the *With* box.

7. Click **OK** in the *AutoCorrect* dialog.

8. Click **OK** in the *Word Options* dialog.

The next time you type the error, Word will automatically correct it for you.

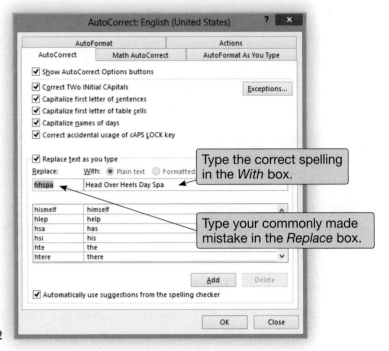

FIGURE WD 5.2

tips & tricks

If you find yourself typing certain long phrases over and over again, you can use the AutoCorrect feature to replace short abbreviations with long strings of text that you don't want to type. For example, you could replace the text *hhspa* with *Head Over Heels Day Spa*. This will not only save you time when typing, but more important, it will ensure accuracy in your documents.

tell me **more**

AutoCorrect does more than just fix spelling errors. From the *AutoCorrect* dialog you can set options to:

▶ Correct accidental use of the Caps Lock key.

▶ Automatically capitalize the first letter in a sentence or the names of days.

▶ Automatically apply character formatting such as bold and italic, and format lists and tables.

Explore the *AutoCorrect* dialog on your own to discover all the options available.

let me try

Open the student data file **wd5-01-SpaProductReport** and try this skill on your own:

1. Display Backstage view.
2. Open the **Word Options** dialog.
3. Display the **Proofing** options and open the **AutoCorrect** dialog.
4. Create an AutoCorrect entry to change **hhspa** to **Head Over Heels Day Spa** when typed.
5. Close the **Word Options** dialog.
6. Place the cursor between the words **at** and **The** in the first paragraph of the document.
7. Type **hhpsa.** Be sure to include the period. Notice Word replaces the text with the entry you created.
8. Save the file as directed by your instructor and close it.

Skill 5.2 Checking Grammar

In addition to checking spelling, the *Spelling & Grammar* command can analyze your document for grammar errors. It searches through your document and displays the errors in the order they are found. Spelling errors display in the *Spelling* task pane and grammar errors are displayed in the *Grammar* task pane. Word displays the original word along with potential corrections for you to select or ignore.

To check a document for grammar errors:

1. Click the **Review** tab.
2. In the *Proofing* group, click the **Spelling & Grammar** button.
3. When Word encounters the first grammar error, the error is displayed in the *Grammar* task pane.
4. Review the grammar suggestions to determine which one is correct:
   - Click a suggestion and click the **Change** button to make the correction.
   - Click **Ignore** to skip the grammar error.
5. A message appears to tell you when the spelling and grammar check is complete. Click **OK** to close the *Grammar* task pane and return to the document.

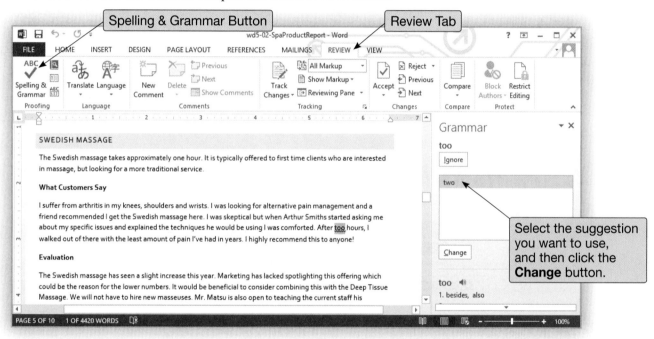

FIGURE WD 5.3

tips & tricks

At the bottom of the task pane, you will see definitions, along with audio pronunciations, of each word to help you make your selection.

another method

To display the *Grammar* task pane, you can also press the F7 key.

let me try

Open the student data file **wd5-02-SpaProductReport** and try this skill on your own:

1. Start the **Spelling & Grammar** check.
2. Correct each grammar error as it is displayed in the task pane.
3. Save the file as directed by your instructor and close it.

Skill 5.3 Using the Thesaurus

When writing documents, you may find you are reusing a certain word over and over again and would like to use a different word that has the same meaning. Microsoft Word's **Thesaurus** tool provides you with a list of synonyms (words with the same meaning) and antonyms (words with the opposite meaning).

To replace a word using the Thesaurus:

1. Place the cursor in the word you want to replace.
2. Click the **Review** tab.
3. In the *Proofing* group, click the **Thesaurus** button.
4. The selected word appears in the *Search for* box of the *Thesaurus* task pane with a list of possible meanings below it. Each possible meaning has a list of synonyms (and, in some cases, antonyms).
5. Point to a synonym (or antonym), and click the arrow that appears to display a menu of options.
6. Click **Insert** on the menu to replace the original word with the one you selected.

Thesaurus Button

Review Tab

Search For Box

Click **Insert** to replace the original word with the one you selected.

FIGURE WD 5.4

tips & tricks

You can look up and replace words with synonyms without opening the *Thesaurus* task pane. Right-click the word you want to replace, point to **Synonyms.** Word lists a number of possible synonyms on the submenu. Click a synonym to replace the original word with the synonym.

another method

To look up a word using the Thesaurus, you can also:

❱ Right-click the word, point to *Synonyms,* and select **Thesaurus...**

❱ With the cursor in the word you want to look up, press ⬆Shift + F7 on the keyboard.

let me try

Open the student data file **wd5-03-SpaProductReport** and try this skill on your own:

1. Select the word **division** in the second sentence of the first paragraph.
2. Using the Thesaurus, replace the word with the synonym **department.**
3. Save the file as directed by your instructor and close it.

word 2013   chapter 5 Working with Reports, References, and Mailings

Skill 5.4 Using the Tabs Dialog

You can quickly add tabs to a document by selecting a tab stop type and clicking on the ruler where you want the tab to appear. Another way to set tabs in your document is through the *Tabs* dialog. From the *Tabs* dialog, you can add new tabs or modify or clear existing tabs.

To set tab stops in the *Tabs* dialog:

1. On the *Home* tab, in the *Paragraph* group, click the **dialog launcher.**
2. In the *Paragraph* dialog box, click the **Tabs...** button.
3. The *Tabs* dialog opens.
4. In the *Tab stop position:* box, type the number of where you want the tab stop to appear.
5. Click a radio button in the *Alignment* section.
6. Click **OK.**

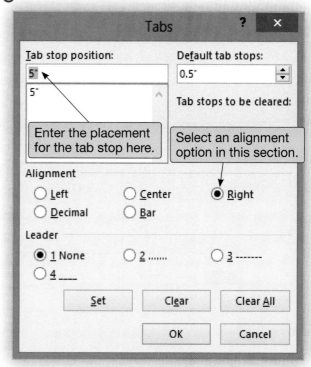

FIGURE WD 5.5

tips & tricks

❯ Click the **Clear All** button to clear all the tabs displayed in the *Tabs* dialog.

❯ To add the tab stop and continue working in the *Tabs* dialog, click the **Set** button instead of **OK.**

another method

To open the *Tabs* dialog, you can double-click a tab stop on the ruler.

let me try

Open the student data file **wd5-04-SpaProductReport** and try this skill on your own:

1. Select the list of services and sales figures in the *Manicures and Pedicures* section.
2. Open the **Paragraph** dialog.
3. Open the **Tabs** dialog.
4. Add a **right tab stop** at **5".**
5. Save the file as directed by your instructor and close it.

Skill 5.5 Adding Tab Leaders

Adding **tab leaders** can make data even easier to read. Tab leaders fill in the space between tabs with solid, dotted, or dashed lines. Using tab leaders helps associate columns of text by leading the reader's eye from left to right.

To add tab leaders:

1. Select the text to which you want to add the leader.
2. On the *Home* tab, in the *Paragraph* group, click the **dialog launcher.**
3. In the *Paragraph* dialog, click the **Tabs...** button.
4. In the *Leader* section of the *Tabs* dialog, select the leader option you want.
5. Click **OK.**

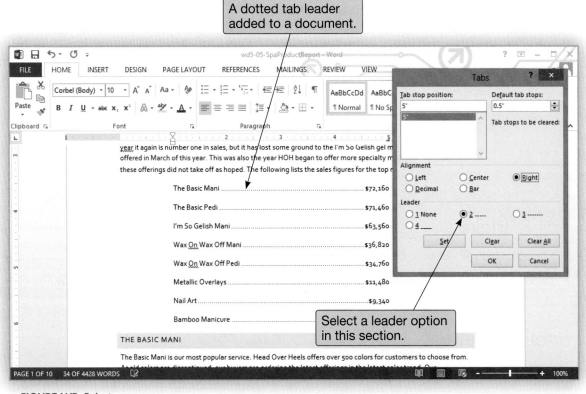

A dotted tab leader added to a document.

Select a leader option in this section.

FIGURE WD 5.6

tips & tricks

When creating a table of contents for your document, use tab leaders to visually link section headings with page numbers.

another method

To open the *Tabs* dialog, you can double-click a tab stop on the ruler.

let me try

Open the student data file **wd5-05-SpaProductReport** and try this skill on your own:

1. Select the list of services and sales figures in the *Manicures and Pedicures* section.
2. Open the **Tabs** dialog.
3. Add a **dotted tab leader** to the text (option **2** in the *Leader* section of the *Tabs* dialog).
4. Save the file as directed by your instructor and close it.

Skill 5.6 Inserting a Table of Contents

If you have a long document with many sections and headings, it is a good idea to include a **table of contents** at the beginning of the document. A table of contents lists the topics and associated page numbers, so your reader can easily locate information. The table of contents is created from heading styles in the document. If you want your document's section titles to display in the table of contents, be sure to apply heading styles to that text.

To insert a table of contents:

1. Verify the insertion point is at the beginning of the document.
2. Click the **References** tab.
3. In the *Table of Contents* group, click the **Table of Contents** button and select an option from the gallery.
4. The table of contents is added to the beginning of the document.

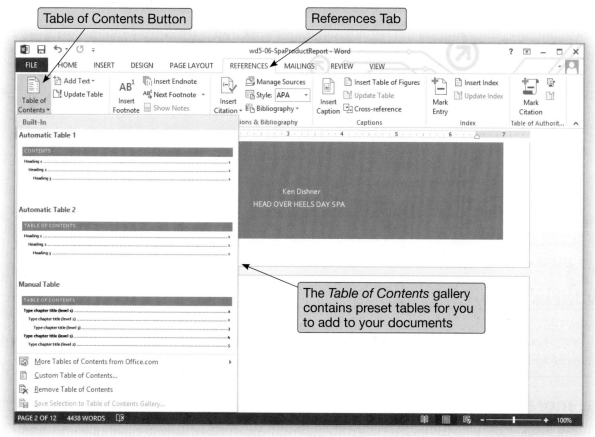

The *Table of Contents* gallery contains preset tables for you to add to your documents

FIGURE WD 5.7

If you make changes to your document after you have inserted a table of contents, you should be sure to update the table of contents to keep the information accurate. To update the table of contents, click the **Update Table** button in the *Table of Contents* group. You can also update the table of contents by clicking on the table of contents and clicking the **Update Table...** button at the top of the control.

To remove a table of contents, click the **Table of Contents** button and select **Remove Table of Contents** at the bottom of the gallery.

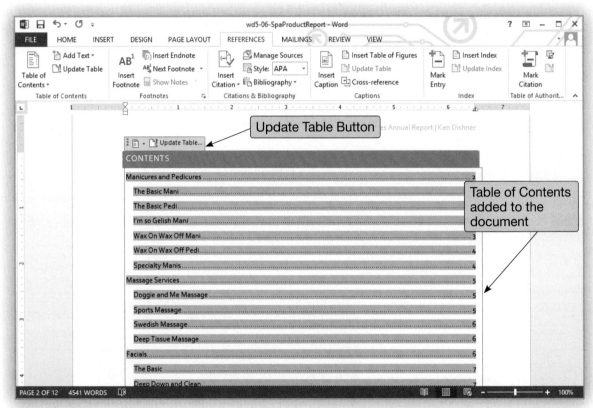

FIGURE WD 5.8

tips & tricks

If you want to add your own customized table of contents, click **Insert Table of Contents...** at the bottom of the gallery. The *Table of Contents* dialog opens. Here you can choose different options for the table of contents, including tab leaders, formats, and page number formatting.

tell me more

A table of contents is typically based on heading styles, but you can create a table of contents based on custom styles or from marked entries.

A table of contents is a building block that is added to the document. When you select the building block, extra controls appear at the top, including the *Table of Contents* and the *Update Table...* buttons.

let me try

Open the student data file **wd5-06-SpaProductReport** and try this skill on your own:

1. Place the cursor on the blank page between the cover page and the beginning of the document.
2. Insert a table of contents based on the **Automatic Table 1** format.
3. Save the file as directed by your instructor and close it.

Skill 5.7 Inserting Footnotes and Endnotes

Footnotes and **endnotes** provide your reader with further information on a topic in a document. They are often used for source references. Footnotes and endnotes are composed of two parts: a **reference mark** (a superscript character placed next to the text) and the associated text. Footnotes appear at the bottom of a page, whereas endnotes are placed at the end of the document.

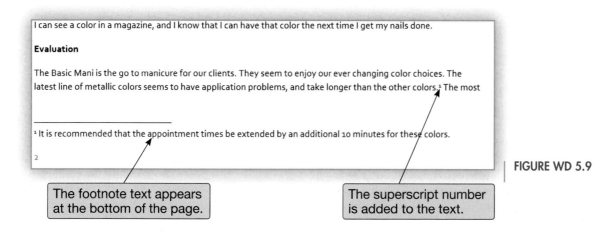

FIGURE WD 5.9

To insert a footnote:

1. Place your cursor where you want the footnote to appear.
2. Click the **References** tab.
3. In the *Footnotes* group, click the **Insert Footnote** button.
4. The superscript number is added next to the text, and the cursor is moved to the footnote area at the bottom of the page.
5. Type the text for your footnote. When you are finished, return to your document by clicking anywhere in the main document area.

To insert an endnote:

1. Place your cursor where you want the endnote to appear.
2. Click the **References** tab.
3. In the *Footnotes* group, click the **Insert Endnote** button.
4. The superscript number is added next to the text, and the cursor is moved the endnote area at the end of the document.
5. Type the text for your endnote.

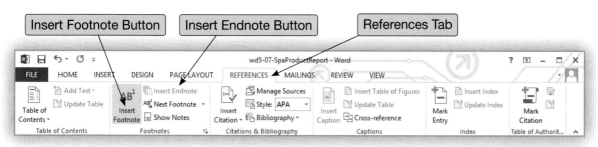

FIGURE WD 5.10

To convert footnotes to endnotes or vice versa, click the **dialog launcher** in the *Footnotes* group. In the *Footnote and Endnote* dialog, click the **Convert...** button, choose an option, and click **OK.**

tips & tricks

Click the **Next Footnote** button to navigate to the next footnote in the document. Click the arrow next to the *Next Footnote* button to display a menu allowing you to navigate to previous footnotes and between endnotes in the document.

To delete a footnote, you must first select the reference mark in the document and press **Delete** on the keyboard. If you select and delete the text of the footnote, the reference mark will remain and the footnote will not be removed from the document.

tell me **more**

Once you have inserted and formatted your first footnote or endnote, Word automatically numbers all subsequent notes in your document for you. If you add a new footnote between two existing footnotes, Word will renumber all the footnotes in the document, keeping them in sequential order.

another **method**

To insert a footnote, you can also click the **dialog launcher** in the *Footnotes* group. In the *Footnote and Endnote* dialog, verify that the **Footnote** radio button is selected and click **Insert.**

let me try

Open the student data file **wd5-07-SpaProductReport** and try this skill on your own:

1. Place the cursor at the end of the third sentence in the first paragraph in the *Evaluation* section under *The Basic Mani* (the sentence ending *and take longer than the other colors* on the third page of the document).
2. Add a footnote that reads: `It is recommended that the appointment times be extended by an additional 10 minutes for these colors.`
3. Save the file as directed by your instructor and close it.

Skill 5.8 Adding a Caption

A **caption** is a brief description of an illustration, chart, equation, or table. Captions can appear above or below the image, and typically begin with a label followed by a number and the description of the image. Captions are helpful when referring to images within paragraphs of text (see Figure 1: An example of a caption).

To add a caption to a figure:

1. Select the figure you want to add the caption to.

2. Click the **References** tab.

3. In the *Captions* group, click the **Insert Caption** button.

4. The *Caption* dialog opens.

5. Click the **Label** arrow and select a figure type.

6. Click the **Position** arrow and select where you want the caption to appear.

7. Type any additional text, such as a description of the figure, in the *Caption* box.

8. Click **OK** to close the dialog and add the caption.

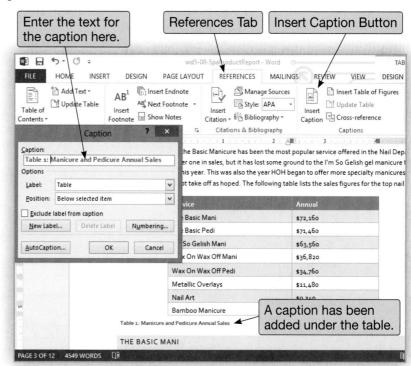

FIGURE WD 5.11

tips & tricks

Word automatically numbers the figures in your document based on the label type. For example, if you have several tables that use the "table" label, those captions will be numbered sequentially. If you have other figures labeled as "figures," those images will be numbered sequentially. If you go back and add a new caption or change the label of an existing caption, Word will renumber the existing captions for you.

tell me **more**

When you add certain types of images or objects to your document, such as a Microsoft Excel chart or an Adobe Acrobat document, you can have Word automatically add a caption to the figure. In the *Insert Caption* dialog, click the **AutoCaption...** button. In the *AutoCaption* dialog, select the type of object you want to automatically add captions to and click **OK.**

let me **try**

Open the student data file **wd5-08-SpaProductReport** and try this skill on your own:

1. Place the cursor in the **sales figures table** in the *Manicures and Pedicures* section.

2. Add a caption to display below the table. The caption should read `Table 1: Manicure and Pedicure Annual Sales`

3. Save the file as directed by your instructor and close it.

Skill 5.9 Selecting a Reference Style

A **reference style** is a set of rules used to display references in a bibliography. These rules include the order of information, when and how punctuation is used, and the use of character formatting, such as italics and bold. The two most common reference styles in use today are *APA, MLA,* and *Chicago;* however, there are a number of other reference styles you can choose from. It is important that you use the correct reference style for the subject of your document.

When creating a bibliography, it is important to use a consistent reference style for your citations. Word makes this easy by allowing you to set the reference style for the entire document at once.

To change the reference style for a document:

1. Click the **References** tab.
2. In the *Citations & Bibliography* group, click the arrow next to *Style* and select a style from the list.

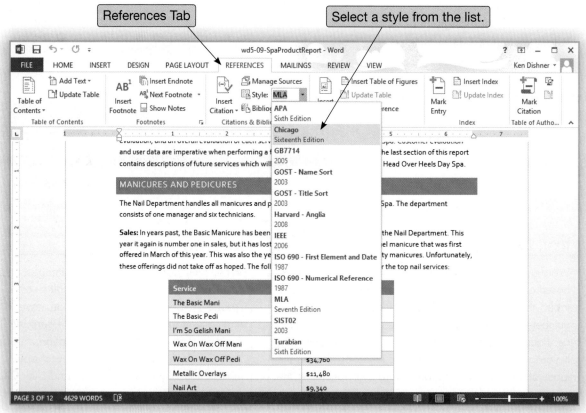

FIGURE WD 5.12

The following table lists the available styles in Word and when they are most commonly used.

STYLE ABBREVIATION	FULL NAME	PURPOSE
APA Sixth Edition	American Psychological Association	Education, psychology, and social sciences
Chicago Sixteenth Edition	The Chicago Manual of Style	Books, magazines, and newspapers
GB7714 2005	NA	Used in China
GOST—Name Sort	Russian State Standard	Used in Russia
GOST—Title Sort	Russian State Standard	Used in Russia
Harvard—Anglia 2008	Harvard reference style	For the specification at Anglia Ruskin University
IEEE 2006	IEEE Citation Reference	Research papers in technical fields
ISO 690—First Element and Date	International Standards Organization	Patents and industry (both print and nonprint works)
ISO 690—Numerical Reference	International Standards Organization	Patents and industry (both print and nonprint works)
MLA Seventh Edition	Modern Language Association	Arts and humanities
SIST02	NA	Used in Asia
Turabian Sixth Edition	Turabian	All subjects (designed for college students)

tips & tricks

When you change the reference style for a document, all citations are automatically updated to use the new style.

tell me more

To see a preview of the source style, click the **Manage Sources** button in the *Citations & Bibliography* group. The preview box at the bottom of the *Manage Sources* dialog shows how the selected reference will appear as a citation and in the bibliography.

let me try

Open the student data file **wd5-09-SpaProductReport** and try this skill on your own:

1. Navigate to the second paragraph of the document. Notice the format of the reference *(Faah)* in the first sentence.
2. Change the reference style for the document to use the **Chicago Sixteenth Edition** style.
3. Notice how the reference has changed to (*Faah 2012*).
4. Save the file as directed by your instructor and close it.

Skill 5.10 Adding Citations to Documents

When you use materials in a document from other sources, such as a book or a journal article, you need to give credit to the original source material. A **citation** is a reference to such source material. Citations include information such as the author, title, publisher, and the publication date.

To add a citation to a document, you must first create the source:

1. Place the cursor where you want to add the citation.
2. Click the **References** tab.
3. In the *Citations & Bibliography* group, click the **Insert Citation** button and select **Add New Source...**
4. In the *Create Source* dialog, click the arrow next to *Type of Source* and select an option.
5. In the *Author* box, type the name of the author.
6. In the *Title* box, type the title of the book or article.
7. In the *Year* box, type the year the book or article was published.
8. Add other information about the source to the appropriate fields.
9. When you are finished, click **OK** to add the citation to the document.

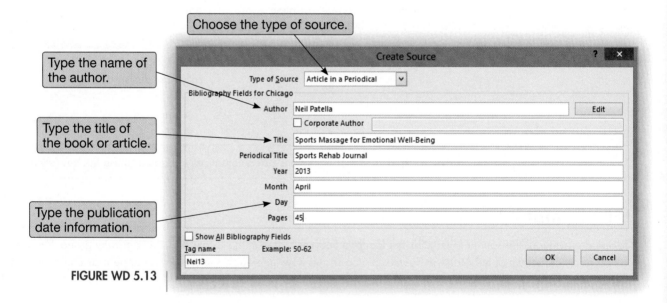

FIGURE WD 5.13

After you have added a new source, it appears on the *Insert Citation* menu. To add the same source to another part of the document, click the **Insert Citation** button and select the source for the citation.

tips & tricks

When you add a citation, the citation appears inside parentheses at the place where you inserted it. A citation includes basic information from the source, including the author, year, title, and pages. A bibliography lists all the citations in a document and includes more of the source information than the citation does.

tell me more

Citations appear in the document as a control. When you click the control, you will see an arrow on the right side. Click the arrow to display a menu for editing the source and the citation. In the *Edit Source* dialog, you can change the information you added when you created the source. In the *Edit Citation* dialog, you can change information specific to the citation, such as page numbers.

let me try

Open the student data file **wd5-10-SpaProductReport** and try this skill on your own:

1. Navigate to the *Sports Massage* section and place the cursor at the end of the first paragraph.

2. Add a new source with the following information:

Type of source	Article in Periodical
Author	Neil Patella
Title	Sports Massage for Emotional Well-Being
Periodical Title	Sports Rehab Journal
Year	2013
Month	April
Pages	45

3. Save the file as directed by your instructor and close it.

Skill 5.11 Creating a Bibliography

A **bibliography** is a compiled list of sources you referenced in your document. Typically, bibliographies appear at the end of a document and list all the sources you marked throughout the document. Microsoft Word 2013 comes with a number of prebuilt bibliography building blocks for you to use. When you select one of these building blocks, Word will search the document and compile all the sources from your document and format them according to the style you chose.

To add a bibliography to a document:

1. Place the cursor at the end of the document.
2. Click the **References** tab.
3. In the *Citations & Bibliography* group, click the **Bibliography** button and select one of the bibliography building blocks.
4. The bibliography is added to the end of the document, listing all the sources referenced in the document.

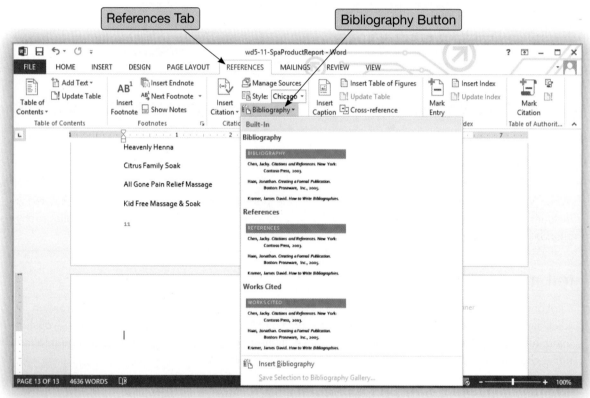

FIGURE WD 5.15

another **method**

To add a simple bibliography, click the **Insert Bibliography** command at the bottom of the *Bibliography* gallery.

let me **try**

Open the student data file **wd5-11-SpaProductReport** and try this skill on your own:

1. Navigate to the end of the document. Place the cursor at the top of the blank page.
2. Add a bibliography using the **References** style.
3. Save the file as directed by your instructor and close it.

Skill 5.12 Marking Entries

When creating long documents, you may want to add an index to the document to help your readers quickly locate specific information. To create an index you must first mark the topics you want to include, and then create the index. When formatting marks are hidden, marked entries look no different from other text in the document. However, when the index is created, Word finds all the marked entries and adds them to the index.

To mark entries:

1. Select the word or phrase you want to add to the index.
2. Click the **References** tab.
3. In the *Index* group, click the **Mark Entry** button.
4. The word or phrase appears in the *Main entry* box.
5. Click the **Mark** button to mark the entry.
6. Click the **Close** button to close the *Mark Index Entry* dialog.

After you mark an entry, Word adds the *XE (Index Entry)* formatting mark to the word and displays all formatting marks in the document, so you can double-check your page layout. However, formatting marks should be hidden before you create and insert the index to make it easier to view your final document.

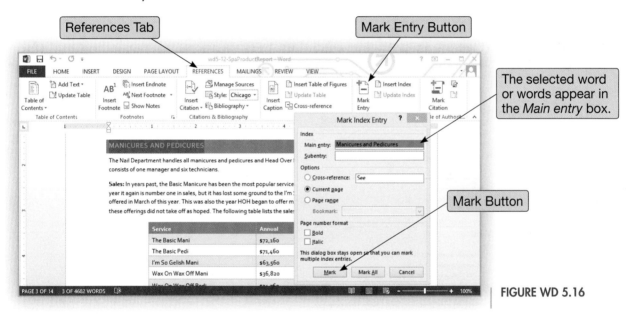

FIGURE WD 5.16

tips & tricks

To add a reference to every instance of a word to the index, click the **Mark All** button in the *Mark Index Entry* dialog.

another method

To open the *Mark Index Entry* dialog, you can also click the **Insert Index** button in the *Index* group. In the *Index* dialog, click the **Mark Entry...** button.

let me try

Open the student data file **wd5-12-SpaProductReport** and try this skill on your own:

1. Select the text **manicures and pedicures** in the first sentence of the *Manicures and Pedicures* section.
2. Mark the text as an entry to use in the index.
3. Save the file as directed by your instructor and close it.

Skill 5.13 Creating an Index

An **index** is a list of topics and associated page numbers that typically appears at the end of a document. Adding an index to your document can help your readers find information quickly.

An index entry can reference a single word, a phrase, or a topic spanning several pages. You can also add cross-references to your index.

To add an index to a document:

1. Place the cursor at the end of the document.
2. Click the **References** button.
3. In the *Index* group, click the **Insert Index** button.
4. The *Index* dialog opens.
5. Click the **Formats** arrow and select a format.
6. Modify the other options until the preview looks the way you want.
7. Click **OK** to insert the index into your document.

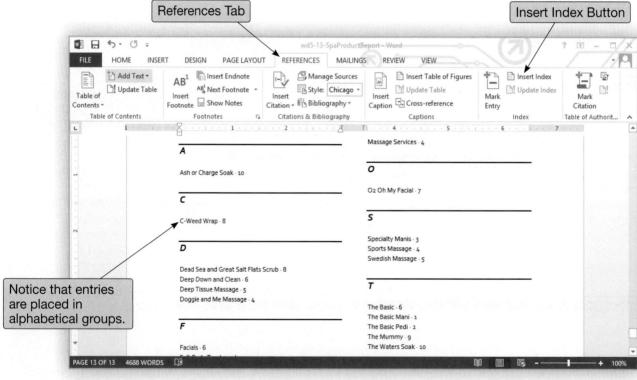

FIGURE WD 5.17

word 2013   chapter 5 Working with Reports, References, and Mailings

tips & tricks

tell me **more**

A cross-reference is an index entry that refers to another entry in the index rather than to a page in the document. Cross-references are often used to direct readers from an uncommon entry to a more frequently used one.

let me **try**

Open the student data file **wd5-13-SpaProductReport** and try this skill on your own:

1. Navigate to the end of the document. Place the cursor at the top of the last page.
2. Insert an index based on the **Modern** format. The entries should display in two columns.
3. Save the file as directed by your instructor and close it.

from the perspective of . . .

GRADUATE STUDENT

When I wrote my first term paper, my professor rejected it informing me that it wasn't formatted correctly and I was using the wrong reference style. I didn't understand. I had typed everything very carefully, but apparently I was supposed to use the APA style and not the MLA style. After that, I started using the reference tools built into Word 2013. Now I can generate a table of contents from headings in my paper, mark entries for my index as I write, and auto-generate the index. Most important, I can set my reference style to use the APA style, add my sources, and create a bibliography in the right style. When I resubmitted my paper, my professor was impressed with how well it was formatted. I got an A!

Skill 5.14 Using Views

By default, Microsoft Word displays documents in Print Layout view, but you can display your documents in a number of other ways. Each view has its own purpose, and considering what you want to do with your document will help determine which view is most appropriate to use.

To switch between different views, click the appropriate icon located in the lower-right corner of the status bar next to the zoom slider.

Read Mode—Use this view when you want to review a document. Read Mode presents the document in an easy-to-read format. In this view, the Ribbon is no longer visible. To navigate between screens, use the navigation buttons on the left and right side of the window.

Print Layout view—Use this view to see how document elements will appear on a printed page. This view will help you edit headers and footers, and adjust margins and layouts.

Web Layout view—Use this view when designing documents that will be viewed on-screen, such as a Web page. Web Layout view displays all backgrounds, drawing objects, and graphics as they will appear on-screen. Unlike Print Layout view, Web Layout view does not show page edges, margins, or headers and footers.

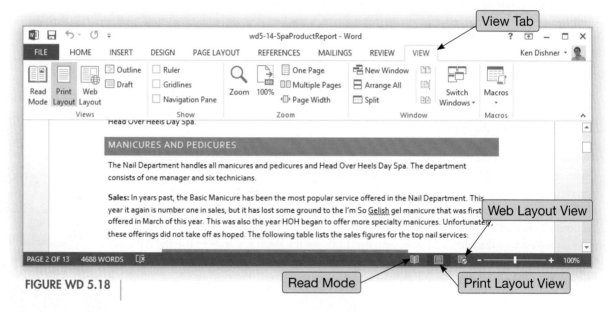

FIGURE WD 5.18

tell me **more**

In previous versions of Word, Outline view and Draft view were accessible from the status bar. In Word 2013, you can now only access these views from the *View* tab:

Outline view—Use this view to check the structure of your document. In Outline view, you can collapse the document's structure to view just the top-level headings or expand the structure to see the document's framework. Outline view is most helpful when you use a different style for each type of heading in your document.

Draft view—Use this simplified layout view when typing and formatting text. Draft view does not display headers and footers, page edges, backgrounds, or drawing objects.

another **method**

To switch views, you also can click the **View** tab and select a view from the *Views* group.

let me **try**

Open the student data file **wd5-14-SpaProduct Report** and try this skill on your own:

1. Switch to **Read Mode.**
2. Switch to **Web Layout** view.
3. Switch back to **Print Layout** view.
4. Close the file.

Skill 5.15 Using Read Mode

Today more and more documents are read on devices such as tablets and smartphones. Word 2013 now includes Read Mode, which is designed for reading documents in electronic format. In Read Mode, documents are displayed as screens rather than pages.

To display a document in Read Mode:

1. Click the **Read Mode** button on the status bar.
2. Click the **Next** button to navigate to the next screen.
3. Click the **Back** button to navigate to the previous screen.

Read Mode comes with specific tools to modify the look of the document as you read. When reading documents electronically, some people prefer a softer screen appearance than black text on a white background, while others prefer reading white text on a black background. Read Mode comes with specific tools to modify the look of the document as you read, including changing the page color.

To change the page color in Read Mode:

1. Click the **View** menu.
2. Point to **Page Color** and select an option:
   - **None**—Displays black text on a white background
   - **Sepia**—Displays black text on a sepia tone background
   - **Inverse**—Displays white text on a black background

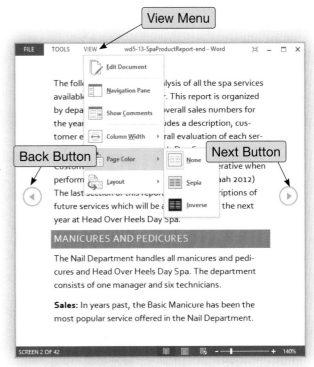

FIGURE WD 5.19

tell me **more**

If you resize the Read Mode window, the text will automatically resize to fit the window. If you make the window smaller, you will notice the number of screens to display increases. If you make the window larger, the number of screens to display decreases.

another **method**

To navigate through pages of a document in Read Mode, you can also use the horizontal scrollbar along the bottom of the window.

let me **try**

Open the student data file **wd5-15-SpaProductReport** and try this skill on your own:

1. Switch to **Read Mode.**
2. Change the color of the page to **Sepia.**
3. Navigate to the next screen in the document.
4. Navigate to the previous screen in the document.
5. Save the file as directed by your instructor and close it.

Skill 5.16 Creating a New Document Using a Template

A **template** is a document with predefined settings that you can use as a pattern to create a new file of your own. Using a template makes creating a fully formatted and designed new file easy, saving you time and effort. There are templates available for letters, memos, résumés, newsletters, and almost any other type of document you can imagine.

To create a new document from a template:

1. Click the **File** tab to open Backstage view.

2. Click **New.** Word 2013 includes a variety of templates that are copied to your computer when you install the application. These templates are always available from the *New* page. Additional templates that you download are also displayed on the *New* page, so your screen may look different from the one in Figure WD 5.20.

3. Click each template preview picture for a brief description of the template.

4. When you find the template you want to use, click the **Create** button.

5. A new document opens, prepopulated with all of the template elements.

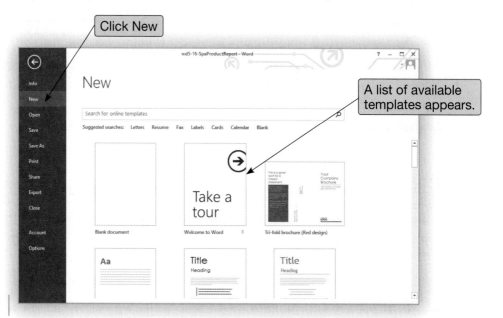

FIGURE WD 5.20

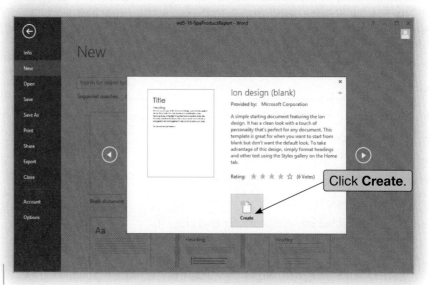

FIGURE WD 5.21

You can search for more document templates online. (You must have an active Internet connection.)

1. Near the top of the *New* page, in the *Search online templates* box, type a keyword or phrase that describes the template you want.

2. Click the **Start searching** button (the magnifying glass image at the end of the *Search online templates* box).

3. The search results display previews of the templates that match the keyword or phrase you entered. To further narrow the results, click one of the categories listed in the *Filter by* pane at the right side of the window. Notice that each category lists the number of templates available.

4. When you find the template you want, click it to display the larger preview with detailed information about the template, and then click **Create.**

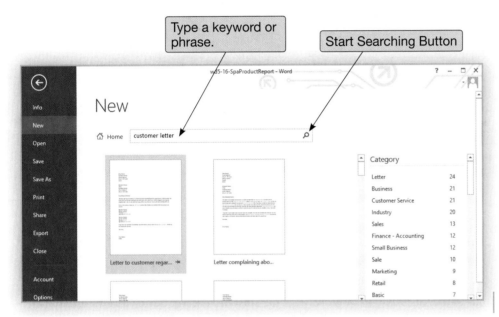

FIGURE WD 5.22

tell me **more**

Some templates include fully formed documents with sample text for you to replace with your own information. Other templates are empty shells based on a certain design. The template includes the proper styles applied to document elements to help you get started in creating well formatted documents using proper desktop publishing rules.

let me try

Open the student data file **wd5-16-Document1** and try this skill on your own:

1. Display the **New** page in Backstage.

2. Search for a template of a **new customer letter.**

3. Create a new document based on the **Thank you letter to new customer** template.

4. Save the new file as directed by your instructor and close it. Close the original file you opened but do not save it.

Skill 5.17 Starting a Mail Merge

Suppose you have a letter you want to send out to 20 recipients, but you want each person's name to appear on the letter, giving it a more personal touch. You could write the letter and save 20 versions—one for each recipient—but this is time-consuming and cumbersome. In Word, you can take a list of names and addresses and merge them with a standard document, creating a personalized document for each name on your list. This process is called a **mail merge.**

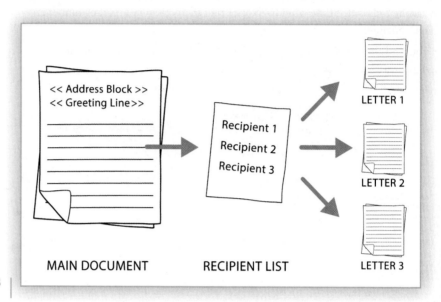

FIGURE WD 5.23

Before you create a mail merge, you first select a main document type. To set up the main document:

1. Click the **Mailings** tab.
2. In the *Start Mail Merge* group, click the **Start Mail Merge** button and select **Letters.**

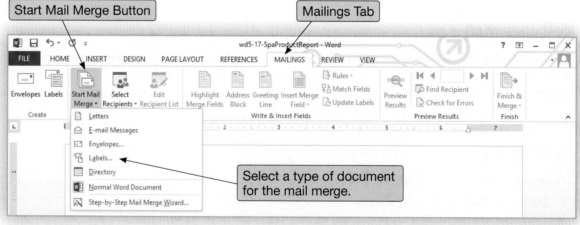

FIGURE WD 5.24

word 2013   chapter 5 Working with Reports, References, and Mailings

tips & tricks

tell me **more**

You can also create a mail merge using the *Mail Merge Wizard,* which will take you through creating the mail merge step by step. To display the *Mail Merge Wizard,* click the **Start Mail Merge** button and select **Step by Step Mail Merge Wizard...**

let me try

Open the student data file **wd5-17-CustomerLetter** and try this skill on your own:

1. Start a new mail merge for a **letter.**
2. Keep this file open for working on the next skill.

from the perspective of . . .

PAROLE OFFICER

I have several form letters that I use to send to my clients when they have a parole violation or have missed a court mandated appointment. Often times, I am sending several letters out to clients at the same time, so I use mail merge to make the process go faster. I keep all my clients' information in an Access database that I use to create the recipients list. I can select which clients to add to the merge and then add the address block and greeting line to the form letter. I print all the letters at once, send them out, and I am done—until the next violation occurs.

Skill 5.18 Selecting Recipients

The **recipients list** for the mail merge is a table of names and address for the people you want to include in the merge. You can import recipients from an existing Access database or Word document, or you can enter the recipients' information in manually.

To select recipients for the mail merge:

1. Click the **Mailings** tab.
2. In the *Start Mail Merge* group, click the **Select Recipients** button.
3. Select **Use an Existing List...**
4. In the *Select Data Source* dialog, select a data source and click **Open.**

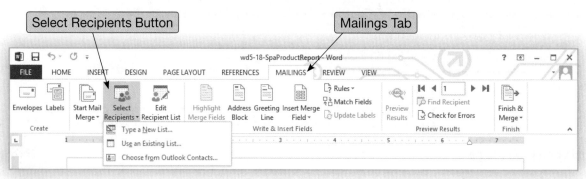

FIGURE WD 5.25

To enter recipients for the mail merge manually:

1. In the *Start Mail Merge* group, click the **Select Recipients** button and select **Type a New List...**
2. In the *New Address List* dialog, enter the information for the recipient in the appropriate boxes.
3. Click the **New Entry** button to add another recipient.
4. Continue adding all the recipients for the mail merge. When you are done, click **OK** to create the list of recipients.

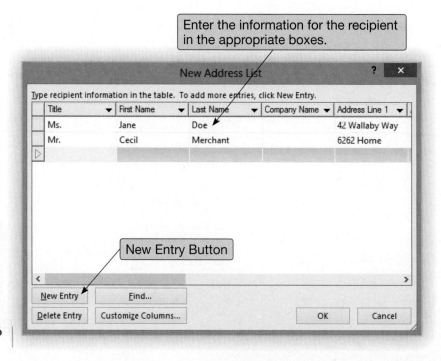

FIGURE WD 5.26

Once you have added a list of recipients, you can then edit the recipients list, making any changes to information that may be incorrect.

To edit the recipients list:

1. On the *Mailings* tab, in the *Start Mail Merge* group, click the **Edit Recipient List** button.

2. Click in any field to change the information for the recipients.

3. Click the checkmark next to a name to deselect it and exclude the recipient from the mail merge.

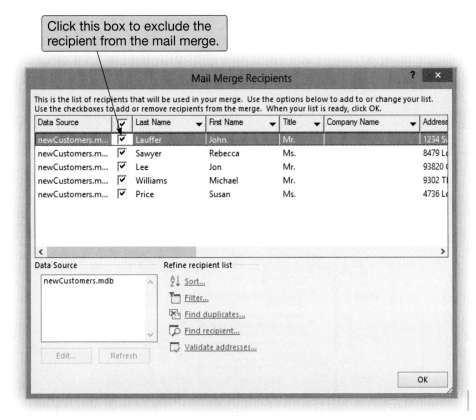

FIGURE WD 5.27

tell me **more**

When you enter contacts manually, Word creates an Access database from the information you entered. The database is then stored on your hard drive in the *My Data Sources* folder in the *My Documents* folder for your user account.

another **method**

You can also add recipients from your Outlook contacts list.

let me **try**

With the document from the previous skill still open, try this skill on your own:

1. Add a list of recipients to the mail merge based on an existing list.

2. Select the **newCustomers** database as the source for the list of recipients. You will find the database in the location where you downloaded your student data files for this book.

3. Keep this file open for working on the next skill.

Skill 5.19 Adding an Address Block

The main document of a mail merge contains the text and merge fields, which appear on every version of the merged document. Merge fields are placeholders that insert specific data from the recipients list you created. If you are writing business letters, you can add an address block merge field where the address for the recipient should appear. An address block will display the name and address of the recipient in the standard business letter format.

To add an address block merge field:

1. Click in the document where you want the merge field to appear.
2. On the *Mailings* tab, in the *Write & Insert Fields* group, click the **Address Block** button.
3. In the **Insert Address Block** dialog, make any changes to the display and click **OK.**

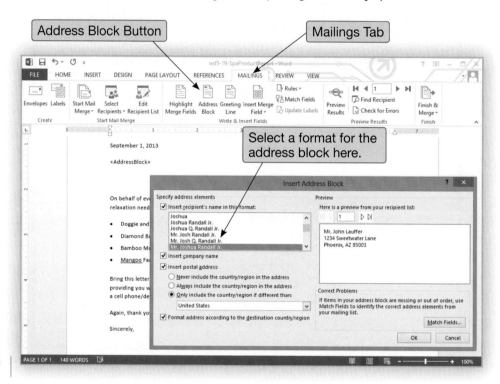

FIGURE WD 5.28

tips & tricks

The *Insert Address Block* dialog includes a preview of how the merge fields will display in the document. Click the **Next** and **Previous** buttons to navigate through the list of recipients to see how each one will display before finalizing your choices.

tell me **more**

The three basic types of merge fields are:

Address Block—Inserts a merge field with the name and address of the recipient.

Greeting Line—Inserts a field with a greeting and the recipient's name.

Merge Fields—Allows you to insert merge fields based on your data source, such as first names, last names, addresses, phone numbers, and e-mail addresses.

let me **try**

With the document from the previous skill still open, try this skill on your own:

1. Place the cursor on the first blank line under the date.

2. Insert an address block using the following format: **Mr. Josh Randall Jr.**

3. Keep this file open for working on the next skill.

Skill 5.20 Adding a Greeting Line

When writing a letter, you should always open with a greeting line personally addressing the reader by name. This is where creating a mail merge can save you a lot of time and effort. When you add a greeting line to a mail merge, you choose the format for the greeting line. Then, Word inserts each name in the recipients list into the greeting line, creating personalized letters without having to create each one individually.

To add a greeting line merge field:

1. Click in the document where you want the merge field to appear.
2. On the *Mailings* tab, in the *Write & Insert Fields* group, click the **Greeting Line** button.
3. In the *Insert Greeting Line* dialog, make any changes to the display and click **OK.**

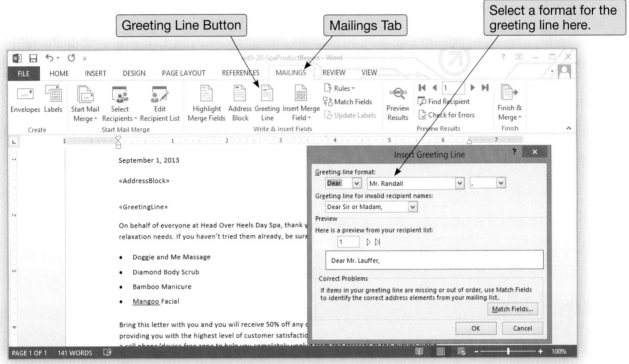

Greeting Line Button

Mailings Tab

Select a format for the greeting line here.

FIGURE WD 5.29

tips & tricks

The *Insert Greeting Line* dialog includes a preview of how the merge fields will display in the document. Click the **Next** and **Previous** buttons to navigate through the list of recipients to see how each one will display before finalizing your choices.

tell me **more**

To add individual merge fields:

1. Click in the document where you want the merge field to appear.
2. Click the **Insert Merge Field** button and select an option to insert.

let me try

With the document from the previous skill still open, try this skill on your own:

1. Place the cursor on the blank line under the address block.
2. Insert a greeting line based on the following format: **Dear Mr. Randall:**
3. Keep this file open for working on the next skill.

Skill 5.21 Previewing and Finishing the Merge

Before you complete the mail merge and print your documents, it is a good idea to review each document created in the merge.

To preview the mail merge:

1. On the *Mailings* tab, in the *Preview Results* group, click the **Preview Results** button.
2. Click the **Next Record** and **Previous Record** buttons to navigate among different documents.

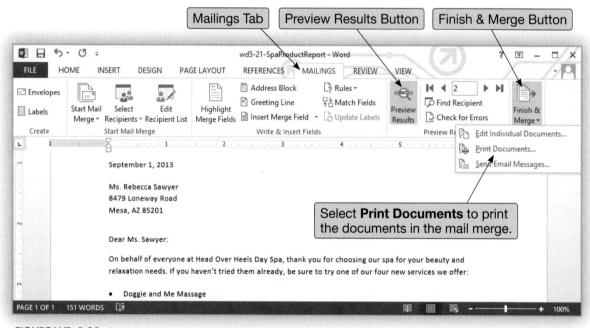

FIGURE WD 5.30

FIGURE WD 5.31

After you have previewed the mail merge, the last step is to finish the merge by printing the documents.

To print the documents in the mail merge:

1. On the *Mailings* tab, in the *Finish* group, click the **Finish & Merge** button and select **Print Documents...**
2. In the *Merge to Printer* dialog, verify the **All** radio button is selected to print all the documents in the merge.
3. Click **OK**.

tips & tricks

Before you finish the merge, click the **Check for Errors** button to review your documents for errors.

tell me **more**

If you want to modify letters individually, click **Edit individual letters...** Then, in the *Merge to New Document* dialog, select the records you want to change and click **OK.** Word opens a new document based on the selected records. Make any changes you want, and then print or save the document just as you would any other file.

If you want to send the document via e-mail, click **Send E-mail Messages...** Enter the subject line and mail format. Select the recipients you want to send the document to and click **OK.**

let me try

With the document from the previous skill still open, try this skill on your own:

1. Preview the mail merge.
2. Navigate through each letter to see how it will display.
3. Print all the letters in the mail merge. **NOTE:** If you are using this in class or in your school's computer lab, check with your instructor about printing permissions before completing this step.
4. Save the file as directed by your instructor and close it.

Skill 5.22 Creating Envelopes

With Word you can create an envelope and print it without leaving the document you are working on. Word's preset formats take care of the measuring and layout for you.

To create and print an envelope:

1. Click the **Mailings** tab.
2. In the *Create* group, click the **Envelopes** button.

FIGURE WD 5.32

3. Type the address of the person you are sending the document to in the *Delivery address* text box.
4. Type your address in the *Return address* text box.
5. Click the **Print** button in the *Envelopes and Labels* dialog.

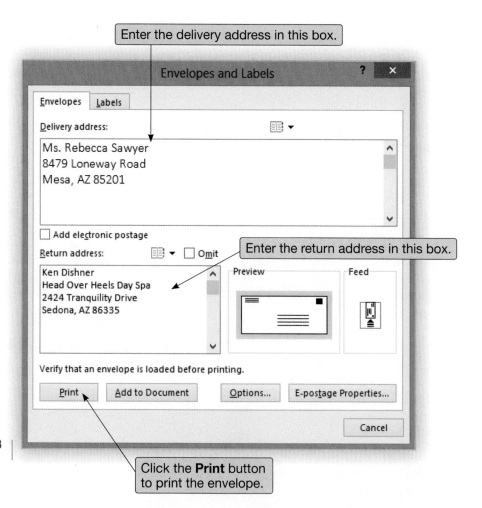

FIGURE WD 5.33

tips & tricks

By default, Word selects a standard envelope size. If your envelope is a different size, you can change the size of the envelope through the *Envelope Options* dialog. In the *Envelopes and Labels* dialog, click the **Options...** button. The *Envelop Options* dialog opens. Click the **Envelope size** arrow and select an envelope size. Click **OK** in the *Envelope Options* dialog.

tell me **more**

When you open the *Envelopes and Labels* dialog, Word searches your document for an address. If it finds what looks like an address, it will copy it directly into the dialog for you. Of course, you can always change this if it's not what you need.

another **method**

To open the *Envelopes and Labels* dialog, you can also click the **Labels** button, and then click the **Envelopes** tab to create an envelope.

let me **try**

Open the student data file **wd5-22-Document1** and try this skill on your own:

1. Open the *Envelopes and Labels* dialog.
2. Add the following delivery address:

   Ms. Rebecca Sawyer

   8479 Loneway Road

   Mesa, AZ 85201

3. Add the following return address:

   Ken Dishner

   Head Over Heels Day Spa

   2424 Tranquility Drive

   Sedona, AZ 86335

4. Send the envelope to the printer. **NOTE:** If you are using this in class or in your school's computer lab, check with your instructor about printing permissions before completing this step.
5. Save the file as directed by your instructor and close it.

Skill 5.23 Creating Labels

Rather than trying to create a document of labels with the correct margin and label size, you can use Word's preset label formats. Before creating your labels, first check the packaging for the manufacturer name and the product name or number.

To create labels:

1. Click the **Mailings** tab.
2. In the *Create* group, click the **Labels** button.

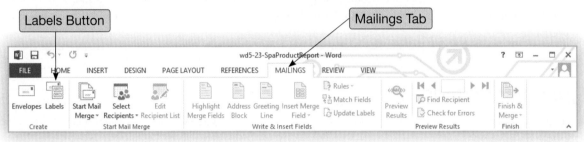

FIGURE WD 5.34

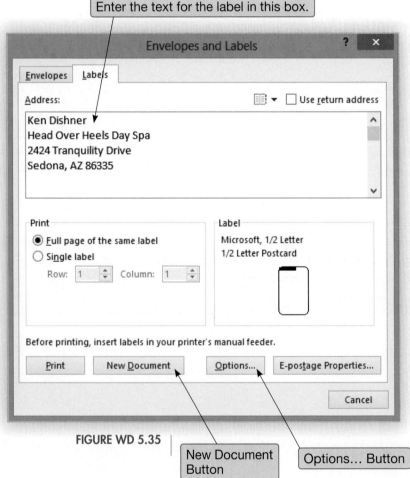

FIGURE WD 5.35

3. The type text for the label in the *Address* box.
4. Click the **Options...** button.
5. Click the **Label vendors** arrow and find the name of the company that made the labels you want to use.
6. Scroll the list of product numbers until you find the one that matches your labels.
7. Click **OK** in the *Label Options* dialog.
8. Click the **New Document** button.

Word creates the document as a table with the proper margins and spacing between cells. The cells in the table are prepopulated with the text you entered in the *Address* box in the *Envelopes and Labels* dialog.

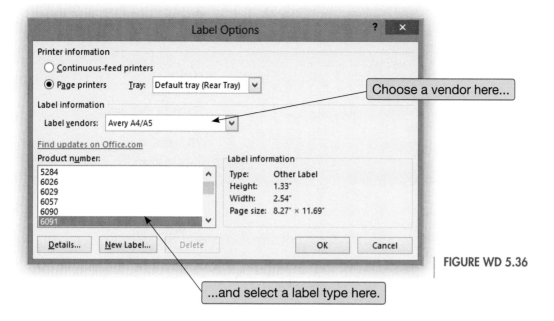

FIGURE WD 5.36

Choose a vendor here...

...and select a label type here.

tips & tricks

If you need to create a page of labels with different text, leave the *Address* box empty, choose the label type, and create the document. Word will create a document of empty labels. Click in each cell and type the text for the labels you want to create.

tell me **more**

You can choose to print a full page of the same label or a single label. Use the full page option if you are printing return address labels that you will need several of. Use the single label option for creating individual labels, such as labels for file folders.

another **method**

To open the *Envelopes and Labels* dialog, you can also click the **Envelopes** button, and then click the **Labels** tab to create a label.

let me **try**

Open the student data file **wd5-23-Document1** and try this skill on your own:

1. Open the *Envelopes and Labels* dialog.
2. Add the following return address:

   Ken Dishner

   Head Over Heels Day Spa

   2424 Tranquility Drive

   Sedona, AZ 86335

3. Open the *Label Options* dialog and select the vendor **Avery A4/A5** and the product number **3651**.
4. Create a new document of labels.
5. Save the file as directed by your instructor and close it.

key terms

AutoCorrect
Thesaurus
Tab leaders
Table of contents
Footnotes
Endnotes
Reference mark
Caption
Reference style
Citation
Bibliography

Index
Read Mode
Print Layout view
Web Layout view
Template
Mail merge
Recipients list
Merge fields
Address block
Greeting line
Labels

concepts review

1. A _____ fills in the space between tabs with solid, dotted, or dashed lines.
   a. border
   b. tab leader
   c. tab marker
   d. none of the above

2. When creating a mail merge, you can add recipients _____.
   a. by typing them in manually
   b. by importing them from an Access database
   c. by importing them from Outlook
   d. all of the above

3. To look up a synonym for a word use the _____.
   a. grammar check
   b. Thesaurus
   c. Dictionary
   d. translate tool

4. When you add a table of contents to a document, the entries created are based on _____.
   a. marked entries
   b. headings
   c. custom styles
   d. all of the above

5. You can add a caption for a _____.
   a. figure
   b. table
   c. neither a nor b
   d. both a and b

6. A _____ appears at the bottom of a page and is composed of two parts: a reference mark (a superscript character placed next to the text) and the associated text.

   a. footnote

   b. endnote

   c. index

   d. citation

7. To view documents optimally on an electronic device, such as a tablet, you should use _____.

   a. Read Mode

   b. Print Layout view

   c. Web Layout view

   d. Draft view

8. A _____ is a set of rules used to display references in a bibliography.

   a. source

   b. reference style

   c. template

   d. citation

9. If you often mistype a word, use Word's _____ to automatically replace the misspelling with the correct spelling as you type.

   a. find and replace commands

   b. spelling check

   c. grammar check

   d. AutoCorrect

10. _____ are placeholders that insert specific data for recipients you added to a mail merge.

   a. Merge fields

   b. Labels

   c. Recipients lists

   d. all of the above

projects

Data files for projects can be found on
www.mhhe.com/office2013skills

skill review 5.1

In this project you will be working on a research paper about alternate assessments for students.

Skills needed to complete this project:

- Checking Grammar (Skill 5.2)
- Using the Thesaurus (Skill 5.3)
- Using the Tabs Dialog (Skill 5.4)
- Adding Tab Leaders (Skill 5.5)
- Inserting a Table of Contents (Skill 5.6)
- Inserting Footnotes and Endnotes (Skill 5.7)
- Selecting a Reference Style (Skill 5.9)
- Adding Citations to Documents (Skill 5.10)
- Creating a Bibliography (Skill 5.11)
- Marking Entries (Skill 5.12)
- Creating an Index (Skill 5.13)
- Using Views (Skill 5.14)

1. Open the **WD2013-SkillReview-5-1** document.
2. Save this document as: **[your initials]WD-SkillReview-5-1**
3. Check for grammar errors in the document.
   a. Click the **Review** tab.
   b. In the *Proofing* group, click the **Spelling & Grammar** button.
   c. The first grammar error found should be **a** instead of **an.** Click the **Change** button in the *Grammar* task pane to fix the error.
   d. The second and third grammar errors found indicate **Behind** should not be capitalized. Click the **Ignore** button to keep the capitalization the same for both instances found.
   e. If Word finds a spelling error on the name **Kettler,** click the **Ignore All** button to keep the spelling of this name throughout the document.
4. Use the Thesaurus to look up synonyms of a word.
   a. Navigate to the beginning of the document.
   b. In the first paragraph under *Introduction,* select the word **pick** in the second sentence.
   c. On the *Review* tab, in the *Proofing* group, click the **Thesaurus** button.
   d. Scroll the list of synonyms, in the *select (v.)* section, point to **choose** and click the **arrow.**
   e. Click **Insert** on the menu.

5. Add an AutoCorrect entry and type the text to see the correction.

   a. Click the **File** tab.

   b. Click **Options.**

   c. In the *Word Options* dialog, click **Proofing.**

   d. Click the **AutoCorrect Options...** button.

   e. In the *Replace* box, type `accomodations`. In the *With* box, type `accommodations`.

   f. Click the **Add** button.

   g. Click **OK** in the *AutoCorrect* dialog. Click **OK** in the *Word Options* dialog.

   h. Place the cursor between the words **of** and **that** in the first sentence of the first paragraph of the document.

   i. Type `accomodations`. Notice Word replaces the misspelled word with the correct spelling you added.

6. Add a new tab through the *Tabs* dialog.

   a. Place the cursor at the beginning of the first paragraph of the document.

   b. Click the **Home** tab.

   c. In the *Paragraph* group, click the **dialog launcher.**

   d. In the *Paragraph* dialog, click the **Tabs...** button.

   e. In the *Tab stop position* box, type `0.5"`.

   f. Verify the alignment of the tab is set to Left and there is no tab leader. Click the **Set** button.

   g. Click **OK** in the *Tabs* dialog.

   h. Press the [Tab] key to indent the paragraph by 0.5".

7. Insert a table of contents.

   a. Place the cursor before the **Introduction** heading.

   b. Click the **Page Layout** tab.

   c. In the *Page Setup* group, click the **Breaks** button and select **Page.**

   d. Place the cursor on the empty line on the newly inserted page.

   e. Click the **References** tab.

   f. In the *Table of Contents* group, click the **Table of Contents** button and select **Automatic Table 2.**

8. Insert a footnote.

   a. Navigate to the *No Child Left Behind* section of the document. Place the cursor after the word **state** in the first sentence.

   b. On the *References* tab, in the *Footnotes* group, click the **Insert Footnote** button.

   c. Type the following text for the footnote: `For this paper the Ohio state standards are employed.`

9. Add a new source and insert a citation.

   a. Navigate to the *Modified Achievement Standards* section. Place the cursor before the period in the second sentence of the last paragraph of the section. This is the sentence ending with *scheduling, presentation format or response format.*

   b. On the *References* tab, in the *Citations & Bibliography* group, click the **Insert Citation** button and select **Add New Source.**

c. In the *Create Source* dialog, select **Journal Article** as the type of source. Enter `Pamela Johnson` as the author. Enter `The Benefits of Administration of Alternate Assessments` as the title. Enter `New Horizons` as the journal name. Enter `2012` for the year.

d. Click **OK** to create the source.

e. Navigate to the *Who Will Benefit* section. Place the cursor before the last period at the end of the second paragraph in the section. This is the sentence ending with *validity of the alternate assessment.*

f. On the *References* tab, in the *Citations & Bibliography* group, click the **Insert Citation** button and select the **Johnson, Pamela** citation.

10. Change the reference style for the document.

a. On the *References* tab, in the *Citations & Bibliography* group, click the **Style** arrow.

b. Select **APA Sixth Edition.**

11. Add a bibliography to the document.

a. Place the cursor at the end of the document.

b. Click the **Page Layout** tab.

c. In the *Page Setup* group, click the **Breaks** button and select **Page.**

d. Click the **References** tab.

e. In the *Citations &Bibliography* group, click the **Bibliography** button and select **References.**

12. Mark and entry for the index.

a. Navigate to the *No Child Left Behind* section. Select **No Child Left Behind Act (NCLB)** in the first sentence of the first paragraph.

b. On the *References* tab, in the *Index* group, click the **Mark Entry** button.

c. In the *Mark Index Entry* dialog, click the **Mark** button.

d. Click the **Close** button.

e. Click the **Home** tab.

f. In the *Paragraph* group, click the **Show/Hide** button to hide formatting marks in the document.

13. Create an index for the document.

a. Navigate to the end of the document and place the cursor on the empty line under the *References* section.

b. Click the **Page Layout** tab.

c. In the *Page Setup* group, click the **Breaks** button and select **Page.**

d. Click the **References** tab.

e. In the *Index* group, click the **Insert Index** button.

f. Click the **Formats** arrow and select **Modern.**

g. Click **OK** to add the index.

14. Display the document in different views.

a. Navigate to the beginning of the document.

b. On the status bar, click the **Read Mode** button.

c. Click **View,** point to **Page Color,** and select **Sepia.**

d. Click the **Next** button to advance to the next page in the document.

e. Navigate through the document using the **Back** and **Next** buttons.

f. On the status bar, click the **Print Layout** button to return to *Print Layout* view.

15. Save and close the document.

In this project you will be creating a mail merge based on a template.

Skills needed to complete this project:

- Creating a New Document Using a Template (Skill 5.16)
- Using the Thesaurus (Skill 5.3)
- Starting a Mail Merge (Skill 5.17)
- Selecting Recipients (Skill 5.18)
- Adding an Address Block (Skill 5.19)
- Adding a Greeting Line (Skill 5.20)
- Previewing and Finishing the Merge (Skill 5.21)

1. Open the **WD2013-SkillReview-5-2** document.
2. Create a new document from a template.
   a. Click the **File** tab.
   b. Click **New.**
   c. In the *Search for online templates* box, type **letter to new client**. Click the **Start searching** button.
   d. Click the **Introductory letter to new client** template. NOTE: You may see two templates with this description. Choose the letter with the following description: *Welcome a new client to your company with this letter template, which encloses information about your services and provides account and contact information.*
   e. Click the **Create** button to create the new document based on the template.
3. Save this document as: **[your initials]WD-SkillReview-5-2**
4. Remove information from the document.
   a. Select the recipient address block (*[Recipient Name], [Title], [Company Name], [Steen Address], [City, ST Zip Code]*. Press the [Delete] key to remove the text.
   b. Delete the **Dear [Recipient Name]:** line.
   c. Delete the last two sentences in the second paragraph (beginning with **Your account manager,**).
5. Insert your own text into the document.
   a. In the first sentence of the first paragraph, delete the [**Company Name**] control. Type **Suarez Marketing**.
   b. In the first sentence of the first paragraph, delete the [**business type**] control. Type **marketing**.
   c. In the last sentence of the third paragraph, delete the [**Company Name**] control. Type **Suarez Marketing**.
   d. Delete the [**Your Name**] control in the salutation. Type **Maria Suarez**.
   e. Delete the [**Title**] control. Type **President**.
   f. Select the company address block at the top of the document. Delete the **Your Name** control and the **Company Name** control. Enter the following information in the company address block at the top of the document:

   Maria Suarez

   Suarez Marketing

   1212 Main St.

   St. Louis MO 63144
   g. Click the **Date** control and select today's date.

6. Use the **Thesaurus** to look up synonyms of a word.

 a. In the first paragraph, select the word **choosing** in the first sentence.

 b. On the *Review* tab, in the *Proofing* group, click the **Thesaurus** button.

 c. In the list of synonyms, point to **selecting** and click the **arrow.**

 d. Click **Insert** on the menu.

7. Start a new mail merge.

 a. Click the **Mailings** tab.

 b. Click the **Start Mail Merge** button and select **Letters.**

8. Add recipients to the mail merge.

 a. On the *Mailings* tab, in the *Start Mail Merge* group, click the **Select Recipients** button and select **Use an Existing List...**

 b. Browse to your student data file location, select the **Clients** file, and click the **Open** button.

 c. In the *Select Table* dialog, select the **Clients** table and click **OK.**

9. Add an address block to the document.

 a. Place the cursor after the zip code in the company address block and press [**Enter**] **twice.**

 b. On the *Mailings* tab, in the *Write & Insert Fields* group, click the **Address Block** button.

 c. In the *Insert recipient's name in this format* box, select the **Josh Randall Jr.** format. Click **OK.**

10. Add a greeting line to the document.

 a. Place the cursor at the beginning of the first paragraph and press ⏎ Enter . Place the cursor on the empty line.

 b. On the *Mailings* tab, in the *Write & Insert Fields* group, click the **Greeting Line** button.

 c. In the *Insert Greeting Line* dialog, click the arrow next to the punctuation under *Greeting line format* and select the **colon (:).** Click **OK.**

11. Preview the merged documents.

 a. On the *Mailings* tab, in the *Preview Results* group, click the **Preview Results** button.

 b. In the *Preview Results* group, click the **Next Record** button to advance through the letters in the mail merge.

12. Print the merged documents.

 a. On the *Mailings* tab, in the *Finish* group, click the **Finish & Merge** button and select **Print Documents...**

 b. Verify the **All** radio button is selected. Click **OK.**

 c. The *Print* dialog opens. Click **OK** to print all the letters in the merge. If you do not want to print the merge, click **Cancel. NOTE:** If you are using this in class or in your school's computer lab, check with your instructor about printing permissions before completing this step.

13. Save and close the document. Close but do not save the original blank document.

In this project you will be adding working on a safety report from the Spring Hills Community.

Skills needed to complete this project:
- Using AutoCorrect (Skill 5.1)
- Checking Grammar (Skill 5.2)
- Using the Thesaurus (Skill 5.3)
- Adding a Caption (Skill 5.8)
- Using the Tabs Dialog (Skill 5.4)
- Adding Tab Leaders (Skill 5.5)
- Inserting a Table of Contents (Skill 5.6)
- Inserting Footnotes and Endnotes (Skill 5.7)
- Marking Entries (Skill 5.12)
- Creating an Index (Skill 5.13)
- Using Views (Skill 5.14)
- Using Read Mode (Skill 5.15)

1. Open the **WD2013-ChallengeYourself-5-3** document.

2. Save this document as: **[your initials]WD-ChallengeYourself-5-3**

3. Add an AutoCorrect entry and type the text to see the correction.

   a. Create an AutoCorrect entry that will change the letters **ghc** to **Green Hills Community** when typed.

   b. Place the cursor between the words **the** and **Outside** on the second line in the first paragraph of the document. Type **ghc.** (Be sure to include the period after the letters). Notice Word changes the text to the entry you just created.

4. Using Word's grammar check, check the documents for any grammar errors and correct the errors that are found. Ignore any spelling errors that appear on names.

5. Use the Thesaurus to look up synonyms of a word.

   a. Select the word **community** in the second sentence of the first paragraph *(Outside our gated community).*

   b. Use the Thesaurus to replace the word **community** with the synonym **neighborhood.**

6. Add a caption to a chart.

   a. Select the chart on page 2.

   b. Add a caption that reads **Figure 1: Top 5 Targeted Electronics**. Have the figure appear below the chart.

7. Add a new tab through the *Tabs* dialog.

   a. Select the list of full-time officers at the bottom of page 3.

   b. Using the *Tabs* dialog, add a **right tab** and the **5"** mark. Include a **dotted tab leader** (option 2).

   c. For each item in the bulleted list, place the cursor between the name and the number of years. Remove the space and press [Tab].

   d. Repeat these steps for the list of part-time officers.

8. Insert a table of contents.

   a. Place the cursor before the document title **Spring Hills Community Safety Strategies** (at the top of the second page).

   b. Add a table of contents based on the **Automatic Table 1** style.

9. Insert a footnote.

   a. Place the cursor at the end of the heading **Basic Tips for Staying Safe.**

   b. Insert a footnote that reads: `Adapted from Dwight Hill's safety presentation.`

10. Mark and entry for the index.

    a. Select the text **top five targeted electronics** at the end of the first paragraph in the *What Electronics Are Being Targeted* section.

    b. Mark the text for use in an index. Close the *Mark Index Entry* dialog.

    c. Hide the formatting marks when you are done.

11. Create an index for the document.

    a. Navigate to the end of the document and add a page break. If necessary, remove the bullet style from the blank line at the top of the new page.

    b. Insert an index based on the **Bulleted** format. Have the index display in one column.

12. Display the document in different views.

    a. Switch to **Read Mode.**

    b. Navigate through the document.

    c. Switch back to **Print Layout** view.

13. Save and close the document.

challenge yourself 5.4

In this project you will be working on a letter for a mail merge from the Greenscapes landscaping company.

Skills needed to complete this project:

- Using AutoCorrect (Skill 5.1)
- Checking Grammar (Skill 5.2)
- Using the Thesaurus (Skill 5.3)
- Using the Tabs Dialog (Skill 5.4)
- Using Views (Skill 5.14)
- Using Read Mode (Skill 5.15)
- Starting a Mail Merge (Skill 5.17)
- Selecting Recipients (Skill 5.18)
- Adding an Address Block (Skill 5.19)
- Adding a Greeting Line (Skill 5.20)
- Previewing and Finishing the Merge (Skill 5.21)

1. Open the **WD2013-ChallengeYourself-5-4** document.

2. Save this document as: `[your initials]WD-ChallengeYourself-5-4`

3. Add an AutoCorrect entry and type the text to see the correction.

   a. Create an AutoCorrect entry that will change the letter **gsc** to **Greenscapes** when typed.

   b. Place the cursor between the words **at** and **thank** on the first line in the first paragraph of the document. Type **gsc,** (Be sure to include the comma after the letters). Notice Word changes the text to the entry you just created.

4. Using Word's grammar check, check the documents for any grammar errors and correct the errors that are found. Ignore any spelling errors.

5. Use the Thesaurus to look up synonyms of a word.

   a. Select the word **picking** in the first sentence of the first paragraph (*for picking us for your lawn care needs.*).

   b. Use the Thesaurus to replace the word **picking** with the synonym **choosing.**

6. Switch views.

   a. Switch to **Read Mode** to review the document.

   b. Switch back to **Print Layout** view.

7. Start a new mail merge for creating letters.

8. Add recipients to the mail merge.

   a. Add recipients to the mail merge based on an existing list.

   b. Browse to your student data file location, and open the **Customers** file as the recipients source.

   c. In the *Select Table* dialog, select the **Customers** table from the database.

9. Add an address block to the document.

   a. Place the cursor on the first empty line under the date.

   b. Add an **address block** to the letter based on the **Mr. Josh Randall Jr.** format.

10. Add a greeting line to the document.

    a. Place the cursor on the empty line under the address block.

    b. Add a greeting line to the letter. Have the field follow the this format:
    Dear Mr. Randall:

11. Preview the merged documents reviewing how each will appear when printed.

12. Print the merged documents.

13. Save and close the document.

on your own 5.5

In this project you will be creating a mail merge letter to job applicants who did not meet the required qualifications.

Skills needed to complete this project:

- Creating a New Document Using a Template (Skill 5.16)
- Using AutoCorrect (Skill 5.1)
- Checking Grammar (Skill 5.2)
- Using the Thesaurus (Skill 5.3)
- Using the Tabs Dialog (Skill 5.4)
- Using Views (Skill 5.14)
- Using Read Mode (Skill 5.15)

- Creating a New Document Using a Template (Skill 5.16)
- Starting a Mail Merge (Skill 5.17)
- Selecting Recipients (Skill 5.18)
- Adding an Address Block (Skill 5.19)
- Adding a Greeting Line (Skill 5.20)
- Previewing and Finishing the Merge (Skill 5.21)
- Creating Envelopes (Skill 5.22)
- Creating Labels (Skill 5.23)

1. Open the **WD2013-OnYourOwn-5-5** document.
2. Search for **template letters about job candidates.** Create a new document based on a template of your choice.
3. Save this document as: **[your initials]WD-OnYourOwn-5-5**
4. Add your own information and remove any information in the template you do not want to use.
5. If the template includes an address block and/or a greeting line, delete those elements from the document.
6. Create an AutoCorrect entry for a word you frequently mistype. If possible, try adding the word to the document by typing the short entry you entered.
7. Using Word's grammar check, check the documents for any grammar errors and correct any errors that are found.
8. Use the Thesaurus to look up a word and replace it with a synonym.
9. Switch to **Read Mode** and read through the document. Switch back to **Print Layout** view.
10. Start a new mail merge for creating letters.
11. Use the *New Address List* dialog to add recipients to the mail merge. Create a list of fictitious job candidates including names and addresses.
12. Add an address block using a format of your choice to the document.
13. Add a greeting line using a format of your choice to the document.
14. Preview the merged documents reviewing how each will appear when printed.
15. Print the merged documents.
16. Save and close the document.

fix it 5.6

In this project you will be working on a paper about behavior modification.

Skills needed to complete this project:
- Using AutoCorrect (Skill 5.1)
- Checking Grammar (Skill 5.2)
- Using the Thesaurus (Skill 5.3)
- Using the Tabs Dialog (Skill 5.4)
- Adding Tab Leaders (Skill 5.5)
- Inserting a Table of Contents (Skill 5.6)
- Inserting Footnotes and Endnotes (Skill 5.7)

- Adding a Caption (Skill 5.8)
- Selecting a Reference Style (Skill 5.9)
- Adding Citations to Documents (Skill 5.10)
- Creating a Bibliography (Skill 5.11)
- Marking Entries (Skill 5.12)
- Creating an Index (Skill 5.13)
- Using Views (Skill 5.14)
- Using Read Mode (Skill 5.15)

1. Open the **WD2013-FixIt-5-6** document.

2. Save this document as: **[your initials]WD-FixIt-5-6**

3. Add an AutoCorrect entry to change the word **behaviour** to **behavior** when typed.

4. Using Word's grammar check, check the documents for any grammar errors and correct the errors that are found.

5. Use the Thesaurus to look up synonyms of a word.

   a. In the fourth sentence of the first paragraph, select the word **first** (*in their first home*).

   b. Using the Thesaurus, replace the word with the synonym **original.**

6. Add new tabs through the *Tabs* dialog.

   a. Navigate to the *V. Collect and evaluate the result* section.

   b. Turn on formatting marks to view the tabs in the section.

   c. Select the all the data in the *Observation Phase* section (from *2/7* to *86%*)

   d. Using the *Tabs* dialog, place a left tab stop at **1"**. Place a center tab stop at **3.5"**. Place a right tab stop at **5"**.

   e. Apply a dotted tab leader to each of the tab stops.

   f. Repeat these steps for the data in the *Implementation Phase* section.

   g. Turn off formatting marks.

7. Navigate to the *I. Identify Target Behavior* section of the document and insert a table of contents based on the **Automatic Table 1** format.

8. Add a footnote after the first sentence in the document that reads: **To protect the identity of the student, I will use the pseudonym Andrew.**

9. Mark and entry for the index.

   a. Navigate to *paragraph B* in the *I. Identify Target Behavior* section of the document.

   b. Select **Language Arts classroom** in the first sentence of the paragraph.

   c. Mark the text for use as an entry in the index.

   d. Hide the formatting marks

10. Add a new blank page to the end of the document and insert an index based on the **Modern** format. Have the entries display in a single column.

11. Display the document in Read Mode to read through the document for accuracy.

12. Save and close the document.

excel 2013

chapter 1

Getting Started with Excel 2013

In this chapter, you will learn the following skills:

- Identify the elements of a Microsoft Excel 2013 workbook
- Navigate a workbook
- Enter and format text, numbers, and dates in cells
- Enter simple formulas
- Understand relative and absolute cell references
- Understand the concept of a function
- Use AutoSum and the Quick Analysis tool to add totals
- Use the status bar to display totals and other values
- Change the zoom level to view more or less of the worksheet
- Create a new workbook from a template
- Arrange multiple workbook windows
- Spell check a worksheet
- Preview and print a worksheet

skills

introduction

This chapter provides you with the basic skills necessary to start working with Excel 2013. The first step is to become familiar with the Excel interface and learn how to navigate a workbook. Next, you'll learn how to enter data and apply simple number and date formats. This chapter introduces the concepts of formulas, functions, and absolute and relative references. Pay close attention to the skill *Understanding Absolute and Relative References*. These concepts are used throughout Excel. You will add totals to worksheet data using the SUM function with a variety of methods including AutoSum and the Quick Analysis tool. To help you start using Excel for your own purposes, you will learn how to create a new workbook from a template and how to manage multiple workbooks at the same time. Finally, the chapter covers how to check a worksheet for spelling errors and how to preview and print.

Skill 1.1 Introduction to Excel 2013

Microsoft Excel 2013 is a spreadsheet program in which you enter, manipulate, calculate, and chart numerical and text data. An Excel file is referred to as a **workbook**, which is a collection of worksheets. Each worksheet (also called a "sheet") is made up of rows and columns of data on which you can perform calculations. It's these calculations that make Excel such a powerful tool.

Some of the basic elements of a Microsoft Excel workbook include:

) **Worksheet**—an electronic ledger in which you enter data. The worksheet appears as a grid where you can enter and then manipulate data using functions, formulas, and formatting. Excel workbooks have one worksheet by default named *Sheet1*. You can rename, add, and delete worksheets as necessary.

) **Row**—a horizontal group of cells. Rows are identified by numbers. For example, the third row is labeled with the number *3*.

) **Column**—a vertical group of cells. Columns are identified by letters. For example, the fourth column is labeled with the letter *D*.

) **Cell**—the intersection of a column and a row. A cell is identified by the **cell address**—its column and row position. For example, the cell at the intersection of column B and row 4 has a cell address of *B4*.

) **Cell Range**—a contiguous group of cells A cell range is identified by the address of the cell in the upper left corner of the range, followed by a colon, and then the address of the cell in the lower right corner of the range. The cell range *B3:D5* includes cells B3, B4, B5, C3, C4, C5, D3, D4, and D5.

) **Formula Bar**—data entry area directly below the Ribbon and above the worksheet grid. Although you can type any data in the formula bar, the *Insert Function* button at the left side of the formula bar was designed to make it easier to create complex formulas.

) **Name Box**—appears at the left side of the formula bar and displays the address of the selected cell. If a group of cells is selected, the *Name* box displays the address of the first cell in the group.

) **Status Bar**—appears at the bottom of the worksheet grid and can display information about the selected data, including the number of cells selected that contain data (count) and the average and sum (total) of the selected values (when appropriate).

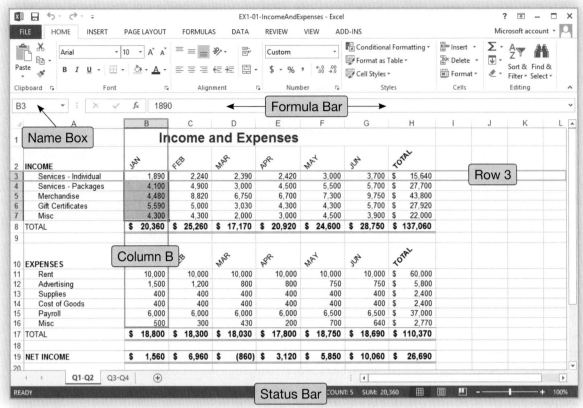

FIGURE EX 1.1

You can use Excel for a wide variety of purposes, from calculating payments for a personal loan, to creating a personal budget, to tracking employee sales and calculating bonuses for your business.

let me try

Open the student data file **EX1-01-IncomeAndExpenses** and explore the Excel workbook on your own:

1. Click the **Q3-Q4** worksheet tab at the bottom of the workbook.
2. Click anywhere in **column B.**
3. Click anywhere in **row 2.**
4. Click cell **B8.**
5. Click the **formula bar.**
6. Click the **Name Box.**
7. Click the **Q1-Q2** worksheet tab.
8. Click the **status bar.**
9. Close the workbook by clicking the **X** in the upper right corner of the window. If Excel asks if you want to save your changes, click **No.**

Skill 1.2 Navigating a Workbook

An Excel 2013 worksheet can include more than one million rows and more than sixteen thousand columns. That's a lot of potential data to navigate! Luckily, most spreadsheets are not quite that large. However, you may encounter workbooks with multiple worksheets and hundreds of rows and columns of data.

The Excel window includes both a **vertical scroll bar** (at the right side of the window) and a **horizontal scroll bar** (at the bottom of the window). Click the arrows at the ends of the scroll bars to move up and down or left and right to see more cells in an individual worksheet. You can also click and drag the scroll box to reposition your view of the spreadsheet. Notice that when you use the scroll bars, the selected cell does not change. Using the scroll bars only changes your view of the worksheet.

The most obvious way to select a cell in a worksheet is to click it with the mouse. Notice that Excel highlights the appropriate column letter and row number to identify the selected cell. When you select a single cell, the cell address appears in the *Name* box in the upper left corner of the spreadsheet, and the cell content appears in the formula bar (immediately below the Ribbon).

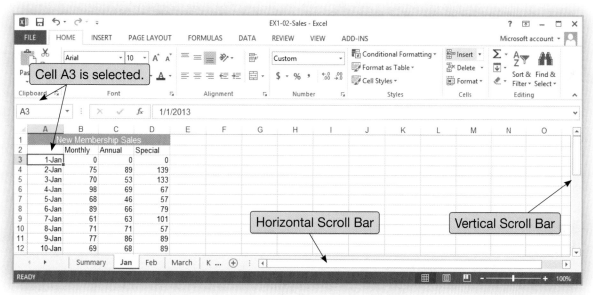

FIGURE EX 1.2

To navigate from cell to cell, use the mouse to click the cell you want to go to. You can also use the arrow keys on the keyboard to navigate around the worksheet.

To select a range of cells, click the first cell in the range and drag the mouse until the cells you want are selected. Release the mouse button. You can also click the first cell in the range, press [Shift], and then click the last cell in the range.

To select an entire row, click the **row selector** (the box with the row number at the left side of the worksheet grid).

To select an entire column, click the **column selector** (the box with the column letter at the top of the worksheet grid).

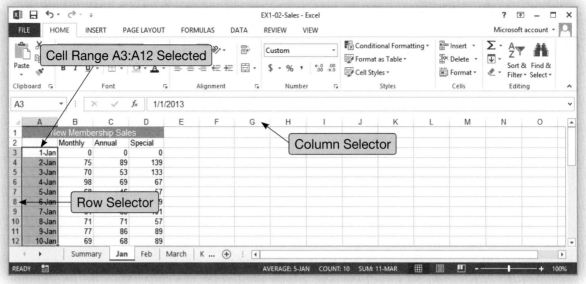

FIGURE EX 1.3

To navigate to another worksheet in the workbook, click the appropriate tab at the bottom of the worksheet grid. If the worksheet tab is not visible, use the navigation arrows located at the left side of the first sheet tab to show one worksheet at a time to the left or the right. These arrows are active only when there are worksheets not visible in your current view.

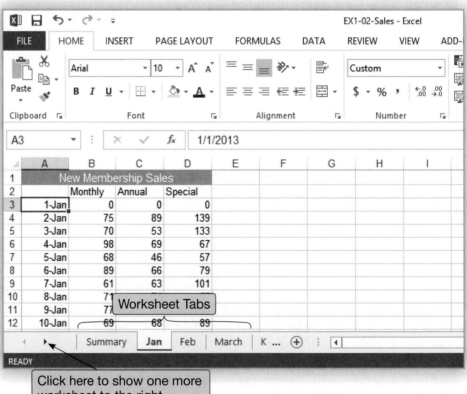

FIGURE EX 1.4

Click here to show one more worksheet to the right.

tips & tricks

To make more worksheets visible at one time, adjust the size of the horizontal scroll bar by clicking the dotted line that appears immediately to the left of the scroll bar. Notice that the cursor shape changes to a double-sided arrow. Click and drag to the right to make the horizontal scroll bar shorter and reveal more worksheet tabs.

another method

Another way to navigate to a specific cell location is to type the cell address in the *Name* box, and then press ⏎Enter .

let me try

Open the student data file **EX1-02-Sales** and try this skill on your own:

1. Select column **A.**
2. Select row **2.**
3. Navigate to the **Summary** worksheet.
4. Select cell **B6.**
5. Move to cell **B7.**
6. Select cells **E3:E5.**
7. Save the file as directed by your instructor and close it.

from the perspective of . . .

SPORTS CLINIC OFFICE MANAGER

I couldn't do my job without Microsoft Excel. All the clinic financial data is kept in Excel spreadsheets, and I use Excel's analysis and formatting tools to visualize our cash flow. Any problem areas are easy to find. We sell rehab equipment directly to our patients, and I also use Excel to track the progress of our orders and sales.

Skill 1.3 Working in Protected View

When you download a workbook from a location that Excel considers potentially unsafe, it opens automatically in Protected View. **Protected View** provides a read-only format that protects your computer from becoming infected by a virus or other malware. Potentially unsafe locations include the Internet, e-mail messages, or a network location. Files that are opened in Protected View display a warning in the **Message Bar** at the top of the window, below the Ribbon.

To disable Protected View, click the **Enable Editing** button in the Message Bar.

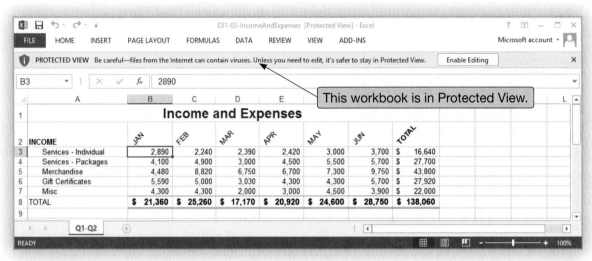

FIGURE EX 1.5

You can also enable editing from the Info page in Backstage.

1. Click the **File** tab to open Backstage.
2. Click **Info.**
3. The Info page provides more information about the file. If you are sure you want to remove it from Protected View, click the **Enable Editing** button.

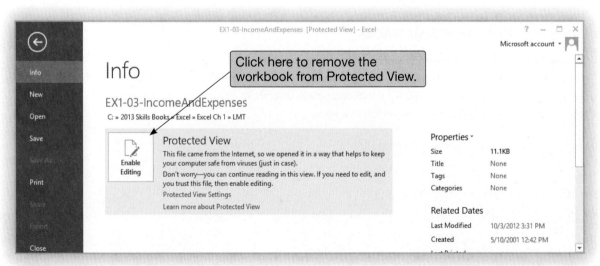

FIGURE EX 1.6

tips & tricks

To learn more about the security settings in Excel 2013, open the Trust Center and review the options. We do not recommend changing any of the default Trust Center settings.

tell me **more**

You can modify the Protected View settings to add or delete specific locations or types of locations.

To review or modify the Protected View settings for Excel:

1. Click the **File** tab.

2. If you are currently in Protected View, the *Info* tab will include a link to go to the Protected View settings. If you are not currently in Protected View, click the **Options** button to open the *Excel Options* dialog.

3. Click **Trust Center,** and then click the **Trust Center Settings** button.

4. The *Trust Center* dialog opens. Click **Protected View** to enable or disable Protected View for different locations, such as the Internet and Outlook attachments.

5. To exempt specific locations from Protected View, click **Trusted Locations,** and add the location you trust (such as secure network locations).

6. Click **OK** to save your changes and close the *Trusted Locations* dialog.

7. Click **OK** again to close the *Excel Options* dialog.

let me **try**

Open the student data file **EX1-03-IncomeAndExpenses** and try this skill on your own:

This workbook came from a trusted source. If the workbook opens in Protected View, disable Protected View and allow editing. Save the file as directed by your instructor and close it.

Skill 1.4 Entering and Editing Text and Numbers in Cells

The most basic task in Excel is entering data in your workbook. Entering numerical data is as easy as typing a number in a cell. Numbers can be displayed as dates, currency values, percentages, or other formats. (Later skills discuss number formatting and using functions and formulas to automate numerical calculations.)

Excel is not just about numbers, though. Without text headers, descriptions, and instructions, your workbook would consist of numbers and formulas without any structure. Adding text headers to your rows and columns creates the structure for you to enter data into your workbook.

To enter data in a cell:

1. Click the cell where you want the data to appear.

2. Type the number or text.

3. Press ⟨← Enter⟩ or ⟨Tab ⭲⟩.
   Pressing ⟨← Enter⟩ after entering text will move the cursor down one cell.
   Pressing ⟨Tab ⭲⟩ will move the cursor to the right one cell.

Excel gives you different ways to edit the data in your worksheet. If you want to change the contents of the entire cell, use **Ready mode**. If you want to change only part of the cell data, use **Edit mode**. The status bar, located at the lower left corner of the Excel window, displays which mode you are in—Ready or Edit.

To use Ready mode to change text:

1. Click the cell you want to change.

2. Type the new contents for the cell.

3. Press ⟨← Enter⟩ or ⟨Tab ⭲⟩ when you are finished.

4. The old contents are completely removed and replaced with what you've typed.

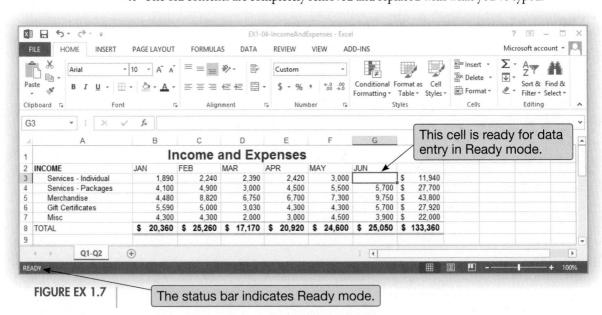

FIGURE EX 1.7

This cell is ready for data entry in Ready mode.

The status bar indicates Ready mode.

To use Edit mode to change text:

1. Double-click the cell you want to change.

2. You should now see a blinking cursor in the cell.

3. Move the cursor to the part of the entry you want to change and make your changes. Use (← Backspace) to delete characters to the left of the cursor; use (Delete) to delete characters to the right of the cursor. You can also click and drag your mouse to select a section of text to delete.

4. Press (← Enter) or (Tab ⇥) when you are finished making your changes.

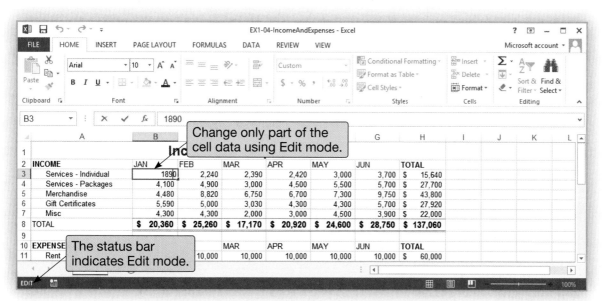

FIGURE EX 1.8

tips & tricks

To add a line break within the cell, press (Alt) while pressing (← Enter).

another method

As you type in a cell, the entry is displayed in the formula bar as well as in the active cell. Clicking the **Enter** icon ✓ next to the formula bar accepts your entry. Clicking the **Cancel** icon ✗ next to the formula bar removes your entry.

let me try

Open the student data file **EX1-04-IncomeAndExpenses** and try this skill on your own:

1. Add the number **3700** to cell **G3.**

2. Add the word **TOTAL** to cell **H2.**

3. Change the text in cell **B3** to **1870.** You can use ready mode or edit mode.

4. Save the file as directed by your instructor and close it.

Skill 1.5 Applying Number Formats

When you first type numbers in a worksheet, Excel applies the General number format automatically. The General format right-aligns numbers in the cells but does not maintain a consistent number of decimal places (43.00 will appear as 43, while 42.25 appears as 42.25) and does not display commas (so 1,123,456 appears as 1123456). For consistency, and to make your worksheet easier to read, you should apply the specific number format that is most appropriate for your data. Excel provides several number formats for you to choose from.

Figure EX 1.9 shows common Excel number formats. All numbers in row 2 contain the number .0567. All numbers in row 3 contain the number 1234. Formatting numbers changes the appearance of the data in your worksheet but doesn't change the numerical values. The formatted number is displayed in the cell, and the actual value is displayed in the formula bar.

> Formula bar displays the full number 0.567 while cell B2 formatted using the Number Style format displays 0.57.

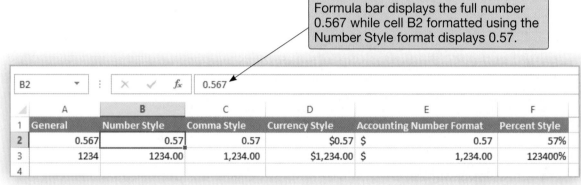

	A	B	C	D	E	F
1	General	Number Style	Comma Style	Currency Style	Accounting Number Format	Percent Style
2	0.567	0.57	0.57	$0.57	$ 0.57	57%
3	1234	1234.00	1,234.00	$1,234.00	$ 1,234.00	123400%
4						

FIGURE EX 1.9

To apply the most common number formats, go to the *Home* tab, *Number* group, and click one of the following buttons:

$ ▾	Click the **Accounting Number Format** button to apply formatting appropriate for monetary values. The Accounting Number Format aligns the $ at the left side of the cell, displays two places after the decimal, and aligns all numbers at the decimal point. Zero values are displayed as dashes (–).
%	Click the **Percent Style** button to have your numbers appear as %. For example, the number .02 will appear as 2%. By default, Percent Style format displays zero places to the right of the decimal point.
,	Click the **Comma Style** button to apply the same format as the Accounting Number Format but without the currency symbol. Comma Style format is a good number format to use if your worksheet includes many rows of numbers, summed in a total row (like a budget or cash flow projection), where too many $ symbols could be distracting. Use Comma Style formatting for all numbers except the total row. Use Accounting Number Format for the total row.

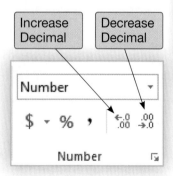

FIGURE EX 1.10

Use *Increase Decimal* and *Decrease Decimal* to increase or decrease the number of digits that appear to the right of the decimal point. For example, if a cell contains the number 1.234 and you click the **Decrease Decimal** button twice, the cell will display 1.2. The formula bar will still display 1.234 because that is the number stored in the worksheet.

For other common number formats, click the **Number Format** arrow above the buttons in the *Number* group to display the *Number Format* menu.

Number—The default Number format shows two decimal places by default (so 43 displays as 43.00) but does not include commas.

Currency—With the Currency format, columns of numbers do not align at the $ and at the decimal as they do with *Accounting Number Format*. Instead, the *Currency* format places the $ immediately to the left of the number.

Percentage—The *Percentage* option on the *Number Format* menu applies the same Percent Style format as clicking the *Percent Style* button.

More Number Formats...—This option opens the *Format Cells* dialog to the *Number* tab, where you can select from even more number formats and customize any format, including adding color, specifying the number of decimal places to display, and setting whether or not negative numbers should be enclosed in parentheses.

tips & tricks

If you type $ before a number, Excel automatically applies the *Currency* number format.

tell me more

On the *Home* tab, in the *Styles* group, click the **Cell Styles** button to expand the *Styles* gallery. At the bottom of the gallery are five number styles. Applying one of these cell styles is the same as applying a number format. However, be aware that applying the Currency cell style actually applies the Accounting Number Format, not the Currency format.

Comma—applies the default Comma Style format with two digits to the right of the decimal.

Comma [0]—applies the Comma Style format but with no digits to the right of the decimal.

Currency—applies the default Accounting Number Format, with two digits to the right of the decimal.

Currency [0]—applies the Accounting Number Format but with no digits to the right of the decimal.

Percent—applies the default Percent Style format.

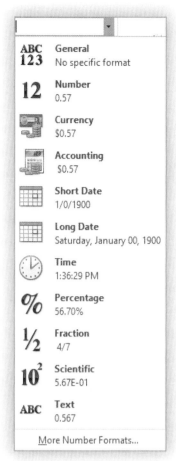

FIGURE EX 1.11
Number Format Menu

another method

When you right-click a cell, these formats are available from the Mini toolbar: Accounting Number Format, Percent style, and Comma style.

The *Increase Decimal* and *Decrease Decimal* buttons are also available from the Mini toolbar.

To apply the Percent Style, you can use the keyboard shortcut Ctrl + ↑ Shift + 5.

let me try

Open the student data file **EX1-05-IncomeAndExpenses** and try this skill on your own:

1. Apply the **Accounting Number Format** to cells **B8** through **H8.**
2. Select cells **B3:H7,** and apply the number format to display the numbers in accounting format without the currency symbol.
3. Select cells **B3:H8.** Modify the number format so no decimal places are visible after the decimal point.
4. Select cells **I3:I7** and change the number format to the default percent format.
5. Save the file as directed by your instructor and close it.

Skill 1.6 Entering Dates and Applying Date Formats

When you enter numbers in a date format such as 9/5/1966 or September 5, 1966, Excel detects that you are entering a date and automatically applies one of the date formats. Excel treats dates as a special type of number, so cells formatted as dates can be used in calculations. There are many types of date formats available, but the underlying number for the date will always be the same.

There are two number formats available from the *Number Format* menu. To apply one of these formats, from the *Home* tab, click the **Number Format** arrow above the buttons in the *Number* group, and then click the format you want:

Short Date format—Applies a simple format displaying the one- or two-digit number representing the month, followed by the one- or two-digit number representing the day, followed by the four-digit year (9/5/1966).

Long Date format—Applies a longer format displaying the day of the week, and then the name of the month, the two-digit date, and the four-digit year (Monday, September 05, 1966).

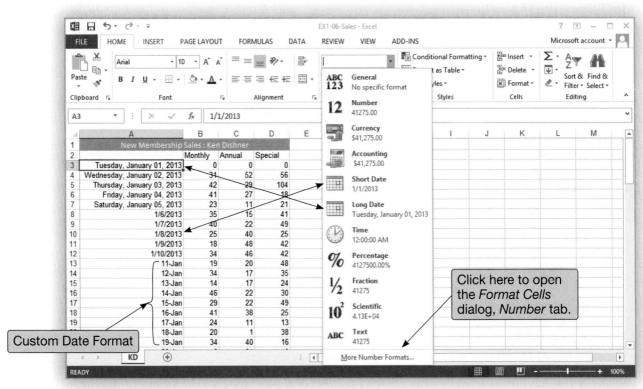

FIGURE EX 1.12

If you would like to use a different date format:

1. Select **More Number Formats...** from the *Number Format* list.

2. In the *Format Cells* dialog, from the *Number* tab, if necessary, click **Date** in the *Category* list. Excel offers a variety of prebuilt date formats to choose from.

3. Notice that as you click each format in the *Type* list, the *Sample* box shows how the active cell will display with the selected format.

4. Click the date format you would like, and click **OK**.

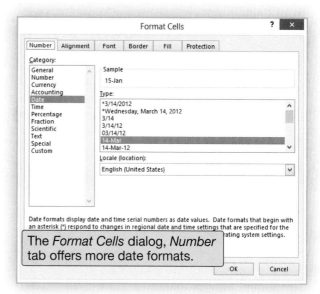

The *Format Cells* dialog, *Number* tab offers more date formats.

FIGURE EX 1.13

tips & tricks

Only dates from January 1, 1900, through December 31, 9999, are stored as numbers. Dates prior to January 1, 1900, are stored as text and cannot be used in calculations. To see the serial number for a date, change the cell format from *Date* to *General* or *Number*. The date will be converted to a "regular" number. For example, December 31, 2009, is the number 40178.

tell me more

Every date format can be expressed as a code. The code for the Short Date format is **m/d/yyy.** The code for the Long Date format is more complicated: **[$ –F800]dddd, mmmm dd, yyyy.** If Excel does not offer the exact date format you want to use, you can modify the date code using the Custom number option.

1. Select **More Number Formats...** from the *Number* list.

2. In the *Format Cells* dialog, from the *Number* tab, click **Custom** in the *Category* list.

3. The *Custom* list includes the code for every number format offered. Click the code for the format closest to the format you want, and then make adjustments to the code in the *Type* box. The *Sample* box shows how the number format will look in your worksheet.

4. Click **OK** to apply your new custom number format.

let me try

Open the student data file **EX1-06-Sales** and try this skill on your own:

1. Select cells **A3:A9** and apply the **Long Date** format.

2. Select cells **A10:A16** and apply the **Short Date** format.

3. Select cells **A17:A23** and apply the date number format to display dates in the format similar to **14-Mar.**

4. Save the file as directed by your instructor and close it.

Skill 1.7 Inserting Data Using AutoFill

Use the **AutoFill** feature to fill a group of cells with the same data or to extend a data series. With AutoFill, you can copy the same value or formula to a group of cells at once. This is much more efficient than using copy and paste over and over again.

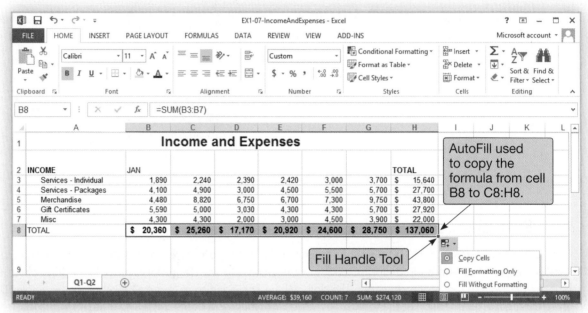

FIGURE EX 1.14

If you have a group of cells with similar data in a series, AutoFill can extend the series automatically. A **data series** is any sequence of cells with a recognizable pattern:

The easiest way to use AutoFill is to use the **Fill Handle tool** to fill data up or down in a column or to the left or right in a row.

To use the Fill Handle tool:

1. Enter the data you want in the first cell.

2. If you want to fill a series of cells with that same value, skip to step 5.

3. Enter the second value of the series in an adjacent cell.

4. Select the cell(s) you want to base the series on. (Click the first cell. Then holding [Shift] click the last cell you want to select.)

FIGURE EX 1.15

5. Click and drag the **Fill Handle** in the direction you want to fill the series. As you drag the Fill Handle, a tool tip appears displaying the value of the highlighted cell.

6. Release the mouse button when you have highlighted the last cell you want to fill.

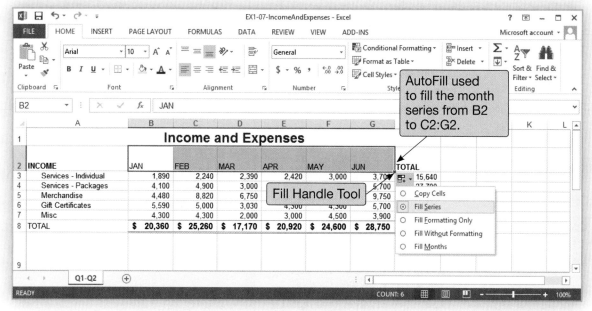

FIGURE EX 1.16

Excel attempts to detect automatically if the data appear to be a series. Sometimes, however, the series doesn't fill with the data you expect or want. To change the type of data Auto-Fill inserts, click the **AutoFill Options** button ⊞▾ and select a different option. From the *AutoFill Options* button, you can choose to copy the cells or fill the series. By default, Excel includes formatting when copying or filling a series; however, you can choose to copy only the cell formatting or to fill or copy the data series without formatting.

tips & tricks

Use AutoFill to enter repetitive data in your worksheet to avoid errors from entering data manually.

tell me **more**

The Fill Handle tool can be used to fill a series of dates by month as well as year. For example, if you start the series with Jan-2013 and Feb-2013, the Fill Handle will fill in the next cells with Mar-2013, Apr-2013, May-2013, etc. When the series reaches Dec-2013, the next cell will be filled in with Jan-2014. If you are filling a series of dates, the AutoFill Options button will give you the options to fill by day, weekday, month, or year.

another **method**

▶ You can also use the *Fill* command from the Ribbon. First, select the cells you want to fill. On the *Home* tab, in the *Editing* group, click the **Fill** button and select the type of fill you want: **Down, Right, Up, Left, Across Worksheets…, Series…,** or **Justify.**

▶ Pressing Ctrl + D will fill the selected cell(s) with the value from the cell above it.

▶ Pressing Ctrl + R will fill the selected cell(s) with the value from the cell to the left of it.

let me try

Open the student data file **EX1-07-IncomeAndExpenses** and try this skill on your own:

1. Select cell **B8** (the total income for January) and use AutoFill to copy the formula and formatting to cells **C8:H8.**

2. Select cell **B2** (Jan) and use AutoFill to complete the month series through cell **G2.**

3. Save the file as directed by your instructor and close it.

Skill 1.8 Entering Simple Formulas

A **formula** is an equation used to calculate a value. A formula can perform a mathematical calculation, such as displaying the sum of **35** + **47,** or a formula can calculate a value using cell references, such as displaying a value equal to the value of another cell (= **B3**) or calculating an equation based on values in multiple cells (= **B3** + **B4**).

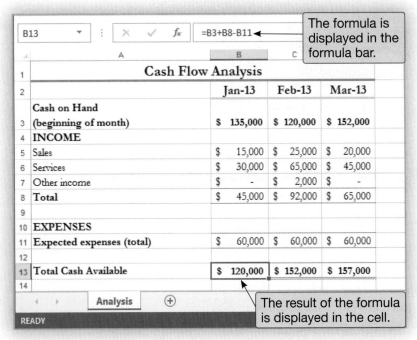

The formula is displayed in the formula bar.

The result of the formula is displayed in the cell.

FIGURE EX 1.17

When you select a cell that contains a formula, the cell displays the value and the formula bar displays the formula.

You can edit the formula in the formula bar, or you can double-click the cell to edit the formula directly in the cell. Notice that when you edit the formula, any referenced cells are highlighted in the same color as the cell reference in the formula.

FIGURE EX 1.18

To enter a formula:

1. Click the cell in which you want to enter the formula.

2. Press [=].

3. Type the formula.

4. To add a cell reference to a formula, you can type the cell address or click the cell. If you are in the middle of typing a formula and you click another cell in the worksheet, Excel knows to add that cell reference to the formula instead of moving to it.

5. Press ⟵ Enter .

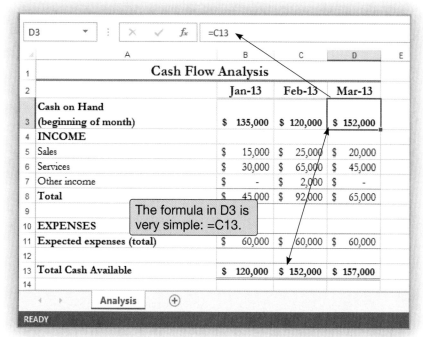

FIGURE EX 1.19

tell me **more**

When you enter a formula with more than one mathematical operation, the formula is not necessarily calculated from left to right. Excel calculations follow the mathematical rules called the order of operations (also called precedence).

The rules state that mathematical operations in a formula are calculated in this order:

1. Exponents and roots

2. Multiplication and division

3. Addition and subtraction

Adding parentheses around part of a formula will override the order of operations, forcing Excel to perform the calculation within the parentheses first.

4 + (5 * 2) = 14—Excel calculates 5 * 2 first (10) and then adds 4.

(4 + 5) * 2 = 18—Excel calculates 4 + 5 first (9), and then multiples by 2.

4 + 5 ^ 2 = 29—Excel calculates 5 to the 2nd power first (25), and then adds 4.

(4 + 5) ^ 2 = 81—Excel calculates 4 + 5 first (9), and then raises that number to the 2nd power.

another **method**

To enter a formula, you can click the **Enter** button ✓ to the left of the formula bar.

let me **try**

Open the student data file **EX1-08-CashFlow** and try this skill on your own:

1. In cell **B13,** enter a formula to calculate total cash available: cash on hand (**B3**) + total income (**B8**) – total expenses (**B11**).

2. In cell **D3,** enter a formula to make the cash on hand for March (**D3**) equal to the total cash available at the end of February (**C13**).

3. Save the file as directed by your instructor and close it.

Skill 1.9 Understanding Absolute and Relative References

A cell's address, its position in the workbook, is referred to as a **cell reference** when it is used in a formula. In Excel, the $ character before a letter or number in the cell address means that part of the cell's address is *absolute* (nonchanging). Cell references can be relative, absolute, or mixed.

❱ A **relative reference** is a cell reference that adjusts to the new location in the worksheet when the formula is copied.

❱ An **absolute reference** is a cell reference whose location remains constant when the formula is copied.

❱ A **mixed reference** is a combination cell reference with a row position that stays constant with a changing column position (or vice versa).

> Relative reference—A1
>
> Absolute reference—$A$1
>
> Mixed reference with absolute row—A$1
>
> Mixed reference with absolute column—$A1

Here's how relative and absolute references work:

When you type a formula into a cell, it uses *relative* references by default. Excel calculates the position of the referenced cell *relative* to the active cell. For example, if cell B15 is the active cell and you type the formula =**B13,** Excel displays the value of the cell that is up two rows from the active cell.

If you add another row to your worksheet, shifting the position of cell B15 to cell B16, Excel automatically adjusts the reference in the formula to reflect the new cell address that is up one row from the current position.

If you copy the formula =**B13** from cell B15 and paste it into cell C15, the pasted formula will update automatically to =**C13** to reflect the cell address that is up two rows from the new position.

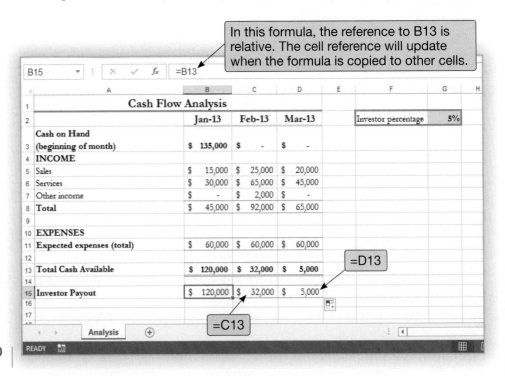

FIGURE EX 1.20

If you cut and paste the formula, Excel assumes that you want the formula to maintain its previous value and treats the formula as if it had included absolute references, pasting the formula exactly as it was.

But what if you don't want the cell reference to adjust? For example, cell G2 contains a value that you want to use in calculations for multiple cells in a row. If you were to copy the formula **=B13*G2** from cell B15 to cell C15, the formula would update to **=C13*H2** (not what you intended) because both of the cell references are *relative.* Instead, you want the reference to cell G2 to be *absolute,* so it does not update when you copy it. If you use the formula **=B13*$G$2** instead and copy it from cell B15 to cell C15, the pasted formula will only update the relative reference **B13.** The absolute reference **$G$2** will remain constant. The formula in cell C15 will be **=C13*$G$2.**

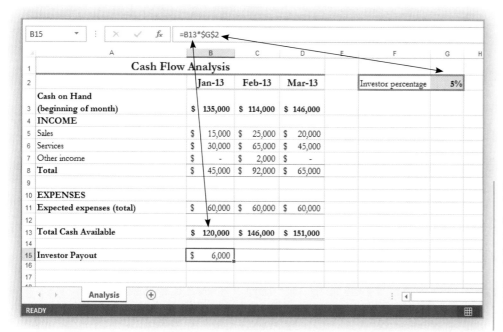

FIGURE EX 1.21
The relative reference to cell B13 will update to the new relative cell position when the formula is copied. The absolute reference to cell G2 will not. When the formula is copied to cell C15, it will be =C13*$G$2.

another method

Another way to change the cell reference type is to select the cell reference in the formula bar, and then press (F4) to cycle through the various reference types until you find the one you want (absolute, mixed with absolute row, mixed with absolute column, and then back to relative).

let me try

Open the student data file **EX1-09-CashFlow** and try this skill on your own:

1. Enter a formula in cell **B15** to calculate the investor payout: total cash available **(B13)** * investor percentage **(G2).** Be sure to use an absolute reference to G2.

2. Use AutoFill to copy the formula to cells **C15:D15.** If you entered the formula in B15 correctly, the reference to G2 will remain constant.

3. Save the file as directed by your instructor and close it.

Skill 1.10 Using Functions in Formulas

Functions are preprogrammed shortcuts for calculating equations. Functions can simplify a straightforward computation such as figuring the total of a list of values. They can also calculate the answer to a complicated equation such as figuring the monthly payment amount for a loan.

Most functions require you to provide input called the **arguments**. For example, when writing a formula using the SUM function to calculate the total of a list of values, each value or range of values to be included in the calculation is an argument. Multiple arguments are separated by commas [,].

This formula will calculate the total of the values in cells B5 through B7:

SUM(B5,B6,B7)

In this example, each cell reference is an argument.

An easier way to write the arguments for this formula is:

SUM(B5:B7)

In the second example, the function requires only one argument—the cell range containing the values. Both formulas will return the same total value.

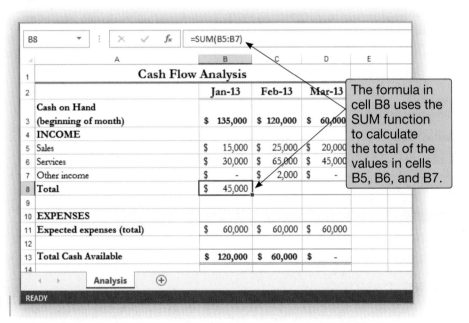

FIGURE EX 1.22

The easiest way to enter a formula using a simple function like SUM is to type the formula directly in the cell or the formula bar. Begin the formula by typing (=), and then type the function name. After the function name, type (() followed by the function arguments, separated by commas, and then ()). Press (←Enter) to complete the formula.

tell me **more**

You can also enter functions in formulas using AutoSum, Formula AutoComplete, and the *Function Arguments* dialog. These methods are covered in later skills.

let me **try**

Open the student data file **EX1-10-CashFlow** and try this skill on your own:

In cell **B8,** enter a formula using the SUM function to calculate the total of cells **B5** through **B7.** Save the file as directed by your instructor and close it.

excel 2013   chapter 1 Getting Started with Excel 2013

Skill 1.11 Using AutoSum to Insert a SUM Function

If your spreadsheet includes numerical data organized in rows or columns, **AutoSum** can enter totals for you. When you use AutoSum, Excel enters the SUM function arguments using the most likely range of cells based on the structure of your worksheet. For example, if you use AutoSum at the bottom of a column of values, Excel will assume that you want to use the values in the column as the function arguments. If you use AutoSum at the end of a row of values, Excel will use the values in the row.

To insert a SUM function using AutoSum:

1. Select the cell in which you want to enter the function.
2. On the *Home* tab, in the *Editing* group, click the **AutoSum** button.
3. Excel automatically inserts a formula with the SUM function, using the range of cells contiguous to (next to) the selected cell as the arguments for the function. You can increase or decrease the range of cells selected by clicking and dragging the corner of the highlighted cell range
4. Press ⏎ Enter to accept the formula.

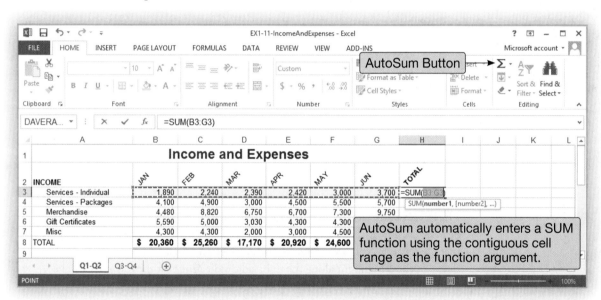

FIGURE EX 1.23

another **method**

▸ AutoSum is also available on the *Formulas* tab, in the *Function Library* group.

▸ You can also click the **AutoSum** button arrow and select **SUM** from the list.

▸ Another way to use the AutoSum function is to select a range of cells, and then click the **AutoSum** button. Excel will insert the SUM function in the next available (empty) cell.

let me **try**

Open the student data file **EX1-11-IncomeAndExpenses** and try this skill on your own:

1. If necessary, select cell **H3**.
2. Use AutoSum to enter a formula using the SUM function to calculate the total of cells **B3:G3**.
3. Save the file as directed by your instructor and close it.

Skill 1.12 Calculating Totals with the Quick Analysis Tool

The **Quick Analysis tool** is a new feature in Excel 2013 to help you easily apply formatting, create charts, and insert formulas based on the selected data. In this skill, we will focus on creating totals with the Quick Analysis tool. You will learn to use the other features of this tool in later skills.

To use the Quick Analysis tool to calculate totals:

1. Select the range of cells. Verify that there are empty cells below or to the right of the selection (where the totals will be inserted).

FIGURE EX 1.24

Empty Row for Totals   Quick Analysis Tool Button

2. The Quick Analysis tool button appears near the lower right corner of the selected range. Click the **Quick Analysis tool** button, and then click the **Totals** tab.

3. Click the first **Sum** button to insert totals below the selected cells. Notice that live preview displays the totals as you hover the cursor over the **Sum** button before clicking.

The images in the *Totals* tab of the Quick Analysis tool show where the formulas will be inserted. The first set of buttons shows a blue highlight along the bottom, indicating that the formulas will be inserted below the selected range. The second set of buttons shows a yellow highlight along the right side, indicating that the formulas will be inserted to the right of the selected range.

FIGURE EX 1.25

4. Excel inserts formulas using the SUM function into the empty cells below the selected range.

B8	▼ :	× ✓ *fx*	=SUM(B3:B7)					

	A	B	C	D	E	F	G	H
1			**Income and Expenses**					
2	**INCOME**	*JULY*	*AUG*	*SEPT*	*OCT*	*NOV*	*DEC*	*TOTAL*
3	Services - Individual	1,890	2,240	2,390	2,420	3,000	5,000	$ 16,940
4	Services - Packages	4,100	4,900	3,000	4,500	5,500	8,000	$ 30,000
5	Merchandise	4,480	8,820	6,750	6,700	8,500	15,000	$ 50,250
6	Gift Certificates	5,590	5,000	3,030	4,300	6,000	9,000	$ 32,920
7	Misc	4,300	4,300	2,000	3,000	4,500	3,900	$ 22,000
8	TOTAL	$ 20,360	$ 25,260	$ 17,170	$ 20,920	$ 27,500	$ 40,900	$ 152,110
9								

Formulas inserted by the Quick Analysis tool.

FIGURE EX 1.26

tips & tricks

If the Quick Analysis tool button is not visible, move your mouse cursor over the selected cell range, without clicking. This action should make the button appear.

let me try

Open the student data file **EX1-12-IncomeAndExpenses** and try this skill on your own:

1. If necessary, select the cell range **B3:H7**.
2. Click the **Quick Analysis tool** button, and then click the **Totals** tab.
3. Click the first **Sum** button to insert totals in the empty row beneath the selected cell range.
4. Save the file as directed by your instructor and close it.

Skill 1.13 Using the Status Bar

The **status bar** appears at the bottom of the Excel window and displays information about the current worksheet. By default, the status bar displays whether you are in Ready or Edit mode and information about the selected cells (such as the number of cells selected, the sum of the values in the selected cells, or the average of the values in the selected cells). You can customize the status bar to show other information about the worksheet, the minimum or maximum value in the selected cells, and whether Caps Lock is on or off.

To change the information shown on the status bar:

1. Right-click anywhere on the status bar.
2. The *Customize Status Bar* menu appears. Options with checkmarks next to them are currently active. Options without a checkmark are not currently active.
3. Click an item on the menu to add it to or remove it from the status bar display.

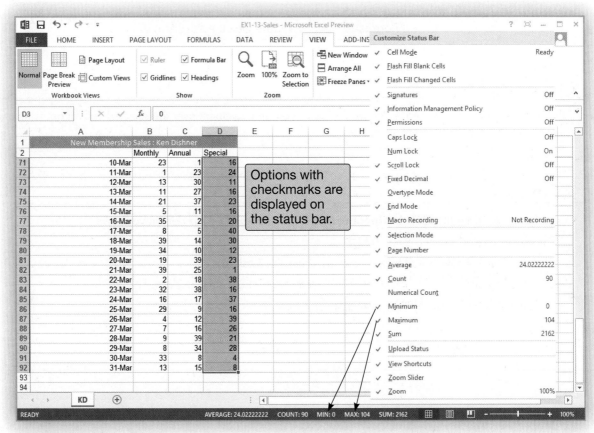

Options with checkmarks are displayed on the status bar.

FIGURE EX 1.27

let me try

Open the student data file **EX1-13-Sales** and try this skill on your own:

1. If necessary, select cells **D3:D92**.
2. Right-click anywhere on the status bar.
3. Click **Minimum** to add a checkmark.
4. Click **Maximum** to add a checkmark.
5. Click anywhere to dismiss the menu.
6. Note the minimum and maximum values displayed on the status bar.
7. Save the file as directed by your instructor and close it.

Skill 1.14 Changing the Zoom Level

If you are working with a large spreadsheet, you may find that you need to see more of the spreadsheet at one time or that you would like a closer look at a cell or group of cells. You can use the **zoom slider** in the lower-right corner of the window to zoom in and out of a worksheet, changing the size of text and images on screen. As you move the slider, the zoom level displays the percentage the worksheet has been zoomed in or zoomed out. Zooming a worksheet only affects how the worksheet appears on screen. It does not affect how the worksheet will print.

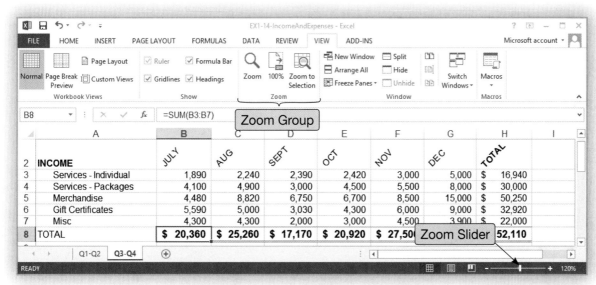

FIGURE EX 1.28

To zoom in on a worksheet, making the text and graphics appear larger:

> Click and drag the zoom slider to the right.
> Click the **Zoom In** button on the slider.

To zoom out of a worksheet, making the text and graphics appear smaller:

> Click and drag the zoom slider to the left.
> Click the **Zoom Out** button on the slider.

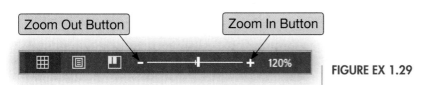

FIGURE EX 1.29

On the *View* tab, the *Zoom* group includes buttons for two of the most common zoom options:

> Click the **Zoom to Selection** button to zoom in as close as possible on the currently selected cell(s).
> Click the **100%** button to return the worksheet back to 100% of the normal size.

You can also change the zoom level through the *Zoom* dialog.

1. On the *View* tab, in the *Zoom* group, click the **Zoom** button.
2. In the *Zoom* dialog, click the radio button for the zoom option you want, and then click **OK**.

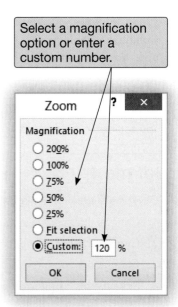

FIGURE EX 1.30

from the perspective of . . .

ACCOUNTING FIRM INTERN

My boss works on two 24″ monitors. She always has her files set at 150% or higher because she has the room to spread the worksheet across two large monitors. I work on a laptop with a 15″ screen. When I open her files, I can only see part of the worksheet until I set the zoom level back to 100%. It is harder to see details when the zoom level is set lower, but for me, it's more important to see the whole worksheet without having to scroll.

tips & tricks

When you save a workbook, Excel saves the zoom setting. However, if you change the zoom level and then close the workbook without making any other changes, Excel will not warn you about saving your change. The next time you open the workbook, it will be back to the zoom level that was set at the time the workbook was last saved.

another method

You can also open the *Zoom* dialog by clicking the zoom level number that appears at the right side of the zoom slider.

let me try

Open the student data file **EX1-14-IncomeAndExpenses** and try this skill on your own:

1. Change the zoom level to 110%.
2. Change the zoom level back to 100%.
3. Change the zoom level to 90%.
4. Save the file as directed by your instructor and close it.

Skill 1.15 Creating a New Workbook Using a Template

A **template** is a file with predefined settings that you can use as a starting point for your workbook. Using an Excel template makes creating a new workbook easy and results in a professional appearance. Many templates use advanced techniques that you may not have learned yet—but you can take advantage of them in a template where someone else has created the workbook framework for you. Templates are available for every imaginable task: from creating budgets to tracking exercise to calculating your grade point average.

To create a new workbook using a template:

1. Click the **File** tab to open Backstage view.
2. Click **New.** Excel 2013 includes a variety of templates that are copied to your computer when you install the application. These templates are always available from the *New* page. Additional templates that you download are also displayed on the *New* page, so your screen may look different than the one in Figure EX 1.31.
3. Click a template picture to open the template preview including a brief description of the template.
4. You can cycle through the template previews by clicking the arrows that appear on either side of the preview.
5. When you find the template you want to use, click the **Create** button.
6. A new workbook opens, prepopulated with all of the template elements.

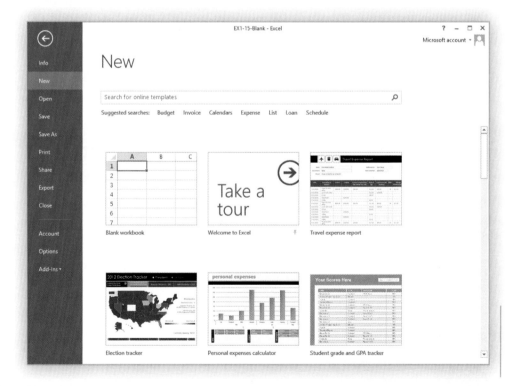

FIGURE EX 1.31
Templates stored on your computer appear on the *New* page.

You can search for more workbook templates online. (You must have an active Internet connection.)

1. Near the top of the *New* page, in the *Search online templates* box, type a keyword or phrase that describes the template you want.
2. Click the **Start searching** button (the magnifying glass image at the end of the *Search online templates* box).

3. The search results display previews of the templates that match the keyword or phrase you entered. To further narrow the results, click one of the categories listed in the *Filter by* pane at the right side of the window. Notice that each category lists the number of templates available.

4. When you find the template you want, click it to display the larger preview with detailed information about the template, and then click **Create.**

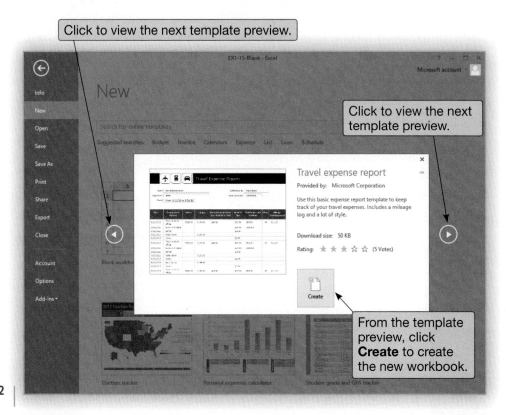

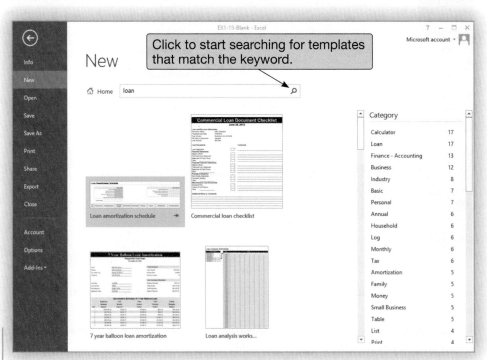

from the perspective of . . .

COLLEGE STUDENT

I thought Excel was only for business. It's not! I found some really useful templates—one for tracking my day-to-day expenses and another one to help me budget my expenses for the semester. And even though some of the templates look fancy and complicated, I find that I can use them easily by reading the instructions and taking a little bit of time to personalize the data with my own information.

tips & tricks

Many Excel templates have a special worksheet labeled Settings, Instructions, or something similar. Be sure to read all of the instructions before entering data.

let me try

Open the student data file **EX1-15-Blank** and try this skill on your own:

1. Click the **File** tab.
2. Click **New.**
3. Click the **Travel expense report** template. If the *Travel expense report* template does not appear on your *New* page, search for it using the *Search online templates* feature. You may find more than one template named *Travel expense report.* Select one that appeals to you.
4. Click **Create.**
5. Save the file as directed by your instructor and close it.

Skill 1.16 Arranging Workbooks

If you are working with multiple workbooks, you may want to arrange them so you can see them all at the same time. You can arrange workbooks so they are tiled, horizontally, vertically, or in cascading windows.

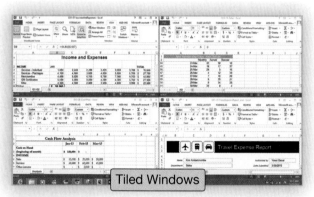

FIGURE EX 1.34

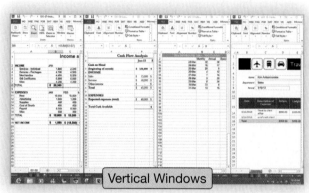

FIGURE EX 1.36

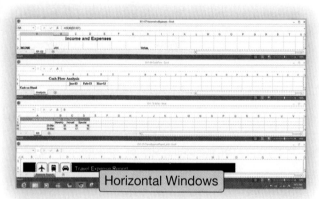

FIGURE EX 1.35

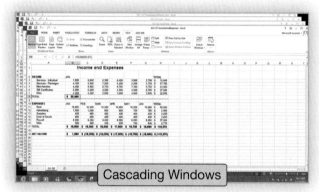

FIGURE EX 1.37

To change the arrangement of workbooks:

1. On the *View* tab, in the *Window* group, click the **Arrange All** button.

2. In the *Arrange Windows* dialog, select an arrangement option:

   - **Tiled**—places the windows in a grid pattern

   - **Horizontal**—places the windows in a stack one on top of the other

   - **Vertical**—places the windows in a row next to each other

   - **Cascade**—places the windows in a staggered, overlapping, diagonal arrangement

3. Click **OK.**

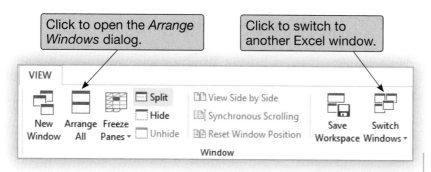

FIGURE EX 1.38

To switch between workbooks, you can:

❭ Click anywhere in the workbook you want to make active.

❭ On the *View* tab, in the *Window* group, click the **Switch Windows** button, then click the name of the workbook you want.

To undo the arrangement and put the workbooks back in separate windows, maximize any of the workbooks by clicking the **Maximize** button on the title bar.

tell me **more**

If you have two workbooks with similar data, you may want to compare their data row by row. Excel's *Compare Side by Side* feature allows you to compare two workbooks at the same time. When you compare workbooks, the *Synchronous Scrolling* feature is on by default. This feature allows you to scroll both workbooks at once. If you scroll the active workbook, the other workbook will scroll at the same time, allowing you to carefully compare data row by row.

1. Open the workbooks you want to compare.
2. On the *View* tab, in the *Window* group, click the **View Side by Side** button.
3. The two workbooks are displayed one on top of the other.
4. Scroll the active window to scroll both workbooks at once.
5. Click the **View Side by Side** button again to restore the windows to their previous positions.

let me **try**

Open any four Excel workbooks. Practice changing the window arrangement and switching back and forth between the Excel windows. Save the file as directed by your instructor and close it.

Skill 1.17 Checking Spelling

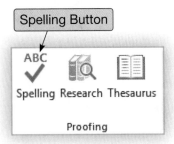

Spelling Button

FIGURE EX 1.39

Regardless of the amount of work you put into a workbook, a spelling error or typo can make the entire workbook appear sloppy and unprofessional. All the Office applications include a built-in spelling checker. In Excel, the *Spelling* command analyzes the current worksheet for spelling errors. It presents any errors it finds in a dialog box, enabling you to make decisions about how to handle each error or type of error in turn.

To check a worksheet for spelling errors:

1. On the *Review* tab, in the *Proofing* group, click the **Spelling** button.
2. The first spelling error appears in the *Spelling* dialog box.
3. Review the spelling suggestions and then select an action:

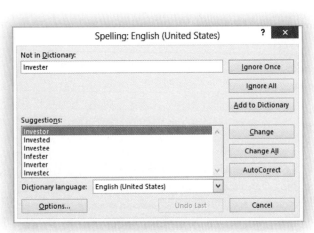

FIGURE EX 1.40

- Click **Ignore Once** to make no changes to this instance of the word.
- Click **Ignore All** to make no changes to all instances of the word.
- Click **Add to Dictionary** to make no changes to this instance of the word and add it to the spelling checker dictionary, so future uses of this word will not show up as misspellings. When you add a word to the dictionary, it is available for all the Office applications.
- Click the correct spelling in the *Suggestions* list, and click **Change** to correct just this instance of the misspelling in your worksheet.
- Click the correct spelling in the *Suggestions* list, and click **Change All** to correct all instances of the misspelling in your worksheet.

4. After you select an action, the spelling checker automatically advances to the next suspected spelling error.
5. When the spelling checker finds no more errors, it displays a message telling you the check is complete. Click **OK** to close the dialog and return to your worksheet.

tips & tricks

Whether or not you use the Spelling tool, you should always proofread your files. Spelling checkers are not infallible, especially if you misuse a word yet spell it correctly—for instance, writing "bored" instead of "board."

If you misspell a word often, the next time the spelling checker catches the misspelling, use this trick: Click the correct spelling in the *Suggestions* list and then click the *AutoCorrect* button. Now, when you type the misspelled version of the word, it will be corrected automatically as you type.

another method

To open the *Spelling* dialog, you can also press F7.

let me try

Open the student data file **EX1-17-CashFlow** and try this skill on your own:

Spell check the worksheet and correct any errors you find. Save the file as directed by your instructor and close it.

Skill 1.18 Previewing and Printing a Worksheet

In Excel 2013, all the print settings are combined in a single page along with a preview of how the printed file will look. As you change print settings, the preview updates. To preview and print the current worksheet:

1. Click the **File** tab to open Backstage view.

2. Click **Print.**

3. At the right side of the page is a preview of how the printed file will look. Beneath the preview there is a page count. If there are multiple pages, use the *Next* and *Previous* arrows to preview all the pages in the file. You can also use the scroll bar to the right to scroll through the preview pages.

4. Set the number of copies to print by changing the number in the *Copies* box.

5. Click the **Print** button to send the file to your default printer

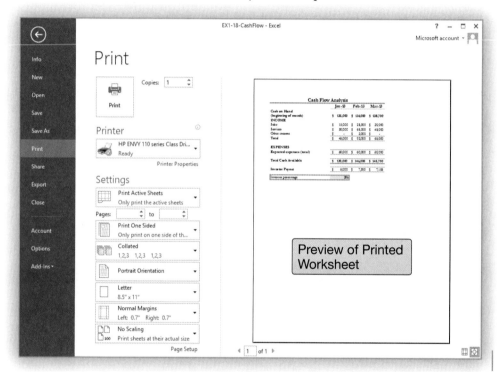

FIGURE EX 1.41

tips & tricks

Add the *Quick Print* command to the Quick Access Toolbar so you can print with a single mouse click. If you do not need to change the default print settings, you can click the *Quick Print* button instead of going through the *Print* tab in Backstage view.

another method

To open the *Print* page in Backstage view, you can use the keyboard shortcut (Ctrl) + (P).

let me try

Open the student data file **EX1-18-CashFlow** and try this skill on your own:

1. Preview how the worksheet will look when printed.

2. If you can, print the worksheet and compare the printed page to the preview.

3. Save the file as directed by your instructor and close it.

key terms

Workbook
Worksheet
Row
Column
Cell
Cell address
Cell range
Formula bar
Name box
Status bar
Vertical scroll bar
Horizontal scroll bar
Row selector
Column selector
Protected View
Message Bar
Ready mode
Edit mode
General number format
Accounting Number Format
Percent Style format
Comma Style format
Number format

Currency format
Short Date format
Long Date format
AutoFill
Data series
Fill Handle tool
Formula
Order of operations (precedence)
Cell reference
Relative reference
Absolute reference
Mixed reference
Function
Argument
AutoSum
Quick Analysis tool
Zoom slider
Template
Tiled window arrangement
Horizontal window arrangement
Vertical window arrangement
Cascade window arrangement

concepts review

1. A new Excel 2013 workbook has _____ worksheet(s).

   a. one

   b. two

   c. three

   d. four

2. The cell D4 refers to the cell at:

   a. The intersection of row D and column 4

   b. The intersection of column D and row 4

   c. The first cell on the D4 worksheet

   d. None of the above

3. Which of these dates uses the Long Date format?

   a. 1/1/2000

   b. January 1, 2000

   c. 01/01/2000

   d. Saturday, January 1, 2000

4. Formulas begin with which character?

   a. $

   b. @

   c. =

   d. *

5. Which of these cell references is an absolute reference?

   a. $G2

   b. G2

   c. $G$2

   d. None of the above

6. Which of these formulas uses a function?

   a. =B4

   b. =B4 + B5

   c. =SUM(B4:B5)

   d. =B4*B5

7. AutoSum is located:

   a. On the *Home* tab, in the *Editing* group

   b. On the *Insert* tab, in the *Formulas* group

   c. On the *Home* tab, in the *Formulas* group

   d. On the *Insert* tab, in the *Tables* group

8. The zoom slider is located:

   a. At the lower right corner of the status bar

   b. On the *View* tab, in the *Zoom* group

   c. In the *Zoom* dialog

   d. On the Ribbon

9. The keyboard shortcut to begin the spelling checker is:

   a. F5

   b. F7

   c. F4

   d. F9

10. Which of these tasks can you **not** perform in Backstage?

   a. Enable Editing when a workbook is in Protected View

   b. Preview how a workbook will look when printed

   c. Create a new workbook from a template

   d. None of the above

skill review 1.1

The workbook for this project generates client bills from staff hours in multiple worksheets. In this project, you will complete the worksheet for staff member Marshall to calculate the daily bill, the total billable hours per week, and the total weekly bill. The worksheet for staff member Stevens has been completed. You may use it for reference as necessary.

Skills needed to complete this project:

- Navigating a Workbook (Skill 1.2)
- Working in Protected View (Skill 1.3)
- Entering and Editing Text and Numbers in Cells (Skill 1.4)
- Applying Number Formats (Skill 1.5)
- Entering Dates and Applying Date Formats (Skill 1.6)
- Inserting Data Using AutoFill (Skill 1.7)
- Understanding Absolute and Relative References (Skill 1.9)
- Entering Simple Formulas (Skill 1.8)
- Calculating Totals with the Quick Analysis Tool (Skill 1.12)
- Previewing and Printing a Worksheet (Skill 1.18)

1. Open the start file **EX2013-SkillReview-1-1** and resave the file as:
 `[your initials]EX-SkillReview-1-1`

2. If the workbook opens in Protected View, click the **Enable Editing** button in the Message Bar at the top of the workbook so you can modify the workbook.

3. Explore the workbook. If you accidentally make changes while exploring, press Ctrl + Z to undo the change.

 a. Click the worksheet tab labeled *Stevens Hours.*

 b. If necessary, use the vertical scroll bar to scroll down so you can see both weeks' of billable hours. (If necessary, use the vertical scroll bar again to return to the top of the worksheet).

 c. Click cell **B3** (the cell displaying the staff member's last name, Stevens). This is the cell at the intersection of column B and row 3.

  i. Note that the column B and row 3 selector boxes highlight.

  ii. Note that the status bar displays *Ready,* indicating that you are in Ready mode.

  iii. On the *Home* tab, in the *Number* group, look at the *Number Format* box at the top of the group. Note that the format for this cell is General.

  iv. Double-click cell **B3** to switch to Edit mode. Note that the status bar now displays *Edit,* and the blinking cursor appears within the cell. If you needed to, you could edit the text directly in the cell.

 d. Press Esc to exit Edit mode and return to Ready mode.

e. Press <kbd>← Enter</kbd> twice to move to cell **B5** (the cell displaying the staff member's billable rate). This cell is formatted with the Accounting Number Format number format.

   i. Look in the *Number Format* box and note that the format for this cell is *Accounting.*

   ii. On the *Home* tab, in the *Styles* group, look in the *Cell Styles* gallery, and note that the cell style *Currency* is highlighted. (If the Cell Styles gallery is collapsed on your Ribbon, click the **Cell Styles** button to display it.)

f. Click cell **B10** (the cell displaying the number of hours for Monday, January 14). This cell is formatted with the Comma Style number format.

   i. Look in the *Number Format* box and note that the format for this cell is also *Accounting.*

   ii. On the *Home* tab, in the *Styles* group, look in the *Cell Styles* gallery, and note that the cell style *Comma* is highlighted for this cell. (If the Cell Styles gallery is collapsed on your Ribbon, click the **Cell Styles** button to display it.)

   iii. Note the style differences between cell **B5** (Accounting Number Format) and cell **B10** (Comma Style format).

g. Click cell **B8** (the cell displaying the date 1/14/2013). This cell is formatted using the Short Date format. Note that the *Number Format* box displays *Date.*

h. Double-click cell **B16.**

   i. Note that the status bar now displays *Edit,* indicating that you are in Edit mode.

   ii. This cell contains a formula to calculate the daily bill for Monday, January 14:
=B14*$B$5

   iii. Note that cells B14 and B5 are highlighted with colors matching the cell references in the formula.

   iv. Note that the reference to cell B5 is an absolute reference ($B$5).

i. Press <kbd>Esc</kbd> to exit Edit mode.

j. Double-click cell **B14.**

   i. Note that once again the status bar displays *Edit,* indicating that you are in Edit mode.

   ii. This cell contains a formula using the SUM function to calculate the total billable hours for Monday, January 14:

    =SUM(B10:B13)

   iii. In this case, the SUM function uses a single argument B10:13 to indicate the range of cells to total.

   iv. Note that the cell range B10:B13 is highlighted with the color matching the argument in the SUM function formula.

   v. Note that the reference to the cell range B10:B13 uses relative references.

k. Press <kbd>Esc</kbd> to exit Edit mode.

l. Press <kbd>Tab ⇄</kbd> to move to cell **C14.** Look in the formula bar and note that this cell contains a similar formula to the one in cell B14:

=SUM(C10:C13)

m. Press <kbd>→</kbd> to move through cells **D14** through **H14.** Note the formula in the formula bar for each cell.

n. Did you notice that the cell references in the formulas in cells C14 through H14 all use relative references?

4. Now you are ready to complete the worksheet for David Marshall. Navigate to the *Marshall Hours* worksheet by clicking the **Marshall Hours** worksheet tab.

5. The staff member's last name is spelled incorrectly. Navigate to cell **B3** and edit the text so the last name is spelled correctly (Marshall—with two Ls). Use Edit mode.

   a. Double-click cell **B3.**

   b. Edit the text to: Marshall

   c. Press ⟵ Enter to accept your changes.

6. The billable rate amount is missing. Navigate to cell **B5** and enter the rate (**150**). Use Ready mode.

   a. Click cell **B5.**

   b. Type: 150

   c. Press ⟵ Enter .

7. Modify the billable rate to use the Accounting Number Format.

   a. Press ↑ to return to cell **B5.**

   b. On the *Home* tab, in the *Number* group, click the **Account Number Format** button.

8. The dates are missing from the timesheet. Enter the first date, January 14, 2013.

   a. Click cell **B8.**

   b. Type: 1/14/2013

   c. Press ⟵ Enter .

9. Use AutoFill to complete the dates in the timesheet.

   a. Click cell **B8.**

   b. Click the **Fill Handle** tool, and drag to cell **H9.** Release the mouse button.

10. Change the date format to the 1/14/2012 format.

   a. The cell range B8:H9 should still be selected. If not, click cell **B8,** press and hold ⟨↑ Shift⟩, click cell **H9,** and then release the ⟨↑ Shift⟩ key.

   b. On the *Home* tab, in the *Number* group, expand the *Number Format* list, and click **Short Date.**

11. Use the Quick Analysis tool to enter total hours for each day.

   a. Select cells **B10:H13.** Click cell **B10,** hold down the left mouse button and drag the mouse to cell **H13.** Release the mouse button. The cell range B10 through H13 should now appear selected.

   b. The Quick Analysis tool button should appear near the lower right corner of the selected cell range. (If the Quick Analysis tool button is not visible, move your mouse cursor over the selected cell range again, without clicking. This action should make the button appear.) Click the **Quick Analysis tool** button, and then click **Totals.**

   c. Click **Sum** (the first option).

12. Format the hours billed section to use the Comma Style number format. Be sure to include the total row.

   a. Select cells **B10:H14.** Try another method: Click cell **B10,** press and hold ⟨↑ Shift⟩, click cell **H14,** and release the ⟨↑ Shift⟩ key.

   b. On the *Home* tab, in the *Number* group, click the **Comma Style** button.

13. Enter a formula in cell **B16** to calculate the daily bill for Monday, January 14. The formula should calculate the total billable hours for the day (cell B14) times the billable rate (B5).

   a. Click cell **B16.**

   b. Type: =

   c. Click cell **B14.**

   d. Type: *

   e. Click cell **B5.**

   f. Press $\boxed{F4}$ to change the cell reference **B5** to an absolute reference (**$B$5**).

   g. Press $\boxed{\leftarrow\text{Enter}}$.

   h. The formula should look like this: **=B14*$B$5**

14. Use AutoFill to copy the formula to the remaining days in the timesheet.

   a. Click cell **B16** again.

   b. Click the **AutoFill handle.** Hold down the left mouse button and drag to cell **H16.** Release the mouse button.

   c. The formulas in cells C16 through H16 should look like this:

◢	C	D	E	F	G	H
16	=C14*$B$5	=D14*$B$5	=E14*$B$5	=F14*$B$5	=G14*$B$5	=H14*$B$5

FIGURE EX 1.42

Notice that when AutoFill copied the formula, it updated the relative reference (B14) to reflect the new column position, but it did not change the relative reference ($B$5).

15. Now you can calculate the bill total for the week.by summing the daily bill amounts. Enter a formula using the SUM function with the cell range **B16:H16** as the argument.

   a. Click cell **B17.**

   b. Type: =SUM(B16:H16)

   c. Press $\boxed{\leftarrow\text{Enter}}$.

16. Preview how the worksheet will look when printed.

   a. Click the **File** tab to open Backstage.

   b. Click **Print** to display the print preview.

17. Save and close the workbook.

skill review 1.2

In this project you will create a new workbook to track the cost of books for your college classes. For each book, you will enter the purchase price, the potential sell-back price, and the cost difference. You will calculate totals using AutoSum. You will then create a new workbook from a template, and practice changing the zoom level and arranging the workbooks. Skills needed to complete this project:

- Entering and Editing Text and Numbers in Cells (Skill 1.4)
- Navigating a Workbook (Skill 1.2)
- Inserting Data Using AutoFill (Skill 1.7)
- Applying Number Formats (Skill 1.5)
- Using the Status Bar (Skill 1.13)
- Using AutoSum to Insert a SUM Function (Skill 1.11)

- Entering Simple Formulas (Skill 1.8)
- Creating a New Workbook Using a Template (Skill 1.15)
- Checking Spelling (Skill 1.17)
- Arranging Workbooks (Skill 1.16)
- Changing the Zoom Level (Skill 1.14)

1. Start a new blank Excel workbook. Save the file as:
   `[your initials]EX-SkillReview-1-2`
2. The new workbook opens with one sheet (Sheet1). Cell A1 is selected.
3. In cell A1, type the title for the worksheet: `Textbooks`
4. Enter data in the worksheet as follows:

	A	B	C	D	E
1	Textbooks				
2					
3	Book	Cost	Value	Difference	
4	Book 1	80.25	40.00		
5	Book 2	74.89	28.00		
6	Book 3	95.26	45.00		
7	Book 4	52.50	25.00		
8					

FIGURE EX 1.43

5. Use AutoFill to add two additional books to the list.
   a. Click cell **A4,** hold down the left mouse button and drag the mouse to cell **A7.** Release the mouse button. The cell range A4 through A7 should now appear selected.
   b. Click the **Fill Handle** tool (located at the lower right corner of the selected cell range).
   c. Drag down to cell **A9,** and release the mouse button.
   d. Excel adds Book 5 and Book 6 to the list.
6. Book 5 cost $65.00 and can be sold for $30.00. Book 6 cost $110.00 and can be sold for $45.00. Add this data to the worksheet.
   a. Click cell **B8** and type: 65
   b. Press → and type: 30
   c. Click cell **B9** and type: 110
   d. Press Tab and type: 45
   e. Press ← Enter.
7. Modify the **status bar** to display the minimum value.
   a. Right-click anywhere on the **status bar.**
   b. Click **Minimum** to add a checkmark.
   c. Click anywhere to dismiss the menu.
8. Use the status bar to check the total value of the books and the minimum value.
   a. Click cell **C4.** Press and hold ↑ Shift and click cell **C9.** Release the ↑ Shift key.
   b. Look at the status bar and find the *Sum* value (**213.00**).
   c. Look at the status bar and find the *Min* value (**25.00**).

9. Use **AutoSum** to calculate total cost and total value. The totals should be placed in cells **B10** and **C10.**

   a. Click cell **A10** and type: Total

   b. Press Tab ⇆.

   c. Cell **B10** should be selected. Press and hold ↑ Shift and click cell **C10.** Release the ↑ Shift key.

   d. On the *Home* tab, in the *Editing* group, click the **AutoSum** button.

10. Change the number format for the cost and value numbers to the Accounting Number Format.

   a. Click cell **B4.** Press and hold ↑ Shift. Click cell **C10.** Release ↑ Shift.

   b. On the *Home* tab, in the *Number* group, click the **Accounting Number Format** button.

11. Enter a formula in cell **D4** to calculate the difference between the cost and the value for Book1. The formula will use only relative references because in the next step, you will use AutoFill to copy the formula down the column.

   a. Click cell **D4.**   d. Type: –

   b. Type: =   e. Click cell **C3.**

   c. Click cell **B2.**   f. Press ← Enter.

12. Use AutoFill to copy the formula to calculate the difference for books 2 through 6 and the total.

   a. Click cell **D4.**

   b. Click the **AutoFill handle.** Hold down the left mouse button and drag to cell **D10.** Release the mouse button.

13. Save the workbook. Do not close it or exit Excel.

14. Create a new file from a template called *Student grade and GPA* tracker.

   a. Click the **File** tab to open Backstage.

   b. Click **New.**

   c. Open a new file based on the *Student grade and GPA tracker* template. (This step may require an active Internet connection.)

      i. The *Student grade and GPA tracker* template may appear in the list of templates automatically. If it does not, you will need to search for it. In the *Search online templates* box, type: student grade tracker

      ii. Click the template preview.

      iii. Click **Create.**

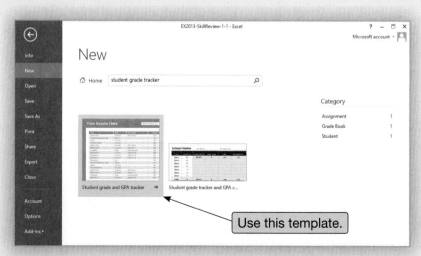

FIGURE EX 1.44

15. The new workbook based on the *Student grade and GPA tracker* template opens. This is a complex workbook using many advanced techniques. The good news is that you don't have to understand how this workbook was created in order to use it.

    a. The workbook includes four worksheets. The first worksheet, *Score Tracker,* lists all assignments the student has completed. Navigate to the other worksheets by clicking each of the sheet tabs and review the content of each. When you are finished, return to the first sheet, *Score Tracker,* by clicking that worksheet tab.

    b. Click cell **C4** (the cell displaying the text *Modern French*).

    c. Click the arrow that appears at the right side of the cell. The list of available classes appears. If you were using this template to actually create your own grade and GPA tracker, this list would display your classes. But where does this list come from?

    d. Click the **Settings** tab to go to the *Settings* worksheet.

    e. Note the classes listed in cells C9:C15. These are the same classes displayed in the list you saw in the *Score Tracker* sheet.

    f. Change the *Modern French* class name to *Conversational Latin.*

        i. Click cell **C9.** Verify that the status bar displays Ready to indicate that you are in Ready mode.

        ii. Type: `Conversational Latin`

        iii. Press `← Enter`.

    g. Use the spelling checker to verify that you did not misspell *Conversational Latin.*

        i. On the *Review* tab, in the *Proofing* group, click the **Spelling** button.

        ii. Excel should display an informational alert box asking if you want to continue checking spelling from the beginning of the sheet. Click **Yes.**

        iii. If you didn't make any spelling mistakes, Excel will display a message telling you that the spell check is complete. If you did make a mistake, select the correct spelling in the *Suggestions* list and click the **Change** button. Continue correcting mistakes until Excel tells you the spell check is complete. Click **OK.**

    h. Now return to the *Score Tracker* sheet and see how your change affected the list. The workbook template author used an advanced technique to create the relationship between the list of classes in the *Settings* sheet and the data entry drop-down list used in the *Score Tracker* sheet. At this stage, you do not need to understand how this was created, but you should understand how the data change on one sheet affects the data in the other sheet.

        i. Click the **Score Tracker** sheet tab. (You could also click the **Score Tracker** button near the top of the *Settings* worksheet.)

        ii. Click cell **C4** again (which still displays *Modern French*).

        iii. Expand the list by clicking the arrow.

        iv. Note the new entry at the top of the list—*Conversational Latin.*

        v. Click **Conversational Latin** to replace the text in the cell.

16. If you think you might like to come back to this workbook later for your personal use, this is a good point to save it. Be sure not to close the file. Use the file name: `[Your Initials]GradesAndGPA`

17. You should still have two workbooks open: the textbooks workbook from the beginning of the project and the grades and GPA workbook based on the template. Arrange the workbooks so you can see both at the same time.

    a. On the *View* tab, in the *Window* group, click the **Arrange All** button.

    b. In the *Arrange Windows* dialog, click the **Vertical** radio button. Click **OK.**

18. The grades and GPA workbook should be active. If not, click the title bar for that window. Review the *Your Performance* sheet and change the zoom level to 75% so you can see more of the data at once.

   a. Click the **Your Performance** tab.

   b. On the *View* tab, in the *Zoom* group, click the **Zoom** button.

   c. In the *Zoom* dialog, click the **75%** radio button for the zoom option you want. Click **OK**.

   d. Navigate to the *Score Tracker* worksheet again, and note that changing the zoom level of the *Your Performance* sheet did not affect the *Score Tracker* sheet.

19. Close both workbooks. If you made changes to the grades and GPA workbook and you plan to continue using it, be sure to save the changes.

challenge yourself 1.3

In this project, you will complete the timesheet for David Marshall which you worked on in Skill Review 1.1. You will need to enter and format missing dates, correct a data entry mistake, apply number formatting, and enter formulas to calculate the total billable hours per day, the daily total for each day, and the bill total for the week.

Skills needed to complete this project:

- Working in Protected View (Skill 1.3)
- Navigating a Workbook (Skill 1.2)
- Entering and Editing Text and Numbers in Cells (Skill 1.4)
- Applying Number Formats (Skill 1.5)
- Entering Dates and Applying Date Formats (Skill 1.6)
- Inserting Data Using AutoFill (Skill 1.7)
- Understanding Absolute and Relative References (Skill 1.9)
- Entering Simple Formulas (Skill 1.8)
- Calculating Totals with the Quick Analysis Tool (Skill 1.12)
- Previewing and Printing a Worksheet (Skill 1.18)

1. Open the start file **EX2013-ChallengeYourself-1-3** and resave the file as: **[your initials] EX-ChallengeYourself-1-3**

2. If the workbook opens in Protected View, enable editing so you can make changes to the workbook.

3. Verify that the *Marshall Hours* worksheet is active.

4. If necessary, scroll to the bottom of the worksheet so you can see the empty timesheet beginning on **row 20.**

5. The dates are missing from the timesheet. Enter the date 1/21/2013 in cell **B21.**

6. Use **AutoFill** to complete the dates in cells **C21:H21.**

7. Change the date format for **B21:H21** to the Short Date format.

8. The hours reported for the Proctor client on Friday (cell F26) are incorrect. Change the number in cell **F26** to: 6

9. Use the **Quick Analysis** tool to enter total hours for each day. Use the cell range **B23:H26.** The daily totals should be inserted into the range **B27:H27.**

10. Format the hours billed section to use the **Comma Style** number format. Be sure to include the total row.

11. Enter a formula in cell **B29** to calculate the daily bill for Monday, January 21. The formula should calculate the total billable hours for the day (cell **B27**) times the billable rate (**B5**). Be sure to use an absolute cell reference for the billable rate.

12. Use **AutoFill** to copy the formula to the remaining days in the timesheet (cells **C29:H29**).

13. Calculate the bill total for the week.by summing the daily bill amounts. In cell **B30**, enter a formula using the **SUM** function. The function argument should be the range of cells representing the daily bill totals (**B29:H29**).

14. Preview how the worksheet will look when printed.

15. Save and close the workbook.

challenge yourself **1.4**

In this project you will work with a college budget spreadsheet. You will change a few values in the budget, modify number formats, and calculate totals and the difference between expected income and expenses. You will then create a new budget workbook from a template, and practice changing the zoom level and arranging the workbooks.

Skills needed to complete this project:

- Working in Protected View (Skill 1.3)
- Entering and Editing Text and Numbers in Cells (Skill 1.4)
- Navigating a Workbook (Skill 1.2)
- Using AutoSum to Insert a SUM Function (Skill 1.11)
- Calculating Totals Using the Quick Analysis Tool (Skill 1.12)
- Using the Status Bar (Skill 1.13)
- Applying Number Formats (Skill 1.5)
- Understanding Absolute and Relative References (Skill 1.9)
- Entering Simple Formulas (Skill 1.8)
- Checking Spelling (Skill 1.17)
- Creating a New Workbook Using a Template (Skill 1.15)
- Arranging Workbooks (Skill 1.16)
- Changing the Zoom Level (Skill 1.14)

1. Open the start file **EX2013-ChallengeYourself-1-4** and resave the file as: `[your initials]EX-ChallengeYourself-1-4`

2. If the workbook opens in Protected View, enable editing so you can make changes to the workbook.

3. Make the following changes to the *Budget* worksheet:

   a. Change the *Utilities* item to `Electric` (cell **B12**).

   b. Change the Insurance value from *90* to `60` (cell **B19**).

4. The worksheet is missing formulas to calculate totals. Enter formulas using the **SUM** function to calculate the following totals. Use any of the methods you learned in this chapter.

   a. Enter a formula in cell **C7** to calculate the total monthly income.

   b. Enter a formula in cell **C24** to calculate the total monthly expenses.

   c. Enter a formula in cell **F16** to calculate the total semester expenses.

   d. Use the **status bar** to verify that the formula is calculating the correct total for each cell range.

5. Cell **F18** displays the number of months in the semester. Change the number format in this cell to the **Number** format with no numbers showing after the decimal (so the number appears as **4** instead of **$4.00**).

6. The number format in the *Semester Expenses* section does not match the number format in the other sections of the worksheet. Change the number format for cells **F11:F16** to the **Accounting Number Format.**

7. Review the formulas in the *Discretionary Income* section.

   a. Cells **F4:F6** should contain references to the cells where you just entered the formulas to calculate totals. Add the appropriate formula to cell **F6** to reference the value in cell **F16** (the total semester expenses).

   b. The semester is four months long, so the formulas in cells **F4** and **F5** should multiply the total monthly income and total monthly expenses by four. Correct the formulas in cells **F4** and **F6.** Use an absolute reference to the value in cell **F18** (the number of months in the semester).

8. Use spelling checker to find and correct any spelling errors in the *Budget* worksheet.

9. Save the workbook. Do not close it or exit Excel.

10. Create a new file from a template called *Personal Expenses Calculator.* If you do not see this template, search for it using the search phrase *personal expenses.*

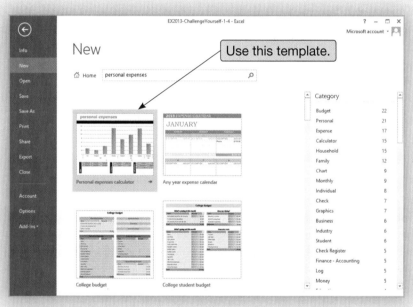

FIGURE EX 1.45

11. Explore the worksheets in this workbook.

12. If you think you might like to come back to this workbook later for your personal use, this is a good point to save it. Be sure not to close the file. Use the file name:
    [Your Initials]PersonalExpenses

13. You should still have two workbooks open: the college budget workbook from the beginning of the project and the personal expenses workbook based on the template. Arrange the workbooks so you can see both at the same time.

    a. Try different arrangements until you find the one that works best for you.

    b. Practice moving back and forth between the two workbooks.

14. Make the personal budget workbook active and navigate to the *Dashboard* worksheet. Modify the zoom to **80%.**

15. Close both workbooks. If you made changes to the personal budget workbook and you plan to continue using it, be sure to save the changes.

on your own 1.5

For Spring Break, you've decided to take a seven-day road trip. Use this Excel workbook to calculate the number of miles you will drive each day and the gas cost for each day. Use the techniques you've learned in this chapter to calculate the total miles and the total gas cost. Don't forget to end the trip at the same location you started! You may want to use the Internet to look up mileage, MPG (miles per gallon), and gas price information.

Skills needed to complete this project:

- Navigating a Workbook (Skill 1.2)
- Working in Protected View (Skill 1.3)
- Entering and Editing Text and Numbers in Cells (Skill 1.4)
- Entering Dates and Applying Date Formats (Skill 1.6)
- Inserting Data Using AutoFill (Skill 1.7)
- Understanding Absolute and Relative References (Skill 1.9)
- Entering Simple Formulas (Skill 1.8)
- Calculating Totals with the Quick Analysis Tool (Skill 1.12)
- Using AutoSum to Insert a SUM Function (Skill 1.11)
- Applying Number Formats (Skill 1.5)
- Checking Spelling (Skill 1.17)

1. Open the start file **EX2013-OnYourOwn-1-5** and resave the file as:
   `[your initials]EX-OnYourOwn-1-5`

2. If the workbook opens in Protected View, click the **Enable Editing** button in the Message Bar at the top of the workbook so you can modify the workbook.

3. Complete the Trip Details section of the *RoadTrip* worksheet:

   a. Enter the dates of your road trip. Use a date format that includes the day of the week.

   b. Enter a start and end location for each day. Remember—the starting location for each day should be the same as the end location for the previous day. If you use a formula with a relative reference rather than retyping the location name for each start location, you can use AutoFill to complete the start location column. Consider using a formula to ensure that the final end location is the same as the first start location.

   c. Look up and enter the miles between each location. Use an appropriate number format for the *Number of Miles* column. (Hint: Use *mapquest.com* or *maps.google.com* to look up the mileage between locations.)

4. Enter your car information including the MPG (miles per gallon). If you don't know your MPG, the government Web site www.fueleconomy.gov has excellent information on average MPG for a variety of car makes, models, and years.

5. Enter the average gas price in your area (or the area of your road trip). Again, the www.fueleconomy.gov Web site has links to this type of information.

6. Enter a formula to calculate the gas cost per mile for your car (gas price per gallon/your car's MPG).

7. Now that you have the gas cost per mile for your car, you can figure the cost of the road trip. Enter a formula to figure the gas cost per day (the number of miles * your gas cost per mile) for the first day of the trip. Be sure to use absolute and relative references as appropriate, so you can use AutoFill to copy the formula to the rest of the cells in the *Gas Cost per Day* column.

8. Apply appropriate number formats to all the cells in the workbook that display costs. Hint: The Accounting Number Format is best for costs that appear in a column. For costs that appear on their own, you may want to use the Currency Style format.

9. Don't forget to spell check the workbook.

10. Save and close the workbook.

fix it 1.6

The workbook for this project tracks how many miles you walked each day for the week of June 2, 2013 through June 8, 2013. Your goal for each day is to walk at least two miles. Use the skills learned in this chapter to fix the workbook.

Skills needed to complete this project:

- Navigating a Workbook (Skill 1.2)
- Working in Protected View (Skill 1.3)
- Entering and Editing Text and Numbers in Cells (Skill 1.4)
- Entering Dates and Applying Date Formats (Skill 1.6)
- Inserting Data Using AutoFill (Skill 1.7)
- Applying Number Formats (Skill 1.5)
- Understanding Absolute and Relative References (Skill 1.9)
- Entering Simple Formulas (Skill 1.8)
- Calculating Totals with the Quick Analysis Tool (Skill 1.12)
- Using AutoSum to Insert a SUM Function (Skill 1.11)
- Checking Spelling (Skill 1.17)

1. Open the start file **EX2013-FixIt-1-6** and resave the file as:
   [your initials] EX-FixIt-1-6

2. If the workbook opens in Protected View, click the **Enable Editing** button in the Message Bar at the top of the workbook so you can modify the workbook.

3. The worksheet is missing a title. Type this title in cell **A1**: Exercise Log

4. The weekly goal should be 2, not 20. Correct the value in cell **D1**.

5. The dates are missing from cells **A5:A10**. Use **AutoFill** to complete the dates for the rest of the week.

6. The exercise log would be more useful if the date showed the day of the week in addition to the date. Change the date format for cells **A4:A10** so the date displays in this format: **Sunday, June 02, 2013.**

7. The mileage for each day should use the Comma Style number format. Correct the number format in cells **C4:C10.**

8. Use one of the skills you learned in this chapter to enter formulas using the **SUM** function in cells **B11** and **C11** to calculate the weekly total minutes and miles.

9. The formulas in the *Under/Over Goal* column aren't quite right. Fix the formula in cell **D4,** and then use **AutoFill** to replace the formulas in cells **D5:D10.**

10. There may be spelling errors. Be sure to use spelling checker before you finish the project.

11. Save and close the workbook.

Formatting Cells

chapter **2**

In this chapter, you will learn the following skills:

- Modify cell data using cut, copy, and paste
- Insert, delete, and merge cells
- Work with text and font attributes
- Apply borders and shading
- Format cells using cell styles
- Copy formatting using Format Painter
- Format cells using conditional formatting
- Modify cell data using find and replace
- Work with the print area

Skill **2.1** Cutting, Copying, and Pasting Cells
Skill **2.2** Using Paste Options
Skill **2.3** Using Undo and Redo
Skill **2.4** Wrapping Text in Cells
Skill **2.5** Inserting and Deleting Cells
Skill **2.6** Aligning Cells
Skill **2.7** Merging Cells and Splitting Merged Cells
Skill **2.8** Applying Bold, Italic, and Underline
Skill **2.9** Changing Fonts, Font Size, and Font Color
Skill **2.10** Adding Borders
Skill **2.11** Adding Shading with Fill Color
Skill **2.12** Applying Cell Styles
Skill **2.13** Using Format Painter
Skill **2.14** Applying Conditional Formatting Using the Quick Analysis Tool
Skill **2.15** Applying Conditional Formatting with Data Bars, Color Scales, and Icon Sets
Skill **2.16** Applying Conditional Formatting with Highlight Cells Rules
Skill **2.17** Applying Conditional Formatting with Top/Bottom Rules
Skill **2.18** Removing Conditional Formatting
Skill **2.19** Clearing Cell Content
Skill **2.20** Using Find and Replace
Skill **2.21** Replacing Formatting
Skill **2.22** Setting and Clearing the Print Area

skills

introduction

This chapter focuses on skills for working with cells and cell ranges. You will learn to use the basic *Cut, Copy,* and *Paste* commands to move data and to insert, delete, and merge cells to create a worksheet structure that fits your data. This chapter also covers the essential skills for formatting cells, including in-depth coverage of conditional formatting. Formatting not only enhances a workbook's appearance, but when used properly, it can make the data easier to understand.

Skill 2.1 Cutting, Copying, and Pasting Cells

The *Cut, Copy,* and *Paste* commands are used to move data within a workbook and from one workbook to another. A cell or range of cells that is **cut** is removed from the workbook and stored for later use. The **Copy** command stores a duplicate of the selected cell or range without changing the workbook. The **Paste** command is used to insert copied or cut cells into a workbook.

If you *copy* and paste a cell containing a formula with relative references, Excel will update the references to reflect the new position in the workbook. However, if you *cut* and paste instead, Excel will treat the formula as if it contained absolute references and will not update the cell reference in the formula.

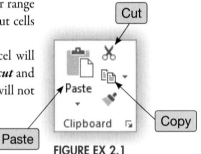

FIGURE EX 2.1

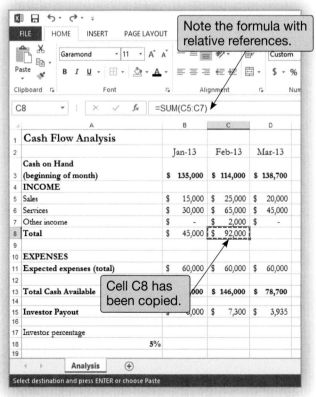

FIGURE EX 2.2

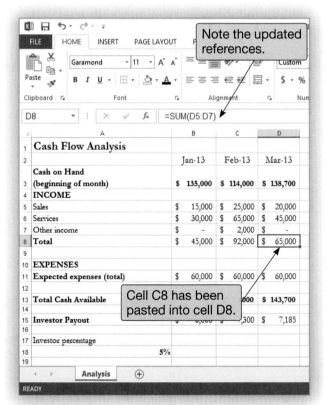

FIGURE EX 2.3

To use *Cut, Copy,* and *Paste:*

1. Select the cell or cells you want to cut or copy.
2. On the *Home* tab, in the *Clipboard* group, click the appropriate button: **Cut** or **Copy.**
3. The selection appears with a flashing dotted line around it, and the cut or copied data are stored temporarily in the computer's memory.
4. Click the cell where you want to paste. If you selected a range of cells to cut or copy, click the cell in the upper-left corner of the area where you want to paste.
5. Click the **Paste** button to paste the cell data and formatting. If the copied or cut cells include formulas, Excel will copy the formulas and update any relative cell references automatically.

These same steps apply whether you are cutting, copying, and pasting text, pictures, charts, or any type of object in an Excel workbook.

If you paste into a cell that contains data, the original cell data will be overwritten. To paste without overwriting existing cells, use the *Insert Copied Cells* or *Insert Cut Cells* command instead.

1. Copy or cut the cells you want to insert.
2. Select the cell where you want to insert.
3. On the *Home* tab, in the *Cells* group, click the **Insert** button arrow and select **Insert Copied Cells** or **Insert Cut Cells.**

tips & tricks

If you insert cut or copied cells into the beginning or end of a data table, be sure to check for formulas that may reference a cell range that does not include the newly inserted cells.

another method

To apply the *Cut, Copy,* or *Paste* command, you can also use the following shortcuts:

❱ **Cut** = Press `Ctrl` + `X`, or right-click and select **Cut.**

❱ **Copy** = Press `Ctrl` + `C`, or right-click and select **Copy.**

❱ **Paste** = Press `Ctrl` + `V`, or right-click and select **Paste.**

let me try

Open the student data file **EX2-01-CashFlow** and try this skill on your own:

1. Copy cell **C7,** and paste to cell **D7.** Note that the formula updated to reflect the new cell range D5:D6.
2. Cut cell **A17,** and paste to cell **B16.** Note that formulas in the workbook that refer to this cell (B14:D14) updated to reflect the new position.
3. Cells **A15:D15** are misplaced. Cut them from their current location and insert them above cell **A6.** Verify that the formulas in cells B8:D8 updated appropriately.
4. Save the file as directed by your instructor and close it.

Skill 2.2 Using Paste Options

When you paste data into Excel, you can use the default *Paste* command to insert the copied data (including formulas and formatting) into the selected cell, or you can select from the paste options to control more precisely what is pasted. The *Paste* button has two parts—the top part of the button pastes the most recent copied or cut data into the current workbook. If you click the bottom part of the button (the *Paste* button arrow), you can control how the item is pasted. Each type of object has different paste options. For example, if you are pasting data that include formulas, you can paste the formulas with or without formatting or just the values without the underlying formulas.

	Paste—The default paste command that pastes all of the source content and formatting.
	Formulas—Pastes the formulas but none of the formatting. The pasted content will use the cell and number formatting of the cell into which it was pasted.
	Formulas & Number Formatting—Pastes the formulas and number formatting but none of the cell formatting such as font size, borders, and shading.
	Keep Source Formatting—Pastes the content, including formulas, and all formatting from the source.
	No Borders—Pastes the content, including formulas, and all formatting except borders.
	Keep Source Column Widths—Pastes the copied cell, including formulas and all number and cell formatting. Also adjusts the column width to match the width of the source column.
	Transpose—Pastes the rows from the source into columns, and the columns from the source into rows.

When your source includes formulas, you have the option to paste the calculated cell values without pasting the underlying formulas.

	Values—Pastes only the values, not the underlying formula or cell formatting.
	Values & Number Formatting—Pastes only the values, not the underlying formulas. Includes number formatting but not other cell formatting such as borders and shading.
	Values & Source Formatting—Pastes only the values, not the underlying formulas. Includes all formatting from the source.

The final group of paste options provides alternatives to pasting the actual contents of one cell into another.

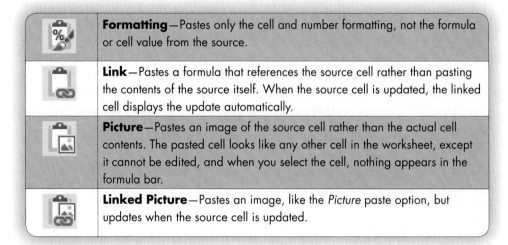

	Formatting—Pastes only the cell and number formatting, not the formula or cell value from the source.
	Link—Pastes a formula that references the source cell rather than pasting the contents of the source itself. When the source cell is updated, the linked cell displays the update automatically.
	Picture—Pastes an image of the source cell rather than the actual cell contents. The pasted cell looks like any other cell in the worksheet, except it cannot be edited, and when you select the cell, nothing appears in the formula bar.
	Linked Picture—Pastes an image, like the *Picture* paste option, but updates when the source cell is updated.

To use the *Paste* button on the Ribbon:

1. On the *Home* tab, in the *Clipboard* group, click the bottom part of the **Paste** button (the **Paste** button arrow) to expand the *Paste Options* menu.

2. Move your mouse over the icon for each paste option to see a live preview of how the paste would look, and then click the paste option you want.

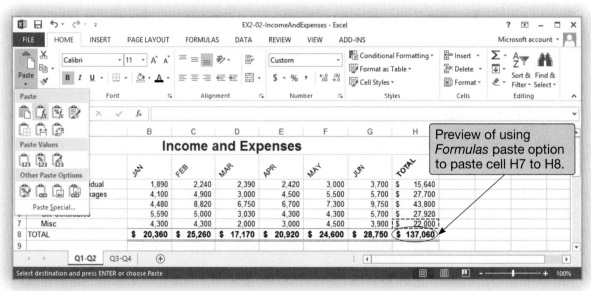

Preview of using *Formulas* paste option to paste cell H7 to H8.

FIGURE EX 2.4

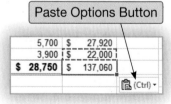

Paste Options Button

FIGURE EX 2.5

To use the keyboard shortcut:

1. Press Ctrl + V.

2. The source is pasted using the default *Paste* option, and the *Paste Options* button appears.

3. Click the **Paste Options** button or press Ctrl to display the *Paste Options* menu. This is the same menu that is available from the *Paste* button on the Ribbon, but moving your mouse over the icons does not show a preview of how the paste would look.

tips & tricks

A useful paste option is *Keep Source Column Widths*. Often, when you paste data into a new worksheet, the default column width is too narrow to display the data. Use the *Keep Source Column Widths* paste option to maintain any column width adjustments you made in the source worksheet.

tell me **more**

If you do not want the *Paste Options* button to appear every time you paste with the keyboard shortcut, you can turn it off:

1. Click the **File** tab to open Backstage.
2. Click **Options** to open the *Excel Options* dialog.
3. Click **Advanced.**
4. In the *Cut, copy, and paste* section near the bottom of the window, click the check box in front of **Show Paste Options button when content is pasted** to remove the checkmark.
5. Click **OK.**

another **method**

You can also access the paste options from the right-click menu. Six of the paste options appear on the right-click menu (*Paste, Values, Formulas, Transpose, Formatting,* and *Paste Link*). To select an option from the full *Paste Options* menu, point to **Paste Special...,** and then click the paste option you want.

let me **try**

Open the student data file **EX2-02-IncomeAndExpenses** and try this skill on your own:

1. Copy cell **H7** and paste only the formula into cell **H8.** Do not paste the original cell formatting.
2. Copy **G17** and paste the formula, formatting, and the source column width into cell **H17.**
3. Save the file as directed by your instructor and close it.

Skill 2.3 Using Undo and Redo

If you make a mistake when working, the **Undo** command allows you to reverse the last action you performed. The **Redo** command allows you to reverse the *Undo* command and restore the file to its previous state. The Quick Access Toolbar gives you immediate access to both these commands.

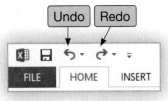

> To undo the last action taken, click the **Undo** button on the Quick Access Toolbar.
> To redo the last action taken, click the **Redo** button on the Quick Access Toolbar.

FIGURE EX 2.6

To undo multiple actions at the same time:

1. Click the **Undo** button arrow to expand the list of your most recent actions.
2. Click an action in the list.
3. The action you click will be undone, along with all the actions completed after that. In other words, your workbook will revert to the state it was in before that action.

tips & tricks

Be careful when using the *Undo* and *Redo* commands in Excel. In other Office applications, undo and redo actions are confined to the file you are currently working on—even if you have multiple files open. However, in Excel, the undo–redo list of actions includes all the open workbooks. This means that if you are working on multiple Excel files at the same time, using the *Undo* command can actually undo an action in one of the other open workbooks.

another method

> To undo an action, you can also press Ctrl + Z.
> To redo an action, you can also press Ctrl + Y.

let me try

Open the student data file **EX2-03-IncomeAndExpenses** and try this skill on your own:

1. Copy cell **H8** and paste into cell **G8.**
2. Look in the formula bar—that's the wrong formula for this cell. Undo the last action.
3. Copy cell **F8** and paste into cell **G8.**
4. Undo the last action.
5. Redo the last action.
6. Save the file as directed by your instructor and close it.

Skill 2.4 Wrapping Text in Cells

When you type text in a cell, the text will appear to continue to the right as far as it can until there is another cell that contains data. At that point, the text will appear to be cut off. You could increase the width of the cell to show all the text, but do you really want the entire column to be that wide? If your worksheet includes cells with more text than will comfortably fit in the cell, you should use the wrap text feature. When wrap text is enabled for a cell, the text in the cell will automatically wrap to multiple lines, just as a paragraph would.

To wrap text in a cell:

> On the *Home* tab, in the *Alignment* group, click the **Wrap Text** button. Notice the button appears selected when text wrapping is active for the cell.

FIGURE EX 2.7

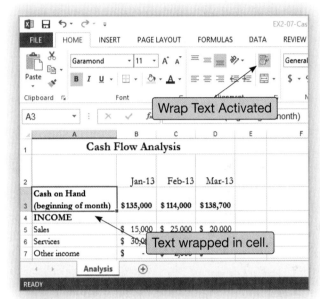

FIGURE EX 2.8

> To turn off text wrapping in a cell, click the **Wrap Text** button again to deselect it.

tips & tricks

The text wrapping feature only works for cells that contain text. If a column is too narrow to display its numerical data, Excel will not wrap it. Instead, the cell will show a series of # symbols, indicating that the cell contains numerical data, but the column is too narrow to display it.

another method

You can also turn on the text wrapping feature from the *Format Cells* dialog.

1. On the *Home* tab, in the *Alignment* group, click the **Alignment Settings** Dialog Box Launcher to open the *Format Cells* dialog.
2. In the *Text control* section, click the **Wrap Text** check box.
3. Click **OK**.

let me try

Open the student data file **EX2-04-CashFlow** and try this skill on your own:

Activate text wrapping for cell **A3.** Save the file as directed by your instructor and close it.

Skill 2.5 Inserting and Deleting Cells

You may find you want to add some extra space or more information into the middle of your worksheet. To do this, you must insert a new cell or group of cells. Any formulas referencing the cell where the insertion takes place will update to reflect the new position of the original cell. Even if the formula uses absolute cell references, it will still update to reflect the updated cell reference.

To insert a cell range, select the range where you want to insert the new cells.

1. If you have a vertical cell range selected, click the **Insert Cells** button and Excel will automatically shift existing cells to the right to make room for the new cells.

2. If you have a horizontal cell range selected, click the **Insert Cells** button and Excel will automatically shift existing cells down to make room for the new cells.

If you want more control over whether cells are shifted to the right or down, use the *Insert* dialog.

1. Select the cell or cell range where you want to insert the new cells.

2. On the *Home* tab, in the *Cells* group, click the **Insert Cells** button arrow.

3. Click **Insert Cells...** to open the *Insert* dialog.

4. Click the **Shift cells right** or **Shift cells down** radio button.

5. Click **OK.**

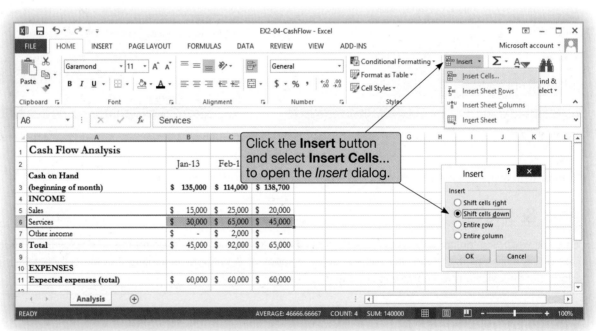

FIGURE EX 2.9

When you insert new cells, the cells will use the same formatting as the cells above (if you shifted cells down) or to the left (if you shifted cells to the right). If you want to use formatting from the cells below or to the left instead, or to insert the cells with no formatting, click the **Insert Options** button that appears at the lower right of the insertion and make a selection from the menu options.

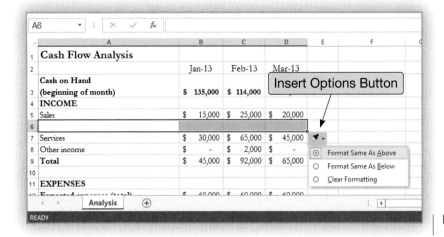

FIGURE EX 2.10

Of course, you can also delete cells. Deleting cells not only deletes the information and formatting in the cell, but also shifts the layout of the worksheet. Even if you delete an empty cell, you shift all the surrounding cells into new positions.

To delete a cell:

1. On the *Home* tab, in the *Cells* group, click the **Delete Cells** button arrow.
2. Click **Delete Cells...** to open the *Delete* dialog.
3. Click the **Shift cells left** or **Shift cells up** radio button.
4. Click **OK.**

tips & tricks

Inserting and deleting cells may have unexpected consequences. Be careful not to delete cells that are referenced in formulas. Even though a new value may shift into the original cell's position, the formula will still be looking for the original cell (now deleted), causing an invalid cell reference error.

another method

Both *Insert...* and *Delete...* commands are available from the right-click menu.

Pressing (Delete) will delete the contents of the cell but not the cell itself.

let me try

Open the student data file **EX2-05-CashFlow** and try this skill on your own:

1. Select cells **A6:D6.**
2. Insert cells so the remaining cells shift down.
3. Delete the inserted cells so the remaining cells shift up.
4. Insert new cells between **A10:D10** and **A11:D11.** Use the formatting from cells A11:D11 for the new cells.
5. Save the file as directed by your instructor and close it.

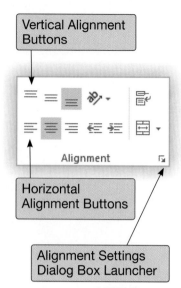

Vertical Alignment Buttons

Horizontal Alignment Buttons

Alignment Settings Dialog Box Launcher

FIGURE EX 2.11

Skill 2.6 Aligning Cells

Alignment refers to how text and numbers are positioned within the cell both horizontally and vertically. By default, cells use the General horizontal alignment. When cells are formatted using the General horizontal alignment, Excel detects the type of content in the cell. Cells that contain text are aligned to the left, and cells that contain numbers are aligned to the right.

To change the horizontal alignment of a cell, click one of the horizontal alignment buttons located on the *Home* tab, in the *Alignment* group: **Align Left, Center,** or **Align Right.**

Excel lets you specify not only alignment horizontally across the cell, but also alignment vertically in the cell. To change the vertical alignment of a cell, click one of the vertical alignment buttons located on the *Home* tab, in the *Alignment* group: **Top Align, Middle Align,** or **Bottom Align.**

These options are also available from the *Format Cells* dialog, *Alignment* tab.

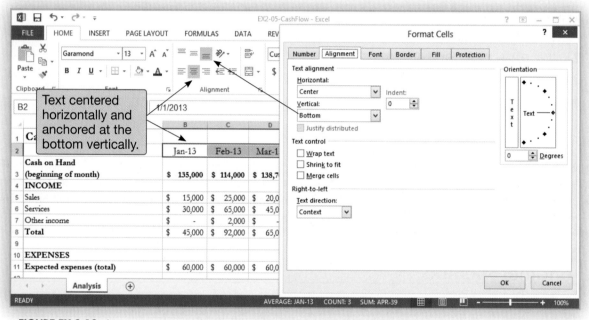

FIGURE EX 2.12

To change alignment using the *Format Cells* dialog:

1. Click the **Alignment Settings Dialog Box Launcher** at the lower right corner of the *Alignment* group.

2. The *Format Cells* dialog opens to the *Alignment* tab.

3. In the *Text alignment* section, expand the **Horizontal** drop-down list and select the option you want.

4. Click **OK.**

You can also change the angle at which the content displays.

❯ On the *Home* tab, in the *Alignment* group, click the **Orientation** button and select one of the options.

❯ From the *Format Cells* dialog, on the *Alignment* tab, in the *Orientation* section, you can change the angle of rotation by clicking one of the dots on the Orientation dial, by clicking and dragging the Orientation dial to the position you want, or by entering the specific degree of rotation in the *Degrees* box.

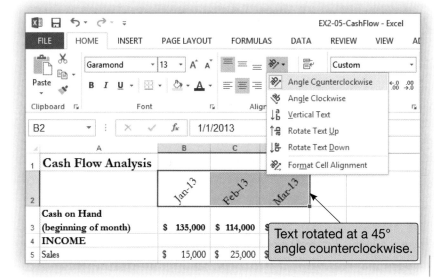

FIGURE EX 2.13

Text rotated at a 45° angle counterclockwise.

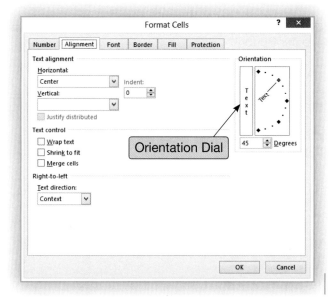

Orientation Dial

FIGURE EX 2.14

tips & tricks

If you have narrow columns of data with descriptive headers, try using one of the orientation options to angle the cells containing the header text.

let me try

Open the student data file **EX2-06-CashFlow** and try this skill on your own:

1. Select cells **B2:D2.**
2. Center the content in each cell horizontally.
3. Center the content in each cell vertically.
4. Change the angle of rotation for these cells to 45°.
5. Save the file as directed by your instructor and close it.

Skill 2.7 Merging Cells and Splitting Merged Cells

Merging cells is one way to control the appearance of your worksheet. You can merge cells to create a header cell across multiple columns of data or center a title across your worksheet. The *Merge & Center* button automatically merges the selected cells and then centers the data from the first cell across the entire merged area. When you merge cells together, Excel will keep only the data in the uppermost left cell. All other data will be lost.

To merge cells and center their content:

1. Select the cells you want to merge, making sure the text you want to keep is in the uppermost left cell.

2. On the *Home* tab, in the *Alignment* group, click the **Merge & Center** button.

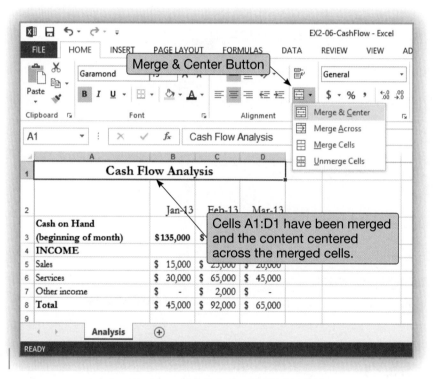

FIGURE EX 2.15

Click the *Merge & Center* button arrow for additional merge commands:

Merge Across—lets you merge cells in multiple rows without merging the rows together. The cells in each row will be merged together, keeping the data in the leftmost cell in each row, but still keeping each row separate.

Merge Cells—lets you merge cells together without centering the data. Like the *Merge & Center* command, *Merge Cells* will combine all the selected cells into one cell, keeping only the data in the uppermost left cell.

Unmerge Cells—splits a merged cell back into its original cells. When the selected cell is a merged cell, clicking the *Merge & Center* button will also undo the merge.

tips & tricks

You cannot really split cells in Excel. You can unmerge a merged cell back into its original cells, but you cannot split a single cell into two new columns or two new rows (like you can with a table in Word or PowerPoint). However, if you have a column of data that you would like to split across multiple cells, you can use the *Text to Columns* command (on the *Data* tab, in the *Data Tools* group).

another method

You can also merge and center cells from the *Format Cells* dialog:

1. On the *Home* tab, in the *Alignment* group, click the **Alignment Settings** Dialog Box Launcher to open the *Format Cells* dialog.
2. On the *Alignment* tab, in the *Text alignment* section, click the **Horizontal** arrow, and select **Center Across Selection** from the drop-down list. (You can also select **Center.** When you merge the cells, it does not matter if the horizontal alignment is *Center Across Selection* or *Center*.)
3. In the *Text control* section, click the **Merge cells** check box.
4. Click **OK.**

To unmerge cells:

1. In the *Format Cells* dialog, on the *Alignment* tab, in the *Text alignment* section, click the **Horizontal** arrow, and select **General** from the drop-down list.
2. In the *Text control* section, click the **Merge cells** check box to uncheck it.
3. Click **OK.**

let me try

Open the student data file **EX2-07-CashFlow** and try this skill on your own:

1. Select cells **A1:D1.**
2. Merge the cells so the text appears centered across the merged cells.
3. Cells **A4:D4** have been merged. Unmerge them.
4. Save the file as directed by your instructor and close it.

Skill 2.8 Applying Bold, Italic, and Underline

You may be familiar with using bold, italic, and underline formatting to emphasize text in a Word document or a PowerPoint presentation. You can use these same techniques in Excel to emphasize cells in your workbook.

To apply bold, italic, and underline formatting:

1. Select a cell or cell range to apply the formatting to all the content in the cell(s). To apply formatting to only part of the content in a cell, double-click the cell to enter Edit mode, and then select the text you want to apply the formatting to.

2. On the *Home* tab, in the *Font* group, click the appropriate button to apply formatting to the selected cell(s).

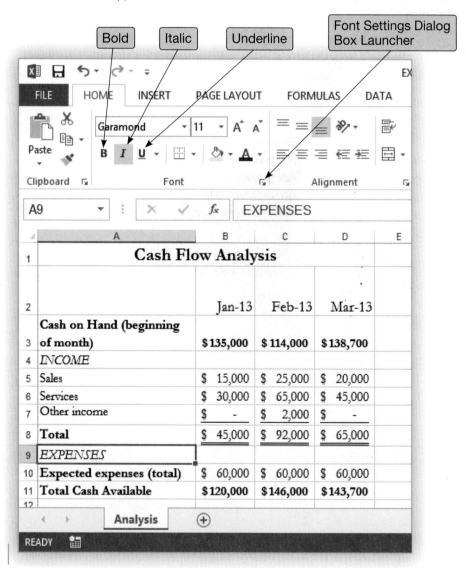

FIGURE EX 2.16

Underline styles used in accounting spreadsheets are slightly different from "regular" underline styles. If you need to apply the accounting style of underline or double underline, do not use the *Underline* button on the Ribbon. Instead, use one of the accounting underline options from the *Format Cells* dialog:

1. On the *Home* tab, in the *Font* group, click the **Font Settings Dialog Box Launcher** to open the *Format Cells* dialog.

2. On the *Font* tab, in the *Underline* section, expand the **Underline** list and select **Single Accounting** or **Double Accounting**.

3. Click **OK**.

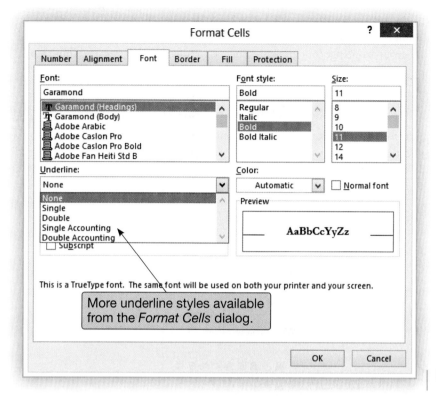

FIGURE EX 2.17

The single and double underline options available when you click the **Underline** button arrow will apply the accounting underline styles only if you recently selected those formats from the *Format Cells* dialog.

tips & tricks

The cell underline formats underline only the content in the cell. The underline does not extend from one edge of the cell to the other. If you want to create an underline that extends across a range of cells without a break in between, use a border instead. (For more information about borders, refer to the skill *Adding Borders*.)

another method

When you right-click a cell, the *Bold* and *Italic* buttons are available on the Mini toolbar.

Bold, italic, and underline font styles are available from the *Format Cells* dialog, *Font* tab.

You can also use the keyboard shortcuts:

❯ Bold: Ctrl + B

❯ Italic: Ctrl + I

❯ Underline: Ctrl + U

let me try

Open the student data file **EX2-08-CashFlow** and try this skill on your own:

1. Apply **Bold** formatting to cells **A3:D3.**

2. Apply the **Single Accounting** underline format to cells **B7:D7.**

3. Apply the **Double Accounting** underline format to cells **B10:D10.**

4. Apply **Italic** formatting to cells **A4** and **A9.**

5. Save the file as directed by your instructor and close it.

Skill 2.9 Changing Fonts, Font Size, and Font Color

A **font,** or typeface, refers to a set of characters of a certain design. The font is the shape of a character or number as it appears on-screen or when printed. Use the commands from the *Home* tab, *Font* group to change font attributes such as font family, font size, and font color.

❱ To change the font, click the **Font** box arrow to expand the list of available fonts, and then select the font you want.

❱ To change the font size, click the **Font Size** box arrow and select the size you want.

❱ To change the font color, click the **Font Color** button arrow to expand the color palette, and then select the color you want.

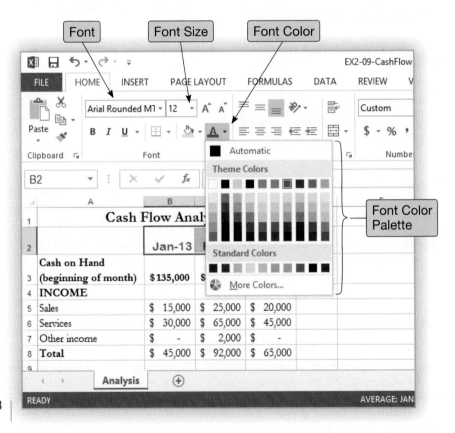

FIGURE EX 2.18

The font color palette is divided into three parts:

1. The top part shows the *Automatic* color choice (black or white, depending on the color of the background).

2. The middle part shows the *Theme Colors* included in the theme that is applied to the workbook. These colors are designed to work together.

3. The bottom part of the palette shows the *Standard Colors* (dark red, red, orange, etc.). These colors are always available, no matter what theme is in use.

tell me **more**

You can pick a custom color by clicking **More Colors**... from the bottom of the font color palette.

another **method**

You can also change the font, font size, or font color by:

❯ Opening the *Format Cells* dialog, clicking the **Font** tab (if necessary), making the font selections you want, and then clicking **OK.**

❯ Right-clicking and making the font, font size, and font color selections you want from the Mini toolbar.

let me **try**

Open the student data file **EX2-09-CashFlow** and try this skill on your own:

1. Select cells **B2:D2.**
2. Change the font to **Arial Rounded MT Bold.** (Bold is part of the font name, not a reference to the font formatting.)
3. Change the font size to **12.**
4. Change the font color to **Blue-Gray, Accent 3** (in the top row of theme colors, the fourth color from the right).
5. Save the file as directed by your instructor and close it.

Skill 2.10 Adding Borders

Add borders to your workbook to emphasize a cell or group of cells. You can use borders to make your workbook look more like a desktop publishing form or to show separation between a column of values and the total row.

To add borders to your workbook:

1. Select the cell(s) you want to add a border to.

2. On the *Home* tab, in the *Font* group, click the **Borders** button arrow and select the border style you want.

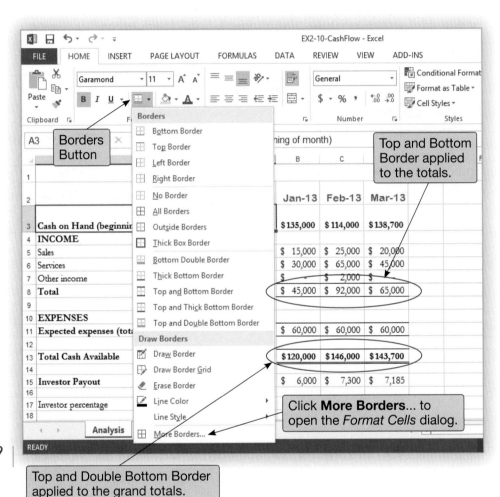

FIGURE EX 2.19

To remove borders:

1. Select the cell(s) you want to remove the borders from.

2. On the *Home* tab, in the *Font* group, click the **Borders** button arrow and select **No Border** from the list of border styles.

For more control over the look of cell borders, select **More Borders...** from the *Borders* menu to open the *Format Cells* dialog. From the *Border* tab, you can specify the line style and color for the border. You can also see a preview of how the border will look.

1. On the *Home* tab, in the *Font* group, click the **Borders** button arrow and select **More Borders...** from the list of border styles.

2. Select a line style from the *Style* section.

3. Expand the **Color** palette and select a color.

4. To add borders around the outside or inside the selected cells, click the appropriate button(s) in the *Presets* section.

5. In the *Border* section, add a border line by clicking the button representing the location of the border or by clicking directly in the area of the preview image where you want the border to appear.

6. Click **OK.**

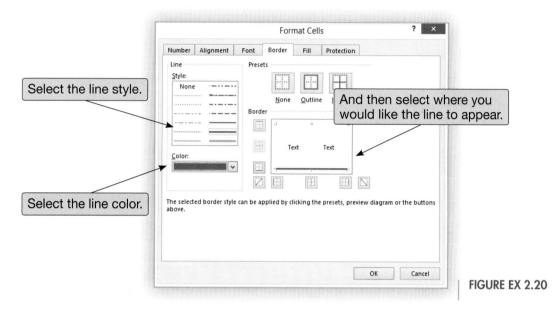

FIGURE EX 2.20

tips & tricks

A properly formatted spreadsheet for accounting purposes should use the cell underline formatting instead of borders on total rows. However, most non-accountant Excel users favor borders above and below total rows instead of using cell underlining.

another method

The *Borders* button displays the most recently used border style. If you want to reuse this style, you can just click the button. You do not need to reselect the border style from the menu again.

The *Borders* button is also available from the Mini toolbar when you right-click a cell.

let me try

Open the student data file **EX2-10-CashFlow** and try this skill on your own:

1. Apply the **Top and Bottom Border** to cells **B8:D8.**

2. Remove the borders from cells **B3:D3.**

3. Add a **Blue-Gray, Accent 3** color, bottom border to cells **B2:D2.** Use the thickest single line style available.

4. Save the file as directed by your instructor and close it.

Skill 2.11 Adding Shading with Fill Color

Another way to emphasize cells in your workbook is to use a **fill color** to change the background color of cells. Fill colors are available in a variety of shades to make it easy to read the cell content. Shading is often used to differentiate alternating rows in a large table or to make the heading row stand out.

To add shading to your workbook:

1. Select the cell(s) you want to add shading to.

2. On the *Home* tab, in the *Font* group, click the **Fill Color** button arrow to display the color palette. The color palette includes colors from the workbook theme as well as a row of standard colors along the bottom. Notice that as you hold the mouse over each color in the palette, a tool tip appears displaying the color name.

3. Click the color you want.

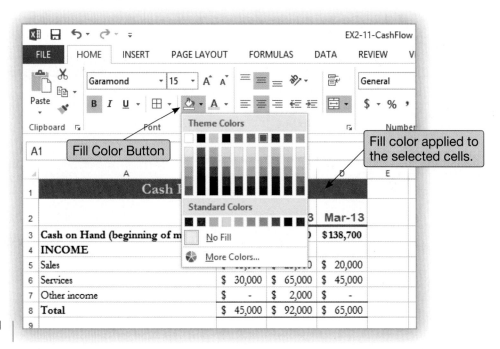

FIGURE EX 2.21

To remove shading:

1. Select the cell(s) you want to remove shading from.

2. On the *Home* tab, in the *Font* group, click the **Fill Color** button arrow to display the color palette.

3. Click **No Fill** to remove the fill color from the selected cells.

tips & tricks

❱ Avoid overusing shading and using too many colors in your workbook. Shading should be used for emphasis and to make the workbook easier to read, not just to make the workbook more colorful.

❱ If you use a dark color for shading, change the font color to white or another light color.

tell me **more**

In the *Format Cells* dialog, options for fill effects and pattern styles are available under the *Fill* tab.

another **method**

Like the *Borders* button, the *Fill Color* button displays the most recently used shading color. If you want to reuse this color, just click the button. You do not need to reselect the color from the Fill Color palette.

The *Fill Color* button is also available from the Mini toolbar when you right-click a cell.

let me **try**

Open the student data file **EX2-11-CashFlow** and try this skill on your own:

1. Add a **Blue-Gray, Accent 3** fill color to cell **A1.** Cells A1:D1 are merged, so you can click anywhere in the merged range to select.

2. Remove the fill color from cell **A17.**

3. Save the file as directed by your instructor and close it.

from the perspective of . . .

HEALTH CLUB OFFICE MANAGER

I use Excel to prepare financial reports for the club owners and their accountant. Proper formatting makes it easier for the owners to read the reports. I would never submit a report without checking for text that appears cut off or titles that aren't centered across columns. And I always use the accounting underline formats instead of borders in my financial reports. Our accountant insists on it!

Skill 2.12 Applying Cell Styles

A **cell style** is a combination of effects that can be applied at one time. Styles can include formatting such as borders, fill color, font size, and number formatting.

Excel includes an extensive gallery of prebuilt cell styles. You can use these styles to help visualize your data by consistently applying them to your worksheet. Use text styles such as *Title* for the title of your worksheet and *Calculation* and *Input* to highlight cells used in formulas. The *Total* style applies borders and font formatting appropriate for a total row in a table.

To apply a cell style:

1. Select the cell or cells you want to apply the style to.
2. On the *Home* tab, in the *Styles* group, click the **Cell Styles** button.
3. Click the style you want to apply to your cells.

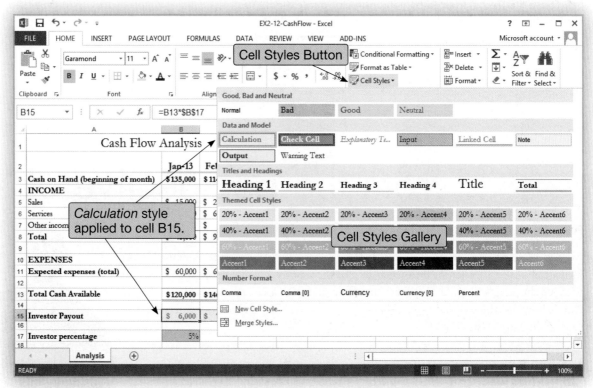

FIGURE EX 2.22

tips & tricks

If you have Live Preview enabled, you can move your mouse over each style in the Cell Styles gallery to see a preview of how that style would look applied to your worksheet.

let me try

Open the student data file **EX2-12-CashFlow** and try this skill on your own:

1. Select cells **A1:D1** (these cells are merged) and apply the **Title** style.
2. Select cells **B13:D13** and apply the **Total** style.
3. Select cells **B15:D15** and apply the **Calculation** style.
4. Select cell **B17** and apply the **Input** style.
5. Save the file as directed by your instructor and close it.

excel 2013   chapter 2 Formatting Cells

Skill 2.13 Using Format Painter

A professional, well-organized workbook uses consistent formatting. Use the **Format Painter** tool to copy formatting from one part of your worksheet to another, rather than trying to recreate the exact combination of font color and size, number formatting, borders, and shading to reuse.

To use *Format Painter:*

1. Select the cell that has the formatting you want to copy.

2. On the *Home* tab, in the *Clipboard* group, click the **Format Painter** button.

3. Click the cell that you want to apply the formatting to. To apply the formatting to a range of cells, click the first cell in the group, hold down the left mouse button, and drag across the cells. Notice that your mouse cursor changes to the *Format Painter* shape. When you reach the last cell in the group, release the mouse button.

4. The formatting is automatically applied to the selected cell(s).

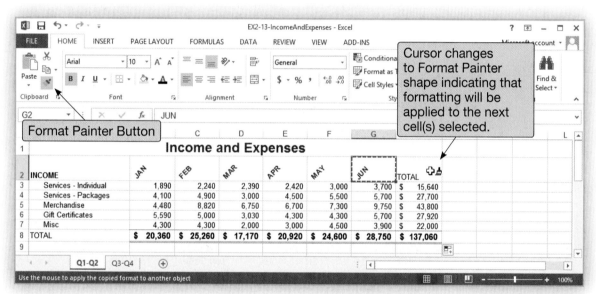

FIGURE EX 2.23

tell me **more**

If you want to apply the formatting to different parts of a worksheet or workbook, double-click the **Format Painter** button when you select it. It will stay on until you click the **Format Painter** button again or press (Esc) to deselect it.

another **method**

To activate *Format Painter,* you can also right-click the cell with formatting you want to copy and click the **Format Painter** button on the Mini toolbar.

let me **try**

Open the student data file **EX2-13-IncomeAndExpenses** and try this skill on your own:

Use **Format Painter** to copy the formatting from cell **G2** and apply it to cell **H2.** Save the file as directed by your instructor and close it.

Skill 2.14 Applying Conditional Formatting Using the Quick Analysis Tool

Conditional formatting provides a visual analysis of data by applying formatting to cells that meet specific criteria (conditions). Excel offers a wide variety of conditional formatting options from the *Conditional Formatting* menu (available on the *Home* tab, in the *Styles* group). However, Excel 2013 offers a new feature from the Quick Analysis tool to quickly apply conditional formatting without opening the menu. The Quick Analysis tool detects whether you've selected numerical or text data and displays only the options appropriate for each type of data. From the Quick Analysis tool, you can also preview conditional formatting before applying it to your data.

To apply conditional formatting with the Quick Analysis tool:

1. Select the cells to which you want to apply conditional formatting.

2. Click the **Quick Analysis** tool button at the lower-right corner of the selection.

3. Notice that Live Preview displays the effect of the conditional formatting on your data as you hover the cursor over each of the formatting options. Review each formatting option before making your selection.

4. Click the button for the type of conditional formatting you want to apply.

5. Some types of conditional formatting apply formatting to all the cells in the selection and are applied automatically when you click the button in the Quick Analysis tool. Other types require a comparison value and will open a dialog where you can specify the value for the rule and select formatting options. Make your selections in the dialog and then click **OK** to apply the conditional formatting.

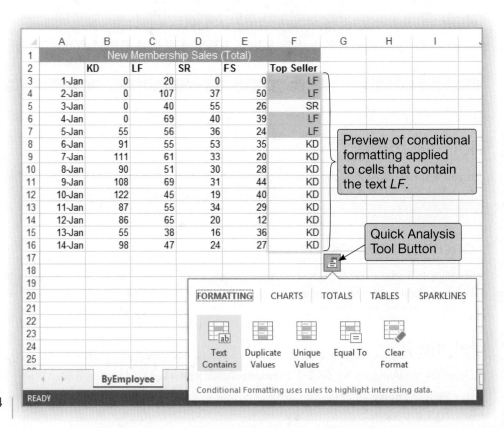

FIGURE EX 2.24

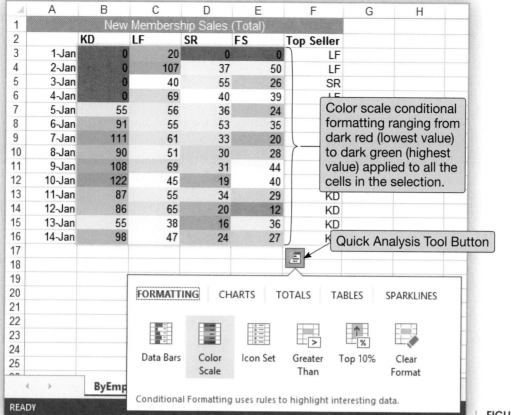

FIGURE EX 2.25

tips & tricks

You should resist the temptation to overuse conditional formatting. Conditional formatting should be used to highlight important data or data trends, not to colorize the entire worksheet.

another method

You can press (Ctrl) + (Q) to open the Quick Analysis tool instead of clicking the *Quick Analysis* tool button.

let me try

Open the student data file **EX2-14-Sales** and try this skill on your own:

1. Use the Quick Analysis tool to apply conditional formatting to cells **F3:F16** to highlight cells containing the text LF. Use the suggested color.

2. Use the Quick Analysis tool to apply conditional formatting to cells **B3:E16** to apply the suggested color scale.

3. Save the file as directed by your instructor and close it.

Skill 2.15 Applying Conditional Formatting with Data Bars, Color Scales, and Icon Sets

Data bars, colors scales, and icon sets can be used to visually represent the value of each cell relative to the other cells in the data selection. These types of conditional formatting apply formatting to all the selected cells.

Data Bars—Display a color bar (gradient or solid) representing the cell value in comparison to other values (cells with higher values have longer data bars).

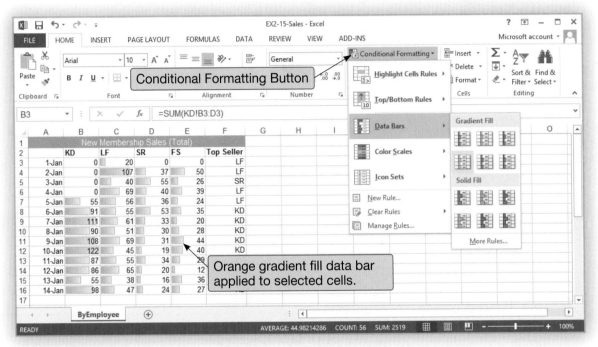

FIGURE EX 2.26

Color Scales—Color the cells according to one of the color scales (e.g., red to green [bad/low to good/high] or blue to red [cold/low to hot/high]).

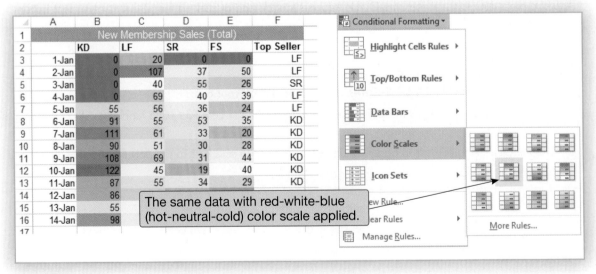

FIGURE EX 2.27

Icon Sets—Display a graphic in the cell representing the cell value in relation to other values.

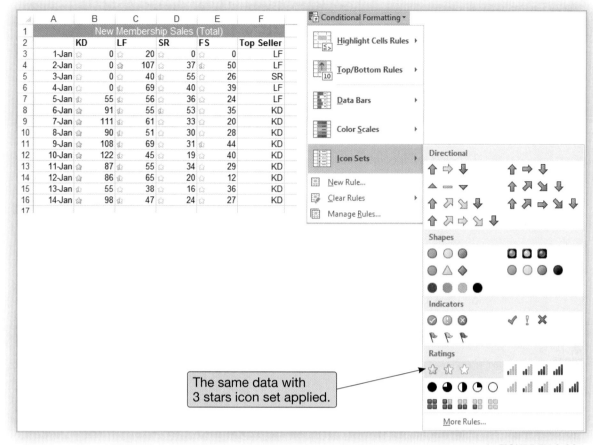

The same data with 3 stars icon set applied.

To apply conditional formatting using data bars, color scales, or icon sets:

1. Select the data you want to apply conditional formatting to.

2. On the *Home* tab, in the *Styles* group, click the **Conditional Formatting** button.

3. From the menu, point to **Data Bars, Colors Scales,** or **Icon Sets,** and then click the specific style of formatting you want. Notice that Live Preview displays the effect of the conditional formatting on your data as you hover the cursor over each of the formatting options.

let me try

Open the student data file **EX2-15-Sales** and try this skill on your own:

Apply conditional formatting to cells **B3:E16** using the orange gradient fill data bar. Save the file as directed by your instructor and close it.

Skill 2.16 Applying Conditional Formatting with Highlight Cells Rules

Conditional formatting with **Highlight Cells Rules** allows you to define formatting for cells that meet specific numerical or text criteria (e.g., greater than a specific value or containing a specific text string). Use this type of conditional formatting when you want to highlight cells based on criteria you define.

To apply *Highlight Cells Rules:*

1. Select the data you want to apply conditional formatting to.
2. On the *Home* tab, in the *Styles* group, click the **Conditional Formatting** button.
3. From the menu, point to **Highlight Cells Rules** and click the option you want.
4. Each option opens a dialog where you can enter a value or date to which the value of each cell will be compared.
5. The default formatting is light red fill with dark red text. To change the formatting, expand the drop-down list in the dialog and select another option.
6. Click **OK** to apply the conditional formatting.

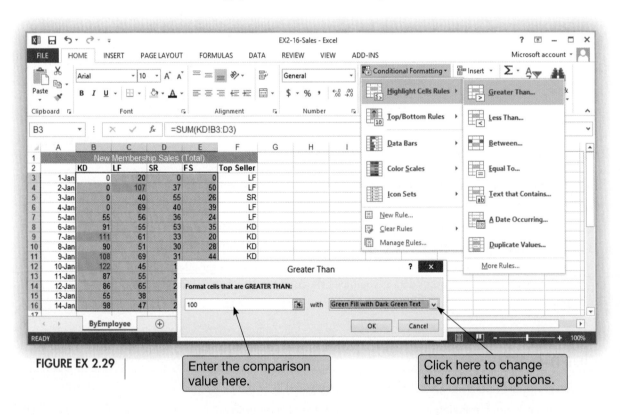

FIGURE EX 2.29

Enter the comparison value here.

Click here to change the formatting options.

tips & tricks

The *Highlight Cells Rules* menu includes an option to highlight duplicate values. This option can be especially helpful when you are trying to find a potential data entry error in a long list of values.

tell me **more**

To highlight unique values (those that are *not* duplicates):

1. Select the data you want to analyze.
2. On the *Home* tab, in the *Styles* group, click the **Conditional Formatting** button.
3. From the menu, point to **Highlight Cells Rules** and click **Duplicate Values...**
4. In the *Duplicate Values* dialog, expand the drop-down box and select **Unique.**
5. Click **OK.**

let me **try**

Open the student data file **EX2-16-Sales** and try this skill on your own:

Apply conditional formatting to cells **B3:E16** so cells with a value greater than 100 are formatted using a green fill with dark green text. Save the file as directed by your instructor and close it.

from the perspective of . . .

HELP DESK COORDINATOR

I love conditional formatting! Every week, each department sends me a spreadsheet of all the help desk calls for each software package we support. I use color scales to identify the software packages with the highest volume of calls. In my spreadsheet that combines the weekly data, I use icon sets to indicate whether the number of calls went up or down for each software package on a week-by-week basis.

Skill 2.17 Applying Conditional Formatting with Top/Bottom Rules

One way to analyze worksheet data is to compare cell values to other cell values. When analyzing a worksheet, you may want to highlight the highest or lowest values or values that are above or below the average. In these cases, use conditional formatting **Top/Bottom Rules**. When you use *Top/Bottom Rules,* Excel automatically finds the highest, lowest, and average values to compare values to, rather than asking you to enter criteria (as you do when using *Highlight Cells Rules*).

To highlight cells with conditional formatting *Top/Bottom Rules:*

1. Select the data you want to apply conditional formatting to.

2. On the *Home* tab, in the *Styles* group, click the **Conditional Formatting** button.

3. From the menu, point to **Top/Bottom Rules** and click the option you want.

4. Each option opens a dialog where you can select the formatting to apply when cells meet the condition. The top and bottom options allow you to modify the threshold to a value other than 10 (top/bottom 10 items and top/bottom 10%).

5. Click **OK** to apply the conditional formatting.

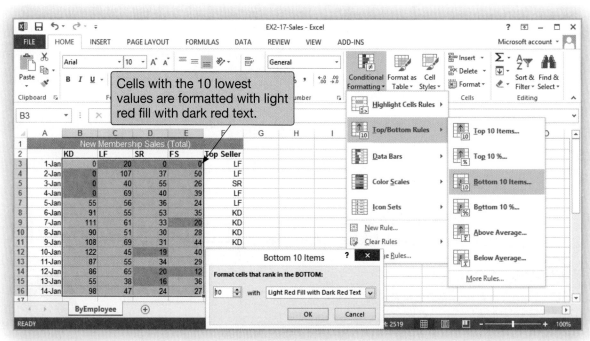

FIGURE EX 2.30

let me try

Open the student data file **EX2-17-Sales** and try this skill on your own:

Apply conditional formatting to cells **B3:E16** so cells with the 10 lowest values are formatted with light red fill and dark red text. Save the file as directed by your instructor and close it.

Skill 2.18 Removing Conditional Formatting

You cannot remove conditional formatting from cells by clearing the data or pressing `Delete` or `← Backspace`. Instead, you must remove the conditional formatting rule from the cells.

To remove conditional formatting:

1. If appropriate, select the cells from which you want to remove conditional formatting.

2. On the *Home* tab, in the *Styles* group, click the **Conditional Formatting** button.

3. Point to **Clear Rules,** and click the option you want from the menu:

   Clear Rules from Selected Cells

   Clear Rules from Entire Sheet

   Clear Rules from This Table (available if the selected cells are part of a table)

   Clear Rules from This PivotTable (available if the selected cells are part of a PivotTable)

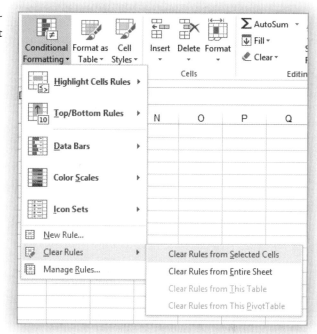

FIGURE EX 2.31

tell me **more**

Through the Conditional Formatting Rules Manager, you can view all of your conditional formatting rules at one time and add, modify, or delete rules. Open the Conditional Formatting Rules Manager from the *Manage Rules...* option at the bottom of the *Conditional Formatting* menu.

another **method**

You can also clear conditional formatting from the Quick Analysis tool:

1. Select the cells from which you want to remove conditional formatting.

2. Click the **Quick Analysis** tool button at the lower-right corner of the selection, and click the **Clear Format** button.

let me **try**

Open the student data file **EX2-18-Sales** and try this skill on your own:

Clear the conditional formatting from cells **F3:F16** without clearing conditional formatting from the rest of the worksheet. Save the file as directed by your instructor and close it.

Skill 2.19 Clearing Cell Content

To remove the contents of a cell without removing the cell from the structure of your workbook, use one of the *Clear* commands. In Excel, when you clear a cell, you remove its contents, formats, comments, and hyperlinks, but the blank cell remains in the worksheet. Clearing a cell does not affect the layout of your worksheet.

To clear a cell:

1. Select the cell you want to clear of formats or contents.
2. On the *Home* tab, in the *Editing* group, click the **Clear** button.
3. Click the command for the type of formatting or contents you want to remove from the cell.

   Clear All—clears all cell contents and formatting and deletes any comments or hyperlinks attached to the cell.

   Clear Formats—clears only the cell formatting and leaves the cell contents, comments, and hyperlinks. The *Clear Formats* command does not remove conditional formatting rules from the cell.

   Clear Contents—clears only the contents (including hyperlinks) and leaves the cell formatting and comments.

   Clear Comments—deletes any comments attached to the cell while leaving the cell contents, formatting, and hyperlinks intact.

   Clear Hyperlinks—removes the hyperlink action from the cell without removing the content or the hyperlink style of formatting.

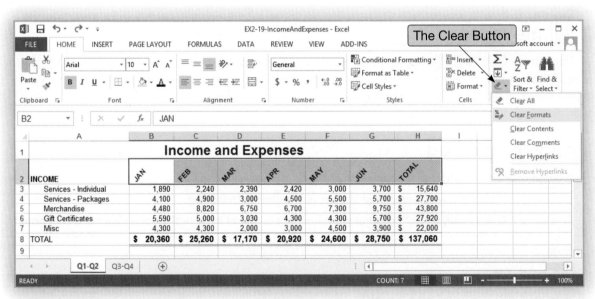

FIGURE EX 2.32

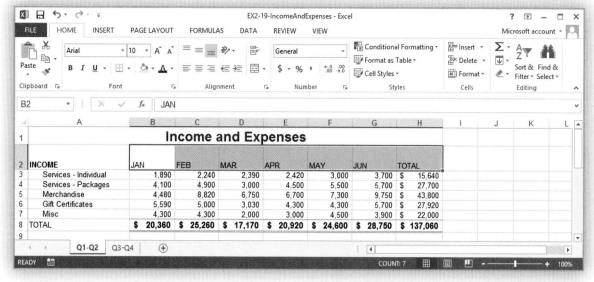

FIGURE EX 2.33
Results after Clearing
Formatting Only

another **method**

To clear the contents of a cell, you can

❯ Right-click the cell and select **Clear Contents** from the menu. Using the right-click method, there are no options to clear formats or comments.

❯ Select the cell and then press (Delete) or (← Backspace) to clear the cell contents but not the cell formatting.

let me **try**

Open the student data file **EX2-19-IncomeAndExpenses** and try this skill on your own:

1. Clear only the formatting from cells **B2:H2** (leaving the content).
2. Clear only the content from cells **B8:H8** (leaving the formatting).
3. Use a single command to clear everything (content and formatting) from cells **B10:H10**.
4. Save the file as directed by your instructor and close it.

Skill 2.20 Using Find and Replace

All of the Microsoft Office applications include **Find** and **Replace** commands that allow you to search for and replace data in your file. In Excel, these commands can be used to find and replace not only text but also numbers in values and formulas in a single worksheet or across an entire workbook.

Before using the *Replace* command, you should use *Find* to make sure the data you are about to replace are what you expect:

1. On the *Home* tab, in the *Editing* group at the far right side of the Ribbon, click the **Find & Select** button.
2. From the *Find & Select* menu, click **Find...**
3. The *Find and Replace* dialog opens, with the *Find* tab on top.
4. Type the word, phrase, or number you want to find in the *Find what* box.
   a. To go to just the first instance, click the **Find Next** button.
   b. To find all instances, click the **Find All** button. When you click *Find All,* Excel displays a list detailing every instance of the data—workbook file name, worksheet name, cell name, cell address, the value of the cell, and the formula (if there is one).

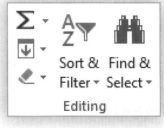

FIGURE EX 2.34

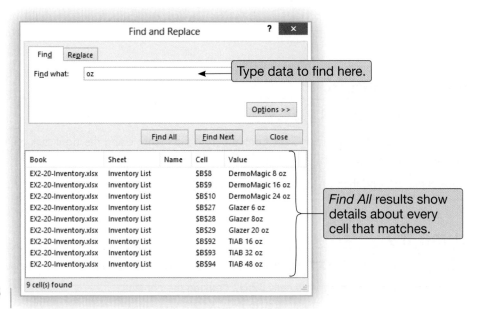

FIGURE EX 2.35

Once you have verified the data you want to replace, switch to the *Replace* tab in the *Find and Replace* dialog:

1. Click the **Replace** tab.
2. Excel keeps the data you typed in the *Find what* box.
3. Now type the replacement text or values in the *Replace with* box.
   a. Click the **Replace** button to replace one instance of the data at a time.
   b. Click the **Replace All** button to replace all instances at once.
4. If you select *Replace All,* Excel displays a message telling you how many replacements were made. Click **OK** to dismiss the message. The results now display details about every cell that was updated with the *Replace* command.
5. Click **Close** to close the *Find and Replace* dialog.

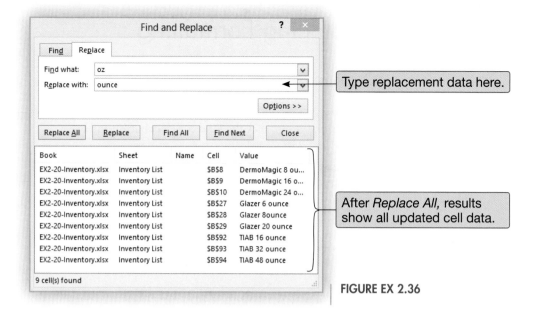

Type replacement data here.

After *Replace All,* results show all updated cell data.

FIGURE EX 2.36

tell me **more**

By default, Excel searches for the data both in cell values and within formulas. If you want to limit the search to only cell values, first click the **Options>>** button in the *Find and Replace* dialog to display the find and replace optional settings. Next, expand the *Look in* list by clicking the arrow, and select **Values.**

another **method**

Use the keyboard shortcut (Ctrl) + (F) to open the *Find and Replace* dialog with the *Find* tab on top.

Use the keyboard shortcut (Ctrl) + (H) to open the *Find and Replace* dialog with the *Replace* tab on top.

let me **try**

Open the student data file **EX2-20-Inventory** and try this skill on your own:

1. Find all instances of the word **oz.**
2. Replace all instances of the word **oz** with **ounce.**
3. Save the file as directed by your instructor and close it.

Skill 2.21 Replacing Formatting

The *Find* and *Replace* commands allow you to find and replace formatting as well as data. This feature is especially helpful when replacing number formats throughout a workbook.

To find and replace formatting:

1. On the *Home* tab, in the *Editing* group, click the **Find & Select** button and select **Replace...** to open the *Find and Replace* dialog.

2. If necessary, click the **Options>>** button to display the find and replace optional settings. Notice that next to the *Find what* and *Replace with* boxes, the preview box displays *No Format Set.*

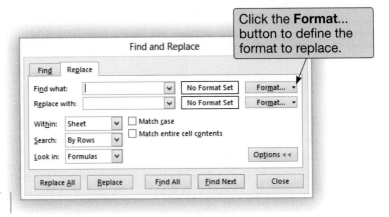

> Click the **Format...** button to define the format to replace.

FIGURE EX 2.37

3. If you want to find specific data, enter it in the *Find what* box. If you do not enter anything, Excel will find all cells with the formatting defined in the next step.

4. Click the **Format...** button next to the *Find what* box to open the *Find Format* dialog where you can define the formatting you want to find. The *Find Format* dialog includes all the tabs and formatting options available in the *Format Cells* dialog. Set the formatting to find just as you would set formatting to apply to cells.

   a. To find all cells formatted using the Accounting Number Format, click the **Number** tab and select **Accounting** in the *Category* list.

   b. Click **OK.**

> Use the *Find Format* dialog to define the format to replace.

FIGURE EX 2.38

5. The preview box now displays the word *Preview* using the formatting you defined. If you included number formatting, *Preview* will appear with an * after it (because the word *Preview* cannot display number formatting).

6. If you want to replace data as well as formatting, enter the replacement data in the *Replace with* box. If you do not enter anything, Excel will modify the formatting and leave the data in each cell unchanged.

7. Click the **Format...** button next to the *Replace with* box and repeat the same process to define the new format you want to use.

   a. To replace the Accounting Number Format with the Currency number format, click the **Number** tab again (if necessary) and select **Currency** in the *Category* list.

   b. You can also change options for the format such as expanding the **Symbol** list and selecting **None** to remove the $ from the format.

   c. Click **OK.**

8. Click **Replace All.**

9. Click **OK** in the message that appears.

10. Click **Close** to close the *Find and Replace* dialog.

another **method**

You can also define the formatting styles to find and replace by picking cells that are already formatted with those attributes.

1. In the *Find and Replace* dialog, click the **Format button arrow** next to the *Find what* box and select **Choose Format from Cell...**

2. The cursor changes to a picker shape ⊹🖋.

3. Click a cell with the formatting attributes you want to find.

4. Click the **Format button arrow** next to the *Replace with* box and select **Choose Format from Cell...**

5. Click a cell with the formatting attributes you want to apply.

6. Click **Replace All.**

7. Click **OK.**

8. Click **Close** to close the *Find & Replace* dialog.

let me **try**

Open the student data file **EX2-21-Inventory** and try this skill on your own:

Using the *Replace* command, find and replace all cells formatted with the Accounting Number Format with the Currency format with no currency symbol. Save the file as directed by your instructor and close it.

Skill 2.22 Setting and Clearing the Print Area

If you do not want to print your entire worksheet, you can set a print area. The **print area** is a range of cells that you designate as the default print selection. If you have defined a print area for your worksheet, it will be the only part of the worksheet that prints.

To set a print area:

1. Select the area you want to print.
2. On the *Page Layout* tab, in the *Page Setup* group, click the **Print Area** button.
3. Click **Set Print Area.**

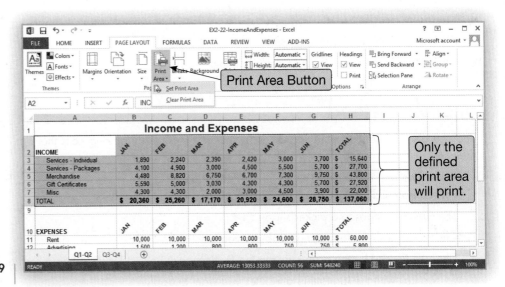

FIGURE EX 2.39

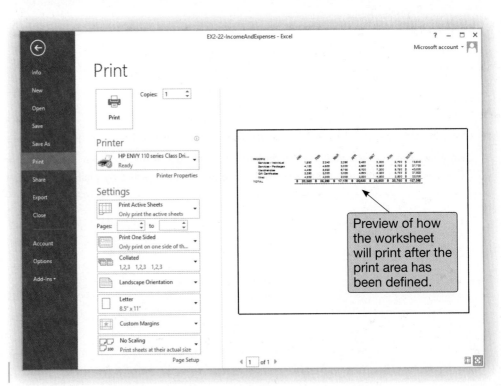

FIGURE EX 2.40

excel 2013   chapter 2 Formatting Cells

When you save the worksheet, the print area is saved as well. To clear a print area:

1. On the *Page Layout* tab, in the *Page Setup* group, click the **Print Area** button.

2. Click **Clear Print Area.**

tips & tricks

Notice that when the print area is selected, the Name box to the left of the address bar displays *Print_Area*. When you define a print area, Excel automatically creates a named range called *Print_Area*.

tell me **more**

You can define more than one print area per worksheet. Select the cells you want in the first print area, and then press (Ctrl) and drag the mouse to select the range of cells for the second print area. Each print area will print on a separate page.

let me try

Open the student data file **EX2-22-IncomeAndExpenses** and try this skill on your own:

1. Preview how the worksheet will look when printed. Notice that a print area has been set to print cells **A2:D19** only.

2. Clear the current print area.

3. Modify the workbook so only the *Income* section of the *Q1-Q2* worksheet (**A2:H8**) will print.

4. Preview how the worksheet will look when printed after the new print area has been set.

5. Save the file as directed by your instructor and close it.

key terms

Cut

Copy

Paste

Undo

Redo

Alignment

General horizontal alignment

Font

Fill color

Cell style

Format Painter

Conditional formatting

Data bars

Color scales

Icon sets

Highlight Cells Rules

Top/Bottom Rules

Find

Replace

Print area

concepts review

1. When you cut and paste a cell containing a formula with relative references, Excel

    a. updates the cell references to the new location.

    b. does not update the cell references to the new location.

    c. treats the formulas as if it contained absolute references.

    d. b and c

2. Which paste option pastes formulas and number formatting but none of the cell formatting?

    a. Values

    b. Formulas

    c. Formulas & Number Formatting

    d. Keep Source Formatting

3. To split a cell into two cells:

    a. On the *Home* tab, in the *Alignment* group, click the **Merge & Center** button and select **Unmerge Cells.**

    b. In the *Format Cells* dialog, on the *Alignment* tab, in the *Text Control* section, click the **Merge cells** box to uncheck it.

    c. On the *Data* tab, in the *Data Tools* group, click the **Text to Columns** button.

    d. You cannot split a cell into two cells; you can only unmerge merged cells.

4. To apply the Double Underline accounting underline format:

    a. Press Ctrl + U.

    b. In the *Font* dialog, on the *Font* tab, expand the **Underline** list and select **Double Accounting.**

    c. On the *Home* tab, in the *Font* group, click the **Underline** button.

    d. On the *Home* tab, in the *Font* group, click the **Underline button arrow** and select **Double Underline.**

5. Clicking the *Borders* button on the Ribbon applies which border style?

    a. None

    b. Outline

    c. Bottom border only

    d. The most recently used border style

6. The keyboard shortcut to open the Quick Analysis tool is

    a. Ctrl + A.

    b. Ctrl + Q.

    c. F7.

    d. F10.

7. To highlight cells with values in the top 10% of the select range, use _____ conditional formatting.

    a. Data bars

    b. Highlight Cells Rules

    c. Top/Bottom Rules

    d. Icon sets

8. You can remove conditional formatting using the

    a. *Clear All* command.

    b. Ctrl + X keyboard shortcut.

    c. Delete key.

    d. *Clear Rules from Selected Cells* command.

9. Selecting a cell and pressing Delete clears

    a. cell content only.

    b. cell content and formatting.

    c. cell content, formatting, and formulas.

    d. cell formatting only.

10. Where is the *Set Print Area* command located?

    a. On the *Page Layout* tab, in the *Page Setup* group

    b. In the *Page Layout* dialog

    c. In the *Print* dialog

    d. On the *Home* tab, in the *Print* group

projects

Data files for projects can be found on
www.mhhe.com/office2013skills

skill review 2.1

In this project you will add formatting to a daily vitamin and supplement plan to make the spreadsheet more attractive and easier to read. Throughout the project, use the *Undo* command (Ctrl + Z) if you make a mistake.

Skills needed to complete this project:

- Using Undo and Redo (Skill 2.3)
- Merging Cells and Splitting Merged Cells (Skill 2.7)
- Applying Cell Styles (Skill 2.12)
- Inserting and Deleting Cells (Skill 2.5)
- Aligning Cells (Skill 2.6)
- Changing Fonts, Font Size, and Font Color (Skill 2.9)
- Using Format Painter (Skill 2.13)
- Adding Borders (Skill 2.10)
- Cutting, Copying, and Pasting Cells (Skill 2.1)
- Wrapping Text in Cells (Skill 2.4)
- Applying Conditional Formatting Using the Quick Analysis Tool (Skill 2.14)
- Applying Conditional Formatting with Data Bars, Color Scales, and Icon Sets (Skill 2.15)
- Applying Conditional Formatting with Highlight Cells Rules (Skill 2.16)
- Removing Conditional Formatting (Skill 2.18)
- Applying Conditional Formatting with Top/Bottom Rules (Skill 2.17)
- Replacing Formatting (Skill 2.21)

1. Open the start file **EX2013-SkillReview-2-1** and resave the file as:
   [your initials]EX-SkillReview-2-1

2. If the workbook opens in Protected View, click the **Enable Editing** button in the Message Bar at the top of the workbook so you can modify the workbook.

3. Merge and center the worksheet title across cells **A1:H1.**

   a. Select cells **A1:H1.**

   b. On the *Home* tab, in the *Alignment* group, click the **Merge & Center** button.

4. Apply the **Title** style to the worksheet title.

   a. If necessary, select the merged cells **A1:H1.**

   b. On the *Home* tab, in the *Styles* group, click the **Cell Styles** button.

   c. Click the **Title** style.

5. There are extra cells to the left of the patient name and total cost. Delete them.

   a. Select cells **B2:B3.**

   b. On the *Home* tab, in the *Cells* group, click the **Delete** button.

6. The patient name would look better aligned at the right side of the cell.

   a. Select cell **B2.**

   b. On the *Home* tab, in the *Alignment* group, click the **Align Right** button.

7. Format the **Patient Name** and **Daily Cost** labels with bolding and the **Blue-Gray, Text 2** font color.

   a. Select cells **A2:A3.**

   b. On the *Home* tab, in the *Font* group, click the **Bold** button.

   c. On the *Home* tab, in the *Font* group, click the **Font Color** button arrow, and select the **Blue-Gray, Text 2** color from the first row of the theme colors.

8. Use *Format Painter* to apply the label formatting to the data table header row (cells **A5:H5**).

   a. If necessary, click cell **A2** or **A3.**

   b. On the *Home* tab, in the *Clipboard* group, click the **Format Painter** button.

   c. Click cell **A5** and drag to cell **H5** to apply the formatting.

9. Add a border beneath the data table header row to separate the titles from the data. The border should be the same color as the font.

   a. If necessary, select cells **A5:H5.**

   b. On the *Home* tab, in the *Font* group, click the **Borders** button arrow, and select **More Borders...**

   c. In the *Format Cells* dialog, on the *Border* tab, expand the **Color** palette, and select the **Blue-Gray, Text 2** color from the first row of the theme colors.

   d. Click the bottom border area of the preview diagram to add the border.

   e. Click **OK.**

10. The data in row 13 are misplaced and belong in the data table. Cut it and insert the cut cells above row 8.

   a. Select cells **A13:H13.**

   b. On the *Home* tab, in the *Clipboard* group, click the **Cut** button.

   c. Click cell **A8.**

   d. On the *Home* tab, in the *Cells* group, click the **Insert** button arrow, and select **Insert Cut Cells.**

11. Apply the *Note* cell style to the note in cell **A12.**

   a. Select cell **A12.**

   b. On the *Home* tab, in the *Styles* group, click the **Cell Styles** button.

   c. Click the **Note** style.

12. The note text is much longer than the width of cell A12, and it looks odd with the cell style applied. Apply text wrapping so all the text is visible within the cell formatted with the *Note* style.

   a. If necessary, select cell **A12.**

   b. On the *Home* tab, in the *Alignment* group, click the **Wrap Text** button.

13. Apply conditional formatting using solid blue data bars to cells **H6:H10** to represent the relative daily cost of each supplement.

   a. Select cells **H6:H10.**

   b. Click the **Quick Analysis** tool button.

   c. Click the **Data Bars** button.

14. Apply conditional formatting using **Highlight Cells Rules** to the cost per bottle data (cells **F6:F10**) to format cells with a value greater than 20 with light red fill with dark red text.

    a. Select cells **F6:F10.**

    b. On the *Home* tab, in the *Styles* group, click the **Conditional Formatting** button.

    c. Point to **Highlight Cells Rules,** and select **Greater Than...**

    d. In the *Greater Than* dialog, type 20 in the *Format cells that are GREATER THAN* box.

    e. Click **OK.**

15. There might be too much conditional formatting in this worksheet. Remove the conditional formatting from cells **G6:G10.**

    a. Select cells **G6:G10.**

    b. On the *Home* tab, in the *Styles* group, click the **Conditional Formatting** button.

    c. Point to **Clear Rules,** and select **Clear Rules from Selected Cells.**

16. You would still like to highlight the least expensive cost per pill. Apply conditional formatting to cells **G6:G10** using **Top/Bottom Rules** to format only the lowest value with green fill with dark green text.

    a. If necessary, select cells **G6:G10.**

    b. On the *Home* tab, in the *Styles* group, click the **Conditional Formatting** button.

    c. Point to **Top/Bottom Rules,** and select **Bottom 10 Items...**

    d. In the *Bottom 10 Items* dialog, type 1 in the *Format cells that rank in the BOTTOM* box.

    e. Expand the formatting list and select **Green Fill with Dark Green Text.**

    f. Click **OK.**

17. Click cell **G11** so the cost per pill data is no longer selected.

18. Find all of the values that use the Accounting Number Format with four digits after the decimal and change the formatting to the Accounting Number Format with two digits after the decimal.

    a. On the *Home* tab, in the *Editing* group, click the **Find & Select** button, and select **Replace...**

    b. In the *Find and Replace* dialog, ensure that there are no values in the *Find what* and *Replace with* boxes.

    c. If necessary, click the **Options>>** button to display the find and replace options.

    d. Click the **Format...** button next to the *Find What* box.

    e. In the *Find Format* dialog, on the *Number* tab, click **Accounting** in the *Category* list. If necessary, change the *Decimal places* value to **4.** Verify that the *Symbol* value is $.

    f. Click **OK.**

    g. Click the **Format...** button next to the Replace with box.

    h. In the *Replace Format* dialog, on the *Number* tab, click **Accounting** in the *Category* list. If necessary, change the *Decimal places* value to **2.** Verify that the *Symbol* value is **$.**

    i. Click **OK.**

    j. Click **Replace All.**

    k. Click **OK.**

    l. Click **Close.**

19. Save and close the workbook.

You want to share your recipe for Greek yogurt with friends, but the spreadsheet is a little rough. Use the formatting skills you learned in this chapter to make the recipe look as good as it tastes.

Throughout the project, use the *Undo* command (Ctrl + Z) if you make a mistake.

Skills needed to complete this project:

- Using Undo and Redo (Skill 2.3)
- Merging Cells and Splitting Merged Cells (Skill 2.7)
- Applying Cell Styles (Skill 2.12)
- Inserting and Deleting Cells (Skill 2.5)
- Using Format Painter (Skill 2.13)
- Changing Fonts, Font Size, and Font Color (Skill 2.9)
- Applying Bold, Italic, and Underline (Skill 2.8)
- Adding Borders (Skill 2.10)
- Using Find and Replace (Skill 2.20)
- Cutting, Copying, and Pasting Cells (Skill 2.1)
- Using Paste Options (Skill 2.2)
- Setting and Clearing the Print Area (Skill 2.22)

1. Open the start file **EX2013-SkillReview-2-2** and resave the file as:
   `[your initials]EX-SkillReview-2-2`

2. Center and merge the recipe title across cells **A1:D1.**

   a. Select cells **A1:D1.**

   b. On the *Home* tab, in the *Alignment* group, click the **Merge & Center** button.

3. Format the title using the **Accent 6** themed cell style.

   a. If necessary, select the merged cells **A1:D1.**

   b. On the *Home* tab, in the *Styles* group, click the **Cell Styles** button.

   c. In the *Themed Cell Styles* section of the gallery, click the **Accent 6** style.

4. Delete cell **B2,** shifting other cells to the left.

   a. Select cell **B2.**

   b. On the *Home* tab, in the *Cells* group, click the **Delete** button arrow and select **Delete Cells...**

   c. Click the **Shift cells left** radio button.

   d. Click **OK.**

5. Use *Format Painter* to copy formatting from the title and apply it to the Ingredients (**A5**) and Directions (**A10**) headers.

   a. Select the merged cells **A1:D1.**

   b. On the *Home* tab, in the *Clipboard* group, double-click the **Format Painter** button.

   c. Click cell **A5.** Notice that *Format Painter* merged cells **A5:D5** and centered the text across the merged cells.

   d. Click cell **A10.** Notice that *Format Painter* merged cells **A5:D5** and centered the text across the merged cells.

   e. On the *Home* tab, in the *Clipboard* group, click the **Format Painter** button again to disable it.

6. The worksheet title should be more prominent than the section headers. Increase the font size to **14** and bold the text.

    a. Select the merged cells **A1:D1.**

    b. On the *Home* tab, in the *Font* group, click the **Font Size** button arrow, and select **14.**

    c. On the *Home* tab, in the *Font* group, click the **Bold** button.

7. Add a bottom border to cells **B6:D6** to separate the headings from the data.

    a. Select cells **B6:D6.**

    b. On the *Home* tab, in the *Font* group, click the **Borders** button arrow and select **Bottom Border.**

8. This recipe is better using organic whole milk. Find and replace all instances of **non fat** with **organic whole.**

    a. On the *Home* tab, in the *Editing* group, click the **Find & Select** button and select **Replace...**

    b. If necessary, display the find and replace options and clear any formats.

        i. Click the **Options>>** button.

        ii. If the button next to the *Find what* box does not display *No Format Set,* click the **Format** button arrow and select **Clear Find Format.**

        iii. If the button next to the *Replace with* box does not display *Not Format Set,* click the **Format** button arrow and select **Clear Replace Format.**

        iv. Click the **Options<<** button to hide the find and replace options.

    c. Type non fat in the *Find what* box.

    d. Type organic whole in the *Replace with* box.

    e. Click the **Replace All** button.

    f. Click **OK.**

    g. Click **Close.**

9. Apply a thick box border around the entire recipe (cells A1:D20).

    a. Select cells **A1:D20.**

    b. On the *Home* tab, in the *Font* group, click the **Borders** button arrow and select **Thick Box Border.**

10. Now that your recipe is formatted, make a copy of it and change the number of servings to **10.** Be sure to retain formulas and column widths.

    a. If necessary, select cells **A1:D20.**

    b. On the *Home* tab, in the *Clipboard* group, click the **Copy** button.

    c. Click cell **F1.**

    d. On the H*ome* tab, in the *Clipboard* group, click the **Paste** button arrow.

    e. Select **Keep Source Column Widths.**

11. Change the value in cell **G2** to **10.**

12. Set the print area so only the original version of the recipe will print. Be sure to preview the printed worksheet.

    a. Select cells **A1:D20.**

    b. On the *Page Layout* tab, it the *Page Setup* group, click the **Print Area** button and select **Set Print Area.**

    c. Click the **File** tab.

    d. Click **Print.**

13. Save and close the workbook.

challenge yourself **2.3**

In this project, you will format a blood pressure report to make it look less like a spreadsheet and more like a form. You will use conditional formatting to highlight important data. Throughout the project, use the *Undo* command ((Ctrl) + (Z)) if you make a mistake.

Skills needed to complete this project:

- Using Undo and Redo (Skill 2.3)
- Adding Shading with Fill Color (Skill 2.11)
- Merging Cells and Splitting Merged Cells (Skill 2.7)
- Applying Cell Styles (Skill 2.12)
- Changing Fonts, Font Size, and Font Color (Skill 2.9)
- Aligning Cells (Skill 2.6)
- Adding Borders (Skill 2.10)
- Using Format Painter (Skill 2.13)
- Applying Bold, Italic, and Underline (Skill 2.8)
- Applying Conditional Formatting with Data Bars, Color Scales, and Icon Sets (Skill 2.15)
- Applying Conditional Formatting with Top/Bottom Rules (Skill 2.17)
- Setting and Clearing the Print Area (Skill 2.22)

1. Open the start file **EX2013-ChallengeYourself-2-3** and resave the file as:
   `[your initials]EX-ChallengeYourself-2-3`
2. If the workbook opens in Protected View, enable editing so you can make changes to the workbook.
3. Select cells **A1:F27** and apply the white fill color.
4. Merge and center the title across cells **A1:F1.**
5. Apply the **Title** cell style to the merged cells.
6. Apply the **Indigo, Accent 6, Lighter 40%** fill color to the merged cells.
7. Change the font color to white.
8. Merge cells **C3:D3** and right align the content in the cell.
9. Apply outside borders to the merged cells.
10. Apply the **20%-Accent 2** cell style to cells **C5:D5.**
11. Apply the same formatting to cells **C8:D8.**
12. Apply outside borders to cells **C5:D6** and cells **C8:D9.**
13. Bold cells **B3, B6, B9,** and B11.
14. Merge cells **C11:D11** and right align the content in the cell.
15. Add outside borders to the merged cells.
16. Apply the **Indigo, Accent 6, Lighter 60%** fill color to cells **A13:F13.**
17. Left align the content in cells **A14:A27.**
18. Add all borders to cells **A14:F27.**
19. Add conditional formatting to cells **E14:E27** using the **3 Arrows (Gray)** icon set.
20. Add conditional formatting to cells **C14:C27** to format values greater than 139 with light red fill with dark red text.
21. Add conditional formatting to cells **C14:C27** to format values between 120 and 139 with yellow fill with dark yellow text.

22. Add conditional formatting to cells **D14:D27** to format values greater than 89 with light red fill with dark red text.

23. Add conditional formatting to cells **D14:D27** to format values between 80 and 89 with yellow fill with dark yellow text.

24. Add a thick box border around cells **A1:F27**.

25. Set cells **A1:F27** as the print area.

26. Preview how the worksheet will look when printed.

27. Save and close the workbook.

challenge yourself **2.4**

In this project you will add formatting to a college budget spreadsheet and rearrange items that are in the wrong categories.

Skills needed to complete this project:
- Using Undo and Redo (Skill 2.3)
- Merging Cells and Splitting Merged Cells (Skill 2.7)
- Applying Cell Styles (Skill 2.12)
- Adding Shading with Fill Color (Skill 2.11)
- Applying Bold, Italic, and Underline (Skill 2.8)
- Cutting, Copying, and Pasting Cells (Skill 2.1)
- Using Paste Options (Skill 2.2)
- Inserting and Deleting Cells (Skill 2.5)
- Using Format Painter (Skill 2.13)
- Applying Conditional Formatting with Data Bars, Color Scales, and Icon Sets (Skill 2.15)
- Wrapping Text in Cells (Skill 2.7)
- Adding Borders (Skill 2.10)

1. Open the start file **EX2013-ChallengeYourself-2-4** and resave the file as: **[your initials]EX-ChallengeYourself-2-4**

2. If the workbook opens in Protected View, enable editing so you can make changes to the workbook.

3. Center and merge the title across cells **B1:F1.**

4. Apply the **Heading 1** cell style to the merged cells.

5. Merge and center the four section titles across the appropriate cells (**Monthly Income, Discretionary Income, Monthly Expenses,** and **Semester Expenses**).

6. Apply cell styles to the section titles as follows:
   a. Monthly Income—**Accent5**
   b. Discretionary Income—**Accent4**
   c. Monthly Expenses—**Accent1**
   d. Semester Expenses—**Accent6**

7. Add the **Brown, Accent 3, Lighter 80%** fill color to cells **B3:C3.**

8. Bold cells **B3:C3.**

9. Copy only the formatting of cells **B3:C3** to the headers in the other sections. (Hint: Copy the cells and use one of the paste options to paste only the formatting.)

10. The line item for lab fees (cells **B21:C21**) is in the wrong category. Cut the cells and paste them above cell **E12,** shifting the other cells down. Do not overwrite the existing data.

11. Delete the empty cells **B21:C21,** shifting the other cells up.

12. Cell F6 has the wrong number format applied. Copy the formatting from cell **F5** and apply it to cell **F6.**

13. Apply conditional formatting to cells **C11:C23** to display an orange gradient data bar in each cell.

14. The text in cell **B21** appears cut-off. Apply text wrapping to the cell.

15. Apply all borders to the following cell ranges: **B3:C7, E3:F7, B10:C24,** and **E10:F16.**

16. Save and close the workbook.

on your own 2.5

In this project, you will add your own data to a worksheet that tracks the original cost and current resell value for textbooks. As you format the worksheet, keep in mind that you want the worksheet to be visually appealing, but you don't want it to look like a circus! Try a variety of formatting options and keep using the *Undo* command until you find the formats you like best.

Skills needed to complete this project:

- Using Undo and Redo (Skill 2.3)
- Adding Shading with Fill Color (Skill 2.11)
- Merging Cells and Splitting Merged Cells (Skill 2.7)
- Applying Cell Styles (Skill 2.12)
- Inserting and Deleting Cells (Skill 2.5)
- Aligning Cells (Skill 2.6)
- Changing Fonts, Font Size, and Font Color (Skill 2.9)
- Using Format Painter (Skill 2.13)
- Adding Borders (Skill 2.10)
- Cutting, Copying, and Pasting Cells (Skill 2.1)
- Applying Conditional Formatting Using the Quick Analysis Tool (Skill 2.14)
- Applying Conditional Formatting with Data Bars, Color Scales, and Icon Sets (Skill 2.15)
- Replacing Formatting (Skill 2.21)
- Wrapping Text in Cells (Skill 2.4)
- Applying Bold, Italic, and Underline (Skill 2.8)
- Applying Conditional Formatting with Highlight Cells Rules (Skill 2.16)
- Applying Conditional Formatting with Top/Bottom Rules (Skill 2.17)

1. Open the start file **EX2013-OnYourOwn-2-5** and resave the file as:
   `[your initials]EX-OnYourOwn-2-5`

2. If the workbook opens in Protected View, click the **Enable Editing** button in the Message Bar at the top of the workbook so you can modify the workbook.

3. Update the data in the workbook with an inventory of textbooks you own. Include the purchase price and estimated resell value for each title.

4. Add and delete cells as necessary.

5. Wrap text if any of your book titles are too long to fit in the cell.

6. Format the worksheet title and data table using cell styles, borders, and fill color. Change fonts, font color, and font size as appropriate.

7. Remember to use *Format Painter* to copy formatting from one part of the worksheet to another.

8. You can also use the *Replace* command if you want to change formatting from one style to another in multiple cells at the same time.

9. Apply conditional formatting to identify the most expensive books and the ones with the highest resell values. Use any type of conditional formatting you'd like.

10. When you are satisfied with the appearance of the worksheet, save and close the workbook.

fix it **2.6**

In this project you will fix a rather unattractive worksheet that was intended for recording walking/running miles and times.

Skills needed to complete this project:

- Using Undo and Redo (Skill 2.3)
- Adding Shading with Fill Color (Skill 2.11)
- Merging Cells and Splitting Merged Cells (Skill 2.7)
- Applying Cell Styles (Skill 2.12)
- Inserting and Deleting Cells (Skill 2.5)
- Changing Fonts, Font Size, and Font Color (Skill 2.9)
- Using Format Painter (Skill 2.13)
- Adding Borders (Skill 2.10)
- Wrapping Text in Cells (Skill 2.4)
- Applying Conditional Formatting Using the Quick Analysis Tool (Skill 2.14)
- Applying Conditional Formatting with Data Bars, Color Scales, and Icon Sets (Skill 2.15)
- Using Find and Replace (Skill 2.20)
- Applying Bold, Italic, and Underline (Skill 2.8)

1. Open the start file **EX2013-FixIt-2-6** and resave the file as:
   [your initials]EX-FixIt-2-6

2. If the workbook opens in Protected View, click the **Enable Editing** button in the Message Bar at the top of the workbook so you can modify the workbook.

3. Begin by removing all the fill color, font colors, and borders from the worksheet. This worksheet has so many different formats, it is probably easier to start from a clean slate.

4. All fonts in the worksheet should be set to **Calibri, 12** point size.

5. Apply appropriate formatting for the title. Consider using a cell style.

6. Add borders and fill color to make the data table easy to follow. Use bold where appropriate to make row and column headers stand out from the data.

7. An entry for June 9 is missing. You walked for 40 minutes that day, and went 3 miles. Insert the data in the appropriate place. (You can copy the formula to calculate miles per hour from one of the other cells.)

8. Apply text wrapping where needed.

9. Apply conditional formatting using data bars to visually compare the distance jogged each day.

10. Ensure that all entries for miles and miles per hour display two digits after the decimal.

11. Ensure that all average calculations display only two digits after the decimal.

12. Find all instances of *walk* and replace with *jog*.

13. Save and close the workbook.

chapter 3

Using Formulas and Functions

In this chapter, you will learn the following skills:

❱ Use a variety of methods to enter functions

❱ Use statistical functions

❱ Use text functions

❱ Use date and time functions

❱ Work with named ranges

❱ Use lookup functions

❱ Use the IF logical function

❱ Use the PMT financial function

❱ Troubleshoot formulas

❱ Display and print formulas

skills

introduction

It is time to go beyond simple formulas. In this chapter you will learn to use the functions built into Excel to compute statistics, modify text, insert dates, work with logical expressions, compute loan payments, and perform table lookups. Also, you will create formulas that reference named ranges and other worksheets for fast replication. Finally, you will learn skills necessary for troubleshooting formulas.

Skill 3.1 Using the Function Arguments Dialog to Enter Functions

In Chapter 1, you learned to enter functions three ways:

1. **Typing the formula directly in the cell or the formula bar.** This method is easiest for simple functions.

2. **Using the *AutoSum* button.** This method works well when your spreadsheet includes numerical data organized in rows or columns. Functions available via AutoSum are limited to simple math and statistical functions (SUM, AVERAGE, COUNT, MIN, and MAX).

3. **Using the Quick Analysis tool.** This method is the easiest way to enter totals for multiple rows or columns of data at once. Like AutoSum, the Quick Analysis tool offers a limited number of functions (SUM, AVERAGE, and COUNT). It has the advantage of including options not available from AutoSum (calculating running totals and calculating the percentage of the overall total for each row or column) and showing a live preview of the totals before you make a selection.

Every function can be entered using its *Function Arguments* dialog. This dialog is different for each function. There are two primary methods for opening the *Function Arguments* dialog.

1. **Select the function from the *Formulas* tab, *Function Library* group.** Each button in this Ribbon group represents a category of functions. Clicking a button displays a menu of functions in that category. Selecting a function opens its *Insert Function* dialog.

2. **Select the function from the Insert Function dialog.** To open the *Insert Function* dialog, on the *Formulas* tab, in the *Function Library* group, click the **Insert Function** button. You can also click the **Insert Function** button to the left of the formula bar.

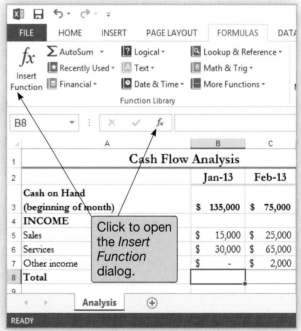

FIGURE EX 3.1

To use the *Insert Function* dialog:

1. Functions in the *Insert Function* dialog are organized in the same categories as the *Function Library* group. By default, the category list will default to the category you last used or it will show the *Most Recently Used* list. To select another category, expand the **Or select a category** list and select the function category you want.

2. Click a function in the *Select a function* box to see a brief description of what it does and the arguments it takes.

3. Click **OK** to open the *Function Arguments* dialog for the selected function.

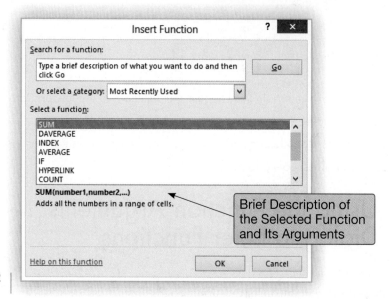

FIGURE EX 3.2

To use the *Function Arguments* dialog:

1. Enter values or cell references in each of the argument boxes as needed by typing or by clicking the cell or cell range in the worksheet. As you click each argument box, a brief description of the argument appears near the bottom of the dialog. The *Function Arguments* dialog also displays a preview of the result of the calculation. This value updates as you add arguments.

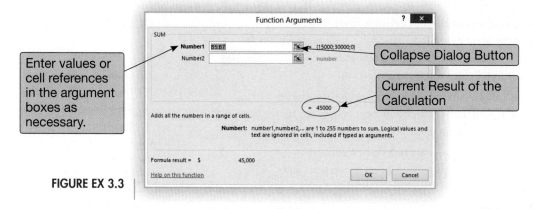

FIGURE EX 3.3

2. If the position of the *Function Arguments* dialog box makes it difficult to click the cell you want, click the **Collapse Dialog** button next to the argument box. The *Function Arguments* dialog collapses to show only the function argument box you are working with. Click the cell to add the reference to the dialog.

3. Click the **Expand Dialog** button to return the *Function Arguments* dialog to its full size.

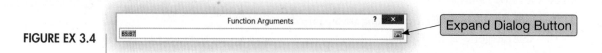

FIGURE EX 3.4

4. When you are finished entering arguments, click **OK.**

tips & tricks

The SUM *Function Arguments* dialog shown in Figure EX 3.3 includes an extra argument box. For functions that calculate a value based on a series of cells, Excel adds a blank argument box each time you enter an argument (up to 256 arguments). Enter values or cell references only in the argument boxes you need.

tell me **more**

If you're not sure of the name of the function you want, open the *Insert Function* dialog and type keywords describing the function in the *Search for a function* box, and then click the **Go** button. The *Or select a category* box changes to *Recommended,* and the *Select a function* box now displays a list of functions that match the keywords you typed.

let me try

Open the student data file **EX3-01-CashFlow** and try this skill on your own:

1. Enter a SUM function in cell **B8** to calculate the total of cells **B5:B7.** Open the *Function Arguments* dialog from the *Formulas* tab, *Function Library* group, **Math & Trig** button. You will have to scroll down the list to find SUM. Because cell B8 is below a list of values, Excel enters that cell range as the function argument for you.

2. Enter a SUM function in cell **C8** to calculate the total of cells **C5:C7.** Use the *Insert Function* dialog. If the SUM function is not listed in the *Select a Function* box, expand the **Or select a category list,** and select either **Math & Trig** or **Most Recently Used.** Again, Excel enters the adjacent cell range as the function arguments for you.

3. Enter a SUM function in cell **E5** to calculate the total of cells **B5:D5.** Use any method you want.

4. Save the file as directed by your instructor and close it.

Skill 3.2 Using Formula AutoComplete to Enter Functions

Formula AutoComplete is a shortcut for entering functions. When you type = and then a letter, Formula AutoComplete displays a list of potential matches (functions and other valid reference names). This is a good method to use if you prefer typing the function arguments, but you need a reminder of what the arguments are or the order in which they should be entered.

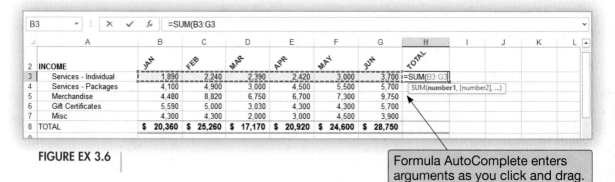

Double-click the function you want.

FIGURE EX 3.5

1. Type = in the cell or the formula bar to begin the formula. Formula AutoComplete displays the list of potential matches.

2. Type more letters to shorten the Formula AutoComplete list.

3. Double-click a function name to enter it in your formula.

4. Enter the expected arguments by typing values or selecting a cell or cell range.

5. Press ⏎ Enter to complete the formula. Excel enters the closing) for you.

	A	B	C	D	E	F	G	H	I	J	K	L
		JAN	FEB	MAR	APR	MAY	JUN	TOTAL				
2	INCOME											
3	Services - Individual	1,890	2,240	2,390	2,420	3,000	3,700	=SUM(B3:G3				
4	Services - Packages	4,100	4,900	3,000	4,500	5,500	5,700	SUM(**number1**, [number2], ...)				
5	Merchandise	4,480	8,820	6,750	6,700	7,300	9,750					
6	Gift Certificates	5,590	5,000	3,030	4,300	4,300	5,700					
7	Misc	4,300	4,300	2,000	3,000	4,500	3,900					
8	TOTAL	$ 20,360	$ 25,260	$ 17,170	$ 20,920	$ 24,600	$ 28,750					

FIGURE EX 3.6

Formula AutoComplete enters arguments as you click and drag.

tips & tricks

When you use Formula AutoComplete, you can click the function name in the ScreenTip to open the Excel help topic for that function.

let me try

Open the student data file **EX3-02-IncomeAndExpenses** and try this skill on your own:

Use Formula Auto Complete to enter a SUM function in cell **H3** to calculate the total of cells **B3:G3**. Save the file as directed by your instructor and close it.

Skill 3.3 Calculating Averages

The **AVERAGE** statistical function is used to calculate the average value of a group of values. Average is calculated by adding the values, and then dividing the sum by the number of values.

A formula using the AVERAGE function looks like this:

=AVERAGE(B3:D3)

The value of this formula is the average of the values of cells B3 through D3: (B3 + C3 + D3)/3.

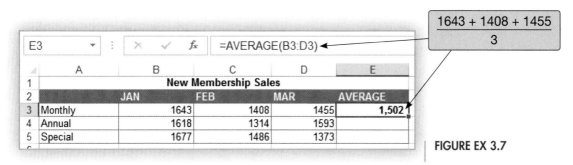

FIGURE EX 3.7

To create a formula with the AVERAGE function, use any of these methods:

) If you prefer typing in the cell or the formula bar, try using Formula AutoComplete.

) If the data are organized in rows or columns, you can use AutoSum. On the *Home* tab, *Editing* group or on the *Formula* tab, *Function Library* group, click the **AutoSum** button arrow and select **Average.**

) If you want to calculate the average for multiple rows or columns at once, use one of the average options in the Quick Analysis tool, *Totals* tab.

) If you prefer using the *Function Arguments* dialog, on the *Formulas* tab, in the *Function Library* group, click the **More Functions** button, point to **Statistical,** and click **AVERAGE.**

tips & tricks

When calculating an average, Excel will ignore empty cells. If you want to include those cells in your average calculations, make sure they have a value of zero.

tell me **more**

What you might think of as the "average" is actually the statistical mean. Average is a general term in statistics that includes **mean** (the sum of a group of values divided by the number of values in the group), **median** (the middle value of a set of values) and **mode** (the value that appears most often in a group of values). In Excel, the AVERAGE function calculates the mean value. Most people say *average* when they really want to calculate the mean value.

let me try

Open the student data file **EX3-03-Sales** and try this skill on your own:

Enter a formula in cell **E3** to calculate the average value of cells **B3:D3.** Use any method you like. Save the file as directed by your instructor and close it.

Skill 3.4 Creating Formulas Using Counting Functions

There are three basic counting functions in Excel. These functions are useful when you need to know how many numbers or items are in a list, or how many rows are missing data for a particular column.

COUNT—Counts the number of cells that contain numbers within a specified range of cells. A formula using the COUNT function looks like this:

=COUNT(G6:G17)

The result of this formula is the number of cells in **G6** through **G17** that contain numerical values. If you want to include cells that contain text, use COUNTA instead.

COUNTA—Counts the number of cells that are not blank within a specified range of cells. Use COUNTA if your cell range includes text data or a mix of text and numbers. A formula using the COUNTA function looks like this:

=COUNTA(B6:B17)

The result of this formula is the number of cells in **B6** through **B17** that contain any data (numerical or text).

COUNTBLANK—Counts the number of blank cells within a specified range of cells. Cells that contain a zero (0) are not considered blank. Use COUNTBLANK to find the number of rows missing values in a column. A formula using the COUNTBLANK function looks like this:

=COUNTBLANK(E6:E17)

The result of this formula is the number of cells in **E6** through **E17** that are blank.

	A	B	C	D	E	H
1	How many different items in our current inventory?			12	=COUNTA(B6:B17)	
2	How many items are on reorder?			2	=COUNT(G6:G17)	
3	How many items are not in stock?			2	=COUNTBLANK(E6:E17)	
4						
5	Inventory ID	Item	Unit Price	Reorder Time in Days	Quantity in Stock	Reorder Level	Quantity in Reorder
6	1094	TIAB sampler	$ 22.00	14	18	5	
7	1095	SPF 15 gel	$ 12.00	5	18	8	
8	1096	SPF 30 gel	$ 19.00	5	16	8	
9	1097	SPF 45 gel	$ 18.00	5	22	8	
10	1098	SPF 60 gel	$ 20.00	5	12	8	
11	1099	Yan Can Shampoo	$ 19.00	21	2	5	20
12	1100	Yan Can Conditioner	$ 7.00	21	28	5	
13	1101	Yan Can Hair Mask	$ 18.00	21	4	5	20
14	1102	Yan Can Mousse	$ 18.00	21		5	
15	1103	Yan Can Gel	$ 15.00	21	1	5	
16	1104	Yan Can Moulding Gel	$ 25.00	21	12	5	
17	1105	Yan Can Masque	$ 20.00	21		5	
18							
19							

FIGURE EX 3.8

To create a formula with COUNT, COUNTA, or COUNTBLANK, use either of these methods:

❯ If you prefer typing in the cell or the formula bar, try using Formula AutoComplete.

❯ If you prefer using the *Function Arguments* dialog, on the *Formulas* tab, in the *Function Library* group, click the **More Functions** button, point to **Statistical,** and click **COUNT, COUNTA,** or **COUNTBLANK.**

To count numbers, you have two additional options:

❯ If the data are organized in rows or columns, you can use AutoSum to enter the COUNT function. On the *Home* tab, *Editing* group or on the *Formula* tab, *Function Library* group, click the **AutoSum** button arrow and select **Count Numbers.**

❯ If you want to count the numbers in for multiple rows or columns at once, use one of the *Count* options in the Quick Analysis tool, *Totals* tab.

tips & tricks

The COUNT and COUNTA functions can take multiple arguments.

COUNTBLANK accepts only a single argument, so if you want to count across a non-contiguous range of cells, you will need to create a formula adding together the results of multiple functions.

=COUNTBLANK(A1:C1)+COUNTBLANK(B10:C15)

let me try

Open the student data file **EX3-04-Inventory** and try this skill on your own:

1. In cell **D1,** enter a formula using a counting function to count the number of items in the inventory (cells **B6:B17**).

2. In cell **D2,** enter a formula using a counting function to count the number of values in the *Quantity in Reorder* column (cells **G6:G17**).

3. In cell **D3,** enter a formula using a counting function to count the number of blank cells in the *Quantity in Stock* column (cells **E6:E17**).

4. Save the file as directed by your instructor and close it.

Skill 3.5 Finding Minimum and Maximum Values

In addition to AVERAGE and the counting functions, there are a few other statistical functions you may find useful in working with day-to-day spreadsheets.

The **MIN** (minimum) statistical function will give you the lowest value in a range of values. The **MAX** (maximum) statistical function will give you the highest value in a range of values. A formula using the MIN or MAX function looks like this:

=**MIN(A3:A6)**

=**MAX(A3:A6)**

	A	B	C	D	E	F	G
1	What is the minimum reorder time?			5	=MIN(D5:D16)		
2	What is the maximum reorder time?			21	=MAX(D5:D16)		
3							
4	Inventory ID	Item	Unit Price	Reorder Time in Days	Quantity in Stock	Reorder Level	Quantity in Reorder
5	1094	TIAB sampler	$ 22.00	14	18	5	
6	1095	SPF 15 gel	$ 12.00	5	18	8	
7	1096	SPF 30 gel	$ 19.00	5	16	8	
8	1097	SPF 45 gel	$ 18.00	5	22	8	
9	1098	SPF 60 gel	$ 20.00	5	12	8	
10	1099	Yan Can Shampoo	$ 19.00	21	2	5	20
11	1100	Yan Can Conditioner	$ 7.00	21	28	5	
12	1101	Yan Can Hair Mask	$ 18.00	21	4	5	20
13	1102	Yan Can Mousse	$ 18.00	21		5	
14	1103	Yan Can Gel	$ 15.00	21	1	5	
15	1104	Yan Can Moulding Gel	$ 25.00	21	12	5	
16	1105	Yan Can Masque	$ 20.00	21		5	
17							

FIGURE EX 3.9

To create a formula with the MIN or MAX function, use any of these methods:

> If you prefer typing in the cell or the formula bar, try using Formula AutoComplete.

> If the data are organized in rows or columns, you can use AutoSum. On the *Home* tab, *Editing* group or on the *Formula* tab, *Function Library* group, click the **AutoSum** button arrow and select **Max** or **Min.**

> If you prefer using the *Function Arguments* dialog, on the *Formulas* tab, in the *Function Library* group, click the **More Functions** button, point to **Statistical,** and click **MAX** or **MIN.**

let me try

Open the student data file **EX3-05-Inventory** and try this skill on your own:

1. In cell **D1,** enter a formula to find the minimum reorder time (cells **D5:D16**).

2. In cell **D2,** enter a formula to find the maximum reorder time (cells **D5:D16**).

3. Save the file as directed by your instructor and close it.

Skill 3.6 Using Date and Time Functions

Excel includes two functions that insert the current date or date and time. The NOW function inserts the current date and time. The TODAY function inserts only the current date. Both of these functions are volatile—that is, they are not constant. They update with the current date or date and time each time the workbook is opened. This is useful if you want to keep track of the last time the workbook was edited or opened.

A formula using the NOW function looks like this:

=NOW()

A formula using the TODAY function looks like this:

=TODAY()

Notice that both of these functions include parentheses, but there are no arguments inside them. These functions do not require arguments.

To create a formula with NOW or TODAY, use either of these methods:

❯ If you prefer typing in the cell or the formula bar, try using Formula AutoComplete.

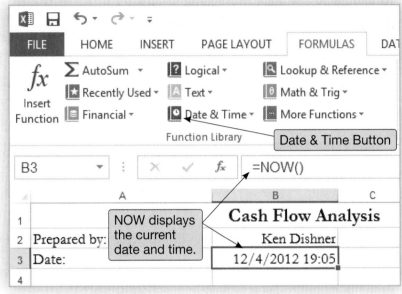

FIGURE EX 3.10

❯ If you prefer using the *Function Arguments* dialog, on the *Formulas* tab, in the *Function Library* group, click the **Date & Time** button and click **NOW** or **TODAY.**

tips & tricks

Both NOW and TODAY use the date and time from your computer's clock. If your computer's clock is wrong, the date and time displayed in your workbook will be wrong as well.

tell me more

If the cell is formatted to use a date format that does not display the time, the result of the NOW and TODAY functions will appear the same. However, the underlying value will still be different. If you change the formatting of the cell to display the time, a cell using the TODAY function will always display a time of 12:00 AM, whereas a cell using the NOW function will display the correct time.

let me try

Open the student data file **EX3-06-CashFlow** and try this skill on your own:

1. Enter a formula in cell **B3** to display only the current date.
2. Modify the formula in cell **B3** to display the current date and time.
3. Save the file as directed by your instructor and close it.

Skill 3.7 Formatting Text Using Functions

Functions can do more than perform calculations. Excel includes a special group of functions to modify text. These text functions are useful for ensuring that text data have a consistent appearance. In functions, text is referred to as a **string** or **text string**.

The most commonly used text functions are:

PROPER—Converts the text string to proper case (the first letter in each word is capitalized). A formula using the PROPER function looks like this:

=PROPER(C2)

UPPER—Converts the text string to all uppercase letters. A formula using the UPPER function looks like this:

=UPPER(D2)

LOWER—Converts the text string to all lowercase letters. A formula using the LOWER function looks like this:

=LOWER(E2)

To create a formula with PROPER, UPPER, or LOWER, use either of these methods:

❱ If you prefer typing in the cell or the formula bar, try using Formula AutoComplete.

❱ If you prefer using the *Function Arguments* dialog, on the *Formulas* tab, in the *Function Library* group, click the **Text** button and click **PROPER, UPPER,** or **LOWER.**

FIGURE EX 3.11

tips & tricks

Typically, when you use one of the text functions, you are left with two groups of cells containing the same data: One group has the original incorrectly formatted text; the second group contains the formulas and displays correctly formatted text. There are two options for managing this:

❱ Hide the columns or rows that contain the original text. For information on hiding rows and columns, refer to the skill *Hiding and Unhiding Rows and Columns.*

❱ Copy the cells containing the text formulas; use one of the *Paste Values* options to paste just the values of the text formulas over the original cells, then delete the cells containing the text formulas. For information on using the *Paste Values* commands, refer to the skill *Using Paste Options.*

let me try

Open the student data file **EX3-07-Customers** and try this skill on your own:

1. Enter a formula in cell **C5** to display the text from cell **C2** so the first letter in each word is capitalized.
2. Enter a formula in cell **D5** to display the text from cell **D2** so all the letters display in upper case.
3. Enter a formula in cell **E5** to display the text from cell **E2** so all the letters display in lower case.
4. Save the file as directed by your instructor and close it.

Skill 3.8 Using CONCATENATE to Combine Text

To **concatenate** means to link items together. You can use the **CONCATENATE** function to combine the text values of cells. For example, if you have two columns for first name and last name, but you need a third column displaying the full name, you can use CONCATENATE to combine the values of the first two columns.

In Figure EX 3.12, the customer name in cell C2 is created by concatenating the values in column B (first name) and column A (last name). The formula looks like this:

=CONCATENATE(B2," ",A2)

The argument in the middle (" ") places a one-space text string between the values of cells B2 and A2.

If you are building a long string from multiple cells, you may want to use the Function Arguments dialog until you become familiar with this function. Of course, you can always type directly in the cell or formula bar and use Formula AutoComplete.

1. On the *Formulas* tab, in the *Function Library* group, click the **Text** button.

2. Click **CONCATENATE**.

3. In the *Function Arguments* dialog, enter each cell reference or text string you want to combine in its own argument. If one of the arguments is a blank space, enter " " in the argument box.

4. Click **OK**.

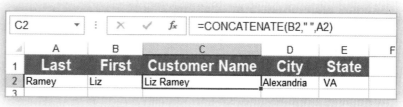

FIGURE EX 3.12

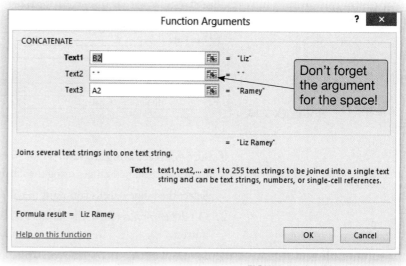

FIGURE EX 3.13

tips & tricks

For sorting purposes, you may want to keep the columns that you concatenate. If you do not want them to display in your worksheet, hide them. Hide the columns or rows that contain the original text. For information on hiding rows and columns, refer to the skill *Hiding and Unhiding Rows and Columns*.

let me try

Open the student data file **EX3-08-Customers** and try this skill on your own:

Enter a formula in cell **C2** to combine the text from cells **B2** and **A2** to display the customer name in the format *Bob Smith*. Don't forget the argument for the space. Save the file as directed by your instructor and close it.

Skill 3.9 Naming Ranges of Cells

Cell references like A4 and J34 do not provide much information about what data the cell contains—they just tell you where the cell is located in the worksheet. However, you can assign names to cells or ranges of cells to give your cell references names that are more user-friendly. These **names** (also called **range names** or **named ranges**) act as a list of short- cuts to the cell locations.

To create a named range:

1. Select the cell or range of cells to which you want to assign a name.
2. Type the name in the *Name* box to the left of the formula bar.
3. Press ← Enter to apply the name to the cell(s).

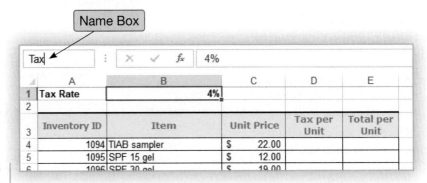

FIGURE EX 3.14

If your worksheet is organized in a table format, with column or row labels, you can automatically create named ranges using the labels as names:

1. Select the range of cells you want to name including the labels.
2. On the *Formulas* tab, in the *Defined Names* group, click the **Create from Selection** button.
3. In the *Create Names from Selection* dialog, click the checkbox to indicate where the names are (*Top row, Left column, Bottom row,* or *Right column*).
4. Click **OK**.

Excel automatically creates named ranges for the groups of cells associated with each label. Because names may not include spaces, Excel will replace the spaces with underscore _ characters. The named ranges will not include the labels. The *Create Names from Selection* command in Figure EX 3.15 will create the following named ranges:

INVENTORY_ID	ITEM	UNIT_PRICE	TAX_PER_UNIT	TOTAL_PER_UNIT
A4:A15	B4:B15	C4:C15	D4:D15	E4:E15

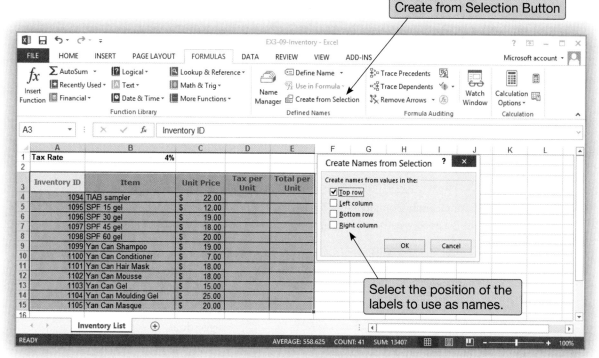

Create from Selection Button

Create Names from Selection

Create names from values in the:
- ☑ Top row
- ☐ Left column
- ☐ Bottom row
- ☐ Right column

Select the position of the labels to use as names.

FIGURE EX 3.15

another **method**

You can also create new names through the *New Name* dialog.

1. On the *Formulas* tab, in the *Defined Names* group, click the **Define Name** button.

2. The selected cell(s) is entered in the *Refers to* box.

3. Type the name you want in the *Name* box. If the cell to the immediate left or immediately above the selected cell appears to include a label, Excel will pre-populate the *Name* box with that text.

4. Click **OK.**

let me **try**

Open the student data file **EX3-09-Inventory** and try this skill on your own:

1. Name cell **B1** as follows: **Tax**

2. Use the *Create from Selection* command to create named ranges for the data table **A4:E15** using the labels in row **3** as the basis for the names.

3. Save the file as directed by your instructor and close it.

Skill 3.10 Working with Named Ranges

Rather than using a range of cells in your formulas, you can use a named range. The name will always refer to the cells, even if their position in the worksheet changes. Using named ranges in your formulas also makes it easier for others to use your workbook. Which formula is easier to understand: =C4*B1 or =C4*Tax?

To use a named range in a formula:

1. Click the cell where you want to enter the new formula.
2. Type the formula, substituting the range name for the cell references.
3. Press ⬅ Enter to accept the formula.

Formula AutoComplete lists named ranges as well as functions. Using the AutoComplete list is a good way to avoid typographical errors and ensure that you enter the name correctly.

The name *Tax* refers to cell B1.

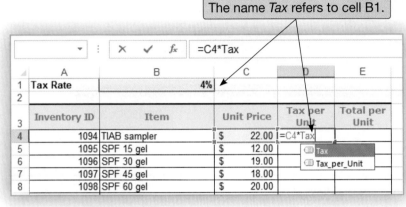

FIGURE EX 3.16

To use Formula AutoComplete with names:

1. Type = (an equal sign) to begin the formula. As you type alphabetical characters, Excel will offer name suggestions.
2. When you find the name you want, double-click it.
3. Excel inserts the name into the formula.

tips & tricks

When you copy and paste a formula containing a named range, the name does not change with the new position in the workbook (similar to using an absolute reference).

If you move a named cell, the name updates with the new cell location automatically.

another method

- On the *Formulas* tab, in the *Defined Names* group, click the **Use in Formula** button to display a list of names in your workbook, and then click one of the names to insert it into your formula.
- You can also click **Paste Names...** from the bottom of the *Use in Formula* list. The *Paste Names* dialog opens and lists all of the names in your workbook. Click a name and then click **OK** to add it to your formula.

let me try

Open the student data file **EX3-10-Inventory** and try this skill on your own:

1. Enter a formula in cell **D4** to calculate the tax. Multiply the item unit price (cell **C4**) * the value in the cell named **Tax**.
2. Copy the formula to cells **D5:D15**. Notice that while the reference to the item unit price updates for each row, the reference to the name *Tax* remains absolute.
3. Save the file as directed by your instructor and close it.

Skill 3.11 Updating Named Ranges with the Name Manager

FIGURE EX 3.17

The **Name Manager** lists all the named ranges used in your workbook, the current value for each, the cells to which the name refers (including the sheet name), the scope of the name (whether it is limited to a specific worksheet or applies to the entire workbook), and comments (if there are any).

To open the Name Manager, on the *Formulas* tab, in the *Defined Names* group, click the **Name Manager** button.

To change the cell or range of cells to which a name refers:

1. Open the Name Manager.

2. Select the name you want to modify.

3. Edit the cell references in the *Refers to* box. You can also click the **Collapse Dialog** button to hide the Name Manager, and then click and drag to select the new cell range. When you are finished, click the **Expand Dialog** button to display the Name Manager again.

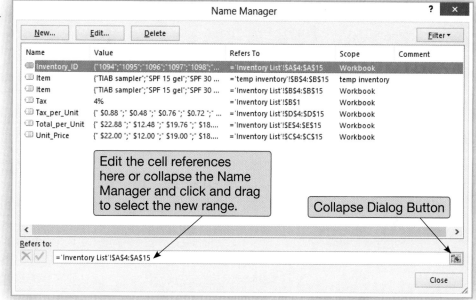

FIGURE EX 3.18

4. Click the checkmark icon to the left of the *Refers to* box to accept the change.

5. Click **Close** to close the Name Manager. If you forgot to save your change, Excel will ask if you want to save the change you made to the cell reference. Click **Yes.**

tell me **more**

When auditing a workbook for errors, you may find it useful to review a list of the defined names in your workbook.

1. Start with a blank worksheet.

2. Select the cell where you want the list to begin.

3. On the *Formulas* tab, in the *Defined Names* group, click the **Use in Formula** button, and select **Paste Names** from the end of the list.

4. The *Paste Name* dialog opens. Click the **Paste List** button.

A two-column list is pasted into Excel. The first column displays the name, and the second column displays the cell or ranges of cells to which the name refers.

let me **try**

Open the student data file **EX3-11-Inventory** and try this skill on your own:

1. Open the Name Manager.

2. Edit the **Inventory_ID** name so it refers to cells **A4:A18** on the *Inventory List* worksheet.

3. Close the Name Manager.

4. Save the file as directed by your instructor and close it.

Skill 3.12 Editing and Deleting Names with the Name Manager

When you copy data, you may find that some of the names in your workbook are repeated. Remember that names must be unique—but only within their scopes. You can have more than one named range with the same name, but only one can belong to the entire workbook. The others are specific to the worksheet in which they are defined.

In Figure EX 3.19, there are two *Item* names. The first is limited in scope to the *temp inventory* worksheet. If you refer to the name *Item* in a formula in any other sheet in the workbook, it will refer to the second name (located on the *Inventory List* worksheet).

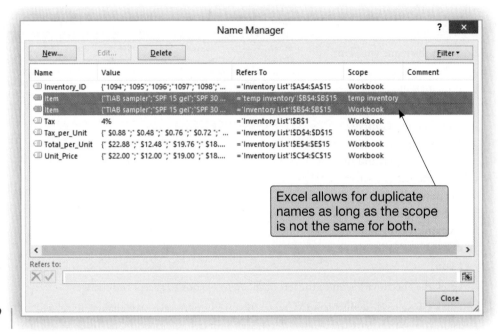

FIGURE EX 3.19

Duplicate names can be confusing. A good practice is to rename duplicates to make them easier to identify and use.

To change a name:

1. Open the Name Manager.
2. Click the name you want to modify, and then click the **Edit** button.
3. The *Edit Name* dialog opens.
4. Type the new name in the *Name* box.
5. Click **OK** to save your changes.
6. Click the **Close** button to close the Name Manager.

When you change a name, Excel automatically updates the name in any formulas that reference that name.

If your workbook includes names you no longer need, you should delete them.

To delete a name:

1. On the *Formulas* tab, in the *Defined Names* group, click the **Name Manager** button.

2. Click the name, and then click the **Delete** button.

3. Excel displays a message asking if you are sure you want to delete the name. Click **OK**.

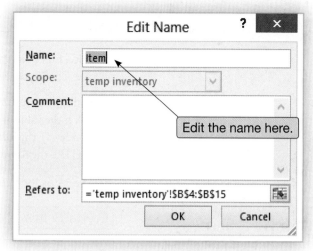

FIGURE EX 3.20

tips & tricks

There are two types of names identified in the Name Manager. **Defined names** are the names you created and names that Excel creates automatically when you define a print area or print titles. Table names are names created automatically when you define a data range as a table. By default, tables are named Table1, Table2, Table3, and so on. To make table names easier to use, consider renaming them through the Name Manager.

let me try

Open the student data file **EX3-12-Inventory** and try this skill on your own:

1. Open the Name Manager.

2. There are two Item names. Rename the one that is limited in scope to the temp inventory list to: **Item_temp**

3. In the Name Manager, review the information about the *Total_Price* name. The name refers to a series of empty cells. You do not need it in this workbook. Delete the **Total_Price** name.

4. Close the Name Manager.

5. Save the file as directed by your instructor and close it.

Skill 3.13 Using the Logical Function IF

The **IF** logical function returns one value if a condition is true and another value if the condition is false. The IF function can return a numerical value or display a text string.

The formula in Figure 3.21 uses the IF function to determine whether or not an item should be ordered. If the value of cell C2 (the quantity in stock) is greater than the value of cell D2 (the reorder level), the formula will return "yes." If the value of cell C2 is not greater than the value of cell D2, the formula will return "no." The formula looks like this:

=**IF(C2>D2,"no","yes")**

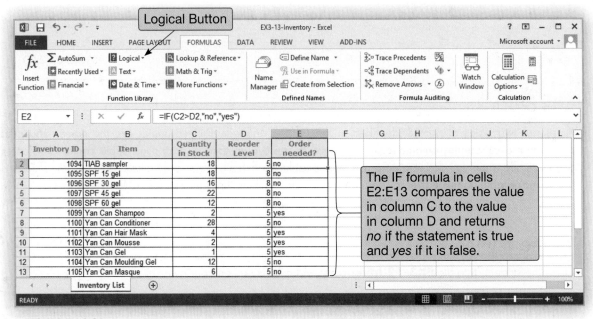

FIGURE EX 3.21

To create a formula using the IF function:

1. Select the cell where you want to enter the formula.

2. On the *Formulas* tab, in the *Function Library* group, click the **Logical** button.

3. Select **IF** to open the *Function Arguments* dialog. IF functions take three arguments as shown in the *Function Arguments* dialog in Figure EX 3.22.

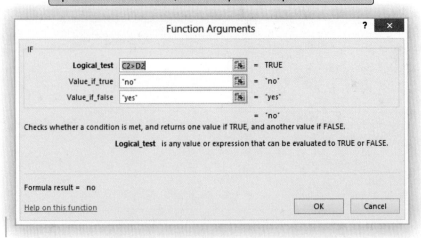

FIGURE EX 3.22

4. Enter the **Logical_test** argument. This argument states the condition you want to test for. The *Logical_test* always includes a comparison operator (=, >, <, etc.).

5. Enter the **Value_if_true** argument. This argument is the text string or value that will be displayed or the formula that will be calculated if the *Logical_test* argument is true.

6. Enter the **Value_if_false** argument. This argument is the text string or value that will be displayed or the formula that will be calculated if the *Logical_test* argument is false.

7. Click **OK.**

tips & tricks

If you use the *Function Arguments* dialog to enter text as the *Value_if_true* or the *Value_if_false* argument, you do not need to include the quotation marks. Excel will add them for you. However, if you type the formula directly in the cell or the formula bar, you must include quotation marks around the text.

let me try

Open the student data file **EX3-13-Inventory** and try this skill on your own:

Enter a formula in cell **E2** using the logical function IF to display **no** if the quantity in stock (cell **C2**) is greater than the reorder level (cell **D2**) and **yes** if it is not. Save the file as directed by your instructor and close it.

from the perspective of . . .

INSTRUCTOR

I use a spreadsheet to keep a grid of class attendance by student and by day. Using formulas and functions for grading gives me the flexibility to add scores, calculate averages, and provide feedback to my students.

Skill 3.14 Calculating Loan Payments Using the PMT Function

One of the most useful financial functions in Excel is **PMT** (payment), which you can use to calculate loan payments. The PMT function is based upon constant payments and a constant interest rate. To calculate a payment using PMT, you need three pieces of information: the interest rate, the number of payments, and the amount of the loan.

PMT(interest rate, number of loan payments, loan principal amount)

Using the values in Figure EX 3.23, the PMT function would look like this:

=PMT(4%/12,36,2500)

The *annual* interest rate is 4%. To calculate monthly payments, the interest rate must be divided by the number of payments per year.

When working with complex functions like PMT, use cell references as arguments rather than entering values directly. This way you can change values in your spreadsheet and see the results instantly without opening the *Function Arguments* dialog again. Using cell references, the PMT function in Figure EX 3.23 looks like this:

=PMT(B4/12,B5,B3)

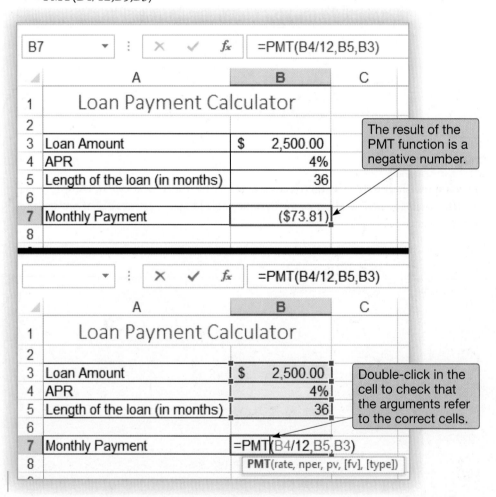

FIGURE EX 3.23

To use the PMT function:

1. Select the cell where you want to enter the formula.

2. On the *Formulas* tab, in the *Function Library* group, click the **Financial** button.

excel 2013   chapter 3 Using Formulas and Functions

3. Select **PMT** from the list to open the *Function Arguments* dialog. PMT takes three required arguments and two optional arguments as shown in Figure EX 3.24.

4. Enter the **Rate** argument. This argument is the interest rate. Usually, interest rate is expressed as an annual rate. If the loan requires a monthly payment, the annual percentage rate (APR) should be divided by 12.

5. Enter the **Nper** argument. This argument is the total number of payments over the life of the loan.

6. Enter the **Pv** argument. This argument is the present value of the loan—how much you owe now (the loan principal).

7. (Optional) The *Fv* argument is future value of the loan. Excel assumes a value of 0 unless you include the argument and specify a different value. If you will make payments on the loan until it is completely paid off, you can leave this argument blank or enter 0.

8. (Optional) The *Type* argument represents when payments will be made during each loan period. Enter 1 if the payment is at the beginning of the period. If you omit this argument, Excel assumes a value of 0 (meaning each payment is at the end of the period).

9. Click **OK.**

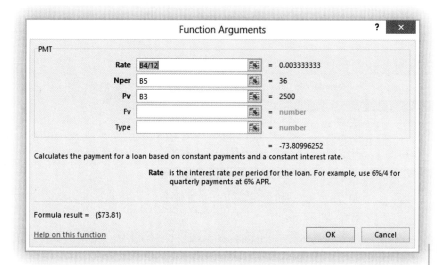

FIGURE EX 3.24

Because the result of the formula is a payment, it is expressed as a negative number. If you want the result expressed as a positive number instead, add a negative symbol before the PMT function: $= -\text{PMT}(B4/12,B5,B3)$.

tips & tricks

It can be helpful to name the cells containing data for the function arguments with the same name as the argument. For example, name the cell with the interest rate **Rate.** Then when you build the PMT function, the cell names match the argument names. It makes creating the function easy.

let me try

Open the student data file **EX3-14-Loan** and try this skill on your own:

Enter a formula in cell **B7** using the PMT function to calculate the monthly loan payment. The annual interest rate is in cell **B4,** the number of monthly payments is in cell **B5,** and the amount of the loan is in cell **B3.** Remember, payments will be monthly, so divide the annual interest rate by 12. Save the file as directed by your instructor and close it.

Skill 3.15 Creating Formulas Referencing Data from Other Worksheets

Cell references are not limited to cells within the same worksheet. You can reference cells in other worksheets in your workbook. This feature is useful when you want to create summary sheets or perform analysis on data from multiple sheets at once.

For example, this formula will display the value of cell B34 from the *Jan* worksheet:

=Jan!B34

To include a reference to a cell from another sheet in your workbook:

1. Click the cell where you want the formula.

2. Type (=).

3. Navigate to the cell you want to reference by clicking the sheet tab and then clicking the cell.

4. Press (← Enter) to complete the formula.

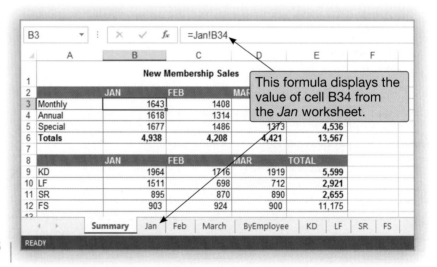

FIGURE EX 3.25

You can also refer to cells in other worksheets within formulas. For example, this formula will calculate the sum of cells B3:D33 from the *KD* worksheet:

=SUM(KD!B3:D33)

To include a reference to another worksheet in a formula:

1. Begin entering the formula as normal.

2. When you want to add a reference to a cell in another sheet, click the sheet tab, then click the cell(s) you want to add to the formula or click and drag to select a cell range.

3. When you are finished with the formula, press (← Enter).

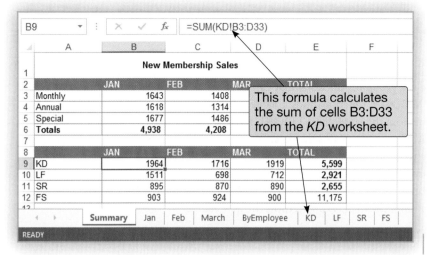

FIGURE EX 3.26

If your workbook includes multiple sheets with the same data structure, you can create a formula that references the same cell(s) on multiple sheets. This is called a **3-D reference**. For example, this formula will calculate the sum of the value of cell D3 on all sheets from KD through FS (sheets KD, LF, SR, and FS).

=SUM(KD:FS!D3)

To add a 3-D reference to a formula:

1. Begin entering the formula as you would normally.

2. Then, when you want to add the 3-D reference, select the sheet tabs for all the sheets you want included and click the specific cell(s) you want.

3. When you are finished with the formula, press (←Enter).

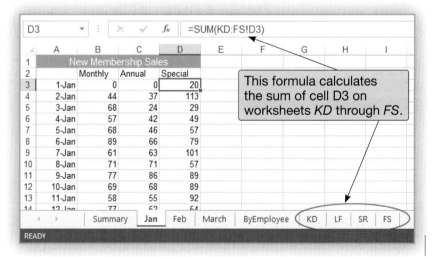

FIGURE EX 3.27

let me try

Open the student data file **EX3-15-Sales** and try this skill on your own:

1. On the *Summary* sheet, in cell **B3,** enter a formula to display the value of cell **B34** from the *Jan* sheet.

2. On the *Summary* sheet, in cell **B9,** enter a formula to calculate the sum of cells **B3:D33** from the *KD* sheet.

3. Go to the *Jan* sheet. Enter a formula using a 3-D reference in cell D3 to calculate the sum of cell **D3** from sheets *KD* through *FS.*

4. Copy that formula to the remaining cells in the column (through cell **D33**). Look at the formulas and note that Excel updated the relative cell reference in each row but did not change the worksheet references.

5. Save the file as directed by your instructor and close it.

Skill 3.16 Finding Data Using the VLOOKUP Function

Excel includes a group of functions that can be used to look up matching values in a cell range. The **VLOOKUP** function finds a value or cell reference in a cell range and returns another value from the same row. VLOOKUP requires you to specify the value you want to find, the cell range that contains the data, and the column that contains the value you want the function to return.

The formula in Figure 3.28 finds the value from cell **B2** in the cell range named **Inventory** and then returns the value from the second column of the range. In other words, VLOOKUP finds the item ID and returns the item name.

=VLOOKUP(B2,Inventory,2,FALSE)

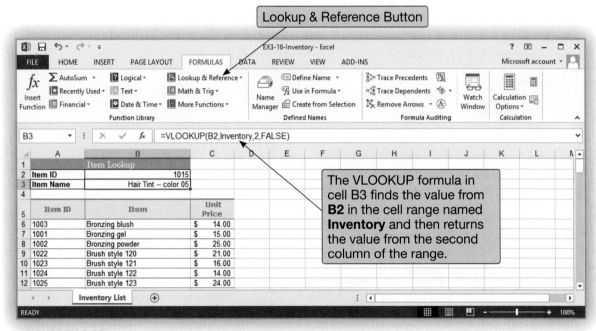

FIGURE EX 3.28

To use the VLOOKUP function:

1. Select the cell where you want to enter the formula.

2. On the *Formulas* tab, in the *Function Library* group, click the **Lookup & Reference** button.

3. Select **VLOOKUP** from the list to open the *Function Arguments* dialog. VLOOKUP takes three required arguments and one optional argument as shown in Figure EX 3.29.

4. Enter the **Lookup_value** argument. Enter the cell reference for which you want to find a corresponding value. In other words, the value you want to look up.

5. Enter the **Table_array** argument. Enter the range of cells (or the range name) that contains the lookup data. If your data include a header row, do not include it in the range used for the *Table_array* argument.

6. Enter the **Col_index_num** argument. This argument is the position of the column in the *Table_array* from which the function should return a matching value. Enter the column number, not the letter or the column heading.

7. (optional) Enter the **Range_lookup** argument. Type **FALSE** if you want to find only an exact match for the value entered in the *Lookup_value* box. If you omit this argument, Excel assumes a value of **TRUE** and will return the value for the closest match in the first column.

8. Click **OK.**

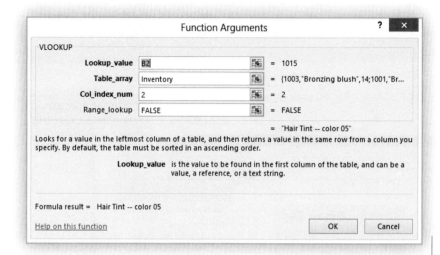

FIGURE EX 3.29

tips & tricks

If you do not specify *False* for the *Range_lookup* argument, make sure the data in the *Table_array* are sorted A–Z by the first column (the lookup column). If your data are not sorted, you may see unexpected results.

tell me **more**

The examples here all use the VLOOKUP function to find corresponding values in different *columns* within the same row (a *vertical* lookup). The HLOOKUP function works similarly, except you use it to find corresponding values in different rows within the same column (a *horizontal* lookup).

Use HLOOKUP when your worksheet uses a horizontal layout—few rows with many columns.

Use VLOOKUP when your worksheet uses a vertical layout—few columns with many rows.

let me **try**

Open the student data file **EX3-16-Inventory** and try this skill on your own:

Enter a formula in cell **B3** using the VLOOUP function to find the item name for the item number listed in cell **A3**. You can use the name **Inventory** for the lookup table. The item names are located in column **2** of the lookup table. Save the file as directed by your instructor and close it.

Skill 3.17 Checking Formulas for Errors

Some worksheet errors are easily identifiable—such as divide by zero errors, which look like this in your worksheet: **#DIV/0!** (because Excel cannot calculate a value to display). Other potential errors, like formulas that leave out part of a cell range, are harder to find yourself. You can use Excel's error checking features to review your worksheet for errors.

Cells that include potential errors are marked with a green triangle in the upper-left corner of the cell. When you click the cell, Excel displays a **Smart Tag** to help you resolve the error.

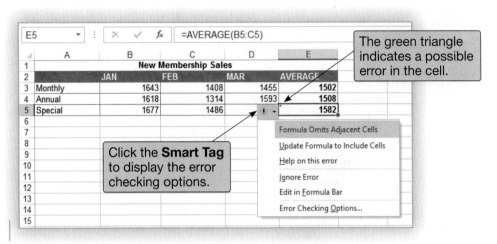

FIGURE EX 3.30

To use Smart Tags to resolve errors in formulas:

1. When a Smart Tag appears, move your mouse over the icon to display a tool tip describing the possible error.
2. Click the **Smart Tag** to display the possible error resolutions.
3. If you want to keep the formula as it is, select **Ignore Error.**
4. If you want to resolve the error, select one of the options:
   - The first option is usually a suggestion of how to resolve the error. Click it to accept Excel's suggestion.
   - Select **Help on this error** to open Microsoft Office Help.
   - Select **Edit in Formula Bar** to manually edit the formula.
   - Select **Error Checking Options...** to open the *Options* dialog and modify the way that Excel checks for errors.
5. Once you have made a selection from the Smart Tag options, the Smart Tag is dismissed.

Error checking is also available from the *Formulas* tab.

The *Error Checking* dialog displays each error it finds, allowing you to resolve or ignore each error in turn.

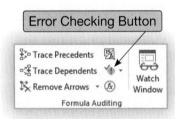

FIGURE EX 3.31

To use error checking to find errors in your worksheet:

1. On the *Formulas* tab in the *Formula Auditing* group, click the **Error Checking** button.
2. The *Error Checking* dialog displays information about the first error. The buttons available in the dialog box will differ, depending on the type of error found.
   - If Excel is able to offer a solution to the error, the dialog will include a button to accept the suggested fix.
   - Click the **Help on this error** button to open Microsoft Office Help.

- Click **Ignore Error** to dismiss the error. Excel will ignore this error until you manually reset ignored errors through Excel *Options*.
- Click **Edit in Formula Bar** to fix the error manually.

4. Click the **Next** button to see the next error in your worksheet.

5. When you have reviewed all errors, Excel displays a message that the error check is complete. Click **OK** to dismiss the message box.

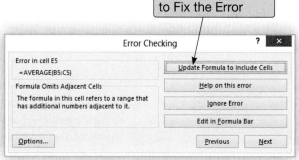

FIGURE EX 3.32

tips & tricks

You can make changes to your worksheet without closing the *Error Checking* dialog. When you click away from the dialog, one of the buttons changes to a *Resume* button and none of the other buttons in the dialog is available. When you are ready to return to error checking, click the **Resume** button.

tell me **more**

If the error is part of a complex formula, Excel may include a *Show Calculation Steps...* button in the *Error Checking* dialog. This button launches the *Evaluate Formula* dialog where you can walk through the formula step by step to try to find the cause of the error.

If the error is related to a reference to another cell, Excel will offer a *Trace Error* button to display precedent and dependent arrows showing dependencies between formulas in your worksheet.

another **method**

You can also start the Error Checking feature by clicking the **Error Checking** button arrow and selecting **Error Checking...**

let me **try**

Open the student data file **EX3-17-Sales** and try this skill on your own:

1. Cell **E5** has an error. Display the **Smart Tag** and accept Excel's suggestion for fixing the error.
2. On the *Formulas* tab, in the *Formula Auditing* group, open the *Error Checking* dialog and check the rest of the worksheet for errors.
3. Review the information about the error and select the option to edit the error in the formula bar.
4. Correct the error and resume error checking until Excel reports that the error check is complete.
5. Save the file as directed by your instructor and close it.

Skill 3.18 Finding Errors Using Trace Precedents and Trace Dependents

In a complex worksheet where formulas often reference each other, an error in one formula can cause a ripple effect of errors throughout the entire workbook. However, finding and fixing the formula that is the root cause of the errors can be difficult. One way to review your workbook for errors is to display the dependencies between formulas.

There are two types of dependencies: precedents and dependents. A **precedent** is the cell containing the formula or value the selected cell refers to. A **dependent** is the cell containing a formula that references the value or formula in the selected cell. On the *Formulas* tab, the *Formula Auditing* group includes commands for displaying and hiding arrows tracing dependencies.

To trace precedents:

1. Select the cell containing the formula for which you want to trace precedents.

2. On the *Formulas* tab, in the *Formula Auditing* group, click the **Trace Precedents** button.

3. Tracer arrows appear pointing from the selected cell to precedent cells.

To trace dependents:

1. Select the cell containing the formula for which you want to trace dependents.

2. On the *Formulas* tab, in the *Formula Auditing* group, click the **Trace Dependents** button.

3. Tracer arrows appear pointing from the selected cell to dependent cells.

Tracer arrows normally appear blue. If the tracer arrow points to a cell that contains an error, the tracer arrow will appear red. If the tracer arrow points to a cell that references a cell in another worksheet or workbook, the arrow will appear black and include a small worksheet icon. Double-click the tracer arrow to open the *Go To* dialog to navigate to the worksheet or workbook that contains the referenced cell.

Figure EX 3.34 shows both precedent and dependent tracer arrows for cell B8. You can see that the precedent arrow changes from blue to red at cell B6. The formula in that cell is the first error. (However, the error itself is not necessarily in that cell. It could be in another cell that B6 refers to.)

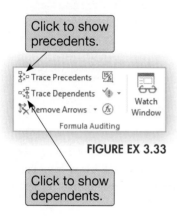

Click to show precedents.

Click to show dependents.

FIGURE EX 3.33

▲	A	B	C	D	E
1	Loan Payment Calculator			My Budget	
2					
3	Loan Amount	$ 27,000.00		Monthly Income	$ 2,800
4	APR	4%		Expenses	$ 2,200
5	Length of the loan (in years)	5 years		Loan	#VALUE!
6	Length of the loan (in months)	#VALUE!		Savings Target (10%)	$ 280
7					
8	Monthly Payment	#VALUE!		Enough left over for savings?	#VALUE!
9					
10					

FIGURE EX 3.34

Red tracer arrows indicate an error.

To remove the tracer arrows from your worksheet, on the *Formulas* tab, in the *Formula Auditing* group, click the **Remove Arrows** button arrow and select the option you want:

) To remove the precedent tracer arrows, select **Remove Precedent Arrows.**

) To remove the dependent tracer arrows, select **Remove Dependent Arrows.**

) To remove all tracer arrows at once, select **Remove Arrows.** Clicking the *Remove Arrows* button instead of the button arrow will also remove all the tracer arrows.

tips & tricks

Tracer arrows cannot identify cells with incorrect values or values of the wrong type (for example, a text value where a number is expected). However, using the tracer arrows may help you find those errors yourself.

tell me more

There may be multiple layers of dependencies in your workbook. Clicking the **Trace Precedents** button or the **Trace Dependents** button once only displays the immediate dependencies. To display tracer arrows from the precedent and dependent cells to their precedents and dependents, click the appropriate button again. Continue clicking the **Trace Precedents** button or the **Trace Dependents** button until you reach the end of the trail.

Selecting **Remove Precedent Arrows** and **Remove Dependent Arrows** removes the tracer arrows one level at a time.

another method

If the selected cell contains an error, you can display tracer arrows by clicking the **Error Checking** button arrow and selecting **Trace Error.**

let me try

Open the student data file **EX3-18-Loan** and try this skill on your own:

1. Show the precedent arrows for cell **B8.**
2. Show the dependent arrows for cell **B8.**
3. Change the value in cell **B5** to: **5** Note that the arrows change color from red to blue.
4. Hide all of the arrows at once.
5. Save the file as directed by your instructor and close it.

Skill 3.19 Displaying and Printing Formulas

How do you troubleshoot a worksheet that is displaying unexpected values? When you look at a worksheet, you see only the results of formulas—cells display the values, not the formulas themselves. When you click a cell, the formula is displayed in the formula bar. But what if you want to view all of the formulas in your worksheet at once?

To display the formulas in the current worksheet instead of values:

> On the *Formulas* tab in the *Formula Auditing* group, click the **Show Formulas** button.

To hide the formulas and display calculated values:

> Click the **Show Formulas** button again.

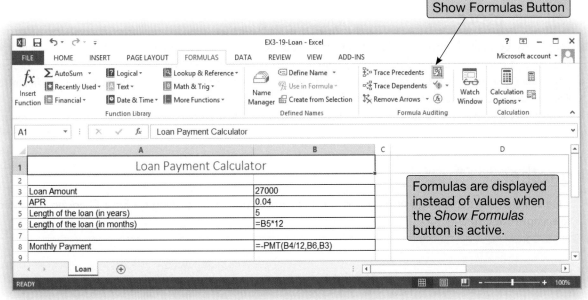

FIGURE EX 3.35

To print a copy of the worksheet with formulas instead of values:

1. First display the formulas in the worksheet by clicking the **Show Formulas** button.
2. Next, print the worksheet:
3. Click the **File** tab.
4. Click **Print.**
5. Click the **Print** button to send the file to your default printer.

tips & tricks

When you show formulas in your worksheet, Excel automatically adjusts the column sizes so the formulas are visible.

another method

The keyboard shortcut to display (or hide) formulas is **Ctrl** + **`** (the ` key is directly to the left of 1 at the top of the keyboard).

let me try

Open the student data file **EX3-19-Loan** and try this skill on your own:

1. Display the formulas in this worksheet.
2. Preview how the worksheet will look when printed.
3. Save the file as directed by your instructor and close it.

Formula AutoComplete
AVERAGE
Mean
Median
Mode
COUNT
COUNTA
COUNTBLANK
MIN
MAX
NOW
TODAY
String
Text string
PROPER
UPPER

LOWER
Concatenate
CONCATENATE
Name
Range name
Named range
Name Manager
Defined name
IF
PMT
3-D reference
VLOOKUP
HLOOKUP
Smart Tag
Precedent
Dependent

concepts review

1. Which of these methods can you use to enter a formula using the AVERAGE function?

   a. Formula Auto Complete

   b. AutoSum

   c. *Function Arguments* dialog

   d. All of the above

2. To count the number of cells that contain text or numerical values, but not blanks, use which function?

   a. COUNT

   b. COUNTALL

   c. COUNTA

   d. COUNTBLANK

3. Which of these functions returns the current date and time?

   a. TIME

   b. DATE

   c. NOW

   d. TODAY

4. What is the definition of *concatenate*?

   a. To link items together

   b. To look up a value

   c. A logical comparison

   d. To convert text to proper case

5. Which of these is **not** an acceptable name for a named range?

   a. BonusRate

   b. Bonus_Rate

   c. Bonus Rate

   d. BONUSRATE

6. Identify the *Value_if_true* argument in this formula: =IF(A1>50,"bonus","no bonus")

   a. A1

   b. 50

   c. bonus

   d. no bonus

7. Identify the *Pv* argument in this formula: =−PMT(B2/12,B3,B4)

   a. B2

   b. B2/12

   c. B3

   d. B4

8. In a PMT function, what is the *Pv* argument?

   a. The interest rate

   b. The present value of the loan

   c. The number of payments

   d. The value of the loan at the end of the loan period

9. A formula to display the value of cell **B2** on the *Sales* worksheet looks like this:

   a. =Sales!B2

   b. =B2,Sales!

   c. =Sales,B2

   d. =Sales(B2)

10. A(n) _____ is the cell containing a formula that references the value or formula in the selected cell.

    a. 3-D reference

    b. argument

    c. precedent

    d. dependent

projects

skill review 3.1

In this project you will complete a staff billing workbook similar to the one you worked on in Chapter 1. This worksheet is more complicated and uses a variety of formulas to calculate information about each staff member's weekly billing and to generate client bills from the staff hours. As you work on the *Marshall Hours* worksheet, you can use the *Luz Hours* or *Stevens Hours* worksheet as a guide. This is a long project. Be sure to save your work often!

Skills needed to complete this project:

- Naming Ranges of Cells (Skill 3.9)
- Using CONCATENATE to Combine Text (Skill 3.8)
- Creating Formulas Referencing Data from Other Worksheets (Skill 3.15)
- Finding Data Using the VLOOKUP Function (Skill 3.16)
- Working with Named Ranges (Skill 3.10)
- Using the Function Arguments Dialog to Enter Functions (Skill 3.1)
- Creating Formulas Using Counting Functions (Skill 3.4)
- Using Formula AutoComplete to Enter Functions (Skill 3.2)
- Calculating Averages (Skill 3.3)
- Finding Minimum and Maximum Values (Skill 3.5)
- Using the Logical Function IF (Skill 3.13)
- Displaying and Printing Formulas (Skill 3.19)
- Using Date and Time Functions (Skill 3.6)
- Checking Formulas for Errors (Skill 3.17)
- Finding Errors Using Trace Precedents and Trace Dependents (Skill 3.18)
- Updating Named Ranges with the Name Manager (Skill 3.11)
- Editing and Deleting Names with the Name Manager (Skill 3.12)
- Calculating Loan Payments Using the PMT Function (Skill 3.14)

1. Open the start file **EX2013-SkillReview-3-1** and resave the file as:
   `[your initials]EX-SkillReview-3-1`

2. If the workbook opens in Protected View, click the **Enable Editing** button in the Message Bar at the top of the workbook.

3. The *Luz Hours* and *Stevens Hours* worksheets are completed, but they contain errors. You'll need to fix the errors before working on the *Marshall Hours* worksheet.

   a. Click the **Luz Hours** sheet tab.

   b. Click cell **C4**.

   c. Notice the #NAME? error. Move your mouse over the **Smart Tag** icon to display a tool tip describing the possible error—*The formula contains unrecognized text*.

   d. The formula =VLOOKUP(C3,BillableRates,4,FALSE) references the named range BillableRates. That name has not yet been defined. That's what is causing the error.

4. Billable rates are kept in the *Rates* worksheet. Create the name **BillableRates** to use in formulas throughout the workbook.

    a. Click the **Rates** sheet tab.

    b. Select cells **A3:D5.**

    c. Type **BillableRates** in the *Name* box.

    d. Press ⏎ Enter .

5. Return to the *Luz Hours* worksheet. Notice all the errors have been fixed. Now you can move on to completing the *Marshall Hours* sheet.

6. Enter a formula in cell **C2** to display Marshall's full name in the format *Bob Smith.* Staff names are kept in the *Rates* worksheet.

    a. Click the **Marshall Hours** sheet tab, and click cell **C2.**

    b. On the *Formulas* tab, in the *Function Library* group, click the **Text** button, and select **CONCATENATE.**

    c. Click the **Rates** sheet tab. If necessary, position the *Function Arguments* dialog so you can click the sheet tabs.

    d. Click cell **C3** to enter the cell reference in the *Text1* argument box.

    e. Press Tab ⇆ to move to the *Text2* argument box.

    f. Type " " to place a space between the first and last names.

    g. Press Tab ⇆ to move to the *Text3* argument box.

    h. Click the **Rates** tab again.

    i. Click cell **B3** to enter the text reference in the *Text3* argument box.

    j. Click **OK.** The completed formula should look like this:

    =CONCATENATE(Rates!C3," ",Rates!B3)

7. Enter a formula in cell **C4** to look up Marshall's current billable rate. Use the employee number as the lookup value.

    a. Click cell **C4.**

    b. On the *Formulas* tab, in the *Function Library* group, click the **Lookup & Reference** button, and select **VLOOKUP.**

    c. Click cell **C3** to enter it in the *Lookup_value* argument box.

    d. Type **BillableRates** in the *Table_array* argument box.

    e. The rates are located in the fourth column of the lookup table. Type **4** in the *Col_index_num* argument box.

    f. Ensure that the function will return only an exact match. Type **false** in the *Range_lookup* argument box.

    g. Click **OK.** The completed formula should look like this:

    =VLOOKUP(C3,BillableRates,4,FALSE)

8. Enter formulas in cells **B17:H17** to calculate the number of clients served each day.

    a. Click cell **B17.**

    b. Type **=COU**

    c. Double-click **COUNT** in the Formula AutoComplete list.

    d. Click cell **B9** and drag to cell **B12.**

    e. Press ⏎ Enter . The completed formula should look like this:

    =COUNT(B9:B12)

    f. Copy the formula in cell **B17** to cells **C17:H17.** Use any method you want.

9. Enter a formula in cell **H19** to calculate the average daily billable hours (B13:H13).

 a. Click cell **H19**.

 b. Type **=AV** and then double-click **AVERAGE** in the Formula AutoComplete list.

 c. Click cell **B13** and drag to cell **H13**.

 d. Press ⏎ Enter. The completed formula should look like this:

 =AVERAGE(B13:H13)

10. Enter a formula in cell **H20** to calculate the total billable hours for the week (B13:H13).

 a. Click cell **H20**.

 b. Type **=SU** and then double-click **SUM** in the Formula AutoComplete list.

 c. Click cell **B13** and drag to cell **H13**.

 d. Press ⏎ Enter. The completed formula should look like this:

 =SUM(B13:H13)

11. Enter a formula in cell **H22** to calculate the lowest daily bill for the week (B15:H15).

 a. Click cell **H22**.

 b. Type **=MIN (** and then click cell **B15** and drag to cell **H15**.

 c. Press ⏎ Enter. The completed formula should look like this:

 =MIN(B15:H15)

12. Enter a formula in cell **H23** to calculate the highest daily bill for the week.

 a. Click cell **H23**.

 b. Type **=MAX(** and then click cell **B15** and drag to cell **H15**.

 c. Press ⏎ Enter. The completed formula should look like this:

 =MAX(B15:H15)

13. Each staff member is required to log a minimum number of billable hours per week. Enter a formula in cell **H3** using an IF statement to display "yes" if the total billable hours for the week (cell H20) is greater than or equal to the required hours (cell H2) and "no" if they are not.

 a. Click cell **H3**.

 b. On the *Formulas* tab, in the *Function Library* group, click **Logical.**

 c. Click **IF.**

 d. If necessary, move the *Function Arguments* dialog to the side so you can see the worksheet data.

 e. In the *Logical_test* argument box, type: **H20>=H2**

 f. In the *Value_if_true* argument box, type: **yes**

 g. In the *Value_if_false* argument box, type: **no**

 h. Click **OK.** The completed formula should look like this:

 =IF(H20>=H2,"yes","no")

14. Display your formulas temporarily to check for accuracy.

 a. On the *Formulas* tab, in the *Formula Auditing* group, click the **Show Formulas** button.

 b. When you are ready to continue, hide the formulas and display formula values by clicking the **Show Formulas** button again.

15. Now that the worksheet for Marshall is complete, you can generate a bill for the Smith client for the week. Click the **Smith Bill** sheet tab.

16. All bills are due thirty days from the date the bill was created. Enter a formula in cell C2 to calculate the due date using the TODAY function.

    a. Double-click cell **C2.**

    b. Type the formula: **=TODAY()+30**

    c. Press ⏎ Enter .

17. Enter formulas to reference the number of hours each staff member billed for Smith.

    a. Click cell **B6** and type = to begin the formula.

    b. Click the **Marshall Hours** sheet, and click cell **J12.**

    c. Press ⏎ Enter . The completed formula should look like this:

        ='Marshall Hours'!J12

    d. Type = to begin the next formula in cell B7.

    e. Click the **Stevens Hours** sheet, and click cell **J12.**

    f. Press ⏎ Enter . The completed formula should look like this:

        ='Stevens Hours'!J12

    g. Type = to begin the next formula in cell B8.

    h. Click the **Luz Hours** sheet, and click cell **J12.**

    i. Press ⏎ Enter . The completed formula should look like this:

        ='Luz Hours'!J12

18. There are errors in the Rate and Bill Amount columns. Use your error checking skills to track down the cause of the error.

    a. On the *Formulas* tab, in the *Formula Auditing* group, click the **Error Checking** button to open the *Error Checking* dialog.

    b. After you've reviewed the first error, click the **Next** button to go to the next error. Continue reviewing each error and clicking **Next** until you receive the message that the error check is complete for the entire sheet. Click **OK.**

19. Did you notice that every error in the worksheet is a "value not available" error? You probably need to dig deeper to find the root cause of the problem.

    a. Click cell **D6** and look at the formula in the formula bar: =B6*C6

    b. Display the Trace Precedent and Trace Dependent arrows for this cell. On the *Formulas* tab, in the *Formula Auditing* group, click both the **Trace Precedents** button and the **Trace Dependents** button.

    c. You can see that the problem appears to start in the precedent cell C6. Hide the arrows for cell **D6** by clicking the **Remove Arrows** button, and then click cell **C6** and click the **Trace Precedents** button.

    d. Notice that one of the precedent arrows for cell C6 refers to another worksheet. Double-click the dashed precedent arrow line.

    e. In the *Go To* dialog, click the worksheet reference and then click the **OK** button.

20. The link takes you to the *Rates* sheet where cells A2:D5 are selected. Notice that the *Name* box displays the name *ClientRates.* (Depending on your screen resolution, the name may be slightly cut-off.) The formula in cell C6 is a lookup formula that uses the named range *ClientRates* as the *Table_array* argument. There are two problems with the definition of the named range: It includes the label row (A2:D2), and it includes the employee number data (A2:A5).

    a. On the *Formulas* tab, in the *Defined Names* group, click the **Name Manager** button.

    b. Click the **ClientRates** name and review the cell range in the *Refers to* box. The range is incorrect. The ClientRates name should refer to cells **B2:D5** on the *Rates* sheet.

c. Edit the range listed in the *Refers to* box to:

```
=Rates!$B$2:$D$5
```

d. Click the **Close** button to close the Name Manager.

e. When Excel asks if you want to save the changes to the name reference, click **Yes.**

21. Now that the total bill amount is computing correctly, you can enter a formula in cell D14 to give the client the option of a monthly payment plan. You are authorized to offer a 6-month payment plan at a 2% annual percentage rate. Use cell references in the formula.

a. If necessary, click the **Smith Bill** sheet.

b. Click cell **D14.**

c. On the *Formulas* tab, in the *Function Library* group, click the **Financial** button.

d. Scroll down the list, and click **PMT.**

e. In the *Function Arguments* dialog, enter the *Rate* argument:

```
D13/12
```

f. Click in the **Nper** argument box, and then click cell **D12** (the number of payments).

g. Click in the **Pv** argument box, and then click cell **D9** (the present value of the loan).

h. In the *Function Arguments* dialog, click **OK.** The completed formula should look like this:

=PMT(D13/12,D12,D9)

i. The monthly payment amount appears as a negative number. That might be confusing to the client. Modify the formula so the result appears as a positive number.

j. Double-click cell **D14** and type **–** between = and **PMT.**

k. Press ⏎ **Enter** . The final formula should look like this:

=–PMT(D13/12,D12,D9)

22. Save and close the workbook.

skill review 3.2

In this project you will edit a worksheet to compute student grades and grade statistics. Be sure to save your work often!

Skills needed to complete this project:

- Using Date and Time Functions (Skill 3.6)
- Using CONCATENATE to Combine Text (Skill 3.8)
- Formatting Text Using Functions (Skill 3.7)
- Creating Formulas Using Counting Functions (Skill 3.4)
- Using Formula AutoComplete to Enter Functions (Skill 3.2)
- Displaying and Printing Formulas (Skill 3.19)
- Using the Logical Function IF (Skill 3.13)
- Using the Function Arguments Dialog to Enter Functions (Skill 3.1)
- Finding Minimum and Maximum Values (Skill 3.5)
- Calculating Averages (Skill 3.3)
- Naming Ranges of Cells (Skill 3.9)
- Finding Data Using the VLOOKUP Function (Skill 3.16)
- Working with Named Ranges (Skill 3.10)
- Checking Formulas for Errors (Skill 3.17)

1. Open the start file **EX2013-SkillReview-3-2** and resave the file as:
   `[your initials]EX-SkillReview-3-2`

2. If the workbook opens in Protected View, click the **Enable Editing** button in the Message Bar at the top of the workbook.

3. Take a look at the two sheets. The first sheet contains the students' names and their scores. The second sheet will be used to look up the letter grade for each student.

4. Enter a function in cell **B3** to display the current date each time the worksheet is opened.

   a. Click cell **B3**.

   b. On the *Formulas* tab, in the *Function Library* group, click the **Date & Time** button.

   c. Click **NOW**.

   d. Click **OK**.

5. The first column should display the full student name. Use CONCATENATE to combine the values from the First Name and Last Name columns.

   a. Click cell **A10**.

   b. On the *Formulas* tab, in the *Function Library* group, click the **Text** button, and select **CONCATENATE**.

   c. Click cell **C10** to enter the cell reference in the *Text1* argument box.

   d. Press (Tab ⇥) to move to the *Text2* argument box.

   e. Type **" "** to place a space between the first and last names.

   f. Press (Tab ⇥) to move to the *Text3* argument box.

   g. Click cell **B10** to enter the text reference in the *Text3* argument box.

   h. Click **OK**. The completed formula should look like this:
      =CONCATENATE(C10," ",B10)

6. Add the PROPER function to the formula so student names do not appear in all upper case.

   a. Double-click cell **A10** to edit the formula.

   b. Create a nested formula by typing **PROPER(** between the = symbol and CONCATENATE.

   c. Type another **)** at the end of the formula.

   d. Press (← Enter). The completed formula should look like this:
      =PROPER(CONCATENATE(C10," ",B10))

7. Copy the formula from cell **A10** to **A11:A28** to fill the list of student names. Use any method you want.

8. Count the number of students to calculate the class size.

   a. Click cell **B2**.

   b. Type **=COU**

   c. Double-click **COUNTA** in the Formula AutoComplete list.

   d. Click cell **A10** and drag to cell **A28**.

   e. Press (← Enter). The completed formula should look like this:
      =COUNTA(A10:A28)

9. Display your formulas to check for accuracy.

   a. On the *Formulas* tab, in the *Formula Auditing* group, click the **Show Formulas** button.

   b. When you are ready to continue, hide the formulas and display formula values by clicking the **Show Formulas** button again.

10. Find out which students have a below C grade at the cut-off point for dropping the class. Enter an IF function in cell **T10** to check if the student's total points divided by the total possible points through the midterm is less than 70% (the lowest percentage for a C grade). Use SUM functions within the IF function. Be sure to use absolute references for the range representing the total possible points. If the student is below a C grade, display **Warning!** in the cell; otherwise leave the cell blank.

   a. Click cell **T10.**

   b. On the *Formulas* tab, in the *Function Library* group, click **Logical.**

   c. Click **IF.**

   d. If necessary, move the *Function Arguments* dialog so you can see the worksheet data.

   e. In the *Logical_test* argument box, type:
   `SUM(D10:S10)/SUM($D$7:$S$7)<70%`

   f. In the *Value_if_true* argument box, type:
   `Warning!`

   g. In the *Value_if_false* argument box, type: `" "`

   h. Click **OK.** The completed formula should look like this:
   =IF(SUM(D10:S10)/SUM($D$7:$S$7)<70%,"Warning!"," ")

11. Fill the IF function in cell **T10** down for all students. Use any method you want.

12. Find the highest score for each assignment.

   a. Click cell **D4.**

   b. Type **=MAX (** and then click cell **D10** and drag to cell **D28.**

   c. Press (← Enter). The completed formula should look like this:
   =MAX(D10:D28)

   d. Copy the formula across the row to cell **AE4.** Use any method you want. Be sure to leave cell T4 blank.

13. Find the lowest score for each assignment.

   a. Click cell **D5.**

   b. Type **=MIN (** and then click cell **D10** and drag to cell **D28.**

   c. Press (← Enter). The completed formula should look like this:
   =MIN(D10:D28)

   d. Copy the formula across the row to cell **AE5.** Use any method you want. Be sure to leave cell T5 blank.

14. Calculate the average score for each assignment.

   a. Click cell **D6.**

   b. Type **=AV** and then double-click **AVERAGE** in the Formula AutoComplete list.

   c. Click cell **D10** and drag to cell **D28.**

   d. Press (← Enter). The completed formula should look like this:
   =AVERAGE(D10:D28)

   e. Copy the formula across the row to cell **AE6.** Use any method you want. Be sure to leave cell T6 blank.

15. Compute the students' total points. Enter a SUM function in cell **AF10** to add all the points across for the first student.

    a. Click cell **AF10.**

    b. Type **=SU** and then double-click **SUM** in the Formula AutoComplete list.

    c. Click cell **D10** and drag to cell **AE10.**

    d. Press ⏎ Enter . The completed formula should look like this:

      =SUM(D10:AE10)

    e. Copy the formula from **AF10** through cell **AF28.** Use any method you want.

16. In cell **AG10,** enter a formula to compute the percentage for the first student. Divide the student's total points by the total possible points. You will be copying this formula, so make sure the reference to the total possible points uses an absolute reference. The formula should look like this:

    =AF10/$AF$7

17. Copy the formula from **AG10** through **AG28.** Use any method you want.

18. The grade scale is stored in the *Grades* worksheet. Before calculating students' final grades, create a named range to use in the formula.

    a. Click the **Grades** sheet tab.

    b. Select cells **B5:C9.**

    c. Type **GradeScale** in the *Name* box.

    d. Press ⏎ Enter .

19. Now you are ready to create a lookup formula to display each student's final letter grade.

    a. Return to the *Scores* sheet, and click cell **AH10.**

    b. On the *Formulas* tab, in the *Function Library* group, click the **Lookup & Reference** button, and select **VLOOKUP.**

    c. Click cell **AG10** to enter it in the *Lookup_value* argument box.

    d. Type **GradeScale** in the *Table_array* argument box.

    e. The rates are located in the second column of the lookup table. Type **2** in the *Col_index_num* argument box.

    f. In this case, you do not want to specify an exact match, as the percentage grades do not match the grade scale percentages exactly An approximate match will return the correct letter grade.

    g. Click **OK.** The completed formula should look like this:

      =VLOOKUP(AG10,GradeScale,2)

20. Fill down for all students. Use any method you want.

21. Before closing the project, check your workbook for errors.

    a. On the *Formulas* tab, in the *Formula Auditing* group, click the **Error Checking** button.

    b. If errors are found, use the error checking skills learned in this chapter to find and fix the errors.

    c. When Excel displays a message that the error check is complete, click **OK.**

22. Save and close the workbook.

challenge yourself **3.3**

In this project you will complete a vehicle shopping workbook to compare the purchase of several vehicles. After completing the project, you can make a copy of the file and use it to compare vehicle purchases you are considering for yourself. Be sure to save your work often!

Skills needed to complete this project:

- Naming Ranges of Cells (Skill 3.9)
- Calculating Averages (Skill 3.3)
- Finding Data Using the VLOOKUP Function (Skill 3.16)
- Working with Named Ranges (Skill 3.10)
- Using the Function Arguments Dialog to Enter Functions (Skill 3.1)
- Using the Logical Function IF (Skill 3.13)
- Calculating Loan Payments Using the PMT Function (Skill 3.14)
- Creating Formulas Referencing Data from Other Worksheets (Skill 3.15)
- Displaying and Printing Formulas (Skill 3.19)
- Finding Errors Using Trace Precedents and Trace Dependents (Skill 3.18)
- Finding Minimum and Maximum Values (Skill 3.5)
- Using Formula AutoComplete to Enter Functions (Skill 3.2)
- Updating Named Ranges with the Name Manager (Skill 3.11)
- Editing and Deleting Names with the Name Manager (Skill 3.12)
- Checking Formulas for Errors (Skill 3.17)

1. Open the start file **EX2013-ChallengeYourself-3-3** and resave the file as:
   `[your initials]EX-ChallengeYourself-3-3`

2. If the workbook opens in Protected View, enable editing so you can make changes to the workbook.

3. The registration fee information in cells **B11:C18** on the *Assumptions* sheet will be used in lookup formulas later in this project. Name the range `RegistrationFees` to make it easier to use later.

4. Return to the *Purchase* worksheet.

5. Calculate the average MPG for each vehicle.

   a. Enter a formula in cell **C11** using the AVERAGE function to calculate the average value of **C9:C10**. Use only one argument.

   b. Copy the formula to the appropriate cells for the other vehicles.

   c. Excel will detect a possible error with these formulas. Use the **SmartTag** to ignore the error. *Hint:* Use the **SmartTag** while cells **C11:F11** are selected and the error will be ignored for all the selected cells.

6. Calculate the registration fee for each vehicle.

   a. Enter a formula in cell **C14** to lookup the registration fee for the first vehicle. Use the vehicle type in cell **C5** as the *Lookup_value* argument. Use the **RegistrationFees** named range as the *Table_array* argument. The registration fees are located in column **2** of the data table. Require an exact match.

   b. Copy the formula to the appropriate cells for the other vehicles.

7. Determine whether or not you will need a loan for each potential purchase.

   a. In cell **C16,** enter a formula using an IF function to determine if you need a loan. Your available cash is located on the *Assumptions* sheet in cell **A3.** If the price of the car is less than or equal to your available cash, display **"no".** If the price of the car is more than your available, cash, display **"yes".** Use absolute references where appropriate—you will be copying this formula across the row.

   b. Copy the formula to the appropriate cells for the other vehicles.

8. Calculate how much you would need to borrow for each purchase.

   a. In cell **C17,** enter a formula to subtract your available cash from the purchase price: Use absolute references where appropriate—you will be copying this formula across the row.

   b. Copy the formula to the appropriate cells for the other vehicles.

9. Calculate the monthly payment amount for each loan.

   a. In cell **C22,** enter a formula using the PMT function to calculate the monthly loan payment for the first vehicle. Use absolute references where appropriate—you will be copying this formula across the row. *Hint:* Don't forget to multiple the number of years by 12 in the *Nper* argument to reflect the number of monthly payments during the life of the loan.

   b. Edit the formula so the monthly payment appears as a positive number.

   c. Copy the formula to the appropriate cells for the other vehicles.

10. Compute the monthly cost of gas.

    a. In cell **C21,** enter a formula to calculate the number of miles you expect to drive each month (*Assumptions* sheet, cell **A5**) / the average MPG for the vehicle (*Purchase* sheet, cell **C11**) * gas price per gallon (*Assumptions* sheet, cell **A6**).

    b. Copy the formula to the appropriate cells for the other vehicles.

    c. If cells **D21:F21** display an error or a value of 0, display formulas and check for errors.

    d. If you still can't find the error, try displaying the precedent arrows.

    e. *Hint:* The references to the cells on the *Assumptions* sheet should use absolute references. If they do not, the formula will update incorrectly when you copy it across the row.

11. Compute the monthly cost of maintenance.

    a. In cell **C23,** enter a formula to calculate the annual maintenance cost (cell **C13**) / 12.

    b. Copy the formula to the appropriate cells for the other vehicles.

12. Compute the monthly cost of insurance.

    a. In cell **C24,** enter a formula to calculate the annual insurance cost (cell **C15**) / 12.

    b. Copy the formula to the appropriate cells for the other vehicles.

13. In cells **C25:F25,** compute the total the monthly cost for each vehicle.

14. Determine which vehicles are affordable.

    a. In cell **C27,** enter a formula using the IF function to display **"yes"** if the total monthly cost (cell **C25**) is less than or equal to the total monthly amount available for vehicle expenses (*Assumptions* sheet, cell **A4**).

    b. Copy the formula to the appropriate cells for the other vehicles.

    c. Display formulas and use the error checking skills learned in this lesson to track down and fix any errors.

15. Complete the Analysis section using formulas with statistical functions. Use named ranges instead of cell references in the formulas.

    a. *Hint:* Select cells **B8:F25** and use Excel's **Create from Selection** command to create named ranges for each row using the labels at the left side of the range as the names.

    b. *Hint:* Open the **Name Manager** and review the names Excel created. Notice that any spaces or special characters in the label names are converted to _ characters in the names.

    c. *Hint:* To avoid typos as you create each formula, try using Formula AutoComplete to select the correct range name.

16. Before finishing the project, check the worksheet for errors.

17. Save and close the workbook.

challenge yourself **3.4**

In this project, you will record data about your completed and planned college courses. You will compute your GPA, college course costs, and various statistics. You will compute your expected college loan payment and count down the days to graduation and paying off the loan. Be sure to save your work often!

Skills needed to complete this project:

- Finding Errors Using Trace Precedents and Trace Dependents (Skill 3.18)
- Finding Data Using the VLOOKUP Function (Skill 3.16)
- Using the Function Arguments Dialog to Enter Functions (Skill 3.1)
- Checking Formulas for Errors (Skill 3.17)
- Creating Formulas Referencing Data from Other Worksheets (Skill 3.15)
- Calculating Loan Payments Using the PMT Function (Skill 3.14)
- Using Date and Time Functions (Skill 3.6)
- Finding Minimum and Maximum Values (Skill 3.5)
- Using Formula AutoComplete to Enter Functions (Skill 3.2)
- Calculating Averages (Skill 3.3)
- Using the Logical Function IF (Skill 3.13)

1. Open the start file **EX2013-ChallengeYourself-3-4** and resave the file as:
    [your initials]EX-ChallengeYourself-3-4

2. If the workbook opens in Protected View, enable editing so you can make changes to the workbook.

3. There are three sheets. Start with the *GPA* sheet.

4. There is at least one error on this sheet. Click the cell that displays an error and use the precedent arrows to find the cause of the error. If the error is caused by missing values in other cells in the worksheet, you will probably fix the error by the end of this project. Hide the arrows before continuing.

5. Enter the formulas for the GPA worksheet as follows.

    a. In cell **B14** compute the cost for the first course by multiplying the unit cost (cell **C11**) by the number of units for the course (cell **G14**). Use absolute references where appropriate.

    b. Fill and copy to compute the cost for each course, both semesters (cells **B15:B16** and **B19:B22**).

6. Lookup the grade points for each letter grade as follows:

 a. In cell **I14,** enter a formula using the VLOOKUP function. Use the cell range **J3:K7** as the *Table_array* argument. The grade points are located in column **2** of this table. Use absolute references where appropriate.

 b. Fill and copy to look up the grade points for each courses, both semesters (cells **I15:I16** and **I19:I22**).

7. Multiply the grade points by the units to calculate the quality points for each course, for both semesters.

 a. In cell **J14,** enter a formula to multiply **I14** (the grade points) * cell **G14** (the units).

 b. Copy the formula to cells **J15:J16** and **J19:J22.**

8. Use AutoSum to calculate totals for cost (cells **B17** and **B23**), units (cells **G17** and **G23**), and quality points (cells **J17** and **J23**) for each semester.

9. In cell **K17,** compute the GPA for the first semester by dividing the total quality points by the total units (**J17/G17**).

10. In cell **K23,** compute the GPA for the second semester using the same formula.

11. Check the worksheet for errors. Is the error you found in step 4 fixed now? (It should be!)

12. Next go to the *Loan* worksheet.

13. In cell **B3,** enter a formula to display the total cost shown in cell **B9** on the *GPA* sheet.

14. Enter a formula in cell **B7** to look up the number of years to pay based on the loan amount show in cell **B3.** Use the data table in cells **G6:H11** as the *Table_array* argument. Do not require an exact match.

15. Now that you have the loan amount and the number of payments, enter a formula using the PMT function in cell **B8** to calculate the payment amount. Allow the payment to display as a negative number.

16. In cell **B10,** enter a formula to display the current date (just the date, not the date and time).

17. Enter a formula in cell **B16** to estimate the date of the last loan payment. Take the number of years to pay (cell **B7**) times **365.3** and add that to the date of the first loan payment (cell **B15**).

18. Enter a formula in cell **B17** to estimate the number of days until the loan is paid off.

19. Complete the *Summary* sheet information.

20. On the *Summary* sheet, in cell **B5,** enter a simple formula to reference the *Cumulative GPA* number from the *GPA* worksheet (**GPA worksheet, cell B5**).

21. Do the same for Total Units (cell **B6**), Total Cost (cell **B8**), and Total Debt (cell **B9**). For Total Debt, reference the Amount Owed number from the *Loan* sheet.

22. Compute the Average Cost Per Unit by dividing the Total Cost (cell **B8**) by the Total Units (cell **B6**).

23. Compute Average Debt Per Unit in the same way.

24. In cell **B14,** enter a formula using a statistical function to calculate the most paid for any semester. Reference cells **B17** and **B23** in the *GPA* sheet. *Hint:* You will need two arguments.

25. In cell **B16,** enter a formula to calculate the average semester cost. Reference cells **B17** and **B23** in the *GPA* sheet. *Hint:* You will need two arguments.

26. In cell **F1,** enter a formula using the IF function to determine if the student met her GPA goal. Display **"yes"** if the goal was met and **"no"** if it was not.

27. In cell **F2,** enter a formula using the IF function to determine if the student met her unit goal. Display **"yes"** if the goal was met and **"no"** if it was not.

28. Before finishing the project, check each worksheet for errors.

29. Save and close the workbook.

on your own 3.5

In this project you will complete a dental plan workbook. Be sure to save your work often!

Skills needed to complete this project:

- Updating Named Ranges with the Name Manager (Skill 3.11)
- Editing and Deleting Names with the Name Manager (Skill 3.12)
- Naming Ranges of Cells (Skill 3.9)
- Working with Named Ranges (Skill 3.10)
- Finding Data Using the VLOOKUP Function (Skill 3.16)
- Using the Function Arguments Dialog to Enter Functions (Skill 3.1)
- Calculating Averages (Skill 3.3)
- Finding Minimum and Maximum Values (Skill 3.5)
- Using Formula AutoComplete to Enter Functions (Skill 3.2)
- Creating Formulas Using Counting Functions (Skill 3.4)
- Using CONCATENATE to Combine Text (Skill 3.8)
- Creating Formulas Referencing Data from Other Worksheets (Skill 3.15)
- Formatting Text Using Functions (Skill 3.7)
- Using Date and Time Functions (Skill 3.6)
- Using the Logical Function IF (Skill 3.13)
- Calculating Loan Payments Using the PMT Function (Skill 3.14)
- Checking Formulas for Errors (Skill 3.17)
- Finding Errors Using Trace Precedents and Trace Dependents (Skill 3.18)
- Displaying and Printing Formulas (Skill 3.19)

1. Open the start file **EX2013-OnYourOwn-3-5** and resave the file as:
`[your initials]EX-OnYourOwn-3-5`

2. If the workbook opens in Protected View, click the **Enable Editing** button in the Message Bar at the top of the workbook so you can modify the workbook.

3. Start with the *Pocket Chart* worksheet. This dental chart is designed to be used to record measurements of the depth of gum pockets around the teeth. Each tooth is identified by number and name. The teeth of the upper and lower jaws are arranged across the worksheet from the patient's right side to the left. Pocket depth measurements have been entered.

4. Enter your name as the patient's name and enter the date of the examination. Do not use a function for the date. (You don't want the value to update every time you open the workbook.)

5. Review the information in the *Look Up* worksheet and assign names as necessary to each of the lookup tables to use in formulas in other worksheets. One of the lookup tables already has a name assigned.

6. Return to the *Pocket Chart* worksheet and complete the patient data.

   a. Use VLOOKUP functions to determine the severity level for each tooth.

   b. Use statistical functions to calculate the smallest pocket depth, the largest pocket depth, and the average pocket depth for the upper and lower teeth sections. Use similar formulas in **O2:O4** to calculate the overall statistical information for the patient (the average, minimum, and maximum pocket depths for both upper and lower teeth).

   c. Count the number of cells missing pocket depth information (blank cells). ***Hint:*** Remember, the COUNTBLANK function accepts only one argument, so you will need to count the blank cells for the upper teeth and the lower teeth and then add those values together.

7. Now switch to the *Treatment Plan* worksheet and fix any errors. ***Hint:*** Display formulas and then use the **Name Manager** to review names and create missing names as needed. Delete any duplicate names you may have accidentally created.

8. Create a formula to display the patient name in the format Bob Smith. Reference the patient name cells from the *Pocket Chart* sheet. Be sure to include a space between the first and last names.

9. Modify the formula that displays the patient name so the name appears in all upper case.

10. Enter a formula to display today's date in cell **I1**.

11. Cells B7:C9 summarize the number of teeth with each severity level. Use this data table to complete the treatment plan. For each treatment, display **"yes"** if the patient meets the requirement below and **"no"** if he does not.

    a. Sonic Toothbrush: Recommend only if the patient has more than five mild pockets.

    b. Scaling & Planing: Recommend only if the patient has more than seven moderate pockets.

    c. Surgery: Recommend only if the patient has more than three severe pockets.

12. Complete the billing information.

    a. Look up the cost of each treatment.

    b. Compute the amount the insurance company will cover for each treatment. Multiply the treatment cost by the insurance company rate. ***Hint:*** Use the HLOOKUP function to find the insurance company rate.

    c. Compute the billable amount for each treatment. If the treatment is recommended, compute the billable amount by subtracting the amount insurance will cover from the cost of the treatment. If the treatment is not recommended, display **"N/A"** instead.

    d. Enter a formula to calculate the total bill for the patient.

13. Enter a formula to compute the monthly payment for the payment plan option. Be sure to display the number as a positive value.

14. Display your formulas and check for errors. Use the error checking skills you learned in this chapter as needed.

15. Save and close the workbook.

fix it **3.6**

In this project, you will correct function mistakes and other formula errors in a workbook designed for planning a large party or event. Be sure to save your work often!

Skills needed to complete this project:

- Checking Formulas for Errors (Skill 3.17)
- Finding Errors Using Trace Precedents and Trace Dependents (Skill 3.18)

- Displaying and Printing Formulas (Skill 3.19)
- Creating Formulas Using Counting Functions (Skill 3.4)
- Finding Minimum and Maximum Values (Skill 3.5)
- Formatting Text Using Functions (Skill 3.7)
- Using CONCATENATE to Combine Text (Skill 3.8)
- Finding Data Using the VLOOKUP Function (Skill 3.16)
- Using the Function Arguments Dialog to Enter Functions (Skill 3.1)
- Using Formula AutoComplete to Enter Functions (Skill 3.2)
- Calculating Averages (Skill 3.3)
- Naming Ranges of Cells (Skill 3.9)
- Working with Named Ranges (Skill 3.10)
- Updating Named Ranges with the Name Manager (Skill 3.11)
- Editing and Deleting Names with the Name Manager (Skill 3.12)
- Using Date and Time Functions (Skill 3.6)
- Using the Logical Function IF (Skill 3.13)
- Creating Formulas Referencing Data from Other Worksheets (Skill 3.15)
- Calculating Loan Payments Using the PMT Function (Skill 3.14)

1. Open the start file **EX2013-FixIt-3-6** and resave the file as:
   `[your initials]EX-FixIt-3-6`

2. If the workbook opens in Protected View, click the **Enable Editing** button in the Message Bar at the top of the workbook so you can modify the workbook.

3. On the *GuestList* sheet, check all the formulas. Cells to check are filled with the light orange color. Most of them need to be corrected.

   a. In the *Name Tag* column, enter a formula to display the guest name in this format: **BILL SMITH**

   b. Correct the function used in cell **A3** to calculate the sum of the values in the *NumAttending* column.

   c. Correct the function used in cell **A4** to count the number of values in the *Street* column.

   d. Correct the function used in cell **A5** to count the number of blank cells in the *NumAttending* column.

   e. Correct the function used in cell **A6** to display the largest value in the *NumAttending* column.

   f. Correct the function used in cell **A7** to display the smallest value in the *NumAttending* column.

4. Use error checking as needed and/or display the formulas on-screen for easy viewing. When you have them right, it should look like Figure EX 3.36.

5. On the *Shopping List* sheet, check all the formulas. Cells to check are filled with the light orange color. Most of them need to be corrected. Many of the problems on this worksheet can be solved by creating named ranges or using a name that already exists.

   a. The formula in cell **B2** uses the wrong function.

   b. The formulas in cells **A9:A23** reference a named range that doesn't exist. There is more than one correct way to fix this problem using the cell range **A5:H18** on the *Places to Shop* worksheet. You can create the named range referenced in the formulas, or you can change the function arguments to reference the cell range instead.

	A	B	C	D	E	F	G	H	I	J
1	**Guest List**									
2										
3	90	Total number of guests attending			cost per invitation	$0.89				
4	65	Count of invitations sent			postage cost	$0.56				
5	6	Count of missing responses			Total cost for purchasing					
6	6	Largest group attending			and mailing invitations	$130.50				
7	1.53	Average number of guests in each group								
8										
9	Title	First Name	Last Name	Name Tag	Street	City	State	Zip	Phone	NumAttending
10	Mr.	Cindy	Jacobs	CINDY JACOBS	417 9th St.	Rocklin	CA	95602	916-598-6952	1
11	Mrs	Larrina	Grande	LARRINA GRANDE	87441 Palace Square	Newcastle	CA	95602	916-741-8526	4
12	Miss	Katherine	Hairless	KATHERINE HAIRLESS	2068 Harry Hill	Auburn	CA	95602	530-888-0805	1
13	Mr	James	Muchley	JAMES MUCHLEY	87543 Baldys Road	Auburn	CA	95602	530-885-6523	1
14	Mr./Mrs	William	Holland	WILLIAM HOLLAND	9225 Marchmont Dr	Saramento	CA	95602	(916)348-9982	2
15	Mr/Mrs	Bethany	Sanchaz	BETHANY SANCHAZ	8852 Jones Lane	Santa Rosa	CA	95602	(707)521-3478	3
16	Mrs	Gerald	Watkins	GERALD WATKINS	446 Chest Ave	San Jose	CA	95602	(415)441-8639	2
17	Mr	Emily	Thatcher	EMILY THATCHER	2275 Oak Park Lane	Rocklin	CA	95602	(916)315-8690	1
18	Mr/Mrs	Louisa	Cater	LOUISA CATER	852 Paly Place	Roseville	CA	95602	(916)789-4470	2
19	Mr.	Harold	Roger	HAROLD ROGER	14 Header Dr	Rocklin	CA	95602	555-1324	

FIGURE EX 3.36

c. The formula in cell **H9** results in the correct value. However, the workbook author copied this formula to the remaining cells in the column and those values are definitely not correct! Fix the formula in cell H9 so you can copy it to cells **H10:H23**. *Hint:* It might be useful to use the name for H8 the tax rate cell (**Tax**) so you don't have to remember to use an absolute reference when referencing it in a formula.

6. If you've fixed the formulas in cells H9:H23 correctly, the formulas in cells **I9:I23** and **G5** should be calculate properly now. However, the formulas in cells **G2:G4** still have errors that need to be fixed.

   a. Correct the function used in cell **G2** to average value of the *Cost* column.

   b. Correct the function used in cell **G3** to display the largest value in the *Cost* column.

   c. Correct the function used in cell **G4** to display the smallest value in the *Cost* column.

7. Use error checking as needed and/or display the formulas on-screen for easy viewing. When you have it right, it should look like Figure EX 3.37.

	A	B	C	D	E	F	G	H	I
1	**Shopping List**								
2	number of different items	15					$241	Average item cost	
3							$1,500	Highest Item Cost	
4							$40	Lowest Item Cost	
5							$3,922.60	Total Cost with Tax	
6									
7	City	Source	Item Description	Quantity	Units	CostperUnit	Cost	Tax	Total Cost
8								9%	
9	Roseville	Super Supermarket	Appetizers	25	pounds	$10.00	$250	$21.25	$271.25
10	Folsom	Sharons Bakery	Cake	1	Each	$350.00	$350	$29.75	$379.75
11	Citrus Heights	The Party Store	Dessert Forks, Cofee spoons	100	each	$0.50	$50	$4.25	$54.25
12	Citrus Heights	The Party Store	Dessert Plates	100	each	$1.00	$100	$8.50	$108.50
13	Citrus Heights	The Party Store	Dinner Plates	100	each	$1.25	$125	$10.63	$135.63
14	Citrus Heights	The Party Store	Dinner Silverware	100	sets	$1.00	$100	$8.50	$108.50
15	Folsom	Flower Power Florist	Flower Arrangements	15	each	$40.00	$600	$51.00	$651.00
16	Roseville	Party Rentals	Glass Coffee Cups and Saucers	50	each	$2.00	$100	$8.50	$108.50
17	Citrus Heights	The Party Store	Glasses	100	each	$1.50	$150	$12.75	$162.75
18	Carmichael	Engravers	Invitations	70	each	$0.89	$62	$5.30	$67.60
19	Sacramento	The Entertainers	Music	1	each	$1,500.00	$1,500	$127.50	$1,627.50
20	Citrus Heights	The Party Store	Napkins	100	each	$0.50	$50	$4.25	$54.25
21	Citrus Heights	The Party Store	Salad Plates	100	each	$0.75	$75	$6.38	$81.38
22	Folsom	Costco - Folsom	Soft Drinks and Water	7	case	$9.00	$63	$5.36	$68.36
23	Citrus Heights	The Party Store	Table Cloths	10	each	$4.00	$40	$3.40	$43.40

FIGURE EX 3.37

8. On the *Summary* sheet, you will be entering all the formulas. Cells to complete are filled with the light orange color.

   a. Cell **B2** should use a function that will update the date to the current date every time the workbook is opened.

   b. Cell **B4** references a named range that doesn't exist. It should reference cell **A4** on the *Guest List* sheet. You can create the named range or edit the formula to reference the cell instead.

   c. Cell **B5** references a named range that doesn't exist. It should reference cell **A3** on the *Guest List* sheet. You can create the named range or edit the formula to reference the cell instead.

   d. Cell **B8** is missing the formula to calculate whether or not the total cost with tax on the *Shopping List* sheet + the total cost for purchasing and mailing invitations on the *Guest List* sheet is greater than the available cash. The cell should display **yes** or **no**.

   e. If the result in cell B8 is *yes,* you should add a formula to cell **B9** to calculate the amount to borrow.

   f. If the result in cell B8 is *yes,* you should add a formula to cell **B10** to calculate the monthly loan payment based on the information in cells B9:B11. Remember to display the monthly payment amount as a positive number.

9. Use error checking as needed and/or display the formulas on-screen for easy viewing. When you have the formulas right, the *Summary* sheet should look like Figure EX 3.38.

	A	B
1	**Party Financing**	
2	As of	12/4/2012
3		
4	# of Invitations	65
5	# of Guests	90
6		
7	Cash Available for Event	$1,800.00
8	Do We Need to Borrow?	yes
9	Amount to Borrow	$2,253.10
10	APR	4.5%
11	# Months to Pay	12
12	Monthly Payment Amount	$192.37
13		

FIGURE EX 3.38

10. Save and close the workbook.

chapter 4

Formatting Worksheets and Managing the Workbook

In this chapter, you will learn the following skills:

- ❱ Insert, delete, and format worksheets
- ❱ Apply themes
- ❱ Insert, delete, and modify rows and columns
- ❱ Modify the worksheet view
- ❱ Manage how the worksheet prints

skills

introduction

As Excel projects get bigger and more complicated, more formatting skills are required. In this chapter, you will learn how to manage the organization and appearance of worksheets for the optimal display of data both on-screen and when printed.

Skill 4.1 Inserting Worksheets

When you create a new workbook, it contains a single worksheet named *Sheet1*. If you need more than one worksheet, you can add more. It is a good practice to keep all related information in the same workbook by adding more worksheets, rather than starting a new workbook.

❱ To add a new worksheet to the end of your workbook, click the **New Sheet** button to the right of the last worksheet tab.

❱ To add a worksheet to the left of the active worksheet, on the *Home* tab, in the *Cells* group, click the **Insert** button arrow, and select **Insert Sheet.**

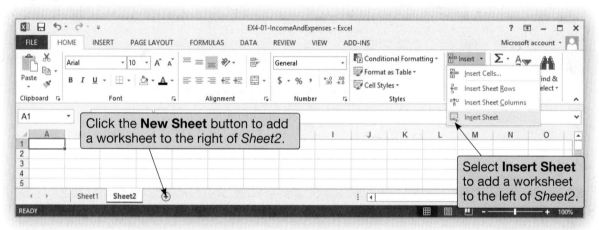

FIGURE EX 4.1

The new sheet is given the name Sheet# (where # is the next number available—for example, if your workbook contains *Sheet1* and *Sheet 2*, the next sheet inserted will be named *Sheet3*).

another **method**

To add a worksheet you can also:
1. Right-click on a sheet tab.
2. Select **Insert...** on the shortcut menu.
   ❱ To insert a blank worksheet, click the **Worksheet** icon in the dialog box.
   ❱ To insert a formatted worksheet, click the **Spreadsheet Solutions** tab, and click any of the template icons.
3. Click **OK.**

let me **try**

Open the student data file **EX4-01-IncomeAndExpenses** and try this skill on your own:
1. Add a new worksheet to the right of the *Sheet1* sheet.
2. Add another new worksheet to the left of the new *Sheet2* worksheet.
3. Save the file as directed by your instructor and close it.

Skill 4.2 Naming Worksheets

When you create a new workbook, Excel automatically includes a worksheet named *Sheet1*. Additional worksheets that you insert are automatically named *Sheet2, Sheet3,* and so forth. It is a good idea to rename your worksheets to something more descriptive. Giving your worksheets descriptive names can help organize multiple worksheets, making it easier for you to find and use information.

To rename a worksheet:

1. Right-click the worksheet tab, and select **Rename.**
2. Excel highlights the sheet name, allowing you to replace it as you type.
3. Type the new sheet name, and press ⏎ Enter .

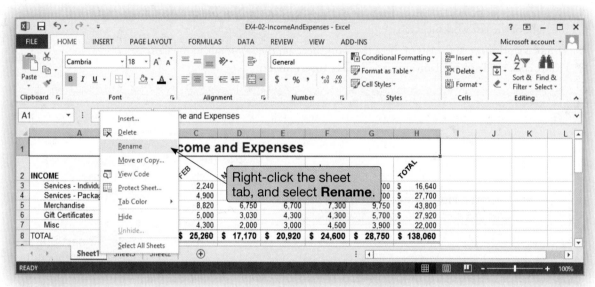

FIGURE EX 4.2

another **method**

You can also use the Ribbon to rename a worksheet.
1. Click the sheet tab you want to rename.
2. On the *Home* tab, in the *Cells* group, click the **Format** button.
3. Click **Rename Sheet.**
4. Type the new sheet name, and press ⏎ Enter .

let me **try**

Open the student data file **EX4-02-IncomeAndExpenses** and try this skill on your own:
1. Rename *Sheet1* using the following name: Q1-Q2
2. Save the file as directed by your instructor and close it.

Skill 4.3 Changing the Color of Sheet Tabs

By default, all the worksheet tabs in Excel are white. If you have many sheets in your workbook, changing the tab colors can help you organize your data.

To change a worksheet tab color:

1. Right-click the sheet tab and point to **Tab Color** to display the color palette.
2. Hover the mouse pointer over each color to preview how the color will look when the worksheet is active.
3. Click the color you want.

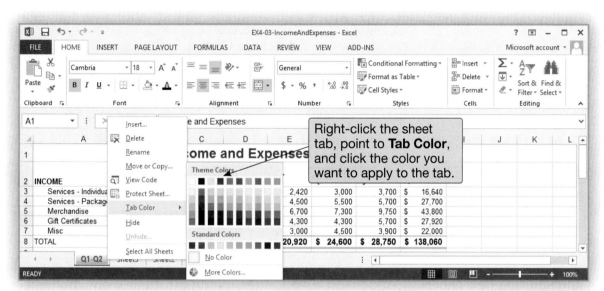

Right-click the sheet tab, point to **Tab Color**, and click the color you want to apply to the tab.

FIGURE EX 4.3

tips & tricks

》 The color palette used for worksheet tab color is the same color palette used for font color, fill color, and border color. The colors available change depending on the theme applied to the workbook.

》 If you have sheets that contain related data, color them using different shades of the same color.

another method

You can also use the Ribbon to change tab color.
1. Click the sheet tab you want to color.
2. On the *Home* tab, in the *Cells* group, click the **Format** button.
3. Point to **Tab Color** to display the color palette.
4. Click the color you want.

let me try

Open the student data file **EX4-03-IncomeAndExpenses** and try this skill on your own:
1. Change the color of the sheet tab for the *Q1-Q2* worksheet to **Dark Blue, Text 2.**
2. Save the file as directed by your instructor and close it.

Skill 4.4 Moving and Copying Worksheets

You can move worksheets around in a workbook, rearranging them into the most logical order.

To move a worksheet within a workbook:

1. Click the worksheet tab and hold down the mouse button.
2. Notice that the mouse pointer changes to the ⬚ shape.
3. Drag the mouse cursor to the position where you want to move the sheet, and release the mouse button.

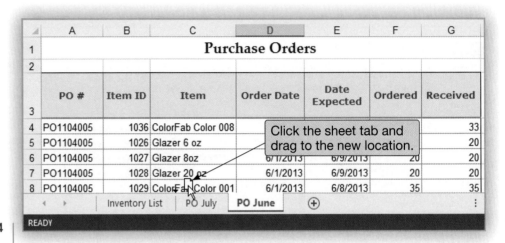

FIGURE EX 4.4

If you want to experiment with worksheet layouts or formulas, you can create a copy of the worksheet in case you want to go back to the original version.

To create a copy of a worksheet:

1. Click the worksheet tab, hold down the mouse button, and press and hold (Ctrl).
2. Notice that the mouse pointer changes to the ⬚ shape.
3. Drag the mouse cursor to the position where you want to insert a copy of the selected sheet, and release the mouse button.

To move or copy a worksheet to another workbook or to a new workbook:

1. Right-click the sheet tab, and select **Move or Copy...** to open the *Move or Copy* dialog.
2. In the *Move or Copy* dialog, expand the **To book** list at the top of the dialog. The *To book* list shows all the Excel workbooks you have open. Click the workbook you want. To move or copy the sheet to a new blank workbook, select **(new book).**
3. The list of sheets in the *Before sheet* box will update to show the sheets available in the workbook you selected. Click the name of the sheet you want to move the selected sheet before. If you want to move the sheet to the end of the workbook, select **(move to end)** in the *Before sheet* box.
4. If you want to create a copy of the selected sheet, instead of moving the original, click the **Create a copy** check box.
5. Click **OK.**

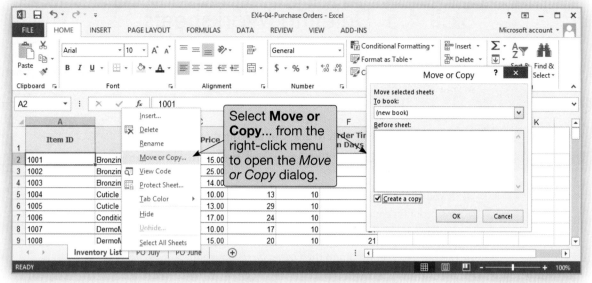

FIGURE EX 4.5

You can use this same method to move or copy worksheets within a workbook by not changing the workbook listed in the *To book* list in the *Move or Copy* dialog.

tips & tricks

Moving a worksheet from one workbook to another deletes the worksheet from the original workbook. Consider copying the worksheet to the second workbook first, and then, once you are confident that formulas work as you intend, delete the worksheet from the original workbook.

tell me **more**

To move or copy more than one worksheet, press (↑ Shift) and click the worksheets you want to move or copy. If the worksheets are not consecutive, then press (Ctrl) instead.

another **method**

You can also open the *Move or Copy* dialog from the Ribbon:
    On the *Home* tab, in the *Cells* group, click the **Format** button, and select **Move or Copy Sheet...**

let me **try**

Open the student data file **EX4-04-PurchaseOrders** and try this skill on your own:
1. Move the *PO June* worksheet so it is positioned before the *PO July* worksheet.
2. Make a copy of the *PO June* worksheet and position it before the *PO July* worksheet.
3. Copy the *Inventory List* worksheet to a new workbook.
4. Save the files as directed by your instructor and close them.

skill 4.4   Moving and Copying Worksheets

Skill 4.5 Deleting Worksheets

If you have multiple copies of the same worksheet in a workbook, be sure to delete the versions you no longer need. It is always a good practice to delete any unnecessary worksheets in your workbook.

To delete a worksheet:

1. Select the sheet you want to delete by clicking the worksheet tab.

2. On the *Home* tab, in the *Cells* group, click the **Delete** button arrow, and select **Delete Sheet.**

3. If you try to delete a sheet that contains data, Excel will display a warning that the sheet may contain data and ask if you are sure you want to permanently remove it from your workbook. Click the **Delete** button to continue and delete the worksheet.

Be careful—you cannot undo the *Delete Sheet* command.

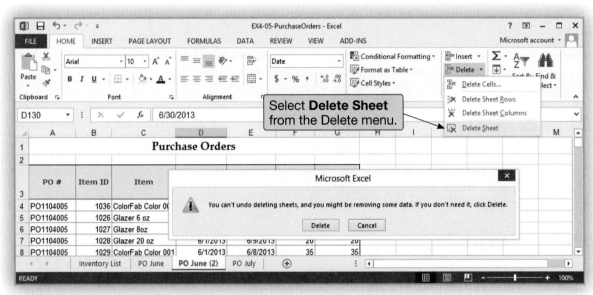

FIGURE EX 4.6

tell me **more**

You can delete multiple worksheets at the same time. First, select all the sheet tabs you want to remove, and then invoke the *Delete Sheet* command.

another **method**

To delete a worksheet you can also right-click on a sheet tab and then select **Delete** from the shortcut menu.

let me try

Open the student data file **EX4-05-PurchaseOrders** and try this skill on your own:
1. Delete the *PO June (2)* worksheet.
2. Save the file as directed by your instructor and close it.

Skill 4.6 Grouping Worksheets

If you have multiple worksheets with the same structure, you can make changes to all of the worksheets at the same time by **grouping** them. This is convenient when you are setting up a series of worksheets with the same row or column headings. When sheets are grouped together, you can also change column widths and formatting, add formulas such as totals, or add headers and footers. Using grouping saves time and ensures that the sheets share a consistent format.

To group worksheets:

1. Click the first worksheet tab.
2. Hold down (⇧ Shift) and click the tab for the last worksheet you want included in the group. If you want to select noncontiguous worksheets (sheets that are not next to each other), press (Ctrl) instead, and then click each sheet tab.
3. Notice that the title bar now includes [Group] after the file name.
4. Make the change you want to the sheet. This same change will be made to all sheets in the group.
5. To ungroup, click any sheet tab that is not part of the group.

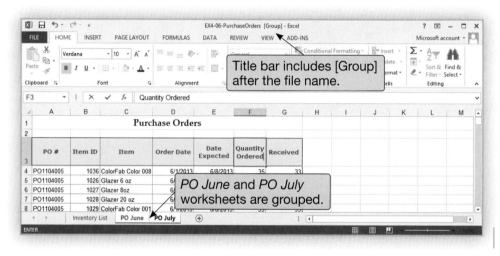

FIGURE EX 4.7

tell me **more**

To group all the sheets in your workbook together, right-click any sheet tab and then click **Select All Sheets.**

To ungroup sheets, right-click one of the grouped sheet tabs and then click **Ungroup.** If all of the sheets in your workbook are grouped together, you must use this method to ungroup them.

let me try

Open the student data file **EX4-06-PurchaseOrders** and try this skill on your own:

1. Group sheets *PO June* and *PO July.*
2. Change the text in cell **F3** to: **Quantity Ordered**
3. Ungroup the sheets.
4. Review cell **F3** in sheets *PO June* and *PO July* to ensure that the change was made to both sheets.
5. Save the file as directed by your instructor and close it.

Skill 4.7 Applying Themes

A **theme** is a unified color, font, and effects scheme. When you apply a theme to the workbook, you ensure that all visual elements work well together, giving the workbook a polished, professional look. When you create a new blank workbook in Excel 2013, the Office theme is applied by default.

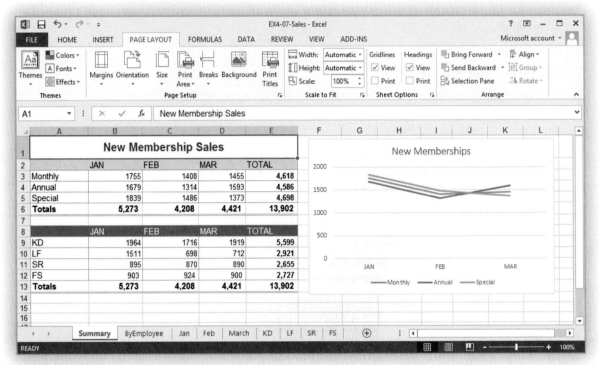

FIGURE EX 4.8

A workbook with the Office theme applied

FIGURE EX 4.9

The same workbook with the Banded theme applied

excel 2013   chapter 4 Formatting Worksheets and Managing the Workbook

To apply a theme to a workbook:

1. On the *Page Layout* tab, in the *Themes* group, click the **Themes** button to expand the gallery.

2. Roll your mouse over each theme in the gallery to preview the formatting changes.

3. Click one of the themes to apply it to your workbook.

From the *Themes* group, you can apply specific aspects of a theme by making a selection from the *Theme Colors, Theme Fonts,* or *Theme Effects* gallery. Applying one aspect of a theme (for example, colors) will not change the other aspects (fonts and effects).

Theme Colors—Limits the colors available from the color palette for fonts, borders, and cell shading. Notice that when you change themes, the colors in the color palette change.

Theme Fonts—Affects the fonts used for cell styles (including titles and headings). Changing the theme fonts does not limit the fonts available to you from the *Font* group on the Ribbon.

Theme Effects—Controls the way graphic elements in your worksheet appear. Chart styles change according to the theme color and effects.

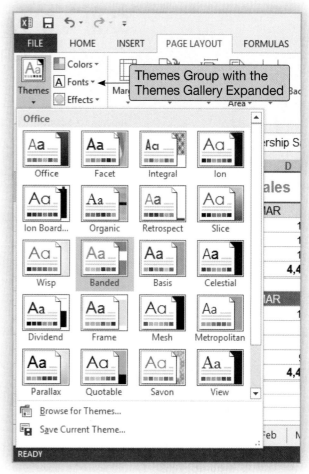

FIGURE EX 4.10

tips & tricks

When you change the workbook theme, the look of the built-in cell styles changes. Be careful, as the change in style may increase the font size, causing some of your data to be too wide for the columns. If you change themes, you may need to adjust some of your column widths or row heights.

let me try

Open the student data file **EX4-07-Sales** and try this skill on your own:

1. If necessary, click the *Summary* sheet tab.
2. Expand the *Themes* gallery and preview how each theme would affect the workbook.
3. Apply the **Banded** theme.
4. Save the file as directed by your instructor and close it.

Skill 4.8 Modifying Column Widths and Row Heights

Some columns in your spreadsheet may be too narrow to display the data properly. If a cell contains text data, the text appears cut off. (If the cell to the right is empty, however, the text appears to extend into the empty cell.) If the cell contains numerical data, Excel displays a series of pound signs (#) when the cell is too narrow to display the entire number. You should adjust the column widths so the spreadsheet is easy to read.

Excel offers an easy way to automatically set columns to the width to best fit the data in the column:

To make the column automatically fit the contents, double-click the right column border.

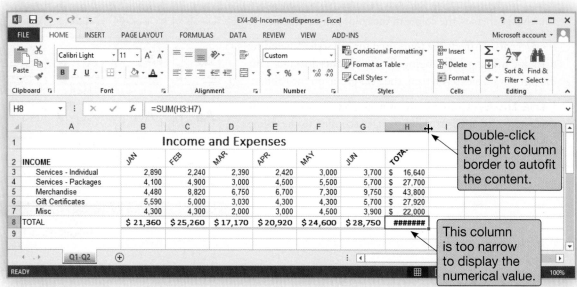

FIGURE EX 4.11

You can also modify column widths manually:

1. Move your mouse over the right column boundary.
2. The cursor will change to a ✛ shape.
3. Click and drag until the column is the size you want, and then release the mouse button.

Rows in Excel are automatically sized to fit the font size. However, if you change the font size or apply a new theme, you may need to modify row heights. Use the same techniques you use for resizing columns:

To make the row automatically fit the contents, double-click the bottom row boundary.

To modify row heights manually:

1. Move your mouse over the bottom row boundary.
2. The cursor will change to a ✛ shape.
3. Click and drag until the row is the size you want, and then release the mouse button.

If your worksheet data are organized in a table format, you should ensure that all columns have the same width. The column width number refers to the number of standard characters that can display in the column.

To specify an exact column width:

1. Select the columns you want to modify. Click the column selector for the first column, press and hold (⇧ Shift), and click the column selector for the last column.
2. On the *Home* tab, in the *Cells* group, click the **Format** button.
3. Select **Column Width...**
4. Enter the value you want in the *Column Width* dialog.
5. Click **OK.**

You can use this same technique to specify a row height. From the *Format* button menu, select **Row Height...** and enter the row height value in the *Row Height* dialog.

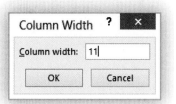

FIGURE EX 4.12

another **method**

You can also apply the *AutoFit* command from the Ribbon:

To autofit a column:
1. Click the column selector for the column you want to resize.
2. On the *Home* tab, in the *Cells* group, click the **Format** button.
3. Click **AutoFit Column Width.**

To autofit a row:
1. Click the row selector for the row you want to resize.
2. On the *Home* tab, in the *Cells* group, click the **Format** button.
3. Click **AutoFit Row Height.**

let me **try**

Open the student data file **EX4-08-IncomeAndExpenses** and try this skill on your own:
1. Autofit column **H** to best fit the data.
2. Autofit row **2** to best fit the data.
3. Select columns **B:G** and change the column width to **11.**
4. Save the file as directed by your instructor and close it.

Skill 4.9 Inserting and Deleting Rows and Columns

You may find you need to add rows or columns of new information into the middle of your workbook. Adding a new row will shift other rows down; adding a new column will shift other columns to the right.

To insert a row:

1. Place your cursor in a cell in the row below where you want the new row.
2. On the *Home* tab, in the *Cells* group, click the **Insert** button arrow and select **Insert Sheet Rows.**
3. The new row will appear above the selected cell.

To insert a column:

1. Place your cursor in a cell in the column to the right of where you want the new column.
2. On the *Home* tab, in the *Cells* group, click the **Insert** button arrow and select **Insert Sheet Columns.**
3. The new column will appear to the left of the selected cell.

When you insert a row or column, a Smart Tag will appear. Click the **Smart Tag** to choose formatting options for the new row or column—**Format Same as Above, Format Same as Below,** or **Clear Formatting** for rows and **Format Same as Left, Format Same as Right,** or **Clear Formatting** for columns.

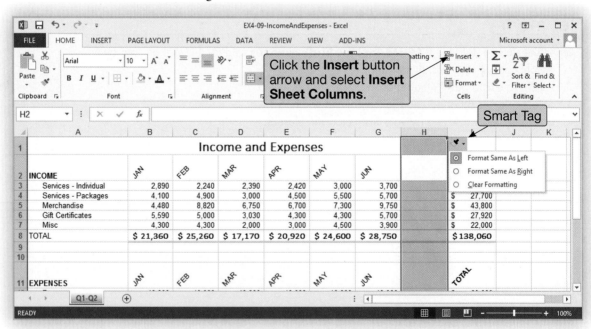

FIGURE EX 4.13

Of course, you can also delete rows and columns. Deleting a row will shift other rows up; deleting a column will shift the remaining columns to the left.

To delete a row:

1. Place your cursor in a cell in the row you want to delete.
2. On the *Home* tab, in the *Cells* group, click the **Delete** button arrow and select **Delete Sheet Rows.**
3. The row will be deleted and the rows below it will shift up.

excel 2013 chapter 4 Formatting Worksheets and Managing the Workbook

To delete a column:

1. Place your cursor in a cell in the column you want to delete.

2. On the *Home* tab, in the *Cells* group, click the **Delete** button arrow and select **Delete Sheet Columns.**

3. The column will be deleted, and columns to the right of the deleted column will shift left.

tips & tricks

Depending on whether you have a cell, a range of cells, a row, or a column selected, the behavior of the *Insert* and *Delete* commands will change. If you have a single cell selected and click the **Insert** button instead of the button arrow, Excel will insert a single cell, automatically moving cells down. However, if you select the entire column first, and then click the **Insert** button, Excel will automatically insert a column.

another method

To insert or delete rows and columns, you can also:
1. Right-click in a cell, then select **Insert...** or **Delete...**
2. In the dialog box, select **Entire row** or **Entire column.**
3. Click **OK.**

You can also select an entire row or column by clicking the row or column selector, then right-click and select **Insert** or **Delete** from the menu. Because you have already selected an entire row or column, Excel will not ask you to specify what you want to insert or delete.

let me try

Open the student data file **EX4-09-IncomeAndExpenses** and try this skill on your own:
1. Insert a new column to the left of column **H.** Format the new column the same as the column to its left.
2. Delete row **10.**
3. Save the file as directed by your instructor and close it.

Skill 4.10 Freezing and Unfreezing Rows and Columns

If you have a large spreadsheet (very wide or very tall), you may want to **freeze** part of the worksheet. By doing this, you can keep column headings and row labels visible as you scroll through your data.

To freeze part of the worksheet, so it is always visible:

1. Arrange the worksheet so the row you want to be visible is the top row or the column you want is the first column visible at the left.

2. On the *View* tab, in the *Window* group, click the **Freeze Panes** button.

   ❯ If you want the first row to always be visible, click **Freeze Top Row.**

   ❯ If you want the first column to always be visible, click **Freeze First Column.**

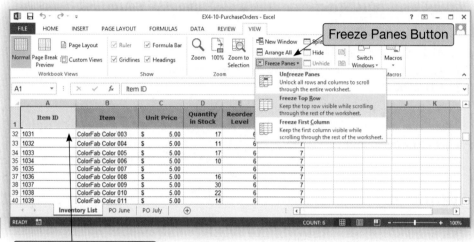

FIGURE EX 4.14

The top row will remain visible as you scroll down the worksheet.

If your worksheet has both a header row and a column of labels in the first column, use the *Freeze Panes* option to freeze the worksheet at the selected cell, so the rows above the cell and the columns to the left of the cell are always visible.

1. Select the cell immediately below the header row and immediately to the right of the label column (usually cell B2).

2. On the *View* tab, in the *Window* group, click the **Freeze Panes** button, and select **Freeze Panes.**

To return your worksheet to normal, click the **Freeze Panes** button and select **Unfreeze Panes.**

let me try

Open the student data file **EX4-10-PurchaseOrders** and try this skill on your own:

1. Verify that the *Inventory List* sheet is selected and the header row (row 1) is visible at the top of the worksheet.
2. Apply the *Freeze Panes* command so the top row will remain visible as you scroll down the worksheet.
3. Save the file as directed by your instructor and close it.

Skill 4.11 Hiding and Unhiding Rows and Columns

When you hide a row or column, the data still remain in your workbook, but they are no longer displayed on-screen and are not part of the printed workbook. Hiding rows can be helpful when you want to print a copy of your workbook for others but do not want to share all the information contained in your workbook.

To hide a row or column:

1. Select any cell in the row or column you want to hide.
2. On the *Home* tab, in the *Cells* group, click the **Format** button.
3. Point to **Hide & Unhide,** and click **Hide Rows** or **Hide Columns.**

To unhide a row or column:

1. Select the rows or columns on either side of the row or column you want to unhide.
2. On the *Home* tab, in the *Cells* group, click the **Format** button.
3. Point to **Hide & Unhide,** and click **Unhide Rows** or **Unhide Columns.**

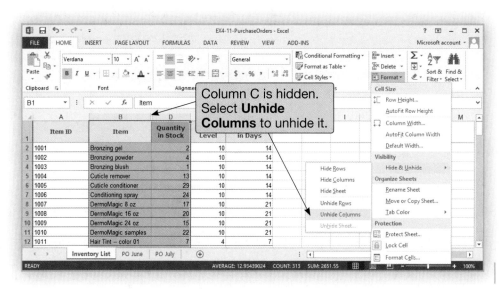

FIGURE EX 4.15

another **method**

The *Hide* and *Unhide* commands are also available from the right-click menu when columns or rows are selected.

let me **try**

Open the student data file **EX4-11-PurchaseOrders** and try this skill on your own:

1. Verify that the *Inventory List* sheet is selected.
2. Hide column **C.**
3. Unhide column **C** without using the *Undo* command.
4. Save the file as directed by your instructor and close it.

Skill 4.12 Splitting Workbooks

In Excel, you can split the worksheet view into two or four panes. Each pane scrolls independently of the other(s), so you can see two (or four) different areas of the worksheet at the same time. This can be especially helpful if you want to compare data in multiple parts of the worksheet at the same time.

To split the worksheet view:

1. Click the cell in the worksheet where you would like to split the view. You can select an entire row or column as the split point.

) If you want to split the worksheet into two horizontal panes, click a cell in column **A**.

) If you want to split the worksheet into two vertical panes, click a cell in row **1**.

) If you want to split the worksheet into four panes, click any cell in the worksheet. The cell you selected will be the top left cell in the pane in the lower-right quadrant.

2. On the *View* tab, in the *Window* group, click the **Split** button.

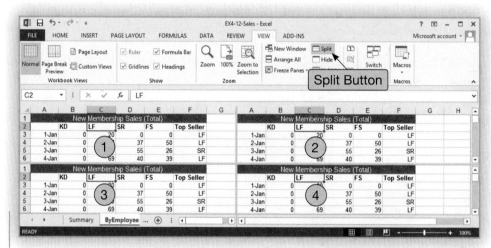

FIGURE EX 4.16
Worksheet split into four panes

To undo the split and return the worksheet to a single view, click the **Split** button again.

tips & tricks

Splitting your worksheet will undo the *Freeze Panes* command.

tell me more

To adjust the size of the panes, click and drag the pane border.

let me try

Open the student data file **EX4-12-Sales** and try this skill on your own:
1. Verify that the *ByEmployee* sheet is selected.
2. Select any cell in the middle of the worksheet, and then split the worksheet into four panes.
3. Save the file as directed by your instructor and close it.

Skill 4.13 Changing the Worksheet View

Excel offers three ways to view a worksheet.

Just as the name implies, **Normal view** is the typical working view. In *Normal* view, Excel shows the aspects of the worksheet that are visible only on-screen. Elements that are visible only when printed (like headers and footers) are hidden.

Page Layout view shows all the worksheet elements as they will print. *Page Layout* view includes headers and footers. You will work with *Page Layout* view when you learn about headers and footers

Page Break Preview view allows you to manipulate where page breaks occur when the worksheet is printed. You will work with *Page Break Preview* view when you learn about inserting page breaks.

To switch between worksheet views, click the appropriate button in the status bar at the bottom of the Excel window, or on the *View* tab, in the *Workbook Views* group, click the button for the view you want.

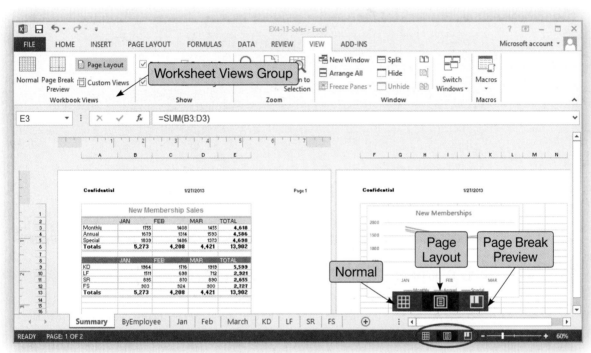

FIGURE EX 4.17
Page Layout view

let me try

Open the student data file **EX4-13-Sales** and try this skill on your own:

1. Verify that the *Summary* sheet is selected.
2. Switch to **Page Break Preview** view.
3. Switch to **Page Layout** view.
4. Save the file as directed by your instructor and close it.

Skill 4.14 Adding Headers and Footers

A **header** is text that appears at the top of every page, just below the top margin; a **footer** is text that appears at the bottom of every page, just above the bottom margin. Typically, headers and footers display information such as dates, page numbers, sheet names, file names, and authors' names.

To add a header or footer to a worksheet from *Page Layout* view:

1. Switch to *Page Layout* view by clicking the **Page Layout** button on the status bar.
2. The header area has three sections with the text *Click to add header* in the center section. Click the header section where you want to add information (left, center, or right).
3. The *Header & Footer Tools Design* contextual tab appears.
4. In the *Header & Footer* group, click the **Header** button and select one of the predefined headers, or click a button in the *Header & Footer Elements* group to add a specific header element such as the sheet name or the current date. Excel inserts the code for the header element. Once you click away from the header, you will see the actual header text.

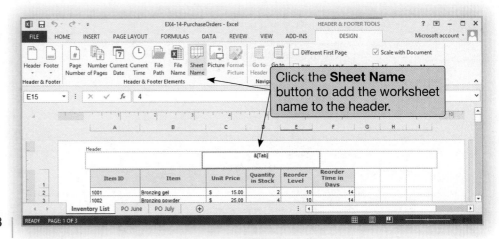

FIGURE EX 4.18

5. In the *Navigation* group, click the **Go to Footer** button to switch to the footer. Add footer elements the same way you add header elements.
6. When you are finished adding your header and footer elements, click anywhere in the worksheet and then switch back to *Normal* view.

Another method for adding headers and footers uses the *Page Setup* dialog. This method will be familiar to users who have worked with older versions of Excel.

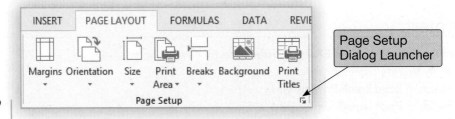

FIGURE EX 4.19

To add a header or footer to a worksheet using the *Page Setup* dialog:

1. On the *Page Layout* tab, in the *Page Setup* group, click the **Page Setup Dialog Launcher** to open the *Page Setup* dialog.
2. Click the **Header/Footer** tab.
3. Click the arrow beneath the Header or Footer area to expand the list of predefined header/footer options. Click the option you want to use.

4. You can also customize the header or footer by clicking the **Custom Header...** or **Custom Footer...** button and adding elements through the *Header* or *Footer* dialog.

5. In the *Header* or *Footer* dialog, click the section you want, and then click one of the header/footer element buttons.

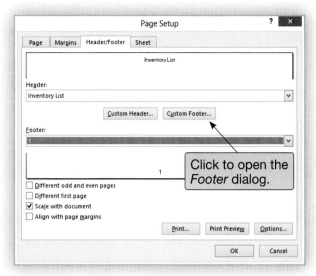

FIGURE EX 4.20

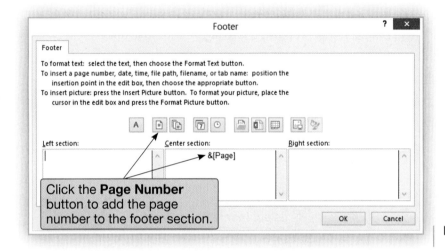

FIGURE EX 4.21

tips & tricks

Page Layout view is not compatible with Freeze Panes. If you have Freeze Panes applied to your worksheet, Excel will warn you before switching to *Page Layout* view. Click **OK** in the message box to continue to *Page Layout* view and undo Freeze Panes.

another method

Another way to add a header or footer to your worksheet is to click the *Insert* tab. In the *Text* group, click the **Header & Footer** button. (The worksheet will automatically switch to *Page Layout* view when you click the *Header & Footer* button.)

let me try

Open the student data file **EX4-14-PurchaseOrders** and try this skill on your own:
1. Verify that the *Inventory List* sheet is active.
2. Add a header that displays the sheet name in the center section.
3. Add a footer that displays the page number in the center section.
4. Click anywhere in the worksheet grid, and then switch back to *Normal* view.
5. Preview how the worksheet will look when printed and note the header and footer.
6. Save the file as directed by your instructor and close it.

Skill 4.15 Inserting Page Breaks

Excel automatically inserts page breaks so columns and rows are not split across pages when you print. However, you may want to control where page breaks happen so your worksheet prints in a more logical order. When the worksheet is in *Normal* view, page breaks appear as faint dotted lines. To view the page breaks more clearly, switch to *Page Break Preview* view.

To manually insert a new page break:

1. Begin by selecting the cell below and to the right of where you want the new page break.
2. On the *Page Layout* tab, in the *Page Setup* group, click the **Breaks** button.
3. Click **Insert Page Break.**
4. A new page break is inserted to the left of the selected column or above the selected row.

When the worksheet is in *Page Break Preview* view, automatic page breaks appear as blue dotted lines and manually inserted page breaks appear as solid blue lines. You can manually move a page break by clicking the page break line, and then dragging to the right or left or up or down. Release the mouse button when the line appears where you want the break. Notice that if you move an automatic page break, the line changes from dotted to solid.

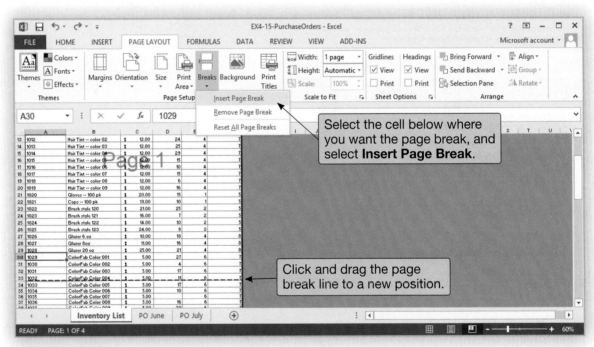

FIGURE EX 4.22
This worksheet is in Page Break Preview view

To remove a manual page break, select any cell adjacent to (to the right of or below) the break, then on the *Page Layout* tab, in the *Page Setup* group, click the **Breaks** button, and click **Remove Page Break.**

excel 2013   chapter 4 Formatting Worksheets and Managing the Workbook

tips & tricks

If you insert a page break but nothing seems to happen, check to see if you have the scaling option set for printing. For example, if you have the worksheet set to print all columns on a single page, inserting a new page break between columns will not appear to have any effect on the worksheet. However, if you remove the scaling option, the new manual page break will appear.

tell me **more**

To remove all the manual page breaks at once, on the *Page Layout* tab, in the *Page Setup* group, click the **Breaks** button, and click **Reset All Page Breaks.**

let me try

Open the student data file **EX4-15-PurchaseOrders** and try this skill on your own:
1. Verify that the *Inventory List* sheet is active.
2. Switch to *Page Break Preview* view and observe the page breaks.
3. Move the page break between pages 1 and 2 to just below **row 29.**
4. Switch back to *Normal* view.
5. Save the file as directed by your instructor and close it.

from the perspective of . . .

WAREHOUSE LOGISTICS SUPERVISOR

Part of our company's "green" initiative is to minimize paper usage for printing. Using Excel's page break controls and layout controls like scaling, page orientation, and margins, we make sure that the reports we *have* to print use as little paper as possible.

Skill 4.16 Showing and Hiding Worksheet Elements

Gridlines are the lines that appear on the worksheet defining the rows and columns. Gridlines make it easy to see the individual cells in your worksheet. By default, gridlines are visible on-screen when you are working in Excel, but they do not print.

Headings are the numbers at the left of rows and the letters at the top of columns. By default, Excel displays the row and column headings on-screen to make it easy to identify cell references but they do not print.

To hide gridlines or headings on-screen:

On the *Page Layout* tab, in the *Sheet Options* group, click the **View** check box under **Gridlines** or **Headings** to remove the checkmark.

To print the gridlines and headings when you print the worksheet:

On the *Page Layout* tab, in the *Sheet Options* group, click the **Print** check box under **Gridlines** or **Headings.**

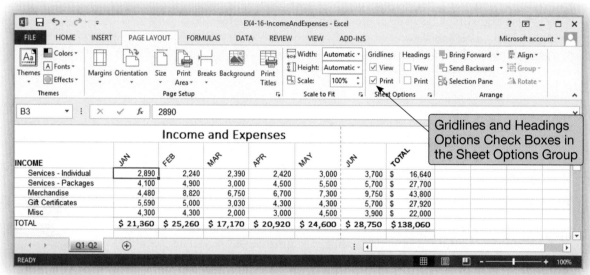

FIGURE EX 4.23

tips & tricks

Hiding gridlines and headings can make your workbook look less like a spreadsheet and more like a form.

another method

To show or hide gridlines and headings on-screen, you can also check or uncheck the appropriate boxes on the *View* tab, in the *Show* group.

let me try

Open the student data file **EX4-16-IncomeAndExpenses** and try this skill on your own:
1. Modify the *Q1-Q2* worksheet so gridlines will print.
2. Modify the *Q1-Q2* worksheet so headings are hidden on-screen.
3. Save the file as directed by your instructor and close it.

Skill 4.17 Changing Worksheet Orientation

Orientation refers to the direction the worksheet prints. It doesn't affect the way the worksheet looks on your computer screen. The default print setting is for **portrait orientation**—when the height of the page is greater than the width (like a portrait hanging on a wall). If your workbook is wide, you may want to use **landscape orientation** instead, where the width of the page is greater than the height.

You can set the worksheet orientation from the *Page Layout* tab on the Ribbon:

1. On the *Page Layout* tab, in the *Page Setup* group, click the **Orientation** button.
2. Click the **Portrait** or **Landscape** option.

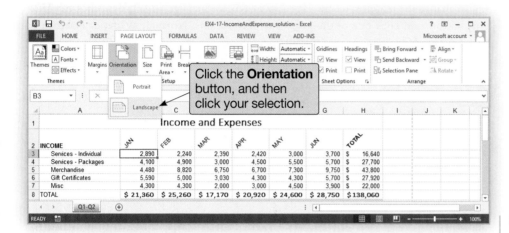

FIGURE EX 4.24

You can also change the worksheet orientation when you print:

1. Click the **File** tab to open Backstage.
2. Click **Print.**
3. In the *Settings* section, click the button displaying the current orientation setting, and then click the orientation setting you want.

tips & tricks

Changing the *Orientation* setting affects only the active worksheet.

another method

You can also use the *Page Setup* dialog box to change the orientation of your worksheet. On the *Page* tab, click the **Portrait** or **Landscape** radio button, and then click **OK.**

let me try

Open the student data file **EX4-17-IncomeAndExpenses** and try this skill on your own:

1. Note the page break line between columns F and G.
2. Change the worksheet orientation to **Landscape.**
3. Note that the page is wider now and the page break line is between columns I and J.
4. Save the file as directed by your instructor and close it.

Skill 4.18 Setting Up Margins for Printing

Margins are the blank spaces at the top, bottom, left, and right of a printed page. You may need to adjust the margins individually for each worksheet in your workbook to ensure they print exactly as you intend. Excel provides three margin settings:

> ⟩ **Normal**—Uses Excel's default margins: 0.75 inch for the top and bottom and 0.7 inch for the left and right.

> ⟩ **Wide**—Adds more space at the top, bottom, left, and right sides.

> ⟩ **Narrow**—Reduces the amount of space at the top, bottom, left, and right sides, so more of your worksheet fits on each printed page.

If none of the automatic margins options is exactly what you want, the *Custom Margins...* option opens the *Page Setup* dialog where you can specify exact margins.

To change the margins, on the *Page Layout* tab, in the *Page Setup* group, click the **Margins** button, and click one of the preset margins options: **Normal, Wide,** or **Narrow,** or click **Custom Margins...** to specify your own values.

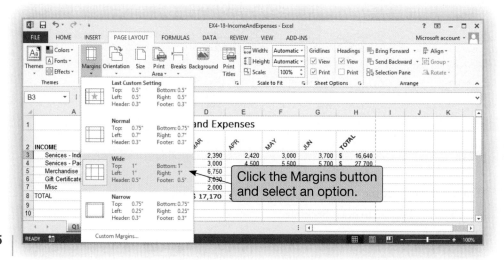

FIGURE EX 4.25

Because you will often want to adjust margins once you are ready to print, Excel allows you to adjust the margins directly from Backstage.

1. Click the **File** tab to open Backstage.

2. Click **Print.**

3. In the *Settings* section, click the button displaying the current margins setting, and then select the option you want.

let me try

Open the student data file **EX4-18-IncomeAndExpenses** and try this skill on your own:
1. Note the page break line between columns I and J.
2. Change the worksheet margins to the **Wide** option.
3. Note the printable area has become smaller and the page break line is between columns H and I.
4. Save the file as directed by your instructor and close it.

Skill 4.19 Scaling Worksheets for Printing

When printing your worksheet, you can set the **scale** and specify that the worksheet prints at a percentage of the original size or at a maximum number of pages wide and/or tall. Each worksheet in the workbook has its own scale settings.

On the *Page Layout* tab, in the *Scale to Fit* group, select the option(s) you want.

❭ Click the **Width** arrow and select the maximum number of pages you want the worksheet to print across.

❭ Click the **Height** arrow and select the maximum number of pages you want the worksheet to print vertically.

❭ Click the **Scale** box and enter a percentage to grow or shrink the worksheet when printed.

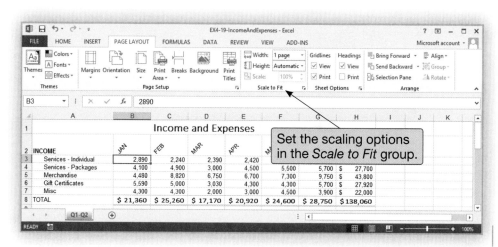

FIGURE EX 4.26

Because you often need to adjust scaling once you are ready to print, Excel has included scaling options on the Print page in Backstage view:

1. Click the **File** tab to open Backstage.

2. Click **Print.**

3. In the *Settings* section, click the button displaying the current scaling setting and select the setting you want to use.

tips & tricks

When scaling your worksheet, be careful not to make the worksheet too small to read.

let me try

Open the student data file **EX4-19-IncomeAndExpenses** and try this skill on your own:

1. If necessary, switch the orientation back to portrait.

2. Set the scaling options so all the columns will print on one page across.

3. Save the file as directed by your instructor and close it.

Skill 4.20 Printing Titles

If your worksheet includes a large table of data that prints on more than one page, you should ensure that the column or row labels print on every page.

To repeat rows and columns on every printed page:

1. On the *Page Layout* tab, in the *Page Setup* group, click the **Print Titles** button.

2. In the *Page Setup* dialog, on the *Sheet* tab, click in the **Rows to repeat at top** box, and then click and drag to select the rows to repeat. You can also type the row reference(s) using the format $1:$1. This example would repeat the first row only. $1:$3 would repeat rows 1 through 3 on every printed page.

3. Click in the **Columns to repeat at left** box, and then click and drag to select the columns to repeat. You can also type the column reference(s) using the format $A:$A. This example would repeat the first column only. $A:$C would repeat columns A through C on every printed page.

4. Click **OK.**

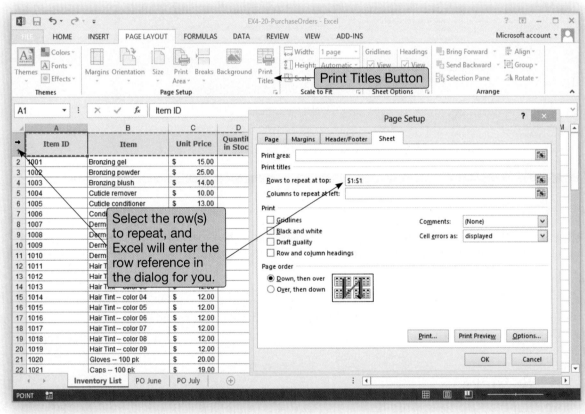

FIGURE EX 4.27

let me try

Open the student data file **EX4-20-PurchaseOrders** and try this skill on your own:

1. Verify that the *Inventory List* worksheet is active.
2. Set row **1** to print on every page.
3. Go to Backstage and preview how the worksheet will look when printed. Verify that the titles from row 1 are included at the top of every page.
4. Save the file as directed by your instructor and close it.

Skill 4.21 Printing Selections, Worksheets, and Workbooks

By default, Excel will print the current, active worksheet. You can change the printing options, however, to print only part of a worksheet or the entire workbook at once.

1. Click the **File** tab to open Backstage.
2. Click **Print.**
3. In the *Settings* section, the first button displays which part of the workbook will print. By default, **Print Active Sheets** is selected. To change the print selection, click the button, and then click one of the other options:

   - **Print Entire Workbook**—Prints all the sheets in the workbook.
   - **Print Selection**—Prints only the selected cells in the active worksheet, overriding any print area definitions in the active worksheet.
   - **Print Selected Table**—Prints the table only (only available if the current selection is within a defined table).

4. If you want to ignore the defined print area, click **Ignore Print Area** at the bottom of the list.
5. Click the **Print** button to print.

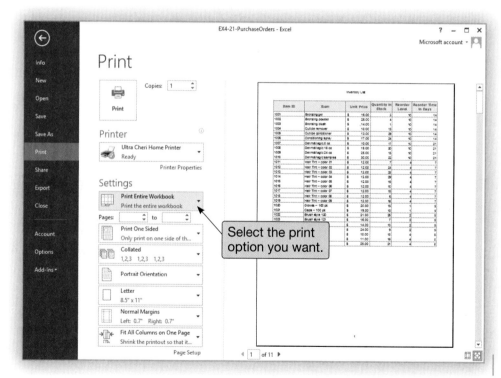

FIGURE EX 4.28

let me try

Open the student data file **EX4-21-PurchaseOrders** and try this skill on your own:
1. Change the print option to print the entire workbook.
2. Verify that all the worksheets in the workbook are included in the print preview.
3. Save the file as directed by your instructor and close it.

key terms

Group

Theme

Theme Colors

Theme Fonts

Theme Effects

Freeze

Normal view

Page Layout view

Page Break Preview view

Header

Footer

Gridlines

Headings

Orientation

Portrait orientation

Landscape orientation

Margins

Scale

concepts review

1. If you delete a worksheet, you can undo the action.

   a. True

   b. False

2. To group worksheets that are not next to each other, select the first worksheet and press the _____ key, and then click the other sheet tabs you want included in the group.

   a. Shift

   b. Alt

   c. Ctrl

   d. None of the above

3. A _____ is a unified color, font, and effects scheme you apply to a workbook.

   a. style

   b. theme

   c. cell format

   d. conditional format

4. To keep column headings as you scroll through a large spreadsheet you should use the _____ command.

   a. Freeze Top Row

   b. Freeze First Column

   c. Split

   d. View Headings

5. When you hide a row or column, the data remain in your workbook. They are no longer displayed on-screen but will be part of the printed workbook.

   a. True

   b. False

6. To display a worksheet in two or four panes, you should _____ the worksheet.

   a. merge

   b. freeze

   c. split

   d. group

7. A _____ is text that appears at the bottom of every page just above the margin.

    a. header

    b. footer

    c. headings

    d. sheet tab

8. _____ are the numbers at the left of rows and the letters at the top of columns.

    a. Headings

    b. Headers

    c. Footers

    d. Gridlines

9. If your worksheet is wide, you may want to use portrait orientation where the height of the page is greater than the width.

    a. True

    b. False

10. If you want more or less white space around your worksheet area when printing, you should adjust the _____.

    a. margins

    b. scaling

    c. orientation

    d. page size

projects

Data files for projects can be found on
www.mhhe.com/office2013skills

skill review 4.1

In this project, you will work on an attendance log for a 16-week college course. For one section of the course, you will set up the sheet to print as an attendance sign-in sheet. For another section, you will set up the sheet to print as an attendance report for the administration office. This is a long project. Be sure to save often!

Skills needed to complete this project:

- Naming Worksheets (Skill 4.2)
- Changing the Color of Sheet Tabs (Skill 4.3)
- Moving and Copying Worksheets (Skill 4.4)
- Grouping Worksheets (Skill 4.6)
- Modifying Column Widths and Row Heights (Skill 4.8)
- Changing the Worksheet View (Skill 4.13)
- Adding Headers and Footers (Skill 4.14)
- Applying Themes (Skill 4.7)
- Splitting Workbooks (Skill 4.12)

- Inserting and Deleting Rows and Columns (Skill 4.9)
- Deleting Worksheets (Skill 4.5)
- Freezing and Unfreezing Rows and Columns (Skill 4.10)
- Hiding and Unhiding Rows and Columns (Skill 4.11)
- Changing Worksheet Orientation (Skill 4.17)
- Setting Up Margins for Printing (Skill 4.18)
- Scaling Worksheets for Printing (Skill 4.19)
- Showing and Hiding Worksheet Elements (Skill 4.16)
- Printing Selections, Worksheets, and Workbooks (Skill 4.21)
- Printing Titles (Skill 4.20)
- Inserting Page Breaks (Skill 4.15)

1. Open the start file **EX2013-SkillReview-4-1** and resave the file as: `[your initials]EX-SkillReview-4-1`

2. If the workbook opens in Protected View, click the **Enable Editing** button in the Message Bar at the top of the workbook.

3. Rename *Sheet1* and change the color of the sheet tab.

   a. Right-click on the *Sheet1* tab, choose **Rename,** and type: `TTH1230`

   b. Press `← Enter`.

   c. Right-click the sheet tab again, point to **Tab Color,** and select **Red, Accent 2, Darker 25%.**

4. Make a copy of the *TTH1230* sheet.

   a. Right-click the sheet tab and select **Move or Copy...** to open the *Move or Copy* dialog.

   b. In the *Before sheet* box, select **Sheet2.**

   c. Check the **Create a copy** check box.

   d. Click **OK.**

5. Name the new sheet **TTH340** and change the tab color.

   a. Right-click the new *TTH1230 (2)* sheet tab, choose **Rename,** and type: `TTH340`

   b. Press `← Enter`.

   c. Right-click the sheet tab again, point to **Tab Color,** and select **Yellow.**

6. Group sheets *TTH1230* and *TTH340* so you can apply formatting changes to both sheets at once.

   a. Click the **TTH1230** sheet tab, press and hold `Ctrl`, and click the **TTH340** sheet tab. Now any changes made to one of the sheets will be made to both sheets.

   b. Verify that [Group] appears in the title bar, indicating that the selected sheets are grouped.

7. Resize **column A** in both worksheets at once to best fit the data by double-clicking the right border of the column heading.

8. Add a header and footer to both worksheets at once.

   a. Switch to *Page Layout* view by clicking the **Page Layout** button on the status bar.

   b. Click in the center section of the header.

c. On the *Header & Footer Tools Design* tab, in the *Header & Footer Elements* group, click the **File Name** button. The code **&[File]** will be entered in the center section of the header. Once you click somewhere else, this will display the name of your file.

d. Click in the right section of the header and type your own name.

e. On the *Header & Footer Tools Design* tab, in the *Navigation* group, click the **Go to Footer** button.

f. Click in the center section of the footer.

g. On the *Header & Footer Tools Design* tab, in the *Header & Footer Elements* group, click the **Sheet Name** button. The code **&[Tab]** will be entered. Once you click somewhere else, this will display the name of the sheet.

h. Click in the right section of the footer.

i. On the *Header & Footer Tools Design* tab, in the *Header & Footer Elements* group, click the **Current Date** button. Once you click somewhere else, this will display the current date.

j. Click in any cell of the worksheet and click the **Normal** button on the status bar.

9. Ungroup the sheets by clicking on any other sheet, such as *Sheet3*. Verify that the same formatting was applied to both sheets and that they are now ungrouped.

10. Apply the **Dividend** theme to the workbook.

   a. On the *Page Layout* tab, in the *Themes* group, click the **Themes** button to display the *Themes* gallery.

   b. Notice that as you hover the mouse pointer over each option in the *Themes* gallery, Excel updates the worksheet to display a live preview of how the theme would affect the worksheet.

   c. Click the **Dividend** option.

11. Select the **TTH1230** sheet. It can be difficult to work with such a wide worksheet. Scroll to the right to see the end of the semester, and you can no longer see the student names. Split the screen into two views of different parts of this worksheet.

   a. Click cell **D1.** On the *View* tab, in the *Window* group, click the **Split** button. Now you can scroll each pane separately, but it is all still the same worksheet. You can drag the split bar to the right or left as needed.

   b. Scroll to show the student names and the last few weeks of the semester on your screen.

   c. Click the **Split** button again to return to normal.

12. Insert a new row to add a new student to the list.

   a. Right-click on the row heading for row number **9** and select **Insert.**

   b. Click the **Insert Options** button that appears immediately below where you right-clicked, and select **Format Same As Below.**

   c. Enter the new student name: **Alloy, Craig**

   d. Enter his student ID #: **1350699**

13. Justin Parry has decided to drop the class. Delete the entire row for Justin by right-clicking on the row heading for row number **23** and selecting **Delete.**

14. Select the **TTH340** sheet. Because this sheet was copied from the 12:30 pm class worksheet, the student names and ID numbers are not those of the students in the 3:40 pm class. Copy the student data from *Sheet3,* and then delete *Sheet3* when it is no longer needed.

   a. Copy the student names and ID numbers from *Sheet3*.

   b. Paste the copied names and ID numbers to the *TTH340* sheet, overwriting the existing student names and ID numbers.

c. Delete *Sheet3* by right-clicking on the sheet name and selecting **Delete.**

d. When Excel displays the message telling you that you can't undo deleting sheets, click the **Delete** button to complete the action.

15. Use the *Freeze Panes* option to keep rows 1:8 and columns A:B visible at all times.

    a. Verify that the *TTH340* sheet is selected, and click cell **C9.**

    b. On the *View* tab, in the *Window* group, click the **Freeze Panes** button, then click the **Freeze Panes** option.

    c. Verify that you selected the correct point at which to freeze panes. Scroll down and to the right. Are rows 1:8 and columns A:B visible regardless of where you scroll?

16. Modify sheet *TTH340* to print as an attendance sign-in sheet.

17. First, hide the student ID numbers by right-clicking on the **column B** heading and selecting **Hide.**

18. Set the page layout options.

    a. On the *Page Layout* tab, in the *Page Setup* group, click the **Orientation** button, and select **Landscape.**

    b. On the *Page Layout* tab, in the *Page Setup* group, click the **Margins** button, and select **Narrow.**

    c. On the *Page Layout* tab, in the *Scale to Fit* group, expand the **Width** list and select **1 page,** and expand the **Height** list and select **1 page.**

    d. On the *Page Layout* tab, in the *Sheet Options* group, click the **Print** check box under **Gridlines.**

19. Print only the part of the worksheet to use as the attendance sign-in sheet.

    a. Select the appropriate cells to print as an attendance sign-in by selecting cells **A1:C29.**

    b. Click the **File** tab, and then click **Print** to display the Print page.

    c. Under *Settings,* click the **Print Active Sheets** button to expand the options, and select **Print Selection.**

    d. If your instructor has directed you to print the attendance sign-in list, click the **Print** button.

    e. Click the **Back** button to exit Backstage.

20. At the end of the semester you will need to print all the attendance records to turn in to the administration office. Let's do this for the *TTH1230* class worksheet.

21. First, complete the worksheet data by entering **P** for present or **A** for absent for each day and student.

22. Hide the attendance sign-in column by right-clicking the **column C** heading and selecting **Hide.**

23. Modify the worksheet so column A and rows 1 through 8 will print on every page.

    a. On the *Page Layout* tab, in the *Page Setup* group, click the **Print Titles** button.

    b. Click in the **Rows to repeat at top** box, and then click and drag with the mouse to select rows **1:8.** When you release the mouse button, you should see $1:$8 in the box.

    c. Click in the **Columns to repeat at left** box, and then click with the mouse to select column **A.** When you release the mouse button, you should see $A:$A in the box.

    d. Click **OK.**

24. Preview how the worksheet will look when printed and make adjustments from the Print page to keep the report to four or fewer pages.

    a. Click the **File** tab to open Backstage, and then click **Print.**

    b. Under *Settings,* click the **Print Selection** button to expand the options, and select **Print Active Sheets.**

    c. Under *Settings,* click the **Fit All Columns on One Page** button to expand the options, and select **No Scaling.**

    d. Note that the current settings will cause the worksheet to print on six pages.

    e. Under *Settings,* click the **Portrait Orientation** button and switch to **Landscape Orientation** instead.

    f. Under *Settings,* click the **Normal Margins** button, and select **Custom Margins...** to set your own margins.

    g. In the *Page Setup* dialog, on the *Margins* tab, change the **Top, Bottom, Left,** and **Right** values to **.5.** Click **OK.**

    h. Under *Settings,* click the **No Scaling** button, and select **Fit All Rows on One Page.**

25. Modify the worksheet page breaks so weeks 1–8 print on the first page and weeks 9–16 print on the second page.

    a. Click the **Back** button to exit Backstage.

    b. If necessary, scroll to the right so columns T:V are visible. Note that the current page break occurs between columns U and V (after week 9).

    c. Click cell **T1.**

    d. On the *Page Layout* tab, in the *Page Setup* group, click the **Breaks** button, and select **Insert Page Break.** This inserts a page break to the left of the selected cell (after week 8).

    e. Click the **File** tab, and then click **Print** to preview how the change will affect the printed pages.

    f. If your instructor has directed you to print the worksheet, click the **Print** button.

    g. Click the **Back** button to exit Backstage.

26. Save and close the workbook.

skill review 4.2

In this project, you will be working with a workbook designed to plan employees' or volunteers' work schedules.

Skills needed to complete this project:

- Naming Worksheets (Skill 4.2)
- Changing the Color of Sheet Tabs (Skill 4.3)
- Applying Themes (Skill 4.7)
- Grouping Worksheets (Skill 4.6)
- Modifying Column Widths and Row Heights (Skill 4.8)
- Splitting Workbooks (Skill 4.12)
- Freezing and Unfreezing Rows and Columns (Skill 4.10)
- Moving and Copying Worksheets (Skill 4.4)
- Hiding and Unhiding Rows and Columns (Skill 4.11)

- Showing and Hiding Worksheet Elements (Skill 4.16)
- Deleting Worksheets (Skill 4.5)
- Changing the Worksheet View (Skill 4.13)
- Adding Headers and Footers (Skill 4.14)
- Changing Worksheet Orientation (Skill 4.17)
- Setting Up Margins for Printing (Skill 4.18)
- Scaling Worksheets for Printing (Skill 4.19)
- Inserting Page Breaks (Skill 4.15)
- Printing Titles (Skill 4.20)
- Printing Selections, Worksheets, and Workbooks (Skill 4.21)

1. Open the start file **EX2013-SkillReview-4-2** and resave the file as: **[your initials]EX-SkillReview-4-2**

2. If the workbook opens in Protected View, click the **Enable Editing** button in the Message Bar at the top of the workbook.

3. Look at the various worksheets. The monthly schedule worksheets need to be named and color coded.

   a. Double-click the tab for **Sheet1,** type **January** and press ⏎ Enter .

   b. Right-click the tab, point to **Tab Color,** and select **Dark Blue, Text 2, Lighter 40%.**

   c. Double-click the tab for **Sheet2,** type **February** and press ⏎ Enter .

   d. Right-click the tab, point to **Tab Color,** and select **Red, Accent 2, Lighter 40%.**

   e. Double-click the tab for **Sheet3,** type **March** and press ⏎ Enter .

   f. Right-click the tab, point to **Tab Color,** and select **White, Background 1, Darker 50%.**

4. Apply a theme to the workbook.

   a. On the *Page Layout* tab, in the *Themes* group, click the **Themes** button. Slide the mouse over different themes and notice the preview of the theme appearance on the worksheet.

   b. Choose the **Facet** theme.

5. The monthly schedule sheets all need formatting. Group them and then format them all at once.

   a. Click the **January** sheet tab, hold down ⇧ Shift , click the **March** sheet tab, and then release ⇧ Shift . Notice the three sheet tabs' appearance has changed to indicate that the three are selected. The *Regular Schedule* tab is not selected.

   b. Verify that the title bar displays [Group]. Any changes you make to the current sheet will be made to all three of the selected sheets, so be very careful.

6. Adjust column widths and row heights to fit the contents and to make the worksheet more readable.

   a. Look in column **A.** If you see ########### it means that the cell content is too wide for the column. Double-click the right column border to autofit the column to the data.

   b. Select all the time columns (**B:U**). Locate the column that is too narrow to display both the *From* time and the *To* time. Double-click the right column border to best fit the column width to the content. All the selected columns will size to match.

   c. Select all the rows (**5:35**).

   d. On the *Home* tab, in the *Cells* group click the **Format** button, and select **Row Height.** In the *Row Height* dialog, change the height value to **18** to make each row a little roomier.

   e. Click **OK.**

7. Ungroup the sheets by clicking on any other sheet, such as the *Regular Schedule* sheet.

   a. Look at the *January, February,* and *March* sheets; they should all have been formatted.

   b. Verify that the sheets are now ungrouped.

8. Select just the **Regular Schedule** sheet. It is hard to work with such a wide worksheet. Scroll to the right to see the night shift and you can no longer see the dates. Split the screen into two views of different parts of this worksheet.

   a. Click cell **G1.** On the *View* tab, in the *Window* group, click the **Split** button. Now you can scroll each pane separately, but it is all still the same worksheet. You can drag the split bar to the right or left as needed.

   b. Scroll to show the morning and night shifts on your screen.

   c. Click the **Split** button again to return to normal.

9. Another way to deal with large worksheets is to freeze panes.

   a. Select any one of the month worksheets.

   b. Select cell **B5.** On the *View* tab, in the *Window* group, click **Freeze Panes,** and select **Freeze Panes.**

   c. Now you can scroll up or down and everything above and to the left of B5 remains visibly frozen on the screen.

   d. Freeze panes must be set on each of the month sheets separately. Grouping does not work for freeze panes. Repeat the freeze panes process for each of the month worksheets.

10. Drag the sheet tab for **Regular Schedule** before the sheet tab for **January** so that *Regular Schedule* is the first worksheet in the workbook.

11. Look closely at the *Regular Schedule* sheet. There are two row numbers missing.

   a. Select the rows before and after the missing rows. Select the entire rows by dragging over the row heading numbers at the far left.

   b. With both rows selected, right-click on the selection, and select **Unhide** to reveal the rows for Tuesdays and Wednesdays.

12. Ensure that the worksheet gridlines will print with the worksheet.

   a. On the *Page Layout* tab, in the *Sheet Options* group, click the **Print** check box under *Gridlines.*

   b. Repeat this process for the *January, February,* and *March* worksheets. (If you group the sheets first, be sure to ungroup them when you are finished.)

13. The *Sheet 4* worksheet is unnecessary. Delete it.

   a. Click the **Sheet 4** tab.

   b. On the *Home* tab, in the *Cells* group, click the **Delete** button arrow and select **Delete Sheet.**

14. Prepare to print your worksheets by adding headers and footers.

   a. Group all the worksheets to save time. This way the headers and footers may be added to all the sheets at once. Verify that all the sheets are selected.

   b. Click the **Page Layout** view button in the lower right of your screen. If you see a message about Freeze Panes being incompatible with *Page Layout* view, click **OK** to continue.

c. Click the **Click to add header** text at the top of any of the pages to add information to the center header section.

d. On the *Header & Footer Tools Design* tab, in the *Header & Footer Elements* group, click the **File Name** button. The code **&[File]** will be entered in the center section of the header. Once you click somewhere else, this will display the name of your file.

e. Click in the right section of the header and enter your own name.

f. On the *Header & Footer Tools Design* tab, in the *Navigation* group, click the **Go to Footer** button.

g. Click in the center section of the footer.

h. On the *Header & Footer Tools Design* tab, in the *Header & Footer Elements* group, click the **Sheet Name** button. The code **&[Tab]** will be entered. Once you click somewhere else, this will display the name of the sheet tab.

i. Click in the right section of the footer and click the **Current Date** button.

j. Click in any cell of the worksheet and click the **Normal** view button in the lower right of your screen.

k. Ungroup the sheets. Right-click on any sheet tab and choose **Ungroup Sheets.**

15. Set up printing options for the *Regular Schedule* sheet.

a. Select the **Regular Schedule** sheet. Click the **File** tab, and then click **Print.**

b. Scroll down to see all the pages for your worksheet. Scroll back up to the first page.

c. Click the **Portrait Orientation** button and select **Landscape.**

d. Click the **Normal Margins** button and select **Narrow.**

e. Click the **No Scaling** button, and select **Fit Sheet on One Page.**

16. The monthly schedules would be easier to read if the morning, afternoon, and night shifts each printed on a separate page in a reasonably large font size.

a. Click the **Back** arrow to return to the worksheet.

b. Group sheets **January:March.**

c. On the *Page Layout* tab, in the *Page Setup* group, click the **Orientation** button, and select **Landscape.**

d. On the *Page Layout* tab, in the *Page Setup* group, click the **Margins** button, and select **Narrow.**

e. Review the current page break. Switch to *Page Break Preview* view if you want by clicking the **Page Break Preview** button at the lower right corner of the status bar.

f. Notice that the schedule just barely requires two pages vertically. On the *Page Layout* tab, in the *Scale to Fit* group, click the **Height** box arrow and select **1 Page.**

g. Click cell **I1.** On the *Page Layout* tab, in the *Page Setup* group, click the **Breaks** button. Select **Insert Page Break.** (Note that you cannot drag the page break lines when the worksheets are grouped. You must use the Ribbon method to insert manual page breaks.)

h. Click in cell **N1.** On the *Page Layout* tab, in the *Page Setup* group, click the **Breaks** button. Select **Insert Page Break.**

i. Click the **Normal** button to return to *Normal* view.

17. The days will only show on the first sheet, so the second and third sheets will make no sense. Set the worksheets so column A will print on every page. You must ungroup the sheets first.

a. Click the **Regular Schedule** sheet to ungroup the sheets, and then click the **January** sheet tab again.

b. On the *Page Layout* tab, in the *Page Setup* group, click **Print Titles** button.

c. In the *Columns to repeat at left* box enter **$A:$A** or click in the box and then click anywhere in column **A**.

d. Click **OK** in the *Page Setup* dialog box.

e. Repeat this process with the **February** and **March** worksheets.

18. Preview how the entire workbook will print. Be sure to verify that column A will print at the left side of the *January, February,* and *March* worksheets.

    a. Click the **File** tab to open Backstage.

    b. Click **Print**.

    c. Click the **Print Active Sheets** button and select **Print Entire Workbook**.

    d. Use the **Next Page** button below the print preview to review how every printed page will look. There should be 10 pages. Note the worksheet name in the footer area at the bottom of each page.

19. Save and close the workbook.

challenge yourself **4.3**

In this project, you will be working with a workbook designed to keep track of loan repayment.

Skills needed to complete this project:

- Naming Worksheets (Skill 4.2)
- Changing the Color of Sheet Tabs (Skill 4.3)
- Moving and Copying Worksheets (Skill 4.4)
- Freezing and Unfreezing Rows and Columns (Skill 4.10)
- Inserting and Deleting Rows and Columns (Skill 4.9)
- Applying Themes (Skill 4.7)
- Grouping Worksheets (Skill 4.6)
- Modifying Column Widths and Row Heights (Skill 4.8)
- Hiding and Unhiding Rows and Columns (Skill 4.11)
- Changing the Worksheet View (Skill 4.13)
- Adding Headers and Footers (Skill 4.14)
- Showing and Hiding Worksheet Elements (Skill 4.16)
- Deleting Worksheets (Skill 4.5)
- Changing Worksheet Orientation (Skill 4.17)
- Printing Titles (Skill 4.20)
- Scaling Worksheets for Printing (Skill 4.19)
- Printing Selections, Worksheets, and Workbooks (Skill 4.21)

1. Open the start file **EX2013-ChallengeYourself-4-3** and resave the file as:
[your initials]EX-ChallengeYourself-4-3

2. If the workbook opens in Protected View, enable editing so you can make changes to the workbook.

3. Change the name of *Sheet1* to **Truck 1.**

4. Change the *Truck 1* sheet tab color to **Blue, Accent 1.**

5. Make a copy of the *Truck 1* sheet, placing it before *Sheet2.*

6. Change the name of the new sheet to **Truck 2.**

7. Change the *Truck 2* sheet tab color to **Green, Accent 6.**

8. Change the values in the *Truck 2* worksheet.

   a. Change the amount borrowed (cell **B3**) to **10,000.**

   b. Change the APR (cell **B5**) to **2%.**

9. Freeze panes so rows **1:8** and columns **A:B** remain in place when you scroll through the worksheet.

10. Delete any extra rows at the bottom of the worksheet where the payment due is 0 (row **45**).

11. Apply the **Retrospect** theme.

12. Switch to the *Truck 1* sheet and delete any extra rows at the bottom of the worksheet where the payment due is 0 (rows **43:45**).

13. Apply the **Metropolitan** theme.

14. Group the *Truck 1* and *Truck 2* worksheets. Make the following changes to both sheets at once.

15. Change the width of the Payment Date column (column **C**) to exactly **17.**

16. Delete the extra column (column **H**).

17. Unhide column **G.**

18. Add header and footer information to the worksheet. (You may allow Excel to remove Freeze Panes.)

    a. Enter your name in the right header section.

    b. Set the left header section to display the sheet name.

    c. Add the page number to the center footer section.

    d. Set the right footer section to display the current date.

19. Hide the gridlines so they do not appear on-screen.

20. Ungroup the sheets.

21. Delete the unused worksheets.

22. Change the page orientation for the *Truck 1* sheet to **Landscape.**

23. Modify the *Truck 1* sheet so row **8** will repeat at the top of every printed page.

24. Scale the *Truck 2* sheet so all columns will fit on one page and all rows will fit on one page.

25. Print preview the entire workbook.

26. Save and close the workbook.

challenge yourself **4.4**

In this project, you will be working with data about automobile emissions and fuel economy. These green car data were downloaded from the Web site https://explore.data.gov/d/9un4-5bz7 and are explained at this Web site: http://www.epa.gov/greenvehicles/Aboutratings.do. The scores range from 0 to 10, where 10 is best. The vehicles with the best scores on both air pollution and greenhouse gas receive the SmartWay designation. These raw data need formatting in order to be usable.

Skills needed to complete this project:

- Changing the Color of Sheet Tabs (Skill 4.3)
- Naming Worksheets (Skill 4.2)

- Inserting Page Breaks (Skill 4.15)
- Moving and Copying Worksheets (Skill 4.4)
- Inserting Worksheets (Skill 4.1)
- Applying Themes (Skill 4.7)
- Grouping Worksheets (Skill 4.6)
- Modifying Column Widths and Row Heights (Skill 4.8)
- Hiding and Unhiding Rows and Columns (Skill 4.11)
- Showing and Hiding Worksheet Elements (Skill 4.16)
- Changing the Worksheet View (Skill 4.13)
- Adding Headers and Footers (Skill 4.14)
- Setting Up Margins for Printing (Skill 4.18)
- Changing Worksheet Orientation (Skill 4.17)
- Scaling Worksheets for Printing (Skill 4.19)
- Inserting and Deleting Rows and Columns (Skill 4.9)
- Printing Titles (Skill 4.20)
- Printing Selections, Worksheets, and Workbooks (Skill 4.21)

1. Open the start file **EX2013-ChallengeYourself-4-4** and resave the file as:
   `[your initials] EX-ChallengeYourself-4-4`

2. If the workbook opens in Protected View, enable editing so you can make changes to the workbook.

3. Color the *all_alpha_10* worksheet tab **Green, Accent 6, Darker 50%** and rename the worksheet **Raw Data.**

4. In the *Raw Data* worksheet, enter page breaks after the first three manufacturers (Acura, Aston Martin, and Audi). There are really too many cars to continue doing this with reasonable effort.

5. Copy the *Raw Data* worksheet. Place the new worksheet at the end of the workbook.

6. Color the worksheet tab **Green, Accent 6, Darker 25%** and name the worksheet **Formatted All.**

7. Remove all the manual page breaks on this worksheet.

8. Add a new worksheet to the end of the workbook.

9. Copy row **1** from the *Formatted All* worksheet and paste it into row **1** in the new worksheet. Use the **Keep Source Column Widths** paste option.

10. Copy all the rows for Cadillac models (rows **298:334**) from the *Formatted All* worksheet to the new sheet.

11. Name the new sheet: **Cadillac** and color the sheet tab the standard color **Red.**

12. Repeat steps 10–13, copying the rows for Honda (rows **842:903**). Name the sheet **Honda** and color the sheet tab the standard color **Blue.**

13. Apply the **Banded** workbook theme.

14. Group the *Formatted All, Cadillac,* and *Honda* worksheets.

15. AutoFit column **L** to best fit the data.

16. Set the column width for columns **M:O** to **5.**

17. Set the row height for row **1** to **70.**

18. Hide the **Underhood ID** and **Stnd Description** columns.

19. Set the worksheet gridlines to print.

20. Cause Excel to insert the sheet name into the center of the footer and your name in the upper-right section of the header.

21. Set **Narrow** margins.

22. Set the worksheet orientation to **Landscape.**

23. Scale the worksheet so all columns will print on one page.

24. Insert a row at the top for entering sheet titles. Merge and center cells **A1:Q1** and apply the **Title** cell style.

25. Ungroup the sheets.

26. Set the worksheet options so rows **1:2** will print on every page. You will need to do this individually for the *Formatted All, Cadillac,* and *Honda* worksheets.

27. Enter the following titles in cell **A1** of each of the worksheets.

    a. Enter the title for the *Formatted All* sheet: **All Models**

    b. Enter the title for the *Cadillac* sheet: **Cadillac Models**

    c. Enter the title for the *Honda* sheet: **Honda Models**

28. Preview how the *Cadillac* worksheets will print and change the scaling so the entire worksheet will print on one page.

29. Using the *Formatted All* worksheet, select all the data for Acura (rows **A3:Q20**). Change the print settings to print just this data.

30. Save and close the workbook.

on your own 4.5

In this project, you will be working with a workbook designed keep track of hobbies.

Skills needed to complete this project:

- Naming Worksheets (Skill 4.2)
- Changing the Color of Sheet Tabs (Skill 4.3)
- Applying Themes (Skill 4.7)
- Inserting and Deleting Rows and Columns (Skill 4.9)
- Modifying Column Widths and Row Heights (Skill 4.8)
- Grouping Worksheets (Skill 4.6)
- Changing the Worksheet View (Skill 4.13)
- Adding Headers and Footers (Skill 4.14)
- Freezing and Unfreezing Rows and Columns (Skill 4.10)
- Inserting Worksheets (Skill 4.1)
- Deleting Worksheets (Skill 4.5)
- Moving and Copying Worksheets (Skill 4.4)
- Changing Worksheet Orientation (Skill 4.17)
- Setting Up Margins for Printing (Skill 4.18)
- Scaling Worksheets for Printing (Skill 4.19)
- Showing and Hiding Worksheet Elements (Skill 4.16)
- Inserting Page Breaks (Skill 4.15)
- Printing Selections, Worksheets, and Workbooks (Skill 4.21)

1. Open the start file **EX2013-OnYourOwn-4-5** and resave the file as:
   `[your initials]EX-OnYourOwn-4-5`

2. If the workbook opens in Protected View, click the **Enable Editing** button in the Message Bar at the top of the workbook so you can modify the workbook.

3. Change the names of the sheets as follows and apply a different tab color to each.

   a. Rename *Sheet1* to **Running**

   b. Rename *Sheet2* to **Football**

   c. Rename *Sheet3* to **Movies**

4. Apply a theme of your choice to the workbook.

5. Add a row at the top of each sheet and enter an appropriate title.

6. Adjust column widths to best fit the data (all worksheets individually).

7. Group the worksheets.

8. Add header and footer elements of your choice to all the worksheets at once.

9. Ungroup the worksheets.

10. Freeze panes to make it easier to work with each worksheet. Add more Oscar and/or Super Bowl data. (Research to find this information on the Web.)

11. Insert a new worksheet after *Running* and enter data about your own hobby or interest.

    a. Name the worksheet and apply a color to the worksheet tab.

    b. Add an appropriate header and/or footer.

    c. If necessary, freeze panes.

12. Delete unused sheets.

13. Rearrange the worksheets in alphabetical order.

14. Make an attractive readable printout of each worksheet. Each should fit neatly on one page or have logical page breaks and print titles when more than one page is required. Only print the worksheets if directed to do so by your instructor.

    a. Set the worksheets' orientation appropriately.

    b. Set appropriate margins.

    c. Scale the worksheets appropriately.

    d. Add manual page breaks if necessary.

    e. Set at least one of the sheets to print with gridlines and at least one to print without gridlines.

    f. For worksheets that print on more than one page, ensure that the label row will be included on every page.

    g. For one worksheet, adjust the print settings to print a useful selection of just some cells that will fit all on one page.

15. Save and close the workbook.

fix it 4.6

In this project, you will fix a number of formatting errors that prevent this gradebook spreadsheet from displaying and printing properly.

Skills needed to complete this project:

- Moving and Copying Worksheets (Skill 4.4)
- Deleting Worksheets (Skill 4.5)
- Inserting and Deleting Rows and Columns (Skill 4.9)
- Modifying Column Widths and Row Heights (Skill 4.8)
- Hiding and Unhiding Rows and Columns (Skill 4.11)
- Changing Worksheet Orientation (Skill 4.17)
- Scaling Worksheets for Printing (Skill 4.19)
- Inserting Page Breaks (Skill 4.15)
- Printing Titles (Skill 4.20)
- Showing and Hiding Worksheet Elements (Skill 4.16)
- Changing the Worksheet View (Skill 4.13)
- Adding Headers and Footers (Skill 4.14)
- Printing Selections, Worksheets, and Workbooks (Skill 4.21)
- Naming Worksheets (Skill 4.2)

1. Open the start file **EX2013-FixIt-4-6** and resave the file as:
   `[your initials]EX-FixIt-4-6`

2. If the workbook opens in Protected View, click the **Enable Editing** button in the Message Bar at the top of the workbook so you can modify the workbook.

3. The *Scores* worksheet should be first in the workbook.

4. This workbook has an unnecessary worksheet. Delete it.

5. There are two unnecessary columns in the middle of the worksheet. Delete them.

6. The *Scores* worksheet has at least one column and one row that do not display the data properly. Resize them to best fit the data.

7. Column **S** should not be visible.

8. Review how the *Scores* worksheet will look when printed. Fix the following issues:

   a. The worksheet should print on no more than two pages, with the page break coming after the midterm grades (before column **T**). (Hint: Try changing the worksheet orientation and adjusting the scaling.)

   b. Columns **A:B** should be included on every printed page.

   c. The worksheet gridlines should print.

   d. The worksheet should have a footer with the word *CONFIDENTIAL* in the center section and the date automatically inserted into the right section.

   e. Only cells **A8:AG28** should be printed.

9. The *Scores* worksheet should be named **Gradebook**.

10. Save and close the workbook.

chapter 5

Adding Charts and Analyzing Data

In this chapter, you will learn the following skills:

❱ Create and format charts

❱ Create and format tables

❱ Sort and filter data

❱ Conduct what-if analysis using Goal Seek and data tables

❱ Create PivotTables and PivotCharts

skills

introduction

This chapter introduces data analysis. You will learn to use charts to visualize data; to use tables and PivotTables to quickly sort, filter, and summarize data; and to conduct what-if analyses using Goal Seek and data tables.

Skill 5.1 Exploring Charts

A **chart** is a graphic that represents numeric data visually. In a chart, the values selected in the worksheet, the **data points**, are transformed into graphic **data markers**. Data markers can be columns, bars, pie pieces, lines, or other visual elements. Related data points, usually in the same row or column, are grouped into a **data series**. Some chart types allow you to plot multiple data series.

Figure EX 5.1 shows a column chart with a single data series—*Services-Individual.* You can tell at a glance that the FEB column is the shortest and, therefore, that February has the fewest sales for individual services.

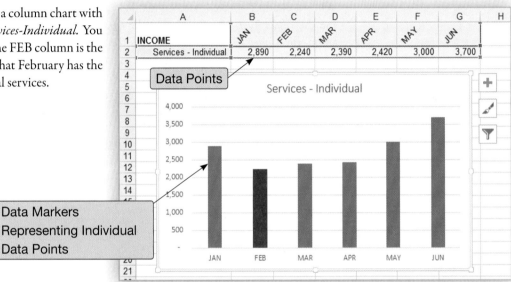

FIGURE EX 5.1

Figure 5.2 is a pie chart using the same data as Figure 5.1. Each individual data point is represented by a piece of the pie. In this chart, it is not as obvious that FEB is the smallest data point.

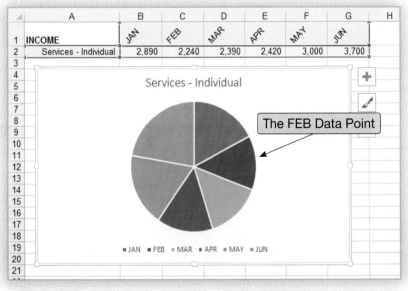

FIGURE EX 5.2

All charts, except pie charts and doughnut charts, plot data along two axes. The **y axis** goes from bottom to top. It is the vertical axis. The **x axis** goes from left to right. It is the horizontal axis. Typically, but not always, values are plotted against the y axis and categories are listed along the x axis.

When working with charts, there are a few other common chart elements you should be familiar with:

❱ The **plot area** is the area where the data series are plotted.

❱ The **chart area** is the area that encompasses the entire chart including the plot area and optional layout elements, such as title and legend.

❱ The **chart title** is a text box above or overlaying the chart. To change the title text, click the box to select it and edit the text directly in the text box. You can also type new text in the formula bar and then press (←Enter).

❱ The **legend** tells you which data point or data series is represented by each color in the chart.

When a chart is selected, two contextual tabs are available: the *Chart Tools Design* tab and the *Chart Tools Format* tab. On the *Chart Tools Format* tab, in the *Current Selection* group, the *Chart Elements* box displays the name of the chart element that is currently selected. This can be helpful if you need to ensure that you have selected the chart area, the plot area, or another chart element. To select a specific chart element, expand the **Chart Elements** list and select the chart element you want to select.

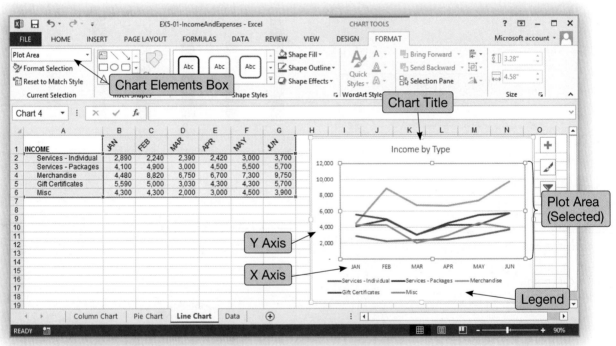

FIGURE EX 5.3

tips & tricks

Because charts make it easier to see trends and relationships, they are an important tool for analyzing data. However, the chart type and formatting can influence how others perceive the data. Be careful that the chart does not present the data in a way that may be misleading.

tell me **more**

If the chart is located on the same worksheet as its data, Excel will highlight that data when you select certain chart elements. For example, select the chart area or the plot area, and Excel highlights the cells containing the data point values in blue, the data series labels in red, and the category labels in purple. If you select a single data series, only that data will be highlighted.

let me **try**

Open the student data file **EX5-01-IncomeAndExpenses** try this skill on your own:

1. Begin with the *Column Chart* sheet. Click any of the data markers to select the entire data series. Use the *Chart Elements* box to verify that you have selected the data series. Observe how the worksheet data are represented by the column data markers.
2. Go to the *Pie Chart* sheet. Select the chart legend. Use the legend to match the pie pieces to the data point values.
3. Go to the *Line Chart* sheet. Select the line representing the Merchandise data series. Observe that when the Merchandise series is selected, cells B4:G4 (the data points) are highlighted in blue.
4. Select the x axis, and then select the y axis. Use the *Chart Elements* list if necessary.
5. Save the file as directed by your instructor and close it.

from the perspective of . . .

COLLEGE STUDENT

I use Excel to track my monthly budget. Before I started using charts, the spreadsheets were just numbers. I knew how much money was going out each month, but I didn't really understand how much of my money I was spending on unnecessary expenses. Once I starting using pie charts, it was obvious that I was spending more on lattes than on transportation! I bought a coffee maker, and now I have a little extra cash each month to put away for a rainy day.

Skill 5.2 Using the Recommended Charts Feature

One trick to working with charts is to select the correct chart type. Excel 2013 makes this easier by recommending specific chart types based on the data you have selected in the worksheet. The recommended charts are available from both the Quick Analysis tool and the *Chart Options* dialog.

To add a recommended chart to a worksheet using the Quick Analysis tool:

1. Select the data you want to visualize as a chart.

2. The Quick Analysis Tool button appears near the lower right corner of the selected range. Click the **Quick Analysis Tool** button, and then click the **Charts** tab.

3. Hover the mouse cursor over each chart type to see a live preview of the chart. Click the button for the chart type you want. Recommended charts may include multiple versions of the same chart type. Check the live preview carefully to ensure that the data display exactly as you want.

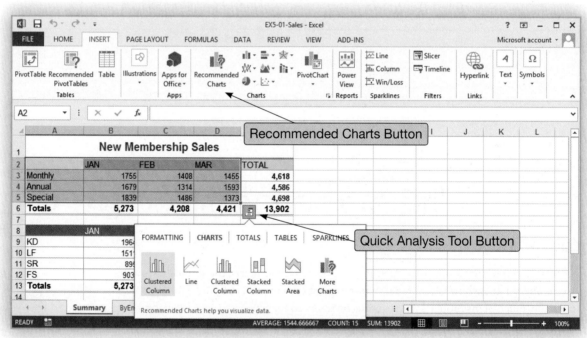

FIGURE EX 5.4

If none of the recommended charts presented in the Quick Analysis tool are precisely what you want, use the *Insert Chart* dialog instead:

1. Select the data for the chart.

2. Click the **Quick Analysis Tool** button.

3. Click the **Charts** tab, and then click the **More Charts** button to open the *Insert Chart* dialog. You can also open the *Insert Chart* dialog from the *Insert* tab, *Charts* group, by clicking the **Recommended Charts** button.

4. The first tab in the *Insert Chart* dialog, *Recommended Charts,* displays the same chart options as the *Charts* tab in the Quick Analysis tool, plus a few more. When you select a chart type, a preview of the chart appears in the right pane of the dialog.

5. Click **OK** to insert the selected chart into the worksheet.

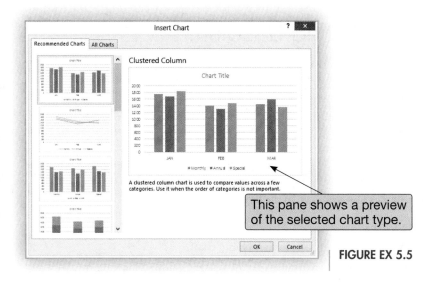

This pane shows a preview of the selected chart type.

FIGURE EX 5.5

FIGURE EX 5.6
A clustered column chart inserted into the worksheet

tips & tricks

The Quick Analysis tool is only available if the data selected for the chart are in contiguous cells—a group of cells that are all next to one another without any cells left out of the group.

let me try

Open the student data file **EX5-02-Sales** and try this skill on your own:
1. If necessary, verify that the *Summary* sheet is active, and cells **A2:D5** are selected.
2. Insert a **Clustered Column** chart based on the first recommended chart type.
3. Save the file as directed by your instructor and close it.

Skill 5.3 Inserting a Column Chart or a Bar Chart

Column charts work best with data that are organized into rows and columns like a table. Data point values are transformed into columns, with the values plotted along the vertical (y) axis. Each row in the table is grouped as a data series. Excel uses the column labels as the categories along the horizontal (x) axis.

In the clustered column chart shown in Figure EX 5.7, each column represents a single data point. The data points are grouped (clustered) together by category. Each data series is represented by a single color as shown in the legend below the chart.

To insert a column chart:

1. Select the data you want to include in the column chart.

2. On the *Insert* tab, in the *Charts* group, click the **Insert Column Chart** button.

3. Click the chart type you want to insert the chart into the worksheet.

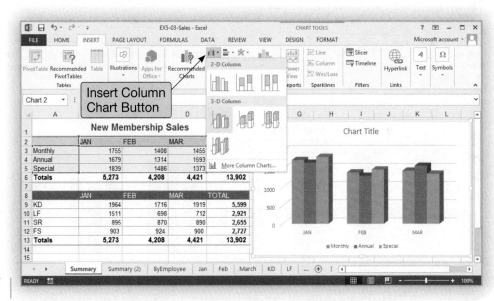

FIGURE EX 5.7

Bar charts are like column charts turned on their side. The categories are displayed on the vertical axis, and the data point values are plotted along the horizontal axis.

The clustered bar chart in Figure EX 5.8 displays the same data as Figure EX 5.7. Each bar represents a single data point. However, in this bar chart, the sales values are plotted along the horizontal axis, grouped into data series by membership type, and the months are displayed along the vertical axis.

To insert a bar chart:

1. Select the data you want to include in the bar chart.

2. On the *Insert* tab, in the *Charts* group, click the **Insert Bar Chart** button.

3. Click the chart type you want to insert the chart into the worksheet.

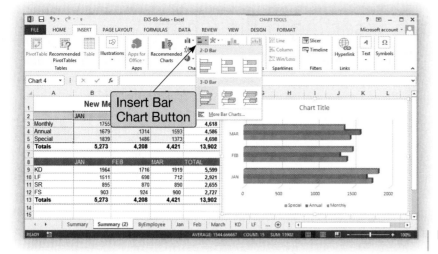

FIGURE EX 5.8

If you don't like the way Excel grouped the data series, you can switch them, making the categories the data series and the data series the categories. On the *Chart Tools Design* tab, in the *Data* group, click the **Switch Row/Column** button. Figure EX 5.9 charts the same data as Figure 5.8 with the rows and columns switched, so the data points are organized into data series by column instead of by row.

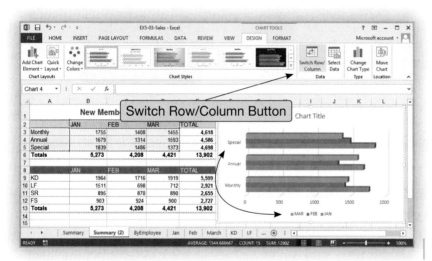

FIGURE EX 5.9

another **method**

You can also insert a column chart or a bar chart from the *Insert Chart* dialog, *All Charts* tab.

let me **try**

Open the student data file **EX5-03-Sales** and try this skill on your own:

1. If necessary, verify that the *Summary* sheet is active, and cells **A2:D5** are selected.
2. Insert a **3-D Clustered Column** chart (the first chart type in the *3-D Column* section of the *Insert Column Chart* menu).
3. Switch to the second sheet, *Summary (2)*, and if necessary, select cells **A2:D5**.
4. Insert a **3-D Clustered Bar** chart (the first chart type in the *3-D Bar* section of the *Insert Bar Chart* menu).
5. Switch the rows and columns in the chart, so the data points are grouped into data series by column.
6. Save the file as directed by your instructor and close it.

skill 5.3   Inserting a Column Chart or a Bar Chart

Skill 5.4 Inserting a Pie Chart

Pie charts represent data as parts of a whole. They do not have x and y axes like column charts. Instead, each value is a visual "slice" of the pie. Pie charts work best when you want to evaluate values as they relate to a total value—for example, departmental budgets in relation to the entire budget, or each employee's bonus in relation to the entire bonus pool.

In Figure EX 5.10, the total sales for each sales person is represented by a slice of the pie.

To add a pie chart:

1. Select the data you want to include in the pie chart.
2. On the *Insert* tab, in the *Charts* group, click the **Insert Pie Chart** button.
3. Click the chart type you want to insert the chart into the worksheet.

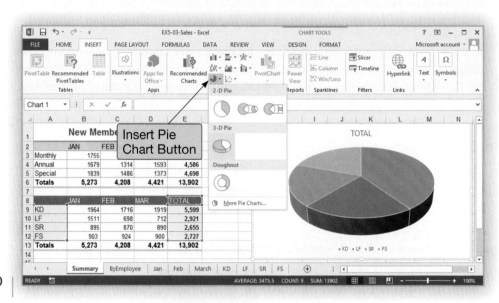

FIGURE EX 5.10

tips & tricks

In an "exploded" pie chart, each slice is slightly separated from the whole. You can "explode" a single slice by clicking it and dragging it away from the rest of the slices. Exploding a single slice of data gives it emphasis.

tell me more

Doughnut charts are similar to pie charts, but they can display more than one series. Each series is represented by a ring around the doughnut. Each data point in the series is represented by a piece of the ring proportional to the total. Doughnut charts can be confusing and are not commonly used.

another method

You can also insert a pie chart from the *Insert Chart* dialog, *All Charts* tab.

let me try

Open the student data file **EX5-04-Sales** and try this skill on your own:
1. If necessary, verify that the *Summary* sheet is active, and cells **A9:A12** and cells **E8:E12** are selected.
2. Insert a **3-D Pie** chart.
3. Save the file as directed by your instructor and close it.

excel 2013   chapter 5 Adding Charts and Analyzing Data

Skill 5.5 Inserting a Line Chart

Line charts feature a line connecting each data point—showing the movement of values over time. Line charts work best when data trends over time are important.

The line chart in Figure EX 5.11 shows sales over a three-month period. Each data series represents a type of membership sales. This type of line chart, called a **line with markers**, includes dots along the line for each data point.

To add a line chart:

1. Select the data you want to include in the line chart. Be sure to include both values and the related cells that represent time segments (dates, calendar quarters, etc.).

2. On the **Insert** tab, in the *Charts* group, click the **Insert Line Chart** button.

3. Click the chart type you want to insert the chart into the worksheet.

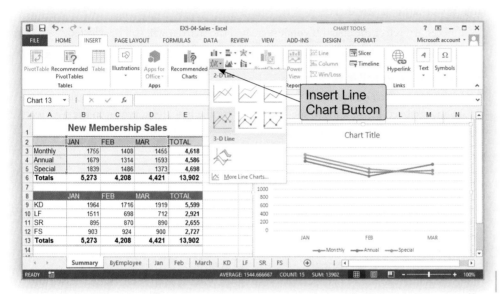

FIGURE EX 5.11

tips & tricks

While line charts are a good choice if the data set has many data points, use a line chart with markers only if there are relatively few data points.

another method

You can also insert a line chart from the *Insert Chart* dialog, *All Charts* tab.

let me try

Open the student data file **EX5-05-Sales** and try this skill on your own:
1. If necessary, verify that the *Summary* sheet is active, and cells **A2:D5** are selected.
2. Insert a **Line with Markers** chart (the first chart type in second row of the *2-D Column* section of the *Insert Line Chart* menu).
3. Save the file as directed by your instructor and close it.

Skill 5.6 Moving a Chart

When you first create a chart, Excel places the chart in the middle of the worksheet. Often, you will need to move the chart so it doesn't cover the worksheet data.

You can move a chart to a new position on the sheet by selecting it and then dragging it anywhere on the worksheet. To move a chart by dragging:

1. Click in the chart area of the chart you want to move. (Be careful not to click in the plot area, or you will move just the plot area instead of the entire chart.) Your mouse cursor will change to the move cursor ✛.

2. With your left mouse button depressed, drag the chart to the new location on the worksheet, and then release the mouse button to "drop" the chart at the new location.

If your chart is large or complex, you may want the chart to appear on its own worksheet. To move a chart to a new sheet:

1. If necessary, select the chart. If you just created the chart, it will still be selected.

2. On the *Chart Tools Design* tab, in the *Location* group, click the **Move Chart** button.

3. The *Move Chart* dialog opens.

4. In the *Move Chart* dialog, click the **New sheet** radio button to move the chart to its own worksheet. If you want to specify a name for the new sheet, type it in the *New sheet* box. To move the chart to an existing worksheet, click the **Object in** radio button, and then select the name of the sheet you want to move the chart to.

5. Click **OK**.

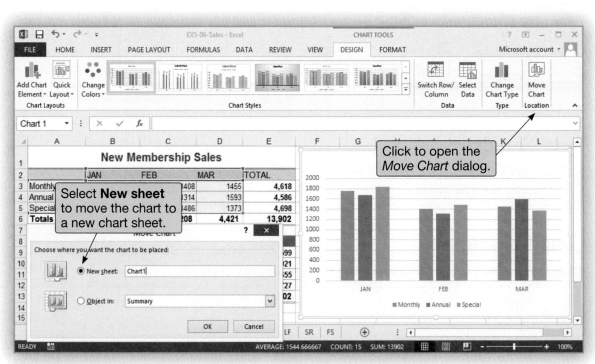

FIGURE EX 5.12

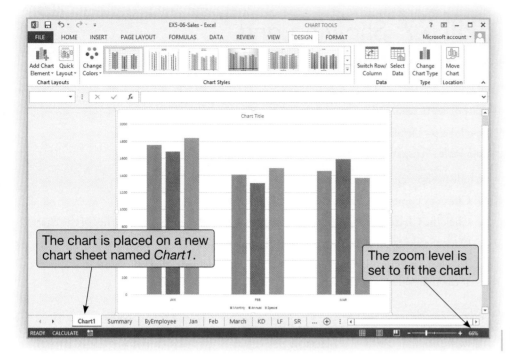

The chart is placed on a new chart sheet named *Chart1*.

The zoom level is set to fit the chart.

FIGURE EX 5.13

When you use the *Move Chart* dialog to move a chart to its own sheet, Excel creates a special type of worksheet called a **chart sheet**. The chart sheet does not include the columns, rows, and cells you are used to seeing in Excel; it contains only the chart object. The new chart sheet automatically changes the zoom level so the entire chart is visible.

tell me **more**

When the chart area is selected, you can resize the chart by clicking one of the resize handles located at the four corners and the middle of each side of the chart area. You cannot resize a chart in a chart sheet.

another **method**

Right-click an empty area of the chart and select **Move Chart...** to open the *Move Chart* dialog.

You can also use the cut, copy, and paste commands to move a chart from one sheet to another.

let me **try**

Open the student data file **EX5-06-Sales** and try this skill on your own:

1. If necessary, select the chart on the *Summary* sheet.
2. Move the chart to the empty area of the worksheet to the right of the data.
3. Move the chart to a new worksheet.
4. Save the file as directed by your instructor and close it.

skill 5.6   Moving a Chart

Skill 5.7 Showing and Hiding Chart Elements

Showing and hiding chart elements such as the chart title, axes, and gridlines can make a chart easier to read. Other common chart elements include:

Data labels—Display data values for each data marker.

Data table—Displays a table of the data point values below the chart.

To hide or show chart elements:

1. Click any empty area of the chart area to select the chart.

2. Click the **Chart Elements** button that appears near the upper right corner of the chart.

3. Click the check boxes to show or hide chart elements.

4. To select a specific placement option for the chart element, click the arrow that appears at the right side of the element name, and then click an option.

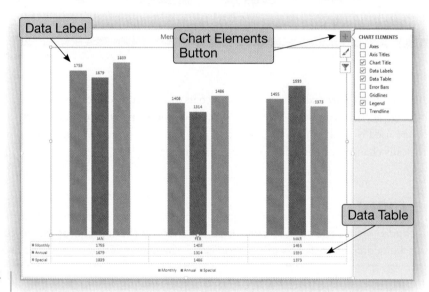

FIGURE EX 5.14

tell me **more**

You can apply a combination of chart elements at once by selecting one of the Quick Layout options from the *Chart Tools Design* tab, *Chart Layouts* group.

another **method**

You can hide or show chart elements and control their appearance and position from the *Chart Tools Design* tab, *Chart Layouts* group. Click the **Add Chart Elements** button, point to the chart element you want, and click an option.

let me **try**

Open the student data file **EX5-07-Sales** and try this skill on your own:

1. If necessary, select the chart on the *Chart1* sheet.
2. Hide the axes.
3. Hide the gridlines
4. Display the data labels at the outside end of each data marker (the top of the columns).
5. Display the data table, including the legend keys.
6. Save the file as directed by your instructor and close it.

Skill 5.8 Applying Quick Styles and Colors to Charts

You can change the style of a chart using the predefined **Quick Styles**. Quick Styles apply combinations of fonts, line styles, fills, and shape effects. You can also change the color scheme from a preset list of colors that coordinate with the workbook theme.

To change the chart style:

1. Select the chart.
2. On the *Chart Tools Design* tab, in the *Chart Styles* group, click the style you want to use, or click the **More** button to see all of the Quick Styles available.
3. To change the color scheme, on the *Chart Tools Design* tab, in the *Chart Styles* group, click the **Change Colors** button and select the color scheme you want.

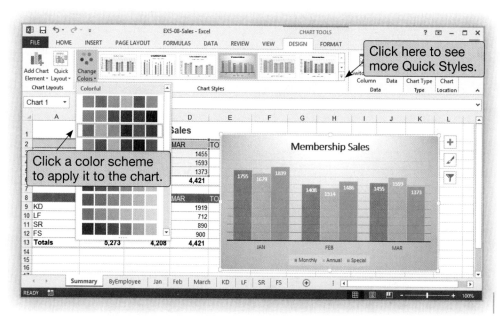

FIGURE EX 5.15

another **method**

Quick Styles and color schemes are also available from the *Chart Styles* button ✎ that appears near the upper right corner of the chart when it is selected.

let me **try**

Open the student data file **EX5-08-Sales** and try this skill on your own:
1. If necessary, select the chart on the *Summary* sheet.
2. Apply the **Style 4** Quick Style.
3. Apply the **Color 3** color scheme from the *Colorful* section.
4. Save the file as directed by your instructor and close it.

Skill 5.9 Changing the Chart Type

Remember that the chart type you select affects the story your chart tells. If you find that your initial chart selection wasn't quite right, you can change the chart type from the *Change Chart Type* dialog without having to delete and recreate the chart.

The **clustered column** chart in Figure EX 5.16 shows a separate column for sales of each membership type per month, but it doesn't depict the total sales for all memberships. By changing the chart type to a **stacked column**, each column now represents the total sales for the month, and individual sales for each membership type are represented by a piece of that column. Using this chart type makes it easier to compare total sales as well as sales for each individual type of membership.

To change the chart type:

1. On the *Chart Tools Design* tab, in the *Type* group, click the **Change Chart Type** button.
2. In the *Change Chart Type* dialog, click a chart type category to display that category in the right pane.
3. Click one of the chart types along the top of the right pane to see the options available, and then click the chart type you want.
4. Click **OK.**

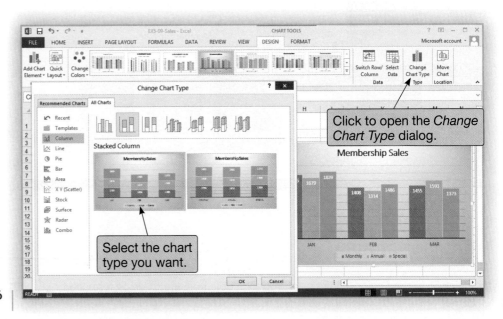

FIGURE EX 5.16

another method

To change the chart type, you can also right-click in the chart area and select **Change Chart Type...**

let me try

Open the student data file **EX5-9-Sales** and try this skill on your own:

1. If necessary, select the chart on the *Summary* sheet.
2. Change the chart type to the first stacked column option.
3. Save the file as directed by your instructor and close it.

excel 2013   chapter 5 Adding Charts and Analyzing Data

Skill 5.10 Filtering Chart Data

Excel 2013 includes a new feature that allows you to hide and show data in a chart without having to filter the source data. The chart in Figure EX 5.17 shows the series options filtered to show just the Monthly and Annual series with a preview of what the chart would look like if the Annual series were the only series option selected.

To filter chart data:

1. Select the chart.
2. Click the **Chart Filters** button that appears near the upper right corner of the chart.
3. Click the check boxes to add or remove data series or categories from the chart.
4. Click the **Apply** button to apply the changes.

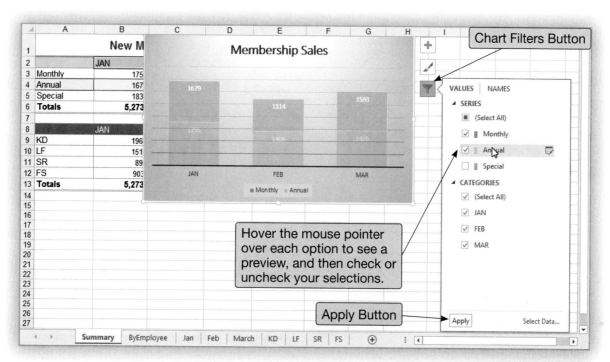

FIGURE EX 5.17

tips & tricks

Notice that when you hover the mouse pointer over the chart filter options, the live preview does not take into account the options that are checked or unchecked. The preview shows what the chart would look like if the highlighted option were the only one checked by dimming all the other series or categories.

let me try

Open the student data file **EX5-10-Sales** and try this skill on your own:

1. If necessary, select the chart on the *Summary* sheet.
2. Filter the chart so only the **Monthly** and **Annual** series are visible.
3. Save the file as directed by your instructor and close it.

Skill 5.11 Converting Data into Tables

In Excel, you can define a series of adjacent cells as a **table**. When you define data as a table, Excel provides a robust tool set for formatting and analyzing the data. In the table, the header row automatically includes filtering and sorting. When you add data to the right of the table, Excel includes the new column in the table automatically.

To define data as a table:

1. Click any cell in the data range. You do not need to select the entire range.
2. On the *Home* tab, in the *Styles* group, click the **Format as Table** button to display the *Table Styles* gallery.
3. Click the style you want to use for your table.
4. Excel will automatically populate the *Format As Table* dialog with the entire data range.
5. Be sure to check the **My table has headers** check box if appropriate.
6. Click **OK** to create the table.

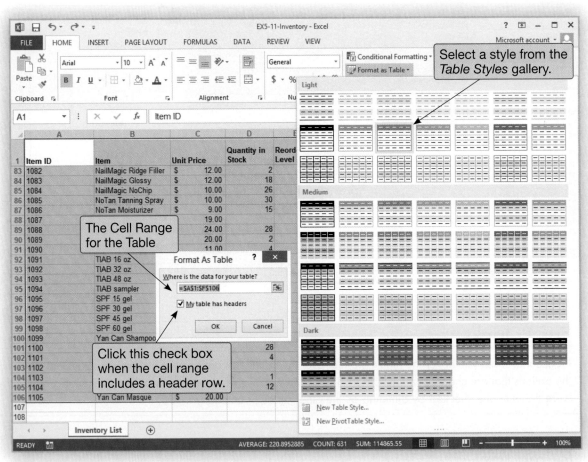

FIGURE EX 5.18

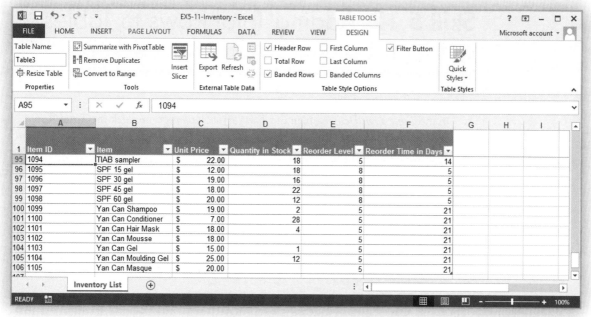

FIGURE EX 5.19
The cell range converted to a table.

tips & tricks

You cannot create a table in a shared workbook. If your workbook contains a table, you will need to convert the table back to a normal cell range before sharing the workbook.

tell me more

One of the most useful features of tables is the ability to reference table column names in formulas. When you enter a formula in a table, you can reference column names by enclosing the column header text in brackets. For example, to add a new column to the table in Figure EX 5.19 to calculate the value of each inventory item, you would enter the formula **[Unit Price]*[Quantity in Stock]** in the first row of the new column. Excel will copy the formula to the remaining cells in the table column automatically.

another method

To insert a table without specifying the table formatting:
1. Select any cell in the data range for the table.
2. On the *Insert* tab, in the *Tables* group, click the **Table** button.
3. Excel will populate the *Insert Table* dialog automatically with the appropriate data range.
4. Be sure to check the **My table has headers** check box if appropriate.
5. Click **OK** to create the table. Excel will format the table with the most recent table style used.

let me try

Open the student data file **EX5-11-Inventory** and try this skill on your own:
1. If necessary, click any cell in the range **A1:F106**.
2. Convert the cell range to a table using table style **Table Style Light 10**.
3. Save the file as directed by your instructor and close it.

Skill 5.12 Adding Total Rows to Tables

If you have data formatted as a table, you can add a **Total row** to quickly calculate an aggregate function such as the sum, average, minimum, or maximum of all the values in the column.

To add a Total row to a table:

1. On the *Table Tools Design* tab, in the *Table Style Options* group, click the **Total Row** check box.

2. In the Total row at the bottom of the table, click the cell where you want to add the function.

3. Click the arrow, and select a function. Excel inserts the formula for you.

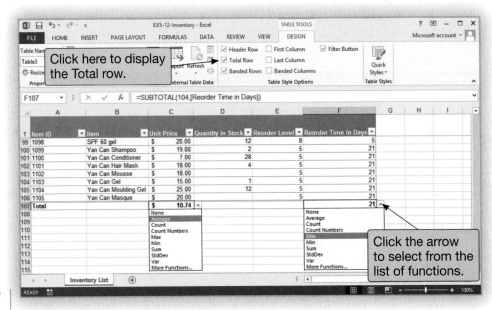

FIGURE EX 5.20

tips & tricks

The **Count** option can be useful when filtering records in a table. Count tells you how many records are included in the filtered table. The Count option from the Total row uses the COUNTA function.

tell me more

When you enable the Total row, the first cell in the Total row displays the word "Total" automatically and the last cell in the Total row calculates the sum of the values in that column (if the column contains numbers).

another method

To add the Total row to the table, right-click any cell in the table, point to **Table,** and click **Total Row.**

let me try

Open the student data file **EX5-12-Inventory** and try this skill on your own:
1. Add a Total row to the table.
2. In the Total row, display the average value for the *Unit Price* column.
3. In the Total row, display the minimum value for the *Reorder Time in Days* column.
4. Save the file as directed by your instructor and close it.

excel 2013 chapter 5 Adding Charts and Analyzing Data

Skill 5.13 Applying Quick Styles to Tables

When you are working with a table, use the *Table Tools Design* tab to apply formatting. This contextual tab is available when you select any cell in the table. From the *Table Styles* gallery, you can select a Quick Style to apply a combination of font colors, fill colors, and banding options. **Banding** applies a fill color to alternating rows or columns, making the table easier to read.

To apply a table Quick Style:

1. Click anywhere in the table.

2. On the *Table Tools Design* tab, in the *Table Styles* group, click the **Quick Styles** button to display the full *Table Styles* gallery. Depending on the width of your Excel window, you may see part of the *Quick Styles* gallery displayed in the Ribbon. In this case, click the **More** button ⤓ to expand the entire gallery.

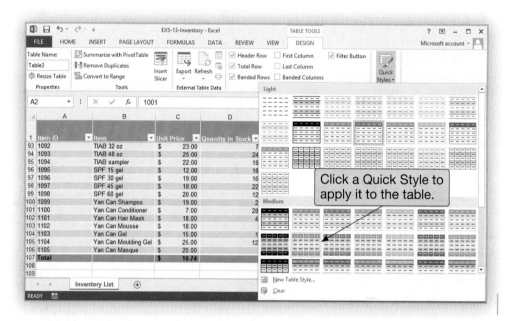

FIGURE EX 5.21

tips & tricks

If your table includes a header row and/or a Total row like the one in Figure EX 5.21, select a style that includes formatting for the first and last rows to help them stand out from the rest of the table.

tell me more

Use the check boxes in the *Table Style Options* group to customize the table formatting by adding or removing banding for rows or columns.

let me try

Open the student data file **EX5-13-Inventory** and try this skill on your own:
1. If necessary, click any cell in the table.
2. Apply the **Table Style Medium 9** Quick Style.
3. Save the file as directed by your instructor and close it.

Skill 5.14 Removing Duplicate Rows from Tables

If you have a large table, it may be difficult to identify rows with duplicate data. Excel includes a tool to find and remove duplicate rows. A "duplicate" can be an exact match, where every cell in the row contains the same data, or you can specify matching data for certain columns only.

To remove duplicate rows from a table:

1. Select any cell in the table.

2. On *Table Tools Design* tab, in the *Tools* group, click the **Remove Duplicates** button.

3. By default, all the columns are selected in the *Remove Duplicates* dialog and Excel will remove duplicates only where the data in the rows are 100 percent identical. To identify duplicate rows where only some of the columns have duplicate data, click the check boxes to uncheck column names. Now Excel will identify rows as duplicates only when the checked columns have the same data.

4. Click **OK** to remove duplicate rows from the table.

5. Excel displays a message box, telling you how many duplicate rows were deleted. Click **OK** to dismiss the message box.

FIGURE EX 5.22

another method

If the data are not formatted as an Excel table, you can access the *Remove Duplicates* command from the *Data* tab, *Data Tools* group.

let me try

Open the student data file **EX5-14-PurchaseOrders** and try this skill on your own:
1. If necessary, click any cell in the table on the *PO July* sheet.
2. Remove duplicate rows where data in all the columns are identical.
3. Save the file as directed by your instructor and close it.

excel 2013   chapter 5 Adding Charts and Analyzing Data

Skill 5.15 Converting Tables to Ranges

Although Excel tables are extremely useful, there are times when you do not want your data formatted as a table. Certain data analysis tools, including creating subtotals and grouping outlines, are not available if data are formatted as a table.

To convert a table to a normal range:

1. On the *Table Tools Design* tab, in the *Tools* group, click the **Convert to Range** button.
2. Excel displays a message box asking if you want to convert the table to a normal range. Click **Yes.**
3. Notice that any table formatting such as banding is still applied to the range.

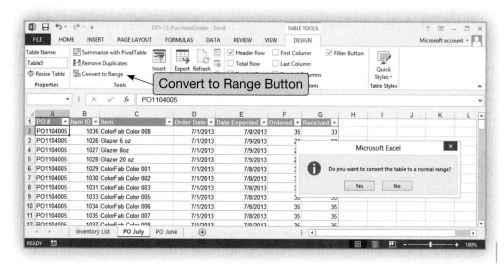

FIGURE EX 5.23

tips & tricks

If you want to use one of the table styles but do not want the data formatted as a table, begin by formatting the range as a table, applying the table style you want, and then convert the table back to a normal range.

another method

You can also right-click anywhere in the table, point to **Table,** and select **Convert to Range.**

let me try

Open the student data file **EX5-15-PurchaseOrders** and try this skill on your own:
1. If necessary, click any cell in the table on the *PO July* sheet.
2. Convert the table to a normal range.
3. Save the file as directed by your instructor and close it.

Skill 5.16 Sorting Data

Sorting rearranges the rows in your worksheet by the data in a column or columns. You can sort alphabetically by text, by date, or by values. Sorting works the same whether or not the data have been formatted as a table.

To sort data:

1. Click any cell in the column you want to sort by.

2. On the *Data* tab, in the *Sort & Filter* group, click the button for the sort order you want:

   〉 $\frac{A}{Z}\downarrow$ sorts text in alphabetical order from A to Z, numbers from smallest to largest, and dates from oldest to newest.

   〉 $\frac{Z}{A}\downarrow$ sorts text in reverse alphabetical order from Z to A, numbers from largest to smallest, and dates from newest to oldest.

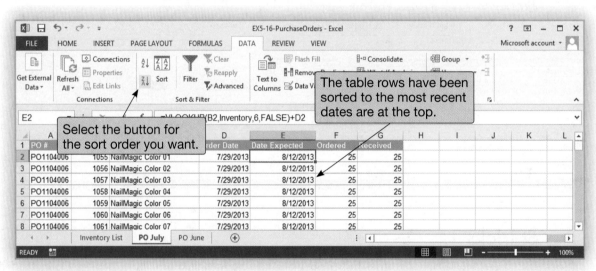

FIGURE EX 5.24

When a table column has been sorted, the column header will display an arrow indicating which way the column has been sorted: **Item ID** ↓↑ An arrow pointing up indicates an A-Z sort order; an arrow pointing down indicates a Z-A sort order.

another **method**

Sort options are also available from the *Home* tab, *Editing* group. Click the **Sort & Filter** button and then select the option you want.

You can also right-click any cell in the column you want to sort by. Point to **Sort,** and select the option you want.

let me **try**

Open the student data file **EX5-16-PurchaseOrders** and try this skill on your own:
1. Verify that the *PO July* sheet is active.
2. Sort the **Date Expected** column so the newest dates are listed first.
3. Go to the *PO June* sheet, and sort the **Item ID** column so the smallest numbers are listed first.
4. Save the file as directed by your instructor and close it.

Skill 5.17 Filtering Data

If your worksheet has many rows of data, you may want to **filter** the data to show only rows that meet criteria you specify. If your data are formatted as a table, filtering is enabled automatically. If your data are not formatted as a table, you must first enable filtering:

1. On the *Home* tab, in the *Editing* group, click the **Sort & Filter** button.
2. Click the **Filter** button to enable filtering. An arrow will appear in each cell of the heading row just as if the data were formatted as a table.

Once filtering is enabled, it works the same whether or not the data have been formatted as a table.

To filter data:

1. Click the arrow at the top of the column that contains the data you want to filter for.
2. At first, all the filter options are checked. Click the **(Select All)** check box to remove all the check marks.
3. Click the check box or check boxes in front of the values you want to filter by.
4. Click **OK.** Excel displays only the rows that include the values you specified.

If the column values are dates, Excel will group the dates in the filter list if possible. You can click a check box to filter for an entire grouping (such as a specific year or month), or you can expand the group by clicking the + and then clicking the check box for specific dates. There may be multiple nested groups of dates, so be sure to continue expanding the date groupings until you find the exact date(s) you want to filter for.

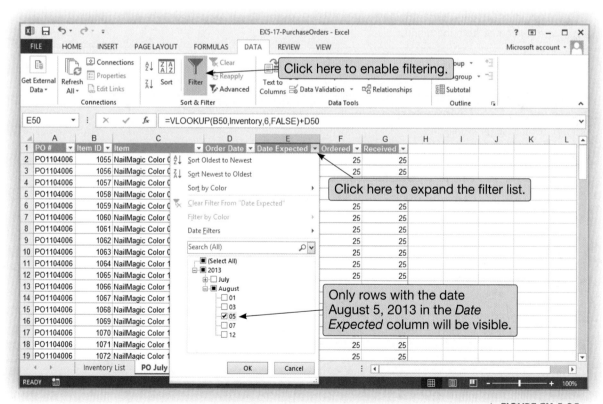

FIGURE EX 5.25

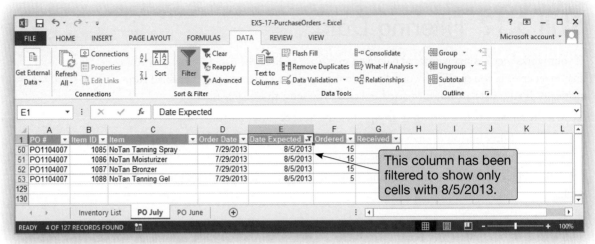

FIGURE EX 5.26

When a filter has been applied to a column, the column header will display a funnel icon:
Date Expected ⟱ To clear the filter, click the funnel icon and select **Clear Filter from 'Name of Column'.**

another method

When filtering is enabled, you can clear the filter and disable filtering from the *Data* tab, *Sort & Filter* group, by clicking the **Filter** button again.

You can also enable or clear filtering from the *Home* tab, *Editing* group, by clicking the **Sort & Filter** button and then making the appropriate choice from the menu.

let me try

Open the student data file **EX5-17-Inventory** and try this skill on your own:

1. Verify that the *PO July* sheet is selected.
2. Filter the **Date Expected** column so only rows with the date **8/5/2013** are shown.
3. Save the file as directed by your instructor and close it.

excel 2013   chapter 5 Adding Charts and Analyzing Data

Skill 5.18 Filtering Table Data with Slicers

A **slicer** is a visual representation of filtering options. You can display multiple slicers and filter the table by multiple values from each. Slicers are only available when the data have been formatted as a table.

To add a slicer:

1. Click anywhere in the table to activate the *Table Tools Design* tab.
2. On the *Table Tools Design* tab, in the *Tools* group, click the **Insert Slicer** button.
3. In the *Insert Slicers* dialog, click the check boxes for the column(s) you want to filter by.
4. Click **OK.**

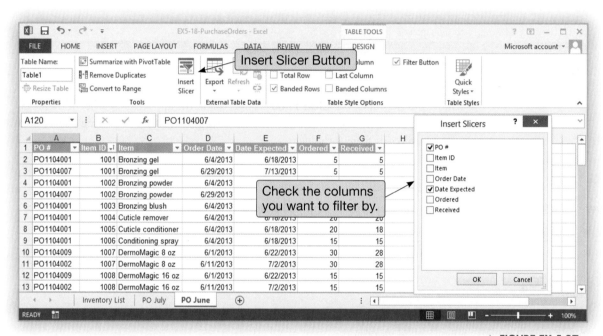

FIGURE EX 5.27

❱ To filter data using a slicer, click the buttons in each slicer to apply filtering to the table.

❱ To display more than one filtering option in a slicer, hold (Ctrl) as you click your selections.

❱ Notice that as you make selections in one slicer, options in the other slicer may become unavailable—indicating that there are no data available for that option under the current filtering conditions.

The table in Figure EX 5.28 has been filtered to show only rows with **PO1104007** in the *PO #* column and **7/4/2013** in the *Date Expected* column. Notice that all other options in the PO # slicer are disabled—which means that only rows with PO # PO1104007 have an expected date of 7/4/2013. However, there are two other options available in the Date Expected slicer—7/6/2013 and 7/13/2013—indicating that PO1104007 has multiple values in the *Date Expected* column.

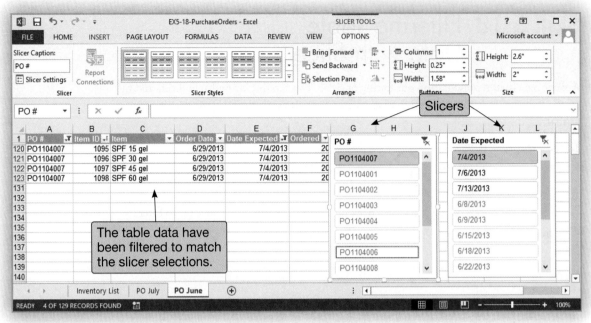

FIGURE EX 5.28

To remove filtering, click the **Clear Filter** 🔻 button in the upper right corner of the slicer. To remove a slicer from the table, click the slicer then press ⌈Delete⌋. Removing a slicer does not clear the filtering from the table.

tips & tricks

Slicers were introduced in Excel 2010 as an easy way to apply filtering to PivotTables. For Excel 2013, Microsoft added this feature to tables.

tell me **more**

❭ To move a slicer, move your mouse pointer over the slicer. When the cursor changes to the move cursor, click and drag the slicer to a new position on the worksheet.

❭ When a slicer is selected, the *Slicer Tools Options* tab becomes available. From this tab, you can apply a style to the slicer and control slicer settings.

let me try

Open the student data file **EX5-18-PurchaseOrders** and try this skill on your own:
1. If necessary, select the *PO June* sheet and click any cell in the table.
2. Add slicers for **PO #** and **Date Expected.**
3. Using the slicers, filter the table to show only rows for **PO # PO1104007** with an expected date of **7/4/2013.**
4. Save the file as directed by your instructor and close it.

Skill 5.19 Inserting Sparklines

Sparklines represent a series of data values as an individual graphic within a single cell. As you update the underlying data series, the Sparklines update immediately.

To add Sparklines to your worksheet using the Quick Analysis tool:

1. Select the data you want to visualize as Sparklines. If you want the Sparklines to appear in empty cells, ensure that there are empty cells to the right of your selection.

2. The Quick Analysis Tool button appears near the lower right corner of the selected range. Click the **Quick Analysis Tool** button, and then click the **Sparklines** tab.

3. Click the button for the Sparkline type you want.

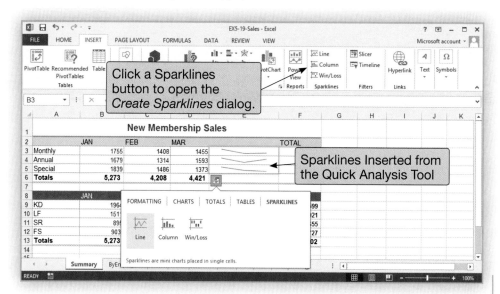

FIGURE EX 5.29

If you do not want Excel to place the Sparklines automatically, or if you are adding Sparklines in a situation where the Quick Analysis tool is not available, use the *Create Sparklines* dialog to specify their location:

1. Select the data range with the data points for the Sparklines.

2. On the *Insert* tab, in the *Sparklines* group, click the button for the type of Sparkline you want to insert: **Line, Column,** or **Win/Loss.**

3. The *Create Sparklines* dialog opens with the selected range added to the *Data Range* box.

4. In the *Location Range* box, enter the cell range where you want the Sparklines to appear. You can type the cell range or click and drag in the worksheet to select the cells.

5. Click **OK** to insert the Sparklines.

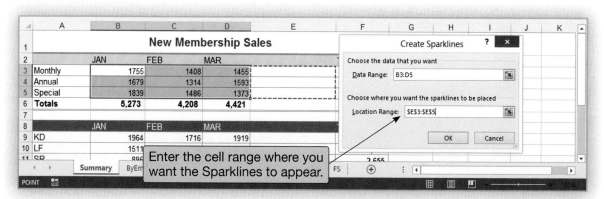

FIGURE EX 5.30

To remove Sparklines, you must select the cells containing the Sparklines, and then on the *Sparkline Tools Design* tab, in the *Group* group, click the **Clear** button.

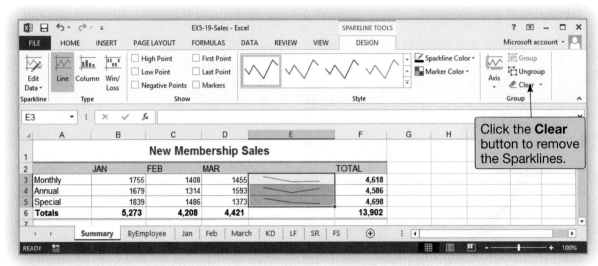

FIGURE EX 5.31

tips & tricks

Sparklines are not actually chart objects—they are charts in the background of the cells. You can add text and other data to the cells that contain Sparklines. You can also extend the Sparklines over multiple cells using the *Merge & Center* commands.

tell me **more**

When cells containing Sparklines are selected, the *Sparkline Tools Design* contextual tab becomes active. From this tab you can customize the look of the Sparklines including emphasizing high or low points, changing the type of Sparkline used, and changing colors.

let me **try**

Open the student data file **EX5-19-Sales** and try this skill on your own:

1. If necessary, select cells **B3:D5** on the *Summary* sheet.
2. Insert Line Sparklines in cells **E3:E6** to visually represent the data in the selected cells.
3. Save the file as directed by your instructor and close it.

Skill 5.20 Analyzing Data with Goal Seek

Excel's **Goal Seek** function lets you enter a desired value (outcome) for a formula and specify an input cell that can be modified in order to reach that goal. Goal Seek changes the value of the input cell incrementally until the target outcome is reached.

To find a value using Goal Seek:

1. Select the outcome cell. (This cell must contain a formula.)

2. On the *Data* tab, in the *Data Tools* group, click the **What-If Analysis** button, and then click **Goal Seek...**

3. Verify that the outcome cell is referenced in the *Set cell* box.

4. Enter the outcome value you want in the *To value* box.

5. Enter the input cell (the cell that contains the value to be changed) in the *By changing cell* box. (This cell must be referenced in the formula in the outcome cell either directly or indirectly and must contain a value, not a formula.)

6. Click **OK.**

7. The *Goal Seek Status* box appears, letting you know if Goal Seek was able to find a solution. Click **OK** to accept the solution, or click **Cancel** to return the input cell to its original value.

In the Goal Seek analysis in Figure EX 5.32, the outcome cell is cell **E15,** the total investor payout for the quarter; the desired outcome value is $25,000; and the input cell is cell **B17,** the investor percentage.

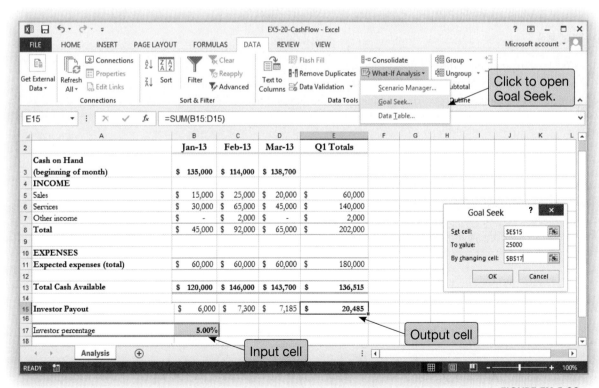

FIGURE EX 5.32

Notice that the formula in cell E15 does not reference cell B17 directly. However, it does reference cells B15:D15, and the formulas in those cells refer to cell B17.

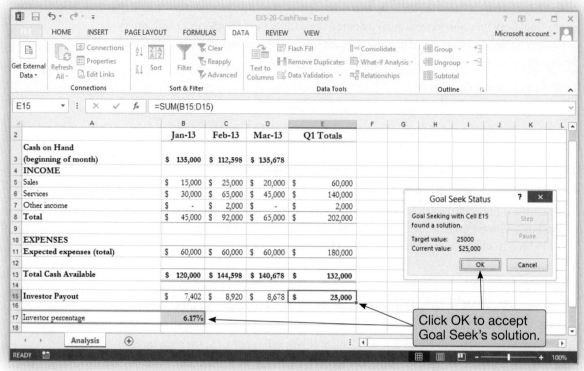

FIGURE EX 5.33

tips & tricks

Goal Seek works best in situations where there is only one variable, such as:
》 Finding the required number of units to sell to reach a sales goal when the price is inflexible.
》 Finding the required percentage to pay an investor when the amount due is inflexible.

let me try

Open the student data file **EX5-20-CashFlow** and try this skill on your own:
1. Use Goal Seek to find a value for cell **B17** that will result in a value of **$25,000** in cell **E15.**
2. If Goal Seek is able to find a solution, accept it.
3. Save the file as directed by your instructor and close it.

Skill 5.21 Analyzing Data with Data Tables

Data tables provide a quick what-if analysis of the effects of changing one or two variables within a formula. The data table is organized with a series of values for the variable(s) in a column or a row or both.

To create a one-variable data table with a column input format:

1. In a column, type the series of values you want to substitute for the variable in your formula.

2. In the cell above and to the right of the first value, type the formula that references the cell you want to replace with the new values.

3. Select the cell range for the data table, beginning with the empty cell above the first value you entered.

4. On the *Data* tab, in the *Data Tools* group, click the **What-If Analysis** button, and click **Data Table...**

5. In the *Data Table* dialog, the input cell is the cell that contains the original value for which you want to substitute the data table values. In this data table, the output values will be listed in a column, so enter the cell reference in the *Column input cell* box.

6. Click **OK.**

In the one-variable data table in Figure EX 5.34, the formula in cell E4 references the loan term in cell **B5**—the *nper* argument for the PMT function. This is the **column input cell** for the data table. The substitute values for cell B5 are listed in cells **D5:D9**.

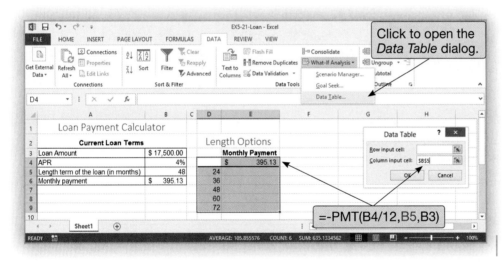

FIGURE EX 5.34

Excel completes the values in the table, using the substitute values in the formula:

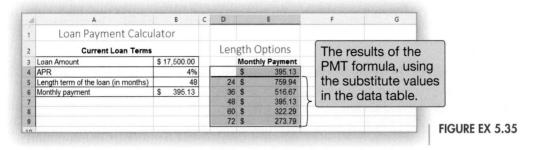

FIGURE EX 5.35

A **two-variable data table** works the same way as a one-variable data table, using inputs for both a column and a row variable. In a two-variable data table, the formula is located in the cell above the column input values and to the left of the row input values.

In the two-variable data table in Figure EX 5.36, the formula in cell E8 references the loan amount in cell **B3**—the *pv* argument for the PMT function. This is the **row input cell** for the data table. The substitute values for cell B3 are listed in cells **F8:I8.** The formula also references the second variable used in the data table, the interest rate in cell **B4**—the *rate* argument for the PMT function. This is the column input cell for the data table. The substitute values for cell B4 are listed in cells **E9:E14.**

In a two-variable data table, you may want to hide the data table formula by changing the cell font color to match the worksheet background. The data table is easier to follow if the cell in the upper left corner of the data table appears blank as shown in Figure EX 5.36. Of course, you can still see the formula in the formula bar.

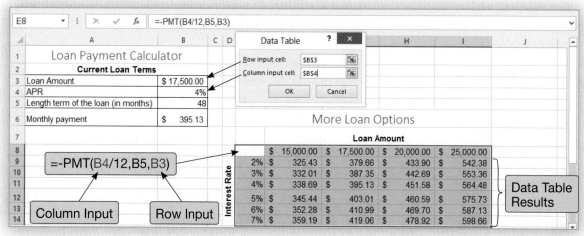

FIGURE EX 5.36

tips & tricks

Use Goal Seek if the result you are looking for is a specific value in a single cell. Use data tables when you want to see multiple possible outcomes based on multiple input options.

let me try

Open the student data file **EX5-21-Loan** and try this skill on your own:

1. If necessary, select the *One Variable* sheet.
2. Insert a one-variable data table in cells **D4:E9** to calculate the monthly loan payment for loan lengths using the following values: **24, 36, 48, 60, 72**
   The formula has been entered for you in cell E4. It references the original loan length in cell **B5.** You will need to enter the substitute values in the data table.
3. Go to the *Two Variables* sheet.
4. Insert a two-variable data table in cells **E8:I14.** The formula in cell E8 has been formatted using the white font color so it appears hidden. Use cell **B3** as the row input cell and cell **B4** as the column input cell for the data table.
5. Save the file as directed by your instructor and close it.

Skill 5.22 Creating PivotTables Using Recommended PivotTables

A **PivotTable** is a special report view that summarizes data and calculates the intersecting totals. PivotTables do not contain any data themselves—they summarize data from a cell range or a table in another part of your workbook.

The easiest way to begin a new PivotTable is to use one of the recommended PivotTables:

1. Select any cell within the table or cell range you want to use for your PivotTable.
2. On the *Insert* tab, in the *Tables* group, click the **Recommended PivotTables** button.
3. Preview each of the options in the *Recommended PivotTables* dialog. Click the one that is closest to how you want your final PivotTable to look.
4. Click **OK** to create the PivotTable in a new worksheet.

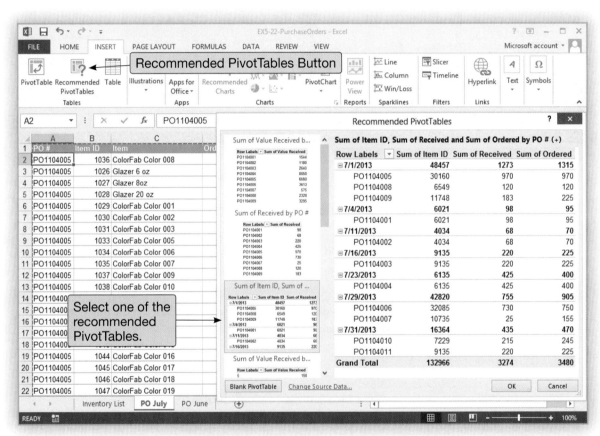

FIGURE EX 5.37

Once the PivotTable is inserted, you can add or remove fields. The *PivotTable Fields* pane shows you the list of available fields—the columns from the PivotTable's data source. In the *PivotTable Fields* pane, check the boxes to add or remove fields from the PivotTable.

❯ Fields that contain text data are added to the Rows section automatically. If there are multiple rows, Excel will attempt to group them in a logical way.

❯ Fields that contain numeric data are added to the Values section automatically. For each row in the PivotTable, Excel summarizes the values in each of the fields listed in the Values section.

You can click and drag the field names to move them between the Filters, Columns, Rows, or Values boxes.

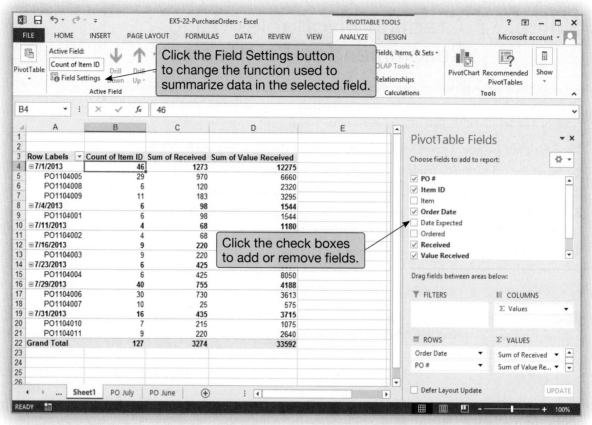

FIGURE EX 5.38

By default, PivotTables calculate totals using the SUM function. To change the calculation type for a field:

1. Click anywhere in the field you want to change.

2. On the *PivotTable Tools Analyze* tab, in the *Active Field* group, click the **Field Settings** button.

3. In the *Value Field Settings* dialog, *Summarize Values By* tab, select the function for the type of calculation you want.

4. Click **OK.**

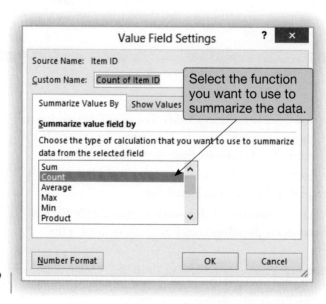

FIGURE EX 5.39

tips & tricks

another method

let me try

Open the student data file **EX5-22-PurchaseOrders** and try this skill on your own:

1. Verify that the *PO July* sheet is active and one of the cells in the data range is selected.
2. Insert a recommended PivotTable, using the **Sum of Item ID, Sum of Received and Sum of Ordered by PO #** option.
3. Add the **Value Received** field to the PivotTable.
4. Remove the **Ordered** field from the PivotTable.
5. Modify the **Item ID** field to use the **COUNT** function instead of the SUM function.
6. Save the file as directed by your instructor and close it.

Skill 5.23 Creating a PivotChart from a PivotTable

A **PivotChart** is a graphic representation of a PivotTable. In a column chart, the category fields are represented along the x (horizontal) axis while the data values are represented along the y (vertical) axis.

To create a PivotChart:

1. Select any cell in the PivotTable.

2. On the *PivotTable Tools Analyze* tab, in the *Tools* group, click the **PivotChart** button.

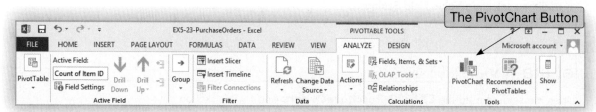

FIGURE EX 5.40

3. Select a chart type from the *Insert Chart* dialog.

4. Click **OK.**

If you need more room to display the PivotChart, you may want to hide the *PivotTable Fields* pane. On the *PivotChart Tools Analyze* tab, in the *Show/Hide* group, click the **Field List** button.

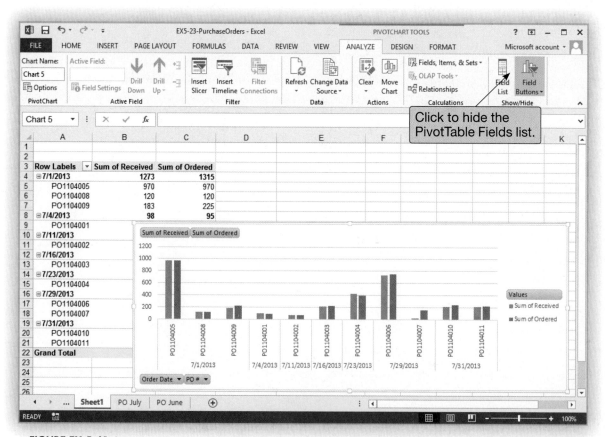

FIGURE EX 5.41

PivotCharts include all the formatting options that regular charts do. You can apply Quick Styles and hide or show chart elements from the *PivotChart Tools Design* tab. You can also resize the PivotChart or move it to its own sheet.

FIGURE EX 5.42
The PivotChart
Tools Design Tab

tell me **more**

To sort or filter the category data in the PivotChart, click the button in the lower-left corner of the PivotChart with the name of the field you want to sort or filter. If your PivotTable used multiple row labels, you will see a button for each.

let me try

Open the student data file **EX5-23-PurchaseOrders** and try this skill on your own:
1. If necessary, click anywhere in the PivotChart in the *Sheet1* worksheet.
2. Insert a PivotChart using the first clustered column chart type.
3. Save the file as directed by your instructor and close it.

key terms

Chart
Data points
Data markers
Data series
Y axis
X axis
Plot area
Chart area
Chart title
Legend
Column charts
Bar charts
Pie charts
Doughnut charts
Line charts
Line with markers
Chart sheet
Data labels

Data table (chart)
Quick Styles
Clustered column chart
Stacked column chart
Table
Total row
Banding
Sort
Filter
Slicer
Sparklines
Goal Seek
Data table (what-if analysis)
Column input cell
Two-variable data table
Row input cell
PivotTable
PivotChart

concepts review

1. Data markers are graphic representations of the values of data points in a chart.
   a. True
   b. False

2. _____ charts represent data as parts of a whole.
   a. Column
   b. Line
   c. Pie
   d. Bar

3. _____ apply combinations of fonts, line styles, fills, and shape effects to charts.
   a. Quick Styles
   b. Quick Layouts
   c. Chart Effects
   d. Chart Templates

4. _____ represent each data series as an individual graphic within a single cell.
   a. Sparklines
   b. Charts
   c. Tables
   d. PivotCharts

5. A Total row can be used to quickly calculate the _____ of all the values in a column.
   a. sum
   b. average
   c. both a and b
   d. neither a nor b

6. When you format data as a table, the header row automatically includes filtering and sorting.
   a. True
   b. False

7. The _____ command lets you enter a designated value for a formula and specify an input cell that can be modified in order to reach that goal.
   a. Scenario
   b. Data Table
   c. Consolidate
   d. Goal Seek

8. _____ rearranges the rows in your worksheet by the data in a column or columns.
   a. Sorting
   b. Filtering
   c. Formatting
   d. Grouping

9. The _____ command provides a quick what-if analysis of the effects of changing a single variable within a formula.

   a. Scenario

   b. Data Table

   c. Consolidate

   d. Goal Seek

10. A _____ is a special report view that summarizes data and calculates the intersecting totals.

   a. PivotTable

   b. Table

   c. Chart

   d. Scenario

Data files for projects can be found on
www.mhhe.com/office2013skills

projects

skill review 5.1

In this project, you will analyze data for an event planning company.

Skills needed to complete this project:

- Converting Data into Tables (Skill 5.11)
- Adding Total Rows to Tables (Skill 5.12)
- Sorting Data (Skill 5.16)
- Filtering Data (Skill 5.17)
- Analyzing Data with Data Tables (Skill 5.21)
- Using the Recommended Charts Feature (Skill 5.2)
- Changing the Chart Type (Skill 5.9)
- Applying Quick Styles and Colors to Charts (Skill 5.8)
- Showing and Hiding Chart Elements (Skill 5.7)
- Moving a Chart (Skill 5.6)
- Analyzing Data with Goal Seek (Skill 5.20)
- Inserting a Pie Chart (Skill 5.4)
- Exploring Charts (Skill 5.1)
- Creating PivotTables Using Recommended PivotTables (Skill 5.22)
- Creating a PivotChart from a PivotTable (Skill 5.23)

1. Open the start file **EX2013-SkillReview-5-1** and resave the file as:
   `[your initials]EX-SkillReview-5-1`

2. If the workbook opens in Protected View, click the **Enable Editing** button in the Message Bar at the top of the workbook.

3. Format the data on the *Table* worksheet into a table using one of the table Quick Styles.

    a. Select all the data including the headings, being careful not to select any blank rows or columns.

    b. On the *Home* tab, in the *Styles* group, click the **Format as Table** button to display the *Table Styles* gallery.

    c. Click the **Table Style Light 2** Quick Style.

    d. Verify that the correct cells will be used. Check the **My table has headers** check box. Click **OK.**

4. Add a Total row to the table to count the number of invitations sent.

    a. On the *Table Tools Design* tab, in the *Table Style Options* group, click the **Total Row** check box.

    b. In the Total row at the bottom of the table, note the total count of guests attending.

    c. In the Total row at the bottom of the table, click in the **Street** column, click the arrow, and select the **Count** function to count the invitations sent.

5. Sort the table by last name in alphabetical order:

    a. Click anywhere in the **Last Name** column.

    b. On the *Data* tab, in the *Sort & Filter* group, click the **A-Z** button.

6. Filter the data in the table to show only guests from the city of Rocklin.

    a. Click the arrow in the **City** column header.

    b. Click the (**Select All**) check box to remove all of the check marks.

    c. Click the check box in front of **Rocklin** to filter for only guests from Rocklin.

    d. Click **OK.** Excel displays only the rows for invitations sent to Rocklin.

7. Switch to work with the *Data Table* worksheet and use a data table to estimate costs for different numbers of attendees. Cell **C19** contains a formula that sums the costs in cells **C3:C16.** The formulas in those cells all refer to the number of guests in cell **C1.**

    a. Select cells **B19:C26** to use as the data table.

    b. On the *Data* tab, in the *Data Tools* group, click the **What-If Analysis** button, and click **Data Table.**

    c. In the *Column input cell* box, type **C1.** Click **OK.**

    d. Review the data table results computing the party costs for the various numbers of guests.

8. Use the recommended charts feature to create a column chart to compare the cost of various size parties.

    a. Select cells **B18:C26.**

    b. Click the **Quick Analysis Tool** button at the lower right corner of the selected range.

    c. Click the **Charts** tab.

    d. Click the **Clustered Column** option.

9. Change the chart to a line chart.

    a. If necessary, click to select the chart.

    b. On the *Chart Tools Design* tab, in the *Type* group, click the **Change Chart Type** button.

    c. In the *Change Chart Type* dialog, click **Line,** and click the first line chart type.

    d. Click **OK.**

10. Format the chart using a Quick Style. On the *Chart Tools Design* tab, in the *Chart Styles* group, click **Style 2.**

11. Display the chart gridlines and hide the data labels.

   a. Click the **Chart Elements** button that appears near the upper right corner of the chart.

   b. Click the **Gridlines** check box to add a checkmark.

   c. Click the **Data Labels** check box to remove the checkmark.

12. Move the chart to its own sheet in the workbook.

   a. On the *Chart Tools Design* tab, in the *Location* group, click the **Move Chart** button.

   b. In the *Move Chart* dialog, click the **New sheet** radio button.

   c. Click **OK.**

13. Use Goal Seek to determine the most you can afford for dinner per person, on a total $6,000 budget for 100 guests.

   a. Switch back to the *Data Table* sheet.

   b. Select the outcome cell **H19** and review the formula.

   c. On the *Data* tab, in the *Data Tools* group, click the **What-If Analysis** button and click **Goal Seek...**

   d. Verify that the outcome cell **H19** is referenced in the *Set cell* box.

   e. Enter the outcome value of **6000** in the *To value* box.

   f. Enter the input cell **F4** in the *By changing cell* box.

   g. Click **OK** to run Goal Seek.

   h. Click **OK** again to accept the Goal Seek solution.

14. Insert a 3-D pie chart to show the breakdown of the per guest costs.

   a. Select cells **G3:H11.**

   b. On the *Insert* tab, in the *Charts* group, click the **Pie** button, and click the **3-D Pie** option.

   c. Move the chart to the right so it does not cover the worksheet data.

   d. Change the chart title to: **Per Guest Cost Breakdown**

15. Create a PivotTable listing the number attending from each city.

   a. Return to the *Table* worksheet.

   b. Click anywhere in the table.

   c. On the *Insert* tab, in the *Tables* group, click the **Recommended PivotTables** button.

   d. Select the option **Sum of NumAttending by City.**

   e. Click **OK.**

16. Create a PivotChart from the PivotTable.

   a. Select any cell in the PivotTable.

   b. On the *PivotTable Tools Analyze* tab, in the *Tools* group, click the **PivotChart** button.

   c. Verify that the Clustered Column chart type is selected in the *Insert Chart* dialog.

   d. Click **OK.**

   e. Click the title and change it to read: **Number of Guests Attending from Each City**

f. Hide the legend by clicking the **Chart Elements** button that appears near the upper right corner of the PivotChart and clicking the **Legend** check box to remove the checkmark.

g. Move the PivotChart to the right so it does not cover the PivotTable.

17. Save and close the workbook.

skill review 5.2

In this project you will analyze real estate data.

Skills needed to complete this project:

- Converting Data into Tables (Skill 5.11)
- Adding Total Rows to Tables (Skill 5.12)
- Sorting Data (Skill 5.16)
- Filtering Data (Skill 5.17)
- Inserting a Line Chart (Skill 5.5)
- Moving a Chart (Skill 5.6)
- Showing and Hiding Chart Elements (Skill 5.7)
- Exploring Charts (Skill 5.1)
- Applying Quick Styles and Colors to Charts (Skill 5.8)
- Creating PivotTables Using Recommended PivotTables (Skill 5.22)
- Inserting Sparklines (Skill 5.19)
- Creating a PivotChart from a PivotTable (Skill 5.23)
- Analyzing Data with Data Tables (Skill 5.21)
- Analyzing Data with Goal Seek (Skill 5.20)

1. Open the start file **EX2013-SkillReview-5-2** and resave the file as:
[your initials]EX-SkillReview-5-2

2. If the workbook opens in Protected View, click the **Enable Editing** button in the Message Bar at the top of the workbook.

3. Format the data on the *Sales Data* worksheet as a table using the **Table Style Medium 5** table style:

a. Select any cell in the data.

b. On the *Home* tab, in the *Styles* group, click the **Format as Table** button to display the *Table Styles* gallery.

c. Click the **Table Style Medium 5** style.

d. Verify that the **My table has headers** check box is checked and that the correct data range is selected.

e. Click **OK.**

4. Add a Total row to the table to display the number of buyers; the average number of bedrooms and bathrooms for each sale; and the average purchase price, interest rate, and mortgage length.

a. On the *Table Tools Design* tab, in the *Table Style Options* group, click the **Total Row** check box.

b. In the Total row at the bottom of the table, click in the **Buyers** column, click the arrow, and select the **Count** function.

c. In the Total row at the bottom of the table, click in the **Bedrooms** column, click the arrow, and select the **Average** function.

d. In the Total row at the bottom of the table, click in the **Bathrooms** column, click the arrow, and select the **Average** function.

e. In the Total row at the bottom of the table, click in the **Purchase Price** column, click the arrow, and select the **Average** function.

f. In the Total row at the bottom of the table, click in the **Rate** column, click the arrow, and select the **Average** function.

g. In the Total row at the bottom of the table, click in the **Mortgage Years** column, click the arrow, and select the **Average** function.

5. Sort the data so the newest purchases appear at the top.

    a. Click anywhere in the **Date of Purchase** column.

    b. On the *Data* tab, in the *Sort & Filter* group, click the **Z-A** button.

6. Filter the data to show only houses sold by **Williman's** with three or more bedrooms.

    a. Click the arrow at the top of the **Agent** column.

    b. Click the (**Select All**) check box to remove all of the checkmarks.

    c. Click the check box in front of **Williman's.**

    d. Click **OK.**

    e. Click the arrow at the top of the **Bedrooms** column.

    f. Click the (**Select All**) check box to remove all of the checkmarks.

    g. Click the check boxes in front of **3, 4,** and **5.**

    h. Click **OK.**

7. Create a line chart showing the purchase prices for houses by date.

    a. Select the **Date of Purchase** data cells. Be careful not to include the column heading. Press and hold [Ctrl] and click and drag to select the **Purchase Price** data cells, again being careful not to include the column heading.

    b. On the *Insert* tab, in the *Charts* group, click the **Insert Line Chart** button.

    c. Select the first line chart type shown.

    d. Click **OK.**

8. Move the chart to its own sheet named *Purchase Prices*.

    a. If necessary, select the chart. On the *Chart Tools Design* tab, in the *Locations* group, click the **Move Chart** button.

    b. In the box type: `Purchase Prices`

    c. In the *Move Chart* dialog, click the **New sheet** radio button.

    d. Click **OK.**

9. Update the chart title and display the data labels as callouts.

    a. Change the chart title to: `Purchase Prices for 3-5 Bedroom Houses`

    b. Click the **Chart Elements** button near the upper right corner of the chart.

    c. Click the **Data Labels** check box to add a checkmark.

    d. Point to **Data Labels,** click the arrow that appears at the right side, and click **Data Callout.**

10. Apply the **Style 15** Quick Style to the chart.

    a. Click the **Chart Styles** button that appears near the upper right corner of the chart.

    b. Scroll to the bottom of the list, and click **Style 15.**

11. Create a PivotTable to summarize the average purchase price of different house types for each agent.

    a. Return to the *Sales Data* worksheet and click anywhere in the table.

    b. Click the **Insert** tab. In the *Tables* group, click the **Recommended PivotTables** button.

    c. Verify that the first recommended PivotTable is **Sum of Purchase Price by Agent.**

    d. Click **OK.**

    e. Select any cell in the **Sum of Purchase Price** column.

    f. On the *PivotTable Tools Analyze* tab, in the *Active Field* group, click the **Field Settings** button.

    g. In the *Summarize value field by* box, select **Average.**

    h. Click **OK.**

    i. Add the **House Type** field to the PivotTable by clicking the check box in the *Fields List* pane. Excel automatically places the *House Type* field in the Rows box and displays the house type data as a subgroup of rows below each agent.

    j. To summarize the house type data for each agent, use the *House Type* field as columns in the PivotTable. Click and drag the **House Type** field from the Rows box to the Columns box in the *PivotTable Fields* pane.

12. Add column Sparklines to the right of the PivotTable.

    a. Select cells **B5:E9** to use as the data for the Sparklines. You do not want to include the grand total column or row.

    b. On the *Insert* tab, in the *Sparklines* group, click the **Column** button.

    c. In the *Create Sparklines* dialog, verify that the cell range **B5:E9** is listed in the *Data Range* box.

    d. Add the range **G5:G9** to the *Location Range* box either by typing the cells range or by clicking and dragging to select it in the worksheet.

    e. Click **OK.**

13. Create a PivotChart from the PivotTable.

    a. Select any cell in the PivotTable.

    b. On the *PivotTable Tools Analyze* tab, in the *Tools* group, click the **PivotChart** button.

    c. Select the first column chart type from the *Insert Chart* dialog. Click **OK.**

    d. Click the **Chart Elements** box near the upper right corner of the PivotChart and click the **Chart Title** check box.

    e. Click the title and change it to: `Average Price by Type of House and Agent`

    f. If necessary, move the PivotChart to another part of the worksheet so it does not cover the PivotTable data.

14. Use the data in the *Loan Worksheet* sheet to run a what-if scenario for a client to show loan payments for a variety of interest rates and loan lengths. This what-if scenario requires a two-variable data table.

    a. Go to the **Loan Worksheet** sheet and familiarize yourself with the formula in cell **B5.** Place close attention to the cell references.

    b. Select cells **B5:E38** to use the payment formula in B5 and the various years and rates as the data table.

    c. On the *Data* tab, in the *Data Tools* group, click the **What-If Analysis** button, and click **Data Table.**

d. In the *Row input cell* box, enter the cell reference for the length of the loan—the *rate* argument from the formula in cell B5: **C2**

e. In the *Column input cell* box, enter the cell reference for the loan interest rate—the *nper* argument from the formula in cell B5: **A2**

f. Click **OK.**

15. Use Goal Seek to determine the most you can afford to borrow, on a $600 per month budget:

a. On the *Loan Worksheet* sheet, select the outcome formula cell, **H4.**

b. On the *Data* tab, in the *Data Tools* group, click the **What-If Analysis** button and click **Goal Seek...**

c. Verify that the outcome cell **H4** is referenced in the *Set cell* box.

d. Enter the outcome value of **600** in the *To value* box.

e. Enter the input cell **H9** in the *By changing cell* box.

f. Click **OK.**

g. Click **OK** again to accept the Goal Seek solution.

h. Notice the loan payment changed to $600 and the amount to borrow was computed to be $111,769.

16. Save and close the workbook.

challenge yourself 5.3

In this project, you will analyze shoe sales data and use what-if analysis to determine your commission potential and your sales goal.

Skills needed to complete this project:

- Converting Data into Tables (Skill 5.11)
- Adding Total Rows to Tables (Skill 5.12)
- Removing Duplicate Rows from Tables (Skill 5.14)
- Filtering Data (Skill 5.17)
- Sorting Data (Skill 5.16)
- Inserting a Line Chart (Skill 5.5)
- Filtering Chart Data (Skill 5.10)
- Moving a Chart (Skill 5.6)
- Filtering Table Data with Slicers (Skill 5.18)
- Creating PivotTables Using Recommended PivotTables (Skill 5.22)
- Creating a PivotChart from a PivotTable (Skill 5.23)
- Showing and Hiding Chart Elements (Skill 5.7)
- Inserting Sparklines (Skill 5.19)
- Analyzing Data with Data Tables (Skill 5.21)
- Analyzing Data with Goal Seek (Skill 5.20)

1. Open the start file **EX2013-ChallengeYourself-5-3** and resave the file as:
   [your initials]EX-ChallengeYourself-5-3

2. If the workbook opens in Protected View, enable editing so you can make changes to the workbook.

3. Convert the shoe sales data in the *Sales* worksheet into a table.

   a. Use the **Table Style Light 9** table style.

   b. Add a Total row to the table and display the average for the *# of Pairs* and the *Price Per Pair* columns.

   c. Delete any rows in the table that have duplicate data in all the columns. There are three.

4. Filter to show just the sales for the **California** region.

5. Sort the table by order date with the newest orders first.

6. Insert a line chart to show the total sale amount for each order by order date.

   a. There was an ordering glitch on April 26 that caused a spike in sales. Apply a filter to the chart to hide orders from that date.

   b. If necessary, move the chart so it does not cover the table data.

7. Add a slicer to the table so you can filter by shoe name. Use the slicer to display data for the **Avone** shoe only. Notice the effect on the chart.

8. Create a PivotTable from the data in the *Sales* worksheet. Use the **Sum of Price Per Pair by Region** recommended PivotTable.

   a. Modify the PivotTable so the Price Per Pair data are averaged, not totaled.

   b. Add the Shoe field to the PivotTable. It should appear in the Rows section below the Region field.

   c. Format all the values in the PivotTable using the Accounting Number Format.

9. Create a column PivotChart based on the PivotTable data. Use the first recommended column chart type.

   a. Hide the chart title and legend.

   b. If necessary, move the PivotChart on the worksheet so it does not cover the PivotChart data.

10. Go to the *By Region* worksheet and add Column Sparklines to the right of the data as appropriate.

11. You have been told that you will receive a commission between 5 and 10 percent. On the *Commission* sheet, make a one-variable data table using cells **A4:B14** to determine how much that commission may be. The column input cell is **A4.**

12. You owe $12,000 in student loans and would like to pay it all off with your commissions. Use *Goal Seek* to determine the amount you must sell (cell **G5**) in order for cell **G3** (your commission) to equal $12,000 so you can fully pay off your student loans. Accept the Goal Seek solution.

13. Save and close the workbook.

challenge yourself 5.4

In this project, the local library has received a significant collection of DVDs as a donation and has asked you to provide an analysis of the titles. They need to decide whether they should keep the collection or sell it to raise money for a new computer.

Skills needed to complete this project:

- Converting Data into Tables (Skill 5.11)
- Adding Total Rows to Tables (Skill 5.12)
- Removing Duplicate Rows from Tables (Skill 5.14)
- Applying Quick Styles to Tables (Skill 5.13)

- Sorting Data (Skill 5.16)
- Filtering Data (Skill 5.17)
- Filtering Table Data with Slicers (Skill 5.18)
- Creating PivotTables Using Recommended PivotTables (Skill 5.22)
- Creating a PivotChart from a PivotTable (Skill 5.23)
- Showing and Hiding Chart Elements (Skill 5.7)
- Analyzing Data with Data Tables (Skill 5.21)
- Analyzing Data with Goal Seek (Skill 5.20)

1. Open the start file **EX2013-ChallengeYourself-5-4** and resave the file as:
   `[your initials]EX-ChallengeYourself-5-4`

2. If the workbook opens in Protected View, enable editing so you can make changes to the workbook.

3. Convert the data on the *Videos* sheet into a table using the style **Table Style Light 1**.

   a. Add a Total row to the table and count the number of movie titles and the average purchase price.

   b. Delete all the duplicate rows. Be careful, there may be duplicate rows with the same movie title, but different data in the other columns. When you are finished, there should be 296 unique titles in the collection.

   c. Change the table style to use the **Table Style Medium 1 Quick Style.**

4. Sort the data in the table alphabetically by category.

5. Filter the table to show only Disney and family movies that are rated G or PG.

6. Create a PivotTable from the table data using the **Sum of Price by Rating** recommend PivotTable.

7. Create a pie PivotChart from the PivotTable.

   a. Display the data labels using the **Best Fit** option.

   b. Hide the chart title.

8. On the *Data Table* worksheet, create a one-variable data table to determine the amount of money that would be raised if 100 DVDs were sold at the various prices listed. Review the formula in cell **C7** to identify the appropriate cell to use as the input cell for the data table.

9. What if the selling price for each DVD is set at $1.50? How many DVDs would the library need to sell to raise $535? Use Goal Seek to find a value for cell **F9** that will result in a value of 535 for cell **F7.**

10. Save and close the workbook.

on your own 5.5

In this project, you will be analyzing data about automobile emissions and fuel economy. These green car data were downloaded from the Web site https://explore.data.gov/d/9un4-5bz7 and are explained at this Web site: http://www.epa.gov/greenvehicles/Aboutratings.do. The scores range from 0 to 10, where 10 is best. The vehicles with the best scores on both air pollution and greenhouse gas receive the SmartWay designation.

Skills needed to complete this project:

- Converting Data into Tables (Skill 5.11)
- Filtering Data (Skill 5.17)

- Filtering Table Data with Slicers (Skill 5.18)
- Sorting Data (Skill 5.16)
- Inserting a Column Chart or a Bar Chart (Skill 5.3)
- Showing and Hiding Chart Elements (Skill 5.7)
- Applying Quick Styles and Colors to Charts (Skill 5.8)
- Changing the Chart Type (Skill 5.9)
- Creating PivotTables Using Recommended PivotTables (Skill 5.22)
- Creating a PivotChart from a PivotTable (Skill 5.23)
- Analyzing Data with Data Tables (Skill 5.21)
- Analyzing Data with Goal Seek (Skill 5.20)

1. Open the start file **EX2013-OnYourOwn-5-5** and resave the file as:
   `[your initials]EX-OnYourOwn-5-5`

2. If the workbook opens in Protected View, click the **Enable Editing** button in the Message Bar at the top of the workbook so you can modify the workbook.

3. The *Data* worksheet contains more than 2,000 rows. That's a lot of data! Use filtering and sorting techniques to display the rows for cars with **8** cylinder engines (*Cyl* column) with an automatic seven-speed transmission (**Auto-7** in the *Trans* column). Narrow the data further to show just four-wheel drives (**4WD** in the *Drive* column). Let's narrow the list down a little bit further and display only cars in the large car class (use the *Veh Class* column). You should end up with six records visible.

4. Sort the data so the cars with the best combination MPG (*Cmb MPG* column) appear at the top.

5. Create a chart comparing the **City MPG, Hwy MPG,** and **Cmb MPG** for the cars shown.

   a. Add and remove chart elements as necessary to make the chart clear and easy to read.

   b. Apply one of the chart Quick Styles.

   c. Try changing the chart to another chart type. Is there another chart type available that's appropriate for the data?

6. Create a PivotTable from the car data to summarize the average City MPG, Hwy, MPG, and Cmb MPG by car class. You may want to start with the **Count of Model by Veh Class** recommended PivotTable and then make changes. Format numbers in the PivotTable as appropriate.

7. Create a PivotChart from the PivotTable data.

8. On the *Commuting Costs* worksheet, create a two-variable data table to calculate the daily cost of gas for a variety of gas prices and a variety of miles driven per day. If you have a daily commute to school or work, use variations on your actual commuting miles in the data table.

   a. The formula to calculate the cost of your daily commute is:
   Commuting miles/your car's MPG*price of gas per gallon

   b. In the data table formula, you can use the MPG in cell B3 or change the value to your car's estimated MPG.

   c. Find a way to hide the data table formula.

   d. Add formatting as appropriate.

9. You're in the market for a new car, and you'd like to reduce your monthly gas costs to around $50. What's the minimum gas mileage you should look for in your new car? Can you use Goal Seek with the data on this worksheet to find an answer?

10. Save and close the workbook.

The staff members of a private college preparatory school have been trying to analyze student data and create what-if scenarios regarding investment decisions. Unfortunately, they've made a mess of this workbook. Can you help them fix it?

Skills needed to complete this project:

- Moving a Chart (Skill 5.6)
- Converting Data into Tables (Skill 5.11)
- Filtering Table Data with Slicers (Skill 5.18)
- Removing Duplicate Rows from Tables (Skill 5.14)
- Adding Total Rows to Tables (Skill 5.12)
- Creating PivotTables Using Recommended PivotTables (Skill 5.22)
- Inserting a Pie Chart (Skill 5.4)
- Changing the Chart Type (Skill 5.9)
- Analyzing Data with Data Tables (Skill 5.21)

1. Open the start file **EX2013-FixIt-5-6** and resave the file as:
   `[your initials]EX-FixIt-5-6`

2. If the workbook opens in Protected View, click the **Enable Editing** button in the Message Bar at the top of the workbook so you can modify the workbook.

3. The data in the *Student Test Data* worksheet has a couple of problems to fix:

   a. The data should be organized alphabetically by subject.

   b. Format the data so the school faculty can use slicers to filter data by month, by subject, or by student or by any combination of the three. Go ahead and display the slicers, but you don't need to apply any filtering.

   c. Find and delete the duplicate records. There should be 90 unique records.

   d. The data should include a Total row to calculate the average score.

4. The faculty members also want a PivotTable to summarize the average scores for each subject for each student by month, but since there wasn't a recommended PivotTable that met their needs exactly, they didn't know how to add one. Go ahead and create the PivotTable for them.

5. The PivotChart on the *Faculty Pivot* sheet should show the size of each department as a proportional part of a whole. A line chart was the wrong choice. Change the chart type to a better choice.

6. The school finance committee has determined that a $14,000 facilities upgrade will be needed in 10 years. An alumnus has donated $10,000. If invested, will it grow to be enough? That depends on the rate of return. On the *Data Table* worksheet, an attempt has been made to use Excel's data table feature to determine the value of the investment after five years at different rates of return. The formula in cell D6 is correct, but something went wrong with the data table. Delete the zeros in cells **D7:D30** and try again. Even if you're not familiar with the PV formula used in cell D6, you should be able to figure this out.

7. Save and close the workbook.

access 2013

chapter 1

Getting Started with Access 2013

In this chapter, you will learn the following skills:

- ❯ Identify the elements of a Microsoft Access 2013 database
- ❯ Use the Navigation Pane to open, organize, and view database objects
- ❯ Understand and view table relationships
- ❯ Understand database object views
- ❯ Navigate records in tables and forms
- ❯ Create new records, enter, edit, find, and move data in tables and forms
- ❯ Delete records in tables and forms
- ❯ Rename and delete database objects
- ❯ Preview and print database objects
- ❯ Export data to other formats
- ❯ Use the Compact & Repair tool
- ❯ Perform a backup

skills

introduction

This chapter is an introduction to the concepts necessary for understanding and working with relational databases. You will learn about the database objects that make up an Access database and how they relate to one another. You will learn to navigate, create, edit, and delete records in tables and forms. You also will learn the importance of database maintenance duties such as compact and repair and creating a backup.

Skill 1.1 Introduction to Access 2013

In the simplest terms, a **database** is a collection of data. An effective database allows you to enter, store, organize, and retrieve large amounts of related data. Access is different from other Microsoft Office applications you may have used. Although you create and work with a single Access database file, inside the file, there are multiple objects. Within each Access database, you create, edit, and save (and delete) objects. The types of objects in an Access database are:

> **Tables**—Store all the database data. They are the essential building blocks of the database. A table looks similar to a spreadsheet. Each row in the table contains all the data for a single **record.** Each column in the table represents a specific data value called a **field.** All records in a table have the same fields.

> Figure AC 1.1 shows the *Appointments* table, which stores the data for each customer appointment.

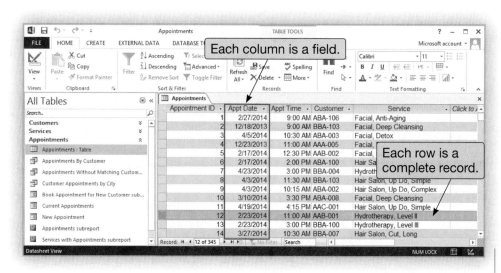

FIGURE AC 1.1

Because Access allows you to relate tables to one another, it is often referred to as a relational database. A **relational database** is a group of tables related to one another by common fields.

> **Forms**—Allow users to input data through a friendly interface. Entering data through a form is easier than entering it directly into a table. All the data entered into a form are stored in the underlying database table(s).

> Figure AC 1.2 shows the *New Appointment* form, which allows a data-entry operator to enter new appointments. When a new appointment is created using this form, a new record is added to the *Appointments* table.

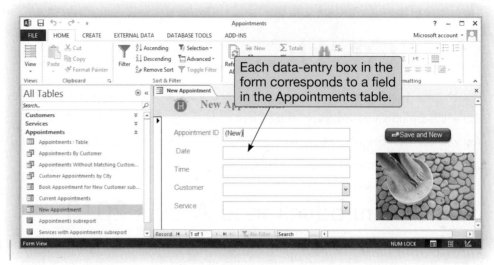

FIGURE AC 1.2

Queries—Extract data from a table or related tables. Queries can also perform actions on tables such as updating data values or deleting data. Query results may look like a table, but they do not store data permanently. The query results are updated dynamically each time the query is run—retrieving data fresh from the table(s) upon which the query is based.

The query in Figure AC 1.3 returns a list of all the appointments for customers who live in a specific city. The query combines data from two tables: *Appointments* and *Customers*.

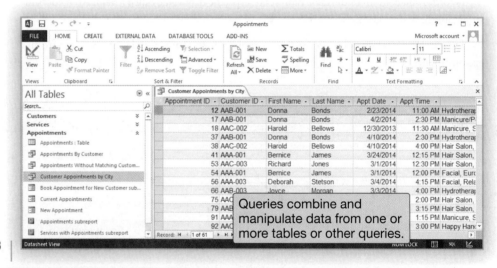

FIGURE AC 1.3

Reports—Display database information for printing or viewing on-screen. Reports do not allow data entry; they are read-only.

The report in Figure AC 1.4, *Services with Appointments subreport*, displays a printable summary of each service and a list of the current appointments for that service (the *subreport*). This report combines data from multiple tables and queries in a format suitable for printing.

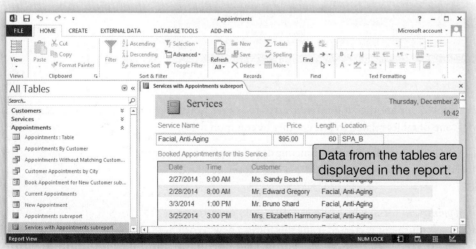

FIGURE AC 1.4

All the database objects are organized in the **Navigation Pane,** which is docked at the left side of the screen. Each database object in the Navigation Pane has a name and an icon representing the type of object.

The Navigation Pane is usually expanded when you open an Access database. If you need more room to work, you can collapse the Navigation Pane by clicking the **Shutter Bar Open/Close** button. To expand the Navigation Pane again, click the **Shutter Bar Open/Close** button.

To open a database object, double-click the object name in the Navigation Pane. The object will appear as a new tab within the Access work area unless it is specifically designed to open in a window format. You can have multiple database objects open at the same time. To navigate from one object to another, click the object tab.

To close an object, click the **X** at the far right side of the object. Be careful not to click the X in the upper right corner of the database window—that will close the database!

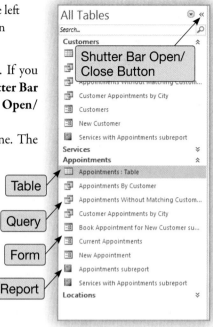

FIGURE AC 1.5

tell me **more**

A fourth type of database object called a Macro is a collection of programming code usually used within forms and reports to create buttons and other user interface elements. You will not work with macros until you are a more experienced Access user.

another **method**

You can also close an open database object by right-clicking the object tab and selecting **Close**.

let me try

If the database is not already open, open the data file **AC1-Appointments** and try this skill on your own:
1. Open the *Appointments* table. (If the Navigation Pane is not open, open it.)
2. Open the *New Customer* form.
3. Close the Navigation Pane.
4. Click the tabs to move back and forth between the *Appointments* table and the *New Customer* form.
5. Close the *New Customer* form.
6. Close the *Appointments* table.
7. Open the Navigation Pane.

Skill 1.2 Working with Security Warnings

When you open a database for the first time, Access may display a security warning in the **Message Bar** at the top of the window, below the Ribbon. Access disables active content such as ActiveX controls and VBA macros to protect your computer from becoming infected by a virus or other malware.

If you trust the source of the database, click the **Enable Content** button in the Message Bar. When you enable active content for a database, Access remembers the setting and you will not see the security warning message the next time you open the database.

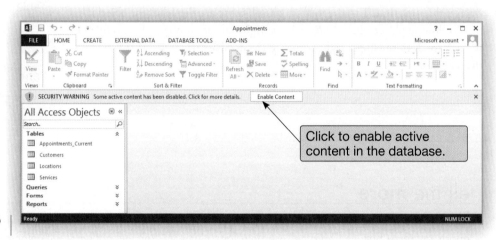

FIGURE AC 1.6

tips & tricks

To learn more about the security settings in Access 2013, open the Trust Center and review the options. We do not recommend changing any of the default Trust Center settings.

another method

You can also enable active content from the Info page in Backstage.

1. Click the **File** tab to open Backstage.
2. Click **Info.**
3. The Info page provides more information about the database. If you are sure you want allow active content, click the **Enable Editing** button.

let me try

If the database is not already open, open the data file **AC1-Appointments** and try this skill on your own:

1. Open the database and enable active content. Once you have done this for the database, you will not see the warning again. If you do not see the warning, you may have enabled active content previously.
2. Close the database and reopen it to confirm that the warning does not appear again.

Skill 1.3 Understanding and Viewing Table Relationships

Remember that Access is a relational database. Objects in your database are related to one another through relationships defined by common fields between tables. Before working with a database, you should understand the underlying database structure—how the tables are related.

For example, a table of customer data might include fields for customer ID, title, first name, last name, and address information. Another table for tracking customer appointments might have fields for appointment ID, appointment date, appointment time, customer, and service. The two tables are related by the data in the *Customer ID* and *Customer* fields, so the database can generate reports combining information from the two tables.

There are three types of relationships: one-to-many, one-to-one, and many-to-many. One-to-many relationships are the most common. In a **one-to-many relationship**, the main table contains a **primary key** field that is included as a field (the **foreign key**) in the secondary table. Thus, one record in the first table can relate to many records in the second table. In Figure AC 1.7, the *Customer ID* field in the *Customers* table is the primary key. Records in the *Appointments* table are related to the *Customers* table through the *Customer* field (the foreign key in the relationship).

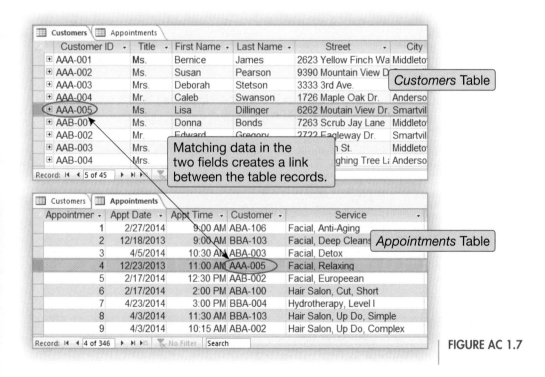

FIGURE AC 1.7

The relationships between primary and foreign key fields are fundamental to understanding and working with any relational database. You will learn more about primary key fields in other skills.

The **Relationships window** provides a visual representation of the relationships in your database.

To open the Relationships window, on the *Database Tools* tab, in the *Relationships* group, click the **Relationships** button.

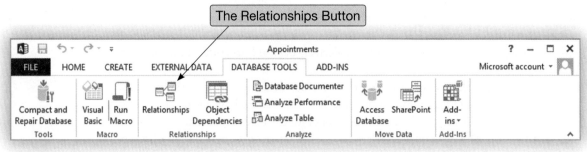

FIGURE AC 1.8

In the Relationships window, each table is represented by a box listing all the fields in the table. Primary key fields are identified with a key icon next to the field name. Lines representing the type of relationship connect related fields. In a one-to-many relationship, the one field in the main table that relates to many records in the secondary table is represented by a 1. The corresponding field in the secondary table is represented by an infinity symbol.

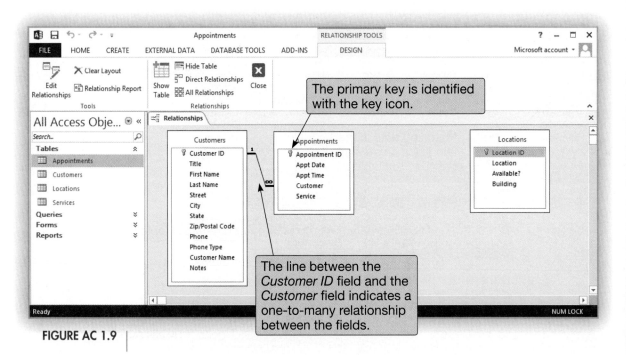

FIGURE AC 1.9

To display a table that isn't already showing in the Relationships window:

1. On the *Relationship Tools Design* tab, in the *Relationships* group, click the **Show Table** button to open the *Show Table* dialog.

2. Double-click the table you want to add to the Relationships window. You can also select the table name and then click the **Add** button in the *Show Table* dialog.

3. When you are finished adding tables to the Relationships window, click the **Close** button to close the *Show Table* dialog.

Figure AC 1.10 shows the effect of adding the *Services* table to the Relationships window. Notice the new lines representing the relationships between the *Appointments* table and the *Services* table and between the *Services* table and the *Locations* table.

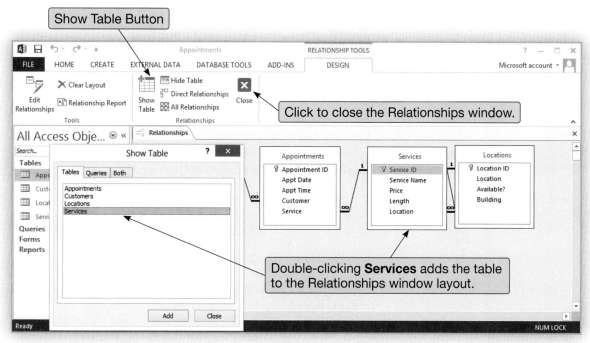

FIGURE AC 1.10

On the *Relationship Tools Design* tab, in the *Relationships* group, click the **Close** button to close the Relationships window.

If you have made changes to the layout of the Relationships window, Access will ask if you want to save the changes. Click **Yes.**

tips & tricks

You can display all the database relationships at once by clicking the **All Relationships** button on the *Relationship Tools Design* tab.

tell me more

To hide a table in the Relationships window:

1. Select the table by clicking it in the Relationships window.
2. On the *Relationship Tools Design* tab, in the *Relationships* group, click the **Hide Table** button.
3. Select the table by clicking it in the Relationships window.

another method

To open the *Show Table* dialog, right-click anywhere in the Relationships window and select **Show Table...** from the shortcut menu.

let me try

If the database is not already open, open the data file **AC1-Appointments** and try this skill on your own:

1. Open the Relationships window.
2. Open the *Show Table* dialog.
3. Show the *Services* table.
4. Close the *Show Table* dialog.
5. Close the Relationships window, saving the layout changes.

Skill 1.4 Organizing Objects in the Navigation Pane

As you have learned, the Navigation Pane lists all the objects in the database. By default, the Navigation Pane displays objects organized by the *Tables and Related Views* category. This category creates a group for each table in the database. The first object listed in the group is the table. Beneath the table, Access lists the other database objects that are dependent on that table. For example, in Figure AC 1.11, the *Customers* group includes the *Customers* table and the queries, forms, and report that use the data stored in that table.

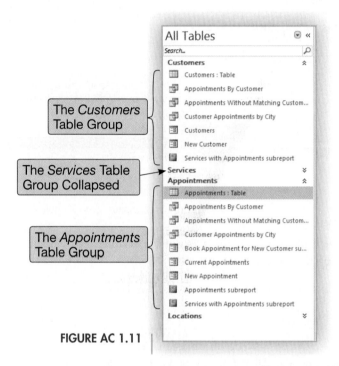

FIGURE AC 1.11

If you are working with the database objects in a single group, it may be helpful to collapse the other groups:

❯ To collapse a group in the Navigation Pane so only the group name is visible, click the **Collapse Group** button ⌃ located at the right side of the group name.

❯ To expand a group, click the **Expand Group** button ⌄.

If you would rather group the database objects by object type, you can change the category by which the Navigation Pane is grouped:

1. Click the top of the Navigation Pane to display the category and group list.

2. In the *Navigate to Category* section, select **Object Type.**

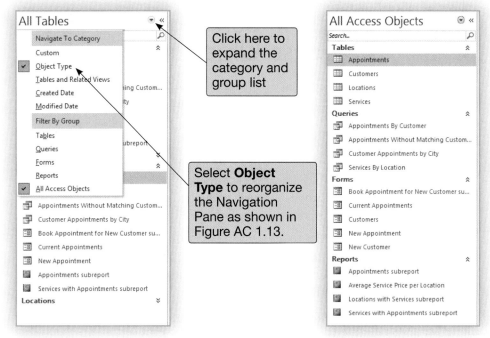

FIGURE AC 1.12　　　　　　　**FIGURE AC 1.13**

Now the Navigation Pane groups all the tables together in one group, all the queries together in another, all the forms together in another, and all the reports together in the final group.

You can also apply a filter to the Navigation Pane to display only a specific group within the category. Click the top of the Navigation Pane, and click an option in the *Filter by Group* section. The groups available vary, depending on the category and the actual objects in your database.

To remove the group filter, click the top of the Navigation Pane again, and select **All Access Objects** in the *Filter by Group* section.

tell me **more**

In addition to grouping the Navigation Pane by the *Tables and Related Views* group and the *Object Type* group, there are three other grouping options:

❱ **Custom**—Groups objects into those you have assigned to the custom group and those that are unassigned.

❱ **Created Date**—Groups database objects by the date they were created.

❱ **Modified Date**—Groups database objects by the date they were last changed.

let me **try**

If the database is not already open, open the data file **AC1-Appointments** and try this skill on your own:

1. Change the Navigation Pane grouping option to **Object Type.**
2. Change the Navigation Pane grouping option to **Tables and Related Views.**

Skill 1.5 Switching between Database Object Views

When you open a database object from the Navigation Pane, it opens in the default view for that object. For examples of each of the default object views, review the figures in the skill *Introduction to Access 2013*.

❱ Tables open in **Datasheet view** where you can enter, sort, and filter data. From Datasheet view you can also add new fields and modify some field properties.

❱ Forms open in **Form view**, which provides a user-friendly interface for entering data. If the form is formatted similar to a table, it will open in a special form Datasheet view. You cannot change the form layout or formatting from these views.

❱ Queries open in **Datasheet view** showing the record set that matches the query criteria. Datasheet view for a query does not allow you to modify fields.

❱ Reports open in **Report view**. which shows a static view of the report. You cannot change the layout or formatting of the report from Report view.

If you want to work on the structure of a database object, you will need to switch to another view. On the *Home* tab, in the *Views* group, click the **View** button arrow, and select the view you want.

You can also switch views from the buttons at the far right side of the status bar. The button representing the current view appears highlighted. The name of the current view appears at the left side of the status bar.

Design view is used to modify the structure of the database object. When you are working with an object in Design view, you see only the structural elements of the object, not the data.

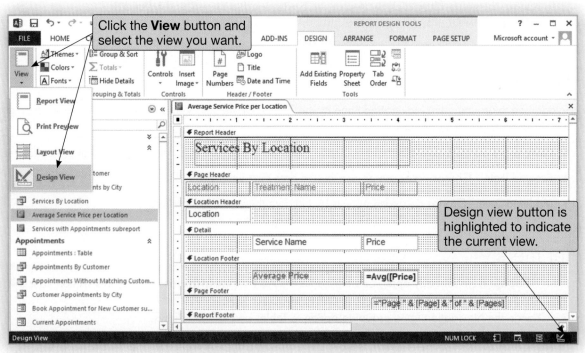

FIGURE AC 1.14
A report in Design view

For queries, Design view gives you a visual grid to create the underlying programming code that defines the parameters and criteria used to generate the resulting dataset. Queries also offer **SQL view** where advanced users can write code directly to build the query.

Forms and reports also offer **Layout view** where you can modify some (but not all) structural elements. The benefit of Layout view is that you can see live data in the object while you work on the object layout.

FIGURE AC 1.15
A report in Layout view

Reports include **Print Preview**, which shows how the report will look when printed. When you are in Print Preview view, only the *Print Preview* tab is available. From this tab, you can adjust print settings and export the report to another file format.

tips & tricks

Table data and query results in Datasheet view are sometimes referred to as **datasheets**.

another method

To switch views you can also right-click the object tab and select the view you want.

let me try

If the database is not already open, open the data file **AC1-Appointments** and try this skill on your own:

1. Open the *Average Price per Location* report from the Navigation Pane. You may need to expand the *Locations* group or the *Reports* group to find the report. It will open in Report view.
2. Switch to Design view.
3. Switch to Layout view.
4. Close the report.

---

skill 1.5   Switching between Database Object Views

Skill 1.6 Navigating Records

Tables, forms, and query results often contain many records and can be difficult to navigate. At the bottom of the datasheet or form window, you'll find navigation buttons to help you move quickly to the beginning or end of the dataset. You can jump to a specific record number or advance through records one at a time.

To navigate among records in a table, form, or query results:

❱ Move to the next record by clicking the **Next Record** button.

❱ Move to the previous record by clicking the **Previous Record** button.

❱ Move to the first record in the dataset by clicking the **First Record** button.

❱ Move to the last record in the dataset by clicking the **Last Record** button.

❱ Move to a specific record number by typing the number in the **Current Record** box, then pressing ⎰←Enter⎱ or ⎰Tab ⇥⎱.

Figure AC 1.16 shows the *Customers* form and the *Customers* table. Both database objects have the same navigation tools even though the form displays only one record at a time while the table datasheet shows all the records.

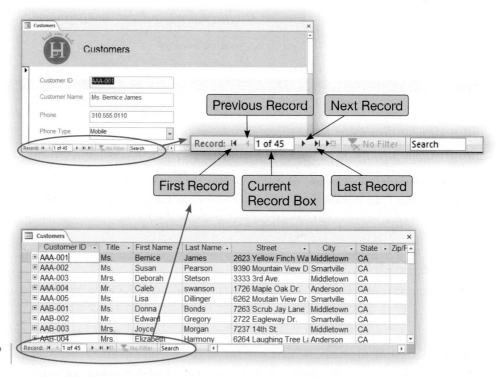

FIGURE AC 1.16

You can use the arrow keys on your keyboard to navigate through fields in a record or between records.

❱ Press ⎰→⎱ to go to the next field in the record.

❱ Press ⎰←⎱ to go to the previous field in the record.

❱ Press ⎰↓⎱ to go to the next record.

❱ Press ⎰↑⎱ to go to the previous record.

❱ Press ⎰Ctrl⎱ + ⎰↑⎱ to go to the first record.

❱ Press ⎰Ctrl⎱ + ⎰↓⎱ to go to the last record.

You can use ⬚Tab⬚ to navigate from field to field and from record to record:

》 Pressing ⬚Tab⬚ moves you from field to field within a record.

》 Pressing ⬚Tab⬚ from the last field in the record will move you to the first field in the next record.

》 If you are on the last record in the dataset, pressing ⬚Tab⬚ will create a new blank record (if creating a new record is allowed).

another **method**

The record navigation commands are also available from the *Home* tab, in the *Find* group. Click the **Go To** button, and then click one of the navigation options from the menu.

let me **try**

If the database is not already open, open the data file **AC1-Appointments** and try this skill on your own:

1. If necessary, open the *Customers* table in Datasheet view.
2. Go to the **last** record.
3. Go to the **previous** record.
4. Go to the **first** record.
5. Go to the **next** record.
6. Go to record number **20.**
7. Close the table.

from the perspective of . . .

PROJECT MANAGER

I inherited a database from the person who had my job before me. I am not a database expert, so before I attempted any data entry, I made sure I understood the structure of the database. I used the Relationships window to see how the tables relate to one another. I also switched the Navigation Pane organization to show the tables and related views, so I could see which forms and reports go with which tables. After spending some time exploring the database objects, I felt much more comfortable about using the database. I'm really glad I didn't jump in and start making changes right away.

Skill 1.7 Creating a New Record in a Table

Data are entered in records—through tables or forms. When entering records in a table, you must use Datasheet view. When you enter data in a table, Access commits the data (saves them) each time you move to a new field or begin a new record.

To enter data in a new record in a table:

1. Open the table in Datasheet view.

2. If the last row of the table is visible, you can enter data by typing in the first field in the next row available for data entry indicated by * in the row selector.

3. If the last row of the table is not visible, insert a new record by clicking the **New (blank) record** button at the bottom of the table, or on the *Home* tab, in the *Records* group, click the **New** button.

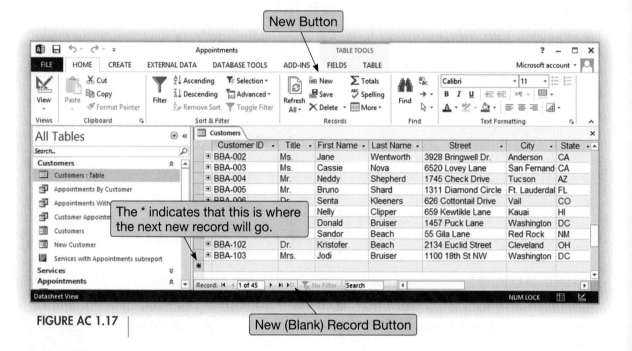

FIGURE AC 1.17

4. Enter the data in the first field of the record. Notice that when you begin entering data, the * changes to a pencil icon to indicate you are writing data to the record.

5. Press Tab or Enter to move to the next field.

6. When you've entered all the data for the new record, press Tab or Enter to start another new record.

Not all fields allow you to enter data by typing.

▸ If a field uses the AutoNumber format, you will not be able to type in that cell of the datasheet. Instead, move to the next cell to begin entering data. Access will populate the AutoNumber field automatically with the next number in sequence.

▸ Some fields require a specific input format (called an input mask). When you enter data in a field that has an input mask, Access will display placeholder characters such as underscores to guide you as you enter data. Access will not let you enter characters that violate the input mask rules (for example, entering a number when a letter is required). The input mask may also include characters that are displayed automatically such as the hyphen in the Customer ID in Figure AC 1.18 or the parentheses around the area code in a phone number.

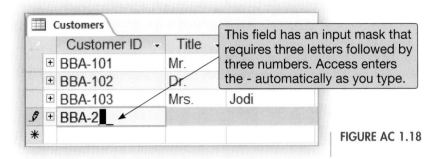

FIGURE AC 1.18

❱ Some fields (called lookup fields) have lists from which you choose values. Click the arrow in the field to display the list of available values and click the value you want.

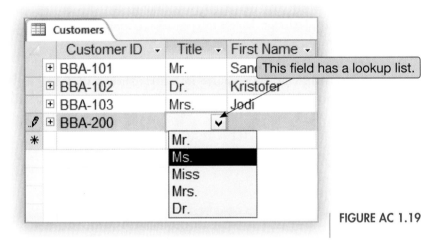

FIGURE AC 1.19

another **method**

Here are other ways to add a new blank record to the table:

❱ On the *Home* tab, in the *Find* group, click the **Go To** button, and select **New.**

❱ Right-click any of the row selector buttons and select **New Record** from the menu.

❱ Use the keyboard shortcut ⌃Ctrl⌃ + ⌃+⌃.

let me **try**

If the database is not already open, open the data file **AC1-Appointments** and try this skill on your own:

1. Open the *Customers* table in Datasheet view.
2. Begin a new record.
3. Enter the customer ID: **BBA-200.** Notice that this field requires a specific format.
4. Select **Ms.** as the title from the lookup list in the next field.
5. Enter data for the remaining fields in the table using a name, address, and phone number of your choice.

Skill 1.8 Creating a New Record in a Form

When you use a form to enter data, you are actually adding data to the underlying table. The form is a more convenient and user-friendly format for entering and editing records. When you enter or edit data in a form, Access commits the data (saves them) each time you move to a new field or begin a new record.

Access offers database designers a wide variety of tools for creating forms, so no two forms may look or behave exactly alike. Some forms are designed for entering new records only and do not allow you to view or edit existing records; other forms are designed for editing existing records and do not allow you to create new ones.

To enter data in a new record in a form:

1. Open the form in Form view.

2. Some forms are designed to automatically open to a new record where you can immediately begin entering data. If necessary, you can start a new blank record by clicking the **New (blank) record** button at the bottom of the form window. Or, on the *Home* tab, in the *Records* group, click the **New** button.

3. Type or select the data in the first field of the record. Notice that when you begin entering data, the * in the record selector changes to a pencil icon to indicate that you are writing data to the record.

4. Press (Tab ⇥) or (← Enter) to move to the next field. The form design determines the tab order— that is, the order in which the Tab key moves from field to field in the form.

5. When you've entered all the data for the new record, press (Tab ⇥) or (← Enter) to start another new record.

New Record Button

FIGURE AC 1.20

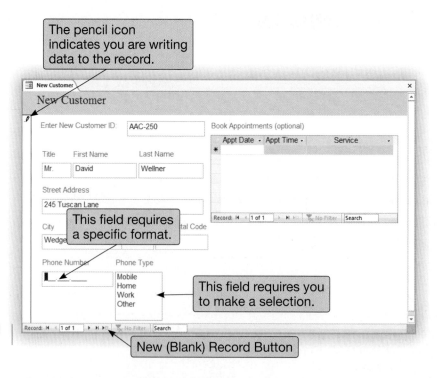

The pencil icon indicates you are writing data to the record.

This field requires a specific format.

This field requires you to make a selection.

New (Blank) Record Button

FIGURE AC 1.21

If the field in the underlying table requires a specific number or format, the form will require that same format. Other fields may present a list of values to choose from, rather than allowing you to enter your own values. For more information about data entry restrictions controlled by the underlying table, refer to the skill *Creating a New Record in a Table*.

Some forms may include interface elements to make it easier for users unfamiliar with Access. The form in Figure AC 1.22 includes a *Save and New* button to help users who may be unfamiliar with Access and think they need to save the record before moving on. You know better. Access saves the data as you enter it in each field in the form.

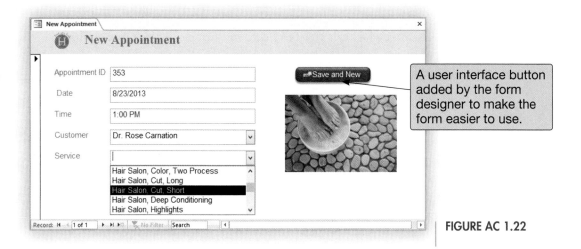

FIGURE AC 1.22

tips & tricks

If one of the fields is a *Long Text* field, you won't be able to use ⟨← Enter⟩ to move to the next field. Pressing ⟨← Enter⟩ will just keep adding blank lines to the text. Use ⟨Tab ⭲⟩ or the mouse to move to the next field.

another method

Here are other ways to enter a new blank record in a form:

❱ On the *Home* tab, in the *Find* group, click the **Go To** button, and select **New.**

❱ Right-click any of the row selector buttons and select **New Record** from the menu.

❱ Use the keyboard shortcut ⟨Ctrl⟩ + ⟨+⟩.

let me try

If the database is not already open, open the data file **AC1-Appointments** and try this skill on your own:

1. Open the *New Appointment* form. Notice that this form automatically opens to a new record.
2. Notice that you cannot enter data in the Appointment ID field. When you begin entering data in the next field in the form, Access will add the next sequential appointment number to this field automatically.
3. Enter the date **8/23/14** and time **1:00 PM** for the appointment. Notice that the form requires specific formats for these fields.
4. Select the customer **Dr. Rose Carnation** and the service **Hair Salon, Cut, Short** from the lists for those fields.
5. Click the **Save and New** button in the form to save the data and start a new record.
6. Close the form.

Skill 1.9 Finding and Replacing Data

Access provides a number of ways to search for information in your database. For a simple search in a table, form, or query, you can use the Search box next to the navigation buttons at the bottom of the datasheet or form.

1. In the Search box, begin typing the letters, numbers, or symbols you want to find.

2. As you type, Access highlights the first field in the first record that matches what you have typed so far.

3. As you continue typing, Access dynamically updates the search result.

FIGURE AC 1.23

If you need to find multiple records that match your search parameters, not just the first one, use the *Find* command. If you have used other Microsoft Office applications, the *Find and Replace* dialog will be familiar to you.

To search for specific records using the *Find* command:

1. Open the database object you want to search. The *Find* command is available for any object in Datasheet view, Form view, Report view, or Layout view.

2. On the *Home* tab, in the *Find* group, click the **Find** button to open the *Find and Replace* dialog.

3. Type the data you want to search for in the *Find What* box.

4. Click **Find Next** to go to the first record that matches the search criteria. Continue clicking **Find Next** until Access displays a message that there are no more records that meet your search criteria.

5. Click the red **X** in the upper right corner of the dialog to close it.

To narrow the search parameters in the *Find and Replace* dialog:

❯ Use the *Look In* list to specify whether to search only in the currently selected field or throughout the entire document (the open database object).

❯ Use the *Match* list to specify a match for the any part of the field, the whole field, or only the beginning of the field.

❯ Use the *Search* list to search only up or down from the current record or to search all the records.

❯ Use the *Match Case* check box to find only records that match the case of your find text. This check box is available even if you are searching for numerical data.

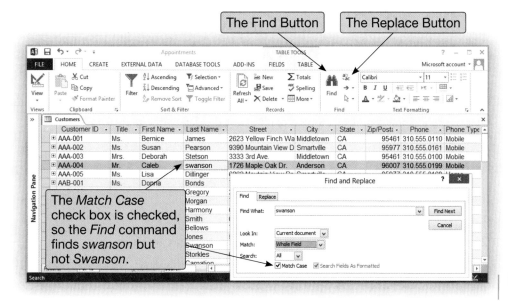

FIGURE AC 1.24

To find and replace data:

1. On the *Home* tab, in the *Find* group, click the **Replace** button. If the *Find and Replace* dialog is already open, click the **Replace** tab.

2. Enter the data to find in the *Find What* box.

3. Enter the data to replace it with in the *Replace With* box.

4. Click the **Replace** button to find and replace just the first instance, or click the **Replace All** button to replace all instances at once.

5. Access warns you that you will not be able to undo this operation. Click **Yes** to continue.

6. Click the red **X** in the upper right corner of the dialog to close it.

FIGURE AC 1.25

tips & tricks

Use wildcards in the *Find and Replace* dialog if you are not sure of the exact data you want to find.

❯ Use an asterisk * when you know the beginning of the search word or phrase, but not the end. For example, B* will find records for Ben, Bob, and Betty.

❯ Use question marks ? in place of specific letters or numbers. For example, B?? will find records for Ben and Bob but not Betty.

let me try

If the database is not already open, open the data file **AC1-Appointments** and try this skill on your own:

1. Open the *Customers* table in Datasheet view.

2. Use the Search box to begin searching for a customer with the first name beginning with *Vivi*. Notice that as you type **v** and then **i**, Access first highlights a record with the word *View* in the *Street* field. Once you finish entering **viv** in the Search box, Access finds the record with *Vivienne* in the *First Name* field.

3. Use the *Find and Replace* dialog to find the record with the text **swanson,** matching the case exactly.

4. Replace all instances of **swanson** with **Swanson.** Be sure to match the case exactly.

5. Close the table.

Skill 1.10 Cutting, Copying, and Pasting Data

The *Cut, Copy,* and *Paste* commands are used to move data within a database object and from one object to another. Data that are **cut** are removed from the database and stored for later use. The **Copy** command stores a duplicate of the data without changing the source. The **Paste** command is used to insert copied or cut data. You are probably familiar with using the *Cut, Copy,* and *Paste* commands in other applications. As expected, you can use these commands in Access during data entry in a table or form.

To use cut or copy and paste data within a table or form:

1. Select the data to be cut or copied.
2. On the *Home* tab, in the *Clipboard* group, click the **Cut** or **Copy** button.
3. Navigate to the record and field where you want to paste the data.
4. Click the **Paste** button.

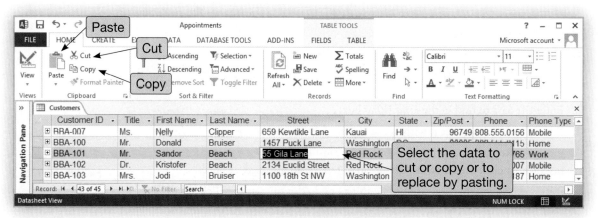

FIGURE AC 1.26

another method

Use the keyboard shortcuts for the *Cut, Copy,* and *Paste* commands:

▶ Cut = Ctrl + X

▶ Copy = Ctrl + C

▶ Paste = Ctrl + V

Use the command from the right-click menu:

▶ The *Cut* and *Copy* commands are available from the menu when you select data then right-click.

▶ To paste, you can right-click within a field and select **Paste.**

let me try

If the database is not already open, open the data file **AC1-Appointments** and try this skill on your own:

1. Open the *Customers* table in Datasheet view.
2. Find the record with the Customer ID **BBA-101.**
3. Copy the data in the *Street* field.
4. Move to the next record (Customer **BBA-102**).
5. Paste into the *Street* field, replacing the existing data.
6. Close the table.

Skill 1.11 Using Undo and Redo

If you make a mistake when working, the **Undo** command allows you to reverse the last action you performed. The **Redo** command allows you to reverse the Undo command and restore the file to its previous state. The Quick Access Toolbar gives you immediate access to both these commands.

To undo the last action taken, click the **Undo** button on the Quick Access Toolbar, or click the **Undo** button arrow and select the action to undo.

If you are working on data entry in Datasheet view or Form view, the *Undo* command is applied to the entire record, not each individual field within the record. If you made multiple changes to the record at the same time, the *Undo* command will reverse all the changes at once. In addition, the *Undo* command can be applied only to the last modified record. If you made changes to multiple records, you are out of luck.

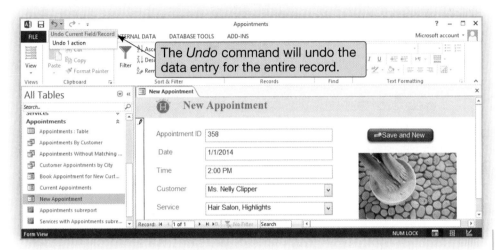

FIGURE AC 1.27

To redo the last action taken, click the **Redo** button on the Quick Access Toolbar.

The *Redo* command is useful mostly when you are working with formatting design elements in forms and reports. It is not available for data entry tasks.

tips & tricks

If you are familiar with using *Undo* and *Redo* in other Office applications, be very careful in Access. There are many actions that cannot be undone. Usually, but not always, Access will warn you before you do something that can't be undone.

another method

Use the keyboard shortcuts:

❯ Undo = Ctrl + Z
❯ Redo = Ctrl + Y

let me try

If the database is not already open, open the data file **AC1-Appointments** and try this skill on your own:

1. Open the *New Appointment* form in Form view.
2. Enter data for a new appointment. Do not continue to another new record.
3. Undo the data entry. Notice that the data entry for the entire record is undone at once.
4. Close the form.

Skill 1.12 Deleting Records

You can delete records. However, if your database has a complex structure, deleting records may not be as simple as the procedures listed below because records in one table may be linked to records in another table. Access will prevent you from deleting records if the deletion would violate the integrity of the database. *You cannot undo a record deletion.*

To delete a record in Datasheet view:

1. Click the record selector so the record you want to delete is selected.
2. On the *Home* tab, in the *Records* group, click the **Delete** button.
3. Access warns you that you cannot undo the deletion. Click **Yes** to continue.

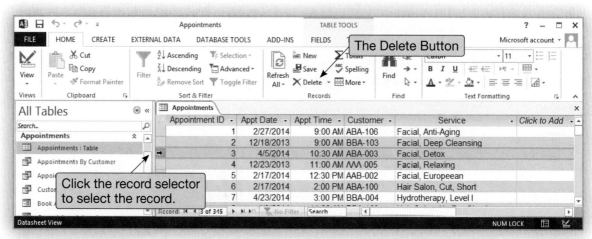

FIGURE AC 1.28

Deleting a record in a form will delete the record in the underlying table.

To delete a record in Form view:

1. Navigate to the record you want to delete.
2. On the *Home* tab, in the *Records* group, click the **Delete** button arrow, and select **Delete Record.**
3. Access warns you that you cannot undo the deletion. Click **Yes** to continue.

another method

> Right-click the record selector and select **Delete Record.**
> Select the record, and press (Delete).
> Select the record and use the keyboard shortcut (Ctrl) + (-).

let me try

If the database is not already open, open the data file **AC1-Appointments** and try this skill on your own:
1. Open the *Appointment* table in Datasheet view.
2. Delete the appointment with the Appointment ID **3.** It should be the third record in the table.
3. Close the table.

Skill 1.13 Checking Spelling

Like other Office applications, Access includes a built-in spelling checker. In Access, the *Spelling* command analyzes the current database object for spelling errors, not the entire database.

To check for spelling errors:

1. On the *Home* tab, in the *Records* group, click the **Spelling** button.
2. The first spelling error appears in the *Spelling* dialog.
3. If you want Access to skip checking spelling for the current field, click the **Ignore '[field name here]' Field** button.
4. Review the spelling suggestions and then select an action:
    - Click **Ignore** to make no changes to this instance of the word or click **Ignore All** to make no changes to all instances of the word.
    - Click the correct spelling in the *Suggestions* list, and click **Change** to correct just this instance of the misspelling or click **Change All** to correct all instances of the misspelling in the current database object or record.
    - Click **Add** to make no changes to this instance of the word and add it to the spelling checker dictionary, so future uses of this word will not show up as misspellings. When you add a word to the dictionary, it is available for all the Office applications.
    - Click **AutoCorrect** to update the AutoCorrect list to automatically autocorrect the misspelling with the selected suggestion when you enter data.
5. After you select an action, the spelling checker automatically advances to the next suspected spelling error.
6. When the spelling checker finds no more errors, it displays a message telling you the check is complete. Click **OK** to close the dialog and return to your worksheet.

Spelling Button

FIGURE AC 1.29

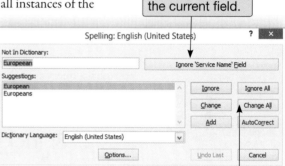

Click to ignore all spelling errors in the current field.

FIGURE AC 1.30

Select an option for each potential spelling error.

tips & tricks

If you are working with a form that shows one record at a time, the spelling checker checks only the current, active record.

another method

To open the *Spelling* dialog, you can use the keyboard shortcut $\boxed{F7}$.

let me try

If the database is not already open, open the data file **AC1-Appointments** and try this skill on your own:
1. Open the *Services* table in Datasheet view.
2. Check for spelling errors, correcting any errors that Access finds.
3. Close the table.

Skill 1.14 Deleting and Renaming Database Objects

FIGURE AC 1.31

When you are in the process of designing your database, you may find that you have database objects you no longer need or that you want to use different names for objects. Access allows you to delete and rename forms, reports, and other database objects.

To delete a database object:

1. Right-click the object name in the Navigation Pane and select **Delete.**

2. Access displays a confirmation message, asking if you want to delete the object. Click **Yes** to delete it or **No** to cancel the delete command.

Be careful! Once you delete a database object, you cannot undo the deletion.

To rename a database object:

1. Right-click the object name in the Navigation Pane and select **Rename.**

2. Type the new object name, and press ⏎ Enter .

Changing the name of a table may have unexpected consequences. Forms and reports based on the table will update automatically to use the new table name. However, queries may not update properly, causing errors not only in the query, but in forms and reports that use the query as well.

tips & tricks

Access will warn you if you try to delete a table that would invalidate relationships. If you are sure you want to delete the table, Access will automatically delete the relationships, and then delete the table. If you do not allow Access to delete the relationships, Access will not delete the table.

another method

You can delete a table or other database object by selecting it in the Navigation Pane, and then on the *Home* tab, in the *Records* group, click the **Delete** button.

FIGURE AC 1.32

let me try

If the database is not already open, open the data file **AC1-Appointments** and try this skill on your own:

1. If necessary, open the Navigation Pane.
2. If necessary, change the Navigation Pane category to **Tables and Related Views.**
3. If there are open database objects, close them all.
4. In the *Customers* group, delete the query *Appointments Without Matching Customers.*
5. In the *Customers* group, rename the form *Customers* to: **Master Customer Form**

Skill 1.15 Exporting Data to Excel or Word

You can export Access data to a variety of other applications, including Microsoft Excel and Microsoft Word. This is helpful if you want to share the data with someone who may not have Access or may not need to see the entire database.

When you export Access data to Word, you are actually exporting to a text format called **Rich Text Format** (or **RTF**). This format can be used with any word processing program, not just Microsoft Word.

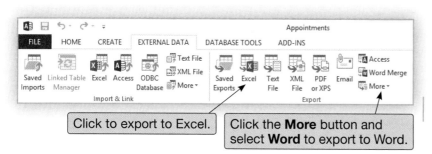

Click to export to Excel.

Click the More button and select Word to export to Word.

FIGURE AC 1.33

To export data to Excel or Word:

1. In the Navigation Pane, click the object you want to export.

2. On the *External Data* tab, in the *Export* group, click the **Excel** button to export to Excel. To export to Word, click the **More** button and select **Word.**

3. Access automatically suggests a file name based on the name of the object you selected. If you want to change the file name or the location of the saved file, click the **Browse...** button and make your changes in the *File Save* dialog.

4. If you are exporting to Word, or if you are exporting a report, the *Export data with formatting and layout.* check box is checked automatically. You do not have the option to uncheck it. If you are exporting to Excel, the box is not checked by default. Be sure to check it if you want to maintain data formats such as dates and currency styles.

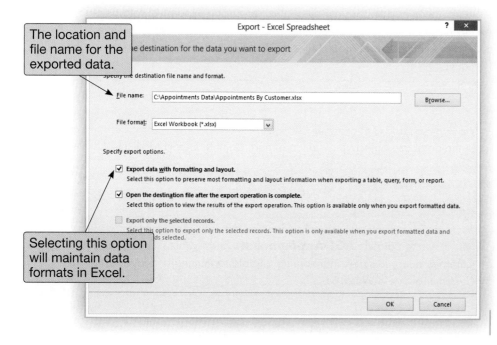

The location and file name for the exported data.

Selecting this option will maintain data formats in Excel.

FIGURE AC 1.34

5. When the *Export data with formatting and layout.* option is checked, you also have the option to check the box to **Open the destination file after the export operation is complete.**

6. If you have a table, query, or form open with specific records selected, you can elect to export only those records. Click the **Export only the selected records.** check box.

7. Click **OK** to begin the export process.

8. After the export is complete, you have the option to save the export steps so you can easily run the same export again later. Check the **Save export steps** check box.

9. Click the **Close** button.

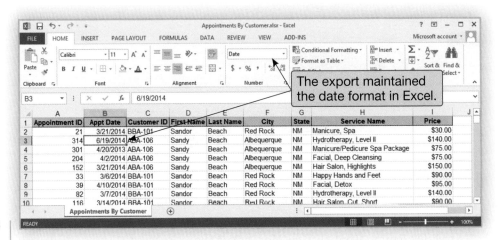

The export maintained the date format in Excel.

FIGURE AC 1.35

tips & tricks

If you save your export specifications, you can run the export again later by clicking the **Saved Exports** button on the *External Data* tab, *Export* group.

tell me more

If you need to import Access data into another database or spreadsheet program, export the data as plain text. This export option allows you to export the data separated by commas, tabs, or other delimiters. It is the most flexible export option. On the *External Data* tab, in the *Export* group, click the **Text File** button. Follow the steps in the wizard to export the data in the text format you need.

another method

In the Navigation Pane, right-click the database object you want to export, point to **Export,** and select the export format you want to use.

let me try

If the database is not already open, open the data file **AC1-Appointments** and try this skill on your own:
1. Export the *Appointments by Customer* query to Excel, maintaining all data formatting and layouts.
2. Export the *Appointments by Customer* query to Word.

Skill 1.16 Exporting Data to a PDF File

You are probably familiar with **PDF** (**Portable Document Format**) files. This type of file can be read by anyone who has the Adobe Reader software installed (which is almost everyone with a computer nowadays). If you need a version of one of your database objects, particularly reports, to look exactly like it would when printed from Access, consider exporting the object to a PDF file.

To export a database object to a PDF file:

1. In the Navigation Pane, click the object you want to export.
2. On the *External Data* tab, in the *Export* group, click the **PDF or XPS** button.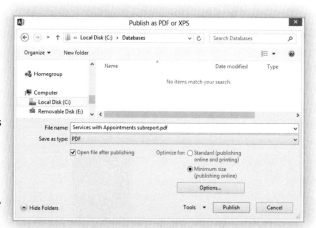
3. In the *Publish as PDF or XPS* dialog, Access automatically suggests a file name based on the name of the object you selected. If necessary, make the location and file name changes in the dialog.
4. Click **Publish.**
5. When you return to Access, the *Export-PDF* window will be open. If you want to save the export steps to repeat again later, check the **Save export steps** check box.
6. Click the **Close** button to close the window.

FIGURE AC 1.36

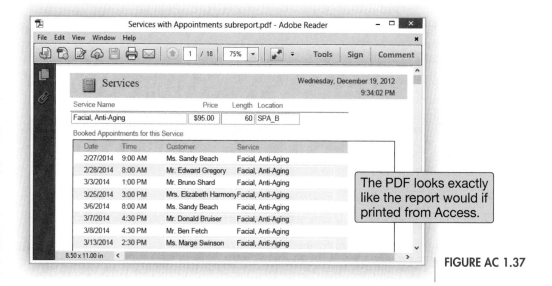

The PDF looks exactly like the report would if printed from Access.

FIGURE AC 1.37

another **method**

In the Navigation Pane, right-click the database object you want to export, point to **Export,** and select **PDF or XPS.**

let me **try**

If the database is not already open, open the data file **AC1-Appointments** and try this skill on your own:

Export the *Services with Appointments subreport* report as a PDF file.

Skill 1.17 Previewing and Printing Database Objects

Normally in Access, reports are the only database objects printed. However, there may be times when you want to print a table, form, or the results of a query. Although these database objects do not have a Print Preview view like reports do, you can still print and preview them from Backstage. From Backstage, Print Preview shows you a reduced version of the active database object as it will appear when printed. Save time and paper by always checking your page layout in Print Preview view before you print.

To preview a database object for printing:

1. Click the **File** tab to open Backstage.
2. Click **Print.**
3. On the *Print* page, click the **Print Preview** button.

FIGURE AC 1.38

4. Access switches to Print Preview view.
5. Before printing, you should ensure that the data fit on the printed page the way you want.
    a. On the *Print Preview* tab, in the *Zoom* group, click the **Two Pages** button or click the **More Pages** button and select **Four Pages, Eight Pages,** or **Twelve Pages.** This lets you preview how the printed data will break across pages.
    b. If the object you are printing has many columns or is wider than 8.5 inches, switch the page orientation from portrait to landscape. On the *Print Preview* tab, in the *Page Layout* group, click the **Landscape** button.
6. To print, click the **Print** button located at the far left side of the *Print Preview* tab.
7. The *Print* dialog opens. From the *Print* dialog, you can set a range of pages to print, enter the number of copies to print, and choose to print to any printer connected to your computer.
8. Click **OK** in the dialog to print the database object.
9. Click the **Close Print Preview** button at the far right side of the Ribbon to return to your regular Access view.

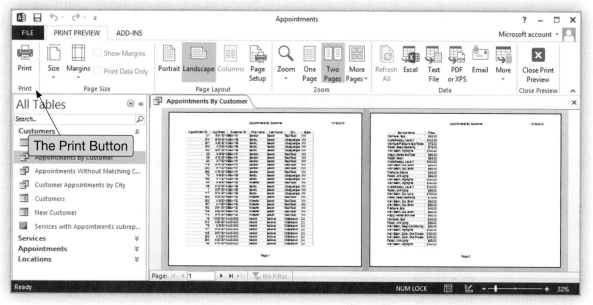

The Print Button

FIGURE AC 1.39

Two-page preview of how the object will look when printed with landscape orientation.

tips & tricks

Access is the only Office application that uses a dedicated Print Preview page. Word, Excel, and PowerPoint incorporate a Print Preview directly into Backstage.

tell me **more**

The Quick Print command prints database objects using all the default print settings.

1. Click the **File** tab.
2. Click **Print.**
3. On the *Print* page, click the **Quick Print** button.

another **method**

To print the current database object using the default print settings, you can also press (Ctrl) + (P). The *Print* dialog will open. Click **OK** to print the database object.

let me try

If the database is not already open, open the data file **AC1-Appointments** and try this skill on your own:

1. Preview how the *Appointments by Customer* query would look if it were printed.
2. Change the orientation to **Landscape.**
3. Change the view to show two pages at once.
4. Close Print Preview.

Skill 1.18 Using Compact and Repair

When you delete records from an Access database, the database maintains space for the deleted data until you compact the database by removing unnecessary file space. Access also creates hidden, temporary database objects that take up database space unnecessarily. The longer your database is in use, the more of these unnecessary temporary objects there are. The **Compact & Repair tool** eliminates these unnecessary database objects for optimum efficiency.

To use the Compact & Repair tool:

1. Click the **File** tab.
2. Backstage opens to the Info page automatically.
3. Click the **Compact & Repair Database** button.

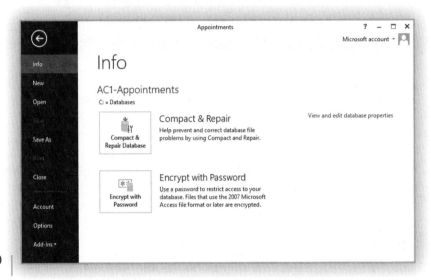

FIGURE AC 1.40

If you need to interrupt the compact and repair process for any reason, press and hold (Esc).

tips & tricks

To help your database run as efficiently as possible, it is a good practice to run the Compact & Repair tool on a regular basis.

tell me more

You can set your database to compact automatically when you close it by changing the database options:

1. Click the **File** tab.
2. Click the **Options** button.
3. Click **Current Database** at the left side of the *Access Options* dialog.
4. Click the check box in front of **Compact on Close.**
5. Click **OK.**

let me try

If the database is not already open, open the data file **AC1-Appointments** and try this skill on your own:

   Run the **Compact & Repair** tool.

Skill 1.19 Backing Up a Database

Remember that the *Undo* function is very limited in Access. If you are about to add a significant amount of data that you may not want to keep, or if you are experimenting with the design of the database, you should create a backup first. By backing up your database, you create a copy of it and preserve the data at a certain point. At any time you can open the backup and restore your data from an earlier stage. Be sure to create a backup of your database before making any major changes to the database structure.

To create a backup of your database:

1. Close and save any open objects.
2. Click the **File** tab.
3. Click **Save As.**
4. Click **Backup Database** in the *Save Database As* section at the right side of the screen.
5. Click the **Save As** button.

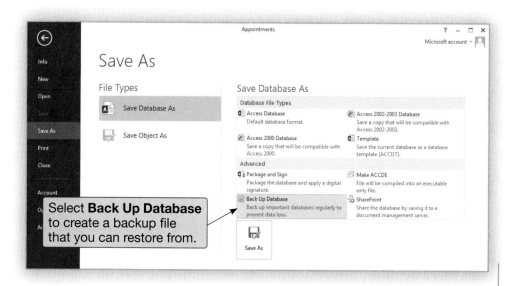

FIGURE AC 1.41

6. The *Save As* dialog box opens.

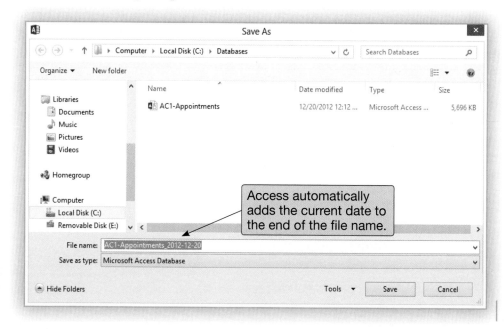

FIGURE AC 1.42

7. If necessary, navigate to the location where you want to save the backup file. Access automatically creates a new file name for the backup using the original file name with the current date.

8. Click **Save** to create the backup file.

To make a copy of the database to experiment with, but not necessarily keep as a backup:

1. Follow the same steps as you would to create a backup, but in the *Save As* page, select **Access Database** in the *Save Database As* section.

2. If necessary, navigate to the location where you want to save the copy. In the *File name* box, enter a name for the database copy.

3. Click **Save** to create the copy.

You are now working on a copy of the database, and any further changes you make will not affect the original.

tips & tricks

To save a copy of the database, you must close all open database objects. If you have any database objects open when you invoke the *Save As* command, Access will offer to close them for you. If any of the open objects have not been saved, Access will also offer to save them for you.

tell me **more**

If you find that you need to restore a database object (such as a table, query, form, or report) from a backup copy, click the *External Data* tab. In the *Import & Link* group, click the **Import Access Database** button to find and restore the database object you want.

If you want to completely replace a database with a backup copy, delete the database file you no longer want and then rename the backup so it has the original file name.

let me try

If the database is not already open, open the data file **AC1-Appointments** and try this skill on your own:

Create a backup of the database.

key terms

Database
Table
Record
Field
Relational database
Form
Query
Report
Navigation Pane
Macro
Message Bar
One-to-many relationship
Primary key
Foreign key
Relationships window
Datasheet view

Form view
Report view
Design view
SQL view
Layout view
Print Preview
Datasheets
Cut
Copy
Paste
Undo
Redo
Rich Text Format (RTF)
PDF (Portable Document Format)
Compact & Repair tool

concepts review

1. _____ are the basic building blocks of a database.
   a. Tables
   b. Forms
   c. Queries
   d. Reports

2. Each row in a table contains all the data for a single _____.
   a. field
   b. form
   c. record
   d. query

3. Each column in a table represents a specific data value called a _____.
   a. field
   b. form
   c. record
   d. query

4. All data entered into a form are stored in the underlying _____.
   a. form
   b. table
   c. All of the above
   d. None of the above

5. You must manually save the record each time you enter data in a table or form.
   a. True
   b. False

6. When you are entering data in a new record in a form, the *Undo* command will _____.

    a. undo only the most recently entered field

    b. undo the entire record at once

    c. undo only formatting and layout changes to the record

    d. do nothing. The *Undo* command does not work in forms.

7. You can undo a record deletion.

    a. True

    b. False

8. To rename a database object, double-click the name in the Navigation Pane and type the new name.

    a. True

    b. False

9. You can export Access data to which of the following file formats?

    a. PDF

    b. PowerPoint

    c. Adobe

    d. All of the above

10. Creating a backup of the database removes unnecessary file space and hidden, temporary objects from your database.

    a. True

    b. False

projects

skill review 1.1

In this project, you will review a database created for the Computer Science department of a local college. They would like your assistance in using Access to keep track of which employees have borrowed items from the department. Become comfortable with the department's database by completing the steps below.

Skills needed to complete this project:

- Introduction to Access 2013 (Skill 1.1)
- Working with Security Warnings (Skill 1.2)
- Backing Up a Database (Skill 1.19)
- Organizing Objects in the Navigation Pane (Skill 1.4)
- Switching between Database Object Views (Skill 1.5)
- Navigating Records (Skill 1.6)
- Creating a New Record in a Table (Skill 1.7)
- Finding and Replacing Data (Skill 1.9)
- Deleting Records (Skill 1.12)
- Creating a New Record in a Form (Skill 1.8)
- Understanding and Viewing Table Relationships (Skill 1.3)
- Exporting Data to Excel or Word (Skill 1.15)
- Deleting and Renaming Database Objects (Skill 1.14)
- Using Compact and Repair (Skill 1.18)

1. Open the start file **AC2013-SkillReview-1-1.**

2. If necessary, enable active content by clicking the **Enable Content** button in the Message Bar.

3. Save a copy of the file to work on.

   a. Click the **File** tab.

   b. Click **Save Database As.**

   c. Verify that *Access Database* is selected in the *Save Database As* section.

   d. Click **Save As.**

   e. If necessary, navigate to the location where you save your personal project files.

   f. In the *File name* box, change the file name to:
      `[your initials]AC-SkillReview-1-1`

   g. Click **Save.**

   h. Enable active content in the new database by clicking the **Enable Content** button in the Message Bar.

4. Use the Navigation Pane.

   a. By default, the Navigation Pane displays the *Tables and Related Views* category. All tables and related objects are visible.

b. Click the top of the Navigation Pane and under the *Filter By Group* section, select **Items.**

c. Observe that the Navigation Pane now displays the title *Items* at the top and only objects related to the *Items* table are visible.

d. Click the top of the Navigation Pane and select the **Object Type** category.

e. Observe that now all database objects are visible in the Navigation Pane, grouped by object type.

5. Open the *Items* table.

a. In the Navigation Pane, double-click the table object named **Items.**

b. Review the fields in this table: *Item ID, ItemName, Description, Category,* and *Cost.*

c. If necessary, use the horizontal scroll bar to view all the fields.

6. Switch views for the *Items* table.

a. Note the state of the *View* button (on the *Home* tab, in the *Views* group). When you are in Datasheet view, the *Views* button displays Design view.

b. On the *Home* tab, in the *Views* group, click the **View** button.

c. Observe that the *View* button has switched to **Datasheet** view to indicate that clicking the button will return you to Datasheet view.

d. Review the field names in Design view.

e. Go back to Datasheet view by clicking the **View** button again.

7. Navigate records in a table.

a. Observe the record navigation buttons at the bottom of the table. Move your mouse over the different arrow buttons and observe the ScreenTips.

b. Observe which record in the table becomes highlighted as you click the following record navigation buttons: **Last record, First record, Next record, Previous record.**

c. Find the *Current Record* box, which indicates the current record number and the total number of records. Click to select the number in the *Current Record* box. Type the number **5** in this box and press (← Enter). The *Current Record* box should now display **5 of 21** and the fifth record in the table should be highlighted.

d. Use the following shortcut keys on your keyboard and observe which field/record becomes highlighted: **Tab, up arrow, down arrow, left arrow, right arrow.** In addition, try holding (Ctrl) while pressing the **up arrow** or **down arrow.**

8. Enter a new record in the *Items* table.

a. Click the **New (blank) record** button at the bottom of the table.

b. Enter the following record into your table, using (Tab ⇆) to move from one field to the next. When you reach the *Category* field, observe that it is a lookup field. Use the **drop-down arrow** to view and select from the available values.

ItemID	ItemName	Description	Category	Cost
ACC1	Accounting 2.0	Accounting software for small businesses	Software	$149.00

9. Find the record with an item ID of **GRA1** and edit the content.

a. Type **GRA1** in the Search box at the bottom of the table.

b. Edit the content in the *ItemName* field to: **Graphics Studio 10.1**

10. Delete the *SPH1* item record.

a. Type **SPH1** in the Search box at the bottom of the table.

b. Click the record selector box at the left side of that row to highlight the entire record.

c. On the *Home* tab, in the *Records* group, click the **Delete** button.

d. Click **Yes** to verify that you want to delete the record.

11. Close the *Items* table by clicking the **X** at the upper right corner of the table. Be careful not to close the Access database instead.

12. Enter a new record in a form.

a. In the Navigation Pane, double-click the form object named **Items Form.**

b. Observe the record navigation buttons at the bottom of the form and note that they are the same as those in the table.

c. Click the **New (blank)** record button at the bottom of the form.

d. Enter the following record into your form, using ⟨Tab ⇥⟩ to move from one field to the next.

ItemID	ItemName	Description	Category	Cost
CAM1	Digital Camera	10 megapixel SLR digital camera	Equipment	$499.00

13. Find and edit the record with the item ID **LAP1.**

a. On the *Home* tab, in the *Find* group, click the **Find** button.

b. Type **LAP1** in the *Find What* box.

c. Click the **Find Next** button.

d. Close the *Find and Replace* dialog by clicking the **X** in the upper right corner of the dialog.

e. The form should now display the *Laptop 1000* item.

f. Click in the *Cost* field and change the value from **$550** to **$450.**

14. Find and delete the record with the item ID **PB03.**

a. On the *Home* tab, in the *Find* group, click the **Find** button.

b. Type **PB03** in the *Find What* box.

c. Click the **Find Next** button.

d. Close the *Find and Replace* dialog by clicking the **X** in the upper right corner of the dialog.

e. The form should now display the *Presentation Basics* item.

f. On the *Home* tab, in the *Records* group, click the **Delete** button arrow, and select **Delete Record.**

g. Click **Yes.**

15. Close the *Items Form* form.

16. Open the *Items* table again.

a. In the Navigation Pane, double-click the table object named **Items.**

b. Observe that the *CAM1* item record you entered in the form was added to the table. It should be listed as the fifth item in the table.

c. Click the **Last record** button at the bottom of the table.

d. Close the *Items* table.

17. Review the table relationships.

a. On the *Database Tools* tab, in the *Relationships* group, click the **Relationships** button.

b. Verify that all table relationships are shown. On the *Relationship Tools Design* tab, in the *Relationships* group, click the **All Relationships** button.

    c. Save the changes to the relationship window layout by clicking the **Save** button on the Quick Access Toolbar.

    d. Close the Relationships window. On the *Relationship Tools Design* tab, in the *Relationships* group, click the **Close** button.

18. Export the *Items* table to Excel.

    a. In the Navigation Pane, if necessary, click the *Items* table once to select it.

    b. On the *External Data* tab, in the *Export* group, click the **Excel** button.

    c. Click the **Browse** button.

    d. If necessary, navigate to the location where you save your personal project files.

    e. In the *File name* box, type:

        `[your initials]AC-SkillReview-1-1-Items`

    f. Click **Save.**

    g. In the *Export–Excel Spreadsheet* window, click **OK.**

    h. Click the **Close** button to finish without saving the export steps.

19. Rename the *Employees* table.

    a. In the Navigation Pane, right-click *Employees* and select **Rename.**

    b. Type: `Staff`

    c. Press `← Enter`.

20. Use Compact & Repair.

    a. Minimize the Access 2013 window and navigate to the folder where you saved this database. Observe the file size.

    b. Return to Access and click the **File** tab.

    c. Click the **Compact & Repair Database** button.

    d. Minimize Access 2013 and look at your database file again. How much did the file size decrease?

21. Back up the database.

    a. If necessary, maximize Access 2013 and click the **File** tab.

    b. Click **Save As.**

    c. In the *Save Database As* section, under *Advanced,* click **Back Up Database,** and click the **Save As** button.

    d. If necessary, navigate to the location where you save your personal project files. Click the **Save** button.

22. Close the database and exit Access.

skill review 1.2

You have just been hired by a small health insurance company in the south Florida area. One of your duties is using Access 2013 to manage the company's list of in-network doctors and covered procedures. Become comfortable with the company's database by completing the steps below.

Skills needed to complete this project:

- Introduction to Access 2013 (Skill 1.1)
- Working with Security Warnings (Skill 1.2)
- Backing Up a Database (Skill 1.19)
- Organizing Objects in the Navigation Pane (Skill 1.4)

- Understanding and Viewing Table Relationships (Skill 1.3)
- Navigating Records (Skill 1.6)
- Deleting Records (Skill 1.12)
- Creating a New Record in a Table (Skill 1.7)
- Cutting, Copying, and Pasting Data (Skill 1.10)
- Using Undo and Redo (Skill 1.11)
- Previewing and Printing Database Objects (Skill 1.17)
- Exporting Data to Excel or Word (Skill 1.15)
- Switching between Database Object Views (Skill 1.5)
- Creating a New Record in a Form (Skill 1.8)
- Finding and Replacing Data (Skill 1.9)
- Checking Spelling (Skill 1.13)
- Exporting Data to a PDF File (Skill 1.16)
- Using Compact and Repair (Skill 1.18)

1. Open the start file **AC2013-SkillReview-1-2.**

2. If necessary, enable active content by clicking the **Enable Content** button in the Message Bar.

3. Save a copy of the file to work on.

   a. Click the **File** tab.

   b. Click **Save Database As.**

   c. Verify that *Access Database* is selected in the *Save Database As* list.

   d. Click **Save As.**

   e. If necessary, navigate to the location where you save your personal project files.

   f. In the *File name* box, change the file name to:
   `[your initials]AC-SkillReview-1-2`

   g. Click **Save.**

   h. If necessary, enable active content in the new database by clicking the **Enable Content** button in the Message Bar.

4. The Navigation Pane is organized using the *Object Type* category. Switch to use the *Tables and Related Views* category instead.

   a. Observe the organization of objects in the Navigation Pane.

   b. Click the top of the Navigation Pane and select the **Tables and Related Views** category.

   c. Observe the changes in the Navigation Pane.

5. Review the table relationships.

   a. On the *Database Tools* tab, in the *Relationships* group, click the **Relationships** button.

   b. Add the *Orders* table to the Relationships window. On the *Relationship Tools Design* tab, in the *Relationships* group, click the **Show Table** button.

   c. In the *Show Table* dialog, double-click **Orders.**

   d. Click the **Close** button to close the *Show Table* dialog.

   e. Save the changes to the relationship window layout by clicking the **Save** button on the Quick Access Toolbar.

   f. Close the Relationships window. On the *Relationship Tools Design* tab, in the *Relationships* group, click the **Close** button.

6. Navigate records in a table.

   a. In the Navigation Pane, double-click the object labeled **Physicians : Table.**

   b. Go to the last record in the table. Click the **Last Record** navigation button at the bottom of the table.

7. Delete the record.

   a. Click the record selector box on the left side of that row to highlight the entire record. Verify that you have selected the record with the physician ID **TW01.**

   b. On the *Home* tab, in the *Records* group, click the **Delete** button.

   c. Click **Yes** to verify that you want to delete the record.

8. Enter a new record in the *Physicians* table.

   a. Click the **New (blank) record** button at the bottom of the table.

   b. Enter the following record into your table, using (Tab ⇥) or (→) to move from one field to the next. When you reach the *City* field, observe that it is a lookup field. Use the **drop-down arrow** to view and select from the available values.

PhysicianID	FirstName	LastName	StreetAddress	City	ZipCode	Phone	MemberCount
JB02	James	Bryant	3091 Main Street	Miami	33143	(305) 555-2122	16

9. Copy the street address from the record with the last name Hartzell to the record with the last name Diggs.

   a. Type **Hartzell** in the Search box at the bottom of the table. Confirm that you have located the record for Heidi Hartzell.

   b. Select the data in the *StreetAddress* field.

   c. On the *Home* tab, in the *Clipboard* group, click the **Copy** button.

   d. Type **Diggs** in the Search box at the bottom of the table. Confirm that you have located the record for Steve Diggs.

   e. Select the data in the *StreetAddress* field.

   f. On the *Home* tab, in the *Clipboard* group, click the **Paste** button.

   g. Confirm that the address for Steve Diggs is now 2204 Plainfield Avenue.

10. Undo the change.

   a. On the Quick Access Toolbar, click the **Undo** button.

   b. Confirm that the address for Steve Diggs is 2860 Godfrey Road again.

11. Preview how the *Physicians* table would look if it were printed from Access.

   a. Click the **File** tab.

   b. Click **Print.**

   c. Click **Print Preview.**

   d. Change the zoom to two pages. On the *Print Preview* tab, in the *Zoom* group, click the **Two Pages** button.

   e. Observe that in portrait orientation, the last column prints on a second page.

   f. Change the orientation to landscape. On the *Print Preview* tab, in the *Page Layout* group, click the **Landscape** button.

   g. Observe that the printed table would now fit on a single page.

   h. Close the print preview by clicking the **Close Print Preview** button at the far right side of the Ribbon.

12. Export the *Physicians* table to Excel. Be sure to include formatting and layout. Open the destination file when the export is complete.

    a. If necessary, select the *Physicians* table by clicking the **Physicians** tab.

    b. On the *External Data* tab, in the *Export* group, click the **Excel** button.

    c. Click the **Browse** button.

    d. If necessary, navigate to the location where you save your personal project files.

    e. In the *File name* box, type:

       `[your initials]AC-SkillReview-1-2-Physicians`

    f. Click **Save.**

    g. Click the **Export data with formatting and layout.** check box.

    h. Click the **Open the destination file after the export operation is complete.** check box.

    i. In the *Export–Excel Spreadsheet* dialog, click **OK.**

    j. Review the exported data in Excel, and then exit Excel and return to Access.

    k. Click the **Close** button to finish without saving the export steps.

13. Close the *Physicians* table by clicking the **X** at the upper right corner of the table. Be careful not to close the Access database instead.

14. Switch views for a form.

    a. In the Navigation Pane, double-click the **PhysiciansForm** form.

    b. Note the state of the *View* button (on the *Home* tab, in the *Views* group). When you are in Form view, the *View* button displays Layout view.

    c. Switch to Layout view. On the *Home* tab, in the *Views* group, click the **View** button.

    d. Observe that the *View* button has switched to Form view to indicate that clicking the button will return you to Form view.

    e. Review the form design in Layout view. Observe that while you can see live data, you cannot edit data in the record. Review the features available on the *Form Layout Tools* tabs.

    f. Switch back to Form view by clicking the **View** button again.

15. Add a new record in a form

    a. Observe the record navigation buttons at the bottom of the form and note that they are the same as those in the table.

    b. Click the **New (blank) record** button at the bottom of the form.

    c. Enter the following record into your form, using $\boxed{\text{Tab}}$ or $\boxed{\rightarrow}$ to move from one field to the next.

PhysicianID	FirstName	LastName	StreetAddress	City	ZipCode	Phone	MemberCount
KS01	Karen	Singer	850 Tyler Street	Miami	33155	(305) 555-2490	21

16. Edit a record in a form

    a. Find the record with a physician ID of **SD01.** Type **SD01** in the Search box at the bottom of the form.

    b. Click inside the *ZipCode* field and change the number from **33304** to **33309.**

    c. Close *PhysiciansForm* by clicking the **X** at the top right of the form.

17. Spell check the *Procedures* table.

    a. In the Navigation Pane, double-click the object labeled **Procedures : Table.**

    b. On the *Home* tab, in the *Records* group, click the **Spelling** button.

    c. The first misspelling found is *Vacine.* Click the **Change** button to accept the suggestion *Vaccine.*

    d. The next misspelling found is *Cardac.* Click the **Change** button to accept the suggestion *Cardiac.*

    e. Click **OK** in the message box telling you that the spelling check is complete.

18. Export the table as a PDF file.

    a. The *Procedures* table should still be open. Confirm that it is the active database object by clicking the **Procedures** tab.

    b. On the *External Data* tab, in the *Export* group, click the **PDF or XPS** button.

    c. If necessary, navigate to the location where you save your personal project files.

    d. In the *File name* box, type:

        `[your initials]AC-SkillReview-1-2-Procedures`

    e. If necessary, click **Open file after publishing** check box so you can review the PDF file.

    f. Click **Publish.**

    g. Observe that the PDF maintains the look of the Access table exactly.

    h. Close the PDF and return to Access.

    i. Click the **Close** button to close the window without saving the export steps.

    j. Close the *Procedures* table by clicking the **X** in the upper right corner of the tab.

19. Use Compact & Repair.

    a. Minimize the Access 2013 window and navigate to the folder where you saved this database. Observe the file size.

    b. Return to Access and click the **File** tab.

    c. Click the **Compact & Repair Database** button.

    d. Minimize Access 2013 and look at your database file again. How much did the file size decrease?

20. Back up the database.

    a. If necessary, maximize Access 2013 and click the **File** tab.

    b. Click **Save As.**

    c. In the *Save Database As* area, under *Advanced,* click **Back Up Database,** and click the **Save As** button.

    d. If necessary, navigate to the location where you save your personal project files. Click the **Save** button.

21. Close the database and exit Access.

challenge yourself **1.3**

In this project, you will work on a database for a small greenhouse. The database contains records of the plants in the greenhouse and the employees who assist with maintenance duties.

Skills needed to complete this project:

- Introduction to Access 2013 (Skill 1.1)
- Working with Security Warnings (Skill 1.2)
- Backing Up a Database (Skill 1.19)
- Switching between Database Object Views (Skill 1.5)

- Creating a New Record in a Table (Skill 1.7)
- Finding and Replacing Data (Skill 1.9)
- Using Undo and Redo (Skill 1.11)
- Deleting Records (Skill 1.12)
- Organizing Objects in the Navigation Pane (Skill 1.4)
- Creating a New Record in a Form (Skill 1.8)
- Understanding and Viewing Table Relationships (Skill 1.3)
- Exporting Data to Excel or Word (Skill 1.15)
- Checking Spelling (Skill 1.13)
- Previewing and Printing Database Objects (Skill 1.17)
- Deleting and Renaming Database Objects (Skill 1.14)
- Using Compact and Repair (Skill 1.18)

1. Open the start file **AC2013-ChallengeYourself-1-3.**

2. If necessary, enable active content by clicking the **Enable Content** button in the Message Bar.

3. Save a copy of the file to work on. Name the file:
   `[your initials]AC-ChallengeYourself-1-3`

4. If necessary, enable active content in the new database by clicking the **Enable Content** button in the Message Bar.

5. Enter and edit data in the *Employees* table.

   a. Open the *Employees* table.

   b. Switch to Design view. Note the field designated as the primary key.

   c. Switch to back to Datasheet view.

   d. Enter the following record into your table and note that the *Position* field is a lookup field.

EmployeeID	FirstName	LastName	Position	WeeklyHours
59267311	Tracy	Seidel	Greenhouse Tech 2	15

   e. Find the record with a *LastName* value of *Rojas*.

   f. Change the *WeeklyHours* value from 35 to **30.**

   g. Undo the change.

   h. Delete the record with an *EmployeeID* of 23605379.

   i. Close the *Employees* table.

6. Enter and edit data in the *EmployeesForm*.

   a. Open the *EmployeesForm*.

   b. Enter the following record into your form:

   c. Close the *EmployeesForm*.

EmployeeID	FirstName	LastName	Position	WeeklyHours
77913350	George	Phillips	Greenhouse Tech 2	20

7. Review table relationships.

   a. Open the Relationships window. Remember the primary key from the *Employees* table? Do you see how that field creates the connection between the *Employees* table and the *Maintenance Log* table?

   b. Close the Relationships window.

8. Export the *Employees* table to Excel. Include layout and formatting. You do not need to save the export steps. Name the file:
   `[your initials]AC-ChallengeYourself-1-3-Employees`

9. Open the *Plants* table and run the spelling checker on the *FlowerColor* field. Correct any spelling errors in the *FlowerColor* field. You can ignore data in the other fields in this table.

10. Preview how the *Plants* table will look when printed. Change the zoom view to see if all the columns will fit on one page when printed in portrait view. If they will not, change to layout orientation.

11. Close the *Plants* table.

12. Open the *Purchases* table, observe that there are no records, and then close the table.

13. Delete the *Purchases* table.

14. Observe the file size of your database. Use the *Compact & Repair Database* command and check the file again. How much did the file size decrease?

15. Create a backup of this database using the default name chosen by Access.

16. Close the database and exit Access.

challenge yourself **1.4**

In this project, you will work with a database for a volunteer organization that ships and administers vaccines to various relief centers all over the world. The database must maintain a list of all approved vaccines and keep track of all shipments made to the relief centers.

Skills needed to complete this project:

- Introduction to Access 2013 (Skill 1.1)
- Working with Security Warnings (Skill 1.2)
- Backing Up a Database (Skill 1.19)
- Organizing Objects in the Navigation Pane (Skill 1.4)
- Understanding and Viewing Table Relationships (Skill 1.3)
- Navigating Records (Skill 1.6)
- Creating a New Record in a Table (Skill 1.7)
- Finding and Replacing Data (Skill 1.9)
- Deleting Records (Skill 1.12)
- Previewing and Printing Database Objects (Skill 1.17)
- Creating a New Record in a Form (Skill 1.8)
- Deleting and Renaming Database Objects (Skill 1.14)
- Exporting Data to Excel or Word (Skill 1.15)
- Using Compact and Repair (Skill 1.18)

1. Open the start file **AC2013-ChallengeYourself-1-4.**

2. If necessary, enable active content by clicking the **Enable Content** button in the Message Bar.

3. Save a copy of the file to work on. Name the file:
   `[your initials]AC-ChallengeYourself-1-4`

4. Change the organization of the Navigation Pane to use the **Tables and Related Views** category.

5. Open the Relationships window and study the table structure of the database.

6. Open the *Vaccines* table and browse the records using the record navigation buttons and keyboard shortcuts.

7. Enter the following record into the *Vaccines* table. Note that the *TargetAudience* field is a lookup field.

VaccineID	VaccineName	TargetAudience
MAL	Malaria	At-risk individuals

8. Find the record with the value **TD** in the *VACCINEID* field and change the value of the *TargetAudience* field from **Adults** to **Teenagers.**

9. Find and delete the record with a *VaccineID* of **LYD.**

10. Preview how the *Vaccines* table would look if it were printed. If necessary, change the orientation to landscape.

11. Close the *Vaccines* table.

12. Open the *VaccinesForm* form and enter the following as a new record:

VaccineID	VaccineName	TargetAudience
DF	Dengue Fever	At-risk individuals

13. Close the *VaccinesForm* form.

14. In the Navigation Pane, rename the **VaccinesForm** form to: **VaccineDetails**

15. Export the *Vaccines* table to Excel. Maintain all formatting and layout. You do not need to save the export steps. Save the exported file as:
[your initials]AC-ChallengeYourself-1-4-Vaccines

16. Observe the file size of your database. Use the **Compact & Repair Database** feature and check the file again. How much did the file size decrease?

17. Create a backup of this database using the default name chosen by Access.

on your own 1.5

You have an extensive movie collection at home. You have realized that Access 2013 is a great tool to help you keep a list of all the movies you own and keep track of which friends and relatives have borrowed your movies. Demonstrate your basic understanding of Access by working with this database.

Skills needed to complete this project:

- Introduction to Access 2013 (Skill 1.1)
- Working with Security Warnings (Skill 1.2)
- Understanding and Viewing Table Relationships (Skill 1.3)
- Navigating Records (Skill 1.6)
- Creating a New Record in a Table (Skill 1.7)
- Creating a New Record in a Form (Skill 1.8)
- Finding and Replacing Data (Skill 1.9)
- Using Undo and Redo (Skill 1.11)
- Deleting Records (Skill 1.12)
- Checking Spelling (Skill 1.13)
- Using Compact and Repair (Skill 1.18)
- Backing Up a Database (Skill 1.19)

1. Open the start file **AC2013-OnYourOwn-1-5.**

2. If necessary, enable active content by clicking the **Enable Content** button in the Message Bar.

3. Save a copy of the file to work on. Name the file:
   `[your initials]AC-OnYourOwn-1-5`

4. Spend some time exploring the structure of the database. Identify the database objects and how they are related to one another. Open and explore the tables and forms without making any data changes.

5. Earlier this week, you acquired four new movies. Add these four movies to your database. You may use real or fake movies, but you must fill in all the fields and ensure your new data are consistent with the ones that are already there. You can enter the new records in a form or table—whichever you prefer.

   a. Use *Undo* if you make a mistake when entering the new records.

   b. Be sure to check your new records for spelling errors.

6. Find the movie with the word *Lincoln* in the title. Change the format to Blu-Ray.

7. You seem to have lost your solar system movie. Find and remove that movie from your database.

8. Make your database file size smaller and create a backup.

fix it 1.6

A local pet store has hired you to fix its database, which keeps track of inventory, customers, and store sales.

Skills needed to complete this project:

- Introduction to Access 2013 (Skill 1.1)
- Working with Security Warnings (Skill 1.2)
- Understanding and Viewing Table Relationships (Skill 1.3)
- Navigating Records (Skill 1.6)
- Finding and Replacing Data (Skill 1.9)
- Cutting, Copying, and Pasting Data (Skill 1.10)
- Deleting Records (Skill 1.12)
- Checking Spelling (Skill 1.13)
- Deleting and Renaming Database Objects (Skill 1.14)
- Exporting Data to Excel or Word (Skill 1.15)
- Exporting Data to a PDF File (Skill 1.16)
- Previewing and Printing Database Objects (Skill 1.17)
- Using Compact and Repair (Skill 1.18)
- Backing Up a Database (Skill 1.19)

1. Open the start file **AC2013-FixIt-1-6.**

2. If necessary, enable active content by clicking the **Enable Content** button in the Message Bar.

3. Save a copy of the file to work on. Name the file:
   `[your initials]AC-FixIt-1-6`

4. The employees can no longer see their forms and reports in the Navigation Pane. Can you help them?

5. Spend some time exploring the structure of the database. Identify the database objects and how they are related to one another. Open and explore the tables and forms without making any data changes.

6. The owner tells you that a former employee would often make data entry errors, and he wants your help in finding and correcting errors in the *Pets* table.

   a. The employee often misspelled the word *terrier*. Find his misspellings and fix them.

   b. The record for the Black Labrador Retriever is missing data in the *MainColor* field. (The color should be *Black*.)

   c. One of the records has the data in the *Breed* and the *MainColor* fields swapped. Find the record and fix it Hint: Find the record with *White* in the *Breed* field. It might be a good idea to cut and paste the breed data and then type the color.

   d. There is also a duplicate record for the Bengal breed. Delete the record with the pet ID **1446011**.

7. Once the data errors are fixed, export the tables to Excel and export the form to a PDF file. Use the following file names:

   a. `[your initials]AC-FixIt-1-6-Pets.xlsx`

   b. `[your initials]AC-FixIt-1-6-Customers.xlsx`

   c. `[your initials]AC-FixIt-1-6-Sales.xlsx`

   d. `[your initials]AC-FixIt-1-6-PetsForm.pdf`

8. The *CustomersReport* report is poorly formatted. Delete it for now. You will need to recreate it at another time.

9. The owner plans on printing the *Customers* table. Make sure it will fit on one page when printed.

10. The owner wonders why the database file size is so large. Help him reduce the file size.

11. Create a backup of the database so you can easily fix the data if these problems crop up again.

chapter 2

Working with Tables

❱ Create a new table in Datasheet view and Design view

❱ Establish the table primary key

❱ Add and delete fields in Datasheet view and Design view

❱ Format fields in Datasheet view and Design view

❱ Work with Attachment fields

❱ Modify field properties in Datasheet view and Design view

❱ Create lookup fields

❱ Create table relationships

skills

introduction

In this chapter you will learn the skills essential for creating well-designed tables. You will learn to create tables from scratch in both Datasheet view and Design view. You will add and rename fields, set field formats, and modify field properties. In Design view, you will add primary keys and apply an input mask to control formatting. Finally, you will create lookup fields and enforce referential integrity in table relationships.

The *Let Me Try* exercises in this chapter use the AC2-Appointments database. You can keep the database open while you work in this chapter, opening and closing database objects as required for each *Let Me Try*.

Skill 2.1 Designing a Table

Remember that Access is a relational database—objects in your database are related to one another through relationships defined by common fields between tables. Take advantage of these relationships, and design your database so information is stored in one table only. For example, a database of customer appointments need not include every detail about each customer. The appointments table should include fields required for the appointment only. Details about customers, services, and staff should be kept in separate, related tables.

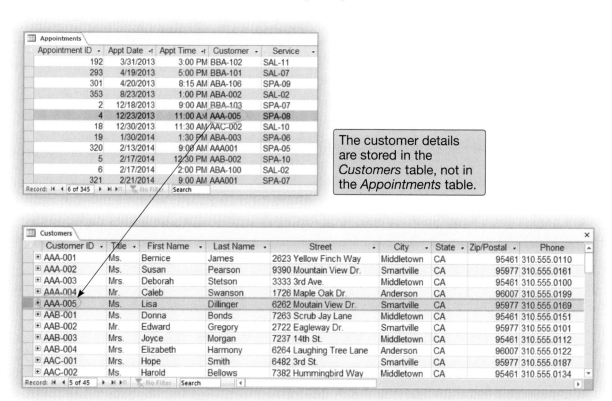

The customer details are stored in the *Customers* table, not in the *Appointments* table.

FIGURE AC 2.1

Storing each unique piece of data in a single table helps prevent data entry errors. There is only one record for each customer, so every time a new appointment record is created you only need to reference the related field (in this case the *Customer ID* field) rather than entering all the customer information again.

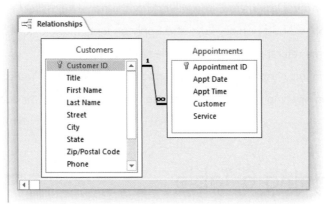

FIGURE AC 2.2
The Relationships window shows the one-to-many relationship between the *Customer ID* field in the *Customers* table and the *Customer* field in the *Appointments* table.

tips & tricks

Keeping repeated data in separate tables where they are stored only once keeps the database file size down, allowing the database to operate more efficiently.

let me try

If the database is not already open, open the data file **AC2-Appointments** and try this skill on your own:

1. Open the *Appointments* table and explore the fields in the table.

2. Open the *Customers* table and explore the fields in the table.

3. Open the Relationships window and review the relationship between the *Appointments* table and the *Customers* table.

4. Close all open database objects.

Skill 2.2 Creating and Saving a Table in Datasheet View

One way to create a new table is to add a blank table and add fields directly in Datasheet view.

1. On the *Create* tab, in the *Tables* group, click the **Table** button to insert a new table.

2. The new table opens in Datasheet view. The first field is automatically added as an AutoNumber field named *ID*.

3. To add a new field, begin typing data for the first record. Access names the first field *Field1*. Access will apply a data type based on what you type. For example, if you type a date, Access will automatically apply the Date/Time data type to the field.

4. Press (Tab ⇥) or (← Enter) to enter data for the next field.

5. Repeat steps 3 and 4 to enter all the data for the first record.

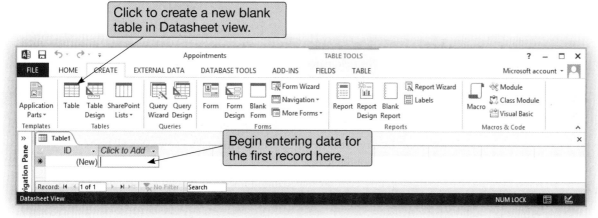

FIGURE AC 2.3

When you create a new database object, you must save the object for the changes to take effect. Access will warn you if you try to close an object that requires saving.

To save a table for the first time:

1. Click the **Save** button on the Quick Access Toolbar.

2. The *Save As* dialog opens.

3. Type a meaningful name in the *Table Name* box.

4. Click **OK**.

FIGURE AC 2.4

another method

To save a database object, you can use the keyboard shortcut (Ctrl) + (S).

let me try

If the database is not already open, open the data file **AC2-Appointments** and try this skill on your own:

1. Create a new table in Datasheet view.

2. Allow Access to create the first AutoNumber field named *ID*.

3. Enter data for the second field: `Bob's Mud Supply`

4. Close the table, saving it with the name: `Vendors`

Skill 2.3 Renaming Fields

When you create a new, blank table in Datasheet view, Access names the fields *Field1*, *Field2*, and so forth by default.

To rename a field, double-click the column header and type the new field name.

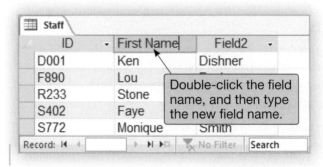

FIGURE AC 2.5

You can also change the field name by modifying the field properties:

1. Click anywhere in the field to select it.

2. On the *Table Tools Fields* tab, in the *Properties* group, click the **Name & Caption** button to open the *Enter Field Properties* dialog.

3. In the *Name* box, type the new field name. This is the name as it will be referenced by other objects in your database.

4. In the *Caption* box, type the field name as it should appear in labels and column headings. If you do not include a caption, Access will use the field name instead.

5. In the *Description* box, type additional information about the field (if necessary).

6. Click **OK.**

7. Save the table.

another **method**

To rename a field:

1. Right-click the field name at the top of the column in Datasheet view and select **Rename Field.**

2. The field name appears highlighted.

3. Type the new name, and press ⏎ Enter .

let me **try**

If the database is not already open, open the data file **AC2-Appointments** and try this skill on your own:

1. Open the *Staff* table in Datasheet view.

2. Rename the *ID* field to: `Staff ID`

3. Rename the *Field1* field to: `First Name`

4. Rename the *Field2* field to: `Last Name`

5. Save the table.

Skill 2.4 Adding Fields in Datasheet View

You can always add a new field to a table by typing data in the blank cell at the end of a record, but what if you want to set up the table without entering data? Use the *Click to Add* heading at the far right side of the table.

To add a new field to a table:

1. At the far right side of the table, there is a column with the header *Click to Add*. Click the arrow to expand the list of available field types.

2. Click the field type you want to add.

3. Access creates a new field with the temporary name highlighted.

4. Type the new field name and then press (← Enter).

   You can also add a new field by clicking the field type you want from the *Table Tools Fields* tab, *Add & Delete* group. If there isn't a button for the data type you want, click the **More Fields** button to expand the *Data Type* gallery.

FIGURE AC 2.6

another **method**

You can also insert a new field by right-clicking any field name and selecting **Insert Field.** A new blank text field is inserted to the left of the field you selected.

let me **try**

If the database is not already open, open the data file **AC2-Appointments** and try this skill on your own:

1. If necessary, open the *Staff* table in Datasheet view.

2. Add a new *Date/Time* field to the far right side of the table.

3. Name the field: **Start Date**

4. Save the table.

Skill 2.5 Using Quick Start to Add Related Fields

FIGURE AC 2.7
Quick Start Section of the
Fields Types Gallery

Almost any table that keeps a list of people or businesses requires separate fields for street address, city, state, zip code, and country. Access makes it easy to insert these commonly used fields in a group. The last section in the *Field Types* gallery, **Quick Start field types**, provides an easy way to add address fields and other common field groups to your table.

To add a *Quick Start* group of fields:

1. The Quick Start fields will be inserted to the left of the selected field. To add them to the far right of the table, click anywhere in the *Click To Add* column.

2. On the *Table Tools Design* tab, in the *Add & Delete* group, click the **More Fields** button.

3. Scroll to the bottom of the *Field Types* gallery to the *Quick Start* section.

4. Click the *Quick Start* option you want.

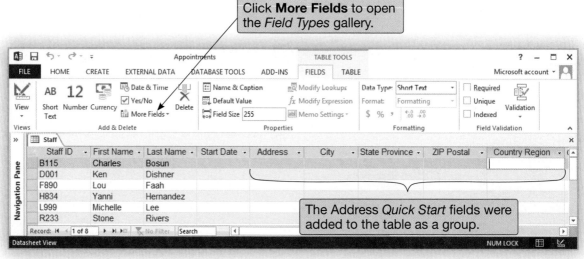

FIGURE AC 2.8

let me try

If the database is not already open, open the data file **AC2-Appointments** and try this skill on your own:

1. If necessary, open the *Staff* table in Datasheet view.

2. Add the **Address** *Quick Start* fields to the table to the right of the *Start Date* field.

3. Save and close the table.

Skill 2.6 Adjusting Table Column Widths

When you insert a new field, it is created with the standard width, which may not be wide enough to display all your data. Adjusting column widths in Datasheet view is similar to working with column widths in Excel.

To use the mouse to change the column size:

1. Move the mouse to the right border of the field header.

2. The cursor changes to a ✛ shape.

3. Click and drag to resize the column width, or double-click the right column border to automatically resize the column to best fit the data.

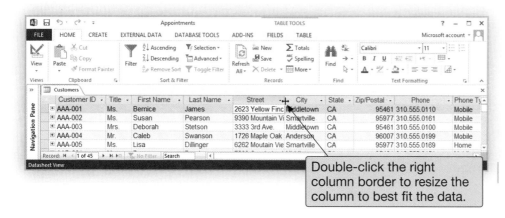

Double-click the right column border to resize the column to best fit the data.

FIGURE AC 2.9

To use the *Column Width* dialog to change the column size:

1. On the *Home* tab, in the *Records* group, click the **More** button, and select **Field Width** to open the *Column Width* dialog.

2. Type the width you want in the **Column Width** box, or click the **Best Fit** button.

3. Click **OK.**

FIGURE AC 2.10

tips & tricks

Do not confuse field size with field width. **Field size** refers to the number of characters the field can hold in the database. **Field width** or column width refers to the number of characters that are visible on screen. This can be a little confusing because Access uses the terms *field width* and *column width* interchangeably.

Refer to the skill *Modifying Field Properties* for more information about working with the Field Size property.

another method

You can also open the *Column Width* dialog by right-clicking the field column header and selecting **Field Width.**

let me try

If the database is not already open, open the data file **AC2-Appointments** and try this skill on your own:

1. If necessary, open the *Customers* table in Datasheet view.

2. Modify the width of the *Street* column to best fit the data.

3. Save and close the table.

Skill 2.7 Creating a Table in Design View

Another way to create a new table is in Design view. In Design view, you create the fields without entering data. You must specify the field name and data type for each field. You also have the option of adding a description.

To create a table in Design view:

1. On the *Create* tab, in the *Tables* group, click the **Table Design** button.
2. Type the name of the first field. Press (Tab).
3. Expand the list of data types, and select the data type you want. Press (Tab) again.
4. Type a useful description of the field. Press (Tab) to go to the next field.
5. Continue adding fields. When you are finished, save the table.

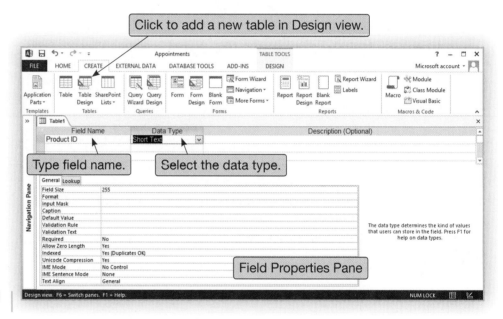

FIGURE AC 2.11

Notice that the Design view window is divided into two panes. The top pane lists the table fields. You may need to use the scroll bar at the right side of the pane to see all the fields. The bottom pane is the **Field Properties pane**. It displays details about the selected field. You will learn more about using the Field Properties pane in other skills.

let me try

If the database is not already open, open the data file **AC2-Appointments** and try this skill on your own:

1. Add a new table in Design view.
2. Name the first field: `Product ID`
3. Make the data type: `Short Text`
4. Add the description: `Internal product ID`
5. Close the table, saving it with the name: `Products`
6. Access asks if you want to designate a primary key. Click **No** to close the table without a primary key.

Skill 2.8 Inserting Fields in Design View

If you are working in Design view, you can always add new fields to the end of the field list by typing a new field name and selecting a data type. You can also insert fields between existing fields.

To insert a new field in Design view:

1. Click the field below where you want to insert the new field.
2. On the *Table Tools Design* tab, in the *Tools* group, click the **Insert Rows** button.
3. Enter the field name and select the data type. Enter a description if you want.
4. When you are finished, save the table.

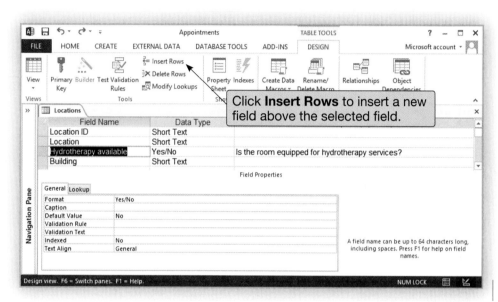

FIGURE AC 2.12

another **method**

You can also right-click the row selector at the left side of the field and select **Insert Rows** to insert a new field row above the selected field.

let me **try**

If the database is not already open, open the data file **AC2-Appointments** and try this skill on your own:

1. If necessary, open the *Locations* table in Design view.
2. Insert a new field above the *Hydrotherapy available* field.
3. Enter the field name: **Stations**
4. Select the data type **Number.**
5. Enter the description: **Number of therapy stations in room**
6. Save the table.

Skill 2.9 Setting the Primary Key

Every Access table should have a primary key defined. The **primary key field** contains data unique to that record. Primary keys are often IDs—product IDs, employee IDs, or record IDs. The primary key is the basis for relationships between tables.

❱ If your data do not already contain a field that is unique for each record, you can add a new field that uses the AutoNumber data type. Using an AutoNumber field ensures that each record has a unique numerical ID.

❱ If your table contains a field that you know is unique for each record (such as a previously established product ID, employee ID, or part number), you can set this field as the primary key.

To set the primary key in a table:

1. In Design view, click the field that is going to be the primary key.

2. On the *Table Tools Design* tab, in the *Tools* group, click the **Primary Key** button.

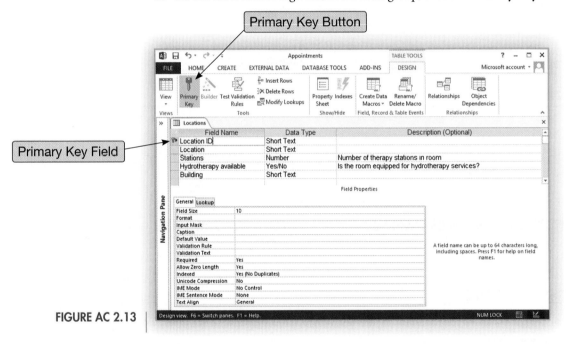

FIGURE AC 2.13

Notice that on the *Table Tools Design* tab, in the *Tools* group, the *Primary Key* button is highlighted to indicate that the selected field is the primary key and a key icon appears in the row selector at the left side of the field.

tips & tricks

Once you establish a field as the primary key, Access automatically sets the *Required* property to *yes* to ensure that each record has a unique primary key.

another method

In Design view, right-click the row selector and select **Primary Key.**

let me try

If the database is not already open, open the data file **AC2-Appointments** and try this skill on your own:

1. If necessary, open the *Locations* table in Design view.

2. Set the *Location ID* field as the primary key.

3. Save the table.

Skill 2.10 Deleting Fields

You can delete fields from both Datasheet view and Design view. When you delete a field, you delete all the data in that field, and the action cannot be undone.

To delete a field in Datasheet view:

1. Click anywhere in the field you want to delete.

2. On the *Table Tools Fields* tab, in the *Add & Delete* group, click the **Delete** button.

3. When Access asks if you if you want to permanently delete the field, click **Yes.**

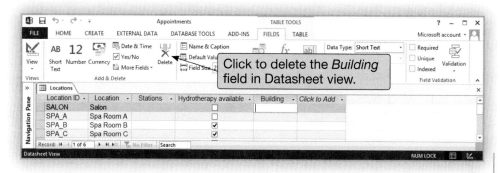

FIGURE AC 2.14

To delete a field in Design view:

1. Click anywhere in the field you want to delete.

2. On the *Table Tools Design* tab, in the *Tools* group, click the **Delete Rows** button.

3. When Access asks if you if you want to permanently delete the field, click **Yes.**

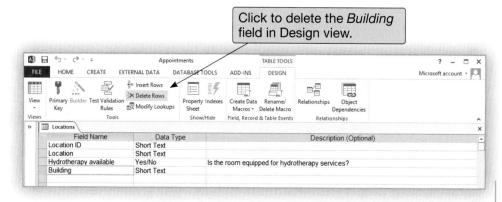

FIGURE AC 2.15

another **method**

▶ In Design view, right-click the row selector to the left of the field name, and select **Delete Rows.**

▶ In Datasheet view, right-click the field name at the top of the column and select **Delete Field.**

▶ In Datasheet view, select the field by clicking the column heading, and then on the *Home* tab, in the *Records* group, click the **Delete** button.

let me **try**

If the database is not already open, open the data file **AC2-Appointments** and try this skill on your own:

1. If necessary, open the *Locations* table in Datasheet view.
2. Delete the *Building* field.
3. Save the table.

4. If necessary, open the *Services* table in Design view.
5. Delete the *Building* field.
6. Save and close the table.

Skill 2.11 Changing Data Type

One key to database efficiency is ensuring that each field is assigned the appropriate data type. For example, you can't run calculations on a field with the Short Text field type, and you can't sort a date field efficiently unless you use the Date/Time field type. Carefully consider the type of data you will include in each field before you decide on the data type.

To change the data type for a field from Datasheet view:

1. Click anywhere in the field you want to change.
2. Click the **Table Tools Fields** tab, in the *Formatting* group, expand the **Data Type** list, and select the data type you want.
3. Save the table to commit the change.

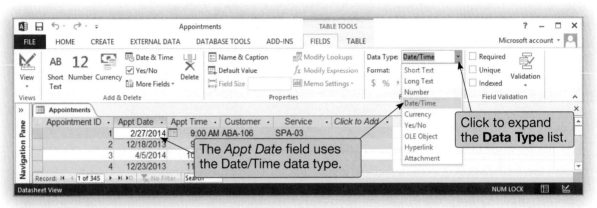

FIGURE AC 2.16

AutoNumber—An *AutoNumber* field is automatically assigned its value by Access. Database users cannot edit or enter data in an *AutoNumber* field. *AutoNumber* fields are often used as a primary key if no other unique field exists in the table.

Short Text—A *Short Text* field can hold up to 255 characters. *Short Text* fields are used for short text data or numbers that should be treated as text.

Long Text—A *Long Text* field holds text and numbers like a *Short Text* field, except you can enter up to 65,535 characters in a *Long Text* field. Text in *Long Text* fields can be formatted using Rich Text Formatting.

Number—A *Number* field holds a numerical value. The default number is described as a long integer, a number between $-2,147,483,648$ and $2,147,483,647$.

Date/Time—A *Date/Time* field stores a numerical value that is displayed as a date and time. The format in which the date and/or time displays is controlled by the Format property. Using the Date/Time data type allows you to sort the field by date.

Currency—A *Currency* field stores a numerical value with a high degree of accuracy (up to four decimal places to the right of the decimal). Access will not round the values stored in currency fields, regardless of the format in which the value displays.

Yes/No—A *Yes/No* field stores a true/false value as a −1 for yes and 0 for no. Yes/No fields can display the words *Yes/No* or *True/False* or a checkbox as shown in Figure AC 2.17.

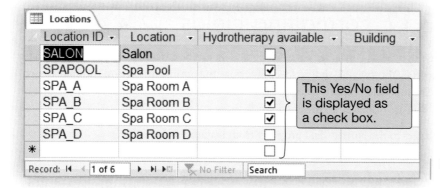

FIGURE AC 2.17

OLE Object—The *OLE Object* data type stores a graphic or file as part of the database. It is maintained in Access 2013 for backward compatibility with databases created prior to Access 2007. In general, you should use the newer Attachment data type instead.

Hyperlink—A *Hyperlink* field stores a Web address or e-mail address. Fields with the Hyperlink data type can be active and set to open the computer's default e-mail program or Web browser populated with the data from the *Hyperlink* field.

Attachment—An *Attachment* field stores files as attachments to records. Attachments can be images, Word documents, or almost any other type of data file.

Calculated Field—A *Calculated* field uses an expression (a formula) to calculate a value.

tips & tricks

In previous versions of Access, the *Short Text* data type was simply *Text* and the *Long Text* data type was *Memo*.

another method

You can also change the data type from Design view:

1. Click in the **Data Type** column for the field that you want to change.
2. Click the **drop-down arrow** to see the list of available data types.
3. Select the appropriate data type for your data.
4. Save the table to commit the change.

let me try

If the database is not already open, open the data file **AC2-Appointments** and try this skill on your own:

1. If it is not already open, open the *Appointments* table in Datasheet view.
2. Change the data type for the *Appt Date* field to **Date/Time.**
3. Save the table.

Skill 2.12 Formatting Fields

When designing a table, you specify what type of data can be entered in each field by selecting the data type. You can also define specific formatting options to control the appearance of data. The **Format field property** does not affect the data stored in the table; it only controls the way the data are displayed to the end user.

To make changes to the Format field property from Datasheet view:

1. Click anywhere in the field you want to format.

2. On the *Table Tools Fields* tab, in the *Formatting* group, expand the **Format** list, and select the format you want. Not all properties are available for all field data types.

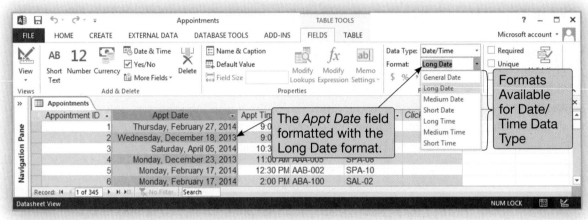

FIGURE AC 2.18

You can quickly apply the Currency, Percent, or Comma number formats by clicking the appropriate button in the *Formatting* group. These formats can be used with AutoNumber, Number, and Currency data types.

❱ The **Currency format** displays a $ symbol before the number and two digits to the right of the decimal place.

❱ The **Percent format** displays the number as a percentage, so .05 displays as 5, and 5 displays as 500. It does not display the % symbol in the table.

❱ The **Comma Style format** displays the , symbol within the number and two digits to the right of the decimal. This is the same as selecting **Standard** from the *Format* list.

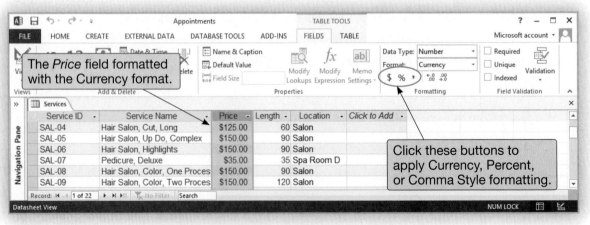

FIGURE AC 2.19

To modify the Format field property in Design view:

1. Click anywhere in the field you want to format.
2. In the Field Properties pane, click in the **Format** property box.
3. Click the arrow at the right end of the box to expand the list of available formats, and select the format you want.

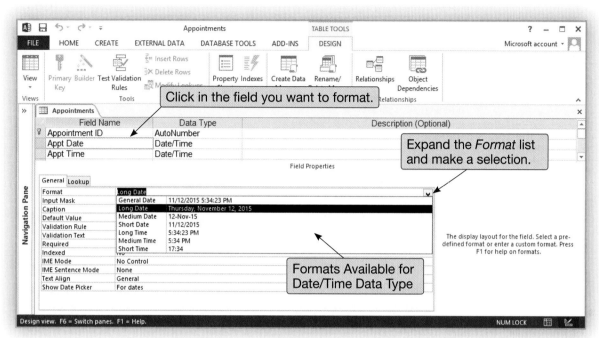

FIGURE AC 2.20

tell me **more**

To increase or decrease the number of digits that appear to the right of the decimal in your *AutoNumber, Number,* and *Currency* fields, on the *Table Tools Fields* tab, in the *Formatting* group, click the **Increase Decimals** or **Decrease Decimals** button.

let me try

If the database is not already open, open the data file **AC2-Appointments** and try this skill on your own:

1. If necessary, open the *Appointments* table in Datasheet view.
2. Apply the **Long Date** format to the *Appt Date* field. Hint: Verify that the data type is **Date/Time** before applying the format.
3. If necessary, expand the column width for the *Appt Date* field so you can see the full date in Datasheet view.
4. If necessary, open the *Services* table in Design view.
5. Apply the **Currency** format to the *Price* field. Change only the formatting, not the data type.
6. Save and close the tables.

Skill 2.13 Modifying Field Properties

You can modify a variety of field properties to control data entry. The Format field property is discussed in detail in the skill *Formatting Fields,* and the Name and Caption properties are covered in the skill *Renaming Fields.* Two other useful properties are the Default Value property, and the Field Size property. Both of these field properties can be modified from either Datasheet view or Design view.

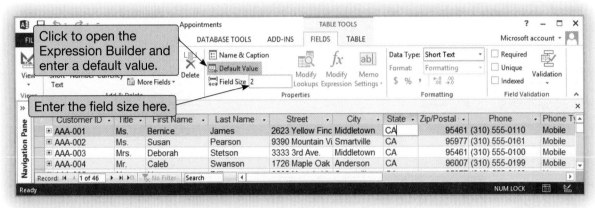

FIGURE AC 2.21

The **Default Value property** adds a preset value to the field. Entering a value in the Default Value property can save time during data entry. For example, if most of your employees live in California, use CA as the default value for the *State* field.

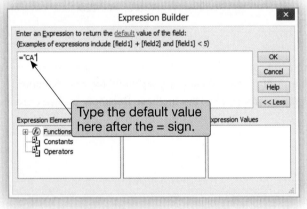

FIGURE AC 2.22

To add a default value in Datasheet view:

1. Select the field to which you want to add a default value.
2. On the *Table Tools Fields* tab, in the *Properties* group, click the **Default Value** button to open the *Expression Builder.*
3. In the *Expression Builder,* enter the numerical value, text, or formula you want to use as the default value for the field. The default value expression always begins with the = sign, which Access adds for you. If the default value is a text string with a space or other special character in it, you must enclose it in quotation marks. If the text is something simple, such as *CA,* you do not need to type the quotation marks. Access will add them for you.
4. Click **OK.**
5. Save the table.

When a field has a default value set, the *Default Value* button appears highlighted. Whenever a new record is created, the default value is entered into this field automatically.

You can also set the default value from Design view:

1. Select the field.
2. In the Field Properties pane, click in the **Default Value** box and type the numerical value, text, or formula you want to use as the default value.
3. If you want to use the *Expression Builder,* click the **Build...** button at the right side of the *Default Value* box.
4. Save the table.

The **Field Size property** limits the number of characters that can be entered in a text field. The default size for a *Short Text* field is 255 (the maximum size for a *Short Text* field). Limiting the field size can ensure that data are entered properly. For example, if you want entries in the *State* field to always use the two-letter state abbreviation, limit the field size to 2.

To modify the Field Size property in Datasheet view:

1. Select the field.

2. On the *Table Tools Fields* tab, in the *Properties* group, type the new field size in the **Field Size** box and press ⏎ Enter .

3. If you are making the field size smaller, Access will warn you that the smaller size may result in data loss, as Access will delete any data in the field that exceeds the new field size limit. Click **Yes** to continue with the change.

4. Save the table.

To modify the Field Size property in Design view, follow the same steps, entering the new field size value in the **Field Size** box in the Field Properties pane.

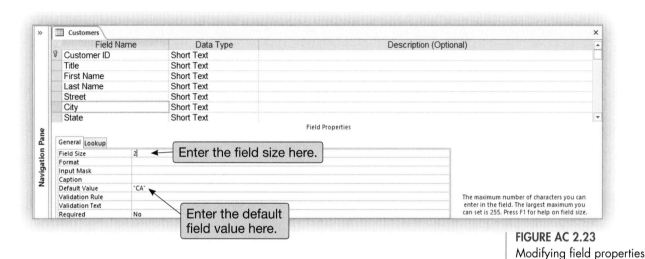

FIGURE AC 2.23
Modifying field properties in Design view

tips & tricks

You cannot limit the size of *Long Text* fields.

tell me **more**

If the selected field is a *Long Text* field, the *Memo Settings* button controls two properties exclusive to *Long Text* fields:

⟩ Rich Text Formatting allows you to add text formatting.

⟩ Append Only saves a history of changes made to the text in the field.

let me **try**

If the database is not already open, open the data file **AC2-Appointments** and try this skill on your own:

1. If necessary, open the *Customers* table in Datasheet view.

2. Set the **Default Value** property for the *State* field to **CA**.

3. Switch to Design view.

4. Change the **Field Size** property for the *State* field to **2**.

5. Save the table.

Skill 2.14 Applying an Input Mask from Design View

One of the keys to an effective database is consistent data entry. An **input mask** forces users to enter data in a consistent format. Input masks are only available from the Design view Field Properties pane. The *Input Mask Wizard* offers a variety of common input masks including phone number and date and time formats.

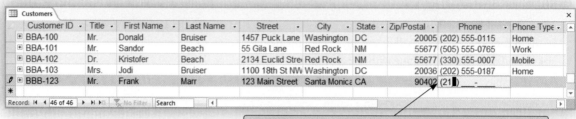

FIGURE AC 2.24 | The *Phone* field has the Phone input mask applied.

To apply one of the sample input masks to a field:

1. With the table open in Design view, click the field you want to apply the input mask to.

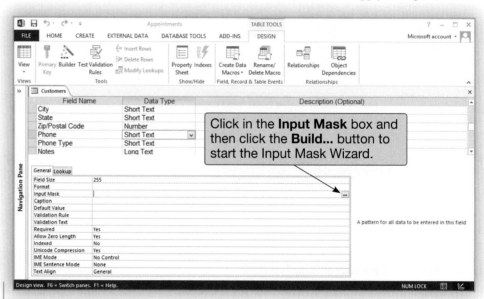

Click in the **Input Mask** box and then click the **Build...** button to start the Input Mask Wizard.

FIGURE AC 2.25

FIGURE AC 2.26

2. Click the **Input Mask** box in the Field Properties pane.

3. Click the **Build...** button to open the *Input Mask Wizard*.

4. Click **Yes** when Access prompts you to save the table.

5. Click the input mask format you want.

6. To test the format, click in the **Try It** box, and type a sample to see how the input mask will affect data entry as shown in Figure AC 2.26.

7. Click **Next**.

8. Click **Next** again to continue without making any customizations to the input mask as shown in Figure AC 2.27.

9. In the next step, you specify how Access will store the data—with or without the input mask symbols. Unless you truly need the symbols stored in the database, select the second option as shown in Figure AC 2.28. This will help reduce the size of the database. Click **Finish.** You can also click **Next** and then click **Finish** on the final step of the wizard.

10. Save the table.

FIGURE AC 2.27

FIGURE AC 2.28

tips & tricks

❯ The Input Mask property is available for *Short Text* or *Date/Time* data type fields only. If you want to use the Social Security input mask, use the Short Text data type for the field that stores the social security numbers.

❯ If the field has a format specified through the Format property, the format takes precedence over the input mask format.

let me try

If the database is not already open, open the data file **AC2-Appointments** and try this skill on your own:

1. If necessary, open the *Customers* table.

2. Switch to Design view.

3. Apply the **Phone** input mask format to the *Phone* field. Do not change default format or placeholder characters. Store the data without the symbols.

4. Save the table.

5. Switch to Datasheet view and enter a new record in the *Customers* table, using any customer information you want. The *Customer ID* field has an input mask applied that requires three letters followed by three numbers. Input in the *Phone* field is controlled by the input mask you applied in step 3.

Skill 2.15 Working with Attachment Fields

One of the most useful enhancements to recent versions of Access is the ability to create **Attachment fields** to store files as attachments to records. Attachments can be pictures, Word documents, or almost any other type of data file. For security reasons, Access will not allow program files (for example, .exe or .bat files) or any files greater than 256 MB as attachments.

To add an *Attachment* field from Datasheet view:

1. At the far right side of the table, there is a column with the header *Click to Add.* Click the arrow to expand the list of available field types, and click **Attachment.**

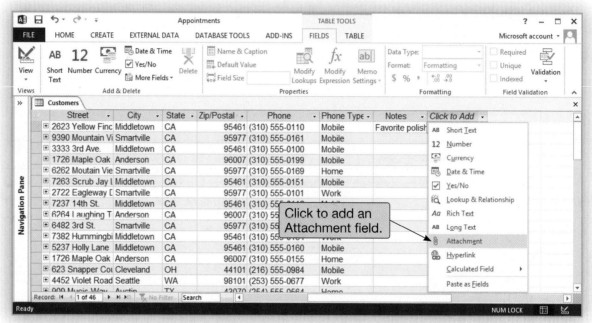

FIGURE AC 2.29

2. Notice that you cannot rename the *Attachment* field. It is designated by a paperclip icon. (You can, however, rename the field in Design view.)

FIGURE AC 2.30

To add an attachment:

1. Double-click the *Attachment* field in the record to which you want to add the attachment.
2. The *Attachments* dialog opens.
3. Click the **Add...** button and browse for the file you want to add.
4. Double-click the file to add it, or click the file once, and then click the **Open** button.
5. Click **OK** to save the attachment and close the *Attachments* dialog.

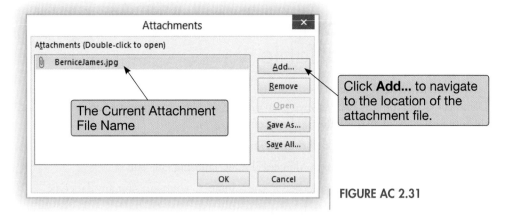

FIGURE AC 2.31

The number next to the attachment icon in each record tells you how many attachments there are. Records can have multiple attachments in a single *Attachment* field.

FIGURE AC 2.32

tips & tricks

Attachment fields cannot be changed to another data type.

tell me **more**

The attachment is not visible in the table. However, when you start working with forms and reports, the attachment is available for display in those database objects.

let me **try**

If the database is not already open, open the data file **AC2-Appointments** and try this skill on your own:

1. If necessary, open the *Customers* table in Datasheet view.
2. Add an *Attachment* field at the far right of the table.
3. Add the JPEG image file **BerniceJames** to the customer record for Bernice James. The image file is located with your student data files for this chapter.
4. Save the table.

Skill 2.16 Adding a Total Row to a Table

New to recent versions of Access is the ability to add a Total row to any database object in Datasheet view. From the **Total row**, you can quickly calculate an aggregate function such as the sum or average of all the values in the column.

Sum—Calculates the total of all the numerical values in the column.

Average—Calculates the average numerical value, ignoring null values.

Count—Counts the number of items in the column. Count works for any data type.

Maximum—Returns the largest numerical value.

Minimum—Returns the smallest numerical value.

Standard Deviation—Calculates the statistical standard deviation for numeric field types only.

Variance—Calculates the statistical variance for numeric field types only.

To add a Total row to a datasheet:

1. On the *Home* tab, in the *Records* group, click the **Totals** button.

2. In the Total row at the bottom of the datasheet, click the column where you want to add a total.

3. Click the arrow, and select the function you want to use.

4. Save the table.

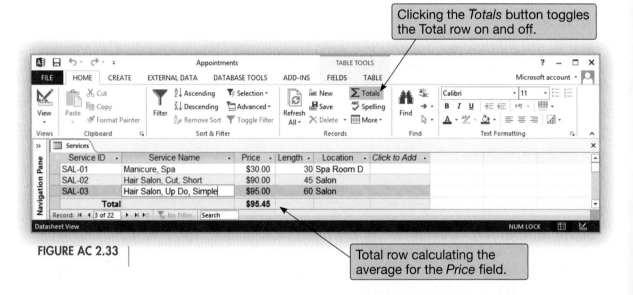

Clicking the *Totals* button toggles the Total row on and off.

Total row calculating the average for the *Price* field.

FIGURE AC 2.33

let me try

If the database is not already open, open the data file **AC2-Appointments** and try this skill on your own:

1. If necessary, open the *Services* table in Datasheet view.

2. Display the Total row.

3. Use the Total row to calculate the average of the values in the *Price* field.

4. Save the table.

Skill 2.17 Adding a Lookup Field from Another Table

A **lookup field** allows the user to select data from a list of items. One type of lookup list presents values from a field in another table or a query. Whether you begin with a new field or modify the data type for an existing field, the process using the *Lookup Wizard* is the same.

To create a new lookup field from Datasheet view:

1. On the *Table Tools Fields* tab, in the *Add & Delete* group, click the **More Fields** button.
2. From the *Basic Types* section of the *Field Types* gallery, click **Lookup & Relationship.**
3. The *Lookup Wizard* opens.

To create a new lookup field from Design view, type the name for the new field to expand the **Data Type** list, and select **Lookup Wizard...** to open the *Lookup Wizard.*

To modify an existing field to use a lookup list:

1. Open the table in Design view.
2. Select the field you want to change to use a lookup list.
3. Expand the **Data Type** list, and select **Lookup Wizard...** to open the *Lookup Wizard.*

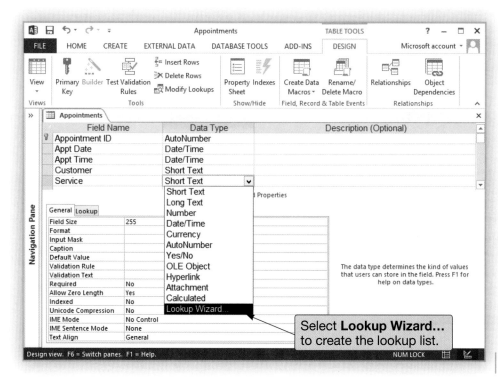

FIGURE AC 2.34

FIGURE AC 2.35

To add the lookup field using the *Lookup Wizard:*

1. The first step of the wizard asks you to determine where your lookup list data will come from. The **I want the lookup field to get the values from another table or query.** radio button is selected by default. Click **Next** to go to the next step.

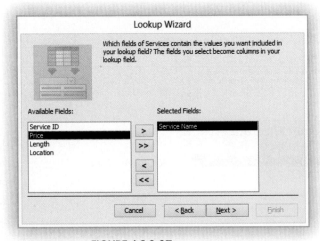

FIGURE AC 2.36

2. Click the name of the table or query that includes the field you want to use for your lookup field values. Click **Next.**

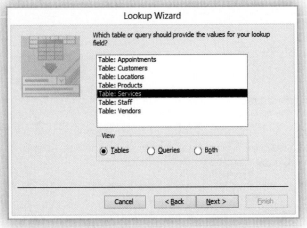

FIGURE AC 2.37

3. Double-click each field name you want to include in the lookup. When you have selected all the fields you want, click **Next.** If you do not select the primary key field, Access will include it automatically.

4. If you want items in the lookup list sorted in a particular order, select the field to sort by. The sort order is ascending by default. Click the **Ascending** button if you want to switch the sort order to descending. Click **Next.**

FIGURE AC 2.38

5. By default, the **Hide key column (recommended)** check box is checked. This hides the primary key in the lookup list.

6. Adjust the column width as necessary to display the values in the lookup list. Click and drag the right border of the column header to make the column wider or narrower. You can double-click the right column border to autofit the column to the data. Click **Next** to continue.

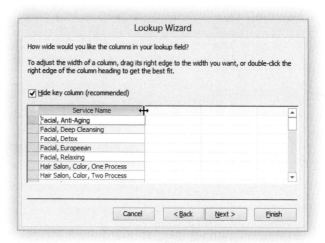

FIGURE AC 2.39

7. If you are modifying an existing field, Access keeps the original field name. If this is a new field, Access gives the field a generic field name such as *Field1*. You should change the name of the new field to something more meaningful.

8. Click the **Enable Data Integrity** check box to require that only values from the lookup list are allowed in the field.

9. Verify that the **Restrict Delete** radio button is selected to prevent any deletions in the table containing the lookup values that would invalidate data in the table containing the lookup field.

10. Click the **Finish** button to add the new lookup field to the table.

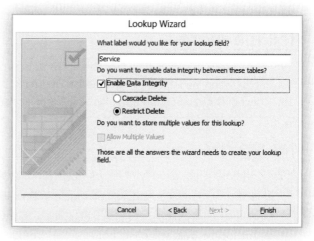

FIGURE AC 2.40

---

skill 2.17   Adding a Lookup Field from Another Table

11. Access will prompt you to save the table so table relationships can be created. Click **Yes.**

Switch to Datasheet view to test the new lookup field. You may need to adjust the column width to display the lookup data properly.

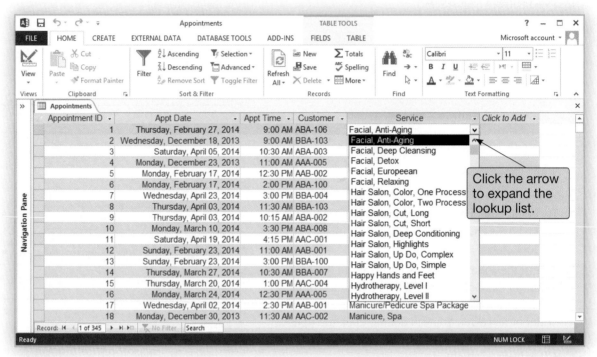

FIGURE AC 2.41

The lookup list in the *Service* field is limited to values in the *Service Name* field in the *Services* table. This prevents data entry errors and ensures data integrity between the two tables.

tell me **more**

When you create a lookup field that references data in another table, Access automatically creates a one-to-many relationship between the table that contains the list data (the "one") and the table that includes the lookup list (the "many"). This concept is discussed further in the skill *Creating Relationships*.

let me try

If the database is not already open, open the data file **AC2-Appointments** and try this skill on your own:

1. If necessary, open the *Appointments* table in Design view.
2. Modify the *Service* field to use a lookup list with the following parameters:
   a. The lookup data will come from the *Services* table.
   b. Include the *Service Name* field in the lookup list.
   c. Sort the lookup list by the *Service Name* field.
   d. Hide the key column and adjust the lookup column width as necessary to display the data.
   e. Enforce data integrity.
   f. Do not allow deletions in the *Services* table that would violate the integrity of records in the *Appointments* table.
3. Save the table.

from the perspective of . . .

SMALL BUSINESS OWNER

I use an Access database to keep track of business contacts, inventory, sales, and customers. When I first set up the database, I included all the customer information with every record in the sales table. Later, when I tried to analyze my sales records to find repeat customers, I realized my mistake. There were multiple records for the same customer, but with the customer information entered slightly differently in each. I know that Cindy Williams and Cynthia Williams are the same person, but Access doesn't. I had to bring in a temp to pull out the customer information into a separate table and make sure the sales records were referencing the correct customers. If I had designed the tables the right way in the first place, I could have saved a lot of time and money. Now my sales table uses a lookup field to add customer data. No more mistakes!

Skill 2.18 Adding a Lookup Field from a List

Lookup fields are useful for fields that reference a specific list of items. A lookup field does not need to reference data in another table or query. You can enter your own values to create a custom list.

To review the procedures for creating new lookup fields, refer to the skill *Adding a Lookup Field from another Table.*

To modify an existing field to use a lookup field with values you specify:

1. Open the table in Design view.
2. Click the field you want to modify to use a lookup list.
3. Click the **Data Type** drop-down arrow and select **Lookup Wizard...**

4. The first step of the wizard asks you to determine where your lookup list data will come from. Click the **I will type in the values that I want.** radio button. Click **Next** to go to the next step.

FIGURE AC 2.42

5. First, enter the number of columns you want in your lookup list.
6. Press (Tab ⇆) to go to the first cell in the first blank column.
7. Type the values in the table exactly as you want them to appear in the lookup field. Click and drag the right border of the column header to make the column wider or narrower. You can double-click the right column border to autofit the column to the data. Click **Next** to continue.

FIGURE AC 2.43

8. Access will keep the original field name. If you want to change it, type a new name.

9. If you want to restrict data entry to only items in the list, click the **Limit To List** check box.

10. Click the **Finish** button to complete the lookup list.

Switch to Datasheet view to test the new lookup field. You may need to adjust the column width to display the lookup data properly.

FIGURE AC 2.44

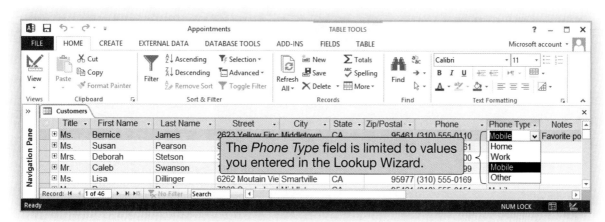

FIGURE AC 2.45

tell me **more**

If the field you want to change to a lookup field uses the *Date/Time* or *Currency* data type, you will need to change the data type to *Number* before you can modify it to be a lookup field.

let me **try**

If the database is not already open, open the data file **AC2-Appointments** and try this skill on your own:

1. If necessary, open the *Customers* table.
2. Switch to Design view.
3. Modify the *Phone Type* field to use a lookup list with the following values: **Home, Work, Mobile, Other**.
4. Limit the lookup list to values in the list.
5. Save the table.

Skill 2.19 Creating Relationships

When a lookup field in one table references values in a field in another table, Access will automatically create a one-to-many relationship between the tables for you. In other cases, you may need to manually create a relationship between two tables.

To view and define relationships between tables:

1. Open the Relationships window. On the *Database Tools* tab, in the *Relationships* group, click the **Relationships** button.

2. To create a new relationship, click the primary key field name in the primary table and drag to the related field name in the secondary table.

3. Review the relationship in the *Edit Relationships* dialog, and then click the **Create** button.

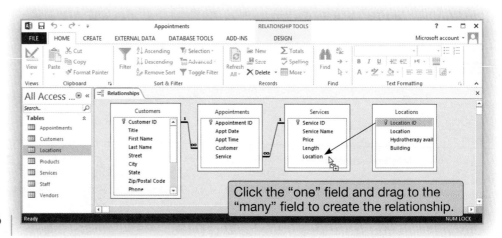

FIGURE AC 2.46

Enforcing **referential integrity** ensures that related database records remain accurate. If a relationship has *Enforce Referential Integrity* checked, then the tables will conform to the following rules:

❯ You cannot add a record to the secondary table without an associated record in the primary table.

❯ You cannot make changes to the primary table that would cause records in the secondary table to become unmatched.

❯ You cannot delete records from the primary table if there are related records in the secondary table.

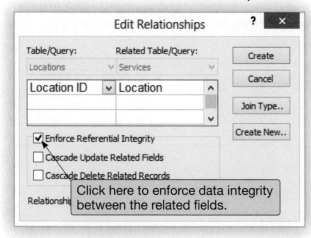

FIGURE AC 2.47

To enforce referential integrity in a relationship:

1. Double-click the relationship line to open the *Edit Relationships* dialog.

2. Click the **Enforce Referential Integrity** check box.

3. Click **OK**.

Notice the change to the relationship line. The 1 indicates the "one" table in the one-to-many relationship. The infinity symbol indicates the "many" table. When these symbols appear, you know that the relationship has referential integrity enforced.

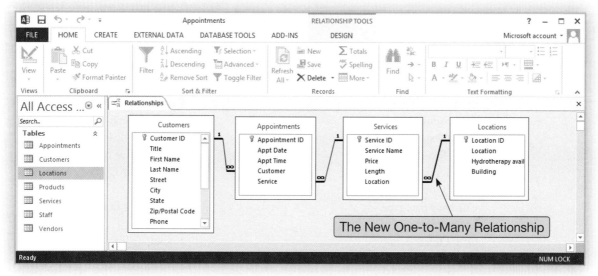

FIGURE AC 2.48

tell me **more**

To delete the relationship between two tables, right-click the relationship line, and select **Delete.**

another **method**

To open the *Edit Relationships* dialog, you can also:

❯ Double-click any field name showing in the Relationships window.

❯ Double-click any empty area of the Relationships window.

When you open the *Edit Relationships* dialog with either of these methods, you will need to select the primary table from the *Table/Query* list at the left side of the dialog. When you make a selection, Access will populate the dialog with the existing relationships.

let me **try**

If the database is not already open, open the data file **AC2-Appointments** and try this skill on your own:

1. If necessary, save and close all open database objects.
2. Open the Relationships window.
3. If necessary, show the *Locations* table and the *Services* table.
4. Create a new relationship between the *Location ID* field in the *Locations* table and the *Location* field in the *Services* table.
5. Enforce data integrity between the two fields.
6. Close the Relationships window, saving the layout changes.

key terms

Quick Start field types
Field Properties pane
Primary key field
AutoNumber data type
Short Text data type
Long Text data type
Number data type
Date/Time data type
Currency data type
Yes/No data type
OLE Object data type
Hyperlink data type
Attachment data type

Calculated Field data type
Format field property
Currency format
Percent format
Comma Style format
Default Value property
Field Size property
Input mask
Attachment field
Total row
Lookup field
Referential integrity

concepts review

1. A well-designed database _____.

   a. repeats important data in multiple tables

   b. stores each unique piece of data in only one table

   c. uses the AutoNumber data type for primary key fields

   d. Both B and C

2. Users can enter and edit data in an AutoNumber field.

   a. True

   b. False

3. To rename a field, _____.

   a. click the column header, and type the new field name

   b. double-click the column header, and type the new field name

   c. right-click the column header, select **Rename Field,** and type the new field name

   d. Both B and C

4. A table's primary key must _____.

   a. use the AutoNumber data type

   b. be linked to other tables

   c. be unique for every field

   d. Be named *ID*

5. To include a photo image with each record in a table, use a field with this data type:

   a. Photo

   b. Attachment

   c. Hyperlink

   d. Memo

6. The Currency field format is the same as the Currency data type.

   a. True

   b. False

7. The Percent field format displays the % symbol in the data table.

   a. True

   b. False

8. To control the number of characters a user can enter into a table field, use _____.

   a. the Field Size property

   b. the Field Width property

   c. the Long Text data type

   d. Rich Text Formatting

9. An input mask _____.

   a. creates a relationship between two tables

   b. modifies the field Format property

   c. changes the field data type to Short Text

   d. forces users to input data in a consistent format

10. If two tables have referential integrity enforced, _____.

   a. you cannot add a record to the secondary table without an associated record in the primary table

   b. you cannot make changes to the primary table that would cause records in the secondary table to become unmatched

   c. Both A and B

   d. None of the above

projects

Data files for projects can be found on
www.mhhe.com/office2013skills

skill review 2.1

In this project, you will continue to work with the Computer Science department database from the *Chapter 1 Skill Review 1.1*. It uses Access to manage employees and various items that are loaned to students and faculty. You will create two new tables in this database: one for the companies that the department frequently purchases from and another with a list of classrooms.

Skills needed to complete this project:

- Designing a Table (Skill 2.1)
- Creating and Saving a Table in Datasheet View (Skill 2.2)
- Renaming Fields (Skill 2.3)
- Changing Data Type (Skill 2.11)
- Adding Fields in Datasheet View (Skill 2.4)
- Using Quick Start to Add Related Fields (Skill 2.5)
- Adjusting Table Column Widths (Skill 2.6)
- Applying an Input Mask from Design View (Skill 2.14)
- Adding a Lookup Field from Another Table (Skill 2.17)
- Formatting Fields (Skill 2.12)
- Modifying Field Properties (Skill 2.13)
- Adding a Total Row to a Table (Skill 2.16)
- Working with Attachment Fields (Skill 2.15)
- Deleting Fields (Skill 2.10)
- Creating a Table in Design View (Skill 2.7)
- Setting the Primary Key (Skill 2.9)
- Inserting Fields in Design View (Skill 2.8)
- Adding a Lookup Field from a List (Skill 2.18)
- Creating Relationships (Skill 2.19)

1. Open the start file **AC2013-SkillReview-2-1**.
2. If necessary, enable active content by clicking the **Enable Content** button in the Message Bar.
3. Save a copy of the file to work on named:
   `[your initials] AC-SkillReview-2-1`
4. Create a table in Datasheet view to store vendor company data.

   a. On the *Create* tab, in the *Tables* group, click the **Table** button.

   b. You are now in the Datasheet view of a new table. Notice that Access has created a new field named *ID* with the AutoNumber data type.

   c. Create the next field by typing `Greg's College Supplies` in the cell directly underneath the **Click to Add** heading.

d. Press `Tab ⇥` to go to the next field in this record.

e. Create another new field by typing: **www.gregscollegesupplies.com**

f. Press `Tab ⇥` again.

g. Go to the next row in the table and enter another record with the following:

Cindy's Business Supplies
www.cindysbusinesssupplies.com

5. Rename the fields.

   a. Right-click the **ID** field heading, and click **Rename Field.**

   b. Type **VendorID** and press `← Enter`.

   c. Repeat the process for **Field1,** renaming it: **CompanyName**

   d. Repeat the process for **Field2,** renaming it: **WebSite**

6. The data type for the *WebSite* field is *Short Text*. Change it to **Hyperlink.**

   a. Click the **WebSite** column header to select the field.

   b. On the *Table Tools Fields* tab, in the *Formatting* group, expand the **Data Type** list, and select **Hyperlink.**

7. Add a new field to the table to store phone numbers.

   a. Click the arrow next to the **Click to Add** heading in the last available field, and select **Short Text.**

   b. Type **Phone** to overwrite the default field name *Field1.*

8. Add a group of related fields using *Quick Start.*

   a. Click the cell underneath the last **Click to Add** heading.

   b. On the *Table Tools Fields* tab, in the *Add & Delete* group, click the **More Fields** button.

   c. Scroll down and select **Address** from the *Quick Start* category.

   d. Observe the five new fields. Type the following data into these new fields:

Address	City	StateProvince	ZipPostal	CountryRegion
370 Pine St	Phoenix	Arizona	85018	USA
900 Finch Way	Phoenix	Arizona	85013	USA

9. Resize all of the columns in this table to the best fit possible by double-clicking the right edge of their field headings.

10. Save the table.

   a. On the Quick Access Toolbar, click the **Save** button.

   b. In the *Save As* dialog, type **Vendors** in the *Table Name* box.

   c. Click **OK.**

11. Switch to Design view.

   a. On the *Home* tab, in the *Views* group, click the **View** button to switch to Design view.

   b. Observe that when you created the new table, Access automatically assigned the *VendorID* field as the primary key.

12. Add an input mask to the new *Phone* field to force users to enter data in the (206) 555-1212 format.

   a. Select the **Phone** field by clicking anywhere in that row.

   b. In the Field Properties pane, click the **Input Mask** box, and then click the **Build...** button to start the *Input Mask Wizard.*

c. The first input mask sample is the phone number format you want. Test it by typing any sample phone number in the *Try It* box. Click **Next** to continue.

d. Click the **Next** button to continue without making any changes to the input mask or the placeholder character.

e. Verify that the radio button to store the data without the symbols is selected, and click **Next.**

f. Click **Finish.**

g. Observe that the Input Mask box now displays the input mask format: **!\(999") "000\-0000;;_**

h. Switch back to Datasheet view by clicking the **Datasheet View** button at the lower right part of the status bar.

i. When Access prompts you to save the table, click **Yes.**

j. Under this field heading, enter the following phone numbers: **(623) 555-6810** for Greg's and **(623) 555-8200** for Cindy's. Notice how the input mask adds the correct characters to the phone number and will prevent you from typing any character other than a number.

13. Close the *Vendors* table. If Access prompts you to save the changes to the table, click **Yes.**

14. Create a *CompanyName* lookup field in the *Items* table using values from the *Vendors* table.

a. Open the *Items* table in Datasheet view.

b. Click the arrow next to the **Click to Add** heading in the last available field, and select **Lookup & Relationship.**

c. In the *Lookup Wizard,* verify that the **I want the lookup field to get the values from another table or query.** radio button is selected, and click **Next.**

d. Select **Table: Vendors** as the table that will provide the values for your lookup field, and click **Next.**

e. From the *Available Fields* list, select the **CompanyName** field and click the single > button to add it to the right. Click **Next.**

f. Click the arrow to expand the **1** list and choose **CompanyName** as the sort field. Observe that even though you added only the *CompanyName* field to the lookup list, Access included the *VendorID* field (the primary key) automatically. Click **Next.**

g. Verify that the **Hide key column (recommended)** check box is checked and that the two companies you entered in the table earlier appear in the lookup field preview. Click **Next.**

h. In the last screen, type **CompanyName** as the label for this new field.

i. Limit data entry to the values in the list by clicking the **Enable Data Integrity** check box.

j. Click **Finish.**

k. Use this new lookup field to add *CompanyName* values for the first three records. Choose **Greg's** for the first two and **Cindy's** for the third.

15. Notice that many of the columns in the table are too narrow and the data are not fully visible.

a. Resize the *ItemName* and *CompanyName* columns to the best fit possible by double-clicking the right edge of their field headings.

b. Resize the *Description* column to be exactly **45** wide.

  i. Click the **Description** column header to select the field.

  ii. On the *Home* tab, in the *Records* group, click the **More** button, and select **Field Width.**

  iii. In the *Column Width* dialog, type **45** in the *Column Width* box.

  iv. Click **OK.**

16. Modify the *Cost* field to use the **Currency** format.

  a. Click the **Cost** column header to select the field.

  b. On the *Table Tools Fields* tab, in the *Formatting* group, click the **Apply Currency Format** button.

  c. Notice that the *Format* box now displays *Currency*.

17. Modify the size of the *ItemID* field.

  a. Click the **ItemID** field heading.

  b. On the *Table Tools Fields* tab, in the *Properties* group, type **4** in the *Field Size* box. Press ⟵ Enter .

  c. Click **Yes** to continue.

  d. If Access shows additional messages, click **OK** to dismiss each one. Changing the field size to 4 will not delete any data or delete the field.

18. Add a Total row to the datasheet to display the sum of the values in the *Cost* field.

  a. On the *Home* tab, in the *Records* group, click the **Totals** button.

  b. In the new Total row, click the cell in the *Cost* column, expand the list, and select **Sum.**

  c. Observe that the *Totals* button appears highlighted. Click it again, and notice that the button is no longer highlighted and the Total row is hidden.

  d. Click the **Totals** button again. The Total row appears again, still displaying the sum of the values in the *Cost* field.

19. Add an *Attachment* field and an attachment.

  a. Click the arrow next to the **Click to Add** heading in the last available field. Select the **Attachment** option.

  b. Find the record with an ID of **LAS1.**

  c. Double-click the paperclip icon for this record, which is located in the new *Attachment* column you just created.

  d. Click **Add** in the *Attachments* dialog and then find the file named **laser_pointer.jpg** in your student data files folder.

  e. Double-click the file and then click **OK.** Note the **(1)** added to the paperclip icon to indicate that the record has one attachment.

20. Delete the *Location* field from the *Items* table.

  a. Click the **Location** field column heading to select the field.

  b. On the *Table Tools Fields* tab, in the *Add & Delete* group, click the **Delete** button.

  c. Click **Yes** to confirm the deletion.

21. Save and close the *Items* table.

22. Close any open tables. If Access prompts you to save changes, click **Yes.**

23. Create a table in Design view:

  a. On the *Create* tab, in the *Tables* group, click the **Table Design** button.

  b. Type **RoomNo** for the first field name. Press Tab ⇄ .

  c. Accept the default data type, Short Text.

d. With the cursor still in this row, on the *Design* tab, in the *Tools* group, click the **Primary Key** button.

e. Create the following fields in Design view:

FieldName	DataType	Description
Capacity	Number	Maximum number of students
UpgradeDate	Date/Time	Date when the instructor's computer was last upgraded

24. Save the table.

    a. On the Quick Access Toolbar, click the **Save** button.

    b. In the *Save As* dialog, type **Classrooms** in the *Table Name* box.

    c. Click **OK.**

25. Modify field properties and formatting in Design view.

    a. Click anywhere in the **UpgradeDate** row. In the Field Properties pane, click in the **Format** box. Click the arrow to expand the selection list, and select **Medium Date.**

    b. Click anywhere in the **Capacity** field. In the Field Properties pane, click in the **Default Value** box. Type: **40**

26. Add a new lookup field to the *Classrooms* table to use values you enter yourself.

    a. Click in the first empty cell in the **Field Name** column and type: **Type**

    b. Press [Tab ⇄] or click in the **Data Type** cell. Expand the selection list, and select **Lookup Wizard...**

    c. In the *Lookup Wizard,* click the **I will type in the values I want,** radio button. Click **Next.**

    d. Use only 1 column and enter the following three values:

        Auditorium

        Computer Lab

        Lecture Room

    e. Click **Next,** and verify that **Type** is the label for the lookup field.

    f. Limit data entry to the values in the list by clicking the **Limit to List** check box.

    g. Click **Finish.**

27. Save and close the table.

28. Review the relationship between the *Vendors* table and the *Items* table.

    a. Open the Relationships window. On the *Database Tools* tab, in the *Relationships* group, click the **Relationships** button.

    b. Show all tables. On the *Relationship Tools Design* tab, in the *Relationships* group, click the **All Relationships** button.

    c. There is a relationship between the *VendorID* field in the *Vendors* table and the *CompanyName* field in the *Items* table. This relationship was created when you created the *CompanyName* lookup field in the *Items* table.

    d. Double-click the line connecting the two field names to open the *Edit Relationships* dialog.

    e. Look at the *Relationship Type* box near the bottom of the dialog and note that the relationship type is one-to-many.

    f. Verify that entries in the *CompanyName* field will have matching entries in the *VendorID* field by noting that the **Enforce Referential Integrity** check box is checked.

    g. Click **OK.**

29. Create a new relationship between the *EmployeeID* field in the *Employees* table and the *EmployeeID* field in the *Loans* table.

   a. Click the **EmployeeID** field in the *Employees* table and drag it to the **EmployeeID** field in the *Loans* table.

   b. The *Edit Relationships* dialog opens.

   c. Click the **Enforce Referential Integrity** check box.

   d. Click **Create.**

   e. Observe the new line connecting the *Employees* table and the *Loans* table.

30. Close the Relationships window. If Access prompts you to save changes to the layout, click **Yes.**

31. Close the database and exit Access.

skill review 2.2

In this project you will continue working with the health insurance database from *Chapter 1, Skill Review 1.2.* You will create two new tables in this database: one that contains a list of all the patients and another for the in-network hospitals that are affiliated with this insurance company.

Skills needed to complete this project:

- Designing a Table (Skill 2.1)
- Creating and Saving a Table in Datasheet View (Skill 2.2)
- Renaming Fields (Skill 2.3)
- Adding Fields in Datasheet View (Skill 2.4)
- Using Quick Start to Add Related Fields (Skill 2.5)
- Modifying Field Properties (Skill 2.13)
- Adding a Total Row to a Table (Skill 2.16)
- Applying an Input Mask from Design View (Skill 2.14)
- Adjusting Table Column Widths (Skill 2.6)
- Adding a Lookup Field from Another Table (Skill 2.17)
- Changing Data Type (Skill 2.11)
- Deleting Fields (Skill 2.10)
- Working with Attachment Fields (Skill 2.15)
- Creating a Table in Design View (Skill 2.7)
- Setting the Primary Key (Skill 2.9)
- Inserting Fields in Design View (Skill 2.8)
- Formatting Fields (Skill 2.12)
- Adding a Lookup Field from a List (Skill 2.18)
- Creating Relationships (Skill 2.19)

1. Open the start file **AC2013-SkillReview-2-2.**

2. If necessary, enable active content by clicking the **Enable Content** button in the Message Bar.

3. Save a copy of the file to work on named:
   `[your initials] AC-SkillReview-2-2`

4. Create a table in Datasheet view to store hospital data.

    a. On the *Create* tab, in the *Tables* group, click the **Table** button.

    b. You are now in the Datasheet view of a new table. Notice that Access has created a new field named *ID* with the AutoNumber data type.

    c. Create the next field by typing **Miami City Hospital** in the cell directly underneath the *Click to Add* heading.

    d. Press ⟨Tab ⇆⟩ to go to the next field in this record.

    e. Create another new field by typing: **87**

    f. Press ⟨Tab ⇆⟩ again.

    g. Enter two more records in the table with the following data:

Central Lauderdale Hospital	59
West Palm Hospital	61

5. Rename the fields.

    a. Right-click the **ID** field heading, and click **Rename Field.**

    b. Type **HospitalID** and press ⟨← Enter⟩.

    c. Repeat the process for **Field1,** renaming it: **HospitalName**

    d. Repeat the process for **Field2,** renaming it: **MemberVisits**

6. Add a new field to the table to store phone numbers.

    a. Click the arrow next to the **Click to Add** heading in the last available field, and select **Short Text.**

    b. Type **Phone** to overwrite the default field name *Field1.*

7. Add a group of related fields using *Quick Start.*

    a. Click the cell underneath the last *Click to Add* heading.

    b. On the *Table Tools Fields* tab, in the *Add & Delete* group, click the **More Fields** button.

    c. Scroll down and select **Address** from the *Quick Start* category.

    d. Observe the five new fields. Type the following data into these new fields:

Address	City	StateProvince	ZipPostal	CountryRegion
4500 Miami Blvd	Miami	FL	33126	USA
320 Palmer Rd	Ft. Lauderdale	FL	33301	USA
800 Jefferson St	West Palm Beach	FL	33403	USA

8. Modify the size of the *State Providence* field.

    a. Click the **State Providence** field heading.

    b. On the *Table Tools Fields* tab, in the *Properties* group, type **2** in the *Field Size* box. Press ⟨← Enter⟩.

    c. Click **Yes** to continue.

    d. If Access shows additional messages, click **OK** to dismiss each one. Changing the field size to 2 will not delete any data or delete the field.

9. Add a Total row to the datasheet to display the average of the values in the *MemberVisits* field.

    a. On the *Home* tab, in the *Records* group, click the **Totals** button.

    b. In the new Total row, click the cell in the *MemberVisits* column, expand the list, and select **Average.**

c. Observe that the *Totals* button appears highlighted. Click it again, and notice that the button is no longer highlighted and the Total row is hidden.

d. Click the **Totals** button again. The Total row appears again, still displaying the average of the values in the *MemberVisits* field.

10. Save the table.

    a. On the Quick Access Toolbar, click the **Save** button.

    b. In the *Save As* dialog, type **Hospitals** in the *Table Name* box.

    c. Click **OK.**

11. Switch to Design view.

    a. On the *Home* tab, in the *Views* group, click the **View** button to switch to Design view.

    b. Observe that when you created the new table, Access automatically assigned the *HospitalID* field as the primary key.

12. Add an input mask to the new *Phone* field to force users to enter data in the (206) 555-1212 format.

    a. Select the **Phone** field by clicking anywhere in that row.

    b. In the Field Properties pane, click the **Input Mask** box, and then click the **Build...** button to start the *Input Mask Wizard.*

    c. The first input mask sample is the phone number format you want. Test it by typing any sample phone number in the *Try It* box. Click **Next** to continue.

    d. Click the **Next** button to continue without making any changes to the input mask or the placeholder character.

    e. Verify that the radio button to store the data without the symbols is selected, and click **Next.**

    f. Click **Finish.**

    g. Observe that the Input Mask box now displays the input mask format: !\(999") "000\-0000;;_

    h. Switch back to Datasheet view by clicking the **Datasheet View** button at the lower right part of the status bar.

    i. When Access prompts you to save the table, click **Yes.**

    j. Under this field heading, enter the following phone numbers: **(305) 555-1100** for Miami; **(954) 555-2000** for Lauderdale; **(561) 555-6500** for West Palm. Notice how the input mask adds the correct characters to the phone number and will prevent you from typing any character other than a number.

13. Resize all of the columns in this table to the best fit possible by double-clicking the right edge of their field headings.

14. Close the *Hospitals* table. If Access prompts you to save the changes to the table, click **Yes.**

15. Create a *HospitalName* lookup field in the *Physicians* table using values from the *Hospitals* table.

    a. Open the *Physicians* table in Datasheet view.

    b. Click the arrow next to the **Click to Add** heading in the last available field, and select **Lookup & Relationship.**

    c. In the *Lookup Wizard,* verify that the **I want the lookup field to get the values from another table or query.** radio button is selected, and click **Next.**

    d. Select **Table: Hospitals** as the table that will provide the values for your lookup field, and click **Next.**

e. From the *Available Fields* list, select the **HospitalName** field and click the single > button to add it to the right. Click **Next**.

f. Click the arrow to expand the **1** list and choose **HospitalName** as the sort field. Observe that even though you added only the *HospitalName* field to the lookup list, Access included the *HospitalID* field (the primary key) automatically. Click **Next**.

g. Verify that the **Hide key column (recommended)** check box is checked and that the three hospitals you entered in the table earlier appear in the lookup field preview. Click **Next**.

h. In the last screen, type `HopitalName` as the label for this new field.

i. Limit data entry to the values in the list by clicking the **Enable Data Integrity** check box.

j. Click **Finish**.

k. Use this new lookup field to add *HospitalName* values for the first three records. Choose **West Palm Hospital** for the first two and **Central Lauderale Hospital** for the third.

l. Adjust the width of the *HospitalName* field to best fit the data by double-clicking the right edge of the field heading.

16. Modify the *MemberCount* field to use the **Number** data type instead of the *Currency* data type.

a. Click the **MemberCount** column header to select the field.

b. On the *Table Tools Fields* tab, in the *Formatting* group, expand the **Data Type** list, and select **Number.**

c. Notice that the *Format* box no longer displays *Currency*. It is not necessary to specify a format for this field.

17. Delete the *YearsInPractice* field.

a. Click the **YearsInPractice** field column heading to select the field.

b. On the *Table Tools Fields* tab, in the *Add & Delete* group, click the **Delete** button.

c. Click **Yes** to confirm the deletion.

18. Add an *Attachment* field and an attachment to the *Physicians* table.

a. Click the arrow next to the **Click to Add** heading in the last available field. Select the **Attachment** option.

b. Go to the record for **Antonio Gonzalez,** and double-click the paperclip icon, which is located in the new *Attachment* column you just created.

c. Click **Add** in the *Attachments* dialog and then find the file named **Gonzalez.jpg** in your student data files folder.

d. Double-click the file and then click **OK.** Note the **(1)** added to the paperclip icon to indicate that the record has one attachment.

19. Close any open tables. If Access prompts you to save changes, click **Yes.**

20. Create a table in Design view:

a. On the *Create* tab, in the *Tables* group, click the **Table Design** button.

b. Type `MemberID` for the first field name. Press (Tab ⇆).

c. Accept the default data type, *Short Text*. Press (Tab ⇆).

d. Enter the following in the Description: `First letter of last name followed by a randomly generated seven-digit number`

e. With the cursor still in this row, on the *Design* tab, in the *Tools* group, click the **Primary Key** button.

f. Create the following fields in Design view. None of these fields require a description.

FieldName	DataType
FirstName	Short Text
LastName	Short Text
Address	Short Text
City	Short Text
State	Short Text
Zip	Number
DOB	Date/Time

21. Save the table.

    a. On the Quick Access Toolbar, click the **Save** button.

    b. In the *Save As* dialog, type **Patients** in the *Table Name* box.

    c. Click **OK.**

22. Modify field properties and formatting in Design view.

    a. Click anywhere in the **DOB** row. In the Field Properties pane, click in the **Format** box. Click the arrow to expand the selection list, and select **Short Date.**

    b. Click anywhere in the **State** field. In the Field Properties pane, click in the **Default Value** box. Type: **FL**

23. Add a new lookup field to the *Patients* table to use values you enter yourself.

    a. Click in the first empty cell in the **Field Name** column and type: **Gender**

    b. Press ⟨Tab ⇆⟩ or click in the **Data Type** cell. Expand the selection list, and select **Lookup Wizard...**

    c. In the *Lookup Wizard,* click the **I will type in the values I want.** radio button. Click **Next.**

    d. Use only 1 column and enter the following two values:

        Female

        Male

    e. Click **Next,** and verify that **Gender** is the label for the lookup field.

    f. Limit data entry to the values in the list by clicking the **Limit to List** check box.

    g. Click **Finish.**

    h. Save and close the table.

24. Review the relationship between the *Physicians* table and the *Hospitals* table.

    a. Open the Relationships window. On the *Database Tools* tab, in the *Relationships* group, click the **Relationships** button.

    b. Show all tables. On the *Relationship Tools Design* tab, in the *Relationships* group, click the **All Relationships** button.

    c. If necessary, click and drag the **Hospitals** table so you can see the line connecting the *Hospitals* table and the *Physicians* table.

    d. There is a relationship between the *HospitalID* field in the *Hospitals* table and the *HospitalName* field in the *Physicians* table. This relationship was created when you created the *HospitalName* lookup field in the *Physicians* table.

    e. Double-click the line connecting the two field names to open the *Edit Relationships* dialog.

f. Look at the *Relationship Type* box near the bottom of the dialog and note that the relationship type is one-to-many.

g. Verify that entries in the *CompanyName* field will have matching entries in the *VendorID* field by observing that the **Enforce Referential Integrity** check box is checked.

h. Click **OK.**

25. Create a new relationship between the *ProcedureID* field in the *Procedures* table and the *ProcedureID* field in the *Orders* table.

  a. Click the **ProcedureID** field in the *Procedures* table and drag it to the **ProcedureID** field in the *Orders* table.

  b. The *Edit Relationships* dialog opens.

  c. Click the **Enforce Referential Integrity** check box.

  d. Click **Create.**

  e. Observe the new line connecting the *Procedures* table and the *Orders* table.

26. Close the Relationships window. If Access prompts you to save changes to the layout, click **Yes.**

27. Close the database and exit Access.

challenge yourself 2.3

In this project you will continue working with the greenhouse database from *Chapter 1, Challenge Yourself 1.3.* You will add a table to keep track of the fertilizers used in the greenhouse and the plants that use them.

Skills needed to complete this project:

- Designing a Table (Skill 2.1)
- Creating and Saving a Table in Datasheet View (Skill 2.2)
- Renaming Fields (Skill 2.3)
- Adding Fields in Datasheet View (Skill 2.4)
- Changing Data Type (Skill 2.11)
- Deleting Fields (Skill 2.10)
- Inserting Fields in Design View (Skill 2.8)
- Setting the Primary Key (Skill 2.9)
- Adding a Lookup Field from a List (Skill 2.18)
- Adding a Total Row to a Table (Skill 2.16)
- Adding a Lookup Field from Another Table (Skill 2.17)
- Adjusting Table Column Widths (Skill 2.6)
- Using Quick Start to Add Related Fields (Skill 2.5)
- Working with Attachment Fields (Skill 2.15)
- Formatting Fields (Skill 2.12)
- Modifying Field Properties (Skill 2.13)
- Creating Relationships (Skill 2.19)

1. Open the start file **AC2013-ChallengeYourself-2-3.**

2. If necessary, enable active content by clicking the **Enable Content** button in the Message Bar.

3. Save a copy of the file to work on named:
   `[your initials]AC-ChallengeYourself-2-3`

4. Create a new table in Datasheet view using the following data. Allow Access to create the *AutoNumber ID* field for now. Name the table: `Fertilizers`

FertilizerName	NutrientRatio	Price
Monoammonium phosphate	11-52-0	$25
Polymer Coated Urea	44-0-0	$35
Nitrogen Solution	28-0-0	$12

5. If necessary, change the format of the *Price* field to use the **Currency** format.

6. Delete the *ID* field that Access created and add a new primary key field. Switch back and forth between Datasheet view and Design view as necessary, saving the table when prompted to do so by Access.

   a. Delete the **ID** field.

   b. Insert a new field at the beginning of the table. Name the field: `FertID`

   c. Set the Data Type to **Short Text.**

   d. Enter the following three values (in the appropriate record) under the **FertID** field: `MAP1, PCU1, NSO1`

   e. Make the **FertID** field the Primary Key.

7. Add a new lookup field. You can use Datasheet view or Design view, whichever you prefer.

   a. Name the new field: **Form**

   b. The lookup field should display the following four values: **Granule, Liquid, Slow-Release, Organic**

   c. Limit data entry to the values in the list.

   d. Save the changes to the table.

8. Add a Total row in Datasheet view that sums up all the fertilizer prices.

9. Save and close the *Fertilizers* table.

10. Open the *Plants* table and make the following changes:

    a. Add a lookup field named `PreferredFertilizer` to the *Plants* table to reference the *FertilizerName* field in the *Fertilizers* table. The lookup list should be sorted alphabetically by the FertilizerName data. It is not necessary to limit values to the list.

    b. Test this field by choosing any fertilizer for the first three plants.

    c. Resize all the columns in the table to best fit the data.

    d. Add an *Attachment* field. Add the image **geranium.jpg** to the record for the **spotted geranium.**

    e. Change the Format property of the *DatePlanted* field to **Medium Date.**

    f. Set the Default Value property for the *FlowerColor* field to **white** and add a Description for this field that reads: `Main color only. Do not enter multiple colors.`

    g. Save and close the table.

11. Review the table relationships and make the following changes.

    a. Show all the tables in the Relationships window.

    b. Create a one-to-many relationship between the **PlantID** field in the **Plants** table and the **PlantID** field in the **MaintenanceLog** table. Enforce referential integrity.

c. Modify the relationship between the **FertID** field in the **Fertilizers** table and the **PreferredFertilizer** field in the **Plants** table to enforce referential integrity.

d. Close the Relationships window, saving the layout changes.

12. Close the database and exit Access.

challenge yourself **2.4**

In this project you will continue working with the vaccines database from *Chapter 1, Challenge Yourself 1.4.* You will add a table to the database to track volunteer information.

Skills needed to complete this project:

- Designing a Table (Skill 2.1)
- Creating and Saving a Table in Datasheet View (Skill 2.2)
- Renaming Fields (Skill 2.3)
- Adding Fields in Datasheet View (Skill 2.4)
- Using Quick Start to Add Related Fields (Skill 2.5)
- Setting the Primary Key (Skill 2.9)
- Formatting Fields (Skill 2.12)
- Adding a Lookup Field from a List (Skill 2.18)
- Modifying Field Properties (Skill 2.13)
- Working with Attachment Fields (Skill 2.15)
- Adding a Lookup Field from Another Table (Skill 2.17)
- Adjusting Table Column Widths (Skill 2.6)
- Adding a Total Row to a Table (Skill 2.16)
- Changing Data Type (Skill 2.11)
- Creating Relationships (Skill 2.19)

1. Open the start file **AC2013-ChallengeYourself-2-4**.

2. If necessary, enable active content by clicking the **Enable Content** button in the Message Bar.

3. Save a copy of the file to work on named:
[your initials]AC-ChallengeYourself-2-4

4. Create a new table to keep track of volunteer information. Use Datasheet view and/or Design view as appropriate.

a. Name the table: **Volunteers**

b. Enter the following data and fields as shown below. If you use the **Name** *Quick Start* option to add the first name and last name fields be sure to rename them to match the format shown below.

VolunteerID	LastName	FirstName	DOB
R56623	Richardson	Tyra	5/9/80
G33390	Graham	Susan	3/28/72
H58892	Hernandez	Mario	5/11/67

c. Set the **VolunteerID** field as the *Primary Key* field.

d. Set the format of the **DOB** field to **Medium Date**.

    e. Add a lookup field to display the following three values:

        `Clerical, Manager, Nurse`

    f. Name the new lookup field: `Position`

    g. Set the default value of the **Position** field to **Nurse.**

    h. Add a new *Attachment* field. Attach the photo **sgraham.jpg** to the **Susan Graham** record.

5. Save and close the *Volunteers* table.

6. Add a new lookup field named `LeadVolunteer` to the *Locations* table to include both the **FirstName** and **LastName** fields from the *Volunteers* table. Sort the lookup list alphabetically by the **LastName** field. Test this field by choosing employee **Mario Hernandez** for the first location and employee **Susan Graham** for the second. Resize the datasheet column as necessary to best fit the data.

7. Save and close the *Locations* table.

8. Make the following modifications to the *Shipments* table. Work in Datasheet view or Design view as appropriate.

    a. Resize the **DateShipped** and **Cost** columns to best fit the data.

    b. Add a Total row that sums up all the amounts in the **Cost** field.

    c. Change the Data Type of the **Quantity** field from *Text* to **Number.** If Access warns about potential data loss, just click Yes to proceed.

9. Save and close the *Shipments* table.

10. If necessary, modify the table relationships to enforce referential integrity between the *Locations* table and *Volunteers* table relationship. Hint: Display all the tables in the Relationships window if the *Volunteers* table is not visible.

11. Close the Relationships window, saving any layout changes.

12. Close the database and exit Access.

on your own 2.5

In this project, you will continue working with the movie database from *Chapter 1, On Your Own 1.5.* You will create a new table to track and organize your home/vacation movies. These are the movies you recorded with your camcorder, such as your son's first birthday and your vacation in Hawaii.

Skills needed to complete this project:

- Designing a Table (Skill 2.1)
- Creating and Saving a Table in Datasheet View (Skill 2.2)
- Renaming Fields (Skill 2.3)
- Adding Fields in Datasheet View (Skill 2.4)
- Creating a Table in Design View (Skill 2.7)
- Inserting Fields in Design View (Skill 2.8)
- Setting the Primary Key (Skill 2.9)
- Adding a Lookup Field from a List (Skill 2.18)
- Adjusting Table Column Widths (Skill 2.6)
- Adding a Total Row to a Table (Skill 2.16)
- Modifying Field Properties (Skill 2.13)

1. Open the start file **AC2013-OnYourOwn-2-5**.

2. If necessary, enable active content by clicking the **Enable Content** button in the Message Bar.

3. Save a copy of the file to work on named:
   `[your initials] AC-OnYourOwn-2-5`

4. Create a **HomeMovies** table and add at least five fields that you believe are appropriate for this type of collection. At a minimum, you must have:

   a. An ID for each movie. This field will serve as the primary key.

   b. A name for each movie.

   c. The running time for each movie in minutes.

   d. The other two (or more) fields are your choice.

5. Demonstrate your knowledge of lookup fields by creating a value list in one of your fields.

6. Enter data for least four home/vacation movies. They can be real or fictional.

7. Resize columns in Datasheet view if necessary.

8. Calculate the total number of minutes in your home movie collection using a Total row.

9. Modify at least two Field Properties for one or more fields in your table.

10. Close the database and exit Access.

fix it 2.6

In this project, you will continue working with the pet store database from *Chapter 1, Fix It 1.6*. Once again, one of the employees has messed up the database, and it's up to you to fix it. This time, you'll implement a few changes to make it harder for employees to make data entry errors.

Skills needed to complete this project:

- Adding a Lookup Field from a List (Skill 2.18)
- Formatting Fields (Skill 2.12)
- Deleting Fields (Skill 2.10)
- Adding Fields in Datasheet View (Skill 2.4)
- Inserting Fields in Design View (Skill 2.8)
- Working with Attachment Fields (Skill 2.15)
- Adding a Total Row to a Table (Skill 2.16)
- Using Quick Start to Add Related Fields (Skill 2.5)
- Modifying Field Properties (Skill 2.13)

1. Open the start file **AC2013-FixIt-2-6**.

2. If necessary, enable active content by clicking the **Enable Content** button in the Message Bar.

3. Save a copy of the file to work on named: `[your initials] AC-FixIt-2-6`

4. Fix the *Pets* table as follows:

   a. In this store, there are only two types of pets sold: cats and dogs. Edit the **AnimalType** field so that these are the only two choices for this field. Do not allow any other type of animal to be entered.

b. The **Price** field should display the numbers using $ and two decimal places.

c. The store realizes it rarely types in the cage number for each animal it receives. Therefore, remove the **CageNum** field from the table.

d. The store needs to keep vaccination information. Add a new field named **Vaccines** that only accepts a yes or no value.

e. Add another new field that can store photographs and insert the **poodle.jpg** image for the record with the Poodle breed.

f. The store needs to know the total price of its pet inventory. Enable the feature that displays a total row in Datasheet view and show the sum of the prices.

g. Save and close the table.

5. Fix the *Sales* table as follows:

   a. The dates in the *Sales* table should look like this: **30-Jun-10**

   b. Add a new field in Datasheet view using the **Payment Type** *Quick Start* option.

   c. Save and close the table.

6. Fix the *Customers* table as follows:

   a. The default value for the *Newsletter* field should be **1** so that it appears checked every time you create a new record.

   b. The *CustomerID* field should never have a value with more than **4** characters and it should be the primary key.

   c. Save and close the table.

7. Open each table in Datasheet view and look at the columns closely. Two columns need to be larger. Find them and resize them.

8. Close the database and exit Access.

chapter 3

Working with Forms and Reports

In this chapter, you will learn the following skills:

- ❯ Create a variety of forms
- ❯ Create a variety of reports
- ❯ Add controls to forms and reports
- ❯ Resize and arrange controls
- ❯ Add formatting to forms and reports
- ❯ Add header and footer elements
- ❯ Group and total data in a report
- ❯ Modify the page settings and print a report

skills

introduction

In this chapter, you will learn to create a variety of forms and reports, including using the *Form Wizard* and the *Report Wizard*. You will also learn to create a form and a report from scratch in Layout view and add controls, formatting, and header and footer elements. You will work with grouping in reports and calculate totals using the automatic tools in Layout view. Finally, you will use Print Preview view to preview the printed report and make page layout adjustments before printing. The *Let Me Try* exercises in this chapter use the AC3-Appointments database. You can keep the database open while you work in this chapter, opening and closing database objects as required for each *Let Me Try*.

Skill 3.1 Creating a Single Record Form Based on a Table or Query

While you can enter data directly in a table in Datasheet view, a form provides a more user-friendly data entry format. Remember, a form displays data from an underlying table or query and allows database users to enter, edit, and delete data, but it does not contain records or data itself. It is only an interface to the underlying table or query (the **record source**). The easiest form to create is a simple Single Record form. A **Single Record form** displays one record at a time.

To create a Single Record form based on a table or query:

1. In the Navigation Pane, select the table or query record source for your form.
2. On the *Create* tab, in the *Forms* group, click the **Form** button.
3. When you save the form, notice that the default name in the *Form Name* box is the same as the name of the table or query that you based the form on. Type a new name if you want to use something else.

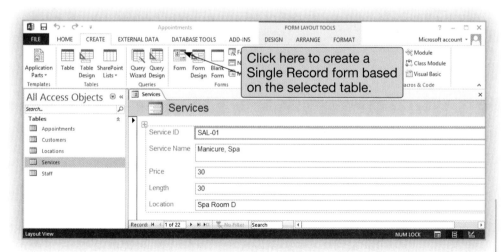

FIGURE AC 3.1
A Single Record form based on the selected table, *Services*

tips & tricks

If Access finds a one-to-many relationship between the table you are basing the form on and another table, Access automatically inserts a Datasheet subform at the bottom of the form. The Datasheet subform displays the records from the related table.

let me try

If the database is not already open, open the data file **AC3-Appointments** and try this skill on your own:
1. Create a Single Record form from the **Services** table.
2. Save the form as: **ServicesForm**
3. Close the form.

Skill 3.2 Creating a Multiple Items Form

Some form types display all the records at once. A **Datasheet form** reproduces the exact look and layout of the table datasheet as a form. A **Multiple Items form** has a similar layout displaying multiple records at once. However, a Multiple Items form is more flexible than a Datasheet form because you can modify the layout and design of a Multiple Items form. Use a Multiple Items form when you need to see multiple records at the same time.

To create a Multiple Items form:

1. In the Navigation Pane, select the table or query record source for your form.

2. On the *Create* tab, in the *Forms* group, click the **More Forms** button, and select **Multiple Items.**

3. When you save the form, notice that the default name in the *Form Name* box is the same as the name of the table or query that you based the form on. Type a new name if you want to use something else.

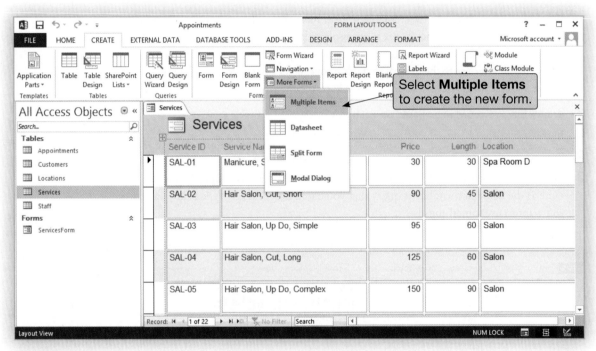

FIGURE AC 3.2
A Multiple Items form based on the selected table, *Services*

let me try

If the database is not already open, open the data file **AC3-Appointments** and try this skill on your own:

1. Create a Multiple Items form from the **Services** table.
2. Save the form as: `ServicesFormMulti`
3. Close the form.

Skill 3.3 Creating a Split Form

A **Split form** combines the convenience of a continuous Datasheet form with the usability of a Single Record form displaying one record at a time. In a Split form, both formats are displayed and work together, so when you navigate records in one section, the other section synchronizes. Use a Split form when you need to see a large group of records at one time while having quick access to an individual record's details.

To create a Split form:

1. In the Navigation Pane, select the table or query record source for your form.
2. On the *Create* tab, in the *Forms* group, click the **More Forms** button, and select **Split Form.**
3. When you save the form, notice that the default name in the *Form Name* box is the same as the name of the table or query that you based the form on. Type a new name if you want to use something else.

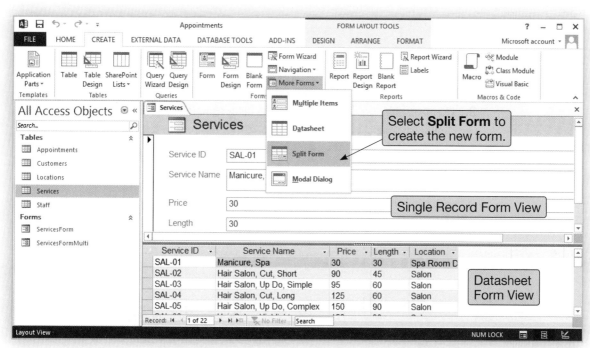

FIGURE AC 3.3
A Split form based on the selected table, *Services*

tips & tricks

The Datasheet form at the bottom of the Split form is not a subform; it is a special form view showing the same dataset.

let me try

If the database is not already open, open the data file **AC3-Appointments** and try this skill on your own:
1. Create a Split form from the **Services** table.
2. Save the form as: `ServicesFormSplit`
3. Close the form.

Skill 3.4 Creating a Form Using the Form Wizard

Another easy way to begin a new form is to use the **Form Wizard**. Instead of automatically creating a form that includes every field in the underlying table, the *Form Wizard* walks you through the steps of creating the form, including selecting fields and a layout. You can use the *Form Wizard* to create a form combining fields from multiple related tables.

To create a new form using the *Form Wizard:*

1. On the *Create* tab, in the *Forms* group, click the **Form Wizard** button.

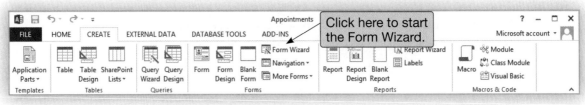

FIGURE AC 3.4

2. The *Form Wizard* opens. The first step is to expand the *Tables/Queries* list and select the underlying table or query for your form.

3. The *Available Fields* box displays all the fields from the table or query you selected. Double-click a field to move it to the *Selected Fields* box or click the field name once to select it and then click the **>** button. Click the **>>** button to add all the available fields with a single click.

4. If you want to include fields from more than one table or query, repeat steps 2 and 3 until you have selected all the fields you want in your form. Click the **Next** button to go to the next step.

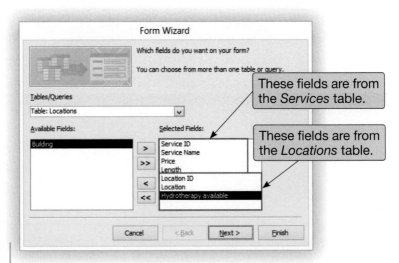

FIGURE AC 3.5

5. If you selected fields from related tables, the next step in the wizard asks how you want to organize the data in the form. To create a form with a subform, in the *How do you want to view your data?* box, select the table that is the "one" part of the one-to-many relationship. The wizard will create a **subform**—a form within the form—to display the related records from the "many" table. Verify that the **Form with subform(s)** radio button is selected, and then click **Next.**

In Figure AC 3.6, the records in the *Locations* table are related to records in the *Services* table in a one-to-many relationship where the record in the *Locations* table is the "one" part of the relationship. The *Form with subform(s)* option will create a Single Record form for each *Locations* record with a subform displaying all the related records from the *Services* table.

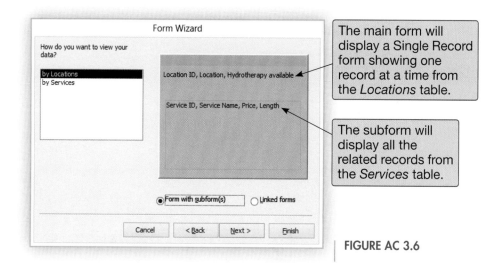

FIGURE AC 3.6

If you selected fields from only one table or query, you will not see this step.

6. The next step asks you to select layout options. If your form includes a subform, select a layout for the subform: **Tabular** or **Datasheet.** If the form does not include a subform, you can select from a list of layout options for the main form: **Columnar, Tabular, Datasheet,** or **Justified.** Click the radio button for the layout option you want, and then click **Next.**

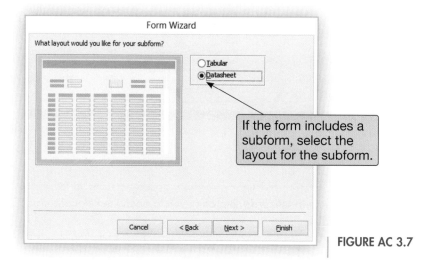

FIGURE AC 3.7

7. Enter a title for the form. If your form includes a subform, enter the title for the subform as well. The subform will be saved as a separate database object. Select whether you want to open the form to view and enter information (Form view) or modify the form's design (Design view).

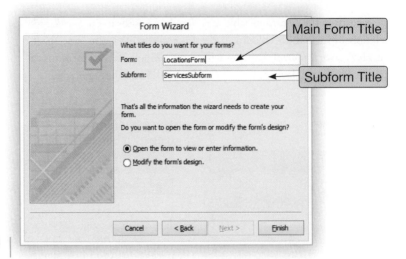

FIGURE AC 3.8

8. Click **Finish** to save the form.

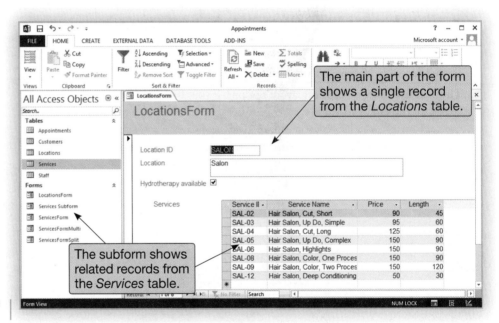

FIGURE AC 3.9

tips & tricks

If you try to combine fields from tables that are not related, the *Form Wizard* will prompt you to open the Relationships window to create the appropriate relationships between the tables.

let me try

If the database is not already open, open the data file **AC3-Appointments** and try this skill on your own:
1. Use the *Form Wizard* to create a new form. Include the **Service ID**, **Service Name**, **Price**, and **Length** fields from the *Services* table and the **Location ID**, **Location**, and **Hydrotherapy available** fields from the *Locations* table.
2. View the data by the *Locations* table, with related data from the *Services* table as a subform.
3. Use the **Datasheet** layout option for the subform.
4. Name the main form: **LocationsForm** and the subform: **ServicesSubform**
5. Close the form.

Skill 3.5 Creating a New Blank Form

One way to start a new form is to begin with a blank form and add fields from tables and queries manually. You can start a new blank form directly in either Layout view or Design view. Layout view may be easier to work with, but if you need to add advanced controls, you'll need to work in Design view instead.

To create a new blank form directly in Layout view, on the *Create* tab, in the *Forms* group, click the **Blank Form** button.

To create a new blank form directly in Design view, on the *Create* tab, in the *Forms* group, click the **Form Design** button.

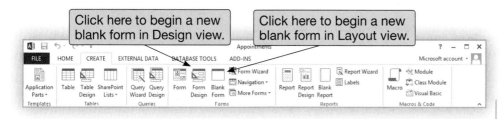

FIGURE AC 3.10

Notice that there are no records in the new form. The new blank form does not have a record source defined. The form is an empty layout until you add controls.

FIGURE AC 3.11
A new blank form in Layout view

tips & tricks

Access will sometimes select a table or query to use as the record source for the form based on the object selected in the Navigation Pane or based on the first table listed in the Navigation Pane. If this is not the record source you want to use for the form, don't worry. The record source will be updated as you add fields.

let me try

If the database is not already open, open the data file **AC3-Appointments** and try this skill on your own:
1. Create a new blank form so it opens directly in Design view.
2. Close the form without saving it.
3. Create a new blank form so it opens directly in Layout view.
4. Save the form as: **TestForm**

Skill 3.6 Adding Fields to a Form in Layout View

If you are starting with a blank form, you will need to add **controls** to display field data. The most common type of control is the **text box control**. Text box controls can display text, numbers, dates, and similar data. A text box control that displays data from a table or query field is called a **bound control** because it is connected (bound) to the field. **Unbound controls** are not connected to field data directly.

Adding a field to a blank form places two controls in a **stacked layout** where an unbound text control, called a **label control**, displays the name of the field to the left of a bound text box control displaying the field data.

To add a field to a form in Layout view:

1. If necessary, on the *Form Layout Tools Design* tab, in the *Tools* group, click the **Add Existing Fields** button to display the *Field List* pane.

2. In the *Field List* pane, click the + in front of the table or query that contains the field(s) you want to add.

3. Double-click a field name to add it to the form. A new bound control is automatically created at the top of the form, along with a label control.

4. To edit the text in a label control, double-click the control to place the cursor within the text. Edit the text normally.

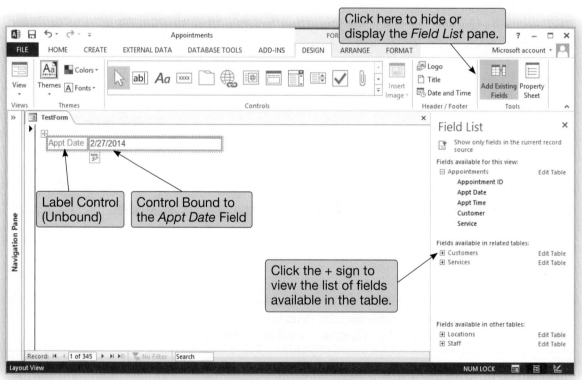

FIGURE AC 3.12

5. To add a second column to the stacked layout, click a field name in the *Field List,* and drag it to the right of the field you just added. Access displays an I-bar shape to indicate where the controls will be placed.

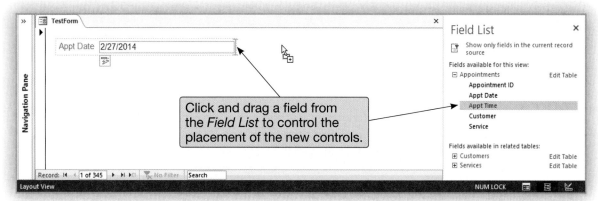

FIGURE AC 3.13

If you double-click the field name instead of dragging it, Access will maintain the single column stacked layout and add the new controls below the currently selected control.

6. Continue adding fields and editing labels until your form is complete. You can add fields to any space in the layout grid using the click-and-drag method. If you look closely, you can see the dotted lines outlining the grid. Use these lines as a guide when you are dragging fields to the layout.

FIGURE AC 3.14

7. Save the form, and then switch to Form view to verify that it looks and behaves as you expect.

FIGURE AC 3.15
The final form in Form view

tips & tricks

tell me **more**

To delete a control, click the control once to select it and then press (Delete) or (← Backspace). If you delete a bound text box control, Access will delete the associated label control as well if there is one.

another **method**

If you prefer working in Design view, you can add fields using the same procedures as described for working in Layout view.

let me **try**

If the database is not already open, open the data file **AC3-Appointments** and try this skill on your own:

1. If necessary, open the *TestForm* form in Layout view. If your database does not include this form, create a new blank form in Layout view and save it as: **TestForm**
2. If necessary, display the *Field List* pane.
3. Add the **Appt Date** field from the *Appointments* table to the form.
4. Add the **Appt Time** field from the *Appointments* table to the form, creating another layout column to the right of the *Appt Time* control.
5. Add the **Customer** field from the *Appointments* table below the *Appt Date* controls.
6. Add the **Last Name** and **First Name** fields from the *Customers* table so they appear below the *Customer* controls.
7. Add the **Service** field from the *Appointments* table so it appears in the same column as the *Appt Time* controls in the same row as the *Last Name* controls.
8. Change the text in the *Appt Date* label control to: **Date**
9. Change the text in the *Appt Time* label control to: **Time**
10. Save the form.
11. Switch to Form view and try adding a new appointment in the form. Notice that when you select a different customer from the *Customer* drop-down list, the values in the *Last Name* and *First Name* bound text box controls update. This is because the *Customer* field in the *Appointments* table is a look-up field referencing the *Customer* table.
12. Close the form.

Skill 3.7 Creating a Basic Report Based on a Table or Query

A report displays data from a table or query in a format suitable for printing. Like forms, reports depend on a record source for their data. Unlike forms, you cannot enter new data into a report. The easiest way to create a new report is to use the *Report* button.

To create a basic report based on a table or query:

1. In the Navigation Pane, select the table or query record source for your report.
2. On the *Create* tab, in the *Reports* group, click the **Report** button.
3. When you save the report, notice that the default name in the *Report Name* box is the same as the name of the table or query that you based the report on. Type a new name if you want to use something else.

In addition to the report title at the upper left side of the report header, the report includes the date and time in the upper-right corner of the header and the page number centered in the page footer.

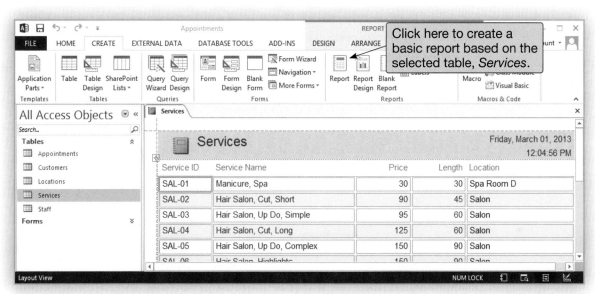

FIGURE AC 3.16
A basic report based on the selected table, *Services*

tips & tricks

The basic report layout is a simple grid with each record displayed as a new row similar to the Multiple Items form. If your report has many columns, this format may not fit on a single page.

let me try

If the database is not already open, open the data file **AC3-Appointments** and try this skill on your own:
1. Create a basic report from the **Services** table.
2. Save the report as: `ServicesReport`
3. Close the report.

Skill 3.8 Creating a Report Using the Report Wizard

The **Report Wizard** walks you step by step through the process of creating a report. The *Report Wizard* allows you to combine fields from more than one table or query and gives you more layout and design options than using the basic *Report* button from the *Create* tab.

To create a report using the *Report Wizard:*

1. On the *Create* tab, in the *Reports* group, click the **Report Wizard** button.

FIGURE AC 3.17

2. The *Report Wizard* opens. The first step is to expand the *Tables/Queries* list and select the underlying table or query for your report.

3. The *Available Fields* box displays all the fields from the table or query you selected. Double-click a field name to move it to the *Selected Fields* box or click the field name once to select it and then click the **>** button. Click the **>>** button to add all the available fields with a single click.

4. If you want to include fields from more than one table or query, repeat steps 2 and 3 until you have selected all the fields you want in your report. Click the **Next** button to go to the next step.

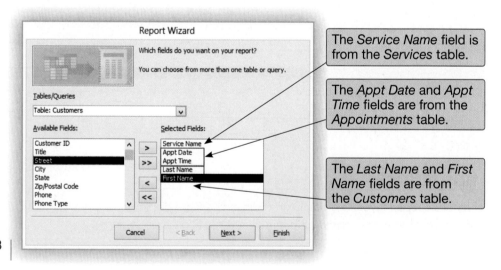

FIGURE AC 3.18

5. If you selected fields from related tables, the next step in the wizard asks how you want to organize the data in the report. Select the table that contains the field you want to use as the main grouping in the report, and then click **Next.** You will have the opportunity to add additional grouping levels in the next step.

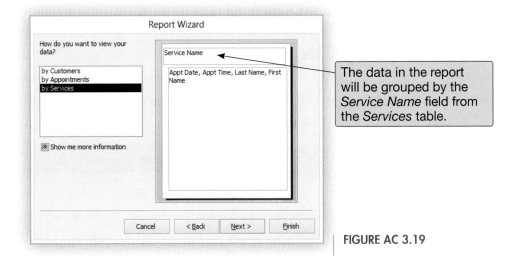

The data in the report will be grouped by the *Service Name* field from the *Services* table.

FIGURE AC 3.19

If you selected fields from only one table or query, you will not see this step.

6. Use grouping levels to organize the data into subgroups by the value of a specific field. Select the field you want to group by and then click the ▶ button. You can add multiple grouping levels and reorder them if necessary using the *Priority* up and down arrows. When you are finished selecting grouping levels, click **Next.**

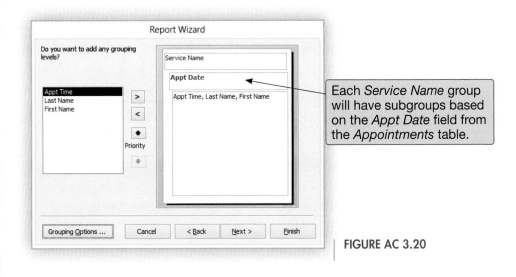

Each *Service Name* group will have subgroups based on the *Appt Date* field from the *Appointments* table.

FIGURE AC 3.20

7. Next, specify how you want the data in each subgroup sorted. Expand the sort level list and select the field you want. You can include up to four fields to sort by. Click **Next.**

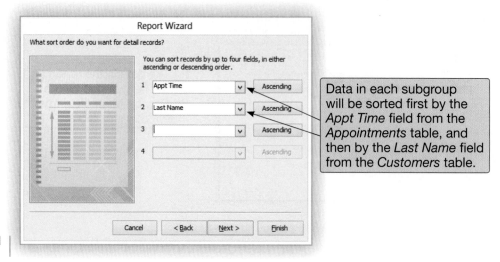

FIGURE AC 3.21

Data in each subgroup will be sorted first by the *Appt Time* field from the *Appointments* table, and then by the *Last Name* field from the *Customers* table.

8. Select the report layout, and select whether you want to print in **Portrait** or **Landscape** orientation. Click **Next.**

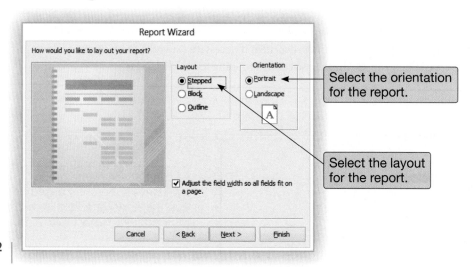

FIGURE AC 3.22

Select the orientation for the report.

Select the layout for the report.

9. Give your report a meaningful title, and choose whether to preview how the report will look when printed (Print Preview view) or to modify its design (Design view).

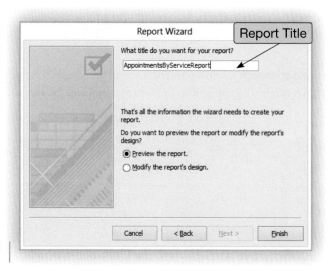

FIGURE AC 3.23

Report Title

10. Click **Finish** to save the report.

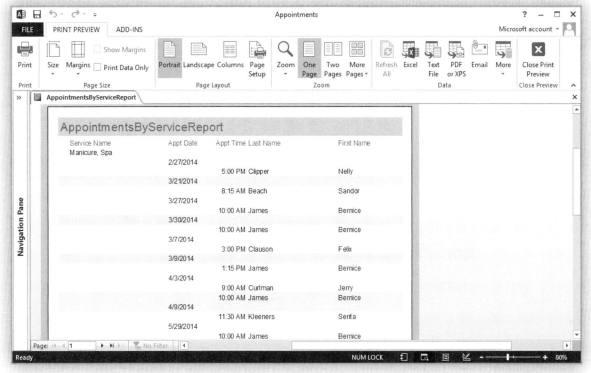

FIGURE AC 3.24
The new report in Print Preview view. Notice how the data are grouped in the report by service name and then by appointment date.

tips & tricks

Use Portrait orientation for reports with few columns; use Landscape orientation for reports with many columns.

tell me more

You can modify your grouping or sorting choices later by editing the report in *Layout* view.

let me try

If the database is not already open, open the data file **AC3-Appointments** and try this skill on your own:

1. Use the *Report Wizard* to create a new report. Include the **Service Name** field from the *Services* table, the **Appt Date** and **Appt Time** fields from the *Appointments* table, and the **Last Name** and **First Name** fields from the *Customers* table.
2. View the report data by the **Services** table.
3. Create subgroups by the **Appt Date** field.
4. Sort each subgroup first by **Appt Time,** and then by **Last Name.**
5. Use the **Stepped** layout and **Portrait** orientation for the report.
6. Name the report: `AppointmentsByServiceReport` and preview it in Print Preview view.
7. Close the report.

Skill 3.9 Creating a New Blank Report

One way to start a new report is to begin with a blank report and add fields from tables and queries manually. You can start a new blank report directly in either Layout view or Design view. Layout view may be easier to work with, but if you need to add advanced controls, you'll need to work in Design view instead.

To create a new blank report directly in Layout view, on the *Create* tab, in the *Reports* group, click the **Blank Report** button.

To create a new blank report directly in Design view, on the *Create* tab, in the *Reports* group, click the **Report Design** button.

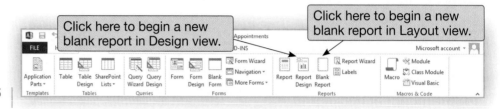

FIGURE AC 3.25

Notice that there are no records in the new report. The new blank report does not have a record source defined. The report is an empty layout until you add controls.

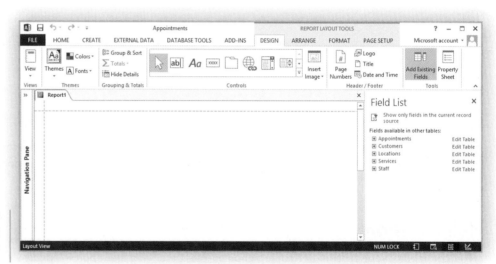

FIGURE AC 3.26
A new blank report
in Layout view

tips & tricks

Access will sometimes select a table or query to use as the record source for the report based on the object selected in the Navigation Pane or based on the first table listed in the Navigation Pane. If this is not the record source you want to use for the report, don't worry. The record source will be updated as you add fields.

let me try

If the database is not already open, open the data file **AC3-Appointments** and try this skill on your own:

1. Create a new blank report so it opens directly in Design view.
2. Close the report without saving it.
3. Create a new blank report so it opens directly in Layout view.
4. Save the form as: **TestReport**

Skill 3.10 Adding Fields to a Report in Layout View

If you are starting with a blank report, you will need to add controls to display field data. By default, blank reports use a **tabular layout** in which the data are arranged similar to a table with the label controls at the top of each column.

To add fields to a report in Layout view:

1. If necessary, on the *Report Layout Tools Design* tab, in the *Tools* group, click the **Add Existing Fields** button to display the *Field List* pane.

2. In the *Field List* pane, click the + in front of the table or query that contains the field(s) you want to add.

3. Double-click a field name to add it. A new label control is automatically created at the top of the report with a bound text box control below it. In Layout view, Access displays values for multiple records in the column.

4. Continue double-clicking fields in the *Field List* to add them to the report.

5. When you are finished adding fields, save the report.

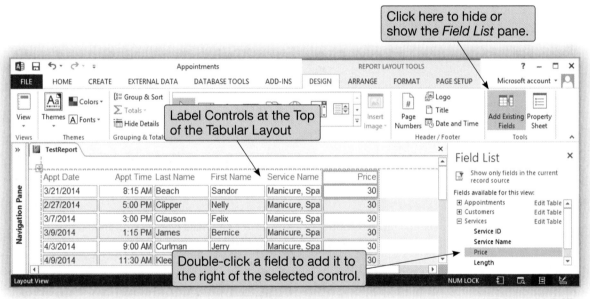

FIGURE AC 3.27

let me try

If the database is not already open, open the data file **AC3-Appointments** and try this skill on your own:

1. If necessary, open the *TestReport* report in Layout view. If your database does not include this report, create a new blank report in Layout view and save it as: **TestReport**
2. If necessary, display the *Field List* pane.
3. From the *Appointments* table, add the **Appt Date** field and then the **Appt Time** field.
4. From the *Customers* table, add the **Last Name** field and then the **First Name** field.
5. From the *Services* table, add the **Service Name** field and then the **Price** field.
6. Save the report

Skill 3.11 Formatting Controls

Once you have created your form or report, it is easy to change formatting in Layout view. Click the control you want to change, and then make your formatting selections from the Ribbon. While these formatting techniques also work in Design view, in Layout view, you can immediately see the formatting change. The formatting options discussed in this skill are available for both forms and reports.

❭ For forms, these commands are found on the *Form Layout Tools Format* tab.

❭ For reports, these commands are found on the *Report Layout Tools Format* tab.

To apply the same formatting to multiple controls at the same time, press Ctrl as you click each control.

From the *Font* group, click the buttons to apply standard text formatting such as **bold,** *italic,* and <u>underline</u>, change the font, font size, or font color, and align text to the left, center, or right side of the control box. You can use *Format Painter* to copy the formatting from one control and apply it to another.

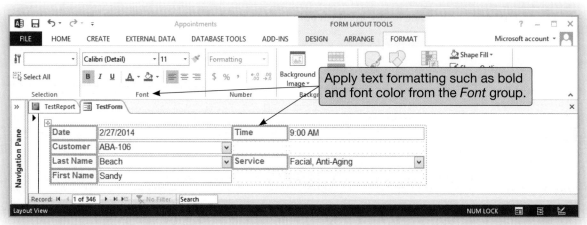

FIGURE AC 3.28

For bound text box controls with the Date/Time data type, you can apply a specific date/time format from the *Format* list in the *Number* group.

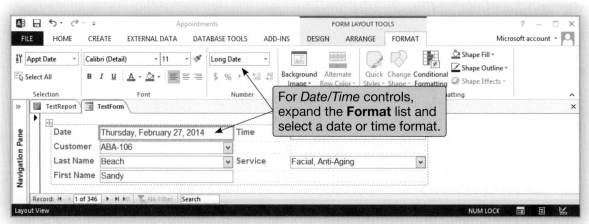

FIGURE AC 3.29

For bound text box controls with the *Number* or *Currency* data type, you can apply specific number formatting from the *Number* group, by clicking the **Apply Currency Format, Apply Percent Format,** or **Apply Comma Number Format** button. More number formats are available from the *Format* list.

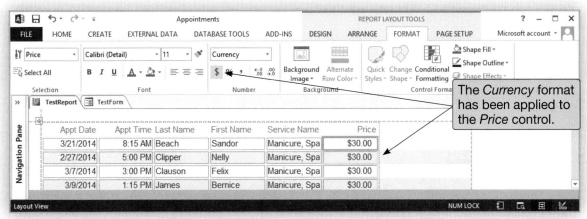

The *Currency* format has been applied to the *Price* control.

FIGURE AC 3.30

another **method**

Common keyboard shortcuts that you may be familiar with in other applications (e.g., Ctrl + B) also work in Access.

let me **try**

If the database is not already open, open the data file **AC3-Appointments** and try this skill on your own:

1. If necessary, open the *TestForm* form in Layout view. If your database does not include this form, create it following the steps in *Skill 3.5: Creating a New Blank Form* and *Skill 3.6: Adding Fields to a Form in Layout View.*
2. Select all the label controls in the form, **bold** them, and apply the **Blue, Accent 1** font color.
3. Apply the **Long Date** format to the **Appt Date** bound text box control.
4. Save the form.
5. If necessary, open the *TestReport* report in Layout view. If your database does not include this report, create it following the steps in *Skill 3.9: Creating a New Blank Report* and *Skill 3.10: Adding Fields to a Report in Layout View.*
6. Apply the **Currency** format to the **Price** bound text box control.
7. Save the report.

Skill 3.12 Applying a Theme

A **theme** is a unified color and font scheme. When you apply a theme to a form or report, you update the look of all the database objects at once. A database can have only one theme applied at a time. Working with themes in Layout view allows you to see the effects of the new theme immediately.

To apply a theme to a form or report in Layout view:

1. On the *Form Layout Tools Design* tab or the *Report Layout Tools Design* tab, in the *Themes* group, click the **Themes** button to expand the gallery.
2. Roll your mouse over each theme to preview the formatting changes.
3. Click one of the themes to apply it.

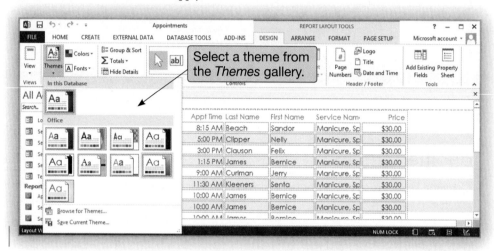

FIGURE AC 3.31

tips & tricks

If you change the theme, you may need to resize some controls to display the data completely.

tell me more

From the *Themes* group, you can apply specific aspects of a theme by making a selection from the *Theme Colors* or *Theme Fonts* gallery.

Theme Colors—Limits the colors available from the color palette for fonts, borders, and shading. Notice that when you change themes, the color palette changes for background colors, fills, outlines, and fonts.

Theme Fonts—Affects the fonts used for titles, label controls, bound controls, and other text in the form. Changing the theme fonts does not limit the fonts available to you from the *Font* list.

another method

Themes are also available from the *Form Design Tools Design* tab, *Themes* group, and the *Report Design Tools Design* tab, *Themes* group. However, you will not see the immediate impact of the theme as you do in Layout view.

let me try

If the database is not already open, open the data file **AC3-Appointments** and try this skill on your own:
1. If necessary, open the *TestReport* report in Layout view.
2. Apply the **Slice** theme.
3. Save the report.

Skill 3.13 Resizing Controls

When designing forms and reports, you should ensure that the controls are sized to fit the data properly. You can change the width and height of controls as necessary. When the control is part of a layout, changing the height of a single control affects all the controls in the row, and changing the width of a single control affects all the controls in the column. For example, in a tabular layout, changing the width of any control in the column will change the width of the entire column.

To change the width of a control in either Layout view or Design view, move the cursor to the right or left edge of the control, and when the cursor changes to ↔ click and drag to the right to make the control wider or to the left to make it smaller. Use the same technique to make rows taller or shorter.

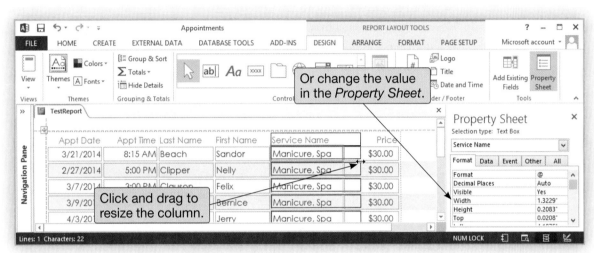

FIGURE AC 3.32

Clicking and dragging to resize controls can be imprecise. Use the *Property Sheet* if you need to specify an exact width or height:

1. On the *Form Layout Tools Design* tab or the *Report Layout Tools Design* tab, in the *Tools* group, click the **Property Sheet** button.

2. Ensure that the correct control is selected from the drop-down list at the top of the *Property Sheet*.

3. If necessary, click the *Property Sheet* **Format** tab.

4. Type the value you want (in inches) in the *Width* and *Height* boxes. Press **Enter** to apply the change.

let me try

If the database is not already open, open the data file **AC3-Appointments** and try this skill on your own:

1. If necessary, open the *TestReport* report in Layout view.
2. Modify the width of the **Service Name** controls (both the label and the bound text box control) so most of the service names are visible on one line (approximately 2.25 inches).
3. Save the report.

Skill 3.14 Moving and Arranging Controls

By default, all controls in a form or a report are included in the control layout. The **control layout** restricts movement of controls to the layout rows and columns ensuring that controls align with one another. Having controls grouped into a control layout makes it easy to add rows and columns to the layout and resize entire layout sections at once.

To rearrange columns in a tabular layout:

1. Click anywhere in the column you want to move.

2. On the *Report Layout Tools Arrange* tab or the *Form Layout Tools Arrange* tab, in the *Rows & Columns* group, click the **Select Column** button. This ensures that you will move the label control along with the bound text box control.

3. Move the mouse pointer over the column. When the cursor changes to ⁺↕↔, click and drag the column to the new location. Access displays an I-bar shape to indicate where the controls will be placed.

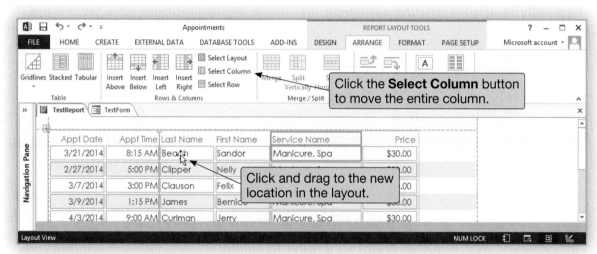

FIGURE AC 3.33
Moving controls in a report in Layout view

In a stacked layout, it is more common to move individual controls rather than an entire column.

1. Select the control or controls you want to move. To move both a bound control and its label control, select both controls by clicking one and pressing (Ctrl) as you click the other.

2. Move the mouse pointer over the selected controls. When the cursor changes to ⁺↕↔, click and drag to the new location. Access highlights the cell in the layout where the control will be placed. When you move multiple controls, Access maintains the relative layout of the controls.

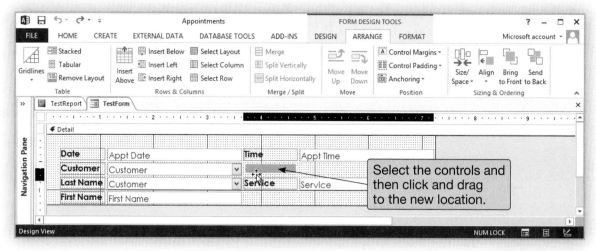

FIGURE AC 3.34
Moving controls in a form in Design view

To add a new empty row or column to the control layout, select a control in the layout, and then click the appropriate button in the *Rows & Columns* group: **Insert Above, Insert Below, Insert Left,** or **Insert Right.**

To remove a row or column from the control layout, right-click anywhere in the row or column, and select **Delete Row** or **Delete Column** from the right-click menu.

tell me **more**

There may be times you want to move a single control outside of the control layout. You must remove the control from the layout before you can manipulate it individually.

❭ In form or report Design view, click the control you want to remove from the control layout. On the *Form Design Tools Arrange* tab or the *Report Design Tools Arrange* tab, in the *Table* group, click the **Remove Layout** button to remove the control from the layout.

❭ The *Remove Layout* command is available in Layout view, but only from the right-click menu. Right-click the control you want to remove from the layout, point to **Layout,** and click **Remove Layout.**

let me **try**

If the database is not already open, open the data file **AC3-Appointments** and try this skill on your own:

1. If necessary, open the *TestReport* report in Layout view.
2. Move the **Service Name** column to place it between the *Appt Time* and *Last Name* columns.
3. Save the report.
4. If necessary, open the *TestForm* form in Layout view.
5. Move the **Service** control and its label control to the layout area directly below the *Appt Time* control and the *Time* label.
6. Save the form.

skill 3.14   Moving and Arranging Controls

Skill 3.15 Adding Design Elements to Form and Report Headers

The **form header** or **report header** is the section directly above the detail section where the data are displayed. Access allows you to add three common design elements to the header quickly and easily: a logo or other small image, a title, and the current date and/or time. While these features are available from both Layout view and Design view, it is much easier to work in Layout view because you will see a live preview of the formatted header.

To add a logo or other small image to the header:

1. On the *Form Layout Tools Design* tab or the *Report Layout Tools Design* tab, in the *Header/Footer* group, click the **Logo** button.

2. In the *Insert Picture* dialog, browse to find the image you want to use as the logo, select the file, and then click the **Open** button.

3. The image is added to the upper-left corner of the header.

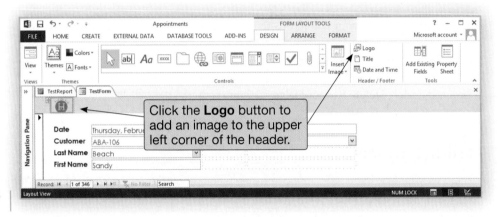

FIGURE AC 3.35

To add a title to the header:

1. On the *Form Layout Tools Design* tab or the *Report Layout Tools Design* tab, in the *Header/ Footer* group, click the **Title** button.

2. An unbound text control with the name of the database object is added to the header, just to the right of the logo (if there is one).

3. To change the title, click in the box and modify the text.

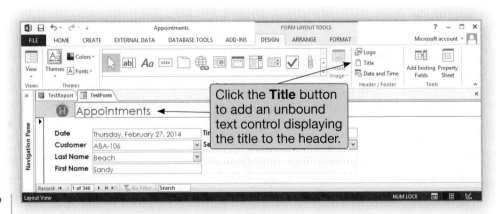

FIGURE AC 3.36

To add the date and/or time to the header:

1. On the *Form Layout Tools Design* tab or the *Report Layout Tools Design* tab, in the *Header/Footer* group, click the **Date and Time** button.

2. The *Date and Time* dialog opens. Check the boxes for the date and/or time formats you want.

3. Click **OK** to add the date and time options you selected to the upper-right corner of the header.

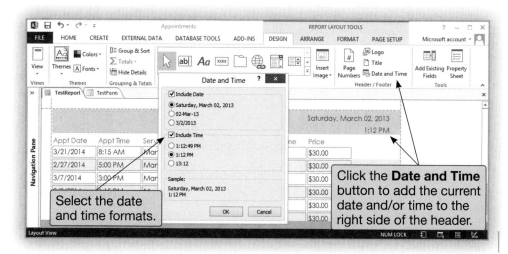

FIGURE AC 3.37

tell me **more**

In Design view, you will not see the actual date and time in the date and time controls. Instead, Design view displays the formulas used in the unbound text controls to calculate the current date and time: =Date( ) and =Time( )

let me **try**

If the database is not already open, open the data file **AC3-Appointments** and try this skill on your own:

1. If necessary, open the *TestForm* form in Layout view.
2. Add the image **SpaLogo** to the form header as a logo. The image file is located with the other data files for this book.
3. Add a title to the form header and change the text to: **Appointments**
4. Save and close the form.
5. If necessary, open the *TestReport* report in Layout view.
6. Add the date and time to the report header using the date format similar to **Saturday, March 02, 2013** and the time format similar to **1:12 PM.**
7. Save the report.

Skill 3.16 Adding Page Numbers to Reports

Because reports are intended for printing, they include additional header and footer sections unavailable in forms. Data in the **page header section** and **page footer section** appear at the top and bottom of every printed page in the report; data in the **report header section** and **report footer section** appear only at the very beginning and the very end of the report.

To add page numbers to the page footer section:

1. On the *Report Layout Tools Design* tab, in the *Header/Footer* group, click the **Page Numbers** button.
2. In the *Page Numbers* dialog, select the page number options you want. Be sure to select the **Bottom of Page (Footer)** radio button to place the page number at the bottom the page.
3. Click **OK** to insert the page numbers.
4. If necessary, scroll down to see the page number at the bottom of the report.

Click the **Page Numbers** button to open the *Page Numbers* dialog.

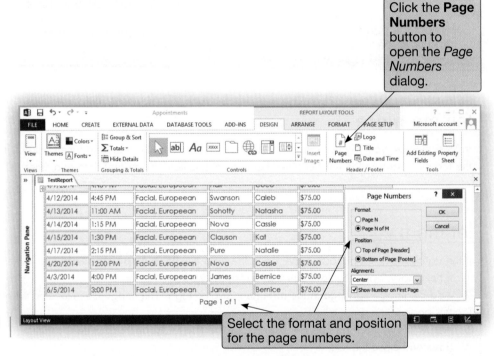

Select the format and position for the page numbers.

FIGURE AC 3.38

tips & tricks

If you use the page number format **Page N of M,** where *N* is the current page number and *M* is the total number of pages, you will always see Page 1 of 1 in Layout view. To test the page number format with the actual number of printed pages, switch to Print Preview view.

let me try

If the database is not already open, open the data file **AC3-Appointments** and try this skill on your own:
1. If necessary, open the *TestReport* report in Layout view.
2. Add automatic page numbers centered at the bottom of the page footer on every page. Use the format page **N of M.**
3. Save the report.

Skill 3.17 Grouping Records in a Report

If you have used the *Report Wizard* to create a report, you should already be somewhat familiar with the concept of grouping. Adding **grouping** organizes the report into sections (groups) by the value of a specific field. Grouping can make a long report much easier to follow. Grouping also allows you to add group-specific headers and footers where you can calculate totals for each group.

To add grouping to a report:

1. On the *Report Layout Tools Design* tab, in the *Grouping & Totals* group, click the **Group & Sort** button to display the *Group, Sort, and Total* pane at the bottom of the report window.

2. Click the **Add a group** button in the *Group, Sort, and Total* pane to display a list of available fields to group by. Click the field you want.

3. Access adds grouping to the report, including a group header for each group with a title. How the data are grouped depends on the type of field you selected. If you selected a date/time field, Access may group the data by year, quarter, month, week, or day. If you selected a text field, Access may group the data by specific text values. The data in Figure AC 3.39 are grouped by the *Appt Date* field by calendar quarter.

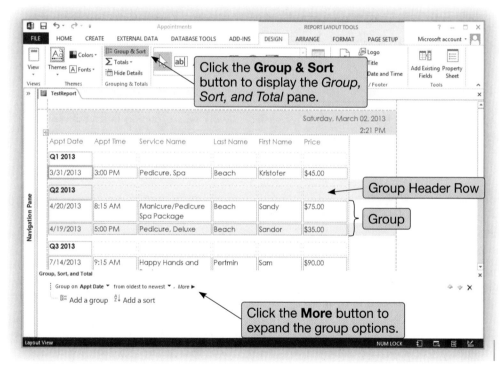

FIGURE AC 3.39

To change the grouping level Access selected:

1. Click the **More** button next to the group you want to change to expand the group options.

2. Click the arrow next to the grouping level description, and select a new option from the menu. In Figure AC 3.40, the grouping option has been changed from **by quarter** to **by month.**

3. To hide the options again, click the **Less** button.

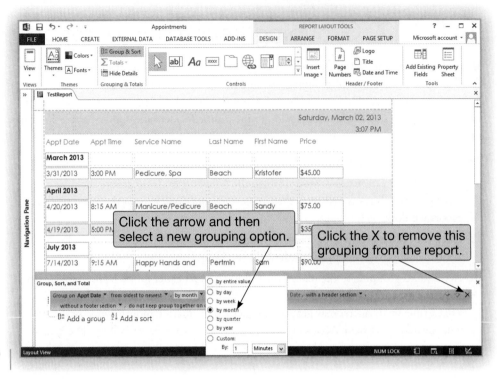

FIGURE AC 3.40

To delete a grouping, click the **X** at the far right side of the group in the *Group, Sort, and Total* pane.

tips & tricks

You can also add groupings from Design view. However, it's always easiest to work with grouping in Layout view so you can preview how the data will look.

let me try

If the database is not already open, open the data file **AC3-Appointments** and try this skill on your own:

1. If necessary, open the *TestReport* report in Layout view.
2. Add grouping by the **Appt Date** field.
3. If necessary, change the width and height of the group header so the group titles are displayed properly. Add formatting of your choice to the group titles to emphasize where each new group begins.
4. Change the grouping level for the *Appt Date* field to **by month.**
5. Save the report.

Skill 3.18 Adding Totals to a Report

Totals in a report display a calculation such as the sum or average of the values in a field or group. The formula to calculate the total is added to the report in a type of control called a **calculated control**—an unbound text box control that contains an expression (a formula). You do not need to know how to add a calculated control, however, in order to add totals to a report. Report Layout view provides a tool that adds totals for you.

To add totals to a report in Layout view:

1. Click any value in the control you want to add a total to.
2. On the *Report Layout Tools Design* tab, in the *Grouping & Totals* group, click the **Totals** button.
3. Select the function you want to use for the total.

Access automatically inserts the new calculated control into the report footer. The calculated control in the report footer calculates a grand total for all the values in the report. If the report includes grouping, Access also adds a calculated control in each group footer to calculate the total for records in that group.

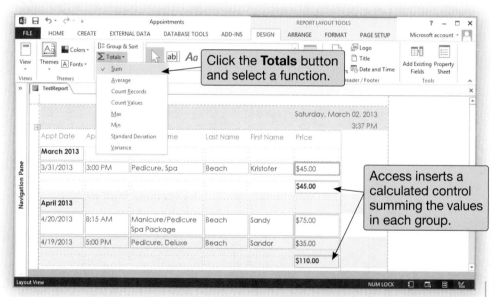

FIGURE AC 3.41

tips & tricks

The *Totals* button is also available on the *Report Design Tools Design* tab, in the *Grouping & Totals* group. However, in Design view, you will not see the total values. Instead, Design view displays the formulas used in the unbound text controls.

let me try

If the database is not already open, open the data file **AC3-Appointments** and try this skill on your own:

1. If necessary, open the *TestReport* report in Layout view.
2. Add totals to the *Price* column to calculate the sum of prices.
3. Adjust the height of the control in the group footer if necessary and bold it to emphasize the group totals.
4. Save the report.

Skill 3.19 Previewing and Printing a Report

Print Preview view shows you exactly how the report will look when it is printed. It is always a good idea to preview the report before printing. There are three main methods for switching to Print Preview view:

> Right-click the report tab, and select **Print Preview.**
> Click the **Print Preview** view button on the status bar.
> On the *Home* tab, in the *Views* group, click the **View** button, and select **Print Preview.**

If the printed report will result in blank pages, Access will display a warning message when you switch to Print Preview view. Click **OK** to dismiss the warning and continue to Print Preview view. You can use Print Preview view to adjust print settings as necessary.

If your report will print on more than one page, it is a good practice to preview the report in a multiple page layout. To preview more than one page at a time, in the *Zoom* group, click the **Two Pages** button or click the **More Pages** button and select an option to see **Four, Eight,** or **Twelve** pages at once.

In Figure AC 3.42, previewing the report two pages at a time shows that the report is just a little bit too wide, causing part of the header to spill over to a second page.

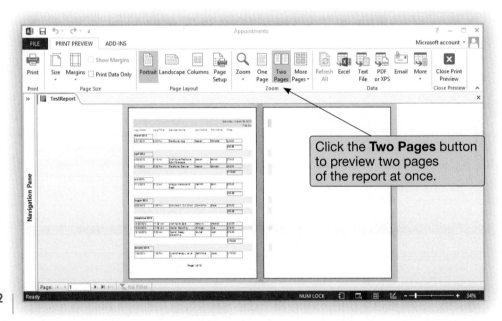

Click the **Two Pages** button to preview two pages of the report at once.

FIGURE AC 3.42

To print the report:

From Print Preview view, click the **Print** button at the far left side of the Ribbon to open the *Print* dialog. In the *Print* dialog you can specify which pages to print and how many copies to print. Click **OK** to send the report to the printer.

To close Print Preview view, click the **Close Print Preview** button at the far right side of the Ribbon.

another **method**

Print options are also available from Backstage.

1. With the report open in any view, click the **File** tab to open Backstage.
2. Click **Print.**
3. Select the print option you want.

    Quick Print sends the report to the printer without opening the *Print* dialog first.

    Print opens the *Print* dialog so you can check the printer settings before printing.

    Print Preview opens the report in Print Preview view.

let me **try**

If the database is not already open, open the data file **AC3-Appointments** and try this skill on your own:

1. If necessary, open the *TestReport* report.
2. Switch to Print Preview view. If you receive a warning that the section width is greater than the page width, click **OK** to dismiss the warning.
3. Change the view to show two pages at once.

from the perspective of . . .

LAWYER

I use Access to track time and billing for my law practice. I use forms to enter client information and to track time spent on each case, and I use reports to generate client invoices. I always check the invoice report in Print Preview view before printing. You never know when an adjustment to a column width will cause the report to spill over to a second page. When that happens, I can usually adjust the margins or switch the page orientation to keep the invoice to no more than one page wide.

Skill 3.20 Controlling the Page Setup of a Report for Printing

When you create a new report from scratch, the default page orientation is **portrait**. This means the height of the page is greater than the width. You may want to change the page orientation to **landscape** to print sideways on the page if your report contains multiple columns of data.

Margins are the blank spaces at the top, bottom, left, and right of the printed page. If your report is just a little bit too wide to fit on one page, try adjusting the margins to a more narrow setting. This will give you more room on the page for printed data.

Use Print Preview view to adjust margins and page orientation for your reports before printing:

1. Switch to Print Preview view.

2. To change the page orientation, in the *Page Layout* group, click the **Portrait** or **Landscape** button.

3. To use a preset margin option, in the *Page Size* group, click the **Margins** button, and select an option: **Normal, Wide,** or **Narrow.**

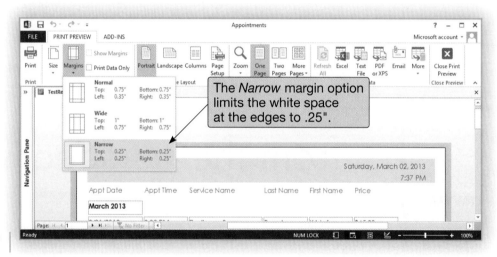

The *Narrow* margin option limits the white space at the edges to .25".

FIGURE AC 3.43

When you switch page orientation or margins, all the visible data in your report may fit on one page, but the report width may still be wider than the page. When that happens, Access will show a warning message that the report may print with blank pages.

FIGURE AC 3.44

To fix this problem:

1. Switch to Design view.

2. In Design view, you can clearly see that the report is wider than it needs to be.

3. Move the mouse pointer to the right side of the report detail section. When the cursor changes to the ✛ shape, click and drag the section boundary to the left to make it smaller. Access will not let you make the section so small that any controls are outside its border.

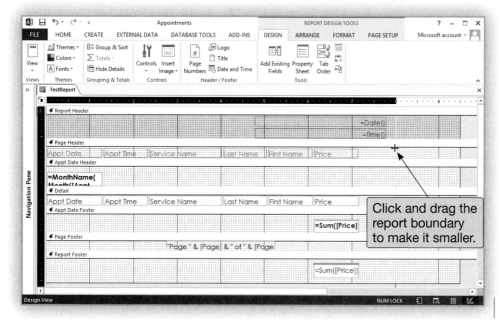

FIGURE AC 3.45

Another way to fix this problem is to allow Access to remove the excess space for you.

1. The green triangle in the report selector box at the upper left corner of the report indicates that there may be a problem. Click it to display the Smart Tag.

2. Hover the mouse pointer over the Smart Tag at the upper right corner of the report to see a description of the problem.

3. Click the **Smart Tag** to see the list of possible solutions.

4. Select **Remove Extra Report Space.**

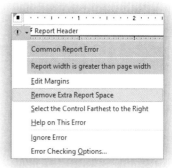

FIGURE AC 3.46

another method

The *Page Setup* tab is also available from Layout view and Design view, but it is best to adjust print settings from Print Preview view.

let me try

If the database is not already open, open the data file **AC3-Appointments** and try this skill on your own:

1. If necessary, open the *TestReport* report in Print Preview view.
2. Change the orientation so the report page is wider than it is tall.
3. Change back to **Portrait** orientation.
4. Change the margins setting to the **Narrow** option.
5. Save and close the report.

key terms

Record source
Single Record form
Datasheet form
Multiple Items form
Split form
Form Wizard
Subform
Control
Text box control
Bound control
Unbound control
Stacked layout
Label control
Report Wizard
Tabular layout

Theme
Theme colors
Theme fonts
Control layout
Form header
Report header
Page header section
Page footer section
Report header section
Report footer section
Grouping
Calculated control
Portrait
Landscape
Margins

concepts review

1. A _____ combines the convenience of a continuous Datasheet form with the usability of a Single Record form displaying one record at a time.

    a. Split form

    b. Datasheet form

    c. Multiple Items form

    d. Subform

2. A _____ is a form within a form that displays records related to the record in the main form.

    a. Split form

    b. Datasheet form

    c. Multiple Items form

    d. Subform

3. A _____ text control displays data from a field.

    a. label

    b. bound

    c. unbound

    d. calculated

4. Click and drag fields from the _____ to add controls to a blank report.

    a. *Property Sheet*

    b. *Field List* pane

    c. *Report Wizard*

    d. none of the above

5. Which of these design elements is not available in forms?

   a. Logo

   b. Date/Time

   c. Title

   d. Page Numbers

6. Page numbers can only be added to a footer section.

   a. True

   b. False

7. A stacked layout places labels across the top, with columns of data (similar to a datasheet or a spreadsheet).

   a. True

   b. False

8. An unbound text box control that contains an expression (formula) is called a(n) _____ control.

   a. calculated

   b. bound

   c. unbound

   d. label

9. Grand totals in a report are added to the _____.

   a. page footer section

   b. report footer section

   c. group footer section

   d. group header section

10. To change the direction a report prints on the page, change the page _____.

   a. margins

   b. orientation

   c. zoom

   d. layout

projects

Data files for projects can be found on
www.mhhe.com/office2013skills

skill review 3.1

In this project, you will continue to work with the Computer Science department database from the *Chapter 2, Skill Review 2.1.* It uses Access to manage employees and various items that are loaned to students and faculty. You will create a variety of forms for entering employee, loan, and item information.

Skills needed to complete this project:

- Creating a Single Record Form Based on a Table or Query (Skill 3.1)
- Creating a Multiple Items Form (Skill 3.2)
- Creating a Split Form (Skill 3.3)
- Creating a Form Using the Form Wizard (Skill 3.4)
- Applying a Theme (Skill 3.12)
- Creating a New Blank Form (Skill 3.5)
- Adding Fields to a Form in Layout View (Skill 3.6)
- Resizing Controls (Skill 3.13)
- Formatting Controls (Skill 3.11)
- Adding Design Elements to Form and Report Headers (Skill 3.15)

1. Open the start file **AC2013-SkillReview-3-1**.
2. If necessary, enable active content by clicking the **Enable Content** button in the Message Bar.
3. Save a copy of the file to work on named:
   [your initials]AC-SkillReview-3-1
4. If necessary, enable active content again.
5. Create a Single Record form using the *Employees* table as the record source.
   a. In the Navigation Pane, select the **Employees** table.
   b. On the **Create** tab, in the *Forms* group, click the **Form** button.
   c. Save the form with the name: **EmployeesForm**
   d. Close the form
6. Create a Multiple Items form using the *Employees* table as the record source.
   a. In the Navigation Pane, select the **Employees** table.
   b. On the **Create** tab, in the *Forms* group, click the **More Forms** button and select **Multiple Items** from the list.
   c. Save the form with the name: **EmployeesFormMulti**
   d. Close the form.
7. Create a Split form using the *Employees* table as the record source.
   a. In the Navigation Pane, select the **Employees** table.
   b. On the **Create** tab, in the *Forms* group, click the **More Forms** button and select **Split Form** from the list.

c. Save the form with the name: `EmployeesFormSplit`

d. Close the form.

8. Create a form using the *Form Wizard* to show items on loan to each employee.

   a. On the *Create* tab, in the *Forms* group, click the **Form Wizard** button.

   b. In the first step of the wizard, select **Table: Employees** from the *Tables/Queries* list box.

   c. Double-click the following fields to add them to the *Selected Fields* box in this order: **EmployeeID, LastName, FirstName**

   d. Expand the *Tables/Queries* list again and select **Table: Loans.**

   e. Double-click the following fields to add them to the *Selected Fields* box below the fields from the *Employees* table: **LoanID, ItemID, LoanDate.**

   f. Click the **Next** button.

   g. Verify that the form will be organized by data in the *Employees* table as a form with a subform. Click **Next.**

   h. Click the **Datasheet** radio button to use the Datasheet layout for the subform. Click **Next.**

   i. Enter the following title in the *Form* box: `EmployeeLoansForm`

   j. Enter the following title in the *Subform* box: `EmployeeLoansSubform`

   k. Verify that the **Open the form to view or enter information** radio button is selected.

   l. Click the **Finish** button. Do not close this form.

9. Apply a theme to the form.

   a. Switch to Layout view.

   b. Click the **Form Layout Tools Design** tab if it is not already selected.

   c. In the *Themes* group, click the **Themes** button. Select the **Wisp** theme.

10. Save and close the form.

11. Create a new blank form in Layout view.

   a. On the *Create* tab, in the *Forms* group, click the **Blank Form** button.

   b. Save the form with the name: `ItemsForm`

12. Add controls to the new *ItemsForm.*

   a. If necessary, display the *Field List* pane. On the *Form Layout Tools Design* tab, in the *Tools* group, click the **Add Existing Fields** button.

   b. If necessary, click the **Show All Tables** link in the *Field List* pane.

   c. Click the + in front of *Items.*

   d. Add the *ItemID* field to the form by double-clicking **ItemID** in the *Field List* pane.

   e. Click the **ItemName** field and drag it to the form to the right of the *ItemID* control. Pay close attention to the placement guide so you drop the new controls to the right of the *ItemID* control, not below it.

   f. Click and drag the **Cost** field to the form so it is placed directly below the *ItemName* field. Make sure the label controls line up in the same column.

   g. Click and drag the **Description** field to the form so it is placed directly below the *Cost* field. Make sure the label controls line up in the same column.

13. Modify the height of the *Description* control so the entire description is visible.

   a. If necessary, click the **Description** text box control to select it.

   b. Click and drag the bottom boundary of the control downward to make the control taller.

14. Apply a font color to all the labels in the form.

   a. Click the **ItemID** label control to select it. Press (Ctrl) and click each of the other label controls. All the label controls should be selected.

   b. On the *Form Layout Tools Format* tab, in the *Font* group, click the **Font Color** button arrow to view the color palette, and click the theme color **Olive Green, Accent 4.**

15. Add a title to the form header.

   a. On the *Form Layout Tools Design* tab, in the *Header/Footer* group, click the **Title** button.

   b. Change the title to: **Items**

16. Save and close the form.

17. Close the database and exit Access.

skill review 3.2

In this project you will continue working with the health insurance database from *Chapter 2, Skill Review 2.2.* You will create the following reports: a report to summarize physician member information by city, an order report summarizing orders by month including the physician and procedure, and a phone contact list for the physicians.

Skills needed to complete this project:

- Creating a Basic Report Based on a Table or Query (Skill 3.7)
- Resizing Controls (Skill 3.13)
- Moving and Arranging Controls (Skill 3.14)
- Grouping Records in a Report (Skill 3.17)
- Adding Totals to a Report (Skill 3.18)
- Formatting Controls (Skill 3.11)
- Applying a Theme (Skill 3.12)
- Previewing and Printing a Report (Skill 3.19)
- Controlling the Page Setup of a Report for Printing (Skill 3.20)
- Creating a Report Using the Report Wizard (Skill 3.8)
- Creating a New Blank Report (Skill 3.9)
- Adding Fields to a Report in Layout View (Skill 3.10)
- Adding Design Elements to Form and Report Headers (Skill 3.15)
- Adding Page Numbers to Reports (Skill 3.16)

1. Open the start file **AC2013-SkillReview-3-2.**

2. If necessary, enable active content by clicking the **Enable Content** button in the Message Bar.

3. Save a copy of the file to work on named:
   [your initials]AC-SkillReview-3-2

4. If necessary, enable active content again.

5. Create a basic report using the *Physicians* table as the data source.

   a. In the Navigation Pane, select the **Physicians** table.

   b. On the *Create* tab, in the *Reports* group, click the **Report** button.

   c. Save the report with the name: **PhysiciansReport**

6. Adjust the column widths to fit the data.

    a. The *PhysciansReport* should still be open in Layout view.

    b. Click anywhere in the **PhysicianID** column.

    c. Click and drag the right boundary of the control to the left to make the control smaller.

    d. Repeat this procedure with all the columns in the report. When you are finished, the page break should appear between the *City* and *ZipCode* fields. You should still be able to read the labels and all values in the table clearly.

7. Move the *City* column so it appears first in the report.

    a. Click the **City** label at the top of the column. On the *Report Layout Tools Arrange* tab, in the *Rows & Columns* group, click the **Select Column** button.

    b. Move the mouse pointer over the column. When the mouse pointer changes to the move shape, , click and drag the entire column to the left. Release the mouse button when the I-bar move indicator appears at the very left side of the report.

8. Add grouping to the report by values in the *City* field.

    a. On the *Report Layout Tools Design* tab, in the *Grouping & Totals* group, click the **Group & Sort** button.

    b. In the *Group, Sort, & Total* pane at the bottom of the report, click **Add a Group,** and then click **City.**

9. Add totals to the report to calculate the total number of members. Calculate totals for each group as well as a grand total for the entire report.

    a. Click any **MemberCount** value.

    b. On the *Report Layout Tools Design* tab, in the *Grouping & Totals* group, click the **Totals** button, and click **Sum.**

10. Adjust the height of the controls displaying the totals.

    a. Click any of the controls displaying the total in one of the group footers.

    b. Drag the bottom boundary down so the entire number is visible.

    c. Scroll to the very bottom of the report.

    d. Click the grand total control immediately above the page number.

    e. Drag the bottom boundary down so the entire number is visible.

11. Apply bold formatting to all the total controls.

    a. Verify that the grand total control is still selected.

    b. Press Ctrl and click any of the group total controls.

    c. On the *Report Layout Tools Format* tab, in the *Font* group, click the **Bold** button.

12. Move the page number control so it is centered in the page footer section.

    a. If necessary, scroll to the bottom of the report so you can see the page number control in the page footer section.

    b. Click the control and drag it to the left so it is below the *Address* field. Be careful not to move the page number control out of the page footer section.

13. Apply a theme to the report. On the *Report Layout Tools Design* tab, in the *Themes* group, click the **Themes** button, and select **Integral.**

14. Adjust the layout settings so the report will print no more than one page wide.

    a. Switch to Print Preview view by right-clicking the report tab and selecting **Print Preview.**

    b. In the *Zoom* group, click the **More Pages** button and click **Four Pages** so you can preview the entire report at once.

c. Observe that in Portrait orientation, the report will print across two pages wide.

d. In the *Page Layout* group, click the **Landscape** button.

e. If the report is still more than one page wide, return to Layout view and repeat step 5 to further adjust the width of the columns until the entire report fits on two pages—one page wide and two pages tall.

f. If you receive a warning that the section width is greater than the page width and the report may print with blank pages, switch to Design view. Click the **Smart Tag** in the upper left corner of the report, and select **Remove Extra Report Space.** Switch back to Print Preview view and verify that this solved the problem.

15. Save and close the report.

16. Use the *Report Wizard* to create a report combining information from the *Orders, Physicians,* and *Procedures* tables.

a. On the *Create* tab, in the *Reports* group, click the **Report Wizard.**

b. Expand the **Tables/Queries** list, and select **Table: Orders.**

c. Double-click the following fields to add them to the *Selected Fields* list in this order: **OrderID** and **OrderDate**

d. Expand the **Tables/Queries** list again, and select **Table: Physicians.**

e. Double-click the following fields to add them to the *Selected Fields* list in this order: **LastName** and **FirstName**

f. Expand the **Tables/Queries** list, and select **Table: Procedures.**

g. Double-click the **ProcedureName** field to add it to the *Selected Fields* list.

h. Click the **Next** button to continue to the next step of the *Report Wizard.*

i. Verify that **by Orders** is selected in the *How do you want to view your data?* box. Click **Next.**

j. Add grouping by order date. Click **OrderDate** in the *Do you want any grouping levels?* box. Observe that Access will group the orders by month Click **Next.**

k. Sort the records in the report by the procedure name. Next to the number **1,** click the arrow and select **ProcedureName** from the list of choices. Click **Next.**

l. Verify that the report will use the **Stepped layout** with **Portrait orientation.** Click **Next.**

m. Enter the following name in the *What title do you want for your report?* box: `OrderDetailsReport`

n. If necessary, click the **Preview the report.** radio button so the report will open in Print Preview view.

o. Click **Finish.**

17. Switch to Layout view so you can make changes to the report.

18. Edit the text in the **OrderDatebyMonth** label in the report header section. Click the label control and change the text to: `Month`

19. Adjust the control widths in the report so all values are visible.

a. Click the **ProcedureName** label control. Press Ctrl and click any value in the column. Click and drag the **right** column border to the **left** to make the column slightly smaller.

b. Click the **OrderID** label control. Press Ctrl and click any value in the column. Click and drag the **left** column border to the **left** to make the column slightly wider so the text in the label control is visible.

    c. Click the **LastName** label control. Press (Ctrl) and click any value in the column. Click and drag the **left** column border to the **right** to make the column slightly smaller.

    d. Click the **Order Date** label control. Press (Ctrl) and click any value in the column. Click and drag the **right** column border to the **right** to make the column slightly wider so the dates are visible.

20. Save and close the report.

21. Create a new blank report and add controls to it.

    a. On the *Create* tab, in the *Reports* group, click the **Blank Report** button.

    b. If necessary, on the *Report Layout Tools Design* tab, in the *Tools* group, click the **Add Existing Fields** button to display the *Field List* pane.

    c. In the *Field List* pane, if necessary, click the **Show all** tables link and then click the + button to expand the *Physicians* table.

    d. Double-click the following fields from the *Physicians* table in order to add them to the report in this order: **LastName, FirstName, Phone**

    e. Adjust column widths as necessary.

    f. Save the report with the name: **PhoneListReport**

22. Add a logo to the report header.

    a. On the *Report Layout Tools Design* tab, in the *Header/Footer* group, click the **Logo** button.

    b. In the *Insert Picture* dialog, navigate to the data files location for this project.

    c. Double-click the **CaduseusLogo** image file.

23. Add a title to the report header.

    a. On the *Report Layout Tools Design* tab, in the *Header/Footer* group, click the **Title** button.

    b. Type: **Phone List**

    c. Press (← Enter).

24. Add page numbers centered in the report page footer.

    a. On the *Report Layout Tools Design* tab, in the *Header/Footer* group, click the **Page Numbers** button.

    b. In the *Page Numbers* dialog, verify that the **Page N** radio button is selected.

    c. Click the **Bottom of Page [Footer]** radio button.

    d. Verify that **Center** is selected from the *Alignment* drop-down list.

    e. Verify that the **Show Number on First Page** check box is checked.

    f. Click **OK**.

25. Save and close the report.

26. Close the database and exit Access.

challenge yourself **3.3**

In this project you will continue working with the greenhouse database from *Chapter 2, Challenge Yourself 2.3*. You will create a variety of forms for entering plant and maintenance information.

Skills needed to complete this project:

- Creating a Single Record Form Based on a Table or Query (Skill 3.1)
- Moving and Arranging Controls (Skill 3.14)
- Creating a Multiple Items Form (Skill 3.2)
- Creating a Split Form (Skill 3.3)
- Adding Fields to a Form in Layout View (Skill 3.6)
- Creating a Form Using the Form Wizard (Skill 3.4)
- Creating a New Blank Form (Skill 3.5)
- Resizing Controls (Skill 3.13)
- Applying a Theme (Skill 3.12)
- Formatting Controls (Skill 3.11)
- Adding Design Elements to Form and Report Headers (Skill 3.15)

1. Open the start file **AC2013-ChallengeYourself-3-3**.
2. If necessary, enable active content by clicking the **Enable Content** button in the Message Bar.
3. Save a copy of the file to work on named:
   [your initials]AC-ChallengeYourself-3-3
4. If necessary, enable active content again.
5. Create a **Single Record form** using the *Plants* table as the record source. Save the form with the name: **PlantsForm**

   a. Move the **DatePlanted** field so it is located directly above the *PurchasePrice* field.

   b. Save and close the form.

6. Create a **Multiple Items Form** using the *Plants* table as the record source. Save the form with the name **PlantsFormMulti** and close it.

7. Create a **Split Form** using the *MaintenanceLog* table as the record source. Save it with the name: **MaintenanceLogFormSplit**

   a. Add the **FirstName** field from the **Employees** table to just below the *EmployeeID* field in the form.

   b. Add the **LastName** field from the **Employees** table to just below the *FirstName* field in the form.

   c. Save and close the form.

8. Use the **Form Wizard** button to create a form showing employee information in the main form with a subform showing related maintenance records.

   a. Add the following fields to the form in this order:

   From the *Employees* table: **EmployeeID, LastName, FirstName, WeeklyHours**

   From the *MaintenanceLog* table: **Date_Time, PlantID, Watered, Inspected, Pruned**

   b. Organize the form by the *Employees* table with data from the *MaintenanceLog* table as a subform.

c. Format the subform as a Datasheet form.

d. Name the main form: `EmployeeWorkLogForm`

e. Name the subform: `WorkLogSubform`

f. Review the form in Form view, and then close it.

9. Create a form from scratch.

   a. Start with a new blank form in Layout view. Save the form with the name:
`MaintenanceTrackingForm`

   b. Add the following fields from the *MaintenanceLog* table to the form in this order:
Date_Time, EmployeeID, PlantID, Watered

   c. Change the **Date_Time** label to: `Date`

   d. If necessary, adjust the width of the labels so all the text is visible.

   e. Add the **Inspected** field to the right of the *Watered* control.

   f. Add the **Pruned** field to the right of the *Inspected* control.

   g. Add the **LastName** field from the *Employees* table to the right of the *EmployeeID* control.

   h. Add the **FirstName** field from the *Employees* table to the right of the *LastName* control

   i. Add the **CommonName** field from the *Plants* table to the right of the *PlantID* field.

   j. If necessary, adjust the width of the labels so all the text is visible.

10. Format the form.

   a. Apply the **Facet** theme to the form.

   b. Change the font color for all the label controls to the theme color **Dark Green, Accent 2.**

   c. Modify the **Date_Time bound text box control** to use the **Long Date** format.

   d. Add the title `Maintenance Log` to the form header.

11. Save the form and close it.

12. Close the database and exit Access.

challenge yourself **3.4**

In this project you will continue working with the vaccines database from *Chapter 2, Challenge Yourself 2.4.* You will create an inventory report and reports to summarize shipments by country and by target audience. Complete the steps below to create and modify these objects.

Skills needed to complete this project:

- Creating a Basic Report Based on a Table or Query (Skill 3.7)
- Resizing Controls (Skill 3.13)
- Moving and Arranging Controls (Skill 3.14)
- Adding Totals to a Report (Skill 3.18)
- Formatting Controls (Skill 3.11)
- Creating a Report Using the Report Wizard (Skill 3.8)
- Creating a New Blank Report (Skill 3.9)
- Adding Fields to a Report in Layout View (Skill 3.10)
- Grouping Records in a Report (Skill 3.17)

- Adding Design Elements to Form and Report Headers (Skill 3.15)
- Adding Page Numbers to Reports (Skill 3.16)
- Applying a Theme (Skill 3.12)
- Previewing and Printing a Report (Skill 3.19)

1. Open the start file **AC2013-ChallengeYourself-3-4.**

2. If necessary, enable active content by clicking the **Enable Content** button in the Message Bar.

3. Save a copy of the file to work on named:
   `[your initials]AC-ChallengeYourself-3-4`

4. If necessary, enable active content again.

5. Create a basic report using the *Vaccines* table as the data source.

   a. Save the report with the name: `InventoryReport`

   b. Adjust the width of the **VaccineID** column so it is just wide enough to display the column label.

   c. Move the page number control in the page footer section so it is centered below the *VaccineName* and *TargetAudience* columns. Be sure to keep the control in the page footer section.

   d. Add a total to the **Inventory** field to calculate the sum of the inventory on hand for all vaccines.

   e. Apply the **Comma** number format to the total control.

   f. If necessary, adjust the height of the total control so the number does not appear cut-off.

   g. Save and close the report.

6. Use the *Report Wizard* to create a report summarizing the vaccine shipments to each country.

   a. Include these fields in the report:

   From the *Shipments* table: **ShipmentID, DateShipped, Quantity**

   From the *Locations* table: **Country**

   From the *Vaccines* table: **VaccineName**

   b. Organize the report data by location.

   c. For each country, group the data by **DateShipped** by month.

   d. Sort the detail records first by **DateShipped,** and then by **VaccineName.**

   e. Use the **Stepped** layout and **Landscape** orientation.

   f. Name the report: `ShipmentsByCountryReport`

   g. Open the report in Print Preview view when the wizard is finished.

   h. Switch to Layout view.

   i. Move the **ShipmentID** column so it appears after the **DateShipped by Month** column.

   j. Modify the column widths so all the data are visible. Use any method you want. Ensure that the labels are completely visible.

   k. Save and close the report.

7. Create a new blank report in Layout view. Save the report with the name:
   `ShipmentsByAudience`

   a. Add the following controls in this order:

   From the *Vaccines* table: **TargetAudience, VaccineName**

   From the *Shipments* table: **ShipmentID, Quantity, Cost**

b. Increase the width of the **TargetAudience** column so the data in the detail section do not wrap.

c. Increase the width of the **VaccineName** column so the data in the detail section do not wrap.

d. Add grouping by the **TargetAudience** field.

e. Add totals to calculate the total quantity and cost for each group. Include a grand total at the end of the report in the report footer.

f. Add bold formatting to the total controls. Don't forget to include the grand total in the report footer.

g. Add a logo to the report header. Use the image file **GlobeLogo** included with the data files for this project.

h. Add the title `Shipments by Target Audience` to the report header.

i. Add the date to the report header. Use the format similar to **03-Mar-13.** Do not include the time.

j. Add page numbers centered in the page footer. Use the format **Page N of M.** Ensure that the page number will be included on the first page of the report.

k. Apply the **Ion** theme to the report.

l. Preview the report and ensure that it will print on one page.

m. Save and close the report.

8. Close the database and exit Access.

on your own 3.5

In this project, you will continue working with the movie database from *Chapter 2, On Your Own 2.5.* You will create forms to enter new movies and loans. You will also create reports to keep a printed record of current loans. Save your changes often as you work through the project.

Skills needed to complete this project:

- Creating a Single Record Form Based on a Table or Query (Skill 3.1)
- Creating a Multiple Items Form (Skill 3.2)
- Creating a Split Form (Skill 3.3)
- Creating a Form Using the Form Wizard (Skill 3.4)
- Creating a New Blank Form (Skill 3.5)
- Adding Fields to a Form in Layout View (Skill 3.6)
- Resizing Controls (Skill 3.13)
- Moving and Arranging Controls (Skill 3.14)
- Applying a Theme (Skill 3.12)
- Formatting Controls (Skill 3.11)
- Adding Design Elements to Form and Report Headers (Skill 3.15)
- Creating a Basic Report Based on a Table or Query (Skill 3.7)
- Creating a Report Using the Report Wizard (Skill 3.8)
- Creating a New Blank Report (Skill 3.9)
- Adding Fields to a Report in Layout View (Skill 3.10)
- Grouping Records in a Report (Skill 3.17)
- Adding Totals to a Report (Skill 3.18)
- Previewing and Printing a Report (Skill 3.19)
- Controlling the Page Setup of a Report for Printing (Skill 3.20)

1. Open the start file **AC2013-OnYourOwn-3-5.**

2. If necessary, enable active content by clicking the **Enable Content** button in the Message Bar.

3. Save a copy of the file to work on named:
   [your initials]AC-OnYourOwn-3-5

4. If necessary, enable active content again.

5. Create three forms: a Single Record form, a Multiple Items form, and a Split form. Use any table you want as the record source for each form.

6. Use the *Report Wizard* to create a form with all the fields from the *Movies* table and a subform displaying all the fields from the *Loans* table.

7. Create a new form in Layout view to use to enter new movie loans. Include any fields you want to create a form that will be easy to use. Resize controls as necessary. Apply a theme to the form. Apply formatting to the label controls so they stand out from the rest of the form. Be sure to add a form title.

8. Create a basic report using the *Borrowers* table as the record source.

9. Use the *Report Wizard* to create a report to summarize loans. At a minimum, include the movie title, borrower, date loaned, and date returned. Organize the report by borrower name. Resize and move controls as necessary. Preview how the report will look when printed and adjust the margins or orientation as you feel necessary.

10. Create another report starting from scratch in Layout view. Use this report to summarize the movie inventory by genre. Calculate the total value of the movies in each genre as well as the total value of all the movies in the collection. Resize controls as necessary. Add formatting to emphasize the labels for each group. Preview how the report will look when printed and adjust the margins or orientation as you feel necessary.

11. Close the database and exit Access.

fix it 3.6

In this project, you will continue working with the pet store database from *Chapter 2, Fix It 2.6*. Once again, the pet store employees tried to work with the database on their own, but their forms and reports need some help.

Skills needed to complete this project:

- Moving and Arranging Controls (Skill 3.14)
- Adding Fields to a Form in Layout View (Skill 3.6)
- Resizing Controls (Skill 3.13)
- Adding Design Elements to Form and Report Headers (Skill 3.15)
- Creating a Split Form (Skill 3.3)
- Adding Fields to a Report in Layout View (Skill 3.10)
- Grouping Records in a Report (Skill 3.17)
- Adding Totals to a Report (Skill 3.18)
- Formatting Controls (Skill 3.11)
- Adding Page Numbers to Reports (Skill 3.16)
- Previewing and Printing a Report (Skill 3.19)
- Controlling the Page Setup of a Report for Printing (Skill 3.20)
- Applying a Theme (Skill 3.12)

1. Open the start file **AC2013-FixIt-3-6.**

2. If necessary, enable active content by clicking the **Enable Content** button in the Message Bar.

3. Save a copy of the file to work on named:
   [your initials]AC-FixIt-3-6

4. If necessary, enable active content again.

5. Fix the *CustomersForm* as follows:

   a. Move the **LastName** controls to the right of the *FirstName* controls.

   b. Move the **ZipCode** controls to the right of the *City* controls.

   c. Move the **Phone** controls up so they are placed below the *ZipCode* controls.

   d. Add the **Newsletter** field to the form, right below the *Phone* control.

   e. Some of the label controls need to be wider. Fix them.

   f. The form is missing the store logo. Use the image file **PetShopLogo** located with the data files for this project.

   g. Save your changes.

6. Fix the *SalesForm* as follows:

   a. Move the **FirstName** controls to the right of the *SaleDate* controls, and then move the **LastName** controls so they appear below the *FirstName* controls.

   b. Move the **PhoneNumber** controls so they appear below the *LastName* controls.

   c. Add the **Breed, MainColor,** and **AgeInMonths** fields to below the *AnimalType* controls.

   d. Some of the label controls need to be wider. Fix them.

   e. The form is missing the store logo. Use the image file **PetShopLogo** located with the data files for this project.

   f. The form is also missing the title: **Sales**

   g. Save your changes.

7. The store owner would like another form for the *Sales* table—one that shows both a datasheet and a single record in one screen. Create this form for her. Name the form: **SalesFormSplit**

8. Fix the *PetsReport* as follows:

   a. The **PetID** field is missing from this report. Add it to the report so it is the first column.

   b. The report should be grouped by animal type with an average age for each group. Adjust the height of the total controls as necessary.

   c. All prices should be formatted using the **Currency** format.

   d. The report is missing the store logo. Use the image file **PetShopLogo** located with the data files for this project.

   e. The report is also missing the title: **Pet Inventory Report**

   f. The report is missing the page numbers. The page number should be centered in the page footer, and it should use the format **Page N.**

   g. Preview the report to make sure it will fit on no more than one page wide. If necessary, make the **MainColor** column narrow enough that the report will fit on one page wide without cutting off the information in the report.

   h. If necessary, switch to Design view and adjust the report width to remove the extra space.

   i. Save your changes.

9. Fix the *Sales* report as follows:

   a. Add the following fields in this order to the right of the *PetID* field.

      From the *Customers* table: **LastName, FirstName, Phone**

      From the *Pets* table: **AnimalType, Breed, Price**

   b. Adjust column widths as necessary so text does not wrap.

   c. The report should be grouped by sale date, by month.

   d. The report should include totals calculating the sum of the values in the **Price** field.

   e. The report is missing the store logo. Use the image file **PetShopLogo** located with the data files for this project.

   f. The report is also missing the title: `Detailed Sales Report`

   g. The report is missing the page numbers. The page number should be centered in the page footer, and it should use the format **Page N.**

   h. Check the report in Print Preview view. Be sure to view multiple pages at once.

   i. Switch to **Landscape** orientation so the report data fits on one page across.

   j. Now the report data fits, but the report is too wide. Switch to Design view and adjust the report width to remove the extra space.

   k. Switch back to Print Preview view to make sure you solved the problem.

   l. Save your changes.

10. The store owner would like all forms and reports to use the **Organic** theme. Apply the theme to all the forms and reports in the database. Save the changes as necessary.

11. Close any open database objects, close the database, and exit Access.

chapter 4

Using Queries and Organizing Information

In this chapter, you will learn the following skills:

❱ Create a simple query

❱ Add criteria to a query

❱ Organize the data in a query

❱ Create Unmatched and Find Duplicate queries

❱ Create a parameter query

❱ Filter and sort data in a datasheet

skills

introduction

This chapter shows you how to find information quickly by using queries, filters, and sorting in Access. You will learn to create a variety of select queries and add criteria. You will also use sorting and filtering techniques to organize data in Datasheet view. The *Let Me Try* exercises in this chapter use the AC4-Appointments database. You can keep the database open while you work in this chapter, opening and closing database objects as required for each *Let Me Try*.

Skill 4.1 Using the Simple Query Wizard

Queries allow you to display and manipulate a subset of data from a table. For example, a table of customer information may include many fields that you don't need on a daily basis. You can use a query to generate a more manageable list displaying just the customer first names, last names, and phone numbers.

Queries can also be used to combine data from related tables into a single database object. For example, if you want a list of appointments including the full customer name, use a query to show fields from both the *Appointments* and *Customers* tables. A query can combine data from both tables because there is a one-to-many relationship between the *Customer* field in the *Appointments* table (which stores the customer ID number) and the *Customer ID* field in the *Customers* table.

Use the Simple Query Wizard to create a simple select query. A **select query** displays data from one or more related tables or queries, based on the fields that you select.

To create a query using the *Simple Query Wizard:*

1. On the *Create* tab, in the *Queries* group, click the **Query Wizard** button.
2. In the *New Query* dialog, **Simple Query Wizard** is selected by default. Click **OK.**

FIGURE AC 4.1

1. Click the **Tables/Queries** drop-down arrow. Click the first table or query that you want to select data from.
2. To add a field to the query, double-click the field name in the *Available Fields* list to add it to the *Selected Fields* list, or click the field name and then click the **>** button.

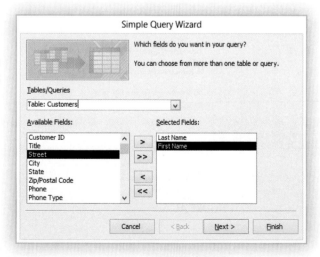

FIGURE AC 4.2

FIGURE AC 4.3

3. To add data fields from another table or query, click the **Tables/Queries** drop-down arrow again. Click the next table or query you want to select data from.

4. Add the field or fields you want to include in the query.

5. When you have added all the fields you want, click **Next.**

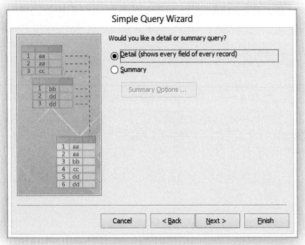

FIGURE AC 4.4

6. The radio button to create a detail query is selected by default. The detail query shows every field you selected for every record. Click **Next.**

FIGURE AC 4.5

7. Give the query a meaningful title.

8. To see the results of the query immediately, verify that the **Open the query to view information.** radio button is selected.

9. Click **Finish.**

Notice that the query results datasheet looks like a table datasheet. It has the same navigation buttons at the bottom. However, the *Table Tools Fields* tab and the *Table Tools Table* tab are not available when you are viewing the query results datasheet. You cannot manipulate the structure of the underlying tables when you are viewing query results.

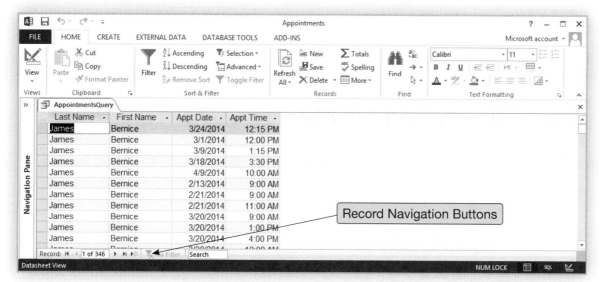

FIGURE AC 4.6
Query results

tips & tricks

You do not need to include the related primary key field and foreign key field(s) in the query.

let me try

If the database is not already open, open the data file **AC4-Appointments** and try this skill on your own:

1. Use the *Simple Query Wizard* to create a select query showing the details for every record in the results. Include these fields in this order: the **Last Name** and **First Name** fields from the *Customers* table and the **Appt Date** and **Appt Time** fields from the *Appointments* table. Select the option to open the query to view information. Use the query title: `AppointmentsQuery`

2. Review the query results, and then close the query.

Skill 4.2 Creating a Query in Design View

You can create a new query from scratch using Design view. The query Design window has two parts. The upper pane shows the tables referenced in the query. The lower pane shows the **query grid** where you specify which fields to include in the query.

To create a select query in Design view:

1. On the *Create* tab, in the *Queries* group, click the **Query Design** button.

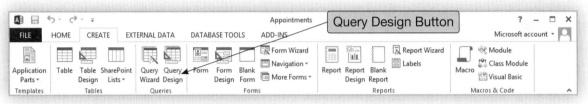

FIGURE AC 4.7

2. The *Show Table* dialog opens. Double-click the name of each table you want to include in the query (or click the table name once, and then click the **Add** button). Click the **Close** button when you have added the tables you want. You must close the *Show Table* dialog before continuing to build the query.

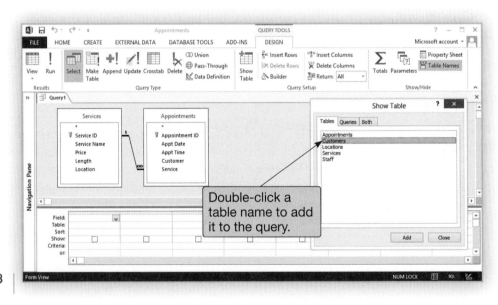

FIGURE AC 4.8

3. A complete field list for each table appears in the upper pane of the query Design window. When a relationship exists between two tables, a line connects the related fields.

- You can adjust the relative size of the two panes in the query Design window by clicking and dragging the horizontal border just above the query grid.
- You can adjust the size of a table box to see more fields by clicking and dragging the bottom boundary of the box downward.
- You can rearrange the table boxes in the upper pane of the query Design window by clicking the box header and dragging the box to a new location (similar to rearranging tables in the Relationships window).

- To remove a table from the query Design window, right-click the table box header and select **Remove Table.**

4. Add fields to the query using one of these methods:
   - Double-click the field name in the field list.
   - Click the field name and drag it to the design grid.
   - Click in an empty cell in the *Field* row of the design grid, expand the list of available fields by clicking the arrow, and click the field name you want.

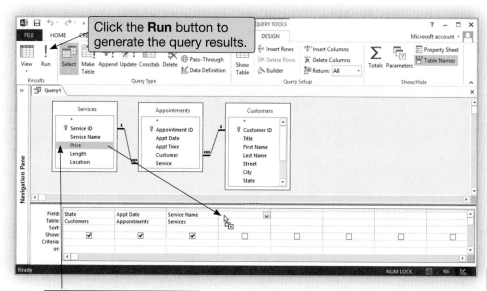

FIGURE AC 4.9

- To rearrange the order of fields in the query, move the mouse pointer to the top of the field column in the grid. When the mouse pointer changes to the ↓ shape, click to select the entire column, and then click and drag the column to the new position in the grid.
- To remove a field from the query grid, move the mouse pointer to the top of the field column in the grid. When the mouse pointer changes to the ↓ shape, click to select the entire column, and then press (Delete).

5. When you have added all the fields you want, run the query by clicking the **Run** button near the left side of the Ribbon (on the *Query Tools Design* tab, in the *Results* group).

6. If you want to use the query again in the future, be sure to save the query, giving it a meaningful name.

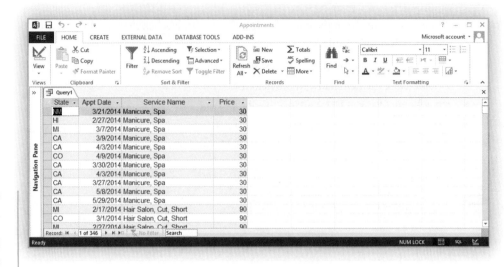

FIGURE AC 4.10
Query results showing fields from the *Customers, Appointments,* and *Services* tables

tips & tricks

If you want to include all the fields from a table in your query, click and drag the asterisk (*) to the field row. Notice that rather than listing each field from the table separately, there is only one field called table.* (where "table" is the name of the table). The * character represents a wildcard. Rather than look for specific field names, the query will look for all the fields in that table. So, if you later add or delete fields, you won't need to change the query design.

another method

You can also view the results of a query by switching to Datasheet view using one of these methods:

- On the *Query Tools Design* tab, in the *Results* group, click the **View** button.
- Click the **View** button arrow, and select **Datasheet View.**
- Right-click the query tab, and select **Datasheet View.**
- Click the **Datasheet View** button in the status bar.

tell me more

To display the *Show Table* dialog again to add other tables to the query, on the *Query Tools Design* tab, in the *Query Setup* group, click the **Show Table** button.

let me try

If the database is not already open, open the data file **AC4-Appointments** and try this skill on your own:

1. Begin a new query in Design view.
2. Add these tables: **Services, Appointments,** and **Customers.**
3. If necessary, adjust the size of the **Customers** table box so you can see the *State* field.
4. Add these fields to the query grid, in this order: **State** from the *Customers* table, **Appt Date** from the *Appointments* table, and **Service Name** and **Price** from the *Services* table.
5. Run the query.
6. Save the query with the name: `ServicesByStateQuery`

Skill 4.3 Adding Text Criteria to a Query

You can refine a select query in Design view so it shows only records that meet specific criteria. **Criteria** are conditions that the records must meet in order to be included in the query results. Each field data type takes a certain type of **criterion**. Text criteria are used for text and hyperlink fields.

To add text criteria to your query:

1. Open the query in Design view.

2. In the *Criteria* row, enter the text you want to match in the column for the appropriate field. For example, to include only records where the state is Colorado, enter the text criterion **"CO"** in the *Criteria* row under the *State* field. If you do not include the quotation marks when you enter text in the *Criteria* row, Access will place the text in quotation marks for you.

3. Run the query to see the results.

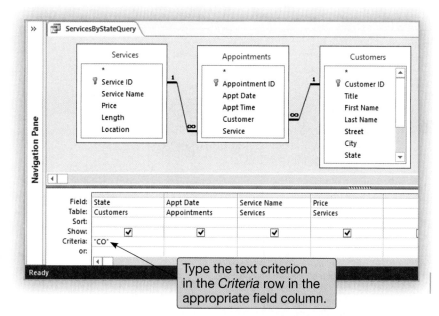

Type the text criterion in the *Criteria* row in the appropriate field column.

FIGURE AC 4.11

State	Appt Date	Service Name	Price
CO	3/3/2014	Manicure/Pedicure Spa Packag	75
CO	3/12/2014	Facial, Deep Cleansing	75
CO	4/6/2014	Facial, Detox	95
CO	3/29/2014	Facial, European	75
CO	4/13/2014	Facial, Relaxing	75
CO	4/14/2014	Hair Salon, Color, One Proces	150
CO	4/1		90
CO	4/1		125
CO	4/1		75
CO	3/		90
CO	3/10/2014	Hydrotherapy, Level III	175
CO	3/18/2014	Facial, Relaxing	75
CO	3/25/2014	Hydrotherapy, Level I	95
CO	4/8/2014	Hair Salon, Up Do, Simple	95
CO	4/9/2014	Manicure, Spa	30

Query results now include only records where the value in the *State* field is CO.

Record: 1 of 15   No Filter   Search

FIGURE AC 4.12

You can use the **wildcard** characters asterisk (*) and question mark (?) and the "like" construction in the query criteria to find inexact text matches. The * wildcard replaces any string of characters. The ? wildcard replaces a single character.

To include all records where the data in the *State* field begins with the letter C followed by one unknown letter, enter the criterion `Like "C?"`. The query in Figure AC 4.13 will return records for CA and CO. (There are no customers from CT in this database.)

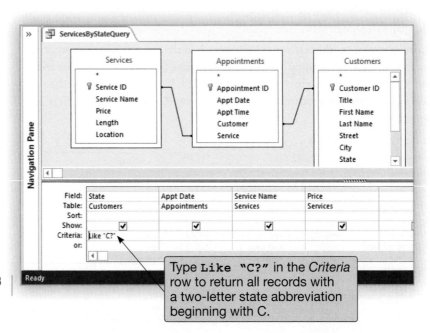

FIGURE AC 4.13

Type `Like "C?"` in the *Criteria* row to return all records with a two-letter state abbreviation beginning with C.

The query results now include records with both CO and CA in the *State* field.

FIGURE AC 4.14

Use the * wildcard instead of the ? wildcard if you're not sure of the exact number of characters you're looking for. The query in Figure AC 4.15 will return records where the data in the *State* field begins with the letter C—including CA, California, CO, and Colorado.

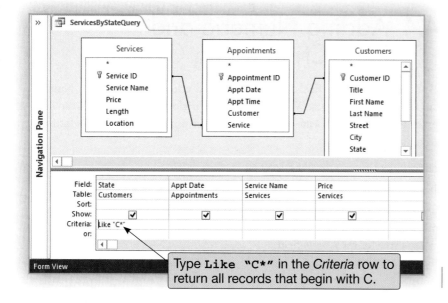

Type **Like "C*"** in the *Criteria* row to return all records that begin with C.

FIGURE AC 4.15

tips & tricks

When you begin typing in the criteria cell, Access may display a list of possible functions you could use if you were building an expression. This can be annoying if you're trying to enter text criteria instead. To prevent this, type the text criteria within quotation marks.

tell me **more**

Wildcard characters are not limited to the beginning of a text string. You can place them at the end or at both the beginning and end of the text.

▶ The criteria construction **Like "*Spa"** will find all records with data that end with the letters "Spa".

▶ The criteria construction **Like "*Spa*"** will find all records with the letters "Spa" anywhere within the data.

▶ The criteria construction **Not Like "*Spa*"** will find all records with data that do not include "Spa" anywhere within the text string.

let me **try**

If the database is not already open, open the data file **AC4-Appointments** and try this skill on your own:

1. If necessary, open the *ServicesByStateQuery* query in Design view. If your database does not include this query, create it following the steps in *Skill 4.2: Creating a Query in Design View*.
2. Add a criterion to the query so the results will include only records where the value of the *State* field is equal to the text CO.
3. Run the query and review the results.
4. Return to Design view and modify the query so the results will include any record where the value of the *State* field begins with the letter C.
5. Run the query and review the results.
6. Save and close the query.

Skill 4.4 Adding Numeric and Date Criteria to a Query

Criteria are not limited to text fields. You can also add criteria to fields with Number, Currency, or Date/Time data types. When entering numeric or date criteria, you can enter values for exact matches, or you can enter an expression using comparison operators to broaden the criteria.

To add numeric or date criteria to your query:

1. Open the query in Design view.

2. In the *Criteria* row, enter the value or the expression in the column for the appropriate field. For example, to find all appointments that are longer than 75 minutes, enter **>75** in the *Criteria* row for the *Length* field.

3. Run the query to see the results.

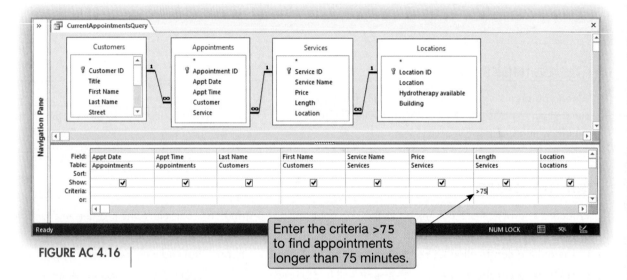

FIGURE AC 4.16

Enter the criteria >75 to find appointments longer than 75 minutes.

FIGURE AC 4.17

Only appointments longer than 75 minutes are included in the query results.

You can also use comparison operators with dates. To find all appointments that are scheduled for January 1, 2014 or later, enter the criterion **>=1/1/2014** in the *Criteria* row for the *Appt Date* field. When you enter dates in the *Criteria* row, Access places # symbols around the date. It is not necessary to type the # symbols yourself.

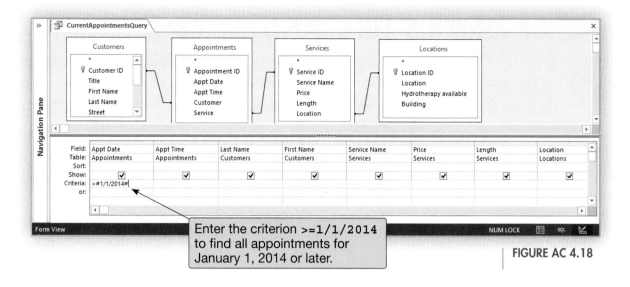

Enter the criterion >=1/1/2014 to find all appointments for January 1, 2014 or later.

FIGURE AC 4.18

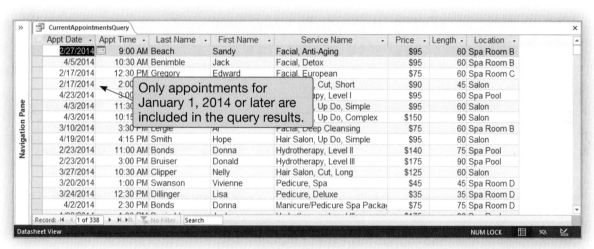

Only appointments for January 1, 2014 or later are included in the query results.

FIGURE AC 4.19

tips & tricks

Common comparison operators are:

>	greater than	<	less than	=	equal to
< >	not equal to	>=	greater than or equal to	<=	less than or equal to

let me try

If the database is not already open, open the data file **AC4-Appointments** and try this skill on your own:

1. If necessary, open the *CurrentAppointmentQuery* query in Design view.
2. Add criteria to limit the query to appointments longer than **75** minutes.
3. Run the query and review the results.
4. Return to Design view and add criteria to show appointments for **January 1, 2014** and later. Be sure to remove the criteria from the *Length* field first.
5. Run the query and review the results.
6. Save the query.

Skill 4.5 Using AND and OR in a Query

You can make a query more specific by limiting query results to records that meet multiple criteria:

▶ To find records that meet two or more conditions in different fields, enter each of the criteria in the *Criteria* row.

▶ To find records that meet more than one condition in the same field, enter both criteria separated by the word *and* in the *Criteria* row.

For example, to find all appointments that meet these conditions—January 1, 2014 or later **AND** March 31, 2014 or earlier **AND** last name is Smith:

Enter >=1/1/2014 and <=3/31/2014 in the *Criteria* row for the *Appt Date* field and enter **Smith** in the *Criteria* row for the *Last Name* field as shown in Figure AC 4.20.

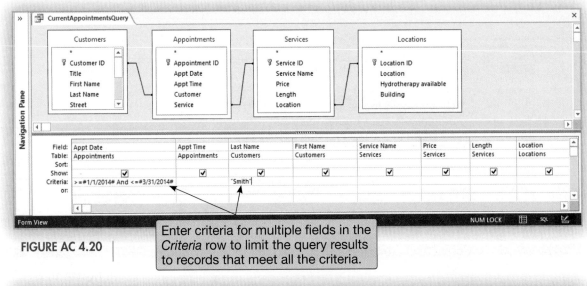

FIGURE AC 4.20

Enter criteria for multiple fields in the *Criteria* row to limit the query results to records that meet all the criteria.

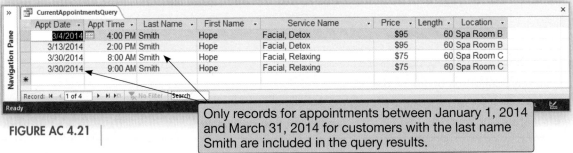

FIGURE AC 4.21

Only records for appointments between January 1, 2014 and March 31, 2014 for customers with the last name Smith are included in the query results.

You can make a query broader by expanding the query results to records that meet any one of multiple criteria. To find records that meet any of the conditions, enter the criteria on separate rows in the query grid:

1. Enter the first criterion in the *Criteria* row.

2. Enter the second criterion in the *or* row (the row immediately below the *Criteria* row).

To find all appointments for customers with the last name Smith or Clauson, enter **Smith** in the *Criteria* row for the *Last Name* field, and then enter **Clauson** in the *or* row for the *Last Name* field as shown in Figure AC 4.22.

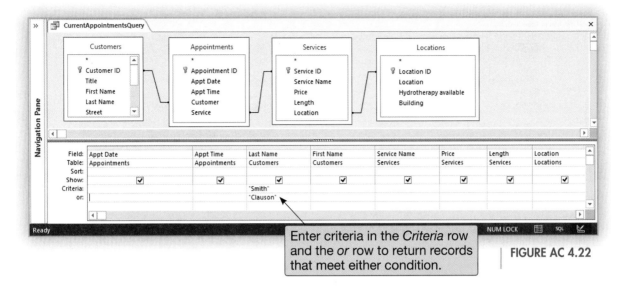

Enter criteria in the *Criteria* row and the *or* row to return records that meet either condition.

FIGURE AC 4.22

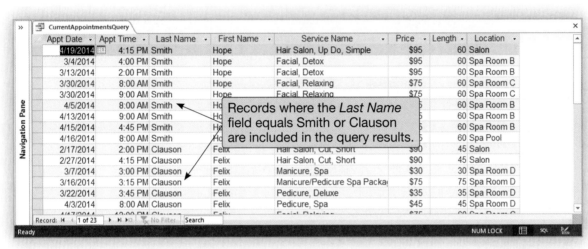

Records where the *Last Name* field equals Smith or Clauson are included in the query results.

FIGURE AC 4.23

Criteria do not need to be in the same field. When using an *or* construction with multiple fields, make sure that each criterion is on its own row. The query shown in Figure AC 4.24 will return records where the value of the *Last Name* field is Smith or the value of the *First Name* field is Caleb.

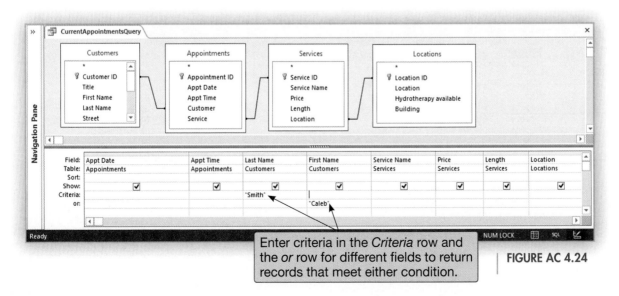

Enter criteria in the *Criteria* row and the *or* row for different fields to return records that meet either condition.

FIGURE AC 4.24

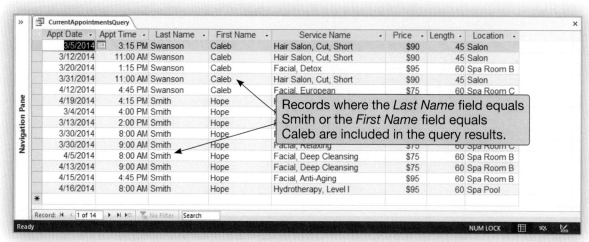

FIGURE AC 4.25

You can combine the *and* and *or* query constructions to create a very precise query. The query in Figure AC 4.26 will return records with appointments between January 1, 2014 and March 31, 2014 for customers with the last name Smith or the first name Caleb. Because the date range criterion is the same for both *or* criteria, it must be repeated in both rows.

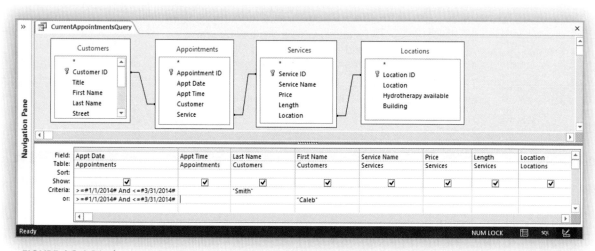

FIGURE AC 4.26

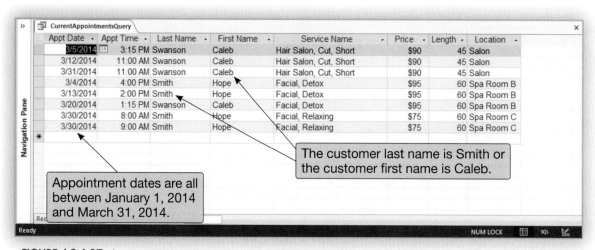

FIGURE AC 4.27

tips & tricks

If your query does not return the records you expect, check the placement of the criteria in the query grid.
- Criteria in the same row make the query more specific.
- Criteria in different rows make the query less specific.
- If you combine the *and* and *or* constructions, don't forget to include the *and* condition in every *or* row.

tell me **more**

You can add more *or* criteria by continuing to add criteria to the rows under the first *or* row.

let me **try**

If the database is not already open, open the data file **AC4-Appointments** and try this skill on your own:
1. If necessary, open the *CurrentAppointmentsQuery* query in Design view.
2. Remove any existing criteria.
3. Add criteria to find appointments between **January 1, 2014** and **March 31, 2014** (inclusive) for any customer with the last name **Smith.**
4. Run the query and review the results.
5. Return to Design view and delete the criteria for the *Appt Date* field.
6. Modify the query criteria to show all appointments for customers with the last name **Smith** or **Clauson.**
7. Run the Query and review the results.
8. Return to Design view and delete the *or* criterion for the *Last Name* field (Clauson).
9. Modify the query criteria to show all appointments for customers with the last name **Smith** or the first name **Caleb.**
10. Run the query and review the results.
11. Return to Design view and limit the query to include results between **January 1, 2014** and **March 31, 2014** (inclusive) for customers with the last name **Smith** or the first name **Caleb.**
12. Run the query and review the results.
13. Save and close the query.

Skill 4.6 Specifying the Sort Order in a Query

Query results may display records in an unexpected order. If you want to control how records are displayed, set the sort order as part of the query design. The sort order will be applied every time the query is run.

To add a sort order to a query:

1. Open the query in Design view.
2. Click in the *Sort* row for the field you want to sort by. Click the arrow to expand the sort options list, and select **Ascending** or **Descending.**
3. Run the query.

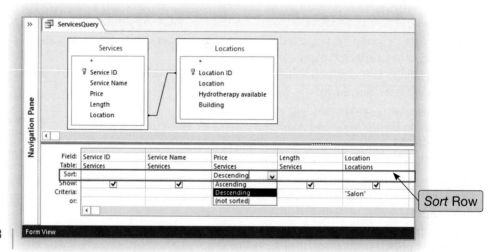

FIGURE AC 4.28

FIGURE AC 4.29

tell me **more**

For more information about sorting, refer to the skill *Sorting Records in a Table.*

let me try

If the database is not already open, open the data file **AC4-Appointments** and try this skill on your own:

1. Open the *ServicesQuery* query in Design view.
2. Set the sort order so the results will display records with the highest price first.
3. Run the query and review the results.
4. Save the query.

Skill 4.7 Hiding and Showing Fields in a Query

If you want to include a field in your query but do not want that field to show in Datasheet view, click the **Show** box to remove the checkmark. By hiding the field, you can use it to define criteria for the query without making the field visible in the final query results.

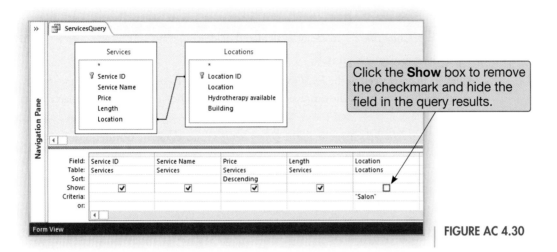

> Click the **Show** box to remove the checkmark and hide the field in the query results.

FIGURE AC 4.30

FIGURE AC 4.31
Query results with the *Location* field hidden

tips & tricks

Run the query to verify that it returns results as you expect before hiding the field.

let me try

If the database is not already open, open the data file **AC4-Appointments** and try this skill on your own:

1. If necessary, open the *ServicesQuery* query in Design view.
2. Notice that the criterion *Salon* is entered for the *Location* field.
3. Run the query and review the results.
4. Return to Design view and hide the **Location** field so it does not appear in the query results.
5. Run the query. Notice that the results are the same, but now the *Location* field is hidden. It was not necessary as every record in the result had the same value.
6. Save and close the query.

Skill 4.8 Adding a Calculated Field to a Query

Database fields generally display the data that are entered into them. However, a **calculated field** displays a value returned by an **expression** (a formula). Expressions can reference fields, mathematical operators, and functions. To create a calculated field using an expression, you can type the formula directly in the query grid or you can use the *Expression Builder* to build the formula.

To use the *Expression Builder* to create a calculated field in a query:

1. Open the query in Design view.

2. Click in an empty cell in the *Field* row in the query grid. If a cell with a field name is selected when you build the expression, you will replace the field with the calculated field.

3. On the *Query Tools Design* tab, in the *Query Setup* group, click the **Builder** button to open the *Expression Builder*.

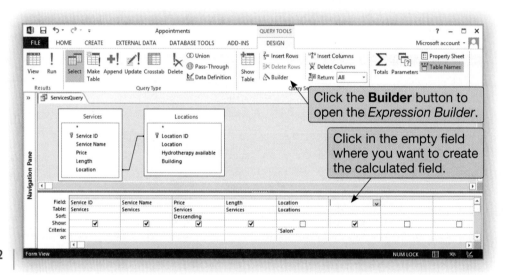

FIGURE AC 4.32

4. The center box in the *Expression Builder* lists fields in the query. In the *Expression Categories* box, double-click the field name to add it to the expression box at the top of the dialog. When referencing a field name in an expression, the field name is always enclosed in brackets.

5. Finish entering the expression. For example, to calculate a 15 percent increase, type *** 1.15** after the field name.

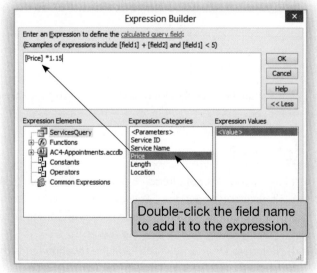

FIGURE AC 4.33

6. Click **OK** to add the expression to the query.

7. Notice that the new calculated field begins with *Expr1:*—this is the temporary name for the field. Click in the field and change **Expr1** to something more meaningful. Be careful not to delete the colon.

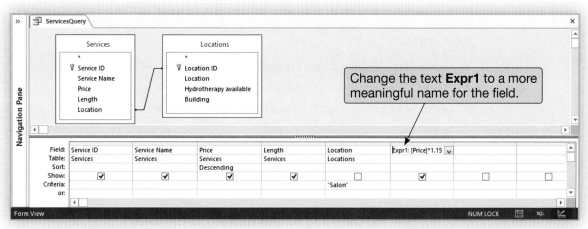

FIGURE AC 4.34

8. Run the query to see the results of the calculated field.

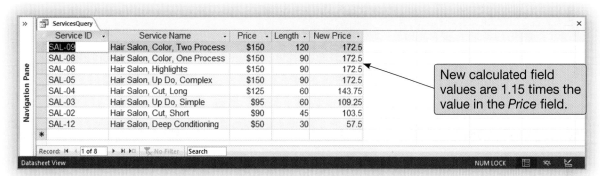

FIGURE AC 4.35

tips & tricks

When you add a calculated field to a query, the field can be used in forms and reports based on that query.

tell me **more**

The *Expression Builder* can be used to create complex expressions including functions similar to those in Excel. You use the *Expression Builder* to create calculated fields in tables and calculated controls in forms and reports.

let me try

If the database is not already open, open the data file **AC4-Appointments** and try this skill on your own:

1. If necessary, open the *ServicesQuery* query in Design view.
2. Add a new calculated field named **New Price** in the first empty column to the right of the *Length* field. The new field should calculate a value that is 1.15 times the value in the *Price* field.
3. Run the query and review the results.
4. Save and close the query.

Skill 4.9 Finding Unmatched Data Using a Query

Use the **Find Unmatched Query Wizard** to create a query that shows records from one table that have no corresponding records in another table. This type of query is useful for scenarios such as finding employees who have no sales records or customers who have no appointments.

To run the *Find Unmatched Query Wizard:*

1. On the *Create* tab, in the *Queries* group, click the **Query Wizard** button.

2. In the *New Query* dialog, click **Find Unmatched Query Wizard,** and click **OK.**

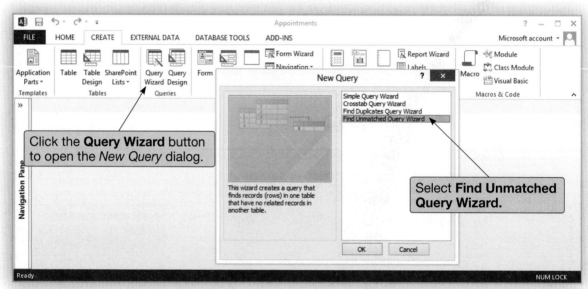

FIGURE AC 4.36

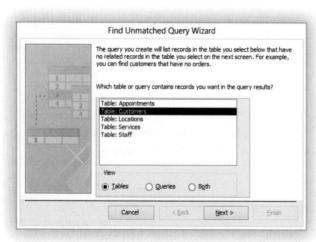

FIGURE AC 4.37

3. First, select the table or query that includes the records you want to match. Click **Next.**

4. Select the table or query that contains the related records. The query will return results from the first table that *do not* have corresponding records in this table. Click **Next**.

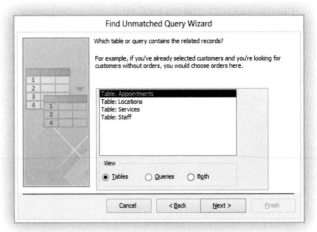

FIGURE AC 4.38

5. Now, find the fields in the two tables that might contain matches. If there is an obvious field (fields with the same name in both tables or fields with an established relationship), Access will automatically suggest it. Click **Next**.

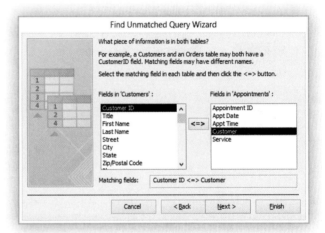

FIGURE AC 4.39

6. Add additional fields that you want to include in the query results. Add the fields that will help identify how the field values are related or fields that you need to identify the records accurately. Click **Next**.

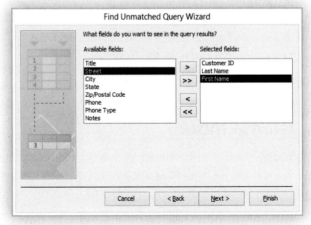

FIGURE AC 4.40

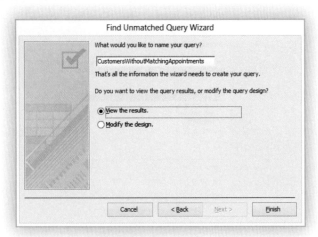

FIGURE AC 4.41

7. Give the query a title, and click **Finish** to view the results.

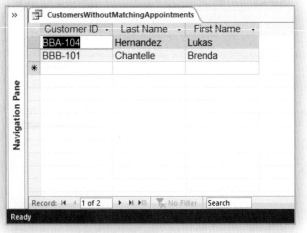

FIGURE AC 4.42

The results of the *Unmatched Query Wizard* display the specified fields from the first table for records that do not have corresponding records in the second table—in this case, the *Customer ID, Last Name,* and *First Name* fields from the *Customers* table where the customer does not have any matching records in the *Appointments* table.

tips & tricks

When selecting the field(s) to search for unmatched values, remember that the fields might be named differently in the two tables. For example, the *CustomerID* field in the *Customers* table might contain the same values as the *Customer* field in the *Appointments* table.

tell me **more**

You can create a select query yourself to find records that are missing data in a particular field. Type **Is Null** in the *Criteria* cell for the field you want to find. When you run the query, the results will show all records that are missing data in that field. To return only records that have data in the field, type **Is Not Null** in the *Criteria* cell instead.

let me **try**

If the database is not already open, open the data file **AC4-Appointments** and try this skill on your own:

1. Create a new query using the *Unmatched Query Wizard* to find records in the **Customers** table without corresponding records in the **Appointments** table. Include the **Customer ID, Last Name,** and **First Name** fields from the *Customers* table in that order. Name the query: **CustomersWithoutMatchingAppointments**
2. View the query results and then close the query.

Skill 4.10 Finding Duplicate Data Using a Query

You can create a query to find all the records that have duplicate values in one or more fields. A **Find Duplicates** query is useful for finding records that may have been entered more than once or for scenarios such as finding all employees who live in the same city (duplicates in the city field) or locating customers who may have duplicate appointments on the same day (duplicates in name and date fields).

To run the *Find Duplicates Query Wizard:*

1. On the *Create* tab, in the *Queries* group, click the **Query Wizard** button.

2. In the *New Query* dialog, click **Find Duplicates Query Wizard.** Click **OK.**

Click the **Query Wizard** button to open the *New Query* dialog.

Select **Find Duplicates Query Wizard.**

This wizard creates a query that finds records with duplicate field values in a single table or query.

FIGURE AC 4.43

3. Select the table or query that you want to search for duplicate values. In Figure AC 4.44, we are selecting a query that includes fields from multiple tables. This allows us to include more useful information in the query results, such as the customer last name and first name. Click **Next.**

FIGURE AC 4.44

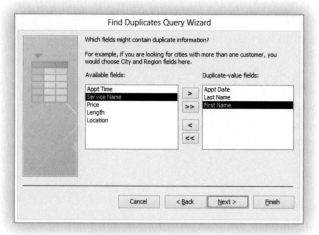

FIGURE AC 4.45

4. Add the field or fields that might contain duplicate values. Click **Next.**

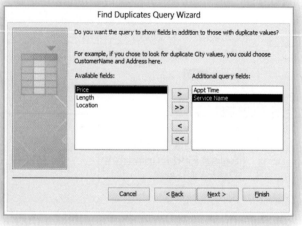

FIGURE AC 4.46

5. Add additional fields that you want to include in the query results. Add the fields that will help identify how the duplicate values are related or provide more information about the results. Click **Next.**

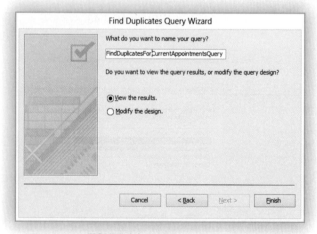

FIGURE AC 4.47

6. Give the query a title, and click **Finish** to view the results.

The results of the *Find Duplicates Query Wizard* display the specified fields from records with duplicate values in the specified fields—in this case, appointments with duplicate values in the *Appt Date, Last Name,* and *First Name* fields. The *Appt Time* and *Service Name* fields are included to provide more information about the possible duplicate appointments.

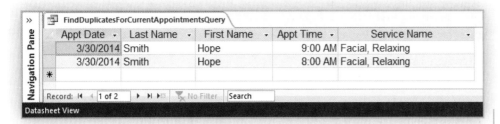

FIGURE AC 4.48

let me try

> If the database is not already open, open the data file **AC4-Appointments** and try this skill on your own:
>
> 1. Create a query using the *Find Duplicates Query Wizard* to find appointments on the same day for the same customer. Use the **CurrentAppointmentsQuery.** Find duplicate values in the **Appt Date, Last Name,** and **First Name** fields. Include the **Appt Time** and **Service Name** fields to provide more information about the appointment. Name the query: `FindDuplicatesForCurrentAppointmentsQuery`
> 2. View the query results and then close the query.

from the perspective of . . .

PERSONAL TRAINER

I use Access to keep track of client appointments and billing. I use queries extensively as the basis for invoices and to create reports for specific clients. The *Unmatched Query Wizard* and the *Find Duplicates Query Wizard* help me create complex queries. As I work through the steps of a wizard, I think about the logic behind the query—considering which table or query contains the fields I want to apply criteria to and which fields I need to include in the results so I can make sense of them.

Skill 4.11 Using a Parameter Query

A **parameter query** is a type of select query that allows the user to provide the criteria. When you create a parameter query, you specify the field or fields that the query will use to limit the records in the results just as you would if you were entering the criteria yourself, but you don't specify the exact criteria. Instead, you enter a prompt that the user will see when the query is run. Then the user can enter the exact value or values to use as the criteria.

To create a parameter query:

1. In Design view, create a select query or open the existing query that you want to change to a parameter query.

2. In the appropriate cell in the *Criteria* row, instead of entering specific criteria, type the prompt the user will see, enclosed in brackets. Ideally, the prompt will give the user direction as to what data to enter. For example, **[Enter Customer Last Name]** or **[Enter Appointment Date]**.

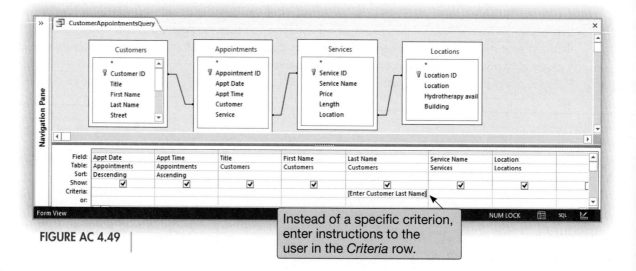

Instead of a specific criterion, enter instructions to the user in the *Criteria* row.

FIGURE AC 4.49

3. Run the query to test it. Notice that before results display, the *Enter Parameter Value* dialog appears with the prompt you created. Enter a value in the box, and then click **OK**.

Type the value to use as the field criterion.

FIGURE AC 4.50

4. The results of the query display only records that match the value you typed in the *Enter Parameter Value* dialog.

In Figure AC 4.51, the query results are limited to records where the value in the *Last Name* field is *Swanson*. Typing **Swanson** in the *Enter Parameter Value* dialog has the same effect as typing **Swanson** in the *Criteria* row for the *Last Name* field.

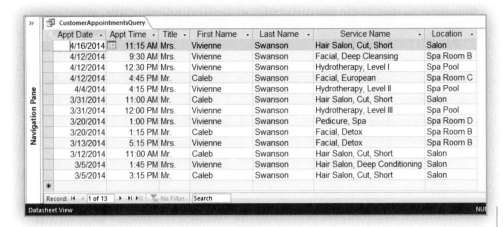

FIGURE AC 4.51

tell me **more**

You can prevent users from entering a parameter input in the wrong data type.

1. On the *Query Tools Design* tab, in the *Show/Hide* group, click the **Parameters** button.
2. The *Query Parameters* dialog opens.
3. In the *Parameter* column, enter the parameter prompt exactly as you entered it in the query grid.
4. In the *Data Type* column, select the appropriate data type.
5. Click **OK.**

Now if a user attempts to use a parameter value with the wrong data type, he or she will see an error message rather than incorrect query results.

let me **try**

If the database is not already open, open the data file **AC4-Appointments** and try this skill on your own:

1. Open the **CustomerAppointmentsQuery** query in Design view.
2. Create a parameter query where the user will enter a value to use as the criterion for the **Last Name** field. Use the prompt **Enter Customer Last Name.** Don't forget to enclose the prompt in brackets.
3. Test the parameter query using the last name **Swanson.**
4. Save and close the query.

Skill 4.12 Filtering Data Using AutoFilter

By applying a **filter** to a database object, you display a subset of records that meet the filter criteria. AutoFilter displays a list of all the unique values in the field. This feature is available for table, queries, and forms. If you have used Microsoft Excel, AutoFilter will be familiar to you.

To filter a datasheet using AutoFilter:

1. Open the database object in Datasheet view.
2. Click the arrow at the top of the column in the column that contains the data you want to filter for.
3. At first, all of the filter options are checked. Click the **(Select All)** check box to remove all the checkmarks.
4. Click the check box or check boxes in front of the values you want to filter for.
5. Click **OK.**

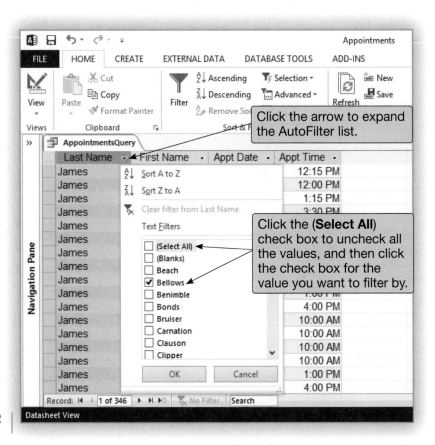

FIGURE AC 4.52

Access displays only the records that include the values you selected. The field that is filtered displays a filter icon next to the arrow in the field header.

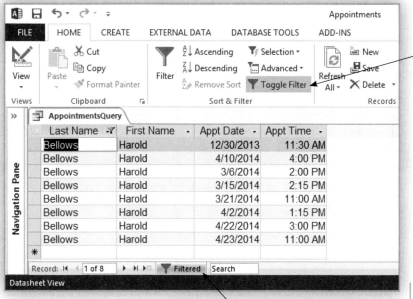

Click the **Toggle Filter** button to toggle back and forth between the filtered view and the unfiltered view.

FIGURE AC 4.53

The highlighted *Filter* button indicates that a filter has been applied to the query.

On the *Home* tab, in the *Sort & Filter* group, click the **Toggle Filter** button to clear the filter. Click the **Toggle Filter** button again to reapply the filter.

Notice that when the database object has a filter applied, the *Filtered* button is highlighted next to the navigation buttons at the bottom of the object. You can also click this button to toggle back and forth between the filtered view and the unfiltered view.

To remove the filter, display the AutoFilter list again, and select the **Clear filter** option. Once you use the *Clear filter* command, you cannot use the *Toggle Filter* or *Filtered* button to show the filter again. You have to recreate it.

Click the **Clear filter** option to remove the filter from the field.

FIGURE AC 4.54

tips & tricks

Filtering with AutoFilter is temporary. When you close the database object, the filter is not saved. If you want a more permanent filter applied to a query, add criteria in Design view instead.

another method

To display the AutoFilter list, on the *Home* tab, in the *Sort & Filter* group, click the **Filter** button.

let me try

If the database is not already open, open the data file **AC4-Appointments** and try this skill on your own:

1. If necessary, open the *AppointmentsQuery* query in Datasheet view. If your database does not include this query, create it following the steps in *Skill 4.1: Using the Simple Query Wizard*.
2. Use AutoFilter to filter the query results to show only records where the last name is **Bellows**.
3. Clear the filter from the field.

Skill 4.13 Filtering Data Using Filter by Selection

If a record that contains the data you want to filter for is visible, you can click the field and use the *Filter by Selection* feature. Besides filtering by matching exact values, you can filter for values that meet broader criteria.

To filter by selection, select the data you want to use as the filter criteria. On the *Home* tab, in the *Sort & Filter* group, click the **Selection** button to view the filtering options available.

❭ The first option is to filter for only records that match the selected field value exactly.

❭ The second option is to filter for all records that do not match the selected field value.

❭ The other options will vary depending on the data type of the selected field. For example:

- A text field will include options to filter for records that contain or do not contain the text in the selected field.
- A numeric field will include options to filter for records that are less than or greater than the selected field value.
- A *Date/Time* field will include options to filter for records that include a date/time on or before or after the selected date.

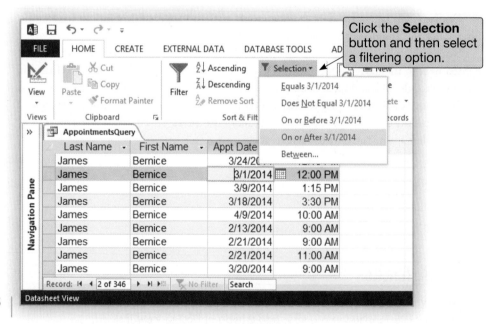

FIGURE AC 4.55

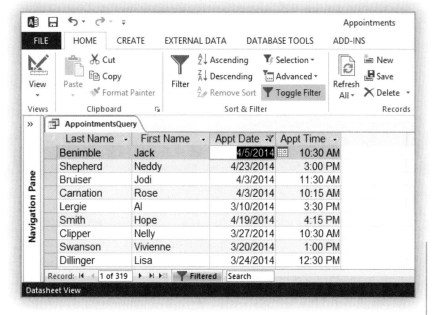

FIGURE AC 4.56
Query results filtered to show only records where the value in the *Appt Date* field is on or after 3/1/2014.

tell me **more**

You can apply filters to more than one field at a time.

To remove all filters from a database object, click the **Advanced Filter Options** button arrow and select **Clear All Filters.**

another **method**

The filter options available by right-clicking a value are more extensive than those available from the *Selection* button menu.

1. Right-click anywhere in the field you want to filter for.
2. Point to the **Filters** option and then click the filter option you want from the submenu. The *Filters* option will include the data type (for example, if the field is a text field, the right-click menu will include *Text Filters;* if it is a date/time field, the right-click menu will include *Date Filters*).
3. When you make a selection from the submenu, a dialog may open, allowing you to enter specific filter criteria.

let me **try**

If the database is not already open, open the data file **AC4-Appointments** and try this skill on your own:

1. If necessary, open the *AppointmentsQuery* query in Datasheet view. If your database does not include this query, create it following the steps in *Skill 4.1: Using the Simple Query Wizard.*
2. Clear any filters that may have been applied to the query results.
3. Filter the query results to show only appointment dates on or after **3/1/2014.** Hint: Use the *Appt Date* field for the second record in the dataset to filter by selection.
4. Clear the filter from the field.

Skill 4.14 Sorting Records in a Datasheet

You can control the order in which records appear in a table, query, or form by using the **Sort** feature. Sorting records in Access is similar to sorting data in Excel.

To sort records:

1. Open the database object in Datasheet view.
2. Click anywhere in the field you want to sort.
3. On the *Home* tab, in the *Sort & Filter* group, click the button for the sort order you want to apply: **Ascending** (A–Z) or **Descending** (Z–A).
4. Save the database object if you want to save the sorting.

You can create multiple levels of sorting by applying the sort command to the fields in the **opposite** order in which you want the sort to appear. For example, if you want records sorted by appointment date and then by appointment time for each date, you would sort by appointment time first, and then sort by appointment date. The first sort level is called the **outermost sort**. The last sort level is called the **innermost sort**. When applying the sort commands, sort the innermost sort first and the outermost sort last. You can have as many sort levels as you want, but remember to begin with the innermost sort and work your way out.

In Figure AC 4.57, the query results are sorted first by dates in the *Appt Date* field, from newest to oldest. This is the outermost sort. The data are then sorted by the *Appt Time* field, from oldest to newest. This is the innermost sort. When creating the sort, we sorted on the *Appt Time* field first, and then applied the sort to the *Appt Date* field.

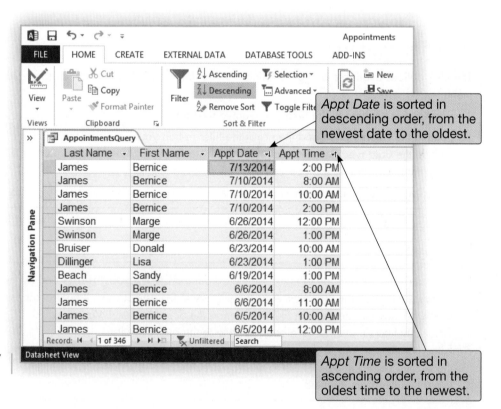

FIGURE AC 4.57

To clear all sorting from the database object, on the *Home* tab, in the *Sort & Filter* group, click the **Remove Sort** button.

tips & tricks

Unlike filters, the sort order you apply to a database object is saved when you save the object.

tell me **more**

The sort options will differ, depending on the data type of the field you are sorting:

> *Text* and *Hyperlink* fields sort alphabetically from *A–Z* or *Z–A*.

> *Number, Currency,* and *AutoNumber* fields sort on their numeric values from *Smallest to Largest* or *Largest to Smallest*.

> *Date/Time* fields sort by time from *Oldest to Newest* or *Newest to Oldest*. If you want to show the most recent records first, use the *Z–A* button (Newest to Oldest).

> *Yes/No* fields are often displayed as check boxes and sort from *Selected to Cleared* or *Cleared to Selected*. A checkmark or "yes" value is the "selected" state.

another **method**

> If the database object is in datasheet format, you can click the arrow at the top of the column you want to sort and select a sort option.

> You can also right-click a field and select a sort option.

let me **try**

If the database is not already open, open the data file **AC4-Appointments** and try this skill on your own:

1. If necessary, open the *AppointmentsQuery* query in Datasheet view. If your database does not include this query, create it following the steps in *Skill 4.1: Using the Simple Query Wizard*.
2. Clear any filters that may have been applied to the query results.
3. Sort the query results by last name, from A–Z.
4. Clear the sort.
5. Sort the query so the results are sorted by date, with the most recent date first, and then by time within each date, with the earliest time first.
6. Save and close the query.

key terms

Select query
Query grid
Criteria
Criterion
Wildcard
Calculated field
Expression

Find Unmatched query
Find Duplicates query
Parameter query
Filter
Outermost sort
Innermost sort

concepts review

1. A _____ displays data from one or more tables or queries, based on the fields that you select.

   a. crosstab query

   b. select query

   c. Find Unmatched query

   d. Find Duplicates query

2. The upper pane in query Design view shows the query grid where you specify which fields to include in the query.

   a. True

   b. False

3. _____ are conditions that the records must meet in order to be included in the query results.

   a. Data

   b. Fields

   c. Criteria

   d. Records

4. Entering < >**80** as the criteria for a query will return results that are _____.

   a. greater than 80

   b. less than 80

   c. equal to 80

   d. not equal to 80

5. To limit query results to only records that meet all the criteria, enter criteria for multiple fields on the *Criteria* row, or enter multiple criteria for the same field separated by the word *And*.

   a. True

   b. False

6. A _____ displays a value returned by an expression.

   a. calculated field

   b. query

   c. formula

   d. parameter query

7. If you want to create a query that shows records from one table that have no corresponding records in another table, use a _____.

    a. parameter query

    b. select query

    c. Find Unmatched query

    d. Find Duplicates query

8. If you wanted to display records of all employees who live in the same city (from the City field in the table), you would use a _____.

    a. parameter query

    b. select query

    c. Find Unmatched query

    d. Find Duplicates query

9. When you create a _____, you specify the field or fields that the query will use, but you don't specify the exact criteria.

    a. parameter query

    b. select query

    c. Find Unmatched query

    d. Find Duplicates query

10. AutoFilter and Filter by Selection settings are saved with the database object.

    a. True

    b. False

projects

Data files for projects can be found on
www.mhhe.com/office2013skills

skill review 4.1

In this project, you will continue to work with the Computer Science department database from *Chapter 3, Skill Review 3.1*. You will add queries to the database to organize the *Employees* table and to manage equipment on loan. You will use sorting and filtering techniques to analyze the *Employees* and *Items* tables.

Skills needed to complete this project:

- Using the Simple Query Wizard (Skill 4.1)
- Adding Text Criteria to a Query (Skill 4.3)
- Specifying the Sort Order in a Query (Skill 4.6)
- Creating a Query in Design View (Skill 4.2)
- Adding Numeric and Date Criteria to a Query (Skill 4.4)
- Hiding and Showing Fields in a Query (Skill 4.7)
- Adding a Calculated Field to a Query (Skill 4.8)
- Finding Unmatched Data Using a Query (Skill 4.9)
- Finding Duplicate Data Using a Query (Skill 4.10)
- Filtering Data Using AutoFilter (Skill 4.12)
- Filtering Data Using Filter by Selection (Skill 4.13)
- Sorting Records in a Datasheet (Skill 4.14)

1. Open the start file **AC2013-SkillReview-4-1.**

2. If necessary, enable active content by clicking the **Enable Content** button in the Message Bar.

3. Save a copy of the file to work on named:
   `[your initials]AC-SkillReview-4-1`

4. Use the **Query Wizard** to create a select query from the *Employees* table.

   a. On the *Create* tab, in the *Queries* group, click the **Query Wizard** button. In the *New Query* dialog, verify that **Simple Query Wizard** is selected. Click **OK.**

   b. Verify that **Table: Employees** is selected in the *Tables/Queries* list. Click the **>>** button to add all the fields to the right. Use the **<** button to remove the *EmployeeID* field from the right side. Click **Next.**

   c. In this step, make sure that **Detail** is selected and click **Next.**

   d. In the last step, type `InstructorsByTenure` for the title. Select the radio button to **Modify the query design** and click **Finish.**

5. Add criteria to the query to return records where the value of the *Position* field is **Adjunct** or **Faculty.**

   a. Type `Adjunct` in the *Criteria* row under the *Position* field. Below that, in the *or* area, type: `Faculty`

   b. Click the drop-down arrow in the *Sort* row under the *LengthOfService* field. Select **Ascending.**

c. Click the **Run** button.

d. Review the query results, and then save and close the query.

6. Create a query in Design view to return records from the *Items* table where the value of the *Category* field is **Software** and the value of the *Cost* field is **greater than or equal to 199**.

    a. On the *Create* tab, in the *Queries* group, click the **Query Design** button. In the *Show Table* dialog, double-click the **Items** table. Click the **Close** button.

    b. Notice the *Items* table in the upper pane of the query Design view window. Double-click each field name in the field list except *ItemID* in order to add them to your query.

    c. Type **Software** in the *Criteria* row under the *Category* field.

    d. Type **>=199** in the *Criteria* row under the *Cost* field.

    e. Uncheck the **Show** box under the *Category* field.

7. Create a calculated field to display a value that is 75% of the *Price* field value.

    a. Next to the *Cost* field, create a new calculated field by typing the following in the *Field* row: **OurCost: [Cost]*0.75**

    b. Click the **Run** button to check your work, and then return to Design view.

    c. On the *Query Tools Design* tab, in the *Query Setup* group, click the **Show Table** button. Double-click the **Loans** table and then click the **Close** button.

    d. Click the **Run** button and observe the new query results.

    e. Save the query with the name: **ExpensiveSoftwareOnLoan**

    f. Close the query.

8. Use the **Unmatched Query Wizard** to find items from the *Items* table that do not have corresponding records in the *Loans* table.

    a. On the *Create* tab, in the *Queries* group, click the **Query Wizard** button. In the *New Query* dialog, click **Find Unmatched Query Wizard** and click **OK**.

    b. Select **Table: Items**. Click **Next**.

    c. Select **Table: Loans**. Click **Next**.

    d. Confirm that Access has selected **ItemID** in both tables and then click **Next**.

    e. Add the following fields to the query by clicking the > button for each: **ItemName, Description, Category**. Click **Next**.

    f. Change the name to **ItemsNotOnLoan** and click **Finish**.

    g. Observe the query results and then close the query.

9. Use the **Find Duplicates Query Wizard** to find employees who have more than one entry in the *Loans* table.

    a. On the *Create* tab, in the *Queries* group, click the **Query Wizard** button. In the *New Query* dialog, click **Find Duplicates Query Wizard** and click **OK**.

    b. Select **Table: Loans**. Click **Next**.

    c. Select **EmployeeID** and add it to the right side by clicking the > button. Click **Next**.

    d. Add all fields by clicking the >> button. Click **Next**.

    e. Change the name to **EmployeeMultipleLoans** and click **Finish**.

    f. Observe the query results and then close the query.

10. Use AutoFilter to filter the *Employees* table to show only records where the value of the *Position* field is **Technician**.

    a. Open the **Employees** table in Datasheet view.

    b. Click the arrow in the **Position** field header. Use the check boxes to make sure that only the **Technician** option is checked. Click **OK** and observe the results.

11. Use *Filter by Selection* to filter the table further to include only employees where the length of service is 10 years or greater.

   a. Click in the *LengthOfService* field for any record where the value is **10.**

   b. On the *Home* tab, in the *Sort & Filter* group, click the **Selection** button.

   c. Click **Greater Than or Equal To 10.**

   d. Save and close the table.

12. Sort the *Items* table so records are organized alphabetically by category and then by cost from smallest to largest.

   a. Open the **Items** table in Datasheet view.

   b. Click anywhere inside the **Cost** field. On the *Home* tab, in the *Sort & Filter* group, click the **Ascending** button.

   c. Click anywhere inside the **Category** field. On the *Home* tab, in the *Sort & Filter* group, click the **Ascending** button.

   d. Save and close the table.

13. Close the database and exit Access.

skill review 4.2

In this project you will continue working with the health insurance database from *Chapter 3, Skill Review 3.2.* You will improve the functionality of the database by creating filters and queries for data most commonly searched for.

Skills needed to complete this project:

- Using the Simple Query Wizard (Skill 4.1)
- Adding Numeric and Date Criteria to a Query (Skill 4.4)
- Using AND and OR in a Query (Skill 4.5)
- Specifying the Sort Order in a Query (Skill 4.6)
- Creating a Query in Design View (Skill 4.2)
- Adding Text Criteria to a Query (Skill 4.3)
- Hiding and Showing Fields in a Query (Skill 4.7)
- Adding a Calculated Field to a Query (Skill 4.8)
- Finding Unmatched Data Using a Query (Skill 4.9)
- Finding Duplicate Data Using a Query (Skill 4.10)
- Using a Parameter Query (Skill 4.11)
- Filtering Data Using AutoFilter (Skill 4.12)
- Sorting Records in a Datasheet (Skill 4.14)

1. Open the start file **AC2013-SkillReview-4-2.**

2. If necessary, enable active content by clicking the **Enable Content** button in the Message Bar.

3. Save a copy of the file to work on named:
   [your initials]AC-SkillReview-4-2

4. Use the **Query Wizard** to create a select query from the *Physicians* table.

   a. On the *Create* tab, in the *Queries* group, click the **Query Wizard** button. In the *New Query* dialog, verify that **Simple Query Wizard** is selected. Click **OK.**

b. Click the **Tables/Queries** drop-down arrow. Select **Table: Physicians.** Click the >> button to add all the fields to the right. Use the < button to remove the *PhysicianID* field from the right side. Click **Next.**

c. In this step, make sure that **Detail** is selected and click **Next.**

d. In the last step, type **PhysiciansByZipCode** for the title. Select the radio button to **Modify the query design** and click **Finish.**

5. Add criteria to the query to limit the query to physicians with the zip code **33176** or **33186.**

   a. Type **33176** in the *Criteria* row under the *ZipCode* field.

   b. Below that, in the *or* row, type: **33186**

   c. Click the drop-down arrow in the **Sort** row under the *LastName* field. Select **Ascending.**

   d. Click the **Run** button and review the query results.

   e. Save and close the query.

6. Create a query in Design view:

   a. On the *Create* tab, in the *Queries* group, click the **Query Design** button. In the *Show Table* dialog, double-click the **Procedures** table. Click the **Close** button.

   b. Notice the *Procedures* table in the upper pane of the query Design view window. Double-click each field name in the field list except *ProcedureID* in order to add them to your query.

   c. Type **Yes** in the *Criteria* row under the *Covered* field.

   d. Type **<=30** in the *Criteria* row under the *ReimbursementAmt* field.

   e. Uncheck the **Show** box under the *Covered* field.

7. Add a calculated field to the query to display the result of a 5% increase in the reimbursement amount.

   a. Next to the *ReimbursementAmt* field, create a new calculated field by typing the following in the *Field* row: **5% Increase:[ReimbursementAmt]*1.05**

   b. Click the **Run** button to check your work and then return to Design view.

8. Add the *OrderDate* field from the *Orders* table to the query.

   a. On the *Query Tools Design* tab, in the *Query Setup* group, click the **Show Table** button. Double-click the **Orders** table and then click the **Close** button.

   b. Double-click the **OrderDate** field in the *Orders* table to add it to the query.

   c. Click the **Run** button and observe the new query results.

   d. Save the query with the name: **CheapCoveredProcedures**

   e. Close the query.

9. Use the **Unmatched Query Wizard** to find records in the *Procedures* table without corresponding records in the *Orders* table.

   a. On the *Create* tab, in the *Queries* group, click the **Query Wizard** button. In the *New Query* dialog, click **Find Unmatched Query Wizard** and click **OK.**

   b. Select **Table: Procedures.** Click **Next.**

   c. Select **Table: Orders.** Click **Next.**

   d. Confirm that Access has matched the **ProcedureID** field in the *Procedures* table and the **Procedure** field in the *Orders* table, and then click **Next.**

   e. Add all of the fields to the query by clicking the >> button. Click **Next.**

f. Change the name to `ProceduresNotOrdered` and click **Finish.**

g. Observe the query results and then close the query.

10. Use the **Find Duplicates Query Wizard** to find records in the *Orders* table with the same values in the *Physician* and *OrderDate* fields.

    a. On the *Create* tab, in the *Queries* group, click the **Query Wizard** button. In the *New Query* dialog, click **Find Duplicates Query Wizard** and click **OK.**

    b. Select **Table: Orders.** Click **Next.**

    c. Select **Physician** and add it to the right side by clicking the **>** button. Do the same for **OrderDate.** Click **Next.**

    d. Add all fields by clicking the **>>** button. Click **Next.**

    e. Change the name to `SameDateOrders` and click **Finish.**

    f. Observe the query results and then close the query.

11. Create a parameter query to allow database users to find records in the *Physicians* table by entering a city name.

    a. On the *Create* tab, in the *Queries* group, click the **Query Design** button. In the *Show Table* dialog, double-click the **Physicians** table. Click the **Close** button.

    b. Notice the *Physicians* table in the upper pane of the query Design view window. Double-click the following field names in order to add them to your query: **FirstName, LastName, City, Phone**

    c. Click the *Criteria* row under the *City* field and type the following: `[Enter the city name]`

    d. Click the **Run** button. In the *Enter Parameter Value* dialog, type: `Miami` and then click **OK.** Observe the query results.

    e. Save the query with the name: `PhysiciansByCity`

    f. Close the query.

12. Filter the *Orders* table to display only records where the procedure is **flu vaccine** or **CBC.**

    a. Open the **Orders** table in Datasheet view.

    b. Click the arrow on the right side of the **Procedure** field header. Use the check boxes to make sure that only the **Flu Vaccine** and **CBC** options are checked. Click **OK** and observe the results.

    c. Save and close the table.

13. Sort the *Physicians* table so the records are sorted alphabetically by city and then by member count for each city.

    a. Open the **Physicians** table in Datasheet view.

    b. Click anywhere inside the **MemberCount** field. On the *Home* tab, in the *Sort & Filter* group, click the **Ascending** button.

    c. Click anywhere inside the **City** field. On the *Home* tab, in the *Sort & Filter* group, click the **Ascending** button.

    d. Save and close the table.

14. Close the database and exit Access.

challenge yourself **4.3**

In this project you will continue working with the greenhouse database from *Chapter 3, Challenge Yourself 3.3.* Improve the functionality of this database by creating filters and queries for information that is commonly searched for.

Skills needed to complete this project:

- Using the Simple Query Wizard (Skill 4.1)
- Creating a Query in Design View (Skill 4.2)
- Adding Text Criteria to a Query (Skill 4.3)
- Adding Numeric and Date Criteria to a Query (Skill 4.4)
- Using AND and OR in a Query (Skill 4.5)
- Specifying the Sort Order in a Query (Skill 4.6)
- Hiding and Showing Fields in a Query (Skill 4.7)
- Adding a Calculated Field to a Query (Skill 4.8)
- Finding Unmatched Data Using a Query (Skill 4.9)
- Filtering Data Using AutoFilter (Skill 4.12)
- Filtering Data Using Filter by Selection (Skill 4.13)
- Sorting Records in a Datasheet (Skill 4.14)

1. Open the start file **AC2013-ChallengeYourself-4-3.**

2. If necessary, enable active content by clicking the **Enable Content** button in the Message Bar.

3. Save a copy of the file to work on named:
   [your initials]AC-ChallengeYourself-4-3

4. Create a new query named: **GreenhouseTechsFT**

   a. Add all the fields from the *Employees* table.

   b. The query should list all employees whose *Position* contains the word **greenhouse** and whose weekly hours are greater than or equal to **30.**

   c. Sort the query by last name.

   d. Add the *MaintenanceLog* table to this query and include the *Date_Time* field after the *WeeklyHours* field.

   e. Run the query to review the results.

   f. Save and close the query.

5. Create a new query named: **MediumSizePlants**.

   a. Add all the fields from the *Plants* table except *ScientificName*.

   b. The query should list all **white** or **yellow** colored plants whose *MaxHeightFeet* is at least **3** and not greater than **5.**

   c. Sort by the query by *MaxHeightFeet* so the shortest plants are listed first.

   d. Run the query to review the results.

   e. Save and close the query.

6. Create a new query named: **RedPlantSale**

   a. Add the following fields from the *Plants* table to the query: **CommonName, FlowerColor, PurchasePrice.**

   b. Select only those plants with a **red** color, but don't show this field in the query results.

    c. Add a calculated field that displays a sale price that is 80 percent of the purchase price. Use the name `SalePrice` for the new field.

    d. Run the query to review the results.

    e. Save and close the query.

7. Use the **Find Unmatched Query Wizard** to create a new query that identifies the plants that have no entry in the *MaintenanceLog*.

    a. Include all fields from the *Plants* table except the *PlantID*.

    b. Name this query: `PlantsMissingMaintenance`

    c. Close the query.

8. Open the **MaintenanceLog** table. Apply a filter that shows only those plants that have been watered and pruned. Save and close the table.

9. Open the **Plants** table. Use sorting (in ascending order) so the records are sorted by flower color and then by the date planted for each color. Save and close the table.

10. Close the database and exit Access.

challenge yourself **4.4**

In this project you will continue working with the vaccines database from *Chapter 3, Challenge Yourself 3.4*. Improve the functionality of this database by creating filters and queries for information that is commonly searched for.

Skills needed to complete this project:

- Using the Simple Query Wizard (Skill 4.1)
- Creating a Query in Design View (Skill 4.2)
- Adding Numeric and Date Criteria to a Query (Skill 4.4)
- Using AND and OR in a Query (Skill 4.5)
- Adding Text Criteria to a Query (Skill 4.3)
- Adding a Calculated Field to a Query (Skill 4.8)
- Specifying the Sort Order in a Query (Skill 4.6)
- Hiding and Showing Fields in a Query (Skill 4.7)
- Finding Unmatched Data Using a Query (Skill 4.9)
- Finding Duplicate Data Using a Query (Skill 4.10)
- Using a Parameter Query (Skill 4.11)
- Filtering Data Using AutoFilter (Skill 4.12)
- Filtering Data Using Filter by Selection (Skill 4.13)
- Sorting Records in a Datasheet (Skill 4.14)

1. Open the start file **AC2013-ChallengeYourself-4-4.**

2. If necessary, enable active content by clicking the **Enable Content** button in the Message Bar.

3. Save a copy of the file to work on named:
    `[your initials]AC-ChallengeYourself-4-4`

4. Create a new query named: `LargeJanShipments`

    a. Add all the fields from the *Shipments* table except *Cost*.

b. Configure the query so it returns only those orders from **1/1/14** to **1/31/14** (inclusive) that have a quantity greater than **75.**

c. Run the query and review the results.

d. Save and close the query.

5. Create a new query named: `YouthShipments`

   a. Add all the fields from the *Vaccines* table.

   b. The query should list the vaccines with a target audience of either children or teenagers.

   c. Add the *Shipments* table to this query and include the *DateShipped* field after the *TargetAudience* field.

   d. Run the query and review the results.

   e. Save and close the query.

6. Create a new query named: `PatientIncrease`

   a. Add all the fields from the *Locations* table.

   b. Add a calculated field named `PatientIncrease` to calculate a patient increase that is 20 percent higher than the current *PatientAvg*.

   c. Sort the query (descending) by this new calculated field.

   d. Hide the *PatientAvg* field from the query results.

   e. Run the query and review the results.

   f. Save and close the query.

7. Use the **Find Unmatched Query Wizard** to create a new query that identifies the vaccines in the *Vaccines* table that have no entry in the *Shipments* table.

   a. Include all fields from the *Vaccines* table except the *TargetAudience*.

   b. Name this query: `VaccinesNotShipped`

   c. Close the query.

8. Use the **Find Duplicates Query Wizard** to find out which Location IDs referenced in the *Shipments* table have received multiple shipments.

   a. Show all fields from the *Shipments* table.

   b. Name this query: `CountriesMultipleShipments`

   c. Close the query.

9. Create a new parameter query that displays all the fields from the *Locations* table. Configure the *Country* field so that it requests the name of the country from the user when the query is run.

   a. Use the user prompt: `Enter country name`

   b. Test the query and save it as: `CountrySearch`

   c. Close the query

10. Open the **Shipments** table. Apply a filter to show only those shipments that have a *VaccineID* of **Rabies.** Save and close the table.

11. Open the **Vaccines** table. Use sorting (in ascending order) so the records are sorted by the target audience and then by vaccine name. Save and close the table.

12. Close the database and exit Access.

on your own 4.5

In this project, you will continue working with the movie database from *Chapter 3, On Your Own 3.5.* Now that you have entered all of your movies, you will search for particular data using queries and filters.

Skills needed to complete this project:

- Finding Unmatched Data Using a Query (Skill 4.9)
- Finding Duplicate Data Using a Query (Skill 4.10)
- Using a Parameter Query (Skill 4.11)
- Using the Simple Query Wizard (Skill 4.1)
- Creating a Query in Design View (Skill 4.2)
- Adding Text Criteria to a Query (Skill 4.3)
- Adding Numeric and Date Criteria to a Query (Skill 4.4)
- Using AND and OR in a Query (Skill 4.5)
- Specifying the Sort Order in a Query (Skill 4.6)
- Hiding and Showing Fields in a Query (Skill 4.7)
- Adding a Calculated Field to a Query (Skill 4.8)
- Filtering Data Using AutoFilter (Skill 4.12)
- Filtering Data Using Filter by Selection (Skill 4.13)
- Sorting Records in a Datasheet (Skill 4.14)

1. Open the start file **AC2013-OnYourOwn-4-5.**
2. If necessary, enable active content by clicking the **Enable Content** button in the Message Bar.
3. Save a copy of the file to work on named: **[your initials]AC-OnYourOwn-4-5**
4. Create at least six queries. Of those six, you must have at least one parameter, one unmatched, and one duplicate query. For the other three select queries, you must demonstrate the use of the following features in a way that creates meaningful/useful queries:

   a. Apply text and numeric criteria, including using wildcards as well as *and* and *or* constructions.

   b. Creation of one calculated field.

   c. Hide a field in the query results

   d. Sort the query results

5. Apply a filter to one table.
6. Apply sorting to one table, demonstrating an understanding of proper use of innermost and outmost sorts.
7. Close the database and exit Access.

In this project, you will continue working with the pet store database from *Chapter 3, Fix It 3.6.* The store is currently having trouble with some queries. Find and fix their problems. Be sure to save the database objects after you make changes.

Skills needed to complete this project:

- Using a Parameter Query (Skill 4.11)
- Adding a Calculated Field to a Query (Skill 4.8)
- Hiding and Showing Fields in a Query (Skill 4.7)
- Adding Numeric and Date Criteria to a Query (Skill 4.4)
- Specifying the Sort Order in a Query (Skill 4.6)
- Adding Text Criteria to a Query (Skill 4.3)
- Using AND and OR in a Query (Skill 4.5)
- Sorting Records in a Datasheet (Skill 4.14)

1. Open the start file **AC2013-FixIt-4-6.**

2. If necessary, enable active content by clicking the **Enable Content** button in the Message Bar.

3. Save a copy of the file to work on named: **[your initials]AC-FixIt-4-6**

4. The **CustomersByPhone** query is not working properly. Fix it so when this query is run, it prompts the user to enter a phone number in order to find a particular customer. Use the prompt: **Enter customer phone number**

5. Fix the **PriceIncrease** query to correctly display a calculated field that increases the pet prices by 10 percent and hides the original pet price. Change the name of the calculated field to: **NewPrice**

6. The **OlderDogSales** query has several problems. Fix it so it correctly displays only dogs that are at least four months of age. Sort the results by pet age from the youngest to the oldest. Then, add the *Sales* table so only those dogs that have been sold are included in the query results. (Hint: Use the criterion **Is Not Null** to find records that are not blank.)

7. Fix the **Customers-W&B** query so only customers whose last names begin with a **W** or a **B** appear in the query results.

8. The *Pets* table is currently being sorted by *Price*. Remove this sort and change it so the data are sorted primarily by animal type, followed by the breeds within each animal type (both ascending).

9. Close the database and exit Access.

powerpoint 2013

chapter 1

Getting Started with PowerPoint 2013

In this chapter, you will learn the following skills:

- Use the different view options
- Navigate between slides
- Create a new presentation from a template
- Add slides to the presentation
- Change the layout of slides
- Add content to slides
- Format text
- Change the layout of text
- Find and replace text

skills

introduction

This chapter provides you with the basic skills necessary to navigate through and edit a basic PowerPoint 2013 presentation. The first step is to become familiar with the different views and how to navigate between and work with slides in the *Normal* view. After you become familiar with PowerPoint's user interface, you will learn how to create a new presentation using one of Microsoft's templates. Once you have the template framework of your presentation, you will add slides and modify the slides in the presentation. Next, you'll learn basic formatting techniques for changing the look of text in a presentation. You will also learn how to find and replace text in a presentation and undo and redo actions.

Skill 1.1 Introduction to PowerPoint 2013

Whether used for a sales pitch or as a teaching tool, a presentation incorporating graphics, animation, sound, and video is much more compelling than paper handouts or a "talking head" lecture. Microsoft Office PowerPoint 2013 enables you to create robust multimedia presentations. A **presentation** is made up of a series of **slides**. Each slide contains content, including text, graphics, audio, and video. You can then manipulate that content by adding transitions, animations, and graphic effects. Before diving in and creating a presentation, you should familiarize yourself with some of PowerPoint's basic features.

When you first start PowerPoint, the presentation is shown in the **working space**, or *Normal* view. You will notice the working space is divided into two areas:

Slides tab—Displays thumbnails of all the slides in the presentation.
Slide pane—Area where you can modify slides, including adding and formatting text, images, SmartArt, tables, charts, and media.

The **Notes pane** is the area where you can type notes about the current slide displayed in the *Slide* pane. The text you type in the *Notes* pane will not appear when you play your presentation. These notes can be printed as handouts for your audience or used by you during your presentation. In previous versions of PowerPoint, the *Notes* pane was displayed by default. In PowerPoint 2013, this has changed so the *Notes* pane is hidden by default. To display the *Notes* pane, click **Notes** button at the bottom of the PowerPoint window.

Each slide contains **placeholders** for you to add content to, including:

Title—Use to display the title of the presentation or the title for the slide.
Subtitle—Use to display the subtitle of the presentation.
Text—Use to add text to a slide. Be sure to keep your points brief, and use bulleted lists to emphasize text.
Tables—Organize information in a table to give your audience a clear picture of your data.
Charts—Use charts to create a visual display of you information.
SmartArt—Use to display lists in a more graphic format, including processes, cycles, hierarchical diagrams, and matrices.
Pictures—Add your own photographs or other images to slides.
Online Pictures—Add clip art or other photographs from online resources, such as *Office.com*, *Bing Image Search,* or your *SkyDrive.*
Video—Add video files from a file or from an online resource.

Presentations can be simple or complex, but they all follow some basic steps:

1. **Plan your presentation**—Decide what you want to include and in what order you want to present the information.
2. **Create your slides**—You can create slides from sophisticated templates, or start with blank slides and add formatting and effects to give your presentation a unique look.
3. **Review and rehearse**—Always check your slides for errors. You can also use special effects to add sizzle to your presentation.
4. **Practice**—Practicing your presentation will give you confidence when it comes time to give it in front of an audience.

FIGURE PP 1.1

tell me **more**

In past versions of PowerPoint, the default aspect ratio for slides was 4:3. In PowerPoint 2013, this default aspect ratio has been changed to widescreen 16:9. A 4:3 slide has a more square appearance, while a 16:9 slide is more rectangular in shape with the width being much longer than the height.

another **method**

To display the *Notes* pane, you can also click the **View** tab. In the *Show* group, click the **Notes** button.

let me **try**

Open the student data file **pp1-01-SpaServices** and try this skill on your own.

1. Click the **Slides** pane.
2. Display the **Notes** pane.
3. Close the file.

Skill 1.2 Designing Presentations

In this book, you will learn the skills needed to create PowerPoint presentations. You will learn to create slides, add text and images, animate objects, and add transitions to slides. You also will learn how to run a presentation using PowerPoint's built-in navigation and presentation tools.

Before you learn the mechanics of creating and giving a presentation, some basic design principles will help you create more effective PowerPoint presentations:

Balance. Distribute the elements on your slides in a balanced layout. Don't crowd the elements to one side or the other.	
Flow. Elements on your slides should guide your audience's eyes from one point to another in a natural progression. Think of reading a line of text on the page. Your eye is naturally led from one word to the next.	
Distinction. If all elements on your slides are the same size, nothing will stand out to your audience. Stress important elements by making them slightly larger than other elements.	
Recurrence. Repeat design elements (such as backgrounds, slide title styles, and bullet styles) throughout a presentation to give your presentation a unified and professional look.	

In addition to these design principles, there are some basic dos and don'ts to follow when designing presentations:

	DO	DON'T
Color choice	Use PowerPoint's built-in color themes.	Use too many colors or colors that do not work well together.
Text amount	Use short bullet points.	Use long paragraphs of text.
Text size	Use large fonts.	Use 10 pt. or 11 pt. fonts.
Animation	Animate important elements for emphasis.	Animate every element on a slide.
Slides	Keep the number of slides to a minimum (10 to 20 slides at the most).	Create a slide for every minor point in the presentation.
Presentation	Make unrehearsed comments.	Read your slides word for word.

tips & tricks

Use the presentation templates available from *Office. com* as a starting point for your presentations. Many of these templates come with built-in styles and slides that incorporate the design principles discussed here. To learn more about PowerPoint templates see Skill 1.5: *Creating a New Presentation Using a Template* later in this chapter.

tell me **more**

Guy Kawasaki, a well-known authority in the software field, developed the ***10/20/30 rule*** for PowerPoint design. This rule states that PowerPoint presentations should have no more than 10 slides, take no longer than 20 minutes, and should not use fonts smaller than 30 points. You can read his blog at http://blog. guykawasaki.com/.

Skill 1.3 Understanding Views

PowerPoint has four main ways to view your presentation: *Normal* view, *Slide Sorter* view, *Reading* view, and *Slide Show* view. Normal view is the view in which you will typically create and edit your content. Slide Sorter view displays thumbnail pictures of the slides in your presentation and is useful in rearranging the order of the slides. Reading view allows you to run your presentation within the PowerPoint application window. Slide Show view displays your slides full screen and allows you to see your presentation the way your audience will see it.

The easiest way to switch between views is to click one of the view buttons located at the right side of the status bar, near the zoom slider.

- Click the **Normal** view button to add or edit content.

- Click the **Slide Sorter** view button to view thumbnails of your presentation.

- Click the **Reading** view button to view your presentation within the current PowerPoint window.

- Click the **Slide Show** view button to view your presentation at full screen as your audience will. To exit *Slide Show* view, press the [Esc] key on the keyboard.

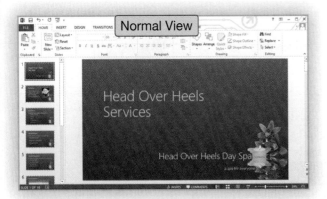

FIGURE PP 1.2

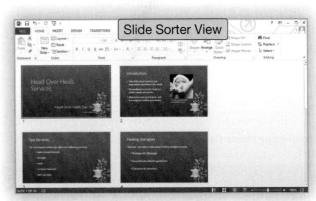

FIGURE PP 1.3

FIGURE PP 1.4

FIGURE PP 1.5

tips & tricks

When you first open a presentation, PowerPoint will display your slides so they fit in the *Slide* pane. The **Zoom slider** (located at the bottom of the PowerPoint window) allows you to change how your slides are displayed in the *Slide* pane. Use the Zoom slider to magnify your slides to check alignment of text and graphics or to see how your slides will appear when you play your presentation.

tell me **more**

In addition to the four main views, PowerPoint also includes the following:

Notes Page view—Allows you to add notes for each slide in your presentation. Each slide appears on its own screen with a large text area for your notes about the slide. The text you type in *Notes Page* view will not appear when you are playing your presentation. However, you can choose to print your notes along with your slides to hand out to your audience.

Master views—Includes *Slide Master* view, *Handout Master* view, and *Notes Master* view. The master views contain universal settings for the presentation. If you want to make changes that will affect the entire presentation, you should use the master view.

another **method**

❭ To switch views, you can also click the **View** tab and click a view button in the *Presentation Views* group.

❭ To switch to *Slide Show* view, you can also click the **Slide Show** tab and click a button in the *Start Slide Show* group.

let me **try**

Open the student data file **pp1-03-SpaServices** and try this skill on your own.

1. Switch to **Slide Sorter** view.
2. Switch to **Reading** view.
3. Switch to **Slide Show** view
4. Switch to **Normal** view.
5. Close the file.

Skill 1.4 Using the Slides Tab

The working space in PowerPoint includes the *Slides* tab to help you navigate between and work with slides. The **Slides tab** displays thumbnails of all your slides. Use the *Slides* tab to quickly navigate between slides, rearrange the slide order, and review and edit content. To make changes to a specific slide, it must first be displayed in the *Slide* pane.

To navigate to a slide using the *Slides* tab:

1. Click the thumbnail of the slide you want to display.
2. The slide appears in the *Slide* pane ready for editing.

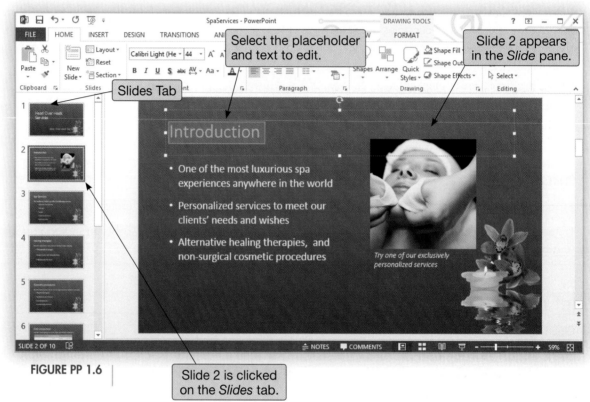

FIGURE PP 1.6

tips & tricks

Clicking in the middle of a text placeholder will select it and prepare it for editing. The placeholder will appear with a dotted line around it and a blinking cursor in the text. If you only want to resize or move the placeholder and not edit the text within it, click the edge of the placeholder. Instead of the dotted line around it, you will see a solid line surrounding the placeholder.

another method

To navigate between slides one slide at a time, you can also:

❯ Click the **Next Slide** and **Previous Slide** buttons on the vertical scroll bar in the *Slide* pane.

❯ Click a slide on the *Slides* tab and press the up and down arrow keys on the keyboard.

let me try

Open the student data file **pp1-04-SpaServices** and try this skill on your own.

1. Using the *Slides* tab, navigate to **Slide 3**.
2. Close the file.

Skill 1.5 Creating a New Presentation Using a Template

A **template** is a file with predefined settings that you can use as a pattern to create a new file of your own. Using a template makes creating a fully formatted and designed new file easy, saving you time and effort. There are templates available for letters, memos, résumés, newsletters, budgets, expense reports, sales presentations, project management databases, and almost any other type of file you can imagine.

To create a new file from a template:

1. Click the **File** tab to open Backstage view.
2. Click **New.** PowerPoint 2013 includes a variety of templates that are copied to your computer when you install the application. These templates are always available from the *New* page. Additional templates that you download are also displayed on the *New* page, so your screen may look different than the one in Figure PP 1.7.
3. Click each template preview picture for a brief description of the template.
4. When you find the template you want to use, click the **Create** button.
5. A new presentation opens, prepopulated with all of the template elements.

FIGURE PP 1.7

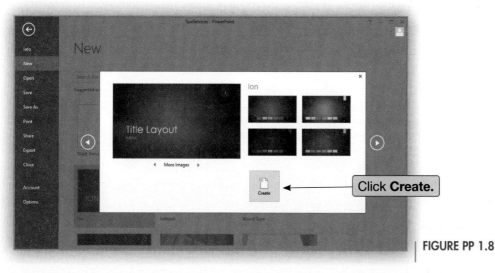

FIGURE PP 1.8

You can search for more presentation templates online. (You must have an active Internet connection.)

1. Near the top of the *New* page, in the *Search online templates* box, type a keyword or phrase that describes the template you want.

2. Click the **Start searching** button (the magnifying glass image at the end of the *Search online templates* box).

3. The search results display previews of the templates that match the keyword or phrase you entered. To further narrow the results, click one of the categories listed in the *Filter by* pane at the right side of the window. Notice that each category lists the number of templates available.

4. When you find the template you want, click it to display the larger preview with detailed information about the template, and then click **Create.**

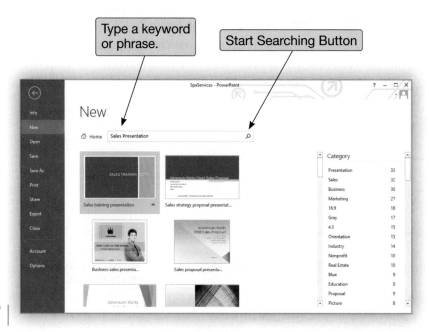

FIGURE PP 1.9

tell me **more**

Some PowerPoint templates are design templates and contain a single slide with all the design elements included. Use one of these templates if you have planned out the content of your presentation. If you know the topic of your presentation but have not outlined the content, there are other presentations that include both the design elements and multiple slides for you to add your content.

let me try

Open the student data file **pp1-05-Presentation** and try this skill on your own.

1. Click the **File** tab.
2. Click **New.**
3. Click the **Ion** template.
4. Click **Create.**
5. Save the file as directed by your instructor and close it.

Skill 1.6 Adding Slides to Presentations

A presentation consists of several slides filled with text and graphics. If you start with a template, your presentation may include several slides ready to add content. But what if you need to add more information to your presentation? How do you add more slides? PowerPoint makes it easy.

To add a slide to a presentation:

1. On the *Home* tab, in the *Slides* group, click the **New Slide** button arrow.
2. Select a slide layout from the *New Slide* gallery.
3. Add your content to the slide.
4. Continue adding and modifying slides until your presentation is complete.

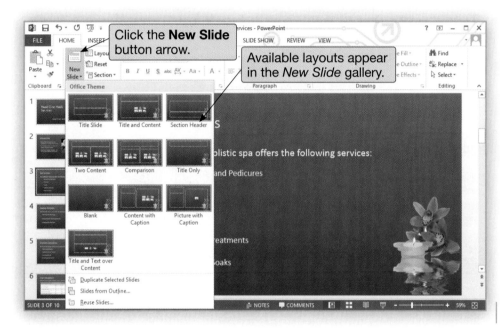

FIGURE PP 1.10

tips & tricks

When you add slides through the *New Slide* gallery, each slide layout includes design elements from the presentation's theme. This helps create a consistent look and feel for the entire presentation. If you switch themes, the look of the new slide layouts will change to match that theme.

tell me more

There are a number of slide layouts for you to choose from, including title only slides, blank slides, title and content slides, comparison content slides, picture with caption slides, and content with caption slides.

another method

To add a slide to a presentation, you can also:

❯ Click the top half of the **New Slide** button.

❯ Press Ctrl + M on the keyboard.

Note: When you use either of these methods, the new slide added to the presentation will use the same layout as the last slide you added.

let me try

Open the student data file **pp1-06-SpaServices** and try this skill on your own.

1. Add a slide to the presentation that uses the **Two Content** layout.
2. Save the file as directed by your instructor and close it.

Skill 1.7 Changing Slide Layouts

After you have created your presentation, you can modify the information displayed on an individual slide. If you add or delete elements, you may want to change the layout of the slide to accommodate the new content. PowerPoint comes with a number of slide layouts for you to use. Choose the one that best suits the content for each slide.

To change the slide layout:

1. Select the slide you want to change.
2. On the *Home* tab, in the *Slides* group, click the **Slide Layout** button.
3. Select a slide layout from the *Slide Layout* gallery.

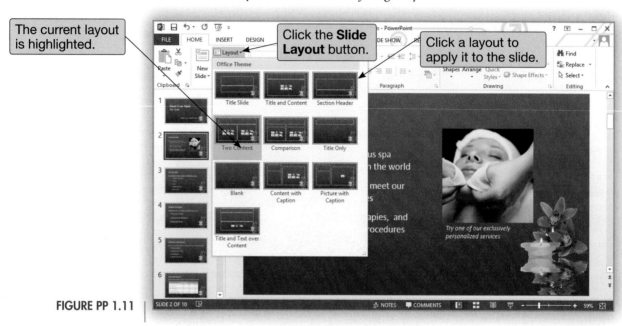

FIGURE PP 1.11

tips & tricks

Once you have selected a new slide layout, you can move and resize placeholders to fit your content. If you have made a number of changes and decide you want to undo your changes, you can revert the slide to its original design. Click the **Reset** button on the *Home* tab in the *Slides* group to return the slide layout to its default layout.

another method

To change the layout of a slide, you can also right-click any area of the *Slide* pane without a placeholder, point to **Layout,** and select a slide layout.

let me try

Open the student data file **pp1-07-SpaServices** and try this skill on your own.

1. Change the layout of **Slide 2** to use the **Two Content** layout.
2. Save the file as directed by your instructor and close it.

Skill 1.8 Adding Text to Slides

A good presentation consists of a balance of text and graphics. It is important to keep text brief. Short, clear points convey your message to your audience better than rambling paragraphs of text. You can add text to slides by using text placeholders and text boxes. **Text placeholders** are predefined areas in slide layouts where you enter text. **Text boxes** are boxes you add to the slide layout to enter text where you want it.

To add text to a text placeholder, click inside the text placeholder and type the text you want to add. Click outside the placeholder to deselect it.

To edit text in a slide placeholder:

1. Click the placeholder with the text you want to change.
2. Click and drag across the text to select it.
3. Type the new text for the placeholder.
4. Click outside the placeholder to deselect it.

To add a text box:

1. Click the **Insert** tab.
2. In the *Text* group, click the **Text Box** button.
3. Click on the slide where you want the text to appear.
4. Type your text.
5. Click outside the text box to deselect it.

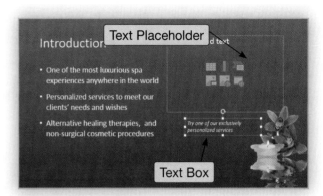

FIGURE PP 1.12

FIGURE PP 1.13

tell me **more**

Text placeholders are a part of the slide layout and cannot be added directly to a slide. You can only add text placeholders to slide layouts in *Slide Master* view. To add a text placeholder, first switch to *Slide Master* view. On the *Slide Master* tab, click the **Insert Placeholder** button and select **Text.** As you can see from the *Insert Placeholder* menu, you can add placeholders for pictures, charts, tables, SmartArt, media, and online images, as well as text.

let me **try**

Open the student data file **pp1-08-SpaServices** and try this skill on your own.

1. Add the text **Head Over Heels Services** to the Title placeholder.
2. Navigate to **Slide 2.**
3. Click **Text Box** to add a text box below the image.
4. Insert the text **Try one of our personalized services** to the text box.
5. Deselect the text box.
6. Save the file as directed by your instructor and close it.

Skill 1.9 Changing the Size of a Placeholder

A **placeholder** is a container on a slide that holds text or other content, such as a table, chart, or image. Placeholders are outlined with a dotted line that does not display in the presentation when it is running. When you resize a placeholder, you resize the content it contains.

To change the size of a placeholder:

1. Point to one of the resize handles on the placeholder.
2. When the mouse changes to the resize cursor , click and drag the mouse:
   - ❱ Drag the mouse toward the center of the placeholder to make it smaller.
   - ❱ Drag the mouse away from the center of the placeholder to make it larger.
3. When the placeholder is the size you want, release the mouse button.

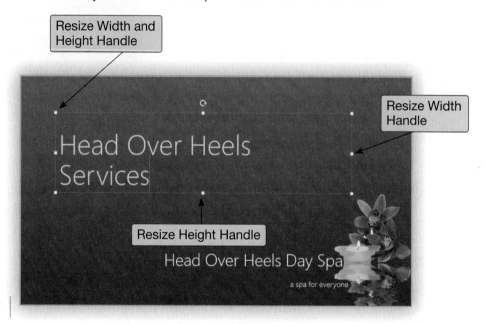

FIGURE PP 1.14

tips & tricks

When using one of the corner resize handles, press [Shift] on the keyboard as you drag the mouse to constrain the aspect ratio of the image and prevent the image from becoming distorted.

tell me **more**

You can only add placeholders from *Slide Master* view. To add a placeholder to a layout, click the **View** tab. In *Master Views* group, click the **Slide Master** button. PowerPoint switches to *Slide Master* view. In the *Master Layout* group, click the **Insert Placeholder** button and select an option.

another **method**

You can also resize a placeholder by entering the width and height of the placeholder in the **Width:** and **Height:** boxes in the *Size* group on the *Format* tab under *Picture Tools*.

let me **try**

Open the student data file **pp1-09-SpaServices** and try this skill on your own.

1. On **Slide 1**, select the Title placeholder with the text *Head Over Heels Services*.
2. Resize the placeholder so the text appears on two lines instead of three.
3. Deselect the placeholder.
4. Save the file as directed by your instructor and close it.

Skill 1.10 Applying Character Effects

When you add text to a slide, it is formatted according to the slide design. But what if you want the text to look different from the preset design? You can call attention to text in your presentation by using the bold, italic, underline, strikethrough, or shadow character effects. Remember, these effects are used to emphasize important text and should be used sparingly.

To add character effects to your text, on the *Home* tab, in the *Font* group:

Bold—click the **Bold** button.
Italic—click the **Italic** button.
Underline—click the **Underline** button.
Shadow—click the **Shadow** button.
Strikethrough—click the **Strikethrough** button.

When text has the bold, italic, underline, shadow, or strikethrough effect applied to it, the button highlights on the Ribbon. To remove the effect, click the highlighted button.

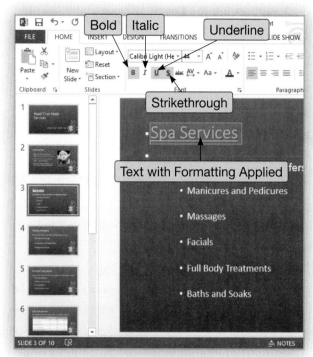

FIGURE PP 1.15

tips & tricks

Character spacing refers to the amount of horizontal space that appears between characters when you type. In some cases, you will want to make the characters closer together to fit better on-screen. In other cases, you will want to make the characters farther apart for a visual effect. To change the spacing of the characters in text, in the *Font* group, click the **Character Spacing** button and select an option.

another method

You can also apply character effects through the *Font* dialog. To open the *Font* dialog, on the *Home* tab, in the *Font* group, click the **dialog launcher.**

To apply character effects, you can also use the following keyboard shortcuts:

❯ **Bold** (Ctrl) + (B)

❯ **Italic** (Ctrl) + (I)

❯ **Underline** (Ctrl) + (U)

To apply the bold or italic effect, you can also:

1. Right-click the text you want to change.
2. Click the **Bold, Italic,** or **Underline** button on the Mini toolbar.

let me try

Open the student data file **pp1-10-SpaServices** and try this skill on your own.

1. On **Slide 1**, select the text **Head Over Heels Services.**
2. Apply the **Bold** formatting to the text.
3. Apply the **Italics** formatting to the text.
4. Apply the **Underline** formatting to the text.
5. Apply the **Shadow** formatting to the text.
6. Save the file as directed by your instructor and close it.

Skill 1.11 Changing Fonts and Font Sizes

A **font**, or typeface, refers to a set of characters of a certain design. The font is the shape of the character or number as it appears on-screen. PowerPoint offers many fonts. **Serif fonts**, such as Cambria and Times New Roman, have an embellishment at the end of each stroke. **Sans serif fonts**, such as Calibri and Arial, do not have an embellishment at the end of each stroke.

To change the font:

1. Select the text to be changed.
2. On the *Home* tab, in the *Font* group, click the arrow next to the **Font** box.
3. Scroll the list to find the new font.
4. Click the font name.

Fonts are measured in **points**, abbreviated "pt." On the printed page, 72 points equal one inch. Different text sizes are used for different slide elements, such as titles, subtitles, and text placeholders.

To change the size of the text:

1. Select the text to be changed.
2. On the *Home* tab, in the *Font* group, click the arrow next to the **Font Size** box.
3. Scroll the list to find the new font size.
4. Click the size you want.

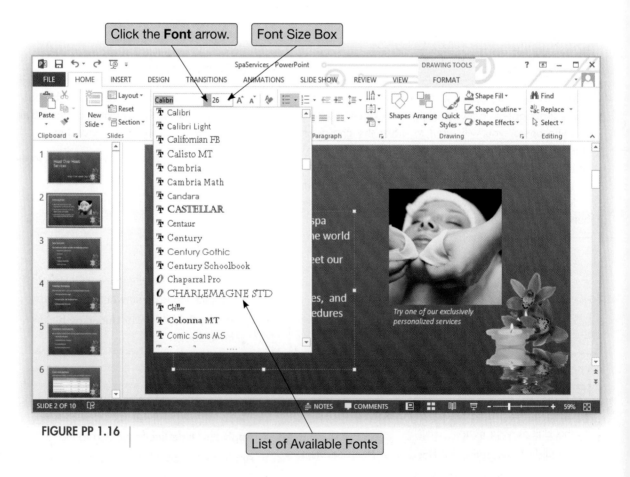

Click the **Font** arrow.

Font Size Box

List of Available Fonts

FIGURE PP 1.16

tips & tricks

When you add text to placeholders, PowerPoint will automatically resize the text to fit within the placeholder. It is a good idea to review the size of similar elements (such as slide titles) to ensure they are the same size.

tell me **more**

When designing a presentation, it is good practice to limit the number of fonts. Using one font for slide titles and a second font for slide text is a good rule to follow. Using multiple fonts in one presentation can be distracting to your audience.

another **method**

To change the font, right-click the text, click the arrow next to the **Font** box on the Mini toolbar, and select an option.

To change the font size, right-click the text, click the arrow next to the **Font Size** box on the Mini toolbar, and select an option.

let me **try**

Open the student data file **pp1-11-SpaServices** and try this skill on your own.

1. Navigate to **Slide 2** and select the text **Introduction.**
2. Change the font to **Calibri Light (Headings).**
3. Change the font size to **44.**
4. Save the file as directed by your instructor and close it.

from the perspective of . . .

TEACHER

Presentations enable me to provide handouts for my students, quickly cover lecture material, and give a professional, visual experience to keep their attention. I can even use presentation software to keep track of notes as I teach my class.

Skill 1.12 Changing the Color of Text

The presentation's theme controls the color of the various slide elements. But what if you want a particular word to stand out on a slide? Adding color to text in your presentation adds emphasis to certain words and helps design elements stand out for your audience. It is important to be selective when adding color to text in your presentation. Using too many colors can often be distracting to your audience, and your message can be lost.

To change the color of the text:

1. Select the text to be changed.
2. On the *Home* tab, in the *Font* group, click the arrow next to the **Font Color** button.
3. Click the color you want.

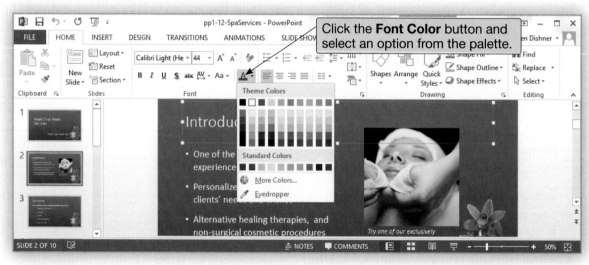

FIGURE PP 1.17

tips & tricks

When you change the color of text, the *Font Color* button changes to the color you selected. Click the **Font Color** button to quickly apply the same color to other text in the presentation.

tell me more

Theme colors are a group of predefined colors that work well together in a document. When you apply a theme in PowerPoint 2013, you can then choose from a number of color variants for applying to slide elements. When you change the color variants in a presentation, the color palette changes and displays only colors that are part of the theme colors. You will learn more about color variants in *Chapter 3: Formatting Presentations*.

another method

To change the color of text, you can also right-click the text, click the arrow next to the **Font Color** button on the Mini toolbar, and select an option.

let me try

Open the student data file **pp1-12-SpaServices** and try this skill on your own.

1. Navigate to **Slide 2** and select the text **Introduction.**
2. Change the font color to **Gray–50%, Accent 6, Lighter 60%.**
3. Save the file as directed by your instructor and close it.

Skill 1.13 Using Format Painter

PowerPoint 2013 gives you the ability to apply complex formatting to objects. If you want to use the same formatting for more than one object, you could select the second object and reapply all the effects to create the final result, or you could use Format Painter to copy the formatting from one object to another.

To use *Format Painter:*

1. Select the object that has the formatting you want to copy.
2. On the *Home* tab, in the *Clipboard* group, click the **Format Painter** button.
3. Click the object that you want to apply the formatting to.
4. The formats are automatically applied to the second object.

If you want to apply the formats more than once, double-click the **Format Painter** button when you select it. It will stay on until you click the **Format Painter** button again or press to deselect it.

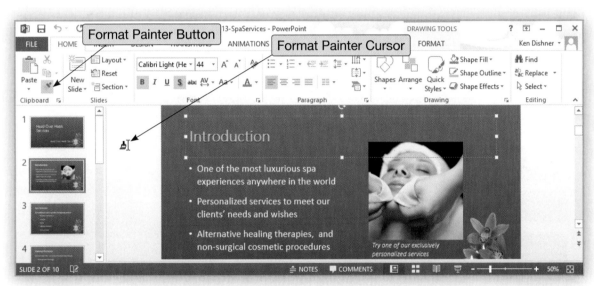

FIGURE PP 1.18

tips & tricks

If you are copying formatting from a text box, click in the text (so the text box appears with a dashed line around it) to copy and paste the formatting of just the text. Select the text box (so it appears with a solid line around it) to copy and paste the formatting of the entire text box.

another method

To activate *Format Painter,* you can also right-click the text with formatting you want to copy and click the **Format Painter** button on the Mini toolbar. If you are copying the formatting on a picture, you will not see the Mini toolbar.

let me try

Open the student data file **pp1-13-SpaServices** and try this skill on your own.

1. Navigate to **Slide 2** and select the text **Introduction.**
2. Click the **Format Painter** button to copy the formatting of the text.
3. Navigate to **Slide 3** and paste the copied formatting to the text **Spa Services.**
4. Save the file as directed by your instructor and close it.

Skill 1.14 Clearing Formatting

After you have applied a number of character formats and effects to text, you may find that you want to return your text to its original formatting. You could perform multiple *Undo* commands on the text, or you could use the **Clear All Formatting** command. The *Clear All Formatting* command removes any formatting that has been applied to text, including character formatting, text effects, and styles, and leaves only plain text.

To remove formatting from text:

1. Select the text you want to remove the formatting from.
2. On the *Home* tab, in the *Font* group, click the **Clear All Formatting** button.

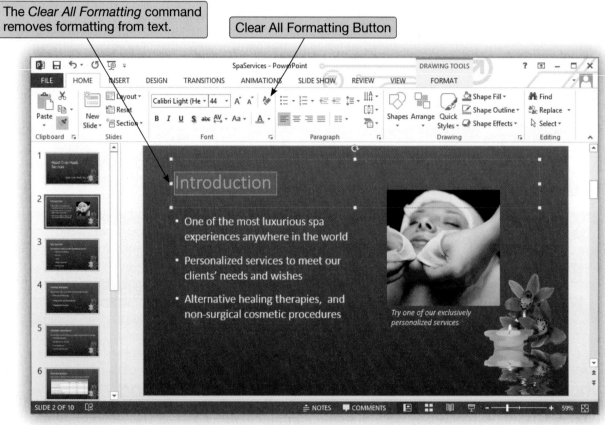

The *Clear All Formatting* command removes formatting from text.

Clear All Formatting Button

FIGURE PP 1.19

tips & tricks

If you clear the formatting from text and then decide that you want to keep the formatting that was removed, you can use the *Undo* command to apply to the previous formatting to the text.

let me try

Open the student data file **pp1-14-SpaServices** and try this skill on your own.

1. On **Slide 1,** select the text **Head Over Heels Services.**
2. Clear all the formatting from the text.
3. Save the file as directed by your instructor and close it.

Skill 1.15 Aligning Text

Text alignment refers to how text is lined up with regard to the left and right edges of a slide.

> **Left alignment** aligns the text on the left side, leaving the right side ragged.
> **Center alignment** centers each line of text relative to the edges of the slide.
> **Right alignment** aligns the text on the right side, leaving the left side ragged.
> **Justified alignment** evenly spaces the words, aligning the text on the right and left sides.

To change the alignment of text:

1. Click in the text you want to change.
2. On the *Home* tab, in the *Paragraph* group, click an alignment button.

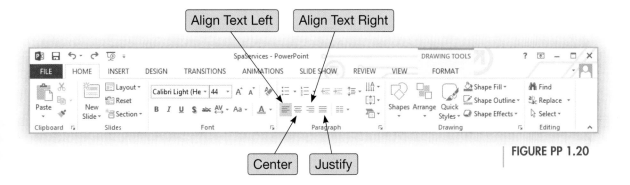

FIGURE PP 1.20

Vertical alignment refers to how text is aligned with regard to the top and bottom of the placeholder. **Top** alignment places the text at the top of the placeholder. **Middle** alignment centers the text vertically in the placeholder. **Bottom** alignment places the text at the bottom of the placeholder.

To change the vertical alignment of text:

1. Click in the text you want to change.
2. On the *Home* tab, in the *Paragraph* group, click the **Align Text** button and select an option: **Top, Middle,** or **Bottom.**

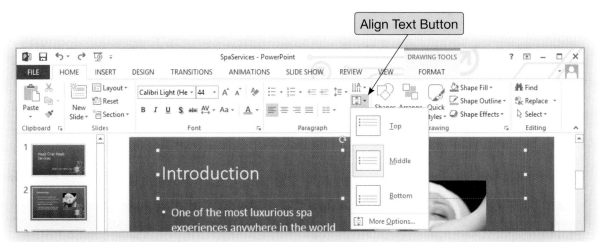

FIGURE PP 1.21

tips & tricks

When creating presentations, it is important to use consistent text alignment on every slide. For example, if a slide's title area is center-aligned, then every title throughout the presentation should also be center-aligned.

tell me **more**

Bulleted and numbered lists are typically left-aligned. When you apply left alignment to a list, the bullets and numbers align vertically, giving your slide a precise, organized appearance.

another **method**

To align text, you can also use the following keyboard shortcuts:

Align Left Ctrl + L
Center Ctrl + E
Align Right Ctrl + R
Justify Ctrl + J

To left-align, center, or right-align text, you can right-click the text and click an alignment button on the Mini toolbar.

let me **try**

Open the student data file **pp1-15-SpaServices** and try this skill on your own.

1. Navigate to **Slide 2** in the presentation.
2. Change the alignment on the text in the title placeholder so it is aligned on left side and in the middle of the placeholder.
3. Change the alignment on the bulleted list so the text is justified and is aligned along the top of the placeholder.
4. Change the alignment on the text in the text box under the picture to be center aligned.
5. Save the file as directed by your instructor and close it.

Skill 1.16 Changing Line Spacing

Line spacing is the white space between lines of text. The default line spacing in Microsoft PowerPoint 2013 is 0.9 lines. This line spacing is a good choice to use for the items on a slide. It is a little tighter vertically than single spacing, giving you more room for text in a placeholder without crowding the text. Other commonly used spacing options include single spacing, double spacing, and 1.5 spacing. When you increase the line spacing, you are adding more white space between the items on the slide.

To change line spacing:

1. Select the text you want to change.
2. On the *Home* tab, in the *Paragraph* group, click the arrow next to the *Line Spacing* button.
3. Select the number of the spacing you want.

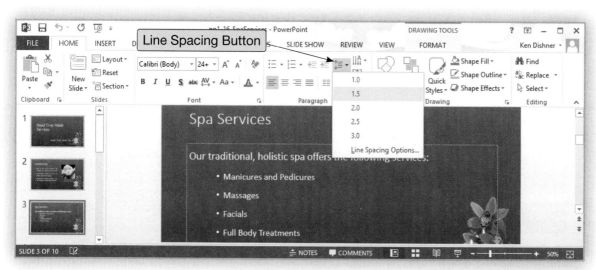

FIGURE PP 1.22

tips & tricks

You can control how much spacing appears before and after text through the *Paragraph* dialog:

1. Click the **Line Spacing** button and select **Line Spacing Options...**
2. In the *Paragraph* dialog, in the *Spacing* section, click the **Before:** and **After:** arrows to adjust the spacing between text.

another method

You can also change line spacing from the *Paragraph* dialog:

1. Click the **Line Spacing** button and select **Line Spacing Options...**
2. In the *Paragraph* dialog, in the *Spacing* section, click the **Line Spacing** arrow and select an option.

let me try

Open the student data file **pp1-16-SpaServices** and try this skill on your own.

1. Navigate to **Slide 3** and select the five items in the bulleted list.
2. Change the line spacing to **2.0**.
3. Save the file as directed by your instructor and close it.

Skill 1.17 Adding Columns to Placeholders

When you add a list to a slide, the items in the list are displayed in a single column. This is fine if you have a few items in the list, but what if your list includes more items than will easily fit in a single vertical column? You can apply **columns** to text, giving you the flexibility of displaying lists across a slide.

To apply columns to text:

1. Select the text placeholder containing the list you want to convert.
2. On the *Home* tab, in the *Paragraph* group, click the **Add or Remove Columns** button and select an option: **One Column, Two Columns,** or **Three Columns.**

    After you have applied the columns to the text placeholder, you can resize the text placeholder, making it wider or shorter to even out the number of items in each column.

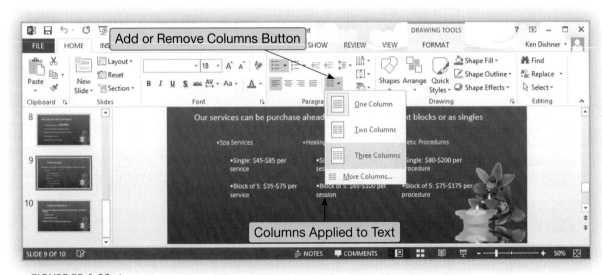

FIGURE PP 1.23

tips & tricks

In the *Columns* dialog, you can increase the number of columns to more than three. You can also control the spacing between the columns of text on the slide. To open the *Columns* dialog, click the **Add or Remove Columns** button and select **More Columns...**

tell me **more**

Applying columns to text is a feature that was introduced in PowerPoint 2007. In older versions of PowerPoint, you needed to create a separate placeholder for each column of text to achieve the same effect. Although this method achieved the same visual effect, it made it cumbersome to add, delete, or reorder items in the placeholders.

let me try

Open the student data file **pp1-17-SpaServices** and try this skill on your own.

1. Navigate to **Slide 9.**
2. Click in the placeholder with the bulleted list.
3. Change the placeholder to have **Three Columns.**
4. Save the file as directed by your instructor and close it.

Skill 1.18 Using Find

The **Find** command in PowerPoint allows you to locate specific instances of text in your presentation. With the *Find* command, you can find instances of a word or phrase throughout a presentation.

To find a word or phrase in a presentation:

1. On the *Home* tab, in the *Editing* group, click the **Find** button.
2. Type the word or phrase you want to find in the *Find what:* box.
3. Click **Find Next** to find the first instance of the word or phrase.
4. Click **Find Next** again to find the next instance.

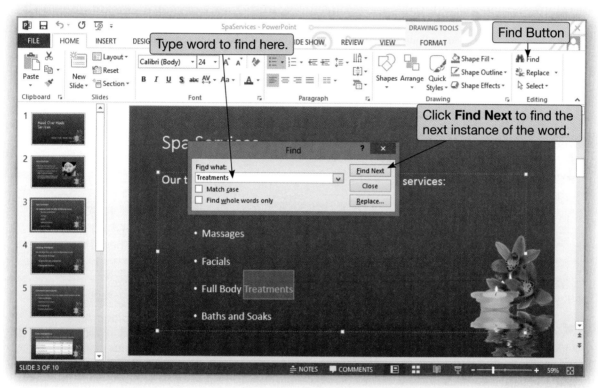

FIGURE PP 1.24

tips & tricks

To find an exact match for how a word is capitalized, select the **Match case** check box.

another method

To open the *Find* dialog, you can also press (Ctrl) + (N) on the keyboard.

let me try

Open the student data file **pp1-18-SpaServices** and try this skill on your own.

Use the **Find** command to find the first instance of the word **treatments** in the presentation.

Skill 1.19 Using Replace

The **Replace** command allows you to locate specific instances of text in your presentation and replace them with different text. With the *Replace* command, you can replace words or phrases one instance at a time or all at once throughout the presentation.

To replace instances of a word in a presentation:

1. On the *Home* tab, in the *Editing* group, click the **Replace** button.
2. Type the word or phrase you want to change in the *Find what:* box.
3. Type the new text you want in the *Replace with:* box.
4. Click the **Find Next** button to find the first instance of the text.
5. Click **Replace** to replace just that one instance of the text.
6. Click **Replace All** to replace all instances of the text.
7. PowerPoint displays a message telling you how many replacements it made. Click **OK** in the message that appears.
8. To close the *Replace* dialog, click the **Close** button.

FIGURE PP 1.25

tips & tricks

The **Replace Fonts** command on the *Replace* menu allows you to quickly change the font for all text in a presentation with another font.

another method

To open the *Replace* dialog, you can also press (Ctrl) + (H) on the keyboard.

let me try

Open the student data file **pp1-19-SpaServices** and try this skill on your own.

1. Open the **Replace** dialog.
2. Replace the first instance of the word **treatments** with **experiences.**
3. Do not change the second instance of the word **treatments.**
4. Close the dialog.
5. Save the file as directed by your instructor and close it.

Skill 1.20 Using Undo and Redo

If you make a mistake when working, the undo command allows you to reverse the last action you performed. The redo command allows you to reverse the undo command and restore the file to its previous state. The Quick Access Toolbar gives you immediate access to both of these commands.

To undo the last action taken, click the **Undo** button on the Quick Access Toolbar.
To redo the last action taken, click the **Redo** button on the Quick Access Toolbar.

To undo multiple actions at the same time:

1. Click the arrow next to the *Undo* button to expand the list of your most recent actions. These actions are listed in the reverse order of how they were done with the most recent action appearing at the top of the list.
2. Click an action in the list.
3. The action you click will be undone, along with all the actions completed after that. In other words, your presentation will revert to the state it was in before that action.

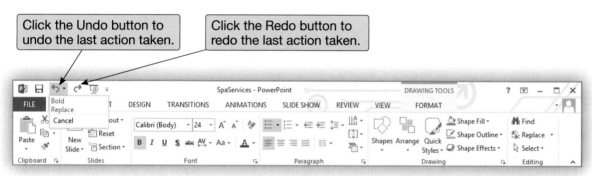

Click the Undo button to undo the last action taken.

Click the Redo button to redo the last action taken.

FIGURE PP 1.26

another method

❯ To undo an action, you can also press (Ctrl) + (Z) on the keyboard.

❯ To redo an action, you can also press (Ctrl) + (Y) on the keyboard.

let me try

Open the student data file **pp1-20-SpaServices** and try this skill on your own.

1. Apply the **Shadow** effect to the text **Head Over Heels Services** on **Slide 1** of the presentation.
2. Use the **Undo** command to remove the effect.
3. Use the **Redo** command to reapply the effect.
4. Save the file as directed by your instructor and close it.

key terms

Presentation
Slides
Working space
Normal view
Slide Sorter view
Reading view
Slide Show view
Zoom slider
Slides tab
Template
Text placeholders
Text boxes
Placeholder
Font

Serif font
Sans serif font
Points
Format Painter
Clear All Formatting
Text alignment
Vertical alignment
Line spacing
Columns
Find
Replace
Undo
Redo

concepts review

1. The final step in designing a presentation is to _____.

   a. create your slides

   b. plan your presentation

   c. practice your presentation

   d. review your presentation

2. The design principle of using elements on your slides to guide your audience's eyes from one point to another in a natural progression is known as _____.

   a. balance

   b. flow

   c. distinction

   d. recurrence

3. To view your presentation as your audience will see it, use _____.

   a. Slide Sorter view

   b. Normal view

   c. Reading view

   d. Slide Show view

4. _____ are predefined areas in slide layouts where you enter text.

   a. Text boxes

   b. Text placeholders

   c. Sections

   d. WordArt

5. A _____ font does not have an embellishment at the end of each stroke.

   a. sans serif

   b. serif

   c. title

   d. body

6. To copy and paste formatting from one object to another use the _____.

  a. Copy and Paste commands

  b. Quick Styles command

  c. Format Painter command

  d. Shape Effects command

7. To align text along the upper edge of a text placeholder, use the _____ command.

  a. Center

  b. Middle

  c. Justify

  d. Top

8. If a list includes more items than will easily fit vertically on a slide, you should use the _____ command to display the items side by side.

  a. Line spacing

  b. Columns

  c. Slide Layout

  d. Arrange

9. Use the _____ command to locate specific instances of text in your presentation.

  a. Find

  b. Replace

  c. Spelling

  d. Thesaurus

10. The keyboard shortcut for reversing the last action you performed is _____.

  a. Ctrl + W

  b. Ctrl + X

  c. Ctrl + Y

  d. Ctrl + Z

projects

skill review 1.1

In this project you will be creating a new presentation from a template for Suarez Marketing. You will add and modify slides, add text, and format text.

Skills needed to complete this project:

- Creating a New Presentation Using a Template (Skill 1.5)
- Adding Text to Slides (Skill 1.8)
- Using the Slides Tab (Skill 1.4)
- Changing Fonts and Font Sizes (Skill 1.11)
- Applying Character Effects (Skill 1.10)
- Changing the Color of Text (Skill 1.12)
- Using Format Painter (Skill 1.13)
- Aligning Text (Skill 1.15)
- Changing Line Spacing (Skill 1.16)
- Using Undo and Redo (Skill 1.20)
- Understanding Views (Skill 1.3)

1. Open the **PP2013-SkillReview-1-1** presentation.
2. Create a new presentation from a template.
   a. Click the **File** tab.
   b. Click **New.**
   c. Click in the **Search for online templates and themes** box at the top of the screen and type **business plan**
   d. Click the **Business plan presentation (Ion green design, widescreen)** template.
   e. Click the **Create** button.
3. Save this presentation as: **[your initials]PP-SkillReview-1-1**
4. Add text to slides.
   a. On **Slide 1,** click in the title placeholder.
   b. Click and drag across the text **Company Name** to select the text.
   c. Type: **Suarez Marketing**
5. Using the Slides tab, click **Slide 2** to display the second slide in the *Slides* pane.
6. Change the font and font size on text.
   a. Select the text **Business Concept.**
   b. On the *Home* tab, in the *Font* group, click the arrow next to the **Font** box and select **Calibri.**
   c. On the *Home* tab, in the *Font* group, click the arrow next to the **Font Size** box and select **48.**
7. Apply character effects to text.
   a. Verify the text *Business Concept* is still selected.

b. In the *Font* group, click the **Bold** button.

c. In the *Font* group, click the **Shadow** button.

8. Change the color of text.

    a. Verify the text *Business Concept* is still selected.

    b. In the *Font* group, click the **Font Color** arrow and select **Purple, Accent 6, Lighter 80%.**

9. Use *Format Painter* to copy and paste formatting.

    a. Verify the text *Business Concept* is still selected.

    b. On the *Home* tab, in the *Clipboard* group, double-click the **Format Painter.**

    c. Apply the formatting to the title of **Slide 4 through Slide 14.**

10. Align text.

    a. On the *Slides* tab, click **Slide 3.**

    b. Select the quote text (**Clearly state your company's long term mission.**)

    c. Type: `To provide the best service with outstanding results.`

    d. On the *Home* tab, in the *Paragraph* group, click the **Center** alignment button.

    e. Delete the text box at the bottom of the slide (*Try to use works that will help . . .*).

11. Change the line spacing.

    a. On **Slide 3,** verify that the cursor is still in the text placeholder you just typed in.

    b. On the *Home* tab, in the *Paragraph* group, click the **Line Spacing** button and select **2.0.**

12. On the *Quick Access Toolbar,* click the **Undo** button.

13. Switch between views.

    a. On the status bar, click the **Slide Sorter** button.

    b. Switch back to *Normal* view by clicking the **Normal** button.

14. Save and close the business plan presentation. Close the blank presentation, but do not save the file.

skill review 1.2

In this project you will be working on a personal fitness presentation. You will add and modify text, change the layout of slides, add a slide to the end of the presentation, and use the *Find* and *Replace* commands.

Skills needed to complete this project:

- Clearing Formatting (Skill 1.14)
- Using the Slides Tab (Skill 1.4)
- Changing Slide Layouts (Skill 1.7)
- Changing the Size of a Placeholder (Skill 1.9)
- Changing Fonts and Font Sizes (Skill 1.11)
- Adding Columns to Placeholders (Skill 1.17)
- Using Find (Skill 1.18)
- Using Replace (Skill 1.19)
- Adding Slides to Presentations (Skill 1.6)
- Adding Text to Slides (Skill 1.8)

- Changing the Color of Text (Skill 1.12)
- Understanding Views (Skill 1.3)

1. Open the **PP2013-SkillReview-1-2** presentation.
2. Save this presentation as: `[your initials]PP-SkillReview-1-2`
3. Clear the formatting from text.

   a. On **Slide 1,** select the text **My Fitness Regimen.**

   b. On the *Home* tab, in the *Font* group, click the **Clear All Formatting** button.

4. Navigate to a slide and change the slide layout.

   a. Using the Slides tab, click **Slide 3** to navigate to that slide.

   b. On the *Home* tab, in the *Font* group, click the **Slide Layout** button and select **Title and Content.**

5. Change the size of a placeholder, change the font, and change the size of text.

   a. On **Slide 3,** click in the bulleted list. Note the size of the placeholder.

   b. Click **Slide 4.**

   c. Click in the bulleted list.

   d. Click and drag a resize handle to resize the placeholder to be the same size as the one on Slide 3.

   e. Select the items in the bulleted list.

   f. On the *Home* tab, in the *Font* group, click the **Font** arrow and select **Century Gothic (Body).**

   g. In the *Font group,* click the **Font Size** arrow and select **28.**

6. Add columns to placeholders.

   a. Click **Slide 5** and click in the bulleted list.

   b. On the *Home* tab, in the *Paragraph* group, click the **Add or Remove Columns** button and select **Two Columns.**

7. Use the *Find* command.

   a. On the *Home* tab, in the *Editing* group, click the **Find** button.

   b. Type: `Regimen` in the *Find what:* box and click the **Find Next** button.

   c. Close the *Find* dialog.

   d. With the word *Regimen* still selected, type **Plan**

8. Use the *Replace* command.

   a. On the *Home* tab, in the *Editing* group, click the **Replace** button.

   b. The word *Regimen* should still be in the *Find what:* box.

   c. Type: `Plan` in the *Replace with:* box.

   d. Click the **Replace All** button.

   e. A message box appears telling you 2 replacements have been made. Click **OK** in the message box.

   f. Close the *Replace* dialog.

9. Add slides to a presentation.

   a. Click **Slide 7.**

   b. On the *Home* tab, in the *Slides* group, click the **New Slide** button arrow and select **Title Only.**

10. Add text to a placeholder.

    a. Click in the title placeholder.

    b. Type: `I can do it!`

11. Change the font size and color.

    a. Select the text you just typed.

    b. On the *Home* tab, in the *Font* group, click the **Font Size** arrow and select **72**.

    c. On the *Home* tab, in the *Font* group, click the **Font Color** arrow and select **Orange, Accent 3**.

12. Switch to *Slide Show* view and then return back to *Normal* view.

    a. Click **Slide 1.**

    b. On the status bar, click the **Slide Show** button.

    c. Press the [Esc] key on the keyboard to return to *Normal* view.

13. Save and close the presentation.

challenge yourself **1.3**

In this project you will be creating a new presentation from a template for presenting a healthy cookbook at a book festival. You will add and format text. Using the Format Painter, you will copy and paste formatting from one slide to another. Finally, you will use the *Undo* and *Redo* commands, and view the presentation in different PowerPoint views.

Skills needed to complete this project:

- Creating a New Presentation Using a Template (Skill 1.5)
- Adding Text to Slides (Skill 1.8)
- Changing Fonts and Font Sizes (Skill 1.11)
- Changing the Color of Text (Skill 1.12)
- Aligning Text (Skill 1.15)
- Using the Slides Tab (Skill 1.4)
- Using Format Painter (Skill 1.13)
- Applying Character Effects (Skill 1.10)
- Changing Line Spacing (Skill 1.16)
- Using Undo and Redo (Skill 1.20)
- Understanding Views (Skill 1.3)

1. Open the **PP2013-ChallengeYourself-1-3** presentation.

2. Create a new presentation from a template.

    a. Search for a **cookbook** template.

    b. Create a new presentation based on the **Fresh food presentation (widescreen).**

3. Save this presentation as: `[your initials]PP-ChallengeYourself-1-3`

4. Add text to slides.

    a. Change the title of the presentation to **Cooking for a Healthier You.**

    b. Change the subtitle to **The Tri-State Book Festival.**

5. Change the font, font size, and font color on text.

   a. Select the text **Cooking for a Healthier You.**

   b. Change the font to **Verdana.**

   c. Change the font size to **48.**

   d. Change the font color to **Red, Accent 4.**

6. Change the alignment of the **subtitle on Slide 1** to be right aligned.

7. Navigate to a slide an add text.

   a. Using the *Slides* tab, navigate to **Slide 2.**

   b. Change the title of the slide to **Why this isn't just another cookbook**

   c. Replace the bullet items with the following:

      - `Original recipes`
      - `Healthy substitutions`
      - `Food metrics`
      - `Life stories`

8. Use the **Format Painter** to copy and paste formatting and then change the size of text.

   a. Copy the formatting from the **presentation title on Slide 1** and apply the formatting to the **title on Slide 2.**

   b. Change the font size to **36.**

9. Apply character effects to text.

   a. Apply the **Italic** character effect to the second word for each item in the bulleted list (**recipes, substitutions, metrics, and stories**)

   b. Apply the **Underline** character effect to the second word for each item in the bulleted list.

10. Change the line spacing on the bulleted list to **1.5** line spacing.

11. **Undo** the line spacing action and then **Redo** the action so the line spacing returns to **1.5.**

12. Switch to **Reading view,** and then switch to **Slide Sorter view.** Switch back to **Normal view.**

13. Save and close the cookbook presentation. Close the blank presentation, but do not save the file.

challenge yourself **1.4**

In this project you will be working on a presentation about personal finance. You will add and modify slides, add and format text, and switch between different PowerPoint views.

Skills needed to complete this project:

- Clearing Formatting (Skill 1.14)
- Using the Slides Tab (Skill 1.4)
- Changing Slide Layouts (Skill 1.7)
- Changing Fonts and Font Sizes (Skill 1.11)
- Changing the Size of a Placeholder (Skill 1.9)
- Using Format Painter (Skill 1.13)
- Adding Columns to Placeholders (Skill 1.17)
- Using Find (Skill 1.18)

- Using Replace (Skill 1.19)
- Adding Slides to Presentations (Skill 1.6)
- Adding Text to Slides (Skill 1.8)
- Changing the Color of Text (Skill 1.12)
- Aligning Text (Skill 1.15)
- Understanding Views (Skill 1.3)

1. Open the **PP2013-ChallengeYourself-1-4** presentation.

2. Save this presentation as: **[your initials]PP-ChallengeYourself-1-4**

3. Clear the formatting from text and change the size of text.

   a. On **Slide 1,** select the text **The basics of smart saving.**

   b. Clear the formatting from the text.

   c. Change the size of the text to **24.**

4. Navigate to a slide and change the slide layout.

   a. Navigate to **Slide 2.**

   b. Change the layout of the slide to **Title and Content.**

5. Change the size of a placeholder, change the font, and change the size of text.

   a. Navigate to **Slide 4** and note the size of the placeholder for the bulleted list.

   b. Navigate to **Slide 3** and change the size of the placeholder to be the same size as the one on Slide 4.

   c. Change the bulleted list items to **Calibri.**

   d. Change the size of the text to **28.**

6. Use the **Format Painter** to copy and paste formatting.

   a. Copy the formatting from the bulleted list on **Slide 3.**

   b. Apply the formatting to the bulleted lists on **Slide 2, Slide 4,** and **Slide 5.**

7. Add columns to placeholders and resize the placeholder.

   a. Change the bulleted list on **Slide 4** to display in two columns.

   b. Resize the placeholder so each column contains four items.

8. Use the **Find** command to find the word **savings** in the presentation.

9. Use the **Replace All** command to replace the phrase **Cut up** with **Freeze.**

10. Add a new blank slide to the end of the presentation.

11. Add a text box to the middle of the newly inserted slide and enter the text **Begin Now!**

12. Change the font size and color and change the alignment of text.

    a. Change the font size to **60.**

    b. Change the color of the text to **Blue, Accent 2.**

    c. Center align the text.

    d. If the text appears on two lines, widen the text box so the text appears on one line.

13. Navigate to **Slide 1.** Switch to **Slide Show** view and then return back to **Normal** view.

14. Save and close the presentation.

In this project you will be creating a presentation from a template on the four steps in creating a PowerPoint presentation. You will add and modify slides, format text, use the *Find* command, and switch between different PowerPoint views.

Skills needed to complete this project:

- Creating a New Presentation Using a Template (Skill 1.5)
- Adding Text to Slides (Skill 1.8)
- Aligning Text (Skill 1.15)
- Adding Slides to Presentations (Skill 1.6)
- Changing Slide Layouts (Skill 1.7)
- Using the Slides Tab (Skill 1.4)
- Changing Fonts and Font Sizes (Skill 1.11)
- Changing the Color of Text (Skill 1.12)
- Using Format Painter (Skill 1.13)
- Applying Character Effects (Skill 1.10)
- Clearing Formatting (Skill 1.14)
- Using Find (Skill 1.18)
- Understanding Views (Skill 1.3)

1. Open the **PP2013-OnYourOwn-1-5** presentation.
2. Create a new presentation from a single slide template based on a design of your choice. Be sure the template only includes one slide.
3. Save this presentation as: **[your initials]PP-OnYourOwn-1-5**
4. On **Slide 1,** add the title **Designing PowerPoint Presentations.** Add the subtitle **4 steps for creating a presentation.**
5. On **Slide 1,** change the alignment of the text in the Title placeholder.
6. Add a new slide with the **Two Content** layout.
7. Add the title **The Four Steps** to the slide.
8. Add the following text to the content placeholder on the left.

   - **Plan your presentation**
   - **Create your slides**
   - **Review and rehearse**
   - **Practice**

9. Change the layout of the slide to the **Title and Content Layout.**
10. Add a **Title and Content** slide for each of the four steps and add the step as the title of the slide.
11. On **Slide 3,** change the font, font size, and color of the text **Plan Your Presentation.**
12. Use the **Format Painter** to copy and paste the formatting to the titles of the other slides in the presentation.
13. Change the title on **Slide 1** to use the same font you used on the other slide titles.
14. Apply character formatting to the subtitle and then clear the formatting on the text.
15. Use the **Find** command to find where the word **practice** appears in the presentation.
16. Display your presentation in the different PowerPoint views.
17. Save and close the designing PowerPoint presentation. Close the blank presentation, but do not save the file.

In this project you will be editing a presentation on team orientation and team building. You will modify slides, add and format text, and switch between different PowerPoint views.

Skills needed to complete this project:

- Clearing Formatting (Skill 1.14)
- Changing the Color of Text (Skill 1.12)
- Applying Character Effects (Skill 1.10)
- Using the Slides Tab (Skill 1.4)
- Changing the Size of a Placeholder (Skill 1.9)
- Aligning Text (Skill 1.15)
- Changing Fonts and Font Sizes (Skill 1.11)
- Using Format Painter (Skill 1.13)
- Changing Slide Layouts (Skill 1.7)
- Adding Text to Slides (Skill 1.8)
- Using Replace (Skill 1.19)
- Understanding Views (Skill 1.3)

1. Open the **PP2013-FixIt-1-6** presentation.
2. Save this presentation as: **[your initials]PP-FixIt-1-6**
3. On **Slide 1,** clear the formatting from the text **Team Orientation.** Change the color of the text to **Blue, Accent 5, Lighter 80%** and apply the **Shadow** character effect.
4. Change the list placeholder on **Slide 3** to be the same size as the list placeholder on Slide 2.
5. Change the list on **Slide 3** to be left aligned.
6. Navigate to **Slide 2.** Change the list to **32 pt. Calibri (Body).**
7. Use **Format Painter** to copy the formatting from the list on Slide 2 and copy it to the lists on **Slides 3, 4,** and **8.**
8. Change the lists on **Slides 2, 4,** and **8** so they are aligned along the top of the placeholder.
9. Change the layout of **Slide 5** to **Title and Content.**
10. Add **Sporting events** as a third item to the list on **Slide 8.**
11. Use the **Replace** command to replace **&** with the word **AND.**
12. Display your presentation in the different PowerPoint views.
13. Save and close the presentation.

chapter 2

Adding Content to Slides

In this chapter, you will learn the following skills:

❱ Add slides and text from a Word Outline

❱ Use the Cut, Copy, and Paste commands

❱ Use the Clipboard

❱ Create bulleted and numbered lists

❱ Add WordArt to Slides

❱ Understand the content placeholder

❱ Add objects to slides including tables, charts, and SmartArt diagrams

❱ Add objects to slides including shapes and pictures

❱ Add audio and video to slides

skills

introduction

This chapter provides you with the skills to add content to presentations. You will learn to quickly fill out a presentation by adding slide content using a Word document. You will then move text around in the presentation using the *Copy* and *Paste* and *Cut* and *Paste* commands. You will apply bulleted and numbered lists to slide content and will add WordArt to slides. You will explore the content placeholder and then add objects to slides through the content placeholders. You will add tables, SmartArt diagrams, online pictures, pictures stored on your computer, and shapes. In addition, you will add audio and online videos to a presentation.

Skill 2.1 Opening a Word Outline as a Presentation

When organizing the content for a presentation, you may find it helpful to write your text in a Word document and then import it into PowerPoint. Use heading styles in the Word document to ensure that the content will convert to a presentation in a uniform manner. Each Heading 1 style becomes the title on the slide, and each Heading 2 style becomes the main text on the slide. After you have saved the Word document, you can then import the content, creating the base slides for your presentation.

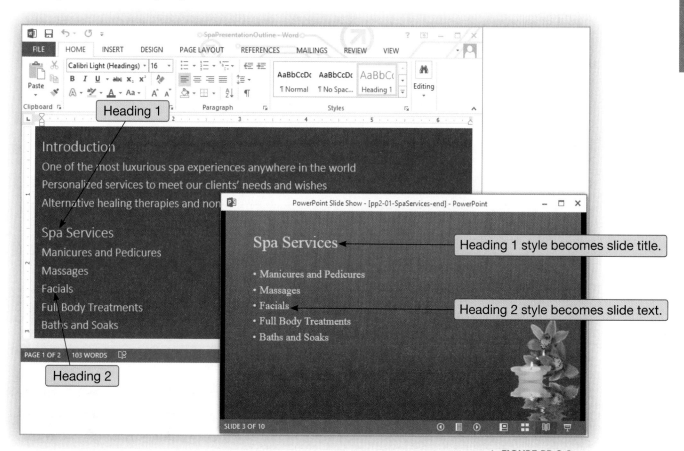

FIGURE PP 2.1

To insert slides from a Word outline:

1. Click in the presentation where you want to insert the slides.
2. On the **Home** tab, in the *Slides* group, click the arrow below the **New Slide** button and select **Slides from Outline...**
3. In the *Insert Outline* dialog, select the file you want to insert.
4. Click the **Insert** button.
5. The slides are added to the presentation based on the heading styles in the Word document.

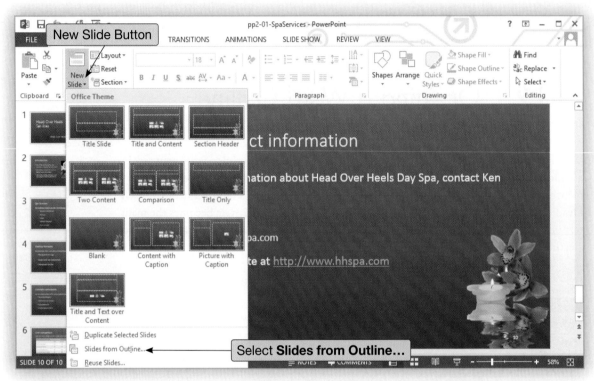

FIGURE PP 2.2

tips & tricks

When you insert an outline, all the slides will use the default slide design. Click the **Layout** button on the *Home* tab to change the layout of a slide. Click the **Design** tab to make any changes to a slide's design.

tell me **more**

You can import many file formats from Word, including Word documents (both .docx and .doc), plain text (.txt), rich text format (.rtf), and HTML (.htm).

let me try

Open the student data file **pp2-01-SpaServices** and try this skill on your own:

1. Open the **Insert Outline** dialog.
2. Navigate to the location where you saved your data files for this book.
3. Insert the **SpaPresentationOutline** into the presentation.
4. Save the file as directed by your instructor and close it.

Skill 2.2 Using the Outline View

When working on a presentation, it's easy to focus on the graphic elements of your slides. Adding graphics, transitions, and animations may seem important, but the foundation of an effective presentation is a focused message. When working with text on slides, it is a good idea to keep the amount of text on each slide balanced and to concentrate on one clear message per slide. The Outline view displays the text from your slides in an outline, allowing you to concentrate on the text aspect of your slides without being distracted by the graphic elements. Use the *Outline* view to enter and edit your text directly in the outline.

To use the *Outline* view:

1. Click the **View** tab.
2. In the *Presentation Views* group, click the **Outline View** button.
3. Click in the text you want to change.
4. Type the new text for the slide. The Slide pane to the right updates with the new text.
5. In the *Presentation Views* group, click the **Normal View** button to return to *Normal* view.

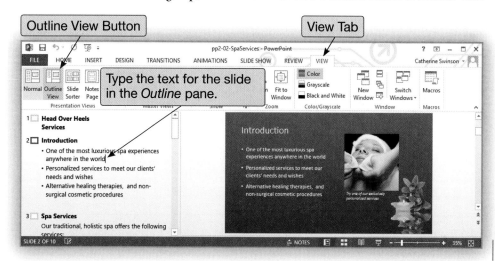

FIGURE PP 2.3

tips & tricks

If your slides include a large amount of text, you can make the *Outline* pane wider to make it easier to write and edit your content. To change the width of the *Outline* pane, place your cursor over the right edge of the pane. When the cursor changes to the resize cursor, click and drag the mouse to the right to make the pane wider or to the left to make the pane narrower.

tell me more

In previous versions of PowerPoint, the *Outline* pane was part of *Normal* view. You could toggle between the *Slides* pane and the *Outline* pane by clicking a tab at the top of the pane.

let me try

Open the student data file **pp2-02-SpaServices** and try this skill on your own:

1. Display the slides in **Outline View.**
2. On **Slide 2,** add the text **anywhere in the world** to the end of the first bullet.
3. Switch back to **Normal view.**
4. Save the file as directed by your instructor and close it.

Skill 2.3 Using Copy and Paste

The **Copy** command places a duplicate of the selected text or object on the **Clipboard** but does not remove it from your presentation. You can then use the **Paste** command to insert the text or object into the same presentation, another presentation, or another Microsoft Office file, such as an Excel workbook or a Word document.

To copy text and paste it into the same presentation:

1. Select the text to be copied.
2. On the *Home* tab, in the *Clipboard* group, click the **Copy** button.
3. Place the cursor where you want to insert the text from the *Clipboard*.
4. On the *Home* tab, in the *Clipboard* group, click the **Paste** button.

These same steps apply whether you are copying and pasting text, pictures, shapes, video files, or any type of object in a presentation.

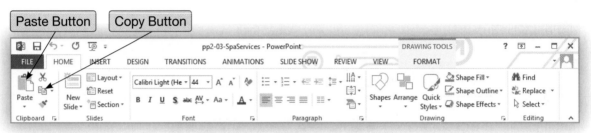

FIGURE PP 2.4

tell me **more**

The *Paste* button has two parts—the top part of the button pastes the topmost contents of the *Clipboard* into the current file. If you click the bottom part of the button (the *Paste* button arrow), you can control how the item is pasted.

Each type of object has different **paste options**. For example, if you are pasting text, you may have options to keep the source formatting, merge the formatting of the source and the current presentation, or paste only the text without any formatting.

another **method**

To apply the *Copy* or *Paste* command, you can also use the following shortcuts:

Copy = Press ⌘ + Ⓒ on the keyboard, or right-click and select **Copy.**

Paste = Press ⌘ + Ⓥ on the keyboard, or right-click and select **Paste.**

let me **try**

Open the student data file **pp2-03-SpaServices** and try this skill on your own:

1. On **Slide 3,** copy the last bullet point on the slide (**Baths and Soaks**).
2. On **Slide 4,** paste the text as the last bullet point on the slide (after *Chiropractic Services*).
3. Save the file as directed by your instructor and close it.

Skill 2.4 Using Cut and Paste

The *Copy* command is great if you want to duplicate content in your presentation, but what if you want to move content from one place to another? The **Cut** command is used to move text and other objects within a file and from one file to another. Text or an object that is cut is removed from the file and placed on the *Clipboard* for later use. You can then use the *Paste* command to insert the text or object into the same presentation, another presentation, or another Microsoft Office file.

To cut text and paste it into the same presentation:

1. Select the text to be cut.

2. On the *Home* tab, in the *Clipboard* group, click the **Cut** button.

3. Place the cursor where you want to insert the text from the *Clipboard*.

4. On the *Home* tab, in the *Clipboard* group, click the **Paste** button.

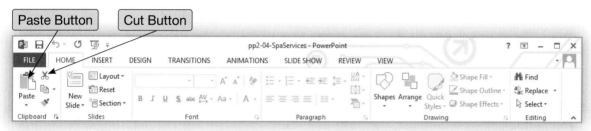

FIGURE PP 2.5

another method

To apply the *Copy* or *Paste* command, you can also use the following shortcuts:

Cut = Press (Ctrl) + (X) on the keyboard, or right-click and select **Cut.**

Paste = Press (Ctrl) + (V) on the keyboard, or right-click and select **Paste.**

let me try

Open the student data file **pp2-04-SpaServices** and try this skill on your own:

1. On **Slide 4,** cut the first bullet point from the slide (**Manicures and Pedicures**).

2. On **Slide 3,** paste the text as the first bullet point on the slide.

3. Save the file as directed by your instructor and close it.

Skill 2.5 Using the Office Clipboard

When you cut or copy items, they are placed on the *Clipboard*. The icons in the *Clipboard* identify the type of document from which each item originated (Word, PowerPoint, Paint, etc.). A short description or thumbnail of the item appears next to the icon, so you know which item you are pasting into your presentation. The *Clipboard* can store up to 24 items for use in the current presentation or any other Office application.

To paste an item from the *Clipboard* into a presentation:

1. Place your cursor where you want to paste the item.
2. On the *Home* tab, in the *Clipboard* group, click the **Clipboard** dialog launcher.
3. The *Clipboard* task pane appears.
4. To paste an item from the *Clipboard* into your presentation, click the item you want to paste.

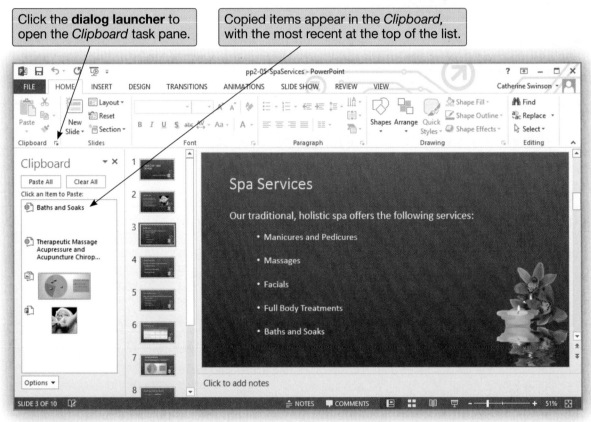

Click the **dialog launcher** to open the *Clipboard* task pane.

Copied items appear in the *Clipboard*, with the most recent at the top of the list.

FIGURE PP 2.6

tips & tricks

The *Clipboard* is common across all Office applications—so you can cut text or an image from a PowerPoint presentation and then paste that text into a Word document or copy a chart from Excel into a PowerPoint presentation.

tell me **more**

❭ To remove an item from the *Clipboard,* point to the item, click the arrow that appears, and select **Delete.**

❭ To add all the items in the *Clipboard* at once, click the **Paste All** button at the top of the task pane.

❭ To remove all the items from the *Clipboard* at once, click the **Clear All** button at the top of the task pane.

another **method**

To paste an item, you can also point to the item in the *Clipboard* task pane, click the arrow that appears, and select **Paste.**

let me **try**

Open the student data file **pp2-05-SpaServices** and try this skill on your own:

1. Display the **Clipboard.**
2. On **Slide 3,** copy the last bullet point on the slide (**Baths and Soaks**).
3. On **Slide 2,** click the picture to select it. Click the **Copy** button to copy it to the *Clipboard.*
4. On **Slide 4,** paste the text you just copied from the *Clipboard* as the last bullet point on the slide (after *Chiropractic Services*).
5. Save the file as directed by your instructor and close it.

Skill 2.6 Adding Bulleted Lists

When you create a PowerPoint presentation, limit each point you want to discuss to a few words. When you give your presentation, you can expand on the information displayed on your slide. This will keep your audience engaged and focused on what you are saying rather than reading your slides.

When you create slides, you will notice that text is organized in bulleted lists. Bulleted lists are used to organize information that does not have to be displayed in a particular order.

To add a bulleted list to a slide:

1. Select the text you want to display in a list.

2. On the *Home* tab, in the *Paragraph* group, click the arrow next to the **Bullets** button.

3. Select a **bullet style** from the gallery.

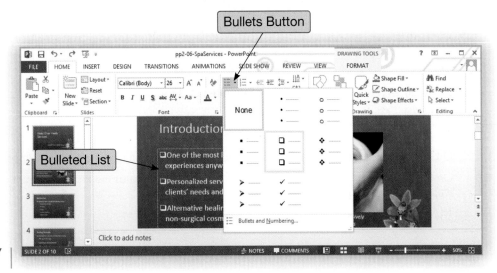

FIGURE PP 2.7

tips & tricks

Sometimes you will want to include subpoints in your bulleted and numbered lists. When a list includes point and subpoints, it is called a multilevel list. In PowerPoint, you can create a multilevel list by demoting and promoting points in lists. To move a point down a level in a list, click the **Increase Indent** button. To move a point up a level in a list, click the **Decrease Indent** button.

another method

To add a bulleted list, you can also right-click the selected text, point to **Bullets,** and select a style from the submenu.

let me try

Open the student data file **pp2-06-SpaServices** and try this skill on your own:

1. Select the three list items on **Slide 2.**
2. Apply the **Hollow Square Bullets** bulleted list style to the items.
3. Save the file as directed by your instructor and close it.

Skill 2.7 Adding Numbered Lists

Numbered lists are used to organize information that must be presented in a certain order, such as step-by-step instructions. When you apply numbering formatting to a list, PowerPoint displays a number or letter next to each list item using the format you chose. You can choose to number lists using Arabic numbers (1, 2, 3), Roman numerals (I., II., III.), or letters (A., B., C.).

To add a numbered list to a slide:

1. Select the text you want to display in a list.
2. On the *Home* tab, in the *Paragraph* group, click the arrow next to the **Numbering** button.
3. Select a **numbering style** from the gallery.

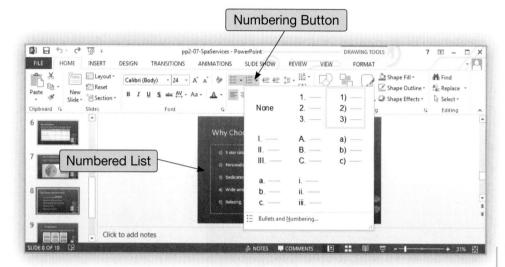

FIGURE PP 2.8

tips & tricks

Sometimes you will want to add more items to an existing list. To add another item to the list, place your cursor at the end of an item and press (←Enter) to start a new line. The list will renumber itself to accommodate the new item.

tell me **more**

To change the numbering list type, click the **Numbering** button arrow and select an option from the *Numbering Library*. You can create new numbered list styles by selecting **Define New Number Format...**

another **method**

To add a numbered list, you can also right-click the selected text, point to **Numbering,** and select a style from the submenu.

let me **try**

Open the student data file **pp2-07-SpaServices** and try this skill on your own:

1. Select the five list items on **Slide 8.**
2. Apply the **1) 2) 3)** numbered list style to the items.
3. Save the file as directed by your instructor and close it.

Skill 2.8 Adding WordArt

Sometimes you'll want to call attention to text that you add to a slide. You can format the text by using character effects, or if you want the text to really stand out, you can use WordArt. WordArt Quick Styles are predefined graphic styles you apply to text. These styles include a combination of color, fills, outlines, and effects. Be sure to limit the use of WordArt to a small amount of text. Overuse of WordArt can be distracting to your audience.

To add WordArt to slides:

1. Click the **Insert** tab.

2. In the *Text* group, click the **WordArt** button and select a Quick Style from the gallery.

3. Begin typing to replace the text "Your Text Here" with the text for your slide.

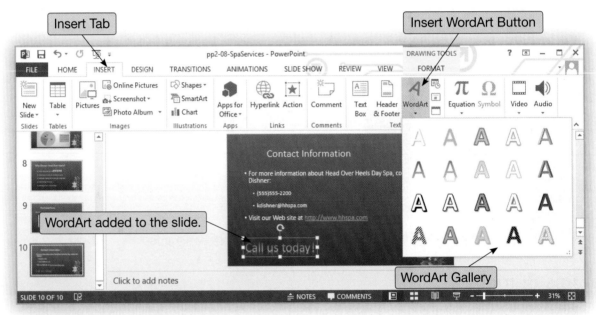

FIGURE PP 2.9

After you have added WordArt to your presentation, you can modify it just as you would any other text. Use the *Font* box and *Font Size* box on the *Home* tab to change the font or font size of WordArt.

tips & tricks

When you add WordArt to a slide, it will appear centered in the middle of the slide. To move the WordArt you added, point to the WordArt and when the cursor changes to the move cursor, click and drag the WordArt to the new location.

let me try

Open the student data file **pp2-08-SpaServices** and try this skill on your own:

1. On **Slide 10**, add WordArt using the **Gradient Fill–Green, Accent 1, Reflection** style.

2. Add the text **Call us today!** in the WordArt style.

3. Move the WordArt so it displays in the lower left corner of the slide.

4. Save the file as directed by your instructor and close it.

Skill 2.9 Understanding the Content Placeholder

A good presentation contains a balance of text, graphics, charts, and other subject matter. The **content placeholder** is a special type of placeholder that gives you a quick way to add a variety of material to your presentations. In PowerPoint, you can add several types of content to your slides through the content placeholder:

To add content to a slide through the content placeholder:

1. Click the icon of the type of content you want to add.
2. The associated dialog or task pane appears.
3. Add the content in the same manner as if you accessed the command from the Ribbon.

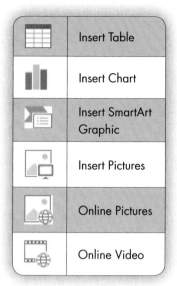

	Insert Table
	Insert Chart
	Insert SmartArt Graphic
	Insert Pictures
	Online Pictures
	Online Video

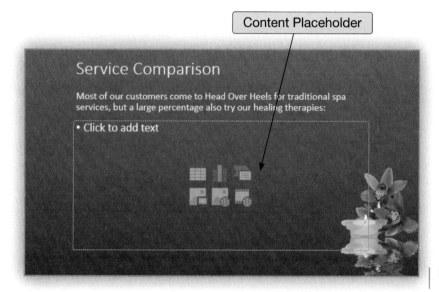

Content Placeholder

FIGURE PP 2.10

tips & tricks

When you add slides to a presentation, you can choose slides that are preformatted with content placeholders. Some slide layouts contain one content placeholder, but other layouts include multiple content placeholders, allowing you to add more than one content type to a slide.

let me try

Open the student data file **pp2-09-SpaServices** and try this skill on your own:

1. Navigate to **Slide 7.**
2. Click the **Insert Chart** icon in the content placeholder. Click **Cancel** to close the dialog.
3. Click the **Online Pictures** icon in the content placeholder.
4. Save the file as directed by your instructor and close it.

Skill 2.10 Creating Tables in Presentations

When you have a large amount of data on one slide, you will want to organize the data so it is easier for your audience to understand. A **table** helps you organize information for effective display. Tables are organized by rows, which display horizontally, and columns, which display vertically. The intersection of a row and a column is referred to as a **cell**. Tables can be used to display everything from dates in a calendar to sales numbers to product inventory.

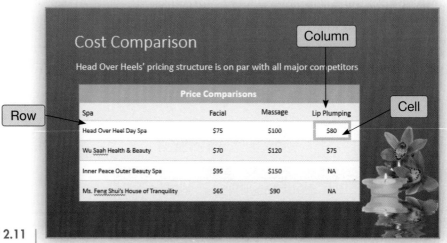

FIGURE PP 2.11

To add a table to a slide:

1. Click the **Insert** tab.
2. Click the **Table** button.
3. Select the number of cells you want by moving the cursor across and down the squares.
4. When the description at the top of the menu displays the number of rows and columns you want, click the mouse.
5. The table is inserted into your presentation.
6. Place the cursor in the cell where you want to enter the data.
7. Type the data just as you would in normal text.
8. Press (Tab ⇄) to move to the next cell and enter more data.
9. Continue pressing (Tab ⇄) until all data are entered.

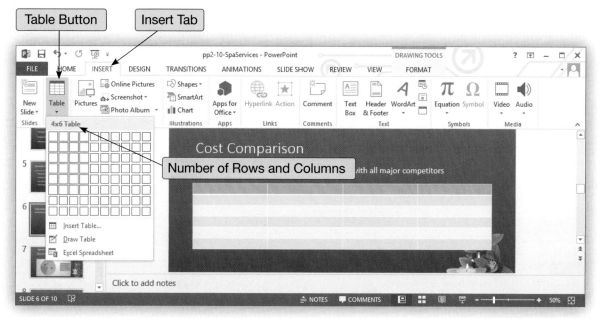

Table Button　　**Insert Tab**

FIGURE PP 2.12

tell me more

When you add a table to a slide, the *Table Tools* contextual tabs display. These tabs contain commands for working with tables. From the *Design* tab, you can modify the rows and columns, apply table styles and effects, and change the table's borders. From the *Layout* tab, you can delete and add rows and columns, change the alignment of text in cells, change the size of cells, and change the size of the table.

another method

To add a table from the *Insert Table* dialog:

❯ Click the **Table** button and select **Insert Table...**

❯ Click the **Insert Table** icon in the content placeholder.

In the *Insert Table* dialog, enter the number of rows and columns for your table. Click **OK** to add the table to the slide.

let me try

Open the student data file **pp2-10-SpaServices** and try this skill on your own:

1. On **Slide 6,** insert a table that has **four columns** and **six rows.**
2. Click in the first cell of the table and type `Cost Comparisons`
3. Click in the second cell of the second row and type `Facial`
4. Press ⟨Tab ⇆⟩ and type `Massage`
5. Press ⟨Tab ⇆⟩ and type `Lip Plumping`
6. Save the file as directed by your instructor and close it.

Skill 2.11 Adding Charts

When creating a PowerPoint presentation, you will want to display your data in the most visual way possible. One way to display data graphically is by using charts. A **chart** takes the information you have entered in a spreadsheet and converts it to a visual representation. In PowerPoint, you can create a wide variety of charts, including bar charts (both stack and 3-D), pie charts, column charts, scatter charts, and line charts.

To add a chart to a presentation:

1. Click the **Insert** tab.
2. In the *Illustrations* group, click the **Add a Chart** button.

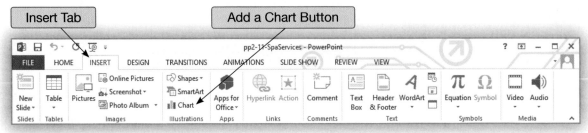

FIGURE PP 2.13

3. In the *Insert Chart* dialog, click a chart type category to display that category in the right pane.
4. Click a chart type in the right pane to select it.
5. Click **OK** to add the chart to the slide.

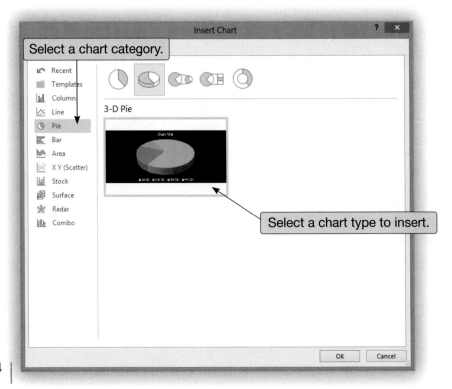

FIGURE PP 2.14

PowerPoint automatically opens the *Chart in Microsoft PowerPoint* dialog. Think of this dialog as a simplified spreadsheet where you can enter the data for your chart. The dialog opens with sample data entered for you.

1. Replace the sample data with your own data.
2. Click the **Close** button to return to PowerPoint to see your finished chart.

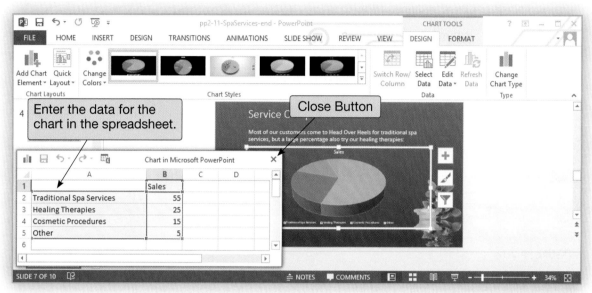

tell me **more**

As you enter data in the *Chart in Microsoft PowerPoint* dialog, PowerPoint will update the chart as you enter data and move from cell to cell in the spreadsheet.

another **method**

To open the *Insert Chart* dialog, you can also click the **Insert Chart** icon in the content placeholder on the slide.

let me **try**

Open the student data file **pp2-11-SpaServices** and try this skill on your own:

1. On **Slide 7,** insert a 3-D **pie chart.**
2. Enter the following information for the chart:

	SALES
Traditional Spa Services	55
Healing Therapies	25
Cosmetic Procedures	15
Other	5

3. Close the **Chart in Microsoft PowerPoint** dialog.
4. Save the file as directed by your instructor and close it.

Skill 2.12 Adding SmartArt

SmartArt is a way to take your ideas and make them visual. Where presentations used to have plain bulleted and ordered lists, now they can have SmartArt. SmartArt images are visual diagrams containing graphic elements with text boxes in which you enter information. Using SmartArt not only makes your presentation look better but helps convey the information in a more meaningful way.

To insert a SmartArt diagram:

1. Click the **Insert** tab.
2. In the *Illustrations* group, click the **Insert a SmartArt Graphic** button.

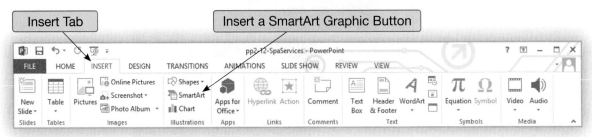

FIGURE PP 2.16

3. In the *Choose a SmartArt Graphic* dialog, click a SmartArt graphic type.
4. Click **OK.**
5. The SmartArt diagram is added to the slide.
6. Each shape in the diagram includes a text placeholder.
7. Click **[Text]** in a shape and enter the text for the item.
8. Enter the text for all the shapes in the diagram.

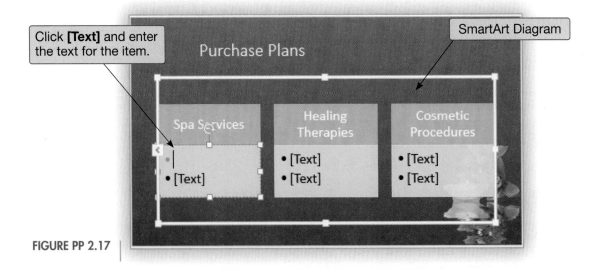

FIGURE PP 2.17

There are eight categories of SmartArt for you to choose from:

List—Use to list items that ***do not*** need to be in a particular order.

Process—Use to list items that ***do*** need to be in a particular order.

Cycle—Use for a process that repeats over and over again.

Hierarchy—Use to show branching, in either a decision tree or an organization chart.

Relationship—Use to show relationships between items.

Matrix—Use to show how an item fits into the whole.

Pyramid—Use to illustrate how things relate to each other with the largest item being on the bottom and the smallest item being on the top.

Picture—Use to show a series of pictures along with text in the diagram.

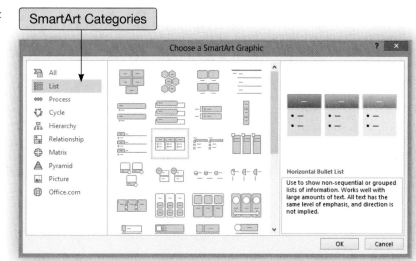

FIGURE PP 2.18

tips & tricks

When choosing a SmartArt diagram, it is important that the diagram type suits your content. In the *Choose a SmartArt Graphic* dialog, click a SmartArt type to display a preview of the SmartArt. The preview displays not only what the diagram will look like, but it also includes a description of the best uses for the diagram type.

another method

To insert a SmartArt diagram, you can also click the **SmartArt** icon in a content placeholder.

let me try

Open the student data file **pp2-12-SpaServices** and try this skill on your own:

1. Navigate to **Slide** 9 and open the **Choose a SmartArt Graphic** dialog.

2. Insert a **Horizontal Bullet List** diagram.

3. Enter the following information in the diagram:

SPA SERVICES	HEALING THERAPIES	COSMETIC PROCEDURES
Single: $45-$85	Single: $75-$110	Single: $80-$200
Block of 3: $35-$75	Block of 3: $65-$100	Block of 3: $75-$175

4. Click outside the diagram to deselect it.

5. Save the file as directed by your instructor and close it.

Skill 2.13 Adding Shapes

A **shape** is a drawing object that you can quickly add to your presentation. The PowerPoint *Shapes* gallery gives you access to a number of prebuilt shapes to add to your presentation. There are a number of types of shapes that you can add to slides, including lines, rectangles, block arrows, equation shapes, stars, banners, and callouts.

To add a shape to a slide:

1. Click the **Insert** tab.
2. In the *Illustrations* group, click the **Shapes** button and select an option from the *Shapes* gallery.
3. The cursor changes to a crosshair.
4. Click anywhere on the presentation to add the shape.

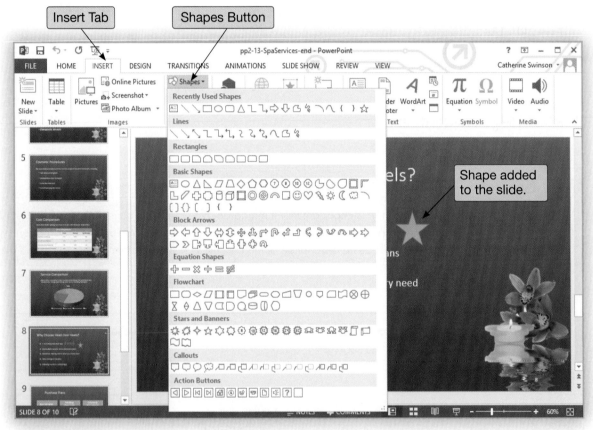

FIGURE PP 2.19

tips & tricks

Once you have added a shape to a presentation, there are a number of ways you can work with it:

» To resize a graphic: click a resize handle (⊡⁻⁻) and drag toward the center of the image to make it smaller or away from the center of the image to make it larger.

» To rotate a graphic: click the rotate handle (⟳) and drag your mouse to the right to rotate the image clockwise or to the left to rotate the image counterclockwise.

» To move a graphic: point to the graphic and when the cursor changes to the move cursor (⟷✛⟷), click and drag the image to the new location.

tell me **more**

When you insert a shape into a presentation, the *Format* tab under *Drawing Tools* displays. This tab is called a contextual tab because it only displays when a drawing object is the active element. The *Format* tab contains tools to change the look of the shape, such as shape styles, effects, and placement on the page.

another **method**

To add a shape, you can also click the **Shapes** button in the *Drawing* group on the *Home* tab.

let me **try**

Open the student data file **pp2-13-SpaServices** and try this skill on your own:

1. Navigate to **Slide 8.**
2. Add a **5-point star** to the slide.
3. Save the file as directed by your instructor and close it.

Skill 2.14 Adding Pictures

Sometimes adding a photograph or an illustration to a slide will convey a message better than text alone. Use the *Insert Picture* dialog to insert pictures you created in another program or downloaded from your smart phone or digital camera into your presentation.

To insert a picture from a file:

1. Click the **Insert** tab.
2. In the *Images* group, click the **Pictures** button.
3. The *Insert Picture* dialog opens.
4. Navigate to the file location, select the file, and click **Insert.**

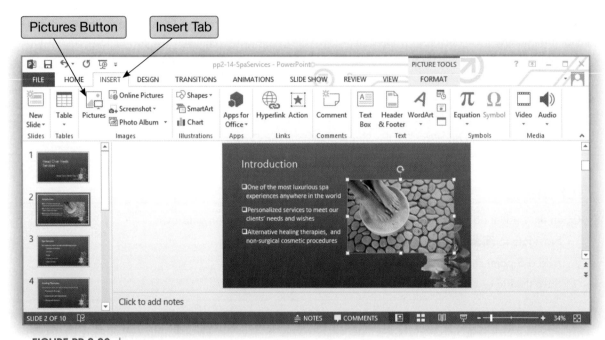

FIGURE PP 2.20

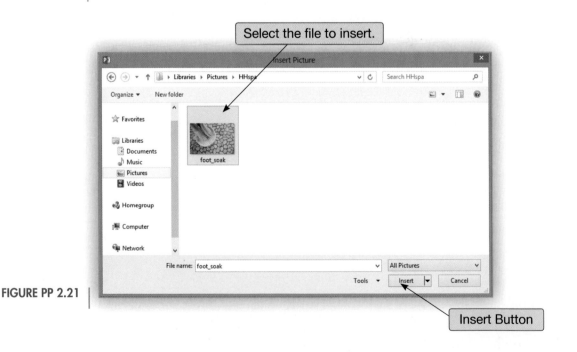

FIGURE PP 2.21

tell me **more**

You can create photograph slide shows including captions using PowerPoint's **Photo Album** feature. On the *Insert* tab, in the *Images* group, click the **Photo Album** button. Use the *Photo Album* dialog to add photos, create captions, and modify the layout. Click the **Create** button to create the photo album as a new presentation.

another **method**

To open the *Insert Picture* dialog, you can also click the **Pictures** icon in the content placeholder.

let me **try**

Open the student data file **pp2-14-SpaServices** and try this skill on your own:

1. Navigate to **Slide 2** and open the **Insert Picture** dialog.
2. Navigate to the location where you saved the data files for this book.
3. Insert the **foot_soak** picture.
4. Save the file as directed by your instructor and close it.

from the perspective of . . .

DENTAL HYGIENIST

In my profession as a dental hygienist, I created a fun presentation showing good oral hygiene habits. First I created all my content in Word and then imported the outline to save time creating all the slides in the presentation. I added information in bulleted lists and tables, and I added a chart to visually display how good hygiene decreases the chance of cavities. I was able to add pictures, music, and videos. My young patients love it.

Skill 2.15 Adding Online Pictures

A new feature in PowerPoint 2013 is the ability to add **online pictures**. You can search for pictures from *Office.com* Clip Art, through a *Bing Image Search,* or from your *SkyDrive*. When you search on *Office.com,* you will be searching through Microsoft Office's royalty-free **clip art** collection. PowerPoint will display results of **clips** for you to use in your presentation. These clips refer to files from another source and include photographs and illustrations. If you use the *Bing Image Search,* you will be searching for images from across the Internet. Searching for images on your *SkyDrive* will return images that you have added to your *SkyDrive* for use in presentation.

To insert clip art from *Office.com:*

1. Click the **Insert** tab.
2. In the *Illustrations* group, click the **Online Pictures** button.

FIGURE PP 2.22

3. The *Insert Pictures* dialog opens.
4. Type a word describing the clip you want to search for in the **Office.com Clip Art** box and click the **Search** button.
5. PowerPoint displays thumbnail results that match the search criteria.
6. Click a thumbnail to select it and click the **Insert** button to add the image to your presentation.

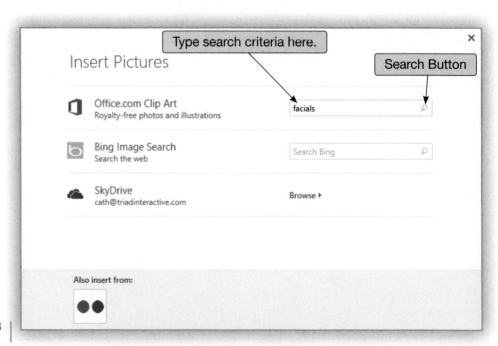

FIGURE PP 2.23

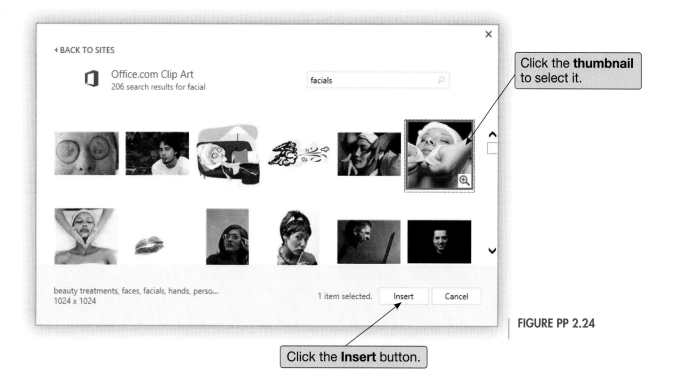

FIGURE PP 2.24

Click the **thumbnail** to select it.

Click the **Insert** button.

tips & tricks

If you use the *Office.com Clip Art* search, all the results that are returned are royalty-free images. This means you can use them freely in your presentation without worry of violating a copyright on an image. If you use the *Bing Image Search*, you will be searching the Internet for images and the results may not include images that are royalty free. You should only use images in your presentations that you know you have the proper rights to use.

tell me **more**

In previous versions of PowerPoint, you searched for clips using the *Clip Art* task pane. In PowerPoint 2013, the *Clip Art* task pane has been replaced with the *Online Pictures* dialog.

another **method**

To open the *Insert Picture* dialog, you can also click the **Online Pictures** icon in the content placeholder.

let me **try**

Open the student data file **pp2-15-SpaServices** and try this skill on your own:

1. Navigate to **Slide 2** and open the **Insert Pictures** dialog.
2. Search **Office.com Clip Art** for images of **facials.**
3. Insert the picture of the **facial with the hands and towel** (the selected thumbnail in Figure PP 2.24).
4. Save the file as directed by your instructor and close it.

Skill 2.16 Adding Online Audio

Sound files, such as music or sound effects, can enhance your slides, making them more engaging to your audience. You can add sounds to your presentation from files you have searched for online or from files you've recorded yourself.

To insert sound files from *Office.com:*

1. Click the **Insert** tab.
2. In the *Media* group, click the **Insert Audio** button and select **Online Audio...**

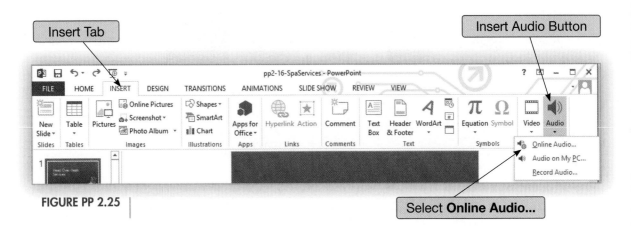

FIGURE PP 2.25

3. The *Insert Audio* dialog opens.
4. Type a word describing the sound file you want to search for in the **Office.com Clip Art** box and click the **Search** button.
5. PowerPoint displays thumbnail results that match the search criteria.
6. Click a thumbnail to select it and click the **Insert** button to add the sound to your presentation.

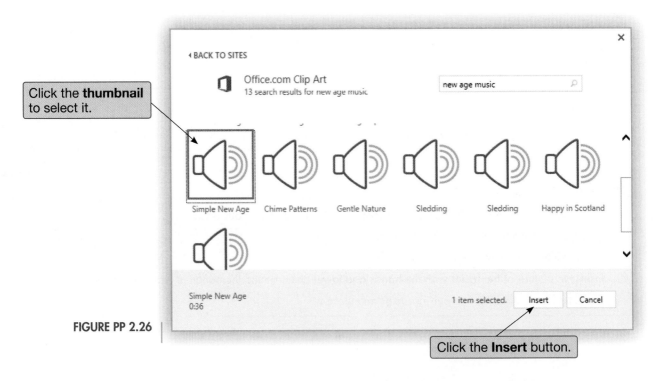

FIGURE PP 2.26

When you add a sound to a slide, the *Audio Tools* contextual tabs display. These tabs contain commands for working with sound objects in PowerPoint:

The *Format* tab allows you to change the look of the sound icon in the presentation, including applying artistic effects and Quick Styles to the icon.

The *Playback* tab provides tools for editing the audio file within PowerPoint. From the *Playback* tab, you can change the slide show volume, fade the audio in and out, loop the sound, and preview the sound.

Audio Tools Playback Tab

Play in Background Button

FIGURE PP 2.27

When you add a sound to a slide, a sound icon is added to the slide. When you run your presentation, this icon will display as part of the slide, and a play bar will display when you rest your pointer over it. To hide the icon, click the **Playback** tab under *Audio Tools.* In the *Audio Options* group, click the **Hide During Show** check box. Click the **Play in Background** button to hide the icon and play bar, play the sound file automatically, and play it across all slides in a continuous loop.

tips & tricks

Rest your mouse over an icon in the *Insert Audio* dialog to hear a sample of the sound file.

tell me **more**

You can also insert sound files from your computer. On the *Insert* tab, in the *Media* group, click the **Insert Audio** button and select **Audio on My PC...** In the *Insert Audio* dialog, browse to find the file you want and click the sound file to select it. Click **Insert** to add the sound file into your presentation.

let me **try**

Open the student data file **pp2-16-SpaServices** and try this skill on your own:

1. On **Slide 1,** open the **Insert Audio** dialog to search for audio files online.
2. Search **Office.com Clip Art** for **new age music.**
3. Insert the **Simple New Age** sound clip.
4. Change the playback settings to have the clip **play in the background.**
5. Save the file as directed by your instructor and close it.

Skill 2.17 Adding Online Video

If you already have digital videos ready to go, you can add them directly into your presentation. But what if you don't have your own videos and you want to include a video in your presentation? PowerPoint includes a built-in **online video** search for you to find videos using Microsoft *Bing* and then add them to your presentation.

To add an online video to a presentation:

1. Click the **Insert** tab.

2. In the *Media* group, click the **Insert Video** button and select **Online Video...**

FIGURE PP 2.28

3. The *Insert Video* dialog opens.

4. Type a word describing the video you want to search for in the **Bing Video Search** box and click the **Search** button.

5. PowerPoint displays thumbnail results that match the search criteria.

6. Click a thumbnail to select it and click the **Insert** button to add the video to your presentation.

FIGURE PP 2.29

When you add a video to a slide, the *Video Tools* contextual tabs display. These tabs contain commands for working with video objects in PowerPoint:

The *Format* tab allows you to change the look of the video frame in the presentation, including applying artistic effects and Quick Styles.

The *Playback* tab provides tools for editing the video file within PowerPoint. From the Playback tab, you can change the video volume, fade the video in and out, loop the video, and preview the video.

tips & tricks

When you add a video to a presentation, it is treated as if it is a picture. You can move and position the video using alignment guides, as well as apply picture Quick Styles from the *Picture Tools Format* tab.

tell me more

You can also insert video files from your computer. On the *Insert* tab, in the *Media* group, click the **Insert Video** button and select **Video on My PC...** In the *Insert Video* dialog, browse to find the file you want and click the video file to select it. Click **Insert** to add the video file into your presentation.

another method

To open the *Insert Picture* dialog, you can also click the **Insert Video** icon in the content placeholder. When you do this, the *Insert Video* dialog includes the option for inserting a video from a file on your PC.

let me try

Open the student data file **pp2-17-SpaServices** and try this skill on your own:

1. On **Slide 4,** open the **Insert Video** dialog to search for video files online.
2. Search **Bing Video Search** for a video showing a **spa facial.**
3. Insert the **How to give a facial spa treatment** video (the selected thumbnail in Figure PP 2.29). If you do not see this clip in your search results, insert a video clip of your choice.
4. Save the file as directed by your instructor and close it.

key terms

Outline view
Copy
Clipboard
Paste
Paste options
Cut
Bulleted lists
Numbered lists
WordArt
Content placeholder

Table
Cell
Chart
SmartArt
Shape
Online picture
Clip art
Clips
Sound files
Online video

concepts review

1. The _____ placeholder is a special type of placeholder that gives you a quick way to add a variety of material to your presentations.

   a. text

   b. slide

   c. content

   d. title

2. _____ are visual diagrams containing graphic elements with text boxes in which you enter information.

   a. SmartArt images

   b. Tables

   c. Charts

   d. Placeholders

3. To copy text to the Clipboard and not remove it from the document, you would use the _____ command.

   a. Copy

   b. Cut

   c. Undo

   d. Redo

4. Text that includes predefined graphic styles, such as shadows, reflections, and glows is known as _____.

   a. SmartArt

   b. shapes

   c. WordArt

   d. fonts

5. If you need to display items in a list in a particular order, use a _____.

   a. bulleted list

   b. numbered list

   c. SmartArt diagram

   d. table

6. To display text thumbnails of your slides to be able to work with the text only, switch to _____.

   a. Slide Sorter view

   b. Slide Show view

   c. Slide Master view

   d. Outline view

7. When creating slides from a Word outline, text with the _____ style applied to it will become the title text for each slide.

   a. Heading 1

   b. Heading 2

   c. Heading 3

   d. Title

8. A _____ is a drawing object that you can quickly add to your presentation and include arrows, lines, rectangles, and callouts.

   a. shape

   b. picture

   c. diagram

   d. chart

9. To hide the sound icon and play an audio file across the entire presentation, click the _____.

   a. Hide During Show check box

   b. Play in Background button

   c. Volume button

   d. No Style

10. A(n) _____ is the intersection of a row and a column in a table.

   a. placeholder

   b. data point

   c. cell

   d. axis

projects

Data files for projects can be found on
www.mhhe.com/office2013skills

skill review 2.1

In this project you will be adding content to a presentation for Suarez Marketing.

Skills needed to complete this project:

- Opening a Word Outline as a Presentation (Skill 2.1)
- Using the Outline View (Skill 2.2)
- Using Cut and Paste (Skill 2.4)
- Adding Numbered Lists (Skill 2.7)
- Adding Shapes (Skill 2.13)
- Understanding the Content Placeholder (Skill 2.9)
- Adding SmartArt (Skill 2.12)
- Creating Tables in Presentations (Skill 2.10)
- Adding Online Pictures (Skill 2.15)
- Adding WordArt (Skill 2.8)
- Adding Online Audio (Skill 2.16)

1. Open the **PP2013-SkillReview-2-1** presentation.
2. Save this presentation as: `[your initials]PP-SkillReview-2-1`
3. Insert slide content from a Word outline.

    a. On the *Home* tab, in the *Slides* group, click the **New Slide** button.

    b. Select **Slides from Outline...**

    c. In the *Insert Outline* dialog, navigate to the location where you saved your data files.

    d. Select the **SuarezMarketingOutline** document and click the **Insert** button.

4. Add text to a slide from *Outline* view.

    a. Click the **View** tab.

    b. In the *Presentation Views* group, click the **Outline View** button.

    c. Place the cursor before **MARIA SUAREZ** on **Slide 1.** Press (←Enter) and move the cursor to the empty line that was added.

    d. Type **PUTTING YOUR NEEDS FIRST**

    e. In the *Presentation Views* group, click the **Normal** button to return to *Normal* view.

5. Cut and paste text from one slide to another.

    a. Navigate to **Slide 3.**

    b. Select the first bullet point: **Provide you with prompt and excellent service to exceed your expectations.**

    c. Click the **Home** tab.

    d. In the *Clipboard* group, click the **Cut** button.

    e. Navigate to **Slide 2,** place the cursor at the end of the bullet point and press (←Enter).

    f. In the *Clipboard* group, click the **Paste** button.

6. Create a numbered list.

    a. Navigate to **Slide 4** and select the bullet points on the slide.

    b. On the *Home* tab, in the *Paragraph* group, click the **Numbering** button and select the **1) 2) 3)** format.

7. Add a shape to a slide.

    a. Navigate to **Slide 5.**

    b. Click the **Insert** tab.

    c. In the *Illustrations* group, click the **Shapes** button and select the **Oval Callout** shape (it is the third option under *Callouts*).

    d. Add the shape to the right of the slide title.

    e. Resize the shape so it more wide than tall. Make the shape larger to fill the space above the text placeholder.

8. Change the layout of a slide to include a content placeholder and add a SmartArt diagram.

    a. Navigate to **Slide 8.**

    b. Click the **Home** tab.

    c. In the *Slides* group, click the **Slide Layout** button and select **Title and Content.**

    d. Roll your mouse over the icons in the placeholder to see the types of content you can add.

    e. Click the **Insert a SmartArt Graphic** icon.

    f. In the *Choose a SmartArt Graphic* dialog, click the **Cycle** category.

    g. Click the **Circle Arrow Process** diagram and click **OK** to add the SmartArt diagram to the slide.

    h. In the top circle, type `Analyze`

    i. In the middle circle, type `Design`

    j. In the bottom circle, type `Implement`

9. Change the layout of a slide to include a content placeholder and add a table.

    a. Navigate to **Slide 9.**

    b. Click the **Home** tab.

    c. In the *Slides* group, click the **Slide Layout** button and select **Title and Content.**

    d. Click the **Insert Table** icon.

    e. In the *Insert Table* dialog, in the *Number of columns* box, type `2`. In the *Number of rows* box, type **4**. Click **OK.**

    f. Enter the following information in the table

Belief	What it means at Suarez
Commitment	Doing everything possible for the client
Teamwork	Working together for success
Trust	Openness and honesty above all

10. Search for a picture online and add it to a slide.

    a. Click the **Insert** tab.

    b. In the *Images* group, click the **Online Pictures** button.

    c. In the *Insert Pictures* dialog, type `teamwork` in the *Office.com Clip Art* box and click the **Search** button.

FIGURE PP 2.30

    d. Click the picture of **Teamwork success celebrated with a high five** (as shown in Figure PP 2.30).

    e. Click the **Insert** button.

    f. Move the picture to the lower right corner of the slide so it doesn't cover up any text in the table.

11. Add WordArt to a slide.

    a. Navigate to **Slide 1.**

    b. Select the **title placeholder** and press Delete.

    c. Click the **Insert** tab.

    d. In the *Text* group, click the **WordArt** button and select the **Fill–White, Text 1, Shadow** option (it is the first option in the first row of the gallery).

    e. Type `Suarez Marketing`

12. Search for an audio file online and add it to the presentation.

    a. Click the **Insert** tab.

    b. In the *Media* group, click the **Insert Audio** button.

    c. Select **Online Audio...**

    d. In the *Insert Audio* dialog, type **techno music** and click the **Search** button.

    e. Select the **Techno pop music** clip and click **Insert.**

    f. On the *Audio Tools Playback* tab, in the *Audio Styles* group, click the **Play in Background** button.

13. Save and close the presentation.

skill review 2.2

In this project you will be modifying the *My Fitness Plan* presentation by adding content.

Skills needed to complete this project:

- Using the Outline View (Skill 2.2)
- Using Copy and Paste (Skill 2.3)
- Adding Bulleted Lists (Skill 2.6)
- Understanding the Content Placeholder (Skill 2.9)
- Adding Charts (Skill 2.11)
- Adding WordArt (Skill 2.8)
- Adding Shapes (Skill 2.13)
- Adding Online Pictures (Skill 2.15)
- Adding Pictures (Skill 2.14)
- Adding Online Audio (Skill 2.16)

1. Open the **PP2013-SkillReview-2-2** presentation.

2. Save this presentation as: **[your initials]PP-SkillReview-2-2**

3. Add text to a slide through *Outline* view

    a. Click the **View** tab.

    b. In the *Presentation Views* group, click the **Outline View** button.

    c. Click next to the square for **Slide 2** on the *Outline* pane.

d. Type **Diet Plan**

e. In the *Presentation Views* group, click the **Normal View** button.

4. Copy and paste text from one slide to another.

  a. Navigate to **Slide 4.**

  b. Select the third bullet point: **Take a nap when possible**.

  c. Click the **Home** tab.

  d. In the *Clipboard* group, click the **Copy** button.

  e. Navigate to **Slide 6.**

  f. Place the cursor after the last bullet point (**Quiet time**) and press ⏎ Enter .

  g. In the *Clipboard* group, click the **Paste** button.

5. Convert a numbered list into a bulleted list.

  a. Navigate to **Slide 7.**

  b. Select the numbered list.

  c. On the *Home* tab, in the *Paragraph* group, click the **Bullets** button arrow.

  d. Select the **Arrow Bullets** option.

6. Add an online picture to a slide.

  a. Click the **Insert** tab.

  b. In the *Images* group, click the **Online Pictures** button.

  c. In the *Office.com Clip Art* box, type **target.** Click the **Search** button.

  d. Select a target image of your choice. Click the **Insert** button.

  e. If necessary, resize the target to fit well on the slide.

7. Add a chart to a slide.

  a. Navigate to **Slide 8.**

  b. Click the **Insert Chart** icon in the content placeholder.

  c. In the *Insert Chart* dialog, select a **Clustered Column** chart (the first option in the *Column* category) and click **OK.**

  d. Delete the **Series 3** column.

  e. Insert the following data for the chart:

	CALORIES CONSUMED	CALORIES BURNED
Sunday	1650	450
Monday	1825	250
Tuesday	1500	200
Wednesday	1900	100
Thursday	1600	350
Friday	1750	400
Saturday	2100	650

  f. Close the **Chart in Microsoft PowerPoint** dialog.

8. Add WordArt to a slide.

  a. Navigate to **Slide 9.**

  b. Click the **Insert** tab.

   c. In the *Text* group, click the **WordArt** button and select the **Fill–Orange, Accent 3, Sharp Bevel** option.

   d. Type `I can do it!`

   e. Click outside the text box to deselect it.

9. Add a shape to a slide

   a. Click the **Insert** tab.

   b. In the *Illustrations* group, click the **Shapes** button and select the **Smiley Face** (it is located in the third row under *Basic Shapes*).

   c. Add the shape on the right side of the slide under the WordArt you added.

10. Add a picture from your computer.

   a. Click the **Insert** tab.

   b. In the *Images* group, click the **Pictures** button.

   c. In the *Insert Picture* dialog, navigate to the location where you saved your data files.

   d. Select the **finish_line** image and click **Insert.**

   e. Move the image so it appears to the left of the WordArt.

11. Add online audio to a slide.

   a. Click the **Insert** tab.

   b. On the *Insert* tab, in the *Media* group, click the **Insert Audio** button.

   c. Select **Online Audio...**

   d. In the *Insert Audio* dialog, type `high five music.`

   e. Select the **High five music** clip and click **Insert.**

   f. On the *Audio Tools Playback* tab, in the *Audio Options* group, click the **Hide During Show** check box.

12. Save and close the presentation.

challenge yourself **2.3**

In this project you will be adding content to a presentation for the Greenscapes landscaping company.

Skills needed to complete this project:

- Opening a Word Outline as a Presentation (Skill 2.1)
- Adding Pictures (Skill 2.14)
- Using the Outline View (Skill 2.2)
- Using Cut and Paste (Skill 2.4)
- Adding Numbered Lists (Skill 2.7)
- Understanding the Content Placeholder (Skill 2.9)
- Adding SmartArt (Skill 2.12)
- Creating Tables in Presentations (Skill 2.10)
- Adding Online Pictures (Skill 2.15)
- Adding WordArt (Skill 2.8)
- Adding Online Audio (Skill 2.16)

1. Open the **PP2013-ChallengeYourself-2-3** presentation.

2. Save this presentation as: **[your initials] PP-ChallengeYourself-2-3**

3. Insert slide content from a Word Outline.

   a. Open the *Insert Outline* dialog.

   b. Navigate to the location where you saved your data files.

   c. Insert the **greenscapesOutline** document.

4. Add a picture from your computer.

   a. Click in the **Title placeholder** on **Slide 1.**

   b. Open the **Insert Picture** dialog.

   c. Navigate to the location where you saved your data files.

   d. Insert the **greenscapes_logo** image.

5. Add text to a slide from *Outline* view.

   a. Switch to **Outline view.**

   b. Add the text **Reduce our carbon footprint** as the last bullet point on **Slide 2.**

   c. Switch back to **Normal view.**

6. Cut and paste text from one slide to another.

   a. On **Slide 5,** select the first bullet point: **Walkways.**

   b. Cut the text and paste it after the last bullet point (**Leaf Removal**) on **Slide 3.**

7. Create a numbered list.

   a. Select the bulleted list on **Slide 3.**

   b. Convert the list to a numbered list using the **1. 2. 3.** format.

8. Change the layout of a slide to include a content placeholder and add a SmartArt diagram.

   a. Change the layout of **Slide 4** to the **Title and Content** layout.

   b. Insert a **Continuous Block Process** SmartArt diagram.

   c. In the box on the left, type **Blow and Rake**

   d. In the middle box, type **Gather and Haul Away**

   e. In the box on the right, type **Compost**

9. Change the layout of a slide to include a content placeholder and add a table.

   a. Change the layout of **Slide 6** to the **Title and Content** layout.

   b. Insert a table with two columns and five rows.

   c. Enter the following information in the table:

SERVICE	PRICE
Lawn Care	$25.00 per service
Lawn Maintenance	$99.00 per treatment
Leaf Removal	$25.00 per hour
Shrub and Tree Maintenance	$125.00 per hour

10. Search for a picture online and add it to a slide.

    a. Change the layout of **Slide 7** to the **Blank** layout.

    b. Search for a picture of a **garden** on *Office.com Clip Art*.

    c. Insert the picture of the landscaped garden and lawn (see Figure PP 2.31)

FIGURE PP 2.31

11. Add WordArt to the slide using the **Fill–Dark green, Accent 2, Outline–Accent 2** style that reads **Thank You.**

12. Search for an audio file online and add it to the presentation.

   a. Search online for **Rainforest music** and add it to the slide.

   b. Have the music play in the background.

13. Save and close the presentation.

challenge yourself **2.4**

In this project you will be adding content to a presentation about emotional intelligence.

Skills needed to complete this project:

- Using the Outline View (Skill 2.2)
- Adding WordArt (Skill 2.8)
- Understanding the Content Placeholder (Skill 2.9)
- Adding Online Pictures (Skill 2.15)
- Adding Online Audio (Skill 2.16)
- Adding Bulleted Lists (Skill 2.6)
- Adding SmartArt (Skill 2.12)
- Using Cut and Paste (Skill 2.4)
- Adding Shapes (Skill 2.13)
- Adding Online Video (Skill 2.17)

1. Open the **PP2013-ChallengeYourself-2-4** presentation.

2. Save this presentation as: `[your initials]PP-ChallengeYourself-2-4`

3. Add text through outline view.

   a. Switch to **Outline view** and add **TO LIFE STRESSORS** to the end of the subtitle on **Slide 1.**

   b. Switch back to **Normal** view.

4. Add WordArt to a slide.

   a. Add WordArt to **Slide 2** using the **Fill–White, Outline–Accent 1, Glow–Accent 1** style that reads **Save the Drama for Your Mama!**

   b. Change the size of the font to **40 pt.**

   c. Move the WordArt so it appears at the top of the slide.

5. Search for a picture online and add it to a slide.

   a. Search for a picture of a **woman screaming** on *Office.com Clip Art*.

   b. Insert the picture of the **Woman with her hands on her head and screaming** (Hint: It has a red background).

6. Search for an audio file online and add it to the presentation.

   a. Search online music from **Sleeping Beauty** and add it to the slide.

   b. Have the music play automatically when the slide loads and have the sound icon hidden during the slide show.

7. Convert the numbered list on **Slide 3** to a bulleted list using the **Hollow Square Bullets** style.

8. Add a SmartArt diagram.

    a. From the *Relationship* category, add a **Basic Venn** SmartArt diagram to **Slide 8.**

    b. Delete the top circle.

    c. In the circle on the left, type `IQ`

    d. In the circle on the right, type `EQ`

9. Cut and paste text from one slide to another.

    a. Select the **last five bullet points** on **Slide 10** (from **Remain Optimistic** to the end).

    b. Cut the bullet points, removing them from the slide and placing them on the Clipboard.

    c. On **Slide 11,** place the cursor after the text **Ways to improve EQ:** and press `← Enter`.

    d. Paste the cut text on to the slide.

10. Add a **12-point star shape** to the upper right corner of **Slide 12.**

11. Search online for a video of **Daniel Goleman and Emotional Intelligence.** Select the **Daniel Goleman Introduces Emotional Intelligence** video and add it to the **Slide 13.** If you do not see this clip in your search results, insert a video clip of your choice.

12. Save and close the presentation.

on your own 2.5

In this project you will be modifying a presentation about creating PowerPoint presentations.

Skills needed to complete this project:

- Adding Bulleted Lists (Skill 2.6)
- Adding Shapes (Skill 2.13)
- Using the Outline View (Skill 2.2)
- Using Cut and Paste (Skill 2.4)
- Adding Numbered Lists (Skill 2.7)
- Creating Tables in Presentations (Skill 2.10)
- Understanding the Content Placeholder (Skill 2.9)
- Adding SmartArt (Skill 2.12)
- Adding Online Pictures (Skill 2.15)
- Adding WordArt (Skill 2.8)
- Adding Online Audio (Skill 2.16)

1. Open the **PP2013-OnYourOwn-2-5** presentation.

2. Save this presentation as: `[your initials]PP-OnYourOwn-2-5`

3. Add a shape of your choice to **Slide 2.**

4. Use **Outline View** to add introductory text for the four steps of creating a presentation.

5. On **Slide 2, select the last four line and convert the lines** to a bulleted list using a bullet style of your choice.

6. Use **Cut** and **Paste** to rearrange the bullet points on **Slide 3** into a more logical order.

7. On **Slide 4,** move the text from the tabbed list into a new table.

8. On **Slide 5,** add a new **cycle SmartArt** diagram of your choice. Include the following points:

   `Review Slides`

   `Set Up Slide Show`

   `Rehearse Timings`

9. On **Slide 6,** search for a picture on **Office.com Clip Art** and add it to the slide. If necessary, resize and move the image to an appropriate place on the slide.

10. Add **WordArt** to the slide in a style of your choice that reads `Practice! Practice! Practice!` Move the WordArt to an appropriate place on the slide.

11. Search online for a piece of background music for the presentation. Add it to **Slide 1** of the presentation and have it play in the background.

12. Save and close the presentation.

fix it **2.6**

In this project you will be modifying a project about team building.

Skills needed to complete this project:

- Using the Outline View (Skill 2.2)
- Using Cut and Paste (Skill 2.4)
- Adding Bulleted Lists (Skill 2.6)
- Understanding the Content Placeholder (Skill 2.9)
- Creating Tables in Presentations (Skill 2.10)
- Adding Charts (Skill 2.11)
- Adding SmartArt (Skill 2.12)
- Adding Shapes (Skill 2.13)
- Adding Online Pictures (Skill 2.15)

1. Open the **PP2013-FixIt-2-6** presentation.

2. Save this presentation as: `[your initials]PP-FixIt-2-6`

3. Use **Outline View** to change the subtitle on **Slide 1** from `A PRIMER` to THE BASICS.

4. On **Slide 3,** cut the first point (**Member introduction**) and paste it as the last bullet point on **Slide 2.**

5. Convert the **numbered list** on **Slide 3** to a bulleted list using the **Filled Round Bullets** style.

6. On **Slide 5,** move the text from the tabbed list into a new table. *Hint:* You can cut the text and then paste it into the table you add. You can then cut and paste each piece of text into the proper cell in the table.

7. On **Slide 6,** create a **pie chart** from the data on the slide. Do not include a title for the chart.

8. On **Slide 7,** add a **Basic Cycle SmartArt diagram.** Include the following points:

    `Specific`

    `Measurable`

    `Attainable`

    `Relevant`

    `Time Bound`

9. At the top of **Slide 7,** add a **horizontal scroll shape.** Double-click the shape and add the text **SMART Review** to the shape. Resize the shape if necessary to better display the text.

10. On **Slide 8,** search for an online picture about team building and add it to content placeholder on the right side of the slide.

11. Save and close the presentation.

chapter 3

Formatting Presentations

In this chapter, you will learn the following skills:

- ❱ Change themes and theme variants
- ❱ Apply slide transitions
- ❱ Change the size of slides in a presentation
- ❱ Change the slide background
- ❱ Modify the look of drawing objects
- ❱ Apply Quick Styles to drawing objects, tables, and pictures
- ❱ Change image alignment, size, and placement
- ❱ Display the ruler and gridlines
- ❱ Add footer information, including slide numbers and the current date
- ❱ Add and modify animations

skills

introduction

This chapter provides you with the skills to modify the look of content in presentations. First, you will change the theme of a presentation and then modify the look of the theme by applying a theme variant. You will apply transitions to all the slides in the presentation and change the slide size and background in a presentation. You will learn about drawing objects and how to change the look of objects by applying Quick Styles, changing the fill color, and modifying the outline.

You will also apply Quick Styles to tables and pictures as well as apply preset picture effects. You will work with images on the slide, changing alignment and using smart guides to move and place images. You will learn to display the ruler and gridlines to help with image placement and sizing. You will add footer content to slides, including slide numbers and the current date. Finally, you will learn how to apply animations, modify animations, and copy animations to other objects using the *Animation Painter*.

Skill 3.1 Changing the Presentation Theme

A **theme** is a group of formatting options that you apply to a presentation. Themes include font, color, and effect styles that are applied to specific elements of a presentation. In Power-Point, themes also include background styles. When you apply a theme, all the slides in the presentation are affected.

To apply a theme to the presentation:

1. Click the **Design** tab.
2. In the *Themes* group, click the **More** button.
3. Select an option in the *Themes* gallery.
4. All the slides in your presentation now use the new theme.

FIGURE PP 3.1

tell me **more**

Although themes are designed to make it easy for you to create a cohesive look for presentations, you may find that the themes available in the Microsoft Office applications are close to what you want but not quite right for your presentation. To create your own version of a theme, all you need to do is change the theme's color, font, or effect styles.

another **method**

To apply a theme, you can also click a theme on the Ribbon without opening the gallery.

let me **try**

Open the student data file **pp3-01-SpaServices** and try this skill on your own:

1. Change the presentation theme to **Ion.**
2. Save the file as directed by your instructor and close it.

Skill 3.2 Using Theme Variants

When you apply a theme, it comes with a set of colors applied to text, the background, and objects in the presentation. But what if you like the layout of a theme, but you don't like the colors? PowerPoint 2013 allows you to choose from a number of theme variants to apply to a presentation. A **theme variant** is a set of color variations you can change for a theme.

To change the theme variant:

1. Click the **Design** tab.
2. In the *Variants* group, select a theme variant option.

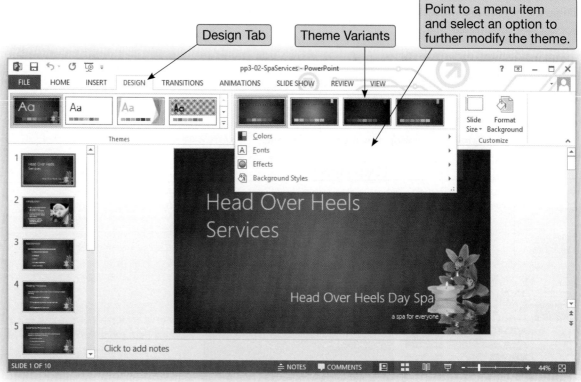

FIGURE PP 3.2

From the *Variants* group, you can change other aspects of the theme:

Color themes—A **color theme** is a set of colors that are designed to work well together in a document. A color theme will change the color of text, tables, and drawing objects in a document.

Font themes—A **font theme** includes default fonts for titles and slide text.

Effects themes—An **effects theme** consists of line and fill effects that you apply to objects on your slides.

Background Styles—Each theme comes with a number of preset background styles you can apply to the presentation. Backgrounds range from light to dark colors and can be a solid color or a gradient.

tips & tricks

When you create a presentation from a template, you can choose the theme variant before you create the new presentation.

let me try

Open the student data file **pp3-02-SpaServices** and try this skill on your own:

1. Change the variant for the theme to use the **purple variant.**
2. Save the file as directed by your instructor and close it.

from the perspective of . . .

RETAIL MANAGER

Working in the marketing field, I need to advertise to clients and present at business meetings. I use Quick Styles to apply formatting, making my presentations look great without a lot of work. With various formatting capabilities such as themes and transitions, I can create exciting presentations that capture the attention of my audience. Whenever I give a presentation, I am always complimented on how nice the presentation looks.

Skill 3.3 Applying Slide Transitions

A **transition** is an effect that occurs when one slide leaves the screen and another one appears. Transitions add movement to your presentation and can keep audiences interested, but remember that overusing transitions can be distracting. Add transitions only where they will improve your presentation.

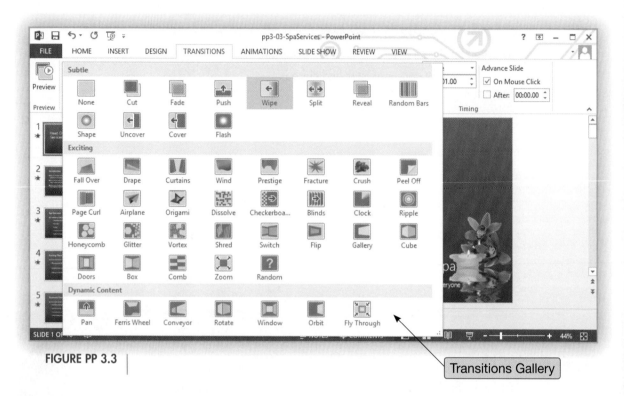

FIGURE PP 3.3

Transitions Gallery

To apply transitions to a slide:

1. Select the slide to which you want to add the transition.
2. Click the **Transitions** tab.
3. In the *Transition to This Slide* group, click the **More** button and select a transition to apply to the slide. PowerPoint automatically previews the transition for you.
4. Click the **Preview** button to play the transition again.
5. To add a sound effect to a slide, click the arrow next to the *Sound* box.
6. To add the same transition to all the slides of a presentation, select the slide with the transition you want to apply, and click the **Apply to All** button.

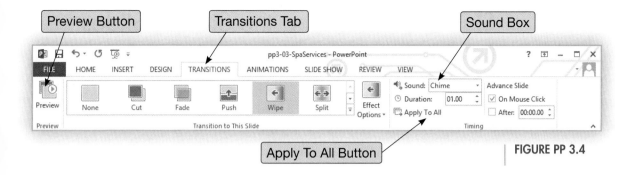

FIGURE PP 3.4

tips & tricks

When you select a transition, PowerPoint applies the default settings for that transition to the slide. You can customize the settings for a transition to create the exact effect you want:

Click the **Effect Options** button to view the different options for the transition. When you select an option, PowerPoint will automatically play a preview of the new transition.

Enter a time in seconds in the *Duration* box or click the up or down arrows to adjust how quickly or slowly the transition happens. Click the **Preview** button to view the new transition speed.

tell me **more**

PowerPoint offers a number of transitions for you to choose from. There are simple fades and dissolves, any number of directional wipes (including shapes and rotations), pushes and covers, stripes and bars, and random transitions. When choosing transitions for your presentation, it is important to keep in mind who your audience will be. If you are presenting in a formal business environment, you will probably want to use more subtle transitions, such as fades and dissolves. If your audience expects more "sizzle" in the presentation, then you may want to choose a complex wipe, such as the Vortex transition.

another **method**

To apply a transition, you can also click a transition in the *Transition to This Slide* group without opening the *Transitions* gallery.

let me **try**

Open the student data file **pp3-03-SpaServices** and try this skill on your own:

1. Apply the **Wipe** transition to the slide.
2. Add the **Chime** sound to the transition.
3. Apply the transition to **all the slides** in the presentation.
4. Save the file as directed by your instructor and close it.

Skill 3.4 Changing the Size of Slides

In past versions of PowerPoint, the default aspect ratio for slides was 4:3. This aspect ratio is square in appearance and does not translate well to widescreen displays. In PowerPoint 2013, this default slide size has been changed to **widescreen 16:9**. If you are working with a presentation or template that was created in an earlier version of PowerPoint, you may want to change the slide size for display on a widescreen display.

To change the size of slides in a presentation:

1. Click the **Design** tab.
2. In the *Customize* group, click the **Slide Size** button and select an option.

FIGURE PP 3.5

tips & tricks

Click **Custom Slide Size...** to open the *Slide Size* dialog where you can manually adjust the size of the slides in a presentation or select from a number of other preset options.

tell me more

If you change your slide size from widescreen (16:9) to standard (4:3), PowerPoint will give you the option of maximizing the content on the new slide size or to reduce the content size to ensure it will fit in the new slide size.

let me try

Open the student data file **pp3-04-SpaServices** and try this skill on your own:

1. Change the slide size for the presentation to **widescreen (16:9).**
2. Save the file as directed by your instructor and close it.

Skill 3.5 Changing the Slide Background

A **background** is the graphic element that fills a slide. Backgrounds can be solid colors, textures, or even images. From the *Format Background* task pane, you can adjust the look of the slide backgrounds.

To change the slide background to a solid color:

1. Click the **Design** tab.
2. In the *Customize* group, click the **Format Background** button.
3. The *Format Background* task pane displays.
4. In the *Fill* section, click the **Solid fill** radio button.
5. Click the **Color** button and select an option from the color palette.
6. Click the **Apply to All** button to change the background for all the slides in the presentation.

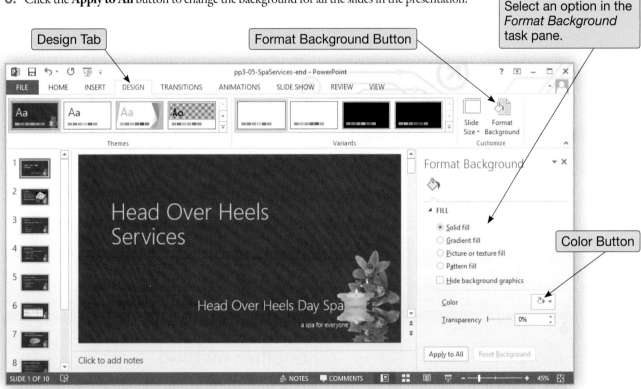

Design Tab

Format Background Button

Select an option in the *Format Background* task pane.

Color Button

FIGURE PP 3.6

tips & tricks

When you select a different background fill option, you will see other controls to adjust the look of the background fill type you selected.

let me try

Open the student data file **pp3-05-SpaServices** and try this skill on your own:

1. Display the **Format Background** task pane.
2. Apply a **solid fill** background using the **Gray–50%, Accent 6, Darker 50%** option (it is the last option in the last row under *Theme Colors*).
3. Apply the background to all the slides in the presentation.
4. Save the file as directed by your instructor and close it.

Skill 3.6 Applying Quick Styles to Drawing Objects

Quick Styles are a combination of formatting that give elements of your presentation a more polished, graphical look without a lot of work. Quick Styles can be applied to **drawing objects**, such as text boxes, shapes, and WordArt, and include a combination of borders, shadows, reflections, and picture shapes, such as rounded corners or skewed perspective. Instead of applying each of these formatting elements one at a time, you can apply a combination of elements at one time using a preset Quick Style.

To apply a Quick Style to a drawing object:

1. Select the drawing object to which you want to apply the Quick Style.
2. Click the **Drawing Tools Format** tab.
3. In the *Shape Styles* group, click the **More** button.
4. In the *Shape Styles* gallery, click a Quick Style to apply it to the drawing object.

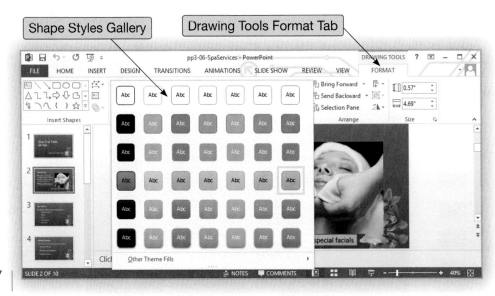

FIGURE PP 3.7

tell me **more**

Drawing objects in PowerPoint include shapes, text boxes, placeholders, and WordArt. When you insert or select a drawing object in a presentation, the *Drawing Tools Format* tab displays. This tab is called a contextual tab because it only displays when a drawing object is the active element. The *Format* tab contains tools to change the look of the selected drawing object, such as shape styles, WordArt styles, sizing, and arrangement options.

another **method**

To apply a Quick Style to a drawing object, you can also click the **Shape Quick Styles** button in the *Drawing* group on the *Home* tab.

To apply a Quick Style to a shape, you can also right-click the shape, click the **Shape Quick Styles** button, and select an option.

let me **try**

Open the student data file **pp3-06-SpaServices** and try this skill on your own:

1. Select the text box under the picture on **Slide 2**.
2. Apply the **Subtle Effect–Gray-50%, Accent 6** Quick Style to the text box (it is the last option in the fourth row of the gallery).
3. Save the file as directed by your instructor and close it.

Skill 3.7 Applying Fill Colors to Drawing Objects

When you add a drawing object to a slide, PowerPoint uses the default object **fill color** from the presentation's theme. But what if you want your object to be a different color? You can customize the fill color for objects from the *Drawing Tools Format* tab.

To change the fill effects on a drawing object:

1. Select the drawing object you want to change.
2. Click the **Drawing Tools Format** tab.
3. In the *Shape Styles* group, click the **Shape Fill** button.
4. Select an option from the color palette.

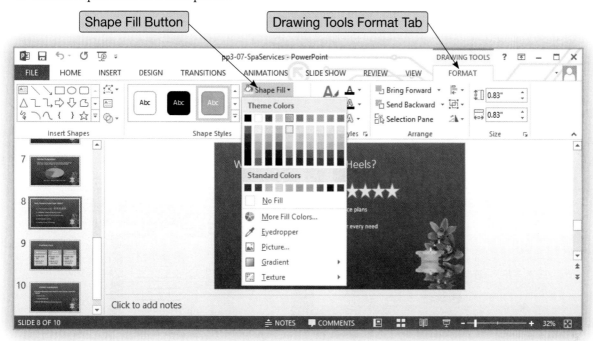

FIGURE PP 3.8

tell me **more**

You can use these same steps to change the fill color on tables. The **Shape Fill** button is located in the *Table Styles* group on the *Table Tools Design* tab.

another **method**

To change the fill color of a drawing object, you can also click the **Shape Fill** button in the *Drawing* group on the *Home* tab.
   To change the fill color of a shape, you can also right-click the shape, click the **Fill** button and select an option.

let me **try**

Open the student data file **pp3-07-SpaServices** and try this skill on your own:

1. Select the five stars on **Slide 8.** Click the **first star** to select it. Press and hold the (↑ Shift) key and click the other four stars to select all five.
2. Apply the **Ice Blue, Accent 1, Lighter 80%** fill color to the stars.
3. Save the file as directed by your instructor and close it.

Skill 3.8 Applying Outlines to Drawing Objects

When you add a drawing object to a slide, PowerPoint uses the default object outline style from the presentation's theme. This may not be the look you want for your drawing object. You can customize the weight and style of outlines for drawing objects from the *Drawing Tools Format* tab.

To change the shape outline of a drawing object:

1. Select the drawing object you want to change.
2. Click the **Drawing Tools Format** tab.
3. In the *Shape Styles* group, click the **Shape Outline** button.
4. Select an option from the color palette to change the color of the outline.
5. Point to **Weight** and select a thickness option for the outline.
6. Point to **Dashes** and select a dash style for the outline.

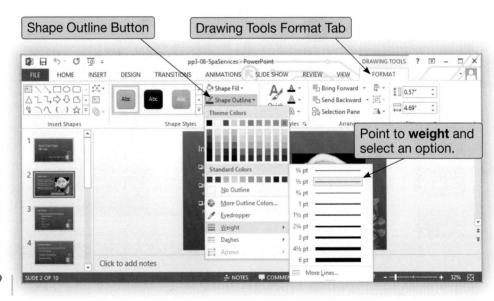

FIGURE PP 3.9

tell me **more**

You can use these same steps to change the outline style on pictures. On the *Picture Tools Format* tab, in the *Picture Styles* group, click the **Picture Border** button to access the same options.

another **method**

To change the outline of a drawing object, you can also click the **Shape Outline** button in the *Drawing* group on the *Home* tab.

To change the outline of a shape, you can also right-click the shape, click the **Outline** button, and select an option.

let me **try**

Open the student data file **pp3-08-SpaServices** and try this skill on your own:

1. Select the text box under the picture on **Slide 2**.
2. Change the outline color for the shapes to **Gray–50%, Accent 6, Darker 50%** (it is the last option in the last row under *Theme Colors*).
3. Change the weight of the outline to **3 pt**.
4. Change the dash style to **Round Dot** style.
5. Save the file as directed by your instructor and close it.

Skill 3.9 Applying Quick Styles to Tables

Just as you can apply complex formatting to drawing objects using Quick Styles, you can also apply complex formatting to tables using Quick Styles for tables. With Quick Styles for tables, you can apply the borders and shading for a table with one command, giving your table a professional, sophisticated look without a lot of work.

To apply a Quick Style to a table:

1. Select the table to which you want to apply the Quick Style.
2. Click the **Table Tools Design.**
3. In the *Table Styles* group, click the **More** button.
4. In the *Table Styles* gallery, click a Quick Style to apply it to the table.

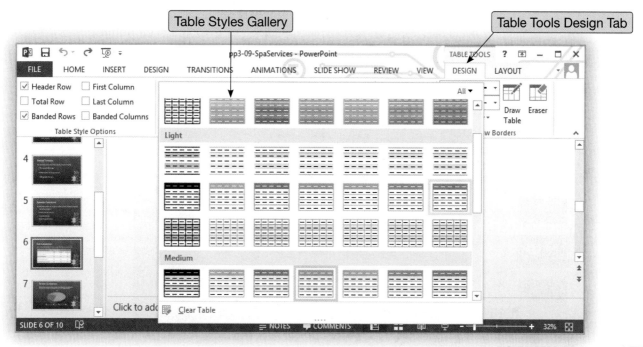

FIGURE PP 3.10

tips & tricks

To remove all formatting from the table, click the **Clear Table** button at the bottom of the *Table Quick Styles* gallery.

tell me **more**

When you insert a table into a presentation, the *Table Tools Design* and *Layout* tabs display. These tabs are called contextual tabs because they only display when a table is the active element. The *Design* tab contains tools to change the look of the table, such as Quick Styles, Word Art, and borders. The *Layout* tab contains tools for changing the structure of a table, including adding and removing rows and columns, resizing the table, and changing the alignment of text.

let me **try**

Open the student data file **pp3-09-SpaServices** and try this skill on your own:

1. Select the table on **Slide 6.**
2. Apply the **Medium Style 1–Accent 6** Quick Style to the table (it is the last option in the first row under *Medium*).
3. Save the file as directed by your instructor and close it.

Skill 3.10 Using the Picture Styles Gallery

When creating a presentation, you want to grab the audience's attention. What makes one presentation stand out from another isn't necessarily the content of the slides, but the images used to convey that content. PowerPoint comes with a number of picture Quick Styles you can apply to pictures, instantly giving them a more sophisticated look. Picture Quick Styles include a combination of graphic effects, such as borders, shadows, 3-D rotation, and reflections.

To apply a picture Quick Style to a picture:

1. Select the picture to which you want to apply the Quick Style.
2. Click the **Picture Tools Format** tab.
3. In the *Picture Styles* group, click the **More** button.
4. In the *Picture Styles* gallery, click a Quick Style to apply it to the picture.

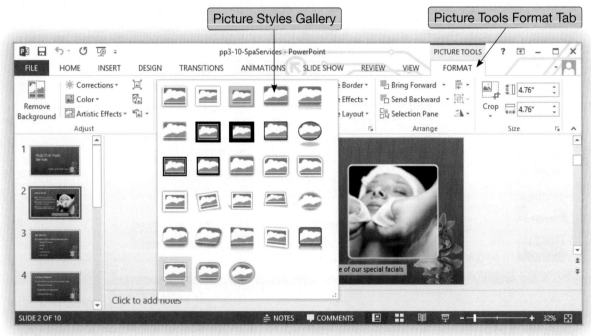

FIGURE PP 3.11

tell me **more**

When you insert a picture into a presentation, the *Picture Tools Format* tab displays. This tab is called a contextual tab because it only displays when a picture is the active element. The *Format* tab contains tools to change the look of a picture, such as applying artistic effects, changing the color, and cropping the image.

another **method**

To apply a Quick Style to a picture, you can also right-click the picture, click the **Picture Quick Styles** button and select an option.

let me **try**

Open the student data file **pp3-10-SpaServices** and try this skill on your own:

1. Select the picture on **Slide 2.**
2. Apply the **Reflected, Bevel White** Quick Style to the picture (it is the third from last option in the gallery).
3. Save the file as directed by your instructor and close it.

Skill 3.11 Applying Preset Picture Effects

PowerPoint allows you to add a number of **picture effects** to images. These effects include shadows, reflections, glows, soft edges, bevels, and 3-D rotation. You can add these effects individually, or you can apply one of PowerPoint's preset effects that include a combination of multiple effects in one style.

To apply preset effects to a picture:

1. Select the picture to which you want to apply the effect.
2. Click the **Picture Tools Format** tab.
3. In the *Picture Styles* group, click the **Picture Effects** button.
4. Point to **Presets** and select a predetermined combination of shape effects.

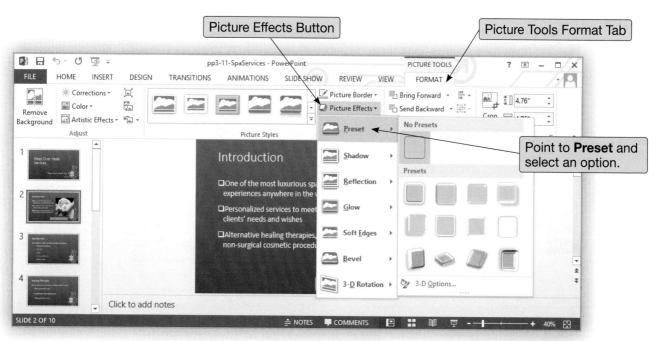

FIGURE PP 3.12

tips & tricks

To apply individual picture effects, point to any other options on the *Picture Effects* menu and select an option.

another method

To change picture effects, you can also click the **Shape Effects** button in the *Drawing* group on the *Home* tab.

let me try

Open the student data file **pp3-11-SpaServices** and try this skill on your own:

1. Select the picture on **Slide 2.**
2. Apply the **Preset 4** picture effects to the picture.
3. Save the file as directed by your instructor and close it.

Skill 3.12 Aligning Objects

When designing a presentation, it is important to place your slide objects so they will have the most impact on your audience. Any objects that appear in a straight line should be aligned to ensure they are precisely placed. You can also distribute objects on a slide ensuring they are evenly spaced.

To align objects on a slide:

1. Select the objects you want to align. To select more than one object, click the first object, press the [Shift] key, click the second object, and release the [Shift] key.

2. Click the **Drawing Tools Format** tab.

3. In the *Arrange* group, click the **Align** button and select an option:

   - The *Align Left, Align Center,* and *Align Right* commands align objects along an invisible vertical line.

   - The *Align Top, Align Middle,* and *Align Bottom* commands align objects along an invisible horizontal line.

   - Click the **Align to Slide** option to align objects along the edges and center of the slide, rather than relative to each other.

   - The *Distribute Horizontally* and *Distribute Vertically* options evenly space the objects on the slide. In order to use these options, the *Align to Slide* option must be active.

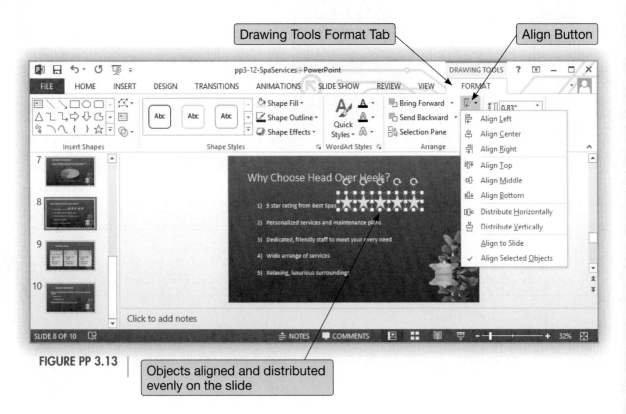

Drawing Tools Format Tab

Align Button

FIGURE PP 3.13

Objects aligned and distributed evenly on the slide

tips & tricks

❯ From the *View* tab you can display gridlines in the *Slide* pane, which is helpful when you have many objects you want to align.

❯ You can use these same steps to align pictures. The **Align** button is located in the *Arrange* group on the *Picture Tools Format* tab.

tell me **more**

A new feature in PowerPoint 2013 is smart guides. Smart guides are dotted lines that appear when you drag an object around a slide. When the object aligns with another object, the smart guide appears letting you know the objects are aligned. To learn more about smart guides, see the *Skill 3.14, Moving Objects Using Smart Guides* in this chapter.

another **method**

To align objects on a slide, you can also click the **Arrange** button on the *Home* tab in the *Drawing* group. Under *Position Objects,* point to **Align,** and select an option.

let me **try**

Open the student data file **pp3-12-SpaServices** and try this skill on your own:

1. Select the five stars on **Slide 8.** Click the first star to select it. Press and hold the (⇧ Shift) key and click the other four stars to select all five.
2. Change the alignment on the shapes to be **middle aligned.**
3. Change the distribution of the shapes so they are evenly spaced **horizontally.**
4. Save the file as directed by your instructor and close it.

Skill 3.13 Changing the Size of Images

When you first add an image to a slide, more than likely it is not the size you want. It will either be too small or too large. You can resize images in a document by either manually entering the values for the size of the picture or by dragging a **resize handle** on the image to resize it.

To resize a picture by manually entering values:

1. Select the picture you want to resize.
2. Click the **Picture Tools Format** tab.
3. In the *Size* group, type a value in the *Width* or *Height* box to resize the picture.
4. Press (←Enter) to resize the picture.

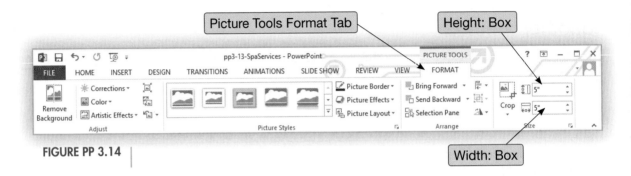

FIGURE PP 3.14

To resize an image using the drag method:

1. Select the picture you want to resize.
2. Point to one of the resize handles on the image.
3. When the mouse changes to the resize cursor, click and drag the mouse:
   - Drag the mouse toward the center of the image to make it smaller.
   - Drag the mouse away from the center of the image to make it larger.
4. When the image is the size you want, release the mouse button.

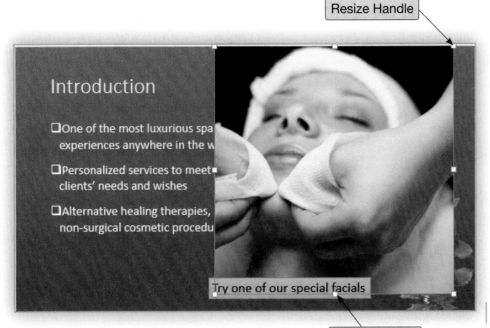

Resize Handle

Resize Handle

FIGURE PP 3.15

tips & tricks

❭ When resizing by dragging, be sure to use one of the resize handles on the four corners of the picture to maintain the aspect ratio of the picture. If you use a resize handle along one of the sides of the picture, you will be resizing the width of the picture only. If you use a resize handle along the top or bottom of the picture, you will be resizing the height of the picture only.

❭ When you enter a value in the *Width* or *Height* box on the Ribbon, the value in the other box will change to maintain the aspect ratio for the picture.

let me try

Open the student data file **pp3-13-SpaServices** and try this skill on your own:

1. Select the picture on **Slide 2.**
2. Click and drag a corner resize handle to make the picture smaller.
3. Manually change the size of the picture to be **5"** in height and **5"** in width.
4. Save the file as directed by your instructor and close it.

Skill 3.14 Moving Objects Using Smart Guides

When you first add an image to a slide, you may find it is not positioned where you want it. You can change the position of images by dragging and dropping the image where you want it on the slide. PowerPoint 2013 now includes smart guides for helping with picture layout. When you drag a picture, you will see horizontal and vertical dotted lines. These lines are the **smart guides.** They appear when the picture's edge is aligned with another object or area on the slide.

To move pictures on a slide:

1. Select the picture you want to move.

2. Rest your mouse over the picture.

3. When the cursor changes to the **move cursor,** click and drag the image to the new location.

4. When a smart guide appears aligning it with the desired element on the slide, release the mouse button to snap the image in place and align it on the slide.

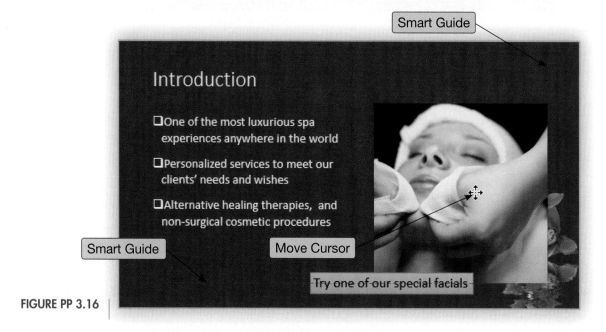

FIGURE PP 3.16

tips & tricks

To turn off smart guides, click the **View** tab. In the *Show* group, click the **dialog launcher.** In the *Grid and Guides* dialog, click the **Display smart guides when shapes are aligned** check box to deselect it.

tell me **more**

PowerPoint also includes drawing guides that are different from smart guides. Drawing guides divide the slide into four quadrants to help you place images on a slide. To turn on drawing guides, click the **View** tab. In the *Show* group, click the **Guides** check box.

let me **try**

Open the student data file **pp3-14-SpaServices** and try this skill on your own:

1. On **Slide 2,** click and drag the image so the right side is aligned with the right margin of the slide and the bottom of the image is aligned with the top of the footer area. Use smart guides to help place the image (see Figure PP 3.16).

2. Save the file as directed by your instructor and close it.

Skill 3.15 Using Gridlines and the Ruler

When you are designing slides in your presentation, aligning placeholders and images can be the difference between a polished presentation and one that looks thrown together. Use PowerPoint's rulers and gridlines as visual tools to check the placement of text and images on your slides. The ruler allows you to control the placement of text in placeholders, including tabs and indents. Gridlines are a series of dotted vertical and horizontal lines that divide the slide into small boxes, giving you visual markers for aligning placeholders and images.

To display gridlines:

1. Click the **View** tab.
2. In the *Show* group, click the **Gridlines** check box to select it.
3. Click the **Gridlines** check box again to hide the gridlines.

To display the ruler:

1. Click the **View** tab.
2. In the *Show* group, click the **Ruler** check box to select it.
3. Click the **Ruler** check box again to hide the ruler.

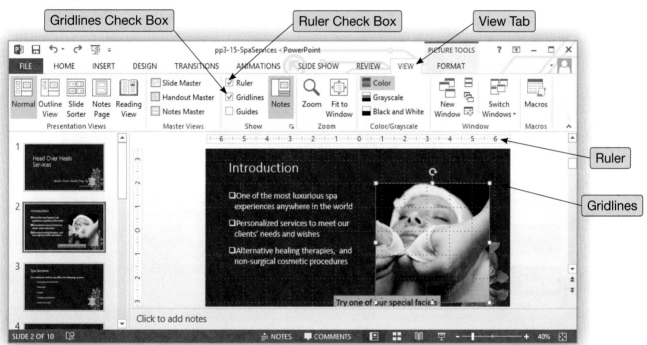

FIGURE PP 3.17

tell me **more**

The grid and ruler are only visible when you are working on the presentation. They do not appear when you show the presentation in *Slide Show* view or when you print handouts.

let me **try**

Open the student data file **pp3-15-SpaServices** and try this skill on your own:

1. Display the **ruler.**
2. Display **gridlines.**
3. Hide the **ruler** and **gridlines.**
4. Save the file as directed by your instructor and close it.

Skill 3.16 Adding Footers

A **footer** is text that appear on every slide. Typically, footers appear at the bottom of the slide, but they can also appear along the side of a slide. Use footers when you want to display the same text on every slide, such as the name of your company.

To add text to the footer of all the slides in a presentation:

1. Click the **Insert** tab.
2. In the *Text* group, click the **Header & Footer** button.

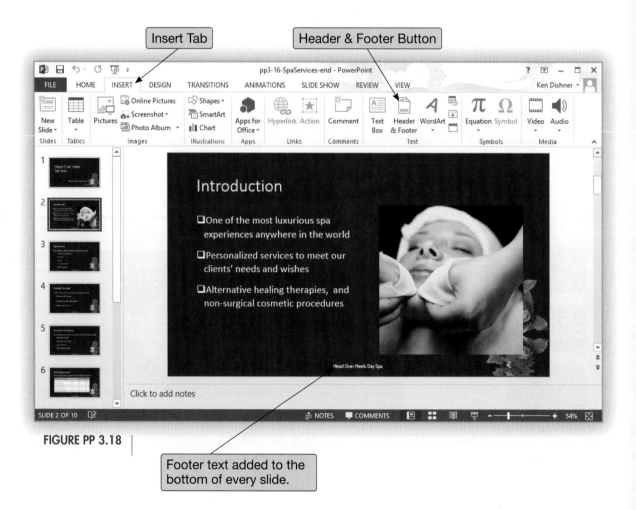

FIGURE PP 3.18

3. On the *Slide* tab of the *Header and Footer* dialog, select the **Footer** check box.
4. Type the text for the footer in the *Footer* text box.
5. Click the **Apply to All** button to add the footer to every slide in the presentation.

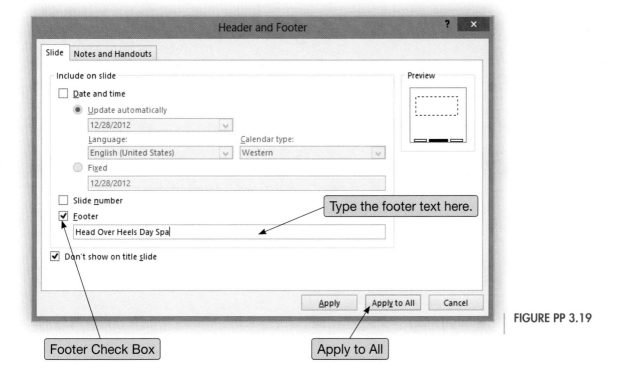

Footer Check Box

Apply to All

FIGURE PP 3.19

tips & tricks

▶ If you do not want your footer to display on the title slide of the presentation, select the **Don't show on title slide** check box.

▶ Click the **Apply** button to add the footer text to only the selected slide.

tell me **more**

Headers appear on the top of every handout. They do not display in the slide show. The footer text you add to slides will appear at the bottom of the handouts.

let me try

Open the student data file **pp3-16-SpaServices** and try this skill on your own:

1. Open the **Header and Footer** dialog.
2. Add a footer to every slide in the presentation except the title slide that reads **Head Over Heels Day Spa.**
3. Save the file as directed by your instructor and close it.

Skill 3.17 Adding the Date to the Footer

It is common practice to include the current date in the footer of slides. You could manually type the date in the footer of each slide and then update the date every time you work on the presentation, or you could add the date to the footer.

To add the date to the footer of a presentation:

1. Click the **Insert** tab.
2. In the *Text* group, click the **Date & Time** button.
3. In the *Header and Footer* dialog, click the **Date and time** check box to select it.
4. Verify the **Update automatically** radio button is selected.
5. Click **Apply to All** to add the date to all the slides in the presentation.

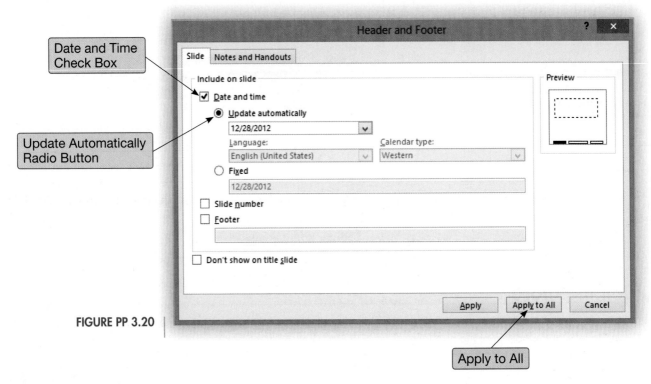

FIGURE PP 3.20

tell me **more**

When you select the **Update automatically** option in the *Header and Footer*, PowerPoint pulls the current date from the computer's system clock and displays the date on the slide. The date is then automatically updated when the computer's date changes.

another **method**

To open the *Header and Footer* dialog, you can also click the **Header & Footer** button in the *Text* group on the *Insert* tab.

let me **try**

Open the student data file **pp3-17-SpaServices** and try this skill on your own:

1. Open the **Header and Footer** dialog.
2. Add the current date to all the slides in the presentation. Have the date update automatically.
3. Save the file as directed by your instructor and close it.

Skill 3.18 Inserting Slide Numbers

When giving a presentation, it is easy to lose track of where you are in it. You can add **slide numbers** to the footer area of each slide to display how far along you are in your presentation. You could manually type the number for each slide in the footer area, but what if you add or delete slides from your presentation? You would have to manually renumber each slide. Instead, you can add slide numbers from the *Header and Footer* dialog; when you add or remove slides, the slide numbers will be updated automatically.

To add slide numbers to the footer of a presentation:

1. Click the **Insert** tab.
2. In the *Text* group, click the **Insert Slide Number** button.
3. In the *Header and Footer* dialog, click the **Slide number** check box.
4. Click **Apply to All** to add slide numbers to all the slides in the presentation.

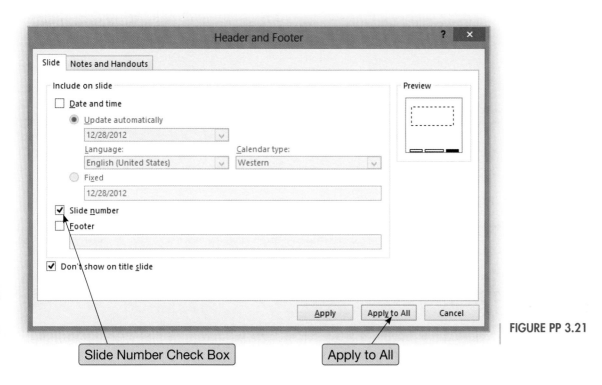

FIGURE PP 3.21

tips & tricks

If you do not want your footer to display on the title slide of the presentation, select the **Don't show on title slide** check box.

let me try

Open the student data file **pp3-18-SpaServices** and try this skill on your own:

1. Open the **Header and Footer** dialog.
2. Add a slide number to every slide in the presentation except the title slide.
3. Save the file as directed by your instructor and close it.

Skill 3.19 Applying Animation Effects

Adding **animations** to slides can help emphasize important points and grab your audience's attention. In PowerPoint you can animate individual objects on a slide, including text, images, charts, tables, and SmartArt.

There are four basic types of animation schemes:

Entrance—Animates the object coming on to the slide; starts with the object not visible and ends with the object visible. Examples of *Entrance* animations include *Fade In, Split, Fly In,* and *Appear.*

Emphasis—Animates the object on the screen. Examples of *Emphasis* animations include *Pulse, Spin, Grow/Shrink,* and *Teeter.*

Exit—Animates the object leaving the slide; starts with the object visible and ends with the object not visible. Examples of *Exit* animations include *Fade, Disappear, Float Out,* and *Wipe.*

Motion Paths—Animates the object along an invisible line. Examples of *Motion Path* animations include *Lines, Arcs,* and *Loops.*

FIGURE PP 3.22

To add an animation to an object:

1. Select the object you want to animate.
2. Click the **Animations** tab.
3. In the *Animation* group, click the **More** button.
4. In the *Animation* gallery, click an option to apply it to the object.

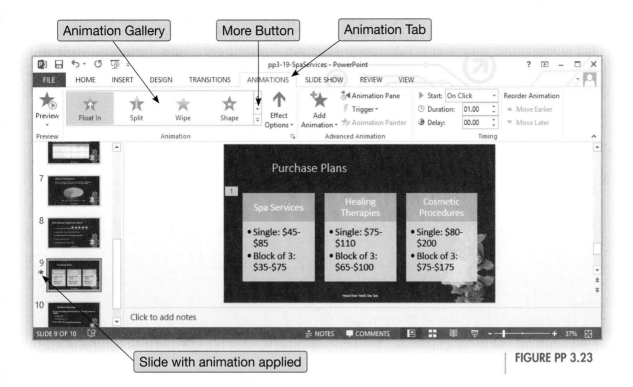

FIGURE PP 3.23

tips & tricks

To remove an animation, select **None** in the gallery.

tell me **more**

A star appears next to the thumbnails in the *Slides* pane that contain animations or transitions.

let me try

Open the student data file **pp3-19-SpaServices** and try this skill on your own:

1. Select the SmartArt diagram on **Slide 9.**
2. Apply the **Float In** animation to the diagram.
3. Save the file as directed by your instructor and close it.

Skill 3.20 Modifying Animations

Although PowerPoint comes with a number of easy-to-use, prebuilt animations, you may find that you want to further customize those animations to better suit your needs. You can adjust the behavior of an animation by adjusting the effect options.

To modify the effect options of an animation:

1. Select the object with the animation you want to modify.
2. Click the **Animations** tab.
3. Click the **Effects Options** button and select an option to change the default behavior of the animation.

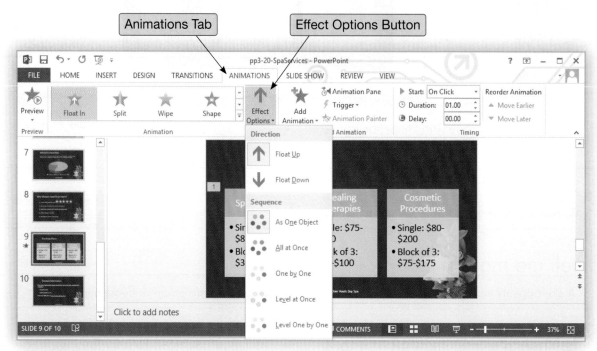

FIGURE PP 3.24

tips & tricks

Click the arrow next to the *Start* box and select when the animation will play—*On Click, With Previous,* or *After Previous.*

let me try

Open the student data file **pp3-20-SpaServices** and try this skill on your own:

1. Select the SmartArt diagram on **Slide 9.**
2. Change the animation effects to have each piece of the diagram float in **one by one.**
3. Save the file as directed by your instructor and close it.

Skill 3.21 Using Animation Painter

Animations can become complex very quickly. You can invest a lot of time working on an animation to get it just right. What if you want to use those same animation effects on another slide? The **Animation Painter** works similarly to the *Format Painter,* but instead of copying and pasting formatting, the *Animation Painter* copies and pastes the animations that have been applied to an object.

To use the *Animation Painter* to copy and paste animations:

1. Select the object that has the animation you want to copy.
2. Click the **Animations** tab.
3. In the *Advanced Animation* group, click the **Animation Painter** button.
4. Click the object to which you want to apply the animation.
5. The animation is automatically applied to the second object.

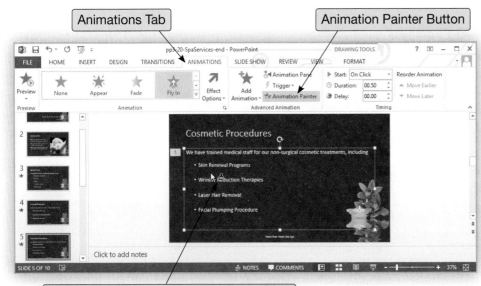

FIGURE PP 3.25

If you want to apply the animation more than once, double-click the **Animation Painter** button when you select it. It will stay on until you click the **Animation Painter** button again or press (Esc) to deselect it.

tips & tricks

To remove an animation, on the *Animations* tab, in the *Animation* group, click the **None** option in the gallery.

let me try

Open the student data file **pp3-21-SpaServices** and try this skill on your own:

1. Select the text placeholder with the animation on **Slide 3.**
2. Use the **Animation Painter** to copy the animation.
3. Apply the animation to the text placeholders on **Slide 4** and **Slide 5.**
4. Save the file as directed by your instructor and close it.

key terms

Theme
Theme variant
Color theme
Font theme
Effects theme
Transition
Widescreen 16:9
Background
Quick styles
Drawing objects
Fill color

Outlines
Picture effects
Resize handle
Smart guides
Ruler
Gridlines
Footer
Slide numbers
Animation
Animation Painter

concepts review

1. The default size for slides is _____.

   a. 3:4

   b. 3:6

   c. 12:4

   d. 16:9

2. To copy and paste animation settings from one object to another, use the _____.

   a. Format Painter

   b. Animation Painter

   c. animation task pane

   d. none of the above

3. Dotted lines that appear when you move an object on a slide that help you align the object with other slide objects are known as _____.

   a. smart guides

   b. guides

   c. gridlines

   d. placeholders

4. A _____ is a combination of formatting settings you apply to objects.

   a. theme colors

   b. Quick Styles

   c. theme effects

   d. theme variants

5. A group of formatting options, including font, color, backgrounds, and effect styles, that you apply to a presentation is known as a _____.

   a. style

   b. theme

   c. Quick Style

   d. variant

6. _____ are a series of dotted vertical and horizontal lines that divide the slide into small boxes, giving you visual markers for aligning placeholders and images.
   a. Gridlines
   b. Guides
   c. Smart guides
   d. Rulers

7. A(n) _____ is an effect that occurs when one slide leaves the screen and another one appears.
   a. animation
   b. transition
   c. slider
   d. video

8. Add an automatic date or slide number to the _____ to have it appear on every slide.
   a. slide placeholder
   b. title
   c. header
   d. footer

9. A _____ is the graphic element that fills a slide.
   a. fill color
   b. drawing object
   c. background
   d. transition

10. A _____ is a set of color variations and backgrounds you can change for a theme.
    a. effects theme
    b. theme variant
    c. color theme
    d. background style

projects

Data files for projects can be found on
www.mhhe.com/office2013skills

skill review 3.1

In this project you will be modifying the look of the marketing presentation from Suarez Marketing.

Skills needed to complete this project:
- Changing the Presentation Theme (Skill 3.1)
- Using Theme Variants (Skill 3.2)
- Changing the Slide Background (Skill 3.5)

- Applying Slide Transitions (Skill 3.3)
- Inserting Slide Numbers (Skill 3.18)
- Applying Quick Styles to Drawing Objects (Skill 3.6)
- Applying Fill Colors to Drawing Objects (Skill 3.7)
- Applying Outlines to Drawing Objects (Skill 3.8)
- Applying Animation Effects (Skill 3.19)
- Modifying Animations (Skill 3.20)
- Using the Picture Styles Gallery (Skill 3.10)
- Aligning Objects (Skill 3.12)
- Changing the Size of Images (Skill 3.13)
- Applying Quick Styles to Tables (Skill 3.9)

1. Open the **PP2013-SkillReview-3-1** presentation.

2. Save this presentation as: **[your initials] PP-SkillReview-3-1**

3. Change the presentation theme and variant.

    a. Click the **Design** tab.

    b. In the *Themes* group, click the **More** button and select the **Ion** theme (the fourth option in the first row under *Office*).

    c. In the *Variants* group, select the **bright blue and green variant** option (the second option in the *Variants* gallery).

4. Change the background of slides in the presentation.

    a. In the *Customize* group, click the **Format Background** button.

    b. In the *Format Background* task pane, select the **Solid fill** radio button under *Fill*.

    c. Click the **Fill Color** button and select **Dark Blue, Background 2** (the third option in the first row under *Theme Colors*).

    d. Click the **Apply to All** button.

    e. Click the **Close** button at the top of the task pane.

5. Apply a slide transition to all the slides in the presentation.

    a. Click the **Transitions** tab.

    b. In the *Transition to This Slide* group, click the **Wipe** transition. If the *Wipe* transition does not appear on the Ribbon, click the **More** button to see all the available transitions.

    c. In the *Timing* group, click the **Apply to All** button.

6. Add slide numbers to the presentation.

    a. Click the **Insert** tab.

    b. In the *Text* group, click the **Insert Slide Number** button.

    c. In the *Header and Footer* dialog, click the **Slide number** check box.

    d. Click the **Apply to All** button.

7. Modify the look of a text box.

    a. Navigate to **Slide 8.**

    b. Select the text box **Our Proven Process.**

    c. On the *Drawing Tools Format* tab, in the *Shape Styles* group, click the **More** button and select **Colored Outline–Lime, Accent 1** (the second option in the first row).

    d. In the *Shape Styles* group, click the **Shape Fill** button and select **Lime, Accent 1, Lighter 60%** (it is the fifth option in the third row of the color palette).

e. In the *Shape Styles* group, click the **Shape Outline** button, point to **Dashes,** and select the **Round Dot** option.

f. In the *Shape Styles* group, click the **Shape Outline** button, point to **Weight,** and select the **4½ pt** option.

8. Apply and modify an animation effect.

a. On **Slide 8,** select the entire **SmartArt** graphic.

b. Click the **Animations** tab.

c. In the *Animations* group, click the **More** button and select the **Wheel** animation effect.

d. Click the **Effect Options** button and select **One by One.**

9. Modify the look, size, and placement of an image on a slide.

a. Navigate to **Slide 9.**

b. Select the image on the slide.

c. On the *Picture Tools Format* tab, in the *Picture Styles* group, apply the **Reflected Rounded Rectangle** Quick Style to the picture (it is the fifth option displayed on the Ribbon). If this option does not appear on the Ribbon, click the **More** button to see all the available Quick Styles.

d. In the *Size* group, type **3.5″** in the *Shape Height* box and press ⏎ Enter .

e. In the *Arrange* group, click the **Align Objects** button. Select **Align Right.** Click the **Align Objects** button again and select **Align Bottom.**

f. In the *Size* group, click the **Shape Height** down arrow three times so the box reads **3.2″.**

10. Apply a Quick Style to a table.

a. On **Slide 9,** select the table.

b. Click the **Table Tools Design** tab.

c. In the *Table Styles* group, click the **More** button. In the *Best Match for Document* section, click the **Themed Style 1–Accent 1** style (it is the second option in the first row of the section).

11. Save and close the presentation.

skill review 3.2

In this project you will be modifying the look of the My Fitness Plan presentation.

Skills needed to complete this project:

- Changing the Presentation Theme (Skill 3.1)
- Using Theme Variants (Skill 3.2)
- Applying Slide Transitions (Skill 3.3)
- Changing the Size of Slides (Skill 3.4)
- Adding Footers (Skill 3.16)
- Adding the Date to the Footer (Skill 3.17)
- Applying Animation Effects (Skill 3.19)
- Modifying Animations (Skill 3.20)
- Using Animation Painter (Skill 3.21)
- Using Gridlines and the Ruler (Skill 3.15)
- Changing the Size of Images (Skill 3.13)

- Using the Picture Styles Gallery (Skill 3.10)
- Applying Preset Picture Effects (Skill 3.11)
- Moving Objects Using Smart Guides (Skill 3.14)

1. Open the **PP2013-SkillReview-3-2** presentation.

2. Save this presentation as: **[your initials] PP-SkillReview-3-2**

3. Change the presentation theme and variant.
   a. Click the **Design** tab.
   b. In the *Themes* group, click the **More** button and select the **Ion Boardroom** theme.
   c. In the *Variants* group, select the **red and orange variant option** (the fourth option in the *Variants* gallery).

4. Apply a slide transition to the first slide in the presentation.
   a. Verify you are on **Slide 1.**
   b. Click the **Transitions** tab.
   c. In the *Transition to This Slide* group, click the **More** button. In the *Exciting* group, click the **Curtains** option.

5. Change the size of slides in the presentation.
   a. Click the **Design** tab.
   b. In the *Customize* group, click the **Slide Size** button and select **Widescreen (16:9).**

6. Add a footer to the presentation.
   a. Click the **Insert** tab.
   b. In the *Text* group, click the **Header & Footer** button.
   c. Select the **Footer** check box.
   d. In the *Footer* text box, type **My Fitness Plan**
   e. Click the **Apply to All** button.

7. Add an automatic date to the presentation.
   a. On the *Insert* tab, in the *Text* group, click the **Date & Time** button.
   b. In the *Header and Footer* dialog, select the **Date and time** check box. Verify the **Update automatically** radio button is selected.
   c. Verify the footer text you added displays in the *Footer* text box. Select the **Footer** check box.
   d. Click the **Apply to All** button.

8. Apply and modify an animation effect.
   a. Navigate to **Slide 2** and select the **text placeholder** with the bulleted list.
   b. Click the **Animations** tab.
   c. In the *Animations* group, click the **Fly In** animation effect.
   d. Click the **Effect Options** button and select **As One Object.**

9. Apply the animation to other slides using the *Animation Painter.*
   a. Select the **text placeholder** on Slide 2 that you applied the animation to.
   b. In the *Advanced Animation* group, double-click the **Animation Painter** button so it will remain active until you turn it off.
   c. Navigate to **Slide 3** and click the **text placeholder** with the bulleted list.
   d. Use the *Animation Painter* to apply the animation to the bulleted lists on **Slides 4, 5, 6,** and **7.**
   e. Press the (Esc) key to turn off the *Animation Painter.*

10. Display gridlines, and the ruler.

    a. Click the **View** tab.

    b. In the *Show* group, click the **Ruler** check box to display the ruler.

    c. In the *Show* group, click the **Gridlines** check box to display gridlines.

11. Change the size and look of an image.

    a. On **Slide 7,** select the image of the target.

    b. Click the **Picture Tools Format** tab.

    c. In the *Size* group, type **4″** in the *Shape Height* box and press ⏎ Enter .

    d. On the *Picture Tools Format* tab, in the *Picture Styles* group, apply the **Drop Shadow Rectangle** Quick Style to the picture (it is the fourth option displayed on the Ribbon). If this option does not appear on the Ribbon, click the **More** button to see all the available Quick Styles.

12. Use smart guides to position an image.

    a. On **Slide 7,** click and drag the image of the target to the left.

    b. When you see a vertical smart guide aligning the left side of the image with the right side of the bulleted list and a horizontal smart guide aligning the bottom of the image with the top of the footer area, release the mouse button.

13. Hide the ruler and gridlines.

    a. Click the **View** tab.

    b. In the *Show* group, click the **Ruler** check box to hide the ruler.

    c. In the *Show* group, click the **Gridlines** check box to hide gridlines.

14. Save and close the presentation.

challenge yourself **3.3**

In this project you will be modifying the look of a presentation for Greenscapes landscaping company.

Skills needed to complete this project:

- Changing the Presentation Theme (Skill 3.1)
- Using Theme Variants (Skill 3.2)
- Changing the Slide Background (Skill 3.5)
- Applying Slide Transitions (Skill 3.3)
- Inserting Slide Numbers (Skill 3.18)
- Applying Animation Effects (Skill 3.19)
- Modifying Animations (Skill 3.20)
- Applying Quick Styles to Tables (Skill 3.9)
- Applying Quick Styles to Drawing Objects (Skill 3.6)
- Applying Fill Colors to Drawing Objects (Skill 3.7)
- Applying Outlines to Drawing Objects (Skill 3.8)
- Aligning Objects (Skill 3.12)
- Changing the Size of Images (Skill 3.13)
- Using the Picture Styles Gallery (Skill 3.10)

1. Open the **PP2013-ChallengeYourself-3-3** presentation.

2. Save this presentation as: **[your initials] PP-ChallengeYourself-3-3**

3. Change the presentation theme to **Integral.**

4. Change the variant to use the **green option** (the second option in the *Variants* gallery).

5. Change the background of slides in the presentation.

   a. Display the **Format Background** task pane.

   b. Change the background to use a **solid fill** with the color **Lime, Accent 1, Lighter 60%** (it is the fifth option in the third row under *Theme Colors*).

   c. Apply the background to all the slides in the presentation.

   d. **Close** the *Format Background* task pane.

6. Apply a **Wipe** slide transition to all the slides in the presentation.

7. Add slide numbers to all the slides in the presentation.

8. Apply and modify an animation effect.

   a. Select the **SmartArt** graphic on **Slide 4.**

   b. Apply the **Float In** animation to the diagram.

   c. Change the **Animation Effect Options** button to use the **One by One** option.

9. Apply a Quick Style to a table.

   a. Select the table on **Slide 6.**

   b. Change the table to use the **Light Style 2–Accent 4** Quick Style (it is the fifth option in the second row under *Light*).

10. Modify the look of a drawing object.

    a. Select the WordArt on **Slide 7** (**Thank You**).

    b. Apply the **Colored Outline–Gold, Accent 4** Quick Style to the object (the fifth option in the first row).

    c. Change the shape fill to **Gold, Accent 3, Lighter 60%** (it is the seventh option in the third row of the color palette).

    d. Change the shape outline weight to **6 pt.**

    e. Use the *Align Objects* menu to center the image horizontally on the slide.

11. Modify the look, size, and placement of an image on a slide.

    a. Select the picture on **Slide 7.**

    b. Change the size of the image to be **5″** in height and **7.47″** in width.

    c. Apply the **Beveled Matte, White** Quick Style to the picture (it is the second option in the *Picture Styles* gallery).

    d. Use the *Align Objects* menu to center the image vertically and horizontally on the slide.

12. Save and close the presentation.

challenge yourself **3.4**

In this project you will be modifying the look of a presentation about emotional intelligence.

Skills needed to complete this project:

- Changing the Presentation Theme (Skill 3.1)
- Using Theme Variants (Skill 3.2)
- Applying Slide Transitions (Skill 3.3)
- Changing the Size of Slides (Skill 3.4)
- Adding the Date to the Footer (Skill 3.17)
- Applying Animation Effects (Skill 3.19)

- Modifying Animations (Skill 3.20)
- Using Animation Painter (Skill 3.21)
- Using Gridlines and the Ruler (Skill 3.15)
- Changing the Size of Images (Skill 3.13)
- Using the Picture Styles Gallery (Skill 3.10)
- Applying Preset Picture Effects (Skill 3.11)
- Moving Objects Using Smart Guides (Skill 3.14)

1. Open the **PP2013-ChallengeYourself-3-4** presentation.
2. Save this presentation as: **[your initials] PP-ChallengeYourself-3-4**
3. Change the presentation theme to **Wisp.**
4. Change the variant to use the one with the **dark background** (the fourth option in the *Variants* gallery).
5. Apply the **Vortex** slide transition to the first slide in the presentation.
6. Change the size of slides in the presentation to be **Widescreen (16:9).**
7. Add an automatic date to all the slides in the presentation.
8. Apply and modify an animation effect.

   a. Select the **text placeholder** with the bulleted list on **Slide 3.**

   b. Apply the **Random Bars** animation effect to the placeholder.

   c. Change the **direction** of the animation from **horizontal** to **vertical.**
9. Use the *Animation Painter* to copy the animation from the text placeholder on **Slide 3** to the text placeholders on **Slide 4, Slide 5, Slide 6, Slide 7, Slide 9, Slide 10,** and **Slide 11.**
10. Display gridlines and the ruler.
11. Change the size and look of an image.

    a. Select the picture on **Slide 2.**

    b. Change the size of the image to be **4.25″** in height and **4.25″** in width.

    c. Apply the **Rounded Diagonal Corner, White** Quick Style to the picture.
12. Click and drag the image so it is center aligned under the title (you will see a vertical smart guide through the middle of the image when it is in the proper place).
13. Hide the ruler and gridlines.
14. Save and close the presentation.

on your own 3.5

In this project you will be modifying the look of a presentation about creating PowerPoint presentations.

Skills needed to complete this project:
- Changing the Presentation Theme (Skill 3.1)
- Using Theme Variants (Skill 3.2)
- Applying Slide Transitions (Skill 3.3)
- Changing the Size of Slides (Skill 3.4)
- Changing the Size of Images (Skill 3.13)
- Moving Objects Using Smart Guides (Skill 3.14)
- Using Gridlines and the Ruler (Skill 3.15)

- Applying Quick Styles to Drawing Objects (Skill 3.6)
- Applying Fill Colors to Drawing Objects (Skill 3.7)
- Applying Outlines to Drawing Objects (Skill 3.8)
- Applying Quick Styles to Tables (Skill 3.9)
- Applying Animation Effects (Skill 3.19)
- Modifying Animations (Skill 3.20)
- Using the Picture Styles Gallery (Skill 3.10)
- Aligning Objects (Skill 3.12)
- Inserting Slide Numbers (Skill 3.18)

1. Open the **PP2013-OnYourOwn-3-5** presentation.
2. Save this presentation as: **[your initials] PP-OnYourOwn-3-5**
3. Apply a theme and variant of your choice to the presentation.
4. Apply a slide transition of your choice to all the slides in the presentation.
5. Change the presentation to use the **Widescreen (16:9)** slide size.
6. Modify a drawing object.
   a. Select the shape on **Slide 2.**
   b. Display the ruler and gridlines if you want.
   c. Resize the shape to fit better on the slide.
   d. Move the shape to the lower right corner of the slide. Use smart guides to align the shape above the slide footer and along the right side of the text placeholder.
   e. Apply a Quick Style of your choice to the shape.
   f. Adjust the look of the shape by changing the fill color and weight and style of the outline.
   g. If you displayed the ruler and gridlines, hide them.
7. Select the table on **Slide 4** and apply a table Quick Style of your choice.
8. Animate the SmartArt diagram on **Slide 5** using an animation of your choice. Change the effects of the animation so each piece of the diagram appears one by one.
9. Modify a picture.
   a. Select the picture on **Slide 6.**
   b. Align the picture so it is centered horizontally on the slide.
   c. Apply a Quick Style of your choice to the picture.
10. Add a slide number to the footer of every slide in the presentation except the title slide.
11. Save and close the presentation.

fix it 3.6

In this project you will be modifying the look of a project about team orientation.

Skills needed to complete this project:
- Changing the Presentation Theme (Skill 3.1)
- Using Theme Variants (Skill 3.2)
- Changing the Size of Slides (Skill 3.4)
- Adding Footers (Skill 3.16)

- Applying Slide Transitions (Skill 3.3)
- Applying Quick Styles to Tables (Skill 3.9)
- Applying Animation Effects (Skill 3.19)
- Modifying Animations (Skill 3.20)
- Using Animation Painter (Skill 3.21)
- Using Gridlines and the Ruler (Skill 3.15)
- Changing the Size of Images (Skill 3.13)
- Applying Quick Styles to Drawing Objects (Skill 3.6)
- Applying Outlines to Drawing Objects (Skill 3.8)
- Aligning Objects (Skill 3.12)
- Using the Picture Styles Gallery (Skill 3.10)
- Aligning Objects (Skill 3.12)

1. Open the **PP2013-FixIt-3-6** presentation.

2. Save this presentation as: **[your initials] PP-FixIt-3-6**

3. Change the presentation theme to **Retrospect.**

4. Change the variant to use the dark gray option (the fourth option in the *Variants* gallery).

5. Change the presentation to use the **Widescreen (16:9)** slide size.

6. Add a footer to every slide in the presentation except the title slide that reads **Team Orientation.**

7. Apply the **Uncover** transition to every slide in the presentation.

8. Apply the **Medium Style 2–Accent 2** table Quick Style to the table on **Slide 5** (it is the third option in the second row under *Medium*).

9. Apply the **Fade** animation effect to the placeholder on **Slide 2.** Change the effects so the text animated as one object.

10. Use the Animation Painter to copy the animation from the text placeholder on **Slide 2** to the text placeholders on **Slide 3, Slide 4,** and **Slide 8.**

11. Modify a drawing object.

    a. Select the scroll shape on **Slide 7.**

    b. Display the ruler and gridlines if you want.

    c. Resize the shape to better fit the text.

    d. Apply the **Light 1 Outline, Colored Fill–Gray–50%, Accent 6** Quick Style to the shape (it is the last option in the third row of the gallery).

    e. Change the weight of the outline on the shape to **1 pt.**

    f. Align the shape so it is centered horizontally on the slide.

12. Change the size and look of an image.

    a. Select the picture on **Slide 8.**

    b. Change the size of the image to be **3″** in height and **4.5″** in width.

    c. Apply the **Reflected Rounded Rectangle** Quick Style to the picture (it is the fifth option in the first row of the *Picture Styles* gallery).

    d. Align the image along the right side of the slide.

    e. If you displayed the ruler and gridlines in step 11, hide them.

13. Save and close the presentation.

chapter 4

Managing and Delivering Presentations

In this chapter, you will learn the following skills:

❱ Delete, reorder, copy, and paste slides

❱ Hide and unhide slides

❱ Add sections

❱ Check for spelling errors

❱ Rehearse timings, use slide show tools, and use Presenter view

❱ Add notes, modify the handout master, and print handouts

❱ Add comments

skills

introduction

This chapter provides you with the skills to give a professional presentation. First, you will learn to change the structure of a presentation by reordering slides, deleting slides, copying and pasting slides, and hiding slides. You will rehearse the slide show using PowerPoint's Rehearse Timings feature. You will then start the presentation, navigate through the slides, and use presentation tools. You will add notes to slides and then use those notes when giving the presentation in *Presenter* view. You will learn to modify and print handouts as well as print the presentation's slides. Finally, you will learn how to add comments to a presentation.

Skill 4.1 Deleting Slides from Presentations

After you have created all the content for your presentation, it is a good idea to carefully review the slides. As you make a final review, you may find that a slide you created is not necessary, and you want to permanently remove it. You can remove an entire slide of content by deleting it from the *Slides* tab.

To delete a slide:

1. On the *Slides* tab, right-click the slide you want to delete.
2. Click **Delete Slide** on the menu that appears.

You can delete multiple slides at once:

1. Click a slide you want to delete and press (↑ Shift) on the keyboard.
2. With the (↑ Shift) key still pressed, click another slide.
3. Notice, all the slides between the two slides you clicked have been selected.
4. Right-click any of the selected slides and select **Delete Slide.**

   If you want to select slides that are not next to each other, press (Ctrl) on the keyboard instead of (↑ Shift) and click each slide you want to delete. Only the slides you clicked are selected.

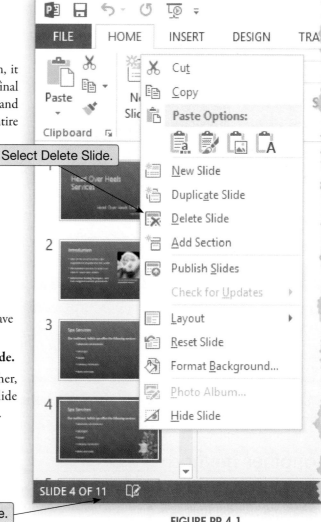

FIGURE PP 4.1

another method

To delete a slide, you can also select the slide and press **Delete** on the keyboard.

let me try

Open the student data file **pp4-01-SpaServices** and try this skill on your own:

1. Delete **Slide 4.**
2. Save the file as directed by your instructor and close it.

Skill 4.2 Changing the Order of Slides

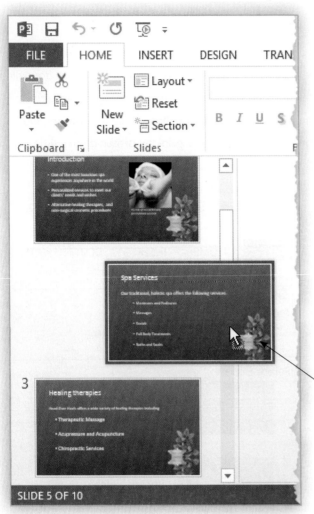

FIGURE PP 4.2

One of the most important aspects of a presentation is the flow of the information. It is important that your slides appear in a logical, grouped order for your audience to fully grasp the message you are presenting. After you have reviewed your presentation, you may find you want to switch the order of some of your slides. You can change the slide order from the *Slides* tab.

To change the slide order from the *Slides* tab:

1. Select the slide you want to move.
2. Click and drag until the gray line appears where you want the slide, and then release the mouse button.

Each slide thumbnail appears with a number next to it indicating its location in the presentation. When you change the order of slides, PowerPoint automatically renumbers the slides for you.

> Click and drag the slide to the new location.

tips & tricks

To select more than one slide to move, select the first slide, press the ⤒ Shift key, and then select the last slide in the set.

another method

To move or copy a slide by dragging, right-click the slide you want to move and drag it to the new location. When you release the mouse button, a menu of options will appear, allowing you to move the slide, copy the slide, or cancel the action.

let me try

Open the student data file **pp4-02-SpaServices** and try this skill on your own:

1. Move **Slide 5** so it appears between **Slide 2** and **Slide 3.**
2. Save the file as directed by your instructor and close it.

Skill 4.3 Hiding Slides

When you practice your presentation, you may find that you want to omit certain slides, but that you do not want to delete them from your presentation in case you need them later. The Hide Slide command allows you to prevent slides from being seen without permanently removing them.

To hide slides:

1. Select the slide you want to hide.
2. Click the **Slide Show** tab.
3. In the *Set Up* group, click the **Hide Slide** button. The button toggles to the "on" state.
4. When a slide is hidden, the thumbnail appears washed out with the hidden slide icon over the slide number in the *Slide* pane.
5. To unhide the slide, click the **Hide Slide** button again.

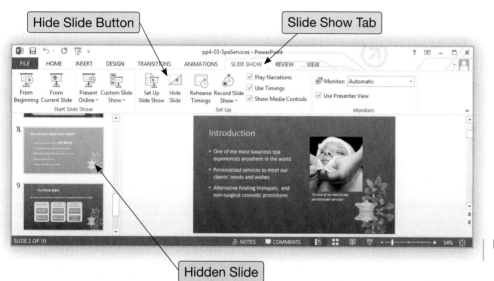

FIGURE PP 4.3

tips & tricks

To unhide a slide during a presentation, right-click any slide, point to **Go to Slide,** and select the slide you want to display. Hidden slides will appear in the list with parentheses around the number. For example, if the third slide in a presentation is hidden, the menu will display the number as (3).

another method

To hide a slide, you can also right-click the slide on the *Slides* tab and select **Hide Slide.** To unhide a slide, right-click the slide and select **Hide Slide** again.

let me try

Open the student data file **pp4-03-SpaServices** and try this skill on your own:

1. Hide **Slide 9.**
2. Unhide **Slide 8.**
3. Save the file as directed by your instructor and close it.

Skill 4.4 Copying and Pasting Slides

You may find when you are creating your presentation that one slide's content and layout are similar to another slide's content and layout that you need to add. Instead of having to recreate all the content for the second slide, you can copy the first slide, paste it into the presentation where you want it to appear, and then change the content you need to change.

To copy and paste slides:

1. Select the slide you want to copy.
2. On the *Home* tab, in the *Clipboard* group, click the **Copy** button.
3. Click the slide that you want to appear before the new slide.
4. Click the **Paste** button.
5. The new slide has been added to the presentation.

The *Paste* button includes a menu of options for pasting slides. You can choose to use the current presentation's theme, keep the formatting for the copied slide, or paste the slide as a picture. If you paste the slide as a picture, it will be inserted as a single image and you will not be able to edit the content.

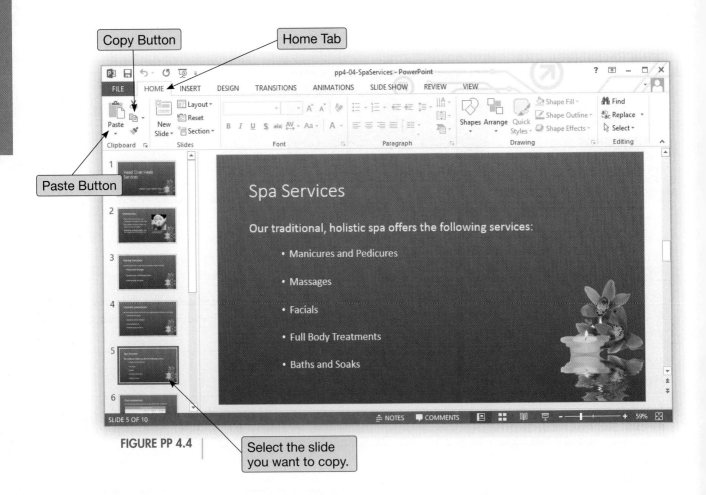

FIGURE PP 4.4

FIGURE PP 4.5

tips & tricks

If you want the copy of the slide to appear directly after the slide you are copying, click the arrow next to the **Copy** button and select **Duplicate.**

Click **Cut** in the *Clipboard* group to copy the slide to the Office *Clipboard* and remove it from its current location in the presentation.

another method

To copy a slide:

▶ Click the arrow next to the **Copy** button and select **Copy.**

▶ Press (Ctrl) + (C) on the keyboard.

▶ Right-click the slide and select **Copy.**

To paste a slide:

▶ Click the arrow below the **Paste** button and select a paste option.

▶ Press (Ctrl) + (V) on the keyboard.

▶ Right-click the slide and select a paste option.

let me try

Open the student data file **pp4-04-SpaServices** and try this skill on your own:

1. Copy **Slide 5.**
2. Paste the copied slide so it appears after **Slide 2.**
3. Save the file as directed by your instructor and close it.

skill 4.4   Copying and Pasting Slides

Skill 4.5 Adding Sections to Presentations

As you work on a presentation and add more slides, you may find it difficult to find a specific slide using the *Slides* tab. Scrolling through 20, 30, or even 40 thumbnails to find the content you are looking for is not a very efficient way to work. PowerPoint 2013 includes the ability to add **sections** to your presentation. You can use sections to create smaller groups of slides within your presentation to help you better organize your work. After you have added sections to your presentation, you can then hide and show the slides' thumbnails by expanding and collapsing the sections.

To add a section to a presentation:

1. On the *Slides* tab, click the thumbnail of the first slide for the section you want to create.

2. On the *Home* tab, in the *Slides* group, click the **Sections** button and select **Add Section.**

3. PowerPoint creates a new section.

4. To collapse the section and hide its slides, click the triangle next to the section name. To expand the section and show the slides, click the triangle again.

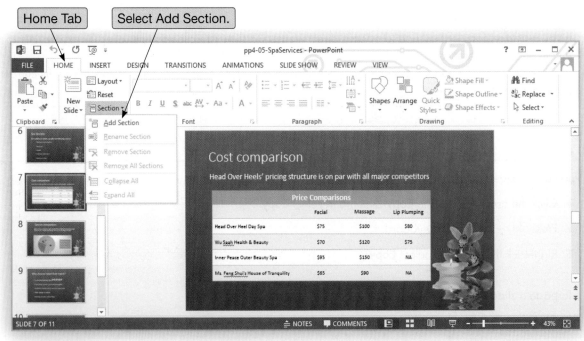

FIGURE PP 4.6

When you first add a section to a presentation, it is given the name *Untitled Section*.

To rename a section:

1. Select the section to rename.
2. Click the **Section** button and select **Rename Section.**
3. In the *Rename Section* dialog, type the name for the section and click **Rename.**

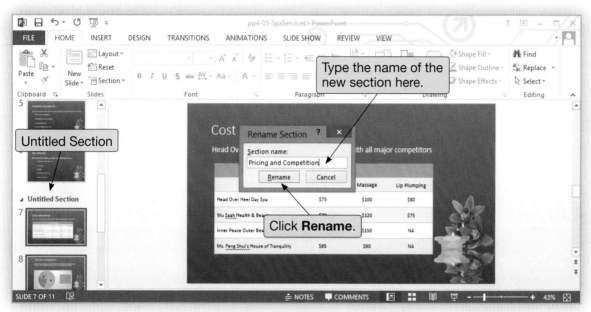

FIGURE PP 4.7

tips & tricks

To remove a section, click the **Section** button and select **Remove Section.** Select **Remove All Sections** to delete all sections in the presentation.

another method

▶ To add a section, you can also right-click a thumbnail on the *Slides* tab and select **Add Section.**

▶ To rename a section, you can also right-click a thumbnail on the *Slides* tab and select **Rename Section.**

▶ You can also expand and collapse sections by double-clicking the section name.

let me try

Open the student data file **pp4-05-SpaServices** and try this skill on your own:

1. Add a new section starting on **Slide 7.**
2. Rename the section **Pricing and Competition.**
3. Save the file as directed by your instructor and close it.

Skill 4.6 Adding Hyperlinks to Slides

A **hyperlink** is text or a graphic that, when clicked, takes you to a new location. You can use hyperlinks to navigate to Web pages, other PowerPoint presentations, custom shows, or any slide in the presentation. When you point to a hyperlink, your mouse cursor turns to a hand, indicating it is something that can be clicked.

Some hyperlinks include ScreenTips. A **ScreenTip** is a bubble with text that appears when the mouse is placed over the link. Add a ScreenTip to include a more meaningful description of the hyperlink.

To add a hyperlink from one slide to another slide in the same presentation:

1. Place the cursor where you want the hyperlink to appear.
2. Click the **Insert** tab.
3. In the *Links* group, click the **Add a Hyperlink** button.

FIGURE PP 4.8

4. The *Insert Hyperlink* dialog opens.
5. Under *Link to* select **Place in This Document.**
6. Select the slide to link to.
7. Type the text for the hyperlink in the *Text to display* box.
8. Click **OK** to insert the hyperlink into your presentation.

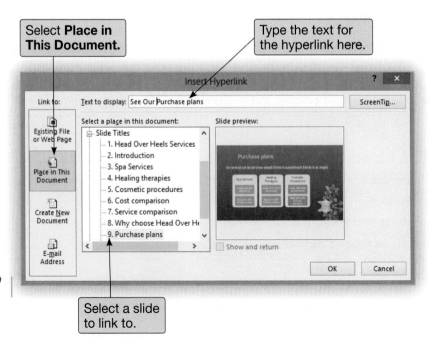

FIGURE PP 4.9

tips & tricks

To remove a hyperlink, first select the hyperlink you want to remove. In the *Links* group, click the **Hyperlink** button. In the *Edit Hyperlink* dialog, click the **Remove Hyperlink** button.

tell me **more**

Hyperlinks do not work in *Normal* view. In order to test your hyperlink, you must be in *Slide Show* view.

another **method**

To open the *Insert Hyperlink* dialog, you can also

❱ Right-click the text or object and select **Hyperlink...** from the menu.

❱ Press Ctrl + K on the keyboard.

let me **try**

Open the student data file **pp4-06-SpaServices** and try this skill on your own:

1. Navigate to **Slide 3** and place the cursor on the blank line at the end of the bulleted list.
2. Open the **Insert Hyperlink** dialog.
3. Add a hyperlink that will navigate to **Slide 9** when clicked. Have the text read **See Our Purchase Plans.**
4. Save the file as directed by your instructor and close it.

Skill 4.7 Checking Spelling

Regardless of the amount of work you put into a presentation, a spelling error or typo can make the entire presentation appear sloppy and unprofessional. All the Office applications include a built-in **spelling checker.** In PowerPoint, the *Spelling* command analyzes your entire presentation for spelling errors. It presents any errors it finds in the *Spelling* task pane, enabling you to make decisions about how to handle each error or type of error in turn.

To check a presentation for spelling errors:

1. Click the **Review** tab. In the *Proofing* group, click the **Spelling** button.

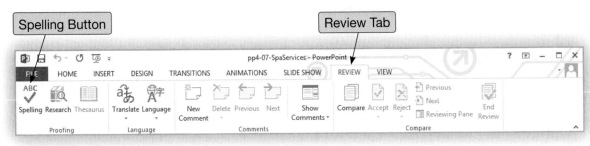

FIGURE PP 4.10

2. The first spelling error appears in the *Spelling* task pane.

3. Review the spelling suggestions and then select an action:

   ❭ Click **Ignore** to make no changes to this instance of the word.

   ❭ Click **Ignore All** to make no changes to all instances of the word.

   ❭ Click **Add** to make no changes to this instance of the word and add it to the main dictionary, so future uses of this word will not show up as misspellings. When you add a word to the main dictionary, it is available for all of the Office applications.

   ❭ Click the correct spelling in the list of suggestions, and click **Change** to correct just this instance of the misspelling in your document.

   ❭ Click the correct spelling in the list of suggestions, and click **Change All** to correct all instances of the misspelling in your document.

4. After you select an action, the spelling checker automatically advances to the next suspected spelling error.

5. When the spelling checker finds no more errors, it displays a message telling you the check is complete. Click **OK** to close the dialog and return to your file.

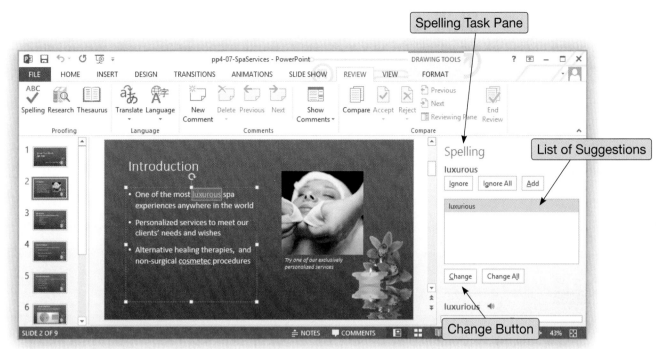

FIGURE PP 4.11

tips & tricks

Whether or not you use the Spelling tool, you should always proofread your files. Spelling checkers are not infallible, especially if you misuse a word yet spell it correctly—for instance, writing "bored" instead of "board."

If you have repeated the same word in a sentence, PowerPoint will flag the second instance of the word as a possible error. In the *Spelling* task pane, the *Change* button will switch to a *Delete* button. Click the **Delete** button to remove the duplicate word.

tell me more

When you select an option in the list of suggestions, PowerPoint displays a list of words that have the same meaning as the selected word along with an audio file of the pronunciation of the word.

another method

To display the *Spelling* task pane, you can also press (F7).

let me try

Open the student data file **pp4-07-SpaServices** and try this skill on your own:

1. Start the spelling checker.
2. Correct any misspellings found in the presentation.
3. Save the file as directed by your instructor and close it.

Skill 4.8 Adding Notes

Speaker notes are hidden notes you can add to slides. They do not appear as part of the presentation. Speaker notes can be used to help remind you to go to a certain slide in the presentation or to mention a specific detail that may not be included on the slide.

To add speaker notes to slides:

1. Click the **Notes** button on the status bar to display the *Notes* pane.
2. Click in the **Notes** pane.
3. Type your note for the slide.

FIGURE PP 4.12

Speaker notes can also be used to create handouts for your audience. You can then print your speaker notes and distribute them to your audience. The Notes view allows you to view how your speaker notes will look when printed. In *Notes* view, the image of the slide appears at the top of the screen and the speaker notes appear directly below the slide. You can add and format text in *Notes* view, but you cannot edit the content of the slides. To switch to *Notes* view, click the **View** tab. In the *Presentation Views* group, click the **Notes Page** button.

another **method**

To display the *Notes* pane, you can also click the **View** tab. In the *Show* group, click the **Notes** button.

let me **try**

Open the student data file **pp4-08-SpaServices** and try this skill on your own:

1. Display the **Notes** pane.
2. Add a note to **Slide 2** that reads **5 Star rating from Best Spas.**
3. Save the file as directed by your instructor and close it.

Skill 4.9 Rehearsing Timings

Timing is an important part of your presentation. For example, you wouldn't want to be part way through explaining the content of a slide and have your presentation advance before you are ready. Before you give your presentation, it is a good idea to rehearse what you will say and set up the timing for the slide show. Use PowerPoint's **Rehearse Timings** feature to synchronize your verbal presentation with your slides.

To use PowerPoint's Rehearse Timing feature:

1. Click the **Slide Show** tab.
2. In the *Set Up* group, click the **Rehearse Timings** button.

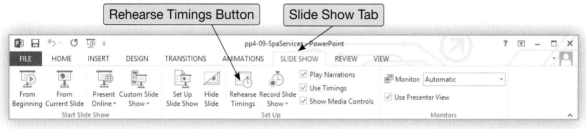

FIGURE PP 4.13

3. When the first slide appears, begin rehearsing your presentation.
4. Click the **Pause** button if you want to stop the timer.
5. Click the **Next** button to advance to the next slide.
6. Continue rehearsing each slide, clicking the **Next** button to advance the slides, until you reach the end of the presentation.
7. At the end of the presentation, you will be asked if you want to keep the timings as part of your slide show. Click **Yes** to include the timings as part of the presentation. If you do not want to keep the timings, click **No.**

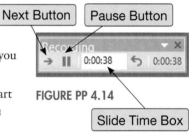

FIGURE PP 4.14

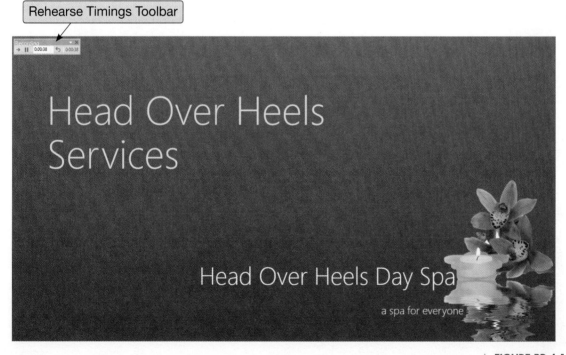

FIGURE PP 4.15

tips & tricks

When you are timing your presentation, be sure to speak slowly and carefully, and to pause slightly before you advance to the next slide.

another method

You can also enter the timing for a slide directly into the *Slide Time* box.

let me try

Open the student data file **pp4-09-SpaServices** and try this skill on your own:

1. Start the **Rehearse Timings** feature.
2. Click the **Next** button to navigate to the next slide.
3. Pause the presentation.
4. Start the timings again.
5. Finish navigating through the presentation using the toolbar.
6. Save the timings.
7. Save the file as directed by your instructor and close it.

from the perspective of . . .

A HEALTH CLUB MANAGER

The first time I gave a presentation to a potential customer, it was a disaster! All my slides were out of order, and I had one slide in the presentation three times. Since then, I've learned to carefully practice my PowerPoint slide shows before presenting them before customers. I can then reorder and delete slides and even hide slides that I don't want to show but want to keep as part of the presentation. I always add notes and then use two screens to show the presentation in *Presenter* view—this helps me stay on track when presenting.

Skill 4.10 Starting the Slide Show

You can choose to start your presentation from the beginning, playing it all the way through. But what if you find you don't have as much time as you originally planned to present? You can also choose to start the presentation from any slide in the presentation.

To start a presentation from the beginning:

1. Click the **Slide Show** tab.
2. In the *Start Slide Show* group, click the **From Beginning** button.

To start a presentation from the current slide:

1. Click the **Slide Show** tab.
2. In the *Start Slide Show* group, click the **From Current Slide** button.

FIGURE PP 4.16

tips & tricks

Another way to start a presentation from the beginning is to select the first slide in the presentation and use any of the methods for playing the presentation from the current slide.

another method

❱ To start a slide show from the current slide, you can also click the **Slide Show** view button on the status bar.

❱ To start the slide show from the beginning, you can also press F5 on the keyboard.

let me try

Open the student data file **pp4-10-SpaServices** and try this skill on your own:

1. Start the slide show from the beginning.
2. Press Esc to exit the slide show.
3. Navigate to **Slide 3.**
4. Start the slide show from the current slide.
5. Press Esc to exit the slide show.
6. Close the file.

Skill 4.11 Navigating the Slide Show

Once you have started the slide show, you will need a way to advance through the slides as you talk. You can use the Rehearse Timings feature to automatically advance the slide show for you. However, if you want the freedom to depart from your script, you will want to navigate the slide show yourself. This table lists commands for navigating a presentation in *Slide Show* view using the mouse and the keyboard:

SLIDE SHOW NAVIGATION		
COMMAND	MOUSE COMMAND	KEYBOARD COMMAND
Next Slide	Left-click on the slide. Right-click and select **Next.**	Press **Enter.** Press the **Spacebar.**
Previous Slide	Right-click and select **Previous.**	Press **Backspace.**
Specific Slide	Right-click and select **See All Slides.** Select the slide.	Press the number of the slide and press **Enter.**
Exit the Presentation	Right-click and select **End Show.**	Press **Escape.**

Right-click Menu

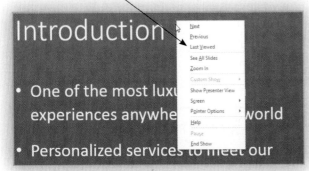

FIGURE PP 4.17

You can also use the Slide Show toolbar, located in the lower-left corner of the slide, to navigate through a presentation.

❱ Click the **Next** button to navigate to the next slide in the presentation.

❱ Click the **Previous** button to navigate to the previous slide in the presentation.

❱ Click the **Zoom** button to magnify a part of a slide.

❱ Click the **Show All Slides** button to display thumbnails of all the slides in the presentation. Click a thumbnail to navigate to that slide.

Previous Button   Next Button   Show All Slides Button

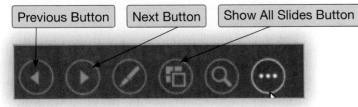

FIGURE PP 4.18

tips & tricks

If you want to see the last slide you viewed, but it is not part of the slide order, right-click the presentation and select **Last Viewed** on the menu.

let me try

Open the student data file **pp4-11-SpaServices** and try this skill on your own:

1. Start the slide show.
2. Navigate to the next slide.
3. Navigate to the previous slide.
4. Navigate to **Slide 6.**
5. Continue navigating through the presentation.
6. When you get to the end, exit the presentation.
7. Close the presentation.

Skill 4.12 Using Presentation Tools

The presentation tools in PowerPoint allow you to write on your slides while you are giving your presentation. You can use the **Pen** tool to underline or circle important points as you discuss them. Use the **Highlighter** tool to add color behind text on slides and emphasize parts of your slides. PowerPoint 2013 also includes a **laser pointer** tool. This tool turns the mouse pointer into a red dot that you can use to call attention to important parts of your slides.

To make notations on slides using the presentation tools:

1. In Slide *Show* view, click the **Pointer Options** button.
2. Select a pointer option: **Laser Pointer, Pen,** or **Highlighter.**
3. Click and drag the mouse to write on the slide or highlight part of the slide.
4. Click the **Pointer Options** button and select **Arrow** to return to the arrow pointer.

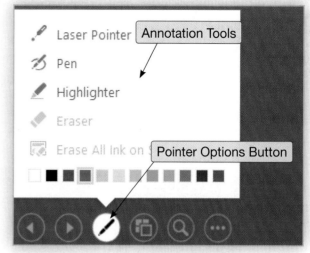

FIGURE PP 4.19

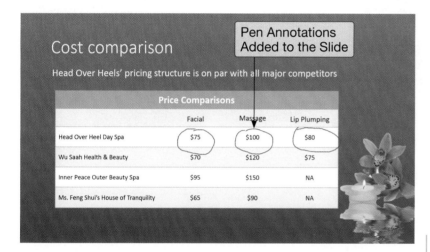

FIGURE PP 4.20

tips & tricks

When you end your presentation, PowerPoint will ask if you want to keep the annotations you added. Click the **Keep** button to include the annotations as part of the presentation. Click the **Discard** button to delete the annotations.

another method

To use presentation tools, you can also right-click the slide, point to **Pointer Options,** and select an option.

let me try

Open the student data file **pp4-12-SpaServices** and try this skill on your own:

1. Start the slide show.
2. Navigate to **Slide 6.**
3. Use the **Pen** tool to circle the three prices for Head Over Heels.
4. Exit the presentation. Do not save the annotations.
5. Close the presentation.

Skill 4.13 Using Presenter View

You can use two monitors to display your presentation. When you use two monitors your audience will see your presentation in *Slide Show* view, while you will see the presentation in **Presenter view.** *Presenter* view allows you to see your notes while you are giving your presentation, making it easier to refer to any notes you have added to slides.

To show a presentation using *Presenter* view:

1. Start the slide show.

2. Click the **Slide Show Options** button and select **Show Presenter View.**

FIGURE PP 4.21

3. *Presenter* view displays with the presentation on the left and a preview of the next slide and your notes for the current slide on the right.

4. Click the **Advance to Next Slide** and **Return to Previous Slide** to navigate through the presentation.

5. Click the **End Slide Show** button to exit the presentation.

FIGURE PP 4.22

tips & tricks

If you need to switch which display shows the presentation and which display shows *Presenter* view, click the **Display Settings** button and select **Swap Presenter View and Slide Show.**

another method

To open *Presenter* view, you can also right-click a slide in *Slide Show* view and select **Show Presenter View.**

To navigate through the slide show, you can use the same keyboard commands you use in *Slide Show* view.

let me try

Open the student data file **pp4-13-SpaServices** and try this skill on your own:

1. Start the slide show from the beginning.
2. Open **Presenter View.**
3. Navigate through the presentation.
4. Exit the slide show.
5. Close the file.

Skill 4.14 Printing Presentations

In PowerPoint 2013, all the print settings are combined in a single page along with a preview of how the printed presentation will look. From the *Print* page in Backstage view, you can preview and print all the slides in your presentation.

To preview and print a presentation:

1. Click the **File** tab to open Backstage view.
2. Click **Print.**
3. Verify that the correct printer name is displayed in the *Printer* section.
4. In the *Settings* section, the last button displays the color options for printing the presentation. By default, *Color* is selected. To change the print selection, click the button, and then click an option: **Color, Grayscale,** or **Pure Black and White.**
5. Click the **Print** button to print.

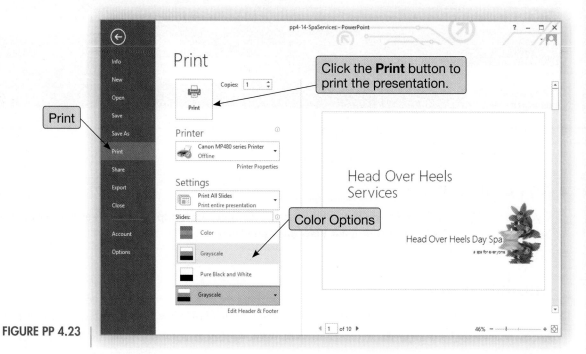

FIGURE PP 4.23

tips & tricks

Click the **Next Page** and **Previous Page** buttons at the bottom of the preview to navigate through your presentation to see how all the slides will appear when printed.

another method

To open the *Print* page in Backstage view, you can use the keyboard shortcut Ctrl + P.

let me try

Open the student data file **pp4-14-SpaServices** and try this skill on your own:

1. Open Backstage view.
2. Display the **Print** page.
3. Change the color of the printed presentation to **Grayscale.**
4. Print the presentation. **NOTE:** If you are using this in class or in your school's computer lab, check with your instructor about printing permissions before completing this step.
5. Close the presentation.

Skill 4.15 Customizing Handout Masters

The **Handout Master** view allows you to modify how the printed version of your presentation will look. When you open the presentation in *Handout Master* view, you will see a preview of the printed page with dotted placeholders for the slides, header, footer, page number, and date.

To open *Handout Master* view:

1. Click the **View** tab.
2. In the *Master Views* group, click the **Handout Master** button.
3. Make any changes to the handout master.
4. Click the **Close Master View** button to return to *Normal* view.

FIGURE PP 4.24

You can show and hide placeholders in *Handout Master* view. When you hide a placeholder, it no longer appears in the *Handout Master* view. To show and hide a placeholder, on the *Handout Master* tab, in the *Placeholders* group, click the placeholder's check box.

Placeholders you can hide and show include:

) **Header**—appears in the upper-left corner of the page. To add header text for a handout, click in the **Header** box and type the text you want to appear in the upper left corner of each handout.

) **Date**—appears in the upper-right corner of the page and displays the date.

) **Footer**—appears in the lower-left corner of the page and displays the text you entered for the footer.

) **Page Number**—appears in the lower-right corner of the page and displays the current number of the printed page (not the slide number).

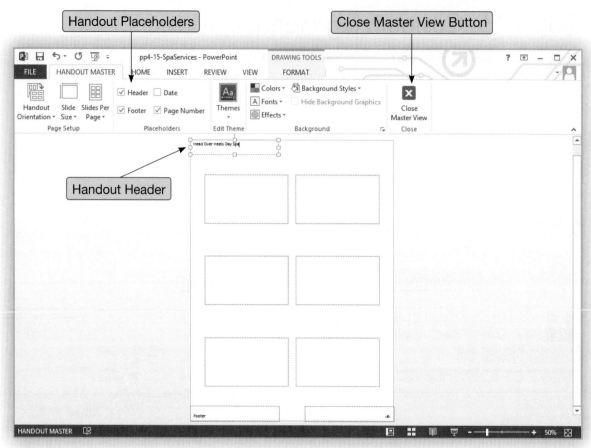

Handout Placeholders

Close Master View Button

Handout Header

FIGURE PP 4.25

tips & tricks

By default, handouts appear in portrait orientation, meaning the page is taller than it is wide. If you want your handouts to appear in landscape orientation (with the page being more wide than tall), in the *Page Setup* group, click the **Handout Orientation** button and select **Landscape.**

another method

To return to *Normal* view, you can also click the **Normal** button on the status bar.

let me try

Open the student data file **pp4-15-SpaServices** and try this skill on your own:

1. Switch to the **Handout Master view.**
2. Add the text **Head Over Heels Day Spa** to the header of the handout.
3. Hide the date on the handout.
4. Close **Handout Master** view.
5. Save the file as directed by your instructor and close it.

Skill 4.16 Printing Handouts

In addition to printing slides, PowerPoint also gives you the ability to print handouts, notes, and an outline of the presentation. A **handout** is a printout of your presentation with anywhere from one to nine slides per page and with areas for taking notes. The **Notes Pages** option will print a copy of the slide with its associated note, if there is one. Select **Outline** when you want to print a text outline of your presentation. As with printing presentations, printing of handouts, notes pages, and outlines are all done from the *Print* page in Backstage view.

To preview and print handouts:

1. Click the **File** tab to open Backstage view.
2. Click **Print.**
3. Verify that the correct printer name is displayed in the *Printer* section.
4. In the *Settings* section, the second button displays the page options for printing the presentation. By default, *Full Page Slides* is selected. To change the print selection, click the button and then select an option.
5. Click the **Print** button to print.

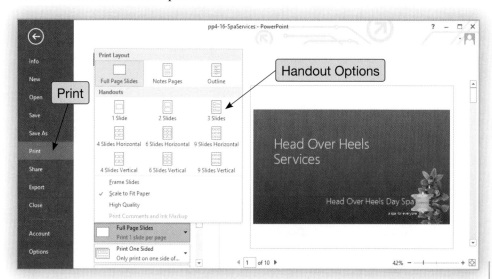

FIGURE PP 4.26

tips & tricks

The Handouts (3 Slides) layout includes lines next to the slide image. This layout is useful if you want to print your presentation for your audience and include an area where they can easily write notes to correspond with each slide.

another method

To open the *Print* page in Backstage view, you can use the keyboard shortcut (Ctrl) + (P).

let me try

Open the student data file **pp4-16-SpaServices** and try this skill on your own:

1. Open Backstage view.
2. Display the **Print** page.
3. Change the print settings to print **3 Slides per page**.
4. Print the presentation. **NOTE:** If you are using this in class or in your school's computer lab, check with your instructor about printing permissions before completing this step.
5. Close the presentation.

Skill 4.17 Adding Comments

Comments are small messages you add to slides that are not meant to be a part of the presentation. Comments are useful when you are reviewing a presentation and want to add messages about changes or errors on a slide.

To insert a comment on a slide:

1. Click the **Review** tab.
2. In the *Comments* group, click the **New Comment** button.
3. The *Comments* task pane appears.
4. Type your comment in the box and click outside the box.

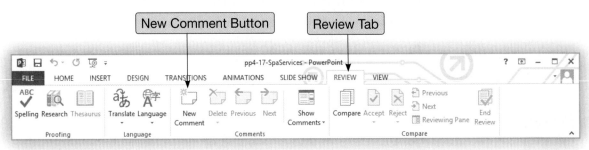

FIGURE PP 4.27

FIGURE PP 4.28

If you do not want your comments to display in the *Slide* pane, you can hide the comments in the presentation. On the *Review* tab, in the *Comments* group, click the bottom half of the **Show Comments** button arrow and select **Show Markup** to hide the comments in the presentation. Click the **Show Markup** option again to show the comments.

FIGURE PP 4.29

tips & tricks

Click the **Delete Comment** button arrow and select an option to delete a specific comment or all comments from the presentation.

When you display the *Comments* task pane, PowerPoint lets you know if other slides in the presentation include comments. Click the **Next** and **Previous** buttons at the top of the task pane to navigate between comments in the presentation.

tell me **more**

You can respond to a specific comment by typing in the *Reply...* box in the comment.

another **method**

To insert a comment, you can also click the **Comments** button on the status bar to display the *Comments* task pane. At the top of the task pane, click the **New** button to add a new comment.

let me **try**

Open the student data file **pp4-17-SpaServices** and try this skill on your own:

1. Navigate to **Slide 2.**
2. Add a new comment to the slide that reads **Make points brief.**
3. Hide the **Comments task pane.**
4. Save the file as directed by your instructor and close it.

key terms

Hide Slide	Pen
Sections	Highlighter
Hyperlink	Laser pointer
SreenTip	Presenter view
Spelling checker	Handout Master
Speaker notes	Handout
Notes view	Notes pages
Rehearse Timings	Comments

concepts review

1. If you want a slide to remain in a presentation but not show by default when you are in Slide Show view, you should _____ the slide.

    a. delete

    b. hide

    c. reorder

    d. cut

2. _____ allows you to give a presentation on two screens, with one screen showing the slide show along with speaker notes and other tools.

    a. Slide Show view

    b. Slide Sorter view

    c. Presenter view

    d. Presentation view

3. A _____ is a printout of your presentation with anywhere from one to nine slides per page and with areas for taking notes.

    a. handout

    b. notes page

    c. handout master

    d. print page

4. When giving a presentation, you can write on slides and save annotations by using PowerPoint's pen options, which include the _____ tool.

    a. pen

    b. laser pointer

    c. highlighter

    d. all of the above

5. To navigate to the next slide in Slide Show view, press _____ on the keyboard.

    a. Enter

    b. Spacebar

    c. Both a and b

    d. Neither a nor b

6. If you want to practice your presentation and record how long you spend on each slide, use the _____ feature.

    a. Slide Show

    b. Presenter view

    c. Rehearse Timings

    d. Record narration

7. Use _____ to create smaller groups of slides within your presentation to help you better organize your work.

    a. sections

    b. slides

    c. Presenter view

    d. none of the above

8. To exit a slide show, press _____ on the keyboard.

    a. Enter

    b. Spacebar

    c. Escape

    d. Backspace

9. _____ are small messages you add to slides for others to read that are not meant to be a part of the presentation.

    a. Notes

    b. Comments

    c. Annotations

    d. None of the above

10. A _____ is text or a graphic that, when clicked, takes you to a new location.

    a. comment

    b. ScreenTip

    c. note

    d. hyperlink

projects

skill review 4.1

In this project you will be working on the structure for the marketing presentation from Suarez Marketing. You will rehearse the presentation and practice navigating through the slide show using the keyboard and mouse. You will add comments, change the handout master, and print handouts for your audience.

Skills needed to complete this project:

- Changing the Order of Slides (Skill 4.2)
- Adding Sections to Presentations (Skill 4.5)
- Hiding Slides (Skill 4.3)
- Adding Hyperlinks to Slides (Skill 4.6)
- Deleting Slides from Presentations (Skill 4.1)
- Checking Spelling (Skill 4.7)
- Adding Notes (Skill 4.8)
- Rehearsing Timings (Skill 4.9)
- Starting the Slide Show (Skill 4.10)
- Navigating the Slide Show (Skill 4.11)
- Customizing Handout Masters (Skill 4.15)
- Printing Handouts (Skill 4.16)
- Adding Comments (Skill 4.17)

1. Open the **PP2013-SkillReview-4-1** presentation.
2. Save this presentation as: **[your initials] PP-SkillReview-4-1**
3. Change the order of slides in a presentation.
   a. Select **Slide 10** in the *Slides* pane.
   b. Click and drag the slide thumbnail down in the list until it appears below the **What Clients Are Saying** slide. The slide should now be the next to the last slide in the presentation.
4. Add section and rename the section.
   a. Select **Slide 10.**
   b. On the *Home* tab, in the *Slides* group, click the **Section** button and select **Add Section.**
   c. Click the **Section** button again and select **Rename Section.**
   d. In the *Section name* box, type **Clients**. Click **Rename.**
5. Hide a slide in a presentation.
   a. Navigate to **Slide 12.**
   b. Click the **Slide Show** tab.
   c. In the *Set Up* group, click the **Hide Slide** button.

6. Add a hyperlink to slides.

    a. Navigate to **Slide 3.**

    b. Click at the end of the second bullet point and press the **Spacebar** one time.

    c. Click the **Insert** tab.

    d. In the *Links* group, click the **Add a Hyperlink** button.

    e. Under *Link to,* click **Place in This Document.**

    f. In the *Select a place in this document* box, click **Slide 10. What Clients Are Saying.**

    g. In the *Text to display* box, delete the text *What Clients Are Saying.* Type `(See the Clients section)`

    h. Click **OK.**

7. Delete a slide from the presentation.

    a. Navigate to **Slide 7.**

    b. Right-click the slide thumbnail and select **Delete Slide.**

8. Check the presentation for spelling errors.

    a. Navigate to **Slide 1.**

    b. Click the **Review** tab.

    c. In the *Proofing* group, click the **Spelling** button.

    d. Click the **Change** button to change the first misspelling from **busines** to **business.**

    e. Click the **Change** button to change the second misspelling from **organisation** to **organization.**

    f. Click the **Change** button to change the third misspelling from **Asociation** to **Association.**

    g. The remaining possible errors are not misspellings. Click the **Ignore** button for each of the remaining possible error in the presentation.

    h. A message box appears when the spell check is complete. Click **OK** in the message box.

9. Add notes to a slide.

    a. Navigate to **Slide 2.**

    b. Click the **Notes** button on the status bar.

    c. Click in the *Notes* pane and type `Talk about client specific needs`

10. Use PowerPoint's Rehearse Timing feature.

    a. Click the **Slide Show** tab.

    b. In the *Set Up* group, click the **Rehearse Timings** button.

    c. When the first slide appears, begin rehearsing your presentation.

    d. Click the **Pause** button if you want to stop the timer.

    e. Click the **Next** button to advance to the next slide.

    f. Continue rehearsing each slide, clicking the **Next** button to advance the slides, until you reach the end of the presentation.

    g. At the end of the presentation, you will be asked if you want to keep the timing as part of your slide show. Click **No.**

11. Start the slide show from the beginning and navigate through the presentation using the mouse.

   a. On the *Slide Show* tab, in the *Start Slide Show* group, click the **From Beginning** button.

   b. To advance to the next slide, click the mouse or click the **Next** button.

   c. To go to the previous slide, click the **Previous** button.

   d. To jump to a specific slide, click the **See All Slides** button and select a slide.

   e. To exit the presentation, click the **Slide Show Options** button and select **End Show.**

12. Unhide a slide.

   a. Navigate to **Slide 11.**

   b. On the *Slide Show* tab, in the *Set Up* group, click the **Hide Slide** button to unhide the slide.

13. Start the slide show from the current slide and navigate through the presentation using the keyboard.

   a. Navigate to **Slide 9.**

   b. On the *Slide Show* tab, in the *Start Slide Show* group, click the **From Current Slide** button.

   c. To advance to the next slide: press ⏎ Enter or the **Spacebar.**

   d. To go to the previous slide: press ← Backspace.

   e. To jump to a specific slide: type the number of the slide and press ⏎ Enter.

   f. To exit the presentation: press Esc.

14. Customize the handout master.

   a. Click the **View** tab.

   b. In the *Master Views* group, click the **Handout Master** button.

   c. Click in the upper left box of the handout header and type `Suarez Marketing Presentation`

   d. Click the **Close Master View** button.

15. Print handouts.

   a. Click the **File** tab.

   b. Click the **Print** button.

   c. Click the second button under *Settings* and select the **3 Slides** option in the *Handouts* section.

   d. Click the **Print** button. **NOTE:** If you are using this in class or in your school's computer lab, check with your instructor about printing permissions before completing this step.

16. Add a comment to a slide.

   a. Navigate to **Slide 9.**

   b. Click the **Review** tab.

   c. In the *Comments* group, click the **New Comment** button.

   d. The *Comments* task pane displays. In the comment box, type `Are the next two slides necessary?` Click below the comment.

   e. Click the **Comments** button on the status bar to close the *Comments* task pane.

17. Save and close the presentation.

In this project you will be working on the structure for a personal fitness plan presentation. You will rehearse the presentation and practice navigating through the slide show in *Presenter* view. You will change the handout master and print handouts for your audience.

Skills needed to complete this project:

- Changing the Order of Slides (Skill 4.2)
- Copying and Pasting Slides (Skill 4.4)
- Deleting Slides from Presentations (Skill 4.1)
- Adding Sections to Presentations (Skill 4.5)
- Hiding Slides (Skill 4.3)
- Checking Spelling (Skill 4.7)
- Adding Notes (Skill 4.8)
- Rehearsing Timings (Skill 4.9)
- Starting the Slide Show (Skill 4.10)
- Navigating the Slide Show (Skill 4.11)
- Using Presentation Tools (Skill 4.12)
- Using Presenter View (Skill 4.13)
- Customizing Handout Masters (Skill 4.15)
- Printing Handouts (Skill 4.16)
- Adding Comments (Skill 4.17)

1. Open the **PP2013-SkillReview-4-2** presentation.

2. Save this presentation as: **[your initials]PP-SkillReview-4-2**

3. Change the order of slides in a presentation.

    a. Select **Slide 4** in the *Slides* pane.

    b. Click and drag the slide thumbnail up in the list until it appears below the **title slide.**

4. Copy and paste a slide.

    a. Select **Slide 8.**

    b. On the *Home* tab, in the *Clipboard* group, click the **Copy** button.

    c. Select **Slide 3.**

    d. In the *Clipboard* group, click the **Paste** button.

5. Delete a slide from the presentation.

    a. Navigate to **Slide 9.**

    b. Right-click the slide thumbnail and select **Delete Slide.**

6. Add sections and rename the sections.

    a. Select **Slide 2.**

    b. On the *Home* tab, in the *Slides* group, click the **Section** button and select **Add Section.**

    c. Click the **Section** button again and select **Rename Section.**

    d. In the *Section name* box, type **Diet and Exercise**. Click **Rename.**

    e. Select **Slide 5.**

f. In the *Slides* group, click the **Section** button and select **Add Section.**

g. Click the **Section** button again and select **Rename Section.**

h. In the *Section name* box, type **Me Time**. Click **Rename.**

i. Select **Slide 8.**

j. In the *Slides* group, click the **Section** button and select **Add Section.**

k. Click the **Section** button again and select **Rename Section.**

l. In the *Section name* box, type **Goals**. Click **Rename.**

m. Click the **triangle** next to the **Me Time** section to hide the slides. Click the **triangle** again to show the slides.

7. Hide a slide in a presentation.

   a. Navigate to **Slide 7.**

   b. Click the **Slide Show** tab.

   c. In the *Set Up* group, click the **Hide Slide** button.

8. Check the presentation for spelling errors.

   a. Navigate to **Slide 1.**

   b. Click the **Review** tab.

   c. In the *Proofing* group, click the **Spelling** button.

   d. Click the **Change** button to change the first misspelling from **bedtim** to **bedtime.**

   e. Click the **Change** button to change the second misspelling from **frend** to **friend.**

   f. Click the **Change** button to change the third misspelling from **massege** to **massage.**

   g. Click the **Change** button to change the fourth misspelling from **triathalon** to **triathlon.**

   h. A message box appears when the spell check is complete. Click **OK** in the message box.

9. Add notes to a slide.

   a. Navigate to **Slide 2.**

   b. Click the **Notes** button on the status bar.

   c. Click in the *Notes* pane and type **Any carbs come from whole grains**

10. Use PowerPoint's Rehearse Timing feature.

   a. Click the **Slide Show** tab.

   b. In the *Set Up* group, click the **Rehearse Timings** button.

   c. When the first slide appears, begin rehearsing your presentation.

   d. Click the **Pause** button if you want to stop the timer.

   e. Click the **Next** button to advance to the next slide.

   f. Continue rehearsing each slide, clicking the **Next** button to advance the slides until you reach the end of the presentation.

   g. At the end of the presentation, you will be asked if you want to keep the timing as part of your slide show. Click **No.**

11. Start the slide show from the beginning and navigate through the presentation using the mouse.

   a. On the *Slide Show* tab, in the *Start Slide Show* group, click the **From Beginning** button.

   b. To advance to the next slide, click the mouse or click the **Next** button.

c. To go to the previous slide, click the **Previous** button.

d. Click the **See All Slides** button and select a **Slide 4.**

e. Click the **Pointer Options** button and select **Pen.**

f. Click and drag the mouse around the bars for **Saturday,** circling the day on the chart.

12. Switch to **Presenter view.**

    a. Click the **Slide Show Options** button and select **Show Presenter View.**

    b. Click the **Advanced to Next Slide** button to move forward in the presentation. Click the **Return to Previous Slide** button to move backward in the presentation.

    c. To exit the presentation, click the **Slide Show Options** button and select **End Show.** In the message box that appears, click the **Discard** button to remove the pen annotation you made.

13. Customize the handout master.

    a. Click the **View** tab.

    b. In the *Master Views* group, click the **Handout Master** button.

    c. Click in the upper left box of the handout header and type `My Fitness Plan`

    d. In the *Placeholders* group, click the **Date** check box to remove the date from the printed handout.

    e. Click the **Close Master View** button.

14. Print handouts.

    a. Click the **File** tab.

    b. Click the **Print** button.

    c. Click the second button under *Settings* and select the **6 Slides** option in the *Handouts* section.

    d. Click the **Print** button. **NOTE:** If you are using this in class or in your school's computer lab, check with your instructor about printing permissions before completing this step.

15. Add a comment to a slide.

    a. Navigate to **Slide 8.**

    b. Click the **Review** tab.

    c. In the *Comments* group, click the **New Comment** button.

    d. The *Comments* task pane displays. In the comment box, type `Add more goals.` Click below the comment.

    e. Click the **Comments** button on the status bar to close the *Comments* task pane.

16. Save and close the presentation.

challenge yourself **4.3**

In this project you will be working on the structure for a presentation for Greenscapes landscaping company. You will rehearse the presentation and practice navigating through the slide show. You will change the handout master and print handouts for your audience.

Skills needed to complete this project:

- Changing the Order of Slides (Skill 4.2)
- Deleting Slides from Presentations (Skill 4.1)
- Adding Sections to Presentations (Skill 4.5)
- Adding Hyperlinks to Slides (Skill 4.6)
- Checking Spelling (Skill 4.7)
- Adding Notes (Skill 4.8)
- Rehearsing Timings (Skill 4.9)
- Starting the Slide Show (Skill 4.10)
- Navigating the Slide Show (Skill 4.11)
- Using Presentation Tools (Skill 4.12)
- Hiding Slides (Skill 4.3)
- Customizing Handout Masters (Skill 4.15)
- Printing Handouts (Skill 4.16)
- Adding Comments (Skill 4.17)

1. Open the **PP2013-ChallengeYourself-4-3** presentation.
2. Save this presentation as: **[your initials] PP-ChallengeYourself-4-3**
3. Move **Slide 5** so it comes after **Slide 1**.
4. Delete **Slide 4.**
5. Add section and rename the section.
   a. Select **Slide 6.**
   b. Add a new section and name it **Pricing**.
6. Add a hyperlink to slides.
   a. Select **Slide 3.**
   b. Place the cursor in the blank line under the numbered list.
   c. Insert a hyperlink to **Slide 7** that reads **See our pricing**.
7. Check the presentation for spelling errors.
   a. Correct the misspellings on the word **maintenance.**
   b. Do not change the suggested misspelling on **greenscapes.**
8. Add notes to a slide.
   a. Navigate to **Slide 2.**
   b. Display the **Notes** pane and add a note the reads **We are certified organic.**
9. Start the **Rehearse Timings** feature. Navigate through the presentation using the toolbar. Do not save the timings.
10. Start the presentation and use presentation tools.
    a. Start the slide show from the beginning.
    b. Navigate through the presentation using the mouse.

c. When you come to the **Specialty Services** slide, use the **Highlighter** tool to highlight **Water landscapes** and **Compost Silos** on the slide.

d. When the slide show ends, do not save the annotations.

11. Hide **Slide 7.**

12. Customize the handout master.

   a. Hide the date on the handout master.

   b. Add the text **Greenscapes Landscaping** to the header.

13. Print handouts.

   a. Change the printing options so three slides appear on each page with lines next to the image of each slide.

   b. Print the handouts. **NOTE:** If you are using this in class or in your school's computer lab, check with your instructor about printing permissions before completing this step.

14. Add a comment to **Slide 7** that reads **This does not belong in the basic customer presentation.**

15. Save and close the presentation.

challenge yourself 4.4

In this project you will be working on the structure for a presentation about emotional intelligence. You will rehearse the presentation and practice navigating through the slide show in *Presenter* view. You will change the handout master and print handouts for your audience.

Skills needed to complete this project:

- Changing the Order of Slides (Skill 4.2)
- Copying and Pasting Slides (Skill 4.4)
- Deleting Slides from Presentations (Skill 4.1)
- Adding Sections to Presentations (Skill 4.5)
- Hiding Slides (Skill 4.3)
- Checking Spelling (Skill 4.7)
- Adding Notes (Skill 4.8)
- Rehearsing Timings (Skill 4.9)
- Starting the Slide Show (Skill 4.10)
- Navigating the Slide Show (Skill 4.11)
- Using Presentation Tools (Skill 4.12)
- Using Presenter View (Skill 4.13)
- Customizing Handout Masters (Skill 4.15)
- Printing Handouts (Skill 4.16)
- Adding Comments (Skill 4.17)

1. Open the **PP2013-ChallengeYourself-4-4** presentation.

2. Save this presentation as: **[your initials]PP-ChallengeYourself-4-4**

3. Move **Slide 3** so it appears below **Slide 6.**

4. Copy **Slide 9** and paste it below **Slide 13.**

5. Delete **Slide 9.**

6. Add sections and rename the sections.

   a. Add a section starting on **Slide 3** named **Emotional Intelligence.**

   b. Add a section starting on **Slide 6** named **The Brain.**

   c. Add a section starting on **Slide 8** named **IQ v. EQ.**

   d. Add a section starting on **Slide 10** named **Improving EQ.**

7. Hide **Slide 5.**

8. Check the presentation for spelling errors and make corrections to the misspellings found. **NOTE:** The spelling error on the title slide should be changed to **Stressors.**

9. Add notes to a slide.

   a. Navigate to **Slide 2.**

   b. Display the **Notes** pane and add a note the reads **Give three examples of overly dramatic situations.**

10. Start the **Rehearse Timings** feature. Navigate through the presentation using the toolbar. Do not save the timings.

11. Start the presentation and use presentation tools.

    a. Start the slide show from the beginning.

    b. Navigate through the presentation using the keyboard.

    c. Use the **Show All Slides** command to navigate to **Slide 4.**

    d. Use the **Highlighter** tool to highlight **'right' emotion, 'right' time, 'right' intensity, 'right' purpose,** and **'right' way** on the slide.

    e. Switch to **Presenter view** and navigate through the presentation.

    f. End the slide show and save the annotations.

12. Customize the handout master by adding the text **Emotional Intelligence** to the upper left corner of the header.

13. Print handouts.

    a. Change the printing options so four slides appear on each page.

    b. Print the handouts. **NOTE:** If you are using this in class or in your school's computer lab, check with your instructor about printing permissions before completing this step.

14. Add a comment to **Slide 5** that reads **This slide is too wordy. Consider rewriting.**

15. Save and close the presentation.

on your own 4.5

In this project you will be modifying a presentation about creating PowerPoint presentations. You will rehearse the presentation and practice navigating through the slide show in *Presenter* view. You will change the handout master and print handouts for your audience.

Skills needed to complete this project:

- Deleting Slides from Presentations (Skill 4.1)
- Changing the Order of Slides (Skill 4.2)
- Checking Spelling (Skill 4.7)
- Adding Hyperlinks to Slides (Skill 4.6)

- Adding Notes (Skill 4.8)
- Rehearsing Timings (Skill 4.9)
- Starting the Slide Show (Skill 4.10)
- Navigating the Slide Show (Skill 4.11)
- Using Presenter View (Skill 4.13)
- Customizing Handout Masters (Skill 4.15)
- Printing Handouts (Skill 4.16)
- Adding Comments (Skill 4.17)

1. Open the **PP2013-OnYourOwn-4-5** presentation.

2. Save this presentation as: **[your initials]PP-OnYourOwn-4-5**

3. Delete the extra slide at the bottom of the presentation.

4. Reorder the slides in the presentation so they follow the four steps outlined on **Slide 2.**

5. Check the presentation for spelling errors and correct any misspellings found.

6. Add hyperlinks from each of the steps on **Slide 2** to its appropriate slide.

7. Add notes for each slide with further talking points about step in creating a presentation.

8. Use the Rehearse Timings feature to practice the presentation. Do not save the timings.

9. Start the slide show from the beginning and navigate through the presentation using the keyboard.

10. Navigate to any slide and start the presentation from the current slide.

11. Switch to **Presenter view** and use the navigation tools to move through the presentation.

12. Customize the handout master to include a header. Change any other options in the handout you want.

13. Print copies of the handouts using a setting of your choice. **NOTE:** If you are using this in class or in your school's computer lab, check with your instructor about printing permissions before selecting **Print.**

14. Add a comment to a slide in the presentation.

15. Save and close the presentation.

fix it 4.6

In this project you will be working on the structure for a presentation about team building. You will practice navigating through the slide show and using annotation tools. You will change the handout master and print handouts for your audience.

Skills needed to complete this project:

- Changing the Order of Slides (Skill 4.2)
- Deleting Slides from Presentations (Skill 4.1)
- Adding Sections to Presentations (Skill 4.5)
- Hiding Slides (Skill 4.3)
- Checking Spelling (Skill 4.7)
- Adding Notes (Skill 4.8)

- Starting the Slide Show (Skill 4.10)
- Navigating the Slide Show (Skill 4.11)
- Using Presentation Tools (Skill 4.12)
- Printing Presentations (Skill 4.14)
- Customizing Handout Masters (Skill 4.15)
- Printing Handouts (Skill 4.16)
- Adding Comments (Skill 4.17)

1. Open the **PP2013-FixIt-4-6** presentation.
2. Save this presentation as: **[your initials] PP-FixIt-4-6**
3. Move **Slide 4** so it appears below **Slide 2.**
4. There is a duplicate slide in the presentation. Delete **Slide 7.**
5. Add a section starting on **Slide 4** named **SMART.**
6. Unhide **Slide 7.**
7. Check the presentation for spelling errors and correct any misspellings found.
8. Start the slide show from the beginning and navigate through the presentation using the mouse. When you get to the **Project Objectives** slide, use the **Pen** tool to circle each objective as it is discussed. End the slide show but do not save the annotations.
9. Print one grayscale copy of all the slides in the presentation (each slide should appear on its own page). **NOTE:** If you are using this in class or in your school's computer lab, check with your instructor about printing permissions before selecting **Print.**
10. Change the handout master so the **date** and **page number** appear on the printed handouts.
11. Print handouts so three slides appear on each page with lines next to the image of each slide. **NOTE:** If you are using this in class or in your school's computer lab, check with your instructor about printing permissions before completing this step.
12. Add a comment to **Slide 7** that reads **Animate this diagram.**
13. Save and close the presentation.

Office 2013 Shortcuts

Office 2013 Keyboard Shortcuts

ACTION	KEYBOARD SHORTCUT
Display Open page in Backstage view	Ctrl + O
Create a new blank file (bypassing Backstage view)	Ctrl + N
Copy	Ctrl + C
Cut	Ctrl + X
Paste	Ctrl + V
Undo	Ctrl + Z
Redo	Ctrl + Y
Save	Ctrl + S
Select All	Ctrl + A
Help	F1
Bold	Ctrl + B
Italic	Ctrl + I
Underline	Ctrl + U
Close Start page or Backstage view	Esc
Close a file	Ctrl + W
Minimize the Ribbon	Ctrl + F1
Switch windows	Alt + Tab

Word 2013 Keyboard Shortcuts

ACTION	KEYBOARD SHORTCUT
Open a new blank Word document	Ctrl + N
Display Open page in Backstage view	Ctrl + O
Open the *Open* dialog	Ctrl + F12
Select All	Ctrl + A
Open Spelling and Grammar task pane	F7
Undo	Ctrl + Z
Redo	Ctrl + Y
Open Navigation task pane with the search results section displayed	Ctrl + F
Open *Find and Replace* dialog with the *Replace* tab displayed	Ctrl + H
Open *Find and Replace* dialog with the *Go To* tab selected	Ctrl + G or F5
Copy	Ctrl + C
Cut	Ctrl + X
Paste	Ctrl + V
Bold	Ctrl + B
Italic	Ctrl + I
Underline	Ctrl + U
Save	Ctrl + S
Open *Save As* dialog	F12
Open *Font* dialog	Ctrl + D
Increase font size	Ctrl + ↑ Shift + >
Decrease font size	Ctrl + ↑ Shift + <
Left align text	Ctrl + L
Center text	Ctrl + E
Right align text	Ctrl + R
Justify text	Ctrl + J
Single line spacing	Ctrl + 1
Double line spacing	Ctrl + 2

ACTION	KEYBOARD SHORTCUT
Show formatting marks	Ctrl + ↑ Shift + 8
Open *Insert Hyperlink* dialog	Ctrl + K
Open Thesaurus pane	↑ Shift + F7
Open Word Help	F1
Insert line break	↑ Shift + ←⏎ Enter
Insert page break	Ctrl + ←⏎ Enter
Insert non-breaking space	Ctrl + ↑ Shift + Space
Copy formatting	Ctrl + ↑ Shift + C
Paste formatting	Ctrl + ↑ Shift + V
Insert an endnote	Alt + Ctrl + D
Insert a footnote	Alt + Ctrl + F
Move the insertion point to the beginning of the document	Ctrl + Home
Move the insertion point to the end of the document	Ctrl + End
Display print page	Ctrl + P
Close a document	Ctrl + W

Excel 2013 Keyboard Shortcuts

ACTION	KEYBOARD SHORTCUT
Open a new blank workbook	Ctrl + N
Display Open page in Backstage view	Ctrl + O
Open the *Open* dialog	Ctrl + F12
Move to cell A1	Ctrl + Home
Save	Ctrl + S
Cut	Ctrl + X
Copy	Ctrl + C
Paste	Ctrl + V
Undo	Ctrl + Z
Redo	Ctrl + Y
Bold	Ctrl + B
Italic	Ctrl + I
Underline	Ctrl + U
Open the Quick Analysis tool	Ctrl + Q
Open the *Find and Replace* dialog with the *Find* tab displayed	Ctrl + F
Open the *Find and Replace* dialog with the *Replace* tab displayed	Ctrl + H
Edit mode (insertion point appears within the cell)	F2
Add a line break within a cell	Alt + ← Enter
Hide row	Ctrl + 9
Hide column	Ctrl + 0
Unhide row	Ctrl + ↑ Shift + 9
Insert dialog (cell, row, or column)	Ctrl + ↑ Shift + =
Insert worksheet	↑ Shift + F11
Insert chart	Alt + F1
Fill selected cell(s) with the value from the cell above it	Ctrl + D
Fill selected cell(s) with the value from the cell to the left of it	Ctrl + R
Open *Insert Function* dialog	↑ Shift + F3

ACTION	KEYBOARD SHORTCUT
Toggle between displaying formulas in cells and showing the formula results	Ctrl + `
Apply percent style	Ctrl + ↑ Shift + 5
Insert the SUM function	Alt + =
Toggle between cell reference states in a formula (absolute, mixed with relative column and absolute row, mixed with absolute column and relative row, relative)	F4
Open Paste Name dialog	F3
Open the Spelling dialog	F7
Open the Print page in Backstage view	Ctrl + P
Close	↑ Shift + F11

Access 2013 Keyboard Shortcuts

ACTION	KEYBOARD SHORTCUT
Open a new blank database	`Ctrl` + `N`
Open an existing database	`Ctrl` + `O`
Go to the next field in the record	`→`
Go to the previous field in the record	`←`
Go to the next record	`↓`
Go to the previous record	`↑`
Go to the first record	`Ctrl` + `↑`
Go to the last record	`Ctrl` + `↓`
Navigate from field to field within a record	`Tab`
Navigate from the last field in the record to the first field in the next record	`Tab`
Create a new blank record from the last record in the dataset	`Tab`
Add a new blank record to a table or form	`Ctrl` + `↑ Shift` + `=`
Cut	`Ctrl` + `X`
Copy	`Ctrl` + `C`
Paste	`Ctrl` + `V`
Undo	`Ctrl` + `Z`
Redo	`Ctrl` + `Y`
Delete a record	`Delete` or `Ctrl` + `-`
Open the *Spelling* dialog	`F7`
Open or close Navigation Pane	`F11`
Open selected object in Design view	`Ctrl` + `← Enter`
Save a database object. If first time saving the object, opens the *Save As* dialog.	`Ctrl` + `S`
Open the *Save As* dialog	`F12`
Open shortcut menu for the selected object	`↑ Shift` + `F10`
Move to preceding cell in a table, query, or form	`↑ Shift` + `Tab`
Insert line break when entering data in a *Short Text* or *Long Text* field	`Ctrl` + `← Enter`

ACTION	KEYBOARD SHORTCUT
Undo changes to current field and all changes if more than one field on current record has been changed.	`Esc`
Switch between Edit mode (insertion point displayed) and Navigation mode	`F2`
Increase selection to add adjacent column to the right	`↑ Shift` + `→`
Increase selection to add adjacent column to the left	`↑ Shift` + `←`
Open *Find and Replace* dialog	`Ctrl` + `F`
Open *Find and Replace* dialog with the Replace tab selected	`Ctrl` + `H`
Find next	`↑ Shift` + `F4`
Open Expression Builder	`Ctrl` + `F2`
Open Zoom window	`↑ Shift` + `F2`
Open or close the Properties window for the selected control	`F4`
Show or hide Field list	`Alt` + `F8`
Open *Page Setup* dialog from Print Preview view	`S`
Open *Print* dialog from Print Preview view	`Ctrl` + `P`
Switch to Form view from Design view	`F5`

PowerPoint 2013 Keyboard Shortcuts

ACTION	KEYBOARD SHORTCUT
Open a new blank presentation	Ctrl + N
Display Open page in Backstage view	Ctrl + O
Open the *Open* dialog	Ctrl + F12
Exit Slide Show view	Esc
Bold	Ctrl + B
Italic	Ctrl + I
Underline	Ctrl + U
Align text left	Ctrl + L
Center text	Ctrl + E
Align text right	Ctrl + R
Justify text	Ctrl + J
Open *Find* dialog	Ctrl + F
Open *Replace* dialog	Ctrl + H
Save	Ctrl + S
Undo	Ctrl + Z
Redo	Ctrl + Y
Cut	Ctrl + X
Copy	Ctrl + C
Paste	Ctrl + V
Open *Insert Hyperlink* dialog	Ctrl + K
Display the Spelling task pane	F7
Duplicate slides	Ctrl + D
Soft return, causes text to wordwrap to the next line	↑ Shift + ←┘ Enter
Open the Print page in Backstage view	Ctrl + P
Open *Save As* dialog	F12
Move to first slide	Home
Move to last slide	End
Move to next slide	Page down or ↓

ACTION	KEYBOARD SHORTCUT
Move to previous slide	`Page up` or `↑`
Move from the slide title to the body placeholder	`Ctrl` + `← Enter`
Start a presentation slide show from the beginning	`F5`
Open Presenter view and start a slide show	`Alt` + `F5`
In Slide Show view, advance to the next slide	`N`, `Space`, `→`, `↓`, `← Enter` or `Page down`
In Slide Show view, go to the previous slide	`P`, `← Backspace`, `←`, `↑`, or `Page up`
In Slide Show view, go to a particular slide	Slide number, `← Enter`
In Slide Show view, open the *All Slides* dialog	`Ctrl` + `S`
In Slide Show view, blanks the screen to black	`B` or `.`
In Slide Show view, blanks the screen to white	`W` or `,`
In Slide Show view, stop or restart an automatic show	`S` or `+`
In Slide Show view, change pointer to pen	`Ctrl` + `P`
In Slide Show view, change pointer to arrow	`Ctrl` + `A`
In Slide Show view, change pointer to laser pointer	`Ctrl` + `L`
In Slide Show view, change pointer to highlighter	`Ctrl` + `I`
In Slide Show view, change pointer to eraser	`Ctrl` + `E`
In Slide Show view, show or hide ink markup	`Ctrl` + `M`
In Slide Show view, erase markings on the screen	`E`
In Slide Show view, zoom in on a slide	`Ctrl` + `=`
In Slide Show view, zoom out on a slide	`Ctrl` + `-`

glossary of key terms

Office 2013 Overview

a

Account page: Page in Backstage view that lists information for the user currently logged in to Office. This account information comes from the Microsoft account you used when installing Office.

b

Backstage: Tab that contains the commands for managing and protecting files, including Save, Open, Close, New, and Print.

c

Contextual tabs: Contain commands specific to the type of object selected and are visible only when the commands might be useful.

e

Enhanced ScreenTip: A ScreenTip that displays the name of the command, the keyboard shortcut (if there is one), and a short description of what the button does and when it is used.

f

File Properties: Information about a file such as the location of the file, the size of file, when the file was created and when it was last modified, the title, and the author. File properties can be found on the Info page in Backstage view.

File tab: Tab located at the far left side of the Ribbon. Opens the Microsoft Office Backstage view.

g

Groups: Subsections of a tab on the Ribbon; organizes commands with similar functions together.

h

Home tab: Contains the most commonly used commands for each Office application.

k

Keyboard shortcuts: Keys or combinations of keys that, when pressed, execute a command.

l

Live Preview: Displays formatting changes in a file before actually committing to the change.

m

Metadata: All the information about a file that is listed under the Properties section of the Info page in Backstage view.

Microsoft Access: A database program. Database applications allow you to organize and manipulate large amounts of data.

Microsoft Excel: A spreadsheet program. Originally, spreadsheet applications were viewed as electronic versions of an accountant's ledger. Today's spreadsheet applications can do much more than just calculate numbers—they include powerful charting and data analysis features.

Microsoft PowerPoint: A presentation program. Such applications enable you to create robust, multimedia presentations.

Microsoft Word: A word processing program. Word processing software allows you to create text-based documents. Word processing software also offers more powerful formatting and design tools, allowing you to create complex documents, including reports, résumés, brochures, and newsletters.

Mini toolbar: Provides access to common tools for working with text. When text is selected and then the mouse is rested over the text, the Mini toolbar fades in.

n

New command: Creates a new file in an Office application without exiting and reopening the program.

o

Office Help: System for searching topics specifically tailored for working with an application.

p

Protected View: Provides a read-only format that protects your computer from becoming infected by a virus or other malware.

q

Quick Access Toolbar: Toolbar located at the top of the application window above the *File* tab. The Quick Access Toolbar gives quick one-click access to common commands.

r

Ribbon: Located across the top of the application window and organizes common features and commands into tabs.

s

ScreenTip: A small information box that displays the name of the command when the mouse is rested over a button on the Ribbon.

Shortcut menus: Menus of commands that display when an area of the application window is right-clicked.

SkyDrive: Microsoft's free cloud storage where you can save documents, workbooks, presentations, videos, pictures, and other files and access those files from any computer or share the files with others.

Start page: Displays when you first launch an application. The Start page gives you quick access to recently opened files and templates for creating new files in each of the applications.

t

Tab: Subsection of the Ribbon; organizes commands further into related groups.

Tags: Keywords used for grouping common files together or for searching.

Word 2013

a

Address block: Merge field that pulls in the address from the list of recipients for a mail merge.

Alignment guides: Horizontal and vertical green lines that appear when an object is dragged and the object's edge is aligned with another element on the page.

Autocorrect: Feature that analyzes each word as it is entered in a document. Each word is compared to a list of common misspellings, symbols, and abbreviations. If a match is found, AutoCorrect automatically replaces the text in the document with the matching replacement entry.

Automatic date stamp: Pulls the current date from the computer's system clock and displays the date in the document.

b

Bibliography: A compiled list of sources referenced in a document.

Bold: Character formatting that gives the text a heavier, thicker appearance.

Building Block: A piece of content that is reusable in any document. Building blocks can be text, such as AutoText, or can include graphics, such as a cover page.

Building Blocks Organizer: Lists the building blocks in alphabetical order by the gallery in which they appear; includes Bibliographies, Cover Pages, Equations, Footers, Headers, Page Numbers, Table of Contents, Tables, Text Boxes, and Watermarks.

Bullet: A symbol that is displayed before each item in a list.

c

Caption: A brief description of an illustration, chart, equation, or table.

Cell: The intersection of a row and column in a table.

Change Case command: Command in Word that manipulates the typed characters, changing how the letters are displayed.

Chart: A graphic that transforms numerical data into a more visual representation.

Citation: A reference to source material in a document. Citations include information such as the author, title, publisher, and the publish date.

Clip art: Illustrations and photographs that are made available through Word to use in documents.

Clipboard: Task pane that displays up to 24 copied or cut items for use in any Office application.

Clips: Images, photographs and scanned material from an external source.

Color theme: A set of colors that complement each other and are designed to work well together.

Column: A group of cells that display vertically in a table.

Copy: Command that places a duplicate of the selected text or object on the *Clipboard* without changing the file.

Cover page: First page in a document that contains brief information about the document, including the title and the date.

Cut: Command that removes the selected text or object from the file and places it on the Office *Clipboard* for later use.

e

Endnotes: References in a document that provide the reader with further information. Endnotes are composed of two parts: a reference mark and the associated text. Endnotes appear at the end of the document.

f

Find: Command that locates specific text or formatting in a document.

Font: Refers to a set of characters of a certain design. The font is the shape of the character or number as it appears on-screen.

Font theme: A set of fonts that complement each other and are designed to work well together.

Footer: Text that appears at the bottom of every page.

Footnotes: References in a document that provide the reader with further information. Footnotes are composed of two parts: a reference mark and the associated text. Footnotes appear at the bottom of a page.

Format Painter: Tool that copies and pastes formatting styles.

Formatting marks: Hidden marks in a document which indicate spaces, paragraphs, tabs, and page breaks.

g

Graphics: Photographs, clip art, SmartArt, or line drawings that can be added to documents, spreadsheet, presentations, and database forms and reports.

Greeting line: Field in the mail merge for the greeting line of a letter. The greeting line uses a set style and pulls in the name for the letter from the list of recipients in the mail merge.

Gridlines: A series of vertical and horizontal lines that divide the page into small boxes, giving you visual markers for aligning graphics, tables, and other elements on the page.

h

Hard page break: Command that forces the text to a new page no matter how much content is on the present page.

Header: Text that appears at the top of every page.

Highlighting: Tool in Word that changes the background color of the selected area to make it stand out on the page.

Hyperlink: Text or a graphic that, when clicked, opens another file or jumps to another place in the document.

i

Index: A list of topics and associated page numbers that typically appears at the end of a document.

Insert Control: Used to quickly add rows and columns to tables. Insert Controls appear when you roll your mouse over the left edge of a row or the top edge of a column.

Italic: Character formatting that makes text slant to the right.

l

Layout Options: Options for changing how objects appear with text—either in line or with text wrapping.

Line spacing: The white space between lines of text.

m

Mail merge: The process of creating several documents based on a main document, merge fields, and a recipients list.

Margins: The blank spaces at the top, bottom, left, and right of a page.

Merge cells: Combines multiple cells in a table into a single cell.

Merge fields: Placeholders that insert specific data from the recipients list you created in a mail merge.

Move cursor: Cursor that appears when the mouse is resting over an object that can be moved. When the move cursor displays, clicking the left mouse button and dragging the mouse will move the object to a new location in the document.

n

Numbered list: List type used to organize information that must be presented in a certain order.

o

Online video: Videos clips located on the Internet that can be accessed by using the *Bing Video Search* in the *Online Video* dialog.

p

Page borders: The decorative graphic element along the top, right, bottom, and left edges of the page. Borders can be simple lines or include 3-D effects and shadows.

Paragraph: Any text separated by a hard return. A hard return refers to pressing the (← Enter) key to create a new paragraph.

Paragraph alignment: How text is aligned with regard to the left and right margins of a document.

Paste: Command that is used to insert text or an object from the *Clipboard* into a file.

Paste options: Options for pasting text and objects in Word. Paste options allow you to choose to keep the source formatting, merge the formatting of the source and the current document, or paste only the text without any formatting.

Points: Measurement for the height of a font. Abbreviated "pt."

Print Layout view: Displays how document elements will appear on a printed page.

Property control: An element that is added to a document to save time entering the same information over and over again. Property controls can be used as shortcuts for entering long strings of text that are difficult to type, such as e-mail addresses, phone numbers, and street addresses.

q

Quick Style: A group of formatting, including character and paragraph formatting, that can easily apply to text, tables, drawings, or other objects.

r

Read Mode: View in Word which is designed for reading documents in electronic format. In Read Mode, documents are displayed as screens rather than pages.

Recipients list: A table of names and address for the people you want to include in a mail merge.

Redo: Reverses the undo command and restores the file to its previous state.

Reference mark: The superscript character placed next to the text for a footnote or endnote.

Reference style: A set of rules used to display references in a bibliography. These rules include the order of information, when and how punctuation is used, and the use of character formatting.

Replace: Used with the *Find* command to replace specified text in a file with new text.

Resize handle: One of the six squares that appear when an object is selected. Clicking and dragging a resize handle toward the center of the object will make the object smaller. Clicking and dragging the resize handle away from the center of the object will make the object larger.

Row: A group of cells that display horizontally in a table.

Ruler: Displays horizontally across the top of the window just below the Ribbon and vertically along the left side of the window. The ruler gives you a quick view of the margins and position of elements in your document.

S

Sans serif fonts: Fonts that do not have an embellishment at the end of each stroke. Includes Calibri and Arial.

ScreenTip: A bubble with text that appears when the mouse hovers over a hyperlink. Typically, a ScreenTip provides a description of the hyperlink.

Serif fonts: Fonts that have an embellishment at the end of each stroke. Includes Cambria and Times New Roman.

Shape: A drawing object that can be quickly added to a document.

SmartArt: Visual diagrams containing graphic elements with text boxes to enter information in.

Sorting: Arranges the rows in a table, worksheet, or datasheet in either ascending (A–Z) or descending (Z–A) alphabetical or numeric order.

Split cells: Divides a cell in a table in Word into multiple cells.

Style set: Formatting options for changing the font and paragraph formatting for an entire document based on styles.

Styles: Complex formatting, including font, color, size, and spacing, that can be applied to Office files.

T

Tab leaders: Element that fills in the space between tab stops with solid, dotted, or dashed lines.

Tab stop: The location along the horizontal ruler that indicates how far to indent text when the *T* key is pressed.

Table: Content element that helps to organize information by rows, which display horizontally, and columns, which display vertically.

Table of contents: Lists the topics in a document and the associated page numbers, so readers can easily locate information.

Template: A file with predefined settings that can be used as a pattern to create a new file.

Text effects: Predefined graphic styles you can apply to text. These styles include a combination of color, outline, shadow, reflection, and glow effects.

Theme: A group of formatting options that is applied to an entire Office file. Themes include font, color, and effect styles that are applied to specific elements in a file.

Thesaurus: Reference tool that provides a list of synonyms (words with the same meaning) and antonyms (words with the opposite meaning) for a selected word or phrase.

U

Underline: Character formatting that draws a single line under the text.

Undo: Reverses the last action performed.

W

Watermark: A graphic or text that appears as part of the page background. Watermarks appear faded so the text that appears on top of the watermark is legible when the document is viewed or printed.

Web Layout view: Displays all backgrounds, drawing objects, and graphics as they will appear on-screen if the document is saved as a Web page.

Word Count: Feature that provides the current statistics of the document you are working on, including the number of pages, number of words, number of characters (with and without spaces), number of paragraphs, and number of lines.

Word wrap: Automatically places text on the next line when the right margin of the document has been reached.

WordArt: Predefined graphic styles that are applied to text. These styles include a combination of color, fills, outlines, and effects.

Z

Zoom slider: Slider bar that controls how large or small the file appears in the application window.

Excel 2013

3-D reference: A formula that references the same cell(s) on multiple sheets.

a

Absolute reference: A cell reference whose location remains constant when the formula is copied. The $ character before a letter or number in the cell address means that part of the cell's address is *absolute* (nonchanging).

Accounting Number Format: Aligns the $ at the left side of the cell, displays two places after the decimal, and aligns all numbers at the decimal point. Zero amounts are displayed as dashes (–).

Alignment: Refers to how text and numbers are positioned within the cell both horizontally and vertically.

Argument: The part of the formula (input) that the function uses to calculate a value.

AutoFill: Feature used to fill a group of cells with the same data or to extend a data series.

AutoSum: Allows you to insert common functions (SUM, AVERAGE, COUNT, MIN, and MAX) with a single mouse click.

Average: A statistical function that is used to calculate the average value of a group of values. A formula using the AVERAGE function looks like this: =AVERAGE(A3:A6)

b

Banding: Applies a fill color to alternating rows or columns, making a table easier to read.

Bar charts: Chart type that works best with data that are organized into rows and columns like a table. The categories are displayed on the vertical (y) axis, and the data points are plotted along the horizontal (x) axis.

c

Cascade window arrangement: Places the windows in a staggered, overlapping, diagonal arrangement.

Cell: The intersection of a row and column in a spreadsheet.

Cell address: The column and row position that defines a cell. For example, the cell at the intersection of column B and row 4 has a cell address of *B4.*

Cell range: A contiguous group of cells. A cell range is identified by the address of the cell in the upper left corner of the range, followed by a colon, and then the address of the cell in the lower right corner of the range. The cell range *B3:D5* includes cells B3, B4, B5, C3, C4, C5, D3, D4, and D5.

Cell reference: A cell's address when it is referred in a formula.

Cell style: A combination of effects that can be applied at one time. Styles can include formatting such as borders, fill color, font size, and number formatting.

Chart: A graphic that represents numeric data visually.

Chart area: Encompasses the entire chart including the plot area and optional layout elements, such as title and legend.

Chart sheet: A special type of worksheet that contains only the chart object.

Chart title: A text box above or overlaying the chart.

Clustered column chart: Chart type where each column represents a single data point. The data points are grouped (clustered) together by category. Each data series is represented by a single color.

Color scales: A conditional formatting style in Excel that colors cells according to one of the color scales (e.g., red to green [bad/low to good/high] or blue to red [cold/low to hot/high]).

Column: A vertical group of cells. Columns are identified by letters. For example, the fourth column is labeled with the letter *D.*

Column charts: Chart type that works best with data that are organized into rows and columns like a table. Data point values are transformed into columns, with the values plotted along the vertical (y) axis. Each row in the table is grouped as a data series. Excel uses the column labels as the categories along the horizontal (x) axis.

Column input cell: The cell that contains the original value for which you want to substitute the data table values when the substitute values are listed in a column.

Column selector: The box with the column letter at the top of the worksheet grid. Clicking this box will select the entire column.

Comma Style format: Number format similar to the *Accounting Number Format,* but without the currency symbol.

Concatenate: Means to link items together.

CONCATENATE: Function used to combine the text values of cells. For example, if you have two columns for first name and last name, but you need a third column displaying the full name, you can use CONCATENATE to combine the values of the first two columns.

Conditional formatting: Provides a visual analysis of data by applying formatting to cells that meet specific criteria (conditions).

Copy: Command that places a duplicate of the selected text or object on the *Clipboard* without changing the file.

COUNT: Counts the number of cells that contain numbers within a specified range of cells. A formula using the COUNT function looks like this: =COUNT(A2:A106)

COUNTA: Counts the number of cells that are not blank within a specified range of cells. Use COUNTA if your cell range includes both numbers and text data. A formula using the COUNTA function looks like this: =COUNTA(B2:B106)

COUNTBLANK: Counts the number of blank cells within a specified range of cells. A formula using the COUNTBLANK function looks like this: =COUNTBLANK(D2:D106)

Currency format: Number format that places the $ immediately to the left of the number, so columns of numbers do not align at the $ and at the decimal as they do with *Accounting Number Format.*

Cut: Command that removes the selected text or object from the file and places it on the Office *Clipboard* for later use.

d

Data bars: A conditional formatting style in Excel that displays a color bar (gradient or solid) representing the cell value in comparison to other values (cells with higher values have longer data bars).

Data labels: Display data values for each data marker in a chart.

Data markers: Columns, bars, pie pieces, lines, or other visual elements in a chart that represent data point values.

Data points: Values from a cell range plotted on a chart.

Data series (AutoFill): A sequence of cells with a recognizable pattern (used with the AutoFill feature).

Data series (chart): A group of related data points plotted on a chart.

Data table (chart): Displays a table of the data point values below the chart.

Data table (what-if analysis): Provides a quick what-if analysis of the effects of changing one or two variables within a formula. The data table is organized with a series of values for the variable(s) in a column or a row or both.

Defined name: The names you created and names that Excel creates automatically when you define a print area or print titles.

Dependent: The cell containing a formula that references the value or formula in the selected cell.

Doughnut charts: Chart type similar to a pie chart with the capability to display more than one series. Each series is represented by a ring around the doughnut. Each data point in the series is represented by a piece of the ring proportional to the total.

e

Edit mode: The data entry method used in Excel to change only part of the cell data by double-clicking the cell, and then moving the cursor within the cell to insert or delete data.

f

Fill color: Solid color that shades a cell.

Fill Handle tool: Appears at the lower-right corner of a selected cell or group of cells and can be used to implement the AutoFill feature.

Filter: Limits the spreadsheet rows displayed to only those that meet specific criteria.

Find: Command that locates specific text, data, or formatting in a spreadsheet.

Font: Refers to a set of characters of a certain design. The font is the shape of the character or number as it appears on-screen.

Footer: Text that appears at the bottom of every page.

Format Painter: Tool that copies and pastes formatting styles.

Formula: An equation used to calculate a value.

Formula AutoComplete: Displays a list of potential matches (functions and other valid reference names) after an = has been typed in a cell in Excel.

Formula bar: Data entry area directly below the Ribbon and above the worksheet grid.

Freeze: Excel command that keeps column headings and row labels visible as you scroll through your data.

Function: Preprogrammed shortcuts for calculating complex equations (like the average of a group of numbers).

g

General horizontal alignment: Default alignment of cells. When cells are formatted using the General horizontal alignment, Excel detects the type of content in the cell. Cells that contain text are

aligned to the left, and cells that contain numbers are aligned to the right.

General number format: Number format that right-aligns numbers in the cells but does not maintain a consistent number of decimal places (43.00 will appear as 43, while 42.25 appears as 42.25) and does not display commas (so 1,123,456 appears as 1123456).

Goal Seek: Feature that lets you enter a desired value (outcome) for a formula and specify an input cell that can be modified in order to reach that goal.

Gridlines: The lines that appear on the worksheet defining the rows and columns.

Group: Multiple worksheets with the same structure that you can make changes to at the same time.

h

Header: Area that appears at the top of every page.

Headings: The numbers at the left of rows and the letters at the top of columns.

Highlight Cells Rules: A conditional formatting style in Excel that allows you to define formatting for cells that meet specific numerical or text criteria (e.g., greater than a specific value or containing a specific text string).

HLOOKUP: Function that finds a value or cell reference in a cell range and returns another value from the same column.

Horizontal scroll bar: The scrollbar located at the bottom of the window. Click the arrows at the ends of the scroll bars to move left and right to see more cells in an individual worksheet.

Horizontal window arrangement: Places the windows in a row next to each other.

i

Icon sets: Conditional formatting style in Excel that displays a graphic in each cell representing the cell value in relation to other values.

IF: Logical function that returns one value if a condition is true and another value if the condition is false. A formula using the IF function looks like this: =IF(TOTAL_SALES > 50000,10%,5%)

l

Landscape orientation: Page orientation where the width of the page is greater than the height.

Legend: A key for a chart defining which data series is represented by each color.

Line charts: Chart type that features a line connecting each data point—showing the movement of values over time.

Line with markers: Line chart type that includes dots along the line for each data point.

Long Date format: Excel date format that displays the day of the week, and then the name of the month, the two-digit date, and the four-digit year (Monday, September 05, 2011).

LOWER: Function that converts the text string to all lowercase letters. A formula using the LOWER function looks like this: =LOWER(E2)

m

Margins: The blank spaces at the top, bottom, left, and right of a page.

MAX: Statistical function that will give the highest value in a range of values. A formula using the MAX function looks like this: = MAX(A3:A6)

Mean: The sum of a group of values divided by the number of values in the group.

Median: The middle value of a set of values.

Message Bar: Displays a warning at the top of the window, below the Ribbon, when a file is opened in Protected View.

MIN: Statistical function that will give the lowest value in a range of values. A formula using the MIN function looks like this: =MIN(A3:A6)

Mixed reference: A combination cell reference with a row position that stays constant with a changing column position (or vice versa).

Mode: The value that appears most often in a group of values.

n

Name: A word or group of words that is assigned to cells or ranges of cells to give your cell references names that are more user-friendly. Also called a named range or a range name.

Name Box: Appears at the left side of the formula bar and displays the address of the selected cell or the name of a named range.

Name Manager: lists all the named ranges used in your workbook, the current value for each, the cells to which the name refers (including the sheet name), the scope of the name (whether it is limited to a specific worksheet or applies to the entire workbook), and comments (if there are any).

Named range: A word or group of words that is assigned to cells or ranges of cells to give your cell references names that are more user-friendly. Also called a name or a range name.

Normal view: The typical working view in Excel. In *Normal* view, Excel shows the aspects of the worksheet that are visible only on-screen. Elements that are visible only when printed (like headers and footers) are hidden.

NOW: Function that inserts the current date and time. A formula using the NOW function looks like this: =NOW()

Number format: An Excel cell format that stores data as numbers and shows two decimal places by default (so 43 displays as 43.00) but does not include commas.

o

Order of operations (precedence): A mathematical rule stating that mathematical operations in a formula are calculated in this order: (1) exponents and roots, (2) multiplication and division, and (3) addition and subtraction.

Orientation: Refers to the direction the worksheet prints.

p

Page Break Preview view: Allows you to manipulate where page breaks occur when the worksheet is printed.

Page Layout view: Shows all the worksheet elements as they will print. *Page Layout* view includes headers and footers.

Paste: Command that is used to insert text or an object from the *Clipboard* into a file.

Percent Style format: Displays numbers as % with zero places to the right of the decimal point.

Pie charts: Chart type that represents data as parts of a whole. Pie charts do not have x and y axes like column charts. Instead, each value is a visual "slice" of the pie.

PivotChart: A graphic representation of a PivotTable.

PivotTable: A special report view that summarizes data and calculates the intersecting totals. In Excel, PivotTables do not contain any data themselves—they summarize data from a range or a table in another part of your workbook.

Plot area: The area of the chart where the data series are plotted.

PMT: Function that can be used to calculate loan payments. The PMT function is based upon constant payments and a constant interest rate. A formula using the PMT function looks like this: =PMT(7%/12,120,250000)

Portrait orientation: Page orientation where the height of the page is greater than the width.

Precedent: The cell containing the formula or value the selected cell refers to.

Print area: A range of cells that you designate as the default print selection.

PROPER: Function that converts the text string to proper case (the first letter in each word is capitalized). A formula using the PROPER function looks like this: PROPER(C2)

Protected View: Provides a read-only format that protects your computer from becoming infected by a virus or other malware.

q

Quick Analysis tool: Feature that helps you easily apply formatting, create charts, and insert formulas based on the selected data.

Quick Styles: A group of formatting, including character and paragraph formatting, that can easily apply to text, tables, drawings, or other objects.

r

Range name: A word or group of words that is assigned to cells or ranges of cells to give your cell references names that are more user-friendly. Also called a name or a named range.

Ready mode: The data entry method used in Excel to change the contents of the entire cell by clicking the cell once and then typing the data.

Redo: Reverses the *Undo* command and restores the file to its previous state.

Relative reference: A cell reference that adjusts to the new location in the worksheet when the formula is copied.

Replace: Used with the *Find* command to replace specified data or formatting in a file with new data or formatting.

Row: A horizontal group of cells. Rows are identified by numbers. For example, the third row is labeled with the number 3.

Row input cell: The cell that contains the original value for which you want to substitute the data table values when the substitute values are listed in a row.

Row selector: The box with the row number at the left side of the worksheet grid. Clicking this box will select the entire row.

S

Scale: Specifies that the worksheet will print at a percentage of the original size or at a maximum number of pages wide and/ or tall.

Short Date format: Excel number format that displays the one- or two-digit number representing the month, followed by the one- or two-digit number representing the day, followed by the four-digit year (9/5/2011).

Slicer: A visual representation of filtering options. You can display multiple slicers and filter by multiple values from each. Slicers are only available when the data have been formatted as a table or PivotTable.

Smart Tag: Icon that appears next to a formula with a potential error and displays a menu for resolving the issue.

Sort: Arranges the rows in a table, worksheet, or datasheet in either ascending (A–Z) or descending (Z–A) alphabetical or numeric order.

Sparklines: Represent a series of data values as an individual graphic within a single cell.

Stacked column chart: Chart type that shows each data point as part of a whole where the column represents the sum of the values in the series. Use a stacked column chart instead of a pie chart when you want the chart to show multiple series.

Status bar: Appears at the bottom of the worksheet grid and can display information about the selected data, including the number of cells selected that contain data (count) and the average and sum (total) of the selected values (when appropriate).

String: Text in a function.

T

Table: A range of cells may be explicitly defined as a table in Excel with additional functionality such as a Total row.

Template: A file with predefined settings that can be used as a pattern to create a new file.

Text String: Text in a function.

Theme: A group of formatting options that is applied to an entire Office file. Themes include font, color, and effect styles that are applied to specific elements in a file.

Theme Colors: Aspect of the theme that limits the colors available from the color palette for fonts, borders, and shading.

Theme Effects: Aspect of the theme that controls how graphic elements appear.

Theme Fonts: Aspect of the theme that controls which fonts are used for built-in text styles. Changing the theme fonts does not limit the fonts available from the *Font* group on the Ribbon.

Tiled window arrangement: Places the windows in a grid pattern.

TODAY: Function that inserts the current date. A formula using the TODAY function looks like this: =TODAY()

Top/Bottom Rules: Excel conditional formatting style that automatically finds and highlights the highest or lowest values or values that are above or below the average in the specified range of cells.

Total row: A row that calculates an aggregate function, such as the sum or average, of all the values in the column. Total rows can be added to defined tables in Excel.

Two-variable data table: Provides a quick what-if analysis of the effects of changing two variables within a formula. The data table is organized with a series of values for the variables in both a column and a row.

U

Undo: Reverses the last action performed.

UPPER: Function that converts the text string to all uppercase letters. A formula using the UPPER function looks like this: UPPER(D2)

V

Vertical scroll bar: The scrollbar located along the right side of the window. Click the arrows at the ends of the scroll bars to move up and down to see more cells in an individual worksheet.

Vertical window arrangement: Places the windows in a stack one on top of the other.

VLOOKUP: Function that finds a value or cell reference in a cell range and returns another value from the same row. A formula using the VLOOKUP function looks like this: = VLOOKUP(D13,LoanRange,7)

W

Workbook: An Excel file made up of a collection of worksheets.

Worksheet: An electronic ledger where you enter data in Excel (also called a sheet). The worksheet appears as a grid made up of rows and columns where you can enter and then manipulate data using functions, formulas, and formatting.

x

X axis: The horizontal axis in a chart. It goes from left to right.

y

Y axis: The vertical axis in a chart. It goes from bottom to top.

z

Zoom slider: Slider bar that controls how large or small the file appears in the application window.

Access 2013

a

Attachment data type: Stores files as attachments to records. Attachments can be images, Word documents, or almost any other type of data file.

AutoNumber data type: Fields with this data type are automatically assigned its value by Access. Database users cannot edit or enter data in an *AutoNumber* field. *AutoNumber* fields are often used as a primary key if no other unique field exists in the table.

b

Bound control: Control that displays a value from a specific field.

c

Calculated control: An unbound text control that contains an expression (formula).

Calculated Field data type: Displays a value returned by an expression (a formula).

Calculated Field (in a query): Displays a value returned by an expression (a formula). The field values are calculated each time the query is run.

Comma Style format: Displays the, symbol within the number and two digits to the right of the decimal.

Compact & Repair tool: Tool that eliminates hidden, temporary database objects that take up database space unnecessarily.

Control layout: Combines multiple controls in your database form or report into a single layout object in one of two formats: tabular or stacked.

Control: Displays data or allows user to enter and edit data in a form or report. Controls can be bound, unbound, or calculated.

Copy: Command that places a duplicate of the selected text or object on the *Clipboard* without changing the file.

Criteria: Conditions that the records must meet in order to be included in the query results. *Criteria* is a plural word that refers to more than one *criterion*.

Criterion: Singular form of the word *criteria*.

Crosstab query: Presents data in a spreadsheet format, allowing you to specify fields to use for column headers and for row headers, and then automatically calculating totals for values in another field as related to the column and row headers.

Currency data type: Fields with this data type store a numerical value with a high degree of accuracy (up to four decimal places to the right of the decimal). Access will not round the values stored in *Currency* fields, regardless of the format in which the value displays.

Currency format: Displays a $ symbol before the number and two digits to the right of the decimal place.

Cut: Command that removes the selected text or object from the file and places it on the Office *Clipboard* for later use.

d

Database: A collection of data. An effective database allows you to enter, store, organize, and retrieve large amounts of related data.

Datasheet form: Form that reproduces the exact look and layout of the table datasheet.

Datasheet view, tables: View to use when entering data in a table or to sort and filter data. By default, tables open in Datasheet view.

Datasheets: Table data and query results displayed in Datasheet view.

Date/Time data type: Fields with this data type store a numerical value that is displayed as a date and time. The format in which the date and/or time displays is controlled by the format property.

Default Value property: Adds a preset value to the field.

Design view, tables: View where you establish the table primary key and table properties as well as specific properties or formatting for individual fields. Use Design view when you want to change the structure or properties of the table.

e

Expression: A formula used in a calculated field in a table or query or a calculated control in a form or report.

f

Field Properties pane: Allows you to set field properties in table Design view.

Field Size property: Limits the number of characters that can be entered in a text field.

Field: Each column in a table in a database.

Filter: Limits the database records displayed to only those that meet specific criteria. Filters are temporary and are not saved with the database object unless they are defined in the object's properties.

Find Duplicates query: Finds duplicate records in a table.

Find Unmatched query: Finds records in one table that do not have matching records in another table.

Foreign key: In a one-to-many relationship, the field in the secondary table that relates to the primary key in the primary table.

Form footer: The section directly below the detail section where the data are displayed in a form.

Form header: The section directly above the detail section where the data are displayed in a form.

Form view: Provides a user-friendly interface for entering data in a database. From Form view, you cannot change the form layout or formatting.

Form Wizard: Wizard that walks you through the steps of creating the form, including selecting fields and a layout. You can use the *Form Wizard* to create a form combining fields from multiple related tables.

Form: Allows database users to input data through a friendly interface.

Format field property: Controls the way the data are displayed to the end user. It does not affect the data stored in the table.

g

Grouping: Feature that organizes records into distinct sections within an Access report.

h

Hyperlink data type: Fields with this data type store a Web address or e-mail address.

i

Innermost sort: In a multilevel sort, the last field the data are sorted on.

Input mask: Ensures that users enter data in a database field in a particular format.

l

Label control: Unbound control that displays the field name or other text.

Landscape: Page orientation where the width of the page is greater than the height.

Layout view: View where you can modify some (but not all) structural elements in a form or report.

Long Text data type: Holds text and numbers like a *Short Text* field, except you can enter up to 65,535 characters in a *Long Text* field. Text in *Long Text* fields can be formatted using Rich Text Formatting. In previous versions of Access, the *Long Text* data type was called the *Memo* data type.

Lookup field: Allows the user to select data from a list of items.

m

Macro: Programming instruction that can be run from within a file. Macros are used to automate data entry and formatting processes and to execute commands from buttons in database forms and reports.

Margins: The blank spaces at the top, bottom, left, and right of a page.

Message Bar: Security warning that displays at the top of the window, below the Ribbon.

Multiple Items form: Displays multiple records at once. The layout and design of a Multiple Items form can be modified.

n

Navigation Pane: Pane that organizes all the objects for a database. The Navigation Pane is docked at the left side of the screen.

Number data type: Fields with this data type hold a numerical value. The default number is described as a *long integer*, a number between –2,147,483,648 and 2,147,483,647.

o

OLE Object data type: Stores a graphic or file as part of the database. It is maintained in Access 2013 for backward compatibility with databases created prior to Access 2007.

One-to-many relationship: A relationship between two database tables where the primary table contains a primary key field that is included as a field (the *foreign key*) in the secondary table. Thus, one record in the first table can relate to many records in the second table.

Outermost sort: In a multilevel sort, the first field the data are sorted on.

p

Page footer: Section that appears at the bottom of every printed page in a report.

Page header: Section that appears at the top of every printed page in a report.

Parameter query: A query with user-controlled criteria input. When the query is run, the user is prompted to enter a value for a specific field (the parameter input) that will be used as the criterion when generating results.

Paste: Command that is used to insert text or an object from the *Clipboard* into a file.

PDF (Portable Document Format): Type of file that can be read by anyone who has the Adobe Reader software installed.

Percent format: Displays the number as a percentage, so .05 displays as 5, and 5 displays as 500. It does not display the % symbol in the table.

Portrait: Page orientation where the height of the page is greater than the width.

Primary key field: The field that contains data unique to each record in a table.

Primary key: In a one-to-many relationship, the field in the main table that is also included in the secondary table.

Print Preview: A specific report view that shows how the database report will appear when printed.

q

Query grid: The lower pane in query Design view where the fields and criteria for the query are defined.

Query: Extracts data from a table or multiple related tables.

Quick Start field types: Provide an easy way to add address fields and other common field groups to your table.

r

Record source: The associated table or query for a database form or report.

Record: Each row in a table in a database.

Redo: Reverses the *Undo* command and restores the file to its previous state.

Referential integrity: The policy that ensures that related database records remain accurate. If a relationship has referential integrity enforced, then no modification can be made to either table that would violate the relationship structure.

Relational database: A database that allows you to relate tables and databases to one another through common fields.

Relationships window: Window that provides a visual representation of the relationships in your database.

Report footer: The section directly below the detail section where the data are displayed in a report.

Report header: The section directly above the detail section where the data are displayed in a report.

Report view: Shows a static view of the database report. You cannot change the layout or formatting of the report from Report view.

Report Wizard: Wizard that walks you step by step through the process of creating a report. The *Report Wizard* allows you to combine fields from more than one table or query and gives you more layout and design options than using the basic *Report* button from the *Create* tab.

Report: Displays database information for printing or viewing on-screen.

Rich Text Format (RTF): Text format can be used with any word processing program, not just Microsoft Word.

s

Select query: Displays data from one or more tables or queries, based on the fields that you select.

Short Text data type: Can hold up to 255 characters. *Short Text* fields are used for short text data or numbers that should be treated as text.

Single Record form: Form that displays one record at a time.

Split form: Combines the convenience of a continuous datasheet form with the usability of a single form displaying one record at a time.

SQL view: Shows the code used to build the query.

Stacked layout: Places the form or report labels at the left side with data to the right (similar to many paper forms or reports).

Subform: A form within the form—to display the related records from the "many" table in a one-to-many relationship.

t

Table: Stores all the database data. Tables are the basic building blocks of the database.

Tabular layout: Places the form or report labels across the top, with columns of data (similar to a datasheet or a spreadsheet).

Text box control: Control that displays text, numbers, dates, and similar data. Text box controls can be bound or unbound.

Theme colors: Aspect of the theme that limits the colors available from the color palette for fonts, borders, and shading.

Theme fonts: Aspect of the theme that controls which fonts are used for built-in text styles. Changing the theme fonts does not limit the fonts available from the *Font* group on the Ribbon.

Theme: A unified font and color scheme applied to the entire database.

Total row: A row that calculates an aggregate function, such as the sum or average, of all the values in the column. Total rows can be added to tables and queries in Datasheet view in Access.

U

Unbound control: A control that is not linked to a field.

Undo: Reverses the last action performed.

W

Wildcard: Special characters used in criteria to substitute for any character. The * wildcard replaces any string of characters. The ? wildcard replaces a single character.

y

Yes/No data type: Fields with this data type store a true/false value as a −1 for yes and 0 for no.

PowerPoint 2013

a

Animation: Movement of an object or text in a presentation. There are four basic types of animation schemes: Entrance, Emphasis, Exit, and Motion Paths.

Animation Painter: Tool that copies and pastes animations from one object to another.

b

Background: The graphic element that fills a slide. Backgrounds can be solid colors, textures, or images.

Bulleted lists: List type used to organize information that does not have to be displayed in a particular order.

c

Cell: The intersection of a row and column in a table.

Chart: A graphic that transforms numerical data into a more visual representation.

Clear All Formatting: Command that removes any formatting that has been applied to text, including character formatting, text effects, and styles, and leaves only plain text.

Clip art: Illustrations and photographs that are made available through PowerPoint to use in presentations.

Clipboard: Task pane that displays up to 24 copied or cut items for use in any Office application.

Clips: Images, photographs and scanned material from an external source.

Color theme: A set of colors that complement each other and are designed to work well together.

Columns: Groups of cells that display vertically in a table.

Comments: A small text note similar to a Post-It note that can be added to a presentation.

Content placeholder: A special type of placeholder that provides a quick way to add a variety of material to presentations, including tables, charts, SmartArt diagrams, pictures, clip art, and videos.

Copy: Command that places a duplicate of the selected text or object on the *Clipboard* without changing the file.

Cut: Command that removes the selected text or object from the file and places it on the Office *Clipboard* for later use.

d

Drawing objects: Objects that when selected display the *Drawing Tools* contextual tab. Drawing objects include text boxes, shapes, and WordArt.

e

Effects theme: A set of line and fill effects that you apply to objects on your slides.

f

Fill color: Solid color that fills a drawing object.

Find: Command that locates specific text in a presentation.

Font: Refers to a set of characters of a certain design. The font is the shape of the character or number as it appears on-screen.

Font theme: A set of fonts that complement each other and are designed to work well together.

Footer: Text that appears on every slide or handout. Typically, a footer appears at the bottom of a slide or handout.

Format Painter: Tool that copies and pastes formatting styles.

g

Gridlines: A series of dotted vertical and horizontal lines that divide the slide into small boxes. Used as visual markers for aligning placeholders and graphics.

h

Handout: A printout of a presentation with one to nine slides per page and with areas for taking notes.

Handout master: Master that controls how the slides in a presentation look when printed.

Hide Slide: Command that hides the slide when in *Slide Show* view, but does not delete the slide in *Normal* view.

Highlighter: Slide show tool used to add color behind text on slides in *Slide Show* view and emphasize parts of a slide.

Hyperlink: Text or a graphic that, when clicked, opens another file or jumps to another place in the presentation.

l

Laser pointer: Slide show tool that turns the mouse pointer into a red dot you can use to call attention to important parts of your slides.

Line spacing: The white space between lines of text.

n

Normal view: The view where content is created and edited. *Normal* view consists of the *Slides* tab, *Slide* pane, and *Notes* pane.

Notes pages: The printed copy of the slide with its associated note.

Notes view: The view where notes are displayed along with slides in a presentation.

Numbered lists: List type used to organize information that must be presented in a certain order.

o

Online picture: Images located on the Internet that can be accessed by searching on *Office.com* Clip Art, through a *Bing Image Search*, or from your SkyDrive.

Online video: Videos clips located on the Internet that can be accessed by using the *Bing Video Search* in the *Online Video* dialog.

Outline view: Displays only the text from the slides in a presentation in an outline format. Use the *Outline* view to enter and edit text directly in the outline.

Outlines: Line that surrounds the shape of a drawing object. You can adjust the weight and style of outlines.

p

Paste: Command that is used to insert text or an object from the *Clipboard* into a file.

Paste options: Options for pasting text and objects in PowerPoint. Paste options allow you to choose to keep the source formatting, merge the formatting of the source and the current document, or paste only the text without any formatting.

Pen: Slide show tool used to underline or circle important points in *Slide Show* view as they are discussed.

Picture effects: Effects including shadows, reflections, glows, soft edges, bevels, and 3-D rotation that you apply to pictures.

Placeholder: A container on a slide that holds text or other content, such as a table, chart, or image.

Points: Measurement for the height of a font. Abbreviated "pt."

Presentation: A multimedia slide show that combines text, images, charts, audio, video, animations, and transition effects to convey information.

Presenter view: View that allows you to see your notes while you are giving your presentation, making it easier to refer to any notes you have added to slides.

q

Quick styles: A group of formatting, including character and paragraph formatting, that can easily apply to text, tables, drawings, or other objects.

r

Reading view: The view that runs the presentation within the PowerPoint application window.

Redo: Reverses the *Undo* command and restores the file to its previous state.

Rehearse Timings: Feature that runs the presentation while recording the time spent on each slide.

Replace: Used with the *Find* command to replace specified text in a file with new text

Resize handle: One of the six squares that appear when an object is selected. Clicking and dragging a resize handle toward the center of the object will make the object smaller. Clicking and dragging the resize handle away from the center of the object will make the object larger.

Ruler: Displays horizontally across the top of the window just below the Ribbon and vertically along the left side of the window. The ruler gives you a quick view of the position of elements on a slide.

s

Sans serif font: Fonts that do not have an embellishment at the end of each stroke. Includes Calibri and Arial.

ScreenTip: A bubble with text that appears when the mouse hovers over a hyperlink. Typically, a ScreenTip provides a description of the hyperlink.

Sections: Smaller groups of slides within a presentation to help better organize the content.

Serif font: Fonts that have an embellishment at the end of each stroke. Includes Cambria and Times New Roman.

Shape: A drawing object that can be quickly added to a presentation.

Slide numbers: Information added to the footer area of each slide to display how far along you are in your presentation. Slide numbers are added through the *Header and Footer* dialog and are automatically updated when slides are added, deleted, or moved.

Slide Show view: The view that displays the slides full-screen and displays the presentation as the audience will see it.

Slide Sorter view: The view that displays a grid of thumbnail pictures of the slides in a presentation, and is useful in rearranging the order of slides in a presentation.

Slides: Units within a presentation. Each slide contains content, including text, graphics, audio, and video.

Slides tab: Displays thumbnails of all the slides in a presentation. Use the *Slides* tab to quickly navigate between slides and rearrange the slide order of slides in a presentation.

Smart guides: Horizontal and vertical dotted lines that appear when an object is dragged and the object's edge is aligned with another element on the slide.

SmartArt: Visual diagrams containing graphic elements with text boxes to enter information in.

Sound files: Music or sound effects that can be added to slides.

Speaker notes: Hidden notes that do not appear as part of the presentation.

Spelling checker: Command that analyzes your entire presentation for spelling errors. It presents any errors it finds in the Spelling task pane, enabling you to make decisions about how to handle each error or type of error in turn.

t

Table: Content element that helps to organize information by rows, which display horizontally, and columns, which display vertically.

Template: A file with predefined settings that can be used as a pattern to create a new file.

Text alignment: Refers to how text is lined up with regard to the left and right edges of a slide.

Text boxes: Boxes that are added to the slide layout to enter text anywhere on the slide.

Text placeholders: Predefined areas in slide layouts where text is entered.

Theme variant: A set of color variations you can change for a theme.

Transition: An effect that occurs when one slide leaves the screen and another one appears.

u

Undo: Reverses the last action performed.

V

Vertical alignment: Refers to how text is aligned with regard to the top and bottom of the placeholder.

W

Widescreen 16:9: Display where the width of the slide is larger than the height of the slide designed for widescreen monitors and projectors. Widescreen 16:9 is the default size for slides.

WordArt: Predefined graphic styles that are applied to text. These styles include a combination of color, fills, outlines, and effects.

Working space: Another name for *Normal* view.

Z

Zoom slider: Slider bar that controls how large or small the file appears in the application window.

photo credits

Page OF–1: © Burazin/Photographer's Choice/Getty
Page OF–14: Stockbytey/Getty Images

Page WD–1: © Burazin/Photographer's Choice/Getty
Page WD–8: © Ocean/Corbis
Page WD–49: Rubberball/Mark Andersen
Page WD–97: Ryan McVay/Getty Images
Page WD–119: Comstock
Page WD–179: Rubberball/Getty Images
Page WD–185: © Ingram Publishing/Alamy

Page EX–1: © Burazin/Photographer's Choice/Getty
Page EX–7: © Design Pics Inc./Alamy
Page EX–28: Burke/Triolo Productions/Brand X/Corbis
Page EX–31: Blend Images/Getty Images
Page EX–71: Rubberball Productions
Page EX–79: © Juice Images/Alamy

Page EX–121: © Ocean/Corbis
Page EX–173: Rubberball Productions
Page EX–199: Lane Oatey/Getty Images

Page AC–1: © Burazin/Photographer's Choice/Getty
Page AC–15: © Jose Luis Pelaez, Inc./Blend Images/Corbis
Page AC–77: Rubberball/Getty Images
Page AC–131: © Blend Images/Alamy
Page AC–175: Rubberball Productions

Page PP–1: © Burazin/Photographer's Choice/Getty
Page PP–17: Comstock
Page PP–59: Rubberball/Mike Kemp
Page PP–81: Mike Kemp/Rubberball/Getty Images
Page PP–130: Ryan McVay/Getty Images

Cover image: © Burazin/Photographer's Choice/Getty

Office Index

Word Index

d

Data
    entering, WD-130–WD-131
    sorting, WD-137
Date content controls, WD-98
Date stamps, automatic, WD-82–WD-83, G-2
Decimal tab stop, WD-57
Decrease Indent button, WD-55
Delete key, WD-5
Deleting
    columns, rows, and cells, WD-133
    footnotes, WD-170
    text, WD-5
Descending order, sorting data in, WD-137
Dictionary, adding words to, WD-8
Different First Page check box, WD-79
Disclaimers, WD-77
Displaying
    gridlines, WD-140
    the ruler, WD-56
Distribute Columns button, WD-134
Distribute Rows button, WD-134
Document Formatting feature, WD-4
Document statistics, WD-24
Documents; *see also under* Formatting
    adding citations to, WD-174–WD-175
    previewing, WD-99
    printing, WD-99–WD-101
    properties of, WD-89
    from templates, WD-182–WD-183
    zooming in, WD-22–WD-23
Double spacing, WD-51
Draft view, WD-180
Dragging, resizing by, WD-115, WD-135
Drawing objects, Quick Styles for, WD-121
Drawing Tools Format tab, WD-124
Duplicated words, WD-10

e

E-mails, mail merge for, WD-191
Editing
    headers, WD-79
    hyperlinks, WD-90–WD-91
    individual letters in mail merges, WD-191
    recipients lists, WD-187
    text, WD-5
Endnotes, G-2
    inserting, WD-170
    in word count, WD-24
Enter key, WD-4, WD-5
Entering
    data in tables, WD-130–WD-131
    text, WD-5, WD-123
Envelope and Labels dialog, WD-193
Envelope Options dialog, WD-193
Envelopes, WD-192–WD-193

f

Figures, adding captions to, WD-171
Files, inserting pictures from,
        WD-118–WD-119
Find and Replace dialog
    finding text with, WD-12, WD-13
    opening, WD-15

Find command, WD-12–WD-13, G-2
Finding text, WD-12–WD-13
Finishing mail merges, WD-190–WD-191
First Line Indent option, WD-55, WD-58
Font Color button, WD-40
Font colors, WD-40
Font dialog, WD-36
    applying text effects from, WD-43
    opening, WD-38
Font sizes, WD-38
Font themes, WD-76, G-2
Fonts, WD-37
    defined, WD-4, WD-37, G-2
    theme, WD-73
    using multiple, WD-37
Footers, WD-80–WD-81, G-3
Footnotes, WD-24, WD-169, WD-170, G-3
Format Painter button, WD-44
Format Painter tool, WD-44, G-3
Format Paragraph dialog, WD-55
Formatting
    documents, WD-73–WD-98
        adding automatic date stamps,
            WD-82–WD-83
        adding cover pages, WD-98
        adding footers, WD-80–WD-81
        adding headers, WD-78–WD-79
        adding page borders, WD-96–WD-97
        adjusting margins, WD-92–WD-93
        applying style sets, WD-74
        applying themes, WD-73
        color themes, WD-75
        creating watermarks, WD-77
        font themes, WD-76
        inserting Building Blocks, WD-86–WD-87
        inserting hyperlinks, WD-90–WD-91
        inserting page breaks, WD-94–WD-95
        inserting page numbers, WD-84–WD-85
        inserting property controls, WD-88–WD-89
    paragraphs, WD-46–WD-58
        adding spaces before and after paragraphs,
            WD-54
        bulleted lists, WD-46
        changing indents, WD-55
        changing line spacing, WD-51
        changing paragraph alignment, WD-50
        displaying the ruler, WD-56
        numbered lists, WD-47
        Quick Styles, WD-48–WD-49
        revealing formatting marks, WD-52–WD-53
        tab stops, WD-57–WD-58
    text, WD-35–WD-45
        applying highlights, WD-41
        applying text effects, WD-42–WD-43
        bold, italic, and underline effects,
            WD-35–WD-36
        changing font colors, WD-40
        changing font sizes, WD-38
        changing fonts, WD-37
        changing text case, WD-39
        Clear Formatting command, WD-45
        Format Painter tool, WD-44
        Quick Styles, WD-48–WD-49
        revealing formatting marks,
            WD-52–WD-53
Formatting marks
    replacing, WD-15
    revealing, WD-52–WD-53
    XE, WD-177
Formatting styles, copying and pasting, WD-44
Full pages of labels, WD-195

g

GB7714 2005 reference style, WD-173
Glow effects, WD-42
Go To tab, WD-15
GOST–Name Sort reference style, WD-173
GOST–Title Sort reference style, WD-173
Graduate students, WD-179
Grammar, checking, WD-7–WD-8, WD-163
Grammar task pane, WD-163
Graphics, WD-122–WD-127
    adding online videos, WD-126–WD-127
    adding WordArt, WD-125
    defined, WD-4, G-3
    inserting shapes, WD-124
    inserting SmartArt, WD-122–WD-123
Greeting lines, WD-188, WD-189, G-3
Gridlines, WD-56, WD-140, G-3
Grow Font button, WD-38
Gutters, WD-93

h

Hanging Indent option, WD-55, WD-58
Hard page breaks, WD-94–WD-95, G-3
Hard returns, WD-4
Harvard–Anglia 2008 reference style, WD-173
Header & Footer Tools Design tab, WD-81
Header font, WD-76
Headers
    adding, WD-78–WD-79
    alignment of, WD-50
    case for, WD-39
    defined, WD-78, G-3
    editing, WD-79
    font sizes for, WD-37
    and title pages, WD-79
Heading rows, table, WD-130
Height
    cells, WD-134
    pictures, WD-115
    tables, WD-134
Help icon, WD-4
Hiding
    chart elements, WD-144
    formatting marks, WD-52–WD-53
Hierarchy SmartArt, WD-122
Highlighting, G-3
    adding, WD-41
    removing, WD-45
Horizontal alignment, WD-50
Hyperlinks, WD-90–WD-91, G-3
    editing, WD-90–WD-91
    removing, WD-90–WD-91

i

Icons, WD-18
IEEE 2006 reference style, WD-173
Increase Indent button, WD-55
Indents, WD-55
Index entries
    adding, WD-179
    marking, WD-177
Indexes, WD-178–WD-179, G-3
Info tab, WD-24
Insert Address Block dialog, WD-188
Insert Controls, WD-132, G-3

Excel Index

Quick Analysis tool for, EX-74–EX-75
removing, EX-81
Top/Bottom Rules for, EX-80
Conditional Formatting Rules Manager, EX-81
Contextual tabs, EX-224
Contiguous cells, EX-201
Converting
data to tables, EX-212–EX-213
tables to ranges, EX-217
Copy command, EX-51–EX-52, EX-207, G-5
Copying
cells, EX-51–EX-52
formulas, EX-116
worksheets, EX-156–EX-157
COUNT function, EX-108, EX-109, G-5
Count option, EX-214
COUNTA function, EX-108, EX-109, G-5
COUNTBLANK function, EX-108, EX-109, G-5
Counting functions, EX-108–EX-109
Create Names from Selection command,
EX-114–EX-115
Create Sparklines dialog, EX-223
Creating
data tables, EX-227–EX-228
named ranges, EX-114–EX-115
PivotCharts, EX-232–EX-233
PivotTables, EX-229–EX-231
workbooks, EX-28–EX-31
Currency [0] cell style, EX-13
Currency cell style, EX-13
Currency format, EX-13, G-5
Custom font color, EX-67
Custom footers, EX-171
Custom headers, EX-171
Custom Margins . . . option, EX-176
Cut command, EX-51–EX-52, EX-207, G-5
Cutting cells, EX-51–EX-52

d

Data, EX-218–EX-233
analyzing, EX-225–EX-228
chart, EX-211
converting, into tables, EX-212–EX-213
editing, EX-10–EX-11
entering, EX-10–EX-11
filtering, EX-211, EX-219–EX-222, G-6
finding, EX-84–EX-85, EX-126–EX-127
inserting, EX-16–EX-17, EX-224
referencing, EX-124–EX-125
replacing, EX-84–EX-85
sorting, EX-218, EX-233, G-8
Sparklines for, EX-223–EX-224
table, EX-221–EX-222
Data bars, EX-76, EX-77, G-5
Data labels, EX-208, G-5
Data markers, EX-197, EX-205, G-5
Data points, EX-197, EX-199, EX-205, G-5
Data series
AutoFill with, EX-16, G-6
for charts, EX-197, EX-199, G-6
dates in, EX-17
grouping of, EX-203
Data tables
for charts, EX-208, G-6
for what-if analysis, EX-227–EX-233, G-6
analyzing data with, EX-227–EX-228
creating PivotCharts, EX-232–EX-233
creating PivotTables, EX-229–EX-231
Goal Seek function vs., EX-228
Date codes, EX-15

Date formats, EX-14–EX-15
Date functions, EX-111
Date patterns, EX-16
Dates
in data series, EX-17
entering, EX-14–EX-15
serial numbers for, EX-15
Decrease Decimal button, EX-13
Defined names, EX-119, G-6
Delete command, EX-165
Delete key, EX-59, EX-83
Delete Sheet command, EX-158
Deleting
cells, EX-59
range names, EX-119
rows/columns, EX-164–EX-165
worksheets, EX-158
Dependencies, EX-130
Dependents, EX-130, EX-131, G-6
Dictionary, adding words to, EX-34
Disabling data filtering, EX-220
Displaying
formulas, EX-132
tracer arrows, EX-130, EX-131
Dollar sign ($), EX-13, EX-20
Doughnut charts, EX-204, G-6
Dragging, moving charts by, EX-206
Duplicate names, for ranges, EX-118–EX-119
Duplicate rows, EX-216
Duplicate values, EX-78

e

Edit mode, EX-10, EX-11, G-6
Editing
data in cells, EX-10–EX-11
formulas, EX-18
and Protected View, EX-8
range names, EX-118–EX-119
Empty cells, AVERAGE function and, EX-107
Enabling
data filtering, EX-219
editing, EX-8
Entering
data in cells, EX-10–EX-11
dates, EX-14–EX-15
formulas, EX-18–EX-20
functions, EX-22, EX-103–EX-106
Error checking, EX-128–EX-129
Errors, EX-128–EX-131
Expand Dialog button, EX-104, EX-117
"Exploded" pie charts, EX-204

f

Fields, in PivotTables, EX-229
Fill color, EX-70–EX-71, G-6
Fill Color button, EX-71
Fill command, EX-17
Fill Handle tool, EX-16, EX-17, G-6
Filtering data, EX-211, EX-219–EX-222, G-6
in charts, EX-211
in PivotCharts, EX-233
with slicers, EX-221–EX-222
Find All button, EX-84
Find and Replace dialog, EX-84, EX-85
Find command, G-6
for data, EX-84, EX-85
for formatting, EX-86, EX-87
Find Format dialog, EX-86–EX-87

Finding
data, EX-84, EX-85, EX-126–EX-127
formatting, EX-86, EX-87
functions, EX-105
values, EX-225
Font color, EX-66–EX-67, EX-70
Font color palette, EX-66
Font size, EX-66–EX-67
Fonts, G-6
changing, EX-66–EX-67
Theme, EX-161, G-8
Footers, EX-170–EX-171, G-6
Format Cells dialog
accounting underline options in, EX-64–EX-65
changing alignment with, EX-60–EX-61
fill effects and pattern styles in, EX-70
merging and centering cells with, EX-63
text wrapping feature in, EX-57
Format Painter, EX-73, G-6
Formats
date, EX-14–EX-15
number, EX-12–EX-13
Formatting; see also Conditional formatting
cells, EX-50–EX-89
adding borders, EX-68–EX-69
adding shading with fill color, EX-70–EX-71
aligning cells, EX-60–EX-61
applying bold, italic, and underline,
EX-64–EX-65
applying cell styles, EX-72
changing fonts, font size, and font color,
EX-66–EX-67
clearing cell content, EX-82–EX-83
Copy command, EX-51–EX-52
Cut command, EX-51–EX-52
Find command, EX-84–EX-85
with Format Painter, EX-73
inserting and deleting cells, EX-58–EX-59
merging and splitting cells, EX-62–EX-63
Paste command, EX-51–EX-52
paste options, EX-53–EX-55
Redo command, EX-56
Replace command, EX-84–EX-85
replacing formatting, EX-86–EX-87
setting and clearing the print area,
EX-88–EX-89
Undo command, EX-56
wrapping text in cells, EX-57
clearing, EX-82
of inserted cells, EX-58
replacing, EX-86–EX-87
of text, EX-112
worksheets, EX-152–EX-179
adding headers/footers, EX-170–EX-171
changing orientation, EX-175
changing tab color, EX-155
changing view, EX-169
freezing and unfreezing rows/columns, EX-166
hiding and unhiding rows/columns, EX-167
inserting and deleting rows/columns,
EX-164–EX-165
inserting page breaks, EX-172–EX-173
modifying column widths and row heights,
EX-162–EX-163
showing and hiding elements, EX-174
Formatting (paste option), EX-54
Formatting Formula AutoComplete shortcut, EX-106, EX-111,
EX-116, G-6
Formula bar
cell reference type in, EX-21
contents of, EX-5, EX-18
defined, EX-3, G-6

Access Index

PowerPoint Index